ANCIENT ECONOMIES OF THE NORTHERN AEGEAN

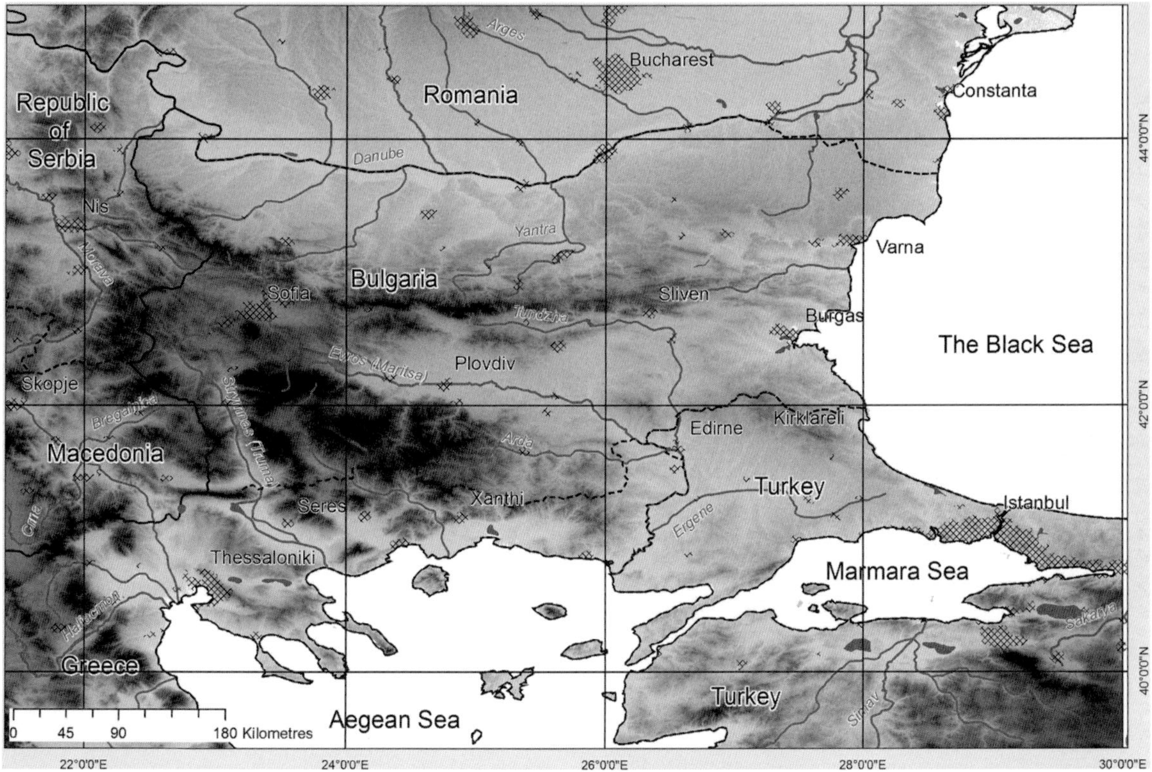

Map 1. The east Balkan and north Aegean area

Ancient Economies of the Northern Aegean

Fifth to First Centuries BC

ZOSIA HALINA ARCHIBALD

OXFORD
UNIVERSITY PRESS

OXFORD
UNIVERSITY PRESS

Great Clarendon Street, Oxford, OX2 6DP,
United Kingdom

Oxford University Press is a department of the University of Oxford. It furthers the University's objective of excellence in research, scholarship, and education by publishing worldwide. Oxford is a registered trade mark of Oxford University Press in the UK and in certain other countries

First Edition published in 2013

Impression: 1

Published in the United States of America by Oxford University Press
198 Madison Avenue, New York, NY 10016, United States of America

British Library Cataloguing in Publication Data
Data available

Library of Congress Control Number: 2013938814

ISBN 978–0–19–968211–9

As printed and bound by
CPI Group (UK) Ltd, Croydon, CR0 4YY

Preface

Most visitors to the northern Aegean today approach it (whether physically or in virtual and abstract terms) from the south, that is, from the Aegean Sea. In this book I have attempted not just to look at this part of southern Europe from the familiar, southerly perspective, but to imagine it from other angles. The chapters are organized to reflect these different approaches, which do deliver different impressions. They are compatible impressions, but nonetheless rather unfamiliar to most Classicists and historians, those of classical antiquity as of more recent times.

I might begin with maps. The map that forms the frontispiece to the book is a unique creation. I could not find a map that provided the physical environment of my story, so it had to be created. Modern national boundaries are powerful drivers of the available geographical information, so most attempts to make use of what is available tend to follow patterns created by convenient, readily accessible parameters. These parameters are of little use when mapping the remote past, which blissfully ignores modern boundaries. Older maps are another matter. Nineteenth-century maps of southern Europe give a far broader perspective, but populate the landscape with unfamiliar names and habits of mind. Travelling about the region certainly helps to provide a better sense of local ecologies; but modern geography conceals as much as it reveals. The great river courses of the east Balkan area have changed their beds and altered the immediate landscape in ways that require big team projects to disentangle. What we see is not what used to be there.

So this book is consciously arranged like a series of successive stage sets, which gradually reveal the full perspective of the remote past. First, there is a preliminary summary, in Chapter 1, intended to explain what the story is about. The players are not just characters and choruses from antiquity, since the story is told through the voices of contemporary historians, geographers, and archaeologists. We need to hear their accounts, but must also manage to discern the fact that they speak in different registers. Modern political configurations of the region have divided up its history into a mass of separate, sometimes quite contradictory interpretations. The stories are not the same, nor are the interpretations compatible. They cannot all be equally valid. Somehow, choices have to be made and readers need to know what these choices are. The introductory chapter tries to see the past through the eyes of a number of key modern personalities, whose research has created much of the modern architecture of the subjects explored here.

Other themes introduced in Chapter 1 are gradually developed in later chapters. Political history is almost always a key component of big narratives; but whose politics may be in question is not easy to discern. The politics of the powerful in southern Europe during the second half of the first millennium BC is both more noticeable than it is in central and southern Greece and less so. The actions of powerful individuals, rulers, princes, and landowners are manifested in all kinds of ways, which also leave visible traces—structures, monuments, public statements, in the form of stone inscriptions and funerary architecture. For a variety of reasons, modern access routes into the region, even today, tend to avoid the inland trajectories that linked the continental heartlands of princes and landowners to coasts and harbours, and thus to the more familiar landmarks and place names of classical maritime itineraries. This may explain why some of these monumental power statements have only been discovered comparatively recently. Yet the stories about the power-holders of the region do survive and can be reinstated, if we find a method by which this can be done.

If we make an effort of imagination to resurrect the landward power-holders of southern Europe, we can begin to see patterns in the geopolitical landscape. The Greco-Persian wars emerge as a significant driver of social and economic changes that refashioned existing hierarchies and thereby introduced new fashions and customs. Understanding the social parameters of the region is therefore the first task to be explored. This cannot, of course, be done without also considering how these social entities have been described and interpreted as modern scholars have sought to gloss and project the disparate evidence about ancient societies in the region into recognizable and coherent social forms. The communities that emerge from historical accounts and archaeological vestiges in Chapter 2 have thus to be made into identifiable economic agents in Chapter 3, before the focus returns in Chapters 4, 5, and 6 towards the ways in which the landscape has become a canvas for human discovery and use.

Most scholarly works on classical antiquity stick to a limited chronology, well supported by ancient literary or other written texts. I have delved much further back into the past. It is no longer uncommon to find ancient historians acknowledging the importance of long-term processes. I want to emphasize this deep perspective. Subsistence patterns in southern Europe have very deep roots indeed, which partly explain the robustness of the mixed agricultural economies that become discernible in rural establishments of the fifth to third centuries BC. The long-term strategies also help to frame the particular events and relationships that provide some of the incidental detail that emerges from my story.

The deeply rooted ecologies of the south-east Balkan and north Aegean area have to be understood in terms of particular communities and traditions. Perhaps the hardest task for any historian who wants to make this region better known is to create the kinds of associations that come so easily to more southerly and easterly locations, whose names echo down the centuries through the poetry of Homer and the rhetoric of orators. The place names of this region are often strange modern ones, and rural mysteries at that. The best kept secret of the east Balkans are its rural retreats. Modernity has gloried in the urban landscape of antiquity, whilst ignoring its equally impressive contributions to the management and construction of the rural landscape.

The scene-setting that each chapter tries to create results in a series of filters through which various historical identifiers–ethnic groups, peoples, archaeological sites, artefacts, and commodities–are viewed in turn. These filters include demography, geology, ecology, languages, and epigraphy. Filters of this kind employ different methods and produce different results, which must nevertheless be factored into the overall narrative of the past. Beyond these filters rises the broader discourse about the nature of ancient societies, their organization and structure. I have tried to keep discussion of social matters firmly in touch with economic ones and have chosen paradigms that seem to reflect the close connection between the material and the social that is such a striking component of any encounter with the artefacts and monuments that these societies created. It makes a very different environment in which to evaluate some of the familiar and established models for conceptualising classical antiquity—including the paradigms invented by Moses Finley; the overriding preoccupation with coastal locations against inland ones; the '*polis*' of the Copenhagen project; 'regionalism', national boundaries.

Handbridge, Chester, May 2013

Acknowledgements

The idea for this book was conceived about five years ago, but it was my colleague at Liverpool, Graham Oliver, who persuaded me, in 2010, that this was the right time to write it. Preparation of the text has coincided with a number of international projects and publications that make this a particularly opportune time to consider the ancient economies of the east Balkan/northern Aegean area as a single entity.

My work has been immensely enhanced by the support and assistance of many people. Figures 6.1 and 6.2 are reproduced with the kind permission of Arthur Muller and Henri Tréziny (Muller 2010, 212 fig. 142; 221 fig. 143, respectively). Map 1 (frontispiece) was specially prepared for this volume in collaboration with Dr Richard Chiverrell, Department of Geography, University of Liverpool. A number of previously published maps and plans have been redrawn, with modifications, by Dr Esme Hammerle. These include Figure 2.1 (map of Macedonia, various sources); Figures 4.1–4.2, which draw on information published in Ghilardi et al. 2008, 113 fig. 2 and figs. p. 122; Figures 4.3, 4.4, and 4.5, which represent, with necessary modifications, parts of the preliminary plans published in Adam-Veleni, Poulaki, and Tzanavari 2003: Tria Platania (p. 58), Komboloi (p. 65) and Vrasna (p. 95). Figure 4.6 has been redrawn, with modifications, from Christov and Lazov's report in *AOR* 2010, 192 fig. 3; Figures 5.5 and 5.6, redrawn, with modifications, from M. Madjarov's reports in *AOR* 2010, 189 fig.1; Figure 4.7 reproduces data presented in *AOR* 2006, 231, map 2; Figure 4.8 reproduces data presented in *AOR* 2010, 241, map 2. Figure 5.3 reproduces the data from Tzvetkova 2008, map 11. I am most grateful to Richard Chiverrell and Esme Hammerle for their assistance; and to Katerina Tzanavari and Mitko Madjarov for their willingness to allow preliminary plans of their projects to be included here.

I would also like to express particular gratitude to Lydia Domaradzka, Lisa Kallet, Jack Kroll, Gavrail Lazov, Evi Margaritis, and Gary Reger, who have given me advanced access to new publications; and to the many friends and colleagues who have either read drafts of different chapters, discussed various aspects of the contents, or otherwise contributed to my perceptions: Alexandru Avram, Alexandre Baralis, Chaido Koukouli-Chrysanthanki, John Davies, Vincent Gabrielsen, Bruce Gibson, Alexey Gotzev, Denver Graninger, Edward Harris, Chryssoula Karadima,

Maria Kostoglou, Jack Kroll, Louisa Loukopoulou, Mitko Madjarov, Dimitris Matsas, Cathy Morgan, Graham Oliver, Maria-Gabriella Parissaki, Selene Psoma, Mustafa Sayar, Milena Tonkova. To Ian I owe much more than gratitude; without him the book could not have been written.

Contents

List of figures, maps and tables

List of abbreviations

Abbreviations for ancient literary sources follow *Oxford Classical Dictionary*[3] (1996), xxix–liv. Abbreviations for epigraphic sources follow *Supplementum Epigraphicum Graecum*, Index XXXVI–XLV (Amsterdam, 1999), 677–688. Abbreviations for periodicals follow *L'Année Philologique*. Other abbreviations are the following:

Adams and Borza	W. L. Adams and E. Borza (eds) (1982), *Philip II, Alexander the Great and the Macedonian Heritage*, Lanham.
AEMΘ	*Το Αρχαιολογικό Έργο στη Μακεδονία και τη Θράκη*
20 Chronia AEMΘ	20 *Χρόνια Το Αρχαιολογικό Έργο στη Μακεδονία και τη Θράκη*, Thessaloniki, 2009.
Agoranomia	P. van Alfen, (ed.) (2006) *Agoranomia: Studies in Money and Exchange Presented to J. H. Kroll*, New York.
Alternatives to Athens	R. Brock and S. Hodkinson (eds) (2000), *Alternatives to Athens. Varieties of Political Organization and Community in Ancient Greece*, Oxford.
Ancient Colonizations	H. Hurst and S. Owen (eds) (2005), *Ancient Colonizations, Analogy, Similarity, and Difference*, London.
AncMac VII	*Ancient Macedonia. VII. Macedonia from the Iron Age to the Death of Philip II. Papers read at the Seventh International Symposium held in Thessaloniki, October 14–18, 2002*, Thessaloniki, 2007.
AOR	*Archeologicheski Razkopki i Prouchvaniya*, Bulgarian Academy of Sciences/Institute of Archaeology and Museum, Sofia.
Aperghis	G. G. Aperghis (2004), *The Seleukid Royal Economy: The Finances and*

	Financial Administration of the Seleukid Empire, Cambridge.
Aphieroma Hammond	Ch. Koukouli-Chrysanthaki (ed.) (1997), *Aphieroma ston N. G. L. Hammond*, Thessaloniki.
Approches	R. Descat (ed.) (2006), *Approches de l'économie hellénistique*. Saint-Bertrand-de-Comminges.
Athenaeus and his World	D. Braund and J. Wilkins (eds) (2000), *Athenaeus and his World, Reading Greek Culture in the Roman Empire*, Exeter.
Austin^2	M. M. Austin (2006), *The Hellenistic World from Alexander to the Roman Conquest. A Selection of Ancient Sources in Translation*. 2nd edn, Cambridge.
Billows	R. A. Billows (1990), *Antigonos the One-Eyed and the Creation of the Hellenistic State*. (*Hellenistic Culture and Society* 4), Berkeley and Los Angeles.
Bouzek and Domaradzka	J. Bouzek and L. Domaradzka (eds) (2005), *The Culture of the Thracians and their Neighbours. Proceedings of the International Symposium in Memory of Prof. Mieczysław Domaradzki, with a Round Table 'Archaeological Map of Bulgaria'*, BAR IS1350, Oxford.
Bresson	A. Bresson (2000), *La cité marchande*, Ausonius 2, Bordeaux.
Bugh ed.	G. Bugh (ed.) (2006), *The Cambridge Companion to the Hellenistic World*, Cambridge.
CAH^2	*Cambridge Ancient History*, new edition, I–. Cambridge, 1970–.
CEHGRW	W. Scheidel, I. Morris, and R. Saller (eds) (2007), *The Cambridge Economic History of the Greco-Roman World*, Cambridge.
CH	M. Jessop-Price (ed.) (1975–), *Coin Hoards*, I–. London.
Clarysse and Thompson	W. Clarysse and D. Thompson (2006), *Counting the People in Hellenistic Egypt*, 2 vols. Cambridge.

Emprunt	L. Migeotte (1984), *L'emprunt public dans les cités grecques: Recueil des documents et analyse critique*, Paris and Québec.
Dossier Pistiros	*Dossier: nouvelles perspectives pour l'étude de l'inscription de Pistiros, BCH* 123 (1999), 1. Études.
Erskine 2003	A. Erskine (ed.) (2003), *A companion to the Hellenistic world,* Malden Mass. and Oxford.
Feyel	Chr. Feyel (2006), *Les artisans dans les sanctuaires grecs aux époques classique et hellénistique à travers la documentation financière en Grèce, BEFAR* 318, Athens.
Fornara	Ch. Fornara (ed.) (1983), *Archaic Times to the end of the Peloponnesian War. Translated Documents of Greece and Rome, Vol. 1,* 2nd edn, Cambridge.
Guerre	J. Andreau, P. Briant, and R. Descat (eds) (2000), *La guerre dans les économies antiques*, Saint-Bertrand de Comminges.
HellEc I	Z. H. Archibald, J. K. Davies, V. Gabrielsen, and G. J. Oliver (eds) (2001), *Hellenistic Economies*, London and New York.
HellEc II	Z. H. Archibald, J. K. Davies, and V. Gabrielsen (eds) (2005), *Making, Moving and Managing: The New World of Ancient Economies, 323–31 BC.*, Oxford.
HellEc III	Z. H. Archibald, J. K. Davies, and V. Gabrielsen, (eds) (2011), *The Economies of Hellenistic Societies,* Oxford.
Horden and Purcell	P. Horden and N. Purcell (2000), *The corrupting sea. A study of Mediterranean history,* Malden Mass and Oxford.
HM I	N. G. L. Hammond (1972), *A History of Macedonia I,* Oxford.
HM II	N. G. L. Hammond, and G. T. Griffith, (1979) *A History of Macedonia II,* Oxford.

HM III	N. G. L. Hammond, and F. W. Walbank (1988), *A History of Macedonia III. 336–167 B.C.*, Oxford.
I. Beroea	Gounaropoulou, L. and M. B. Hatzopoulos (1998), *'Επιγραφὲς Κάτω Μακεδονίας. L. Επιγραφὲς Βέροιας*, Athens.
IGCH	M. Thompson, O. Mørkholm and C. M. Kraay (eds) (1973), *An Inventory of Greek coin hoards*, New York.
IK	*Inschriften griechischer Städte aus Kleinasien*, Bonn, 1972–.
I ThrAeg	L. Loukopoulou, A. Zournatzi, M. G. Parissaki and S. Psoma (2005), *Έπιγραφὲς τῆς Θράκης τοῦ Αἰγαίου μεταξὺ τῶν ποταμῶν Νέστου καὶ Ἕβρου (νομοὶ Ξάνθης Ροδόπης καί Ἑβρου)*, Athens: Κέντρον Έλληνικῆς καί Ρωμαϊκῆς Αρχαιότητος.
Inventory	M. H. Hansen and T. H. Nielsen (eds) (2004), *An Inventory of Archaic and Classical Poleis*, Oxford.
JEH	*Journal of Economic history.*
Manning and Morris	J. Manning and I. Morris (eds) (2005), *The Ancient Economy: Evidence and Models*, Stanford.
Markets, Households, and City-States	D. M. Lewis, E. M. Harris, and M. Woolmer (eds) (2014), *Markets, Households, and City-States in the Ancient Greek Economy,* Cambridge.
Mnimi Lazaridi	*Μνήμη Δ. Λαζαρίδη* (1990), *Πόλις και χώρα στην αρχαία Μακεδονία και Θράκη, Πρακτικά Αρχαιολογικού Συνεδρίου, Καβάλα* 9–11 *Μαΐου*, 1986, Kavalla.
ML	R. Meiggs and A. Lewis (1988 [1969]), *A Selection of Greek Historical inscriptions to the end of the Fifth Century B. C.*, Oxford.
Networks	I. Malkin, Chr. Constantakopoulou, and K. Panagopoulou, (eds) (2009), *Greek and*

	Roman Networks in the Mediterranean, Abingdon and New York.
Les Équidés	A. Gardeisen (ed.) (2005), *Les Équidés dans le monde méditerranéen antique*, Actes du colloque organisé par l'École française d'Athènes, le Centre Camille Jullian, et l'UMR 5140 du CNRS, Athènes 26–28 Novembre 2003, Lattes.
PAA	J. S. Traill (1994–), *Persons of Ancient Athens*, Toronto.
Pistiros I	J. Bouzek, M. Domaradzki and Z. H. Archibald (eds) (1996), *Pistiros I: Excavations and Studies*, Charles University, Prague.
Pistiros II	J. Bouzek, L. Domaradzka and Z. H. Archibald (eds) (2002), *Pistiros II: Excavations and Studies*, Charles University, Prague.
Pistiros III	J. Bouzek, L. Domaradzka and Z. H. Archibald (eds) (2007), *Pistiros III: Excavations and Studies*, Charles University, Prague.
Pistiros IV	J. Bouzek, L. Domaradzka and Z. H. Archibald (eds) (2010), *Pistiros IV. Excavations and Studies*, Charles University, Prague.
Pistiros et Thasos	D. Domaradzki, L. Domaradzka, J. Bouzek, and J. Rostropowicz (eds) (2000), *Pistiros et Thasos : structures économiques dans la péninsule balkanique dans le 1er millénaire av. J.-C.*, Opole.
Reger	G. Reger (1994), *Regionalism and change in the economy of independent Delos, 314–167 B.C.*, Berkeley.
RO	P. J. Rhodes and R. J. Osborne (eds) (2003), *Greek historical inscriptions: 404–323 BC*, Oxford.
Rois, Cités, Nécropoles	A.-M. Guimier-Sorbets, M. B. Hatzopoulos, and Y. Morizot (eds) (2006), *Rois, Cités, Nécropoles. Institutions, rites et monuments en*

	Macédoine, MELETEMATA 45, Athens–Paris.
Roisman and Worthington	J. Roisman and I. Worthington (eds) (2010), *A Companion to Ancient Macedonia*, Malden Mass. and Oxford.
Sboryanovo	T. Stoyanov, with Zh. Mihaylova, K. Nikov, M. Nikolaeva, D. Stoyanova, V. Bonev, and K. Madzharov (forthcoming), *Sboryanovo III. The Thracian City*, Sofia.
SEG	*Supplementum Epigraphicum Graecum.*
SEHHW	M. I. Rostovtzeff (1941), *The social and economic history of the Hellenistic world*, I–III, Oxford.
Settlement life in Ancient Thrace	*Poselishten Zhivot v Drevna Trakya*, I ed. V. Velkov (1979); II ed. V. Velkov (1982); III ed. D. Draganov (1994); IV ed. I. Ilyev (2006).
Stephanèphoros	K. Konuk (ed.) (2012), *Stephanèphoros de l'Économie antique à l'Asie mineure, Hommages à Raymond Descat*, Mémoires 28, Bordeaux.
Thasos, Matières Premières	Ch. Koukouli-Chrysanthaki, A. Muller, S. Papadopoulos (eds) (1999), *Thasos, Protes yles kai technologia apo tous proistorikous Chronous os semera. Thasos, Matières premières et technologie de la préhistoire à nos jours*, Proceedings of the International Colloquium, Limenaria, Thasos, 26–29 September 1995 (École française d'Athènes–18th Ephorate of Prehistoric and Classical Antiquities).
The Customs Law of Asia	M. Cottier, M. H. Crawford, C. V. Crowther, J.-L. Ferrary, B. M. Levick, O. Salomies, and M. Wörrle (2008), *The Customs Law of Asia*, Oxford.
Thrace and the Aegean	A. Fol (ed.) (2002), *Thrace and the Aegean. Eighth International Congress of Thracology, Sofia-Jambol, 25–29 September 2000*, Sofia.

Thrace in the Graeco-Roman World	A. Iakovidou (ed.) (2007), *Η Θράκη στον 'ελληνο- ρωμαϊκο κοσμο. Thrace in the Graeco-Roman World, Proceedings of the Tenth International Congress of Thracology, Komotini-Alexandroupolis, 18–23 October 2005,* Athens.
Tout vendre, tout acheter	V. Chankowski and P. Karvonis (eds) (2012), *Tout vendre, tout acheter. Structures et équipements des marchés antiques*, Scripta Antiqua 42, Bordeaux.
Walbank, *Commentary*	F. W. Walbank (1957, 1967, 1979), *A Historical Commentary on Polybius,* 3 vols, Oxford.
Will, *Histoire Politique*	Éd. Will (1979, 1982), *Histoire politique du monde hellénistique, 323–30 av.J.-C.,* Paris (^{2} vol. 1, 1979; vol. 2, 1982; reprinted with a new preface by P. Cabanes, 2003).

1

Introduction

THE GEOGRAPHY OF NORTH AEGEAN ECONOMIES

A short history of exploration

When Léon Heuzey directed a 'mission' to northern Greece over two years, between 1855 and 1857, he was masterminding a pioneering venture on several counts. This was the first coordinated, scientific project in the region that aimed to document information about important historical locations in a structured way. Heuzey's activities were conducted under the auspices of the École française d'Athènes, founded in 1846, but his project was funded by the Emperor of France, Napoleon III. This generous subvention enabled the first results of his investigations to appear in print promptly, in 1860, with the title: *Le mont Olympe et l'Akarnanie, exploration de ces deux régions*. In the following year, he was active again in the field, with a new programme of excavation close to the township of Palatitsa (now incorporated into the modern city of Vergina), where Heuzey explored traces of a royal palace below a fortified acropolis on the western slopes of the Pierian moutains. The results of these subsequent studies were published, in collaboration with H. Daumet, as *Mission archéologique de Macédoine*, in 1876, including a splendid topographic plan of the ancient remains that he and his team had identified—the palace, cemeteries with individual mound-covered tombs, and the two closest contemporary settlements, called Koutles and Barbes, overlaid on the irregular terrain, broken by ravines, extending from the mountain slopes down to the River Haliakmon. Heuzey's topographic plan has yet to be superseded. The project in the township of Palatitsa, and its immediate environs, was one of the most successful pieces of targeted investigation in the Balkans before the emergence of modern nation states in this area.

The third quarter of the nineteenth century was a critical period in the development of the institutional background of historical research in the

Aegean and its neighbouring mainland and offshore regions. In the 1850s most of the area was still under Ottoman rule, except for the nascent state of Greece, which at that time consisted of the central part of the peninsula, roughly south of Euboia, and the Peloponnese. Research investigations in the Balkans north of the Greek state were thus negotiated with Ottoman officials. Many of the visitors and scholars to the region still thought of journeys around the Aegean as congenial settings rather than targets of investigation. Over the next two decades, both the context of research and approaches to it were transformed. The École française came under the formal scrutiny of the French Académie des Inscriptions et Belles Lettres, and its members were now required to provide regular reports of their activities. The second director of the École française, Albert Dumont, was responsible for setting up guidelines for the training and research objectives of its members, and of the *Bulletin de Correspondence Hellénique*, in 1877, to disseminate research in the eastern Mediterranean. He too travelled widely and published a range of monographs that gather documents and data from different parts of the Balkans, including *Le Balkan et l'Adriatique, Les Bulgares et les Albanais*, in 1874, and *Inscriptions et Monuments figurés de la Thrace*, in 1876. In Sofia, the capital of the newly liberated state of Bulgaria, the first National Museum was mooted alongside the National Library in 1878, although it did not open its doors to the public until 1905, in the former Buyük mosque that still forms the Archaeological Museum's principal interior.[1]

The twilight years of the Ottoman Empire were a fruitful period for ambitious ventures, which aimed to capture geographical and topographical as well as historical data. In the half century prior to the First World War, and in the wake of the subsequent territorial negotiations and population transfers ratified at the Treaty of Lausanne in July 1923, scholarly activities ranged widely over the east Balkans. Some, like G. Perrot, the Czech K. Jireček, or the Austrian Franz Kanitz, operated independently or on behalf of national scientific organizations. Members of the École française were active in the vicinity of Thessaloniki, in the countryside around Plovdiv, in the middle Maritsa valley, as well as in Philippi, Kavala, and Thasos (in addition to Delphi, Argos, Delos and

[1] Leekley and Efstratiou 1980, 69; 148 for the earliest modern discoveries of ancient remains on Olympos; Vokotopoulou 1985 provides a selection of extracts from early travel accounts and reports of monuments and inscriptions by, among others, M. Cousinéry, W. M. Leake, and M. Demitsas, focusing on the remains of Thessaloniki; Ruseva-Slokoska 1993 gives a full account of the foundation of the National Museum in Sofia; see also Nikolov 2006.

elsewhere in central and southern Greece). Members of the British School at Athens developed an active programme in the Thermaic Gulf and in central Macedonia during the period 1911–1918.[2]

Investigations of historical topography were conducted against a background of political uncertainty and periodic insecurity. The success of such projects during this period of immense political upheaval seems astonishing to observers of later generations. The two final decades of the nineteenth and the first twenty years of the twentieth century witnessed the partitioning of the former Ottoman provinces in Europe into new nation states and the emergence of Bulgaria and of the west Balkan polities that were subsumed, after the Second World War, into Yugoslavia.[3] The upland areas were particularly dangerous for foreign travellers, even in peaceful times. Insurgencies and armed conflicts disrupted, but did not put an end to scholarship. Historical investigators sometimes had access to military maps, whose precision was driven by strategic concerns unconnected with scholarly endeavours. But researchers had to have a variety of practical skills that are no longer considered especially useful for a historical or archaeological career. Heuzey's ascent of one of the southern peaks of Mount Olympos provided valuable technical information for mountaineers over the next half century.[4] Transport still retained the timeless rhythms of the pre-modern era. Travel was conducted either on horseback, or on mules, or simply on foot. Carriages were only realistic where there were serviceable metalled roads, which provided access between major towns, but most ancient sites were off the beaten track. An expedition consisted not just of the scholar himself (occasionally herself), but of a whole party of local technicians and guides, who could assist with identification and documentation, as well as informal protection.[5] The strategic interests of various international

[2] Casson provides a list of sites investigated in the east Balkans up to the mid 1920s (1926, x–xiii; Ch. III, Appendix B, pp. 168–74, with map XIX at end). A notable contribution was made by scholars and engineers in the British Salonica Force. Treuil (1996, 410 Carte 1) shows prehistoric sites excavated by the *ÉfA* in the period 1846–1919, including Pylaia, Thermi, and Gona on the eastern shore of the Thermaic Gulf, with Kostievo, Mačkur, Ploska Mogila, in the Hebros valley, Rašov on the right bank of the Tundja, close to the bend near Kabyle; Grandjean and Salviat 2000, 38–41 for Thasos; Waterhouse 1986 and Gill 2011 on students of the British School at Athens.

[3] Glenny 1999, 135–48, 307–402.

[4] Heuzey's description of the ascent assisted in determining which of the peaks was the highest; eventually this was ascertained as that dubbed Venizelos (Baud-Bovy 1921).

[5] Philippa-Touchais (1996, 231, fig. 7) shows a photograph of Polygnotos Kionaris standing beside a *diligence* drawn by a pair of horses, with the archaeologist Charles Picard seated, a horseman in attendance (July 1912, close to Maroneia).

powers in the Mediterranean region gave historical research particular immediacy and relevance in this period.

Economy and environment

Economies, historical or contemporary, involve the manipulation or transformation of material resource. Economic activities also have non-material dimensions, in terms of expertise and technical skills, but these do not exist in isolation. In the remote past, skills were intimately connected with the processing and exchange of commodities. In the second half of the first millennium BC, the range of natural resources exploited in the Balkans—cereals, market gardening, stock rearing, mining, clay extraction for pottery and brick making; leather and other animal by-products; textiles and woodwork, as well as a wide range of foodstuffs—expanded and developed on a considerable scale. These activities built on, and ramified from, the practices of earlier prehistory. The consequences of what took place in the first millennium BC were of critical importance for the economic architecture of early Medieval Europe. Byzantion emerged as a key hub of east Mediterranean trade in the final three centuries of the first millennium BC, reinforcing the north–south trajectory of traffic between southern Europe and the wider Mediterranean, as well as acting as the bridge between Europe and Asia.

Most of this economic activity in the remote past was virtually unknown in the late nineteenth and early twentieth century, when the first systematic investigations of the region's early history effectively began. References to the mines and timber resources of Macedon and Thrace were familiar to readers of Herodotus and Thucydides, and the early fourth-century BC inscription from Olynthos, according to which the Macedonian king Amyntas III affirmed the rights of local Chalkidians to export timber as part of a mutual alliance, was published in 1883.[6] The investigation of Olynthos itself did not begin until the late 1920s and study of the Chalkidian peninsula as a whole has had to wait until the final decades of the twentieth century.

[6] The Thasians drew 80 talents a year from the mine at Skapte Hyle/Syle (Hdt. 6.46.3); the miners of Mount Pangaion were the Satrai, the Pieres, and Odomantoi (Hdt. 7.110, 111, 112–13). The Athenian tyrant Peisistratos took an interest in the mining activities of the area (Ar. *Ath. Pol.* 15.2). The lucrative potential of the mines, and the timber resources of the upland zone, were among the motives behind the Athenian siege of Thasos (Thuc. I.100.2). Thuc. 2.97 for the revenues of the Odrysian kings; alliance of Amyntas III and the Chalcidians: SIG^3 135; Hatzopoulos 1996, II, I; RO 12 (dated 390s–380s BC); Millett 2010, 472–5. Mining resources are discussed in more detail in Ch. 4.

Without close geographical knowledge, any study of economies is bound to be deficient. We need not just to see and comprehend how people in the remote past perceived their environment and utilized what they saw, either for their own use, or for exchange with others. We also need to have some means of evaluating how these transformations operated in space and time; how clay and stone and ores were transformed into bricks, masonry, and metal; which commodities moved by mule and cart to the nearest locality, and which travelled for weeks because they had special value. None of these mechanistic simulations is particularly meaningful unless we take a further step and try to discover why so much human effort was devoted to the cultural manifestations that give the east Balkan regions their distinctive historical character. The environment that we discover, as twenty-first-century observers, was structured through a symbiosis between peoples and their landscapes. This is why Heuzey's grand publications, which marry contours with monumental remains and living communities, still have lasting value.

Since the demise of the Ottoman Empire, the east Balkan region has been trisected by modern state boundaries. The area that constitutes the focus of this book has therefore been explored, by modern scholars, within three different cultural environments (four if we include the FYROM); three or more independent institutional frameworks, operating, for much of the last century, under starkly differing ideological regimes. Until comparatively recently, these regimes constituted separate, virtually vacuum-sealed academic traditions, publishing research in different languages and journals, preoccupied with quite distinct abstract problems, whose direction and colouring was shaped by national Academies of Sciences and national research programmes. The administrative district of Macedonia was incorporated into the Greek state only in 1913, Thrace in 1923. Field research along this coastal strip of the north Aegean has caught up with other parts of Greece only since the 1980s. Mapping of the kind undertaken by Heuzey was resource-intensive and gave way, during the twentieth century, to more geographically restricted projects. In Bulgaria the energetic studies of the early 1900s, expanding over the next half century, were succeeded in the 1950s by new trends, which drew archaeologists and ancient historians away from topographically orientated fieldwork to theoretically inspired approaches, influenced by Soviet historical materialism. The project to map the country's archaeological sites, set out in a programmatic statement by the participants in a national Conference of Archaeological Societies in 1913, generated a series of volumes until the 1960s, then languished, until it was reinstated in a considerably updated form during the 1990s.[7] The Greek local historical societies, whose conscientious accumulation of inscribed stones and other historical remains formed the nucleus of civic museums in the twentieth century, have lacked the institutional capacity to undertake significant topographical projects outside urban centres.[8] Such initiatives seem even less likely today, at a time of economic crisis, than they did a few decades ago.

THE END OF A ROYAL ECONOMY

When Perseus, king of Macedonia, was defeated in open battle towards the end of June 168 BC, the Roman state effectively acquired the power to do with his realm, and with a plethora of Macedonian dependencies, what it wished. By this artless device, the Romans and their Italian allies levered themselves into a permanent footing on the Greek mainland.[9] Until that time, Roman legions or naval ships, and Italian or other allied troops, had been sent on campaign to support specific, short-term political objectives—as well as a vestigial protectorate along the coastline of southern Illyria and northern Epiros, a narrow toe-hold on the Adriatic coast. The victory at Pydna gave the Roman side an unrivalled negotiating advantage. The rules of engagement changed suddenly and dramatically.

There may have been no Italian soldiers stationed in Greece, and no formal or official presence. Yet inter-state decisions were no longer made without the approval of the Roman state. Roman intervention in the administration and internal affairs of the Balkan peninsula over the course of the second century BC provides an unusual opportunity to look closely at the anatomy of this well-watered, generously populated and resourced region. The importance of this juncture in the expansion of Roman power across the eastern Mediterranean attracted responses and reflections from a variety of ancient authors and modern scholarship has accorded it equal prominence. The spotlight of Roman political action soon moved elsewhere, but the concentration of many kinds of evidence, and the unusual conjunction of very different viewpoints, makes this an unrivalled chance to see behind the veil of inter-state preoccupations to the way of life of societies that are at once very

[7] Domaradzki 2005, 261. [8] Loukopoulou 1989, 27–38.

[9] Eckstein 2010, 567–8 and n.3, discusses the Roman understanding of 'empire' *c.*150 BC; cf. also Champion 2007.

much part of what we consider the classical heritage of antiquity and, at the same time, remain enigmatically mysterious.

The extraordinary material world of ancient cultures around the north Aegean shores has shown that these societies enjoyed many of the same traditions as their more southerly counterparts in central and southern Greece. There are many similarities in cult practices, in the athletic and military training of young men, and in farming practices and other forms of subsistence. There are also significant differences, particularly noticeable, to modern eyes at least, in the special treatment of certain members of society after death; and in some forms of social organization, which valued individual leadership and provided institutional mechanisms for identifying leaders, who also had a less immediately apparent but evidently substantive role in ritual. The special training for leadership within these societies is often seen, in modern political analyses, as an autocratic tendency,[10] perhaps because our own societies have been much preoccupied with the failings of leadership, in times when social forms have become remarkably complex. Aside from the rhetoric induced by political disputes, there certainly are some grounds for thinking that the rulers of the north were seen by their contemporaries in other parts of Greece as exceptionally powerful individuals. Such kings could send letters to Greek cities and expect action in return.[11]

Yet the forms of leadership that emerged in the north-east Balkans provided the foundations of the Successor kingdoms of Alexander the Great's realm—arguably among the most successful kingdoms of pre-modern times, since they lasted not only for the three centuries leading up to the Roman Empire, but laid the institutional foundations of the eastern provinces up until the Ottoman conquests.

There is another aspect of leadership in the north-east Balkans that has received less attention, namely the ability to coordinate complex functions. The ancient kingdoms of the Balkans encompassed irregular terrain—mountains draped in thick, impassable forests; distant plains; waterlogged and alluvial coastlines. This topography was hard to exploit effectively without a clearly coordinated set of organizational structures. Historians draw attention to the timber and mineral deposits of the Chalkidic peninsula, of Aegean Thrace or of lower Macedonia. Even today it is far from easy to exploit these resources without systematic planning and coordination. Maps all too easily disguise what the traveller discovers at his or her cost—steep, tortuous roads, rocky, precipitous

[10] Errington 1990, 4–5; *HM II*, 160, 162; Mari 2002, 49 with further refs.

[11] On royal letters see now the volume edited by Yivtach-Firanko, esp. the contributions by Ceccarelli and Harris (see Harris forthcoming).

terrain, and inaccessible coastlines. The valuable timber, mineral, and plant resources could not be accessed without developing a partnership; but coordination was hard to achieve without pyramidal social structures.

What made these kingdoms attractive to ambitious Italian merchants from the second century BC onwards was indigenous success in exploiting these resources, so clearly apparent in the generous provision of gilding, silver ornament, and other decorative elaborations of military apparel. If the conquerors could decapitate the apex of the pyramid, in the same way that human societies replaced the pack leader or bell-weather in a herd of animals, they could enjoy the benefits that the infrastructure of command entailed. It is the economic framework of these northern kingdoms in their heyday before Roman imperial expansion that deserves serious consideration, and what this book seeks to reveal and understand.

Neither Livy, nor his predecessor, Polybius, had much appetite for a dispassionate evaluation of what amounted to asset-stripping on a breath-taking scale (6,000 talents in gold and silver from the royal treasury alone: Plb. 18.35.4).[12] Macedon was, quite literally, dismembered. The anatomy of this process gives us a clear insight into the methods and tactics deployed by Roman commanders and senatorial advisors in order to ensure that the former kingdom's assets either passed directly under Roman control, or could be effectively diverted for later exploitation. We can look back at the evolution of Macedonia's earlier success through the social and cultural connections accumulated over many centuries with its neighbours; and forwards in time beyond the circumstances of military disaster. Although Macedonia's history after Alexander the Great is often seen by historians as one of decline (in terms of manpower as well as resources), there are other ways of looking at the evidence which explain the kingdom's prosperity up until Perseus' defeat. Nor should we assume that provincial status condemned Macedonia to economic stagnation. Rural as well as urban investigations of ancient sites (Fig. 1.1), triggered in part by development work, especially motorway networks, show that the rhythms of economic life were not so simple.

Perseus' defeat may have signalled the end of the Macedonian ruling house, despite subsequent attempts to revive it. In regional terms this was the end of one historical chapter and the opening of another. From the point of view of the region's inhabitants, it was an unlooked-for intrusion that could, indeed had to be accommodated. Whatever the advantages that the Roman authorities enjoyed immediately after Pydna, these

[12] See the analysis in Gruen 1982.

Fig. 1.1. Dion, Macedonia: sanctuary of Isis, second century AD. Dion was first identified for modern scholarly purposes by Colonel William Leake during a reconnoitre in 1806, when he noted the city's fortifications and various still-visible monuments. Léon Heuzey followed in 1855 and 1861. Giorgios Sotiriadis began systematic excavation on behalf of the University of Thessaloniki in 1928, which still sponsors current investigations.

gradually dissipated over time. The Via Egnatia, one of the great arterial highways of the Roman Empire, which began at Dyrrachion on the Adriatic coast, extending across the Pindhos range to Thessalonika on the Thermaic Gulf, and thence parallel with the Aegean shoreline, eventually joined up with Byzantion. It was conceived in the aftermath of experiences during the Second Macedonian War against Perseus' father, Philip V, when Roman troops had trouble moving overland in the mountainous terrain of Pindhos, although the main period of construction probably began in the third quarter of the second century BC. The chief purpose of the road was therefore to convey troops quickly and easily from Italy or the Adriatic coast into the Balkans. Once the road had been built, it reconfigured human dynamics within the continental area. With the extension of Roman power in Illyria, and up to the Danube in the first century BC, the principal theatre of military operations moved northwards, while administrative and commercial traffic dominated the Via Egnatia. Italian and Roman merchants, *negotiatores*, and civic officials, whose names proclaim their high social standing, are documented in cities positioned along the road, such as Edessa, Herakleia Lynkestis, Beroia, and Philippi. There appears to be a direct connection between the route of the Via Egnatia and these social networks.[13]

[13] Walbank 1985 and 2002b; Fasolo 2003; Lolos 2009; cf. also Sève 2005.

The road was of course a creation of the Roman imperial authorities. Yet its course encapsulates the close underlying connections between lower Macedonia and the Aegean coast of Thrace that preceded Roman expansion. A prior route network can be traced back at least to the road built by Persian armies under the Great Kings Dareios and Xerxes in the first two decades of the fifth century BC. The ecology of communities along this coastline presupposes tracks and roads linking settlements on the sea with those farther inland.

CONCEPTUALIZING ROYAL ECONOMIES

Monarchic 'economy' is one of the four forms of economic management identified by the pseudo-Aristotelian pamphlet [Ar.] *Oeconomica*, and the most important of the four in the author's view. This document is really a sketch of what were perceived by some contemporaries as the main fiscal tools of crown authority.[14] It is not therefore the best starting point for understanding the interplay of ambitions, aspirations, and achievements in real time scenarios. Close study of epigraphic documents has made it easier to understand how kings interacted with cities and other political entities in the final three centuries BC. Documents from Macedonia and Thrace are beginning to fit the rulers of these kingdoms into the patterns of policy exhibited by other Hellenistic monarchs.[15]

The Macedonians had a good deal in common, culturally, socially, and economically, not only with their southerly Greek neighbours, but also with their eastern counterparts in Thrace. Before his eventual capture, Perseus was apparently planning to flee to the Odrysian king Kotys (Livy 45.6). Polybius tells us that Kotys was a likeable man, which suggests that he was personally rather better known within Greek and Macedonian circles than the surviving sources imply (27.12; cf. Livy 42.67.3). The Odrysian cavalry played a loyal part in supporting Perseus' forces at Pydna. Moreover, Livy tells us that even before hostilities emerged with Rome, Kotys was (42.29) 'secretly' on the side of Perseus. Notwithstanding Philip V's invasion of central Thrace in 204 BC, both Philip V and Perseus maintained strong relations with the Odrysian princes and their kin, confirmed by at least one known marriage alliance. This

[14] Van Groningen 1933; Descat 2003; Brodersen 2006.

[15] Bringmann and von Steuben 1995, 110–85; 233–34 (Samothrace); pp. 550–51 (Index 5.1, Argeadae; 5.2, Diadochen); Hatzopoulos 1988a; 1996, I, 334–59, 361–9, 371–460, 1999b; Archibald 2010.

acknowledgement opens a new understanding of the 'Balkan' strategy of the last Antigonid rulers.

Kings could impose taxes on their subjects. We know something about the kinds of taxes that Macedonian and Thracian rulers did impose and these provide the outlines of how general revenues were raised on behalf of the central authorities.[16] Tax details nevertheless provide only a starting point. Scholarly interest has focused heavily on military expenditure. The military campaigns of the Macedonian and Thracian kings form the substance of narrative histories, so this bias is not surprising. Economic information appears only sporadically in such accounts.[17] Nevertheless, ancient rulers lacked many of the tools that have been developed since the Middle Ages to regulate the terms of loans, control flows of capital, and, in particular, to enforce fiscal policies. Ultimately, the only sanction a ruler had against a recalcitrant entity was brute force. As Philip II and his later namesake Philip V found, this tactic could be ineffective, if not counter-productive. Cities with strong maritime links could resist military attack, given the right extra-territorial support.[18] Even when vulnerable to arbitrary pressure from central authorities, cities and looser community structures within the east Balkans could and did develop their own economic networks, because of the segmentary nature of ancient trading relationships (see 'Continental trade', below). Rulers might appropriate harbour dues from successful commercial political units, a technique also adopted by Roman authorities when their *portorium* charges were similarly exacted. They did not usually intervene, however, to dictate with whom commerce might be transacted.

The capacity of Macedonian and Thracian rulers to facilitate the provision of scarce resources is an aspect of power that has received far less attention than their military, not to say predatory, activities. The documentary record is rather different for cities within these two kingdoms, as compared with other areas of the eastern Mediterranean, partly because the nature of the relationship between rulers and cities was different in the core areas directly administered by kings. In the case of Macedonia and of the Odrysian kingdom of Thrace, formal negotiations between rulers and cities within their territories (as reflected in inscribed texts) were required principally in cases where the negotiating authorities were in some sense heterodox. Thus we find Amyntas III negotiating an alliance with the Chalkidians of Olynthos in the document referred to

16 See Ch. 2 for more detailed analysis and discussion.

17 See for example the comments of Millett 2010, 472–5.

18 See eg. Avram 2003; Gabrielsen 2007; Archibald forthcoming b/.

above. Similarly, a successor of Kotys I outlined in a decree recorded on the so-called Pistiros inscription the terms on which merchants from Thasos, Apollonia, and Maroneia could operate in the *emporion* of Pistiros and other *emporia*, named and unnamed.[19] Hatzopoulos has characterized the distinction in Macedonian territory as that between the 'Old kingdom' and the 'Macedonian commonwealth'. Yet our modern concepts of Macedonian territory rely far more than we may care to admit on the seemingly arbitrary divisions effected in 167 BC by Aemilius Paullus and his Roman officials (Livy 45.29). From the point of view of their southerly neighbours, the territorial dimensions of the Macedonian and Thracian kingdoms appear to have been unstable, highly dynamic, and altogether rather unclear. What is more, when Thracian rulers were acting in close cooperation with their Macedonian peers, as occurred in the 330s, and again under Philip V and Perseus, much of Thrace south of the Danube also seems to have been aligned with Macedonian policy. This apparent ambiguity about territory means that we need to take a closer look at the nature of territorial power and consider what the relationship was between the region as a whole and the economies of kingdoms, cities, and other entities.

REGIONAL ECONOMIES OF THE NORTH AEGEAN

Exploring regional approaches

It is one thing to consider Macedonia, the template in organizational and political terms for the Hellenistic kingdoms of Alexander the Great's Successors; in what sense, however, do the other parts of the east Balkans constitute a 'region' that can be explored as a coherent economic phenomenon? The area considered in this book explores several heterogeneous political entities, which changed over the time span within its scope. In addition to Macedonia, there were several princely entities in Thrace, including the long-lived Odrysian kingdom, and independent territorial polities, including native ones of the interior, as well as Greek-speaking civic communities along the Aegean and Black Sea coastlines.

Regional approaches to the ecologies of the Mediterranean past have proved to be a fruitful way of enhancing our understanding of historical

[19] *SEG* xliii, 486; xlvi, 872*; xlvii, 1101; Velkov and Domaradzka 1994; Chankowski and Domaradzka 1999; see further Chs. 2 and 5.

economies. A number of different approaches have been pursued in recent studies. Horden and Purcell have used the term 'definite places' as a means of redefining the nexus of human behaviours within four regional zones—the Biqa, southern Etruria, Cyrenaica, and Melos—emphasizing the progressive fragmentation that can, in practice, be discerned as the warp and weft of behavioural patterns. Their focus has been concentrated at least as much on perceptions of difference, as identified by travellers, whether witnesses from remote times, or more recent observers, as it has traced the material imprint of conscious transformations of the landscapes sketched.[20] Reger has identified three separate trajectories along which regional and inter-regional economic connections can be explored, namely geography, ethnicity, and polity.[21] Historians and geographers have not abandoned the conceptual connection between regions as topographic units, and certain cultural forms of expression that coincide with these notional territorial entities. There is, nevertheless, a conscious emphasis in these studies on the complex behavioural patterns that can reinforce a sense of congruence between regions and their inhabitants, either amongst the inhabitants themselves, or as articulated by observers. Fluctuating powers, migrating groups, and graduated changes of cultural practice have served to modify the human and constructed textures of Mediterranean as of other regions, sowing multiplicity and heterogeneity. This heterogeneity has, in turn, provided the fuel for innovation and further cultural transformations. If we accept that changing configurations within a given landscape can become the subject of regional enquiry, it is evident that the boundedness of the region in question can be defined in a variety of ways. The contents of this book provide one framework, following a pattern of interconnections that is especially prominent within the five centuries explored. This framework could in principle be enlarged, to include parts of western Turkey (since the Bosporus was in the first millennium BC, as it remains today, a bridge between Europe and Asia); northwards, to include the Carpathian Basin, as well as the Danube estuary; or westwards, as far as the Adriatic. The connections with these wider territories are acknowledged under different topics in the following chapters. The justification for concentrating on the east Balkans is partly a matter of historical

[20] Horden and Purcell, 53–88; coincidentally, their Map 31A corresponds in essence, if not in the exact contours selected there, with the area covered in these pages; cf. Purcell and Horden 2005; Millett considers that Macedonia ought, in principle, to be a good candidate for such a regional approach (2010, 483).

[21] Reger 2011; cf. also Reger 1994; Oliver 2006a; Elton and Reger 2007, 13–14; Reger 2013a; 2013b.

coherence and partly a reflection of current research, which has exposed the trajectories explored here most clearly. In future other configurations may well be revealed alongside them.

The east Balkan—north Aegean region

In the case of the east Balkans, evidence for the intersection of historical with ecological and economic dynamics is surprisingly rich and varied. We may include the direct political links between the kingdoms of Macedonia and Thrace; those between individual cities; and between cities and kingdoms. Political connections are rather better represented at inter-state level than those of a more local kind.[22] More distant contacts evidently required a more transparent, lasting set of signifiers; hence the production of documents in stone, which record alliances, agreements, and the terms applicable to them. Local exchanges operated within the parameters of various higher-level agreements, so can rarely be tracked in a direct way, except by certain kinds of inorganic objects, or by the existence of routes and tracks that were indispensible to traffic. One of the single most powerful material indications of traffic across this region is the distribution of wine *amphorae* from the island of Thasos.[23] Thasian wine was among the four most widely distributed varieties in the eastern Mediterranean between the fourth and second centuries BC. Current analyses of the volume of this traffic, and of its destinations, suggests that the east Balkan region, from lower Macedonia in the west to the Danube estuary in the far north-east, formed a regular, if fluctuating pattern of recipients and partners for many centuries. The broad parameters conditioning this traffic were shaped by Aegean-wide trading relations. Changes within the large-scale conditions of trade facilitated the emergence of these regional markets in the first place and also determined the demise of this traffic in the second century BC. What did the Thasians exchange for wine? The answers to this question have varied as historians and archaeologists have increasingly refined their knowledge of local production and brought a wider range of activities into consideration. These answers will be reconsidered later in this chapter.

Modern ways of thinking about the history of the Balkan peninsula are strongly shaped by the region's organization in Roman Imperial times. Pausanias, whose *Guide to Greece* is undoubtedly the most complete and

[22] Reger 2011, 368–9; for an earlier analysis of the internal traffic of the Odrysian kingdom, see Archibald 1998.

[23] Tzochev 2010, and forthcoming.

articulate work of scholarship to present Greek culture in its setting during the Imperial period, did not travel farther north than the district of Phocis. His survey of monuments and sanctuaries, both those surviving in his day and those long gone, occasionally refers to people and places outside the purview of his itinerary.[24] Thessaly, Macedonia, Thrace, and Epirus are nevertheless rare entries. The first part of Book 7 of Strabo's *Geography*, which, according to the opening chapter (7.1.1, C289) covered the landmass of the European interior from the River Rhine to the Don and the Sea of Azov, provides a sketch of some prominent peoples within this enormous area, including Germans, Thracians, the inhabitants of the lower Danube, the western approaches of the Black Sea, and Epirus. After 7.7.12, in the midst of a section that explored southern Epirus, culminating in an account of the oracle at Dodona (7.7.9–10), the narrative comes to a halt. The later sections, which explored Macedonia and the southern parts of Thrace, are missing, and the reader must bear in mind that the disconnected fragments that are appended to the surviving sections are little more than citations of the Geographer in other, later authors, and lack the coherence of a sustained exposition. We do not have the guiding hand of a witness, who can offer a distinct narrative, providing a window onto these northern localities, whose formal defeat freed Italians from the burden of any form of tribute at a stroke (Cicero, *de Offic.* 2.76; Pliny *NH* 33.56).

New research directions

Given the fragmentary nature of the written evidence, it has been tempting for historians to limit their investigations to coastal settlements where a representative sample of epigraphic documents can be demonstrated. The difficulty with this approach is that it elides the deep hinterlands that provided the fundamental resource base for such harbour towns.[25]

During the last thirty years the enigmatic pall has begun to lift from our limited modern impressions of this region. Material discoveries, particularly the recovery of intact and extremely wealthy tombs in lower Macedonia and in inland Thrace, have generated popular interest and stimulated much-needed research grants. The new information base is not confined to the socially better-off. Environmental and spatial data

[24] e.g. the pillar and urn commemorating the supposed tomb of Orpheus outside Dion (9.30.7); cf. 6.20.18, 9.17.7, 30.4–12.

[25] See Reger (2013b) for reflections on this very topic.

offer a far broader canvas against which to make sense of the entrances and exits that narrative histories proffer. What is more, new discoveries have not been confined to material culture. Important textual evidence, including the papyrus fragments from one rich burial at Derveni, north-east of Thessaloniki, and a growing body of inscriptions in Greek, offer a rich and articulate resource independent of the kinds of narrative account already referred to.

Much of the scholarly as well as popular interest in the region has been preoccupied with the identities and cultural associations of the communities to which the material evidence and documents belonged. Were the Macedonians Greeks? In what sense did Macedonian and Thracian societies share features in common with their Greek-speaking neighbours to the south? These questions are difficult to answer, because they have been formulated according to fixed assumptions about past identities that are rarely disconnected from questions about identity and ownership in the present. Perhaps these and similar questions need to be reformulated before satisfactory answers can be produced. In the meantime, we may consider the consequences of the dissemination of the Greek language throughout the peninsula and the ways in which this communication tool provided access to a new community of cultural practices, new kinds of knowledge, and above all, a greatly enhanced social network.[26]

The material culture of the Balkans invites economic questions alongside cultural ones. Where did the wealth of these rich northern societies come from? What happened to their wealth once Roman military personnel and administrators had created a new institutional framework for the region's inhabitants? The coastline of the north Aegean and the geological formations of central Thrace contain some of the most significant mineral resources of the eastern Mediterranean that were exploited in antiquity. Mount Pangaion was the single most important source of precious metals in the north Aegean. Competition for its wealth explains why so many different agents attempted to monopolize

[26] 'For my purposes the "Greek world" is, broadly speaking, the vast area (described below) within which Greek was, or became, the principal language of the upper classes. ... In Europe the dividing line began on the east coast of the Adriatic, roughly where the same [19th meridian east of Greenwich] cuts the coast of modern Albania, a little north of Durazzo (the ancient Dyrrachium, earlier Epidamnus); and from there it went east and slightly north, across Albania, Yugoslavia and Bulgaria, passing between Sofia (the ancient Serdica) and Plovdiv (Philippopolis) and joining the Danube at about the point where it turns north below Silistra on the edge of the Dobrudja.' (De Ste Croix, G. E. M. 1981, 7–8). This process was already well under way by the fourth century BC, judging by the widespread evidence of graffiti (See further Ch. 2).

access to it. The proximity of timber for shipbuilding constituted another major attraction. The principal waterways and overland coastal plains enabled corn and human resources to be transported with comparative ease from the continental interior. The same areas were used for intensive horse and cattle rearing, and were therefore among the most valuable sources of large breeds of animal stock. Seen from this perspective, close study of older evidence can yield new information. Nevertheless, some of the innovative cultural phenomena that we now recognize in Macedonia, Thrace, and the Propontis would have been hard to identify without the discoveries of recent decades.

Urban development in the east Balkan region during the late twentieth and start of the twenty-first century makes it easier to understand what the structures of everyday life were like in classical antiquity, in part because modern development also leads to the discovery of ancient remains, but also because we can conceive other ways of landscape use that may be directly applicable to the remote past. The comparative underdevelopment of large parts of the west and east Balkans in early modern and more recent times has encouraged the creation of historical models of settlement in antiquity that make rural and ephemeral forms of community life the dominant ones. This tendency has encouraged a perception that social units in the northern Balkans were fundamentally different from those in the rest of the peninsula and islands. A visitor to the Aegean islands recognizes congruence between the indigenous style of dry stone architecture in picturesque harbour towns and the nucleated pattern of stone paved streets in ancient civic communities. It is rather more difficult to see what the relationship is between modern towns in the Balkan interior and their ancient predecessors. What would such towns have been like? Recent research suggests that although the ecology of the north favoured a rather different set of social configurations from those of central and southern Greece, the observable differences may have been much less marked than the terminology of *poleis* and other forms of community organization imply. Until quite recently many scholars assumed that classical city-states were absent from the north, except for a limited number of 'colonial' foundations strung out around the coast from lower Macedonia to the Black Sea.[27] After all, when geographers of the fifth and fourth centuries BC described these regions, they referred most frequently to *poleis* in the coastal areas and had little to say about what was happening farther inland—or so it appears at first glance.

[27] Compare the description of cities in Macedonia by Papazoglou 1988, 37 and n.1 and Hammond in *HM II*, 61–5 on the one hand, with Hatzopoulos 1996, I, 49–123, esp. 105–23; Hatzopoulos and Paschidis 2004 on the other.

CONTINENTAL TRADE

The ancient coastal harbour towns of the north Aegean (Fig. 2.2) were dominated by a commercial network of Greek-speaking ship-owners, captains, and agricultural producers providing for them. In order to understand the close relationship of the former to the inhabitants of the continental hinterland, whether westwards, towards Macedonia, or northwards, into Thrace, we should begin not with the *periploi* that trace port-to-port traffic, but with Thucydides' analysis of the interdependence between inland communities and coastal ones:

> those who live inland, or off the main trade routes, ought to recognise the fact that, if they fail to support the maritime powers, they will find it much more difficult to secure an outlet for their exports, and to receive in return goods which are imported to them by sea. (Thuc. 1.120.2)

Thucydides put these words into the mouths of the Corinthian delegates to the congress that took place at Sparta in 432 BC, on the eve of the Peloponnesian war. The people whom the Corinthians wanted their fellow delegates to pay special attention to were the Athenians, whose collective policies were consciously intended to restrict traders from Megara. On the other hand, the warning was intended to remind inland cities of the Peloponnese that Corinth was the largest and most active regional exchange centre. Whatever the precise reasons for this celebrated

Fig. 1.2. A fishing boat at anchor on the Sithonia peninsula of Chalkidike.

spat, it was perfectly possible for one state to deny another access to its markets, because commercial transactions between states were predicated on a system of mutual agreements to trade. Individual traders from a partner state could then operate freely under these previously agreed terms.[28]

We think first of all about trading agreements between Greek-speaking states, because much of the surviving written evidence for trading agreements reflects transactions between such partners. However, there is no reason to believe that commercial agreements (*synthēkai*) of this kind were concluded only with Greek-speaking communities. The Greek alphabet was used by many non-Greeks in the Iberian peninsula for a variety of local languages besides Greek, to say nothing of the diffusion of Phoenician scripts. The inland distribution of such scripts makes it clear that the received picture of predominantly coastal users of Greek is false.[29] In the same way, some of the north Aegean and Hellespontine harbours developed an international profile, which allowed traders from many different parts of southern Europe and the Aegean to conduct transactions. Kyzikos and Byzantion became the best-known commercial centres of the northern periphery of the Mediterranean, with an international reputation. Although it is hard to point out documentary evidence of transactions with the cities and communities of the continental interior, the clearest evidence is in the wide, capillary-like distribution of finds that have a distinct commercial profile. Kyzikene electrum staters enjoyed a wide circulation in the Black Sea, continental Thrace, and western Asia Minor. We know much less about its port history. Byzantion, on the other hand, was an entrepôt for inland communities on either side of the Bosporus, as well as a port for ships travelling through the Straits. Much of the direct documentary evidence belongs to the final three centuries BC. But its origins go back to much earlier times (Hdt. 4.144.2).[30] The long-term success of the network of tax stations on both shores of the Bosporus, and of Byzantion in particular, accounts in part for the extraordinary rise of this city. The process by which it began to develop its assets can be traced from the later years of the Peloponnesian war down to the introduction of the Tax Law of Asia in the first century BC. Byzantion began to develop a regional strategy in the fourth century BC, as it gradually loosened the hold previously imposed on it by the Athenian navy. During the third century, Byzantion

[28] Bresson 2000a, 116–30, for a detailed exposition of the political mechanisms and further discussion of this key text.

[29] See the discussion and detailed distribution maps in de Hoz 2010.

[30] See further Chs 2 and 3; Archibald forthcoming b/.

enhanced this strategy by encouraging the 'Northern League' of cities with shared economic interests.

Traffic in antiquity was, for the most part, local traffic. Analyses of transport patterns in Egyptian papyri demonstrate that most journeys were local journeys.[31] In terms of global transport dynamics, even in the early nineteenth century only a tenth of the traffic in commodities travelled by water, because the great majority of journeys involved short distances—carting foodstuffs from fields to barns and mills; fuel to households; livestock to market.[32] This near constant hum of carts and beasts of burden is what made more complex, strategically driven journeys possible. Those who owned animals in the countryside had to invest resource in order to maintain their beasts. Sheep and pigs might be kept on marginal land, but cattle and horses require pasture and water, and are consequently among the most expensive forms of livestock. There was little point in keeping such animals, unless they paid their way. Hiring out cattle and horses for traction or for private travel was the easiest and the most flexible way to maintain them, as commentators for many historical periods agree.[33] Whether we consider the historical narratives of Herodotus, or Thucydides, or Xenophon, or the historians of Alexander the Great; the iconography of royal and civic coins, the imagery of private monuments, or excavated osteological remains, the message that these sources convey is clear. Horses and cattle were highly prominent in the economies of Macedonia and Thrace. They provided these societies with resources in transport and communications that their less well-endowed neighbours could not, indeed did not compete with.

The focus of this book is not on a single political entity or kingdom, but on a network of socially and politically interdependent and interlinked units. The kingdom of Macedonia under the Argead and Antigonid dynasties was politically and culturally orientated not only to its southern neighbours but also north-eastwards, towards Thrace, the Propontis and Black Sea coastline. Argead Macedonian and Odrysian Thracian rulers competed for influence along the Aegean littoral, the principal harbours of which were dominated by wealthy families of merchants and landowners whose primary affiliations were overseas. The affairs of these port cities, and of offshore islands such as Thasos and Samothrace, became deeply engaged with their continental hinterlands. Whilst stressing their pedigree

[31] Adams 2007, 103–4, 119–95; Adams 2012, 218–40.

[32] Archibald (forthcoming a/), citing Braudel 1982, 350–2 on road traffic volumes in Europe between 1800 and the 1820s.

[33] Adams 2007, 281–2, 287–9; cf. Chandezon 2005.

as offshoots from major civic centres in Aegean Greece, these ports conducted close trading relations with their continental neighbours, many of whom spoke local dialects or languages unrelated to Greek. There may well have been a greater degree of shared vocabulary between these communities, particularly along the coastal lowlands, as a result of long-term cultural communication and commodity exchange. Greek was the *lingua franca* of commerce in the region, and those engaged in commerce are likely to have been Greek speakers, whether as bilingual or multilingual agents. There was a stronger incentive for non-Greek speakers to learn Greek than the other way around. This might also explain why the civic histories in these ports seem to reflect little of the commercial activity that is so evident in their material culture and in the tastes and preferences of their non-Greek neighbours. Monoglot Greeks living or working in the port towns had to negotiate with non-Greek speakers through interpreters. This was the experience of Xenophon, who, as an Athenian mercenary captain of a Peloponnesian army, gives a unique insight into the busy comings and goings of Thracian regional administrators and opportunistic commercial travellers, as well as of soldiers of fortune.[34]

A LEARNED QUARTET: MICHAEL ROSTOVTZEFF, ANDREW SHERRATT, VELIZAR VELKOV, AND MANOLIS ANDRONIKOS

The Balkan region has not played a prominent part in handbooks and general studies of ancient Mediterranean economies. Southern Greece, particularly the islands of the southern Aegean, Athens, and the Peloponnese, often appear as case studies. Northern Greece, Macedonia, and the Straits have rarely been included. The inaccessibility of material published in local languages is perhaps partly to blame. A more significant influence on the selection of suitable examples has been the conceptual history of Europe, which has most often been subdivided in a polarized scheme, whether between east and west, or north and

[34] Book 7 of Xenophon's *Anabasis* reveals the permeability of south-eastern Thrace to travellers. Herakleides of Maroneia (*Anab.* 7.3.16–19, 4.2, 5.2, 4–5, 6–8, 9–11, 6.2, 41, 7.41; Stronk 1995, ad loc.) is given a rather dubious profile as a money-grubbing go-between, but this may have more to do with Xenophon's own self-justification than with any basis in reality.

south.[35] Nevertheless, the north has certainly not been neglected by scholarship. Four individuals are singled out here to illustrate the kinds of trajectories that research into the economic history of the region has taken in the last century. Each of them has played a significant role, not only in shaping scholarly perceptions of this sector of the ancient Mediterranean hinterland, but also in developing specific methodologies. These different approaches provide a useful starting point for considering how a history of northern economies can be written.

Rostovtzeff and the grand narrative

Although Michael Rostovtzeff's *Social and Economic History of the Hellenistic World* has more often been invoked, in recent times, as the anti-type, rather than the prototype of scholarship on ancient economies, the example he set of combining different types of data, epigraphic and archaeological, as well as literary and historical, continues to provide a model of the primary resource base with which historians should begin an enquiry of historically remote economies. Indeed, this has even been called 'the only way forward' (Horden and Purcell, 32). The Russian historian gave far more prominence to Macedonia and Thrace in his magisterial history than many subsequent writers on the Aegean area. His knowledge of Cyrillic scripts and of Slav languages made the source material accessible, but this familiarity also made him sensible of the possibilities that the limited evidence available at that time could offer. The problems that historians have since identified with Rostovtzeff's approach have less to do with his materials, and more to do with his conceptual framework. His economic history is couched in a political narrative, which is, in essence, the political history of a subset of the agents concerned:

> The history of the commercial relations between Greece (especially Ionia and Athens) and Thrace is similar [to the Bosporan kingdom]. Thrace exported to Greece through the colonies of the Euxine (Apollonia and Mesembria) and those on the Aegean coast (especially Abdera, Maronea, Aenus, and Amphipolis), large quantities of the same products as were exported from South Russia (chiefly grain and fish) and of metals and timber as well. The imports from Thrace in the early years were probably balanced by exports of wine and olive oil from Greece. But the Greek cities of the Thracian coast very soon became notable centres of wine production,

[35] Horden and Purcell provide an extensive discussion, which has not been superseded in subsequent debates (2000, 9–25).

> and the Thracians themselves were from an early date expert viticulturalists. It is therefore highly probable that from very early times the exports of Greece to the Greek cities of Thrace and to Thrace itself consisted chiefly of olive oil and manufactured goods. (Rostovtzeff, *SEHHW*, 111).

Rostovtzeff assumed that the principal driver in these economic relations was the city of Athens: 'Athens supported, if not created, the Odrysian kingdom, as it had the Bosporan kingdom' (ibid.). This argument needs to be unpicked. The Athenians had the most powerful navy in the Aegean after the Persian Wars, and continued to enforce policies favourable to themselves for much of the fourth as well as the fifth century BC. But there is no evidence that the Athenians helped to create the state entities of Thrace and the Bosporan kingdom. This assumption, which may have more to do with the experience of nineteenth-century imperialist policies in the region than with ancient realities, has been shown to be the weakest part of his interpretation.[36] On the other hand, his appreciation of local ecologies, which included the native domestication of vines and the production of wine, are only beginning to be re-evaluated, with the scientific study of organic remains (see Chapters 6 and 7). He was right to draw attention to the intrinsic advantages of the resource base that was available in the north, and of how these resources were exploited, both independently and in conjunction with traders, who were in many cases Greek traders. Here Rostovtzeff's approach is most clearly in tune with the tenor of current international research programmes in the Black Sea area.[37]

Nevertheless, Rostovtzeff's was a rather complex attitude to these northern regions and his cultural interpretations changed as he moved during the 1920s from his Russian origins, and university post at St. Petersburg, to Yale, via a brief sojourn at Oxford. For Rostovtzeff the Russian professor, the Bosporan kingdom was a deeply oriental place. Subsequently, for Rostovtzeff the exile, it became a place imbued with the Greek genius.[38] Yet the achievements he ascribed to an energetic 'bourgeoisie' form the real focus of criticism by fellow historians, rather than his assumptions about a generalized form of cultural superiority that has yet to receive objective treatment.[39]

[36] Archibald 1998, Ch. 4; Archibald 2001, 380–5; Bresson et al. 2007; and esp. Müller 2010, 19–20; cf. 23–66.

[37] Bresson et al. 2007 and other contributions to the same volume.

[38] Müller 2010, 19 and nn.42–44, citing Bowersock 1993. Rostovtzeff also spent time at the University of Wisconsin in Madison before moving to Yale. (I am grateful to Gary Reger for this additional link in R's North American itinerary).

[39] Horden and Purcell, 32; Archibald 2001, 382; Müller 2010, 19.

In their magnificent and immensely erudite survey of history *of*, not in, the Mediterranean, Horden and Purcell have rejected Rostovtzeff's socio-economic construction as an obsolete relic of early twentieth-century scholarship. Their argument relies partly on a perceived contrast between his 'grandly interactionist' conception and an 'ecologizing' one. Whilst their own approach is avowedly ecological, they reject the tendency of the *Annaliste* school of history, whose practitioners have so consistently attempted to unite geographical with historical approaches, towards 'a somewhat dogmatic substitution of analysis for narrative; statistics for impressions; comparativism and methodological self-consciousness for naïve positivism; and, above all, as befits a broadly sociological approach, a concentration on the anonymous masses instead of conspicuous individuals, and on continuities and regularities instead of rapid changes.'[40]

Rostovtzeff's narrative consciously or unconsciously comprised a deterministic tendency that merges, ironically perhaps, with the geographical determinism that Horden and Purcell have criticized so trenchantly. The Hellenistic world tended to decay in Rostovtzeff's imagination, and the city of Rome reshaped the inner forces of the eastern half of her Empire to prevent decay and restore peace.[41] Whatever we think of the political narrative encapsulated in this vision, it does not begin to describe the economic relationships within the region, even for the latter end of the five centuries under consideration in this book. An economic narrative will not necessarily coincide with the kind of grand political narrative espoused by Rostovtzeff. Ultimately, his single, overarching explanatory theory meant that the historian downplayed the very components that constituted the 'bourgeois' productivity that created material success for the north Aegean.

Had he considered the productive technology that his footnotes and figures illustrate so effectively in the context of more specific, time- and space-limited parameters, later historians might well have paid more serious attention to these material developments and to their irregular distribution in space and time. As it is, the grand historical narrative of political conquest and expansion in the eastern Mediterranean has more often than not been retained, whether out of conviction, or in order to counteract the tendencies towards impersonal patterns to which Horden and Purcell allude, while the clues inherent in the material evidence have been judged less relevant. Before considering the role and significance of productive technologies, an even grander perspective should be considered than the one presented by Rostovtzeff, and on a longer time scale.

[40] Horden and Purcell, 39. [41] Archibald 2001, 380.

Andrew Sherratt's continental merry-go-round

Moses Finley's *The Ancient Economy* promoted the view that long-distance patterns of exchange were comparatively unimportant within the economies of ancient Mediterranean societies. The down-playing of distant exchanges as macro-economic drivers was an argument that mirrored Finley's insistence on social structure as the fundamental operating mechanism of ancient economies.[42] A quarter of a century ago, Finley's low evaluation of material production and exchange seemed convincing to ancient historians, whose theoretical ideas were drawn primarily from cognate work in medieval and early modern history, and not from archaeology or indeed from economics.[43] Discussions of material production and distribution were thus dominated by the 'primitive' nature of agricultural practices; the difficulties of transportation; and the low levels of urban growth (excepting a few large cities), which limited both mechanical production and consumption. Moreover, concern for status discouraged investment, according to this view. The editors and many of the contributors to the new *Cambridge Economic History of the Greco-Roman World* have set out to show that Finley's preoccupation with social status simply avoided fundamental questions about production. This new synthesis encapsulates the emphasis in much recent research not only on per capita growth in the pre-Roman as well as the Roman Imperial Mediterranean world, but also on the nature of demand and patterns of consumption.[44] Although the ghost of Finley still stalks historical narratives,[45] approaches to ancient economies have developed in directions that render the old obsession with 'primitivist' (or substantivist) and 'modernist' credentials no longer relevant. The notion that historians should be obliged either to assume that ancient economies were deeply and fundamentally different from those of later periods, or that they were somehow analogous to more recent times, short-circuits any attempt to understand the dynamics of long-term change and the distinctiveness of specific historical phenomena. Many of the tools of economic transactions that we recognize today, including deeds of sale,

[42] Finley 1985, 44–61, 65–94, 185–6, 177–8 on distance trade; see the Introduction by I. Morris, xx–xxiii; xxviii–xxxi.

[43] Hopkins 1983, xi–xii; reproduced in *CEHGRW*, 4, in order to illustrate the contrast between the Finleyan position and these editors' own views.

[44] *CEHGRW*, esp. 3–6; the nexus between supply and demand is examined most closely by M. Dietler (258–76), A. Möller (362–84), N. Morley (570–91), and W. Jongman (592–618); cf. Bowman and Wilson 2009, 23–60, 213–65.

[45] Andreau 2010, 21.

contracts, loans, bank deposit accounts, and various kinds of taxes, were widespread within the time span examined here. But that rather broad reference frame is where any analogy with more recent times ends.

The conceptual difficulties encountered by historians are rather deeper than what may appear to contemporary onlookers as a minor ideological diversion amongst scholars of equally remote times, whether students of classical antiquity, or the Eurasian Middle Ages. As financial systems in the Atlantic world have seemed to falter alarmingly since 2008, the need for historical perspective has become imperative. Historical memory has acquired a relevance that has often been lacking in conventional analyses of contemporary financial systems.[46] What is less clear is the depth of time that may be relevant for understanding the relationship between present and past economic phenomena. Since the eighteenth-century Enlightenment, politicians, writers, and economists, as well as historians, have used examples from classical antiquity to draw very different conclusions about the relationship between the modern world and its antecedents. The observations of Jean Jacques Rousseau, Karl Marx, and Friedrich Nietzsche, about the value or otherwise of confronting the ancient past with their own eras, could not be more starkly different.[47] One of the reasons why it was possible for commentators to take such different positions was the fact that individual aspects of past economies, whether the existence of slavery, or the extraordinarily creative character of artistic production, were features of classical antiquity considered largely in isolation from other economic phenomena. Karl Marx likened ancient slavery to the 'plantation economy' of the antebellum United States rather than with early modern Europe.[48] This admission shows that nineteenth- and early twentieth-century historians found it difficult to locate ancient slaves into a formal theoretical framework that would help contemporary readers to differentiate between ancient and more recent forms of slavery. Ancient slaves in many cases enjoyed a social intimacy with free men and women that was wholly different from more recent forms of enforced servitude. If we want to think about the significance of slavery within the wider economy, then

[46] Cf. Ferguson 2008, 362: 'When we withdraw banknotes from automated telling machines, or invest portions of our monthly salaries in bonds and stocks, or insure our cars, or remortgage our homes, or renounce home bias in favour of emerging markets, we are entering into transactions with many historical antecedents.'

[47] Morley 2009, 31–9 (on David Ricardo and early modern economists); 50–4, 66–9, 123 (Jean-Jacques Rousseau); 39–44, 146–8, 150–6 (on Karl Marx); 82–3, 88, 92–6, 101–13, 131–2, 142–5 (on Nietzsche).

[48] Morley 2009, 42–3 with discussion, citing K. Marx, *Kapital*, III [1894] in *Marx-Engels Werke*, 25, Berlin, 1983, 795.

slave labour needs to be integrated with free labourers into a broader set of costs and prices, since that is how slaves appear in contracts and other documents relating to specific projects.[49] So a more balanced or a more coherent evaluation of ancient economies would require an integrated approach, one that unites different kinds of social interaction, including economic exchanges.

Is such an attempt doable? After all, surviving data is uneven and fragmentary, and we still lack convincing, widely agreed methods of interpreting the data. Modelling at least provides ways of assessing whether a particular approach makes sense.[50] The outline of an integrated model, one that unites social practices as well as forms of consumption and exchange, has been presented in a series of diagrams by John Davies for the city of Athens during the fifth to fourth centuries BC, in the form of flows of resources within a topological space.[51] As the author readily admits, this model is a simplified scheme, which is intended to make the components clear and comprehensible. Any serious attempt to understand diachronic patterns of exchange requires a far greater integration of the different elements that played a part within the economy of any single community than has ever been attempted by historians of economies, recent or ancient. Davies' model does not try to specify precise chronological boundaries, but rather to characterize the distinctive features of a known historical community over an extended time period of several centuries. Since we lack, for the world of classical antiquity, the kinds of accounting statistics that are considered to provide good enough economic snapshots for contemporary economies, a long view can provide important insights that are not particularly visible within shorter time scales.

Some of the most valuable insights about long-term historical processes in the remote history of the Balkan region have emerged in the work of a prehistorian, Andrew Sherratt, a research student of one of the greatest analytical archaeologists, David Clarke, but an admirer of Gordon Childe. Sherratt consciously aimed to combine Clarke's analytical rigour with Childe's large-scale cultural conceptualizations. In contrast to the majority of scholars, who confined their research to particular sub-regions within the continent of Europe, Sherratt was interested in broad inter- and intra-regional phenomena, as well as localized ones. By enlarging the canvas under investigation, Sherratt was able to detect

[49] See now Feyel 2006, 331, 339–40, 395–438, 442–64, 509–10.
[50] Epstein 2008.
[51] Davies 2005, 142–54, with figures 6.8–6.10, 6.12–6.14.

significant changes within patterns of exchange at considerable distances, which have clear economic implications:

> Mycenaean Greeks maintained links – notoriously ambivalent – with Troy and the local Black Sea routes to the Danube mouth, and also with central and northern Italy.... These two routes (which should be envisaged as multiple-stranded chains of contacts between many different settlements and small polities in fairly broad corridors, based on fluctuating alliances rather than on any imposed authority) must be reckoned as to some degree in competition with each other, or at least as largely incompatible alternatives.... There is a repeated pattern here which is worth making explicit.... When the centre of gravity has been in the eastern Mediterranean, the Danube route has been important; as the focus moves westwards the trans-Alpine routes take over. Two crucial urban centres came to occupy nodal points where the east–west maritime trade routes of the Mediterranean articulate with north–south feeder routes from the interior of the continent: Rome and Constantinople.[52]

Sherratt emphasized that the significance of the two nodes he identified were articulated by continent-wide patterns. This interpretation effectively reverses Finley's proposition that relegated distance exchange to a marginal role. It does not imply that commercial or other transactions played a very large part in terms of overall economic activities. There is no reason to doubt that most forms of economic endeavour were local and related to personal subsistence. The importance of Sherratt's model lies in its successful integration of many separate economic entities into an interrelated network, articulated by a minimal formula of mutually agreed transactions. Such transactions may well have occurred on an irregular basis. What matters is the evidence that these patterns reveal of a continent-wide set of mutual relations, which enabled commodities and people to travel from one end of the network to another. The most visible and incontrovertible evidence of this traffic is amber, whose dissemination in the Aegean area for the south-east of Europe (as in the Adriatic for the west) is represented residually in women's funerary ornaments.[53] Nevertheless, amber is unlikely to have travelled as a single high-value commodity, but was one of a range of northern exports or commodities penetrating into southern Europe, including rare minerals (notably Bactrian gold and Breton or Cornish tin), as well as perishable organic materials, notably furs, exotic pelts, and manufactured items. The disappearance of organic remains from the material record has reduced the visibility of the traffic and the importance of the network

[52] Sherratt 1995, 17–19.
[53] Beck and Bouzek 1993; Kilian-Dirlmeier 2002, 73–5, 227.

as a whole. Sherratt could not demonstrate the political form of the network, or the ways in which it may have been protected or reinforced, but the broader cultural relationships between regions amply support the scheme he postulated.[54] Far from being marginal, these deep trajectories linking continental regions with south-eastern Europe were the essential motors of intra- and extra-continental dynamics. The eastward movement of Celtic mercenary bands during the third and second centuries BC was as much a response to changes in the dynamics of intra-continental commodity transfers as they were to political developments.[55] A web of mutual transactions and obligations linked coastal and inland settlements, which can now be examined in ways that Sherratt did not live long enough to explore, including Horden and Purcell's 'connectivity', as well as Network theory.[56]

Velizar Velkov and settlement history in the Balkans

Velizar Velkov (1928–1993) was both a product of the post-war academic environment and one of the key figures who helped to transform it. A relative of one of the pioneers of Bulgarian archaeology, Ivan Velkov (1891–1958), Velizar Velkov revealed his nascent curiosity in the evolution of settlement types in his postgraduate research dissertation, entitled 'City and village in Thrace and Dacia, fourth to sixth century AD' (1954). He studied at Kliment Ohridski University in Sofia and from 1955 worked at the Institute of Archaeology at the Bulgarian Academy of Sciences and simultaneously as a university assistant professor. He was primarily a classical philologist, promoted to the Chair of Ancient and Medieval History, and directed the Epigraphy Section from 1972 onwards. The publication of a wide variety of Greek and Latin inscriptions furnished a distinguished record in itself. But Velkov had a wider vision. In 1982 he initiated an important series of colloquia on *Settlement Life in Ancient Thrace*. This was a uniquely inspired initiative, which survived him to be continued by a new generation of archaeologists and philologists.[57]

[54] Bauer 2011, 99–103. [55] Sherratt 1995, 20–3; Vagalinski 2010.
[56] *Networks;* Manning 2011; Malkin 2011.
[57] Volumes I and II were edited by V. Velkov; volume III by D. Draganov; and volume IV by Iliya Ilyev; a fifth symposium was convened in 2010 under the chairmanship of Lyudmil Getov, in coordination with Totko Stoyanov, Peter Delev, Kostadin Rabadjiev, Iliya Iliev, and Veneta Handjiyska.

Velkov's principal scholarly focus was, throughout his career, the settlement history of Thrace under the Roman Empire, particularly the period between the fourth and sixth centuries, and the transition to Byzantine rule.[58] The range of information available for this period gave him an acute awareness of the different types of evidence that need to be taken into account in order to provide a coherent and rounded picture of settlement life. Notwithstanding the central role played by the Balkan provinces in the politics of the later Empire, historical narratives were nevertheless of limited use, whereas inscriptions offered a rich and, in many respects, far more nuanced reflection of settlement life in its various permutations. The major civic conurbations, whether imperial foundations (and re-foundations), or veteran colonies, flourished alongside other sites, whose nomenclature implied native origins. The suffixes of many place names, including—*bria—diza,—para*, and occasionally prefixes (notably the *Byzas* that underlies the name Byzantion), indicate the strength of local settlement traditions, as well as the persistence of native linguistic patterns.

The history of these native foundations was not easy to tease out. Most of the epigraphic texts were and are of imperial date, so of little use in clarifying how the educated, propertied families, whose members usually contributed to the cost of such documents, came to wield their influence. Some were immigrants, but many local men could continue to be prominent through grants of Roman citizenship. The views expressed in Velkov's publications of the 1960s and 1970s on the development of civic entities were consistent with the widespread opinion among Balkan scholars that city life, understood as the organization of *poleis* on the Greek model, was a development that post-dated the Macedonian conquest of Thrace.[59]

Karl Marx had promoted the view that slavery in classical antiquity was a defining characteristic of Greek and Roman societies. Although some twentieth-century Marxists, such as G. E. M. de Ste Croix, departed from this all-embracing definition, preferring to identify slavery as the means by which the propertied classes extracted a surplus from their landed wealth, rather than the general means of production in ancient classical societies, these kinds of distinctions were not at all well known in the countries of the Communist bloc.[60] Unlike many of his contemporaries, Velizar

[58] Velkov 1988, 139–277 with further references.

[59] Cf. Velkov 1970, 14 (= 1988, 236). See further Ch. 2 on settlement patterns and types.

[60] On Karl Marx's views on ancient slavery: Morley 2009, 42–3, 151–6; de Ste Croix 1981, 52: 'the most significant distinguishing feature of each social formation, each "mode of production", ... is not so much *how the bulk of the labour of production is done, as how*

Velkov was disinclined to speculate and eschewed theoretical exposition, preferring to explore the available evidence as fully as possible. Since his own systematic investigations ventured into the civic histories of the coastal trading towns of the Black Sea coast, such as Odessos and Mesambria, as well as into classical slavery and mining, it was clear enough to his scholarly eye that no *cordon sanitaire* could realistically be constructed around the coastal communities, isolating these enclaves of foreign contagion from the healthy independence of rural communities in the interior. Whilst he acknowledged that slavery was, in his view, much less widespread in the Balkan heartlands than in the cities of the Aegean, he was well aware of the circumstances that allowed Xenophon's mercenary army to acquire 1,000 slaves, 4,000 oxen, and 10,000 sheep, simply by force of arms (Xen. *Anab.* 7.3.48). It was equally clear to Velkov that Thracian rulers did own slaves and were therefore implicated in the process by which free individuals came to be enslaved as a result of inter-community violence (Xen. *Anab.* 7.7.53).[61] The acquisition of property, including human chattel, far from being a specific characteristic of the slave-owning, corrupt, money-driven world of Greek and Roman cities, was just as much part of native Balkan experience, and by no means confined to the ruling élite. In Xenophon's world, mercenaries, traders, small time husbandmen, and farmers, could and did negotiate their own terms, unconstrained by outside powers. So Marxist attempts to separate the organization of European tribal societies from classical (market-regulated, slave-dominated) ones, in terms of distinct social and economic features, looked rather less convincing to a scholar like Velkov, sensitive to the ambiguities of narratives such as Xenophon's.

An early Byzantine village unit consisted of a dozen or so domestic structures plus units of land that could be assessed for tax purposes.[62] This kind of village might have housed between 75 and 1,000 inhabitants. Nevertheless, many of the named historical locations in ancient written sources referred to settlements that were noticeably larger, involving populations of several thousand. Sites with names terminating in *-bria*,

the dominant propertied classes, controlling the conditions of production, *ensure the extraction of the surplus,* which makes their own leisured existence possible'. Cf. ibid. 52–7; 140; 144–5; 172–3; 256–8; slaves from Thrace: 163, 227; Tacheva 1997, 131–60 with bibliography on Russian and Bulgarian historiography of the topic; Nafissi 2005, 248–56; see further Chs 4 and 5.

[61] Velkov 1964, 125–8 (= Velkov 1988, 113–15); on mining, Velkov 1971. For Velkov's career, see also Delev 2009.

[62] Velkov 1962, 53–4, 65–6 (= Velkov 1988, 202–3, 215–16).

-para, and *–diza* frequently became civic entities over the course of time. How should such sites be compared, at early stages of their development, with Greek municipal governments? International scholarship of the last two decades has greatly enlarged the scope of discussion about 'big' sites, in spite of the lack of a clear ancient nomenclature that might distinguish a hierarchy of agglomerations by size, or by forms of public organization.[63]

Forty years ago, Velkov recognized this problem. Along with other members of the excavation team at Kabyle in the 1970s and 1980s, he could see that the material data did not seem in tune with widespread assumptions about this site, made on the basis of a limited range of literary references. Reported to be among the conquests of Philip II, there was very little evidence at Kabyle of Macedonian authority. On the contrary, the stratified sequence at the eastern gateway of the city, and the burials in the necropolis nearby, pointed to an ephemeral presence at best.[64] Most scholars, of East and West, had assumed that Greek forms of political organization and urban planning were introduced into the Balkans in the wake of the Macedonian conquests. Velkov was beginning to see that this simple explanation was not borne out on the ground. Nor did the burgeoning archaeological discoveries, at Kabyle and elsewhere, suit received or modified Marxist views, which treated evidence of classical Mediterranean culture in the Balkan interior as signs of enforced political exploitation by the ruling élite. A different framework was required for understanding what was happening in this region in the final four centuries BC. The ideological underpinnings of academic perceptions of classical antiquity were beginning to collapse at the same time as the old Communist order of contemporary politics was being superseded. A further complication to perceptions of the Balkan past came in the form of new material discoveries in Macedonia.

Vergina and the Macedonian Kings of Manolis Andronikos

When Manolis Andronikos introduced the plenary session of the Eleventh International Congress of Classical Archaeology on 4 September 1978 in London, he was met not just by a packed hall of scholars, but by journalists and cameramen. It was in London that he unveiled his most recent discoveries that brought to light the unplundered remains of a Macedonian ruler, identified by him as Philip II, and those of his spouse,

[63] See further Chs 2, 3, and 4.

[64] Archibald 1998, 311–16 with further refs; Chs 2, 4, and 5 for full discussion.

which justified every superlative adjective that historians, ancient and modern, had heaped upon the economic success of the kingdom's Argead kings. The peak of Andronikos's career coincided with a new era of communications media, which he was quick to exploit in the promotion of his academic and cultural objectives. His aptitude for communication explains both the epithets that he was given—shaman and showman.[65] The shamanistic qualities have been connected with his initiation of a new debate in Greece about the cultural role of Macedonia's early royal dynasties, both in antiquity and in terms of contemporary heritage.[66]

Much of the intense discussion of Andronikos's discoveries in the Greek press, and the wider controversies about Macedonia's Greek heritage discussed in Hamilakis's biographical chapter on Andronikos have by-passed international audiences. The scientific importance of Andronikos's research was masked, during his lifetime, by the sensationalist tendencies of his media appearances. Beneath the cloud of controversy was a serious programme of investigation. This began with Manolis's first excavations in the royal palace at Vergina under K. A. Rhomaios in 1952, and continued there during the 1960s, in association with Giorgios Bakalakis, after a scholarship to Oxford. Andronikos's first substantial monograph was on the Early Iron Age burials in the vicinity of the palace, published in 1969. A series of inhumations, belonging to men and women, provided the first systematic evidence of the inhabitants of the landscape first mapped by Léon Heuzey almost a century earlier. They revealed a population of men imbued with martial aspirations. Their burials contained a plethora of iron weapons, among the earliest iron objects identified in the region, bronze fittings and ornaments (a metal well-represented in the women's burials too), and a range of other materials, including ivory and amber, the precious stone that played such a key role in Sherratt's intercontinental configurations.

Although he was also involved in excavation at other Macedonian locations, including Verroia, Dion, Kilkis, and the Chalkidic peninsula, the principal focus of Andronikos's later excavations was the palace and the royal burials in the 'Great Tumulus' at Vergina. As the wealth of individual artefacts has emerged from laboratory conservation and museum catalogues, the nature of Macedonian élite lifestyles has become increasingly apparent. Military equipment, some of it of exceptional design, was certainly present, but the overall tenor of mortuary practice,

[65] Hamilakis 2007, 125–68.

[66] Hamilakis 2007; Lane-Fox devotes the introductory chapter to his edited volume on Macedonia entirely to the chronology of the royal tombs at Vergina (Lane-Fox 2011).

and of grave goods, is noticeably different from that of the Early Iron Age burials in the same cemetery, and even from more recently excavated interments of the later sixth century BC. These chronological distinctions reflect significant socio-economic changes in Macedonian communities over the course of the first half of the first millennium BC, including the enrichment of rural foci, the emergence of urban centres, and the self-conscious display of an expanding array of material possessions. The economic development of the modern regional units, or *nomes*, of Macedonia has triggered a vast array of new field investigations, which have produced rich rewards in research terms, much of it still awaiting full study and publication. Alongside town plans, élite country residences, and organic remains of dinner parties, a wide range of inscriptions and other written data has transformed the basis on which historians form their basic ideas about northern communities.

The discoveries of Manolis Andronikos were in the van of this river of change. The social iconography and dinner sets of Macedonia's cavalry class have strong resemblances with the material culture and lifestyles of their peers in Thrace and north-west Anatolia. Unplundered tombs, such as Tomb II at Vergina, and the quantities of grave goods that have emerged in Central Thrace, provide more information than ever before about landowners in the east Balkan region, their cultural tastes and social connections. Such cachets of wealth were not restricted to a narrow, centralized élite, but widely distributed in all regions, as the geographical network of cavalry-type burials demonstrates. Élite tomb distributions in turn prompt a reconsideration of the assumptions that can be made about forms of social control, about the nature of local community organization, and the kinds of social contacts that existed between such landowners and their opposite numbers within the east Balkan region and across the Straits.

The members of our scholarly quartet shared several common features. They were visionaries, able to make connections beyond the specific, localized evidence that they were concerned with. They were all interested in the value of artefacts for the study of long-term history. Each of them grappled with the abstract and conceptual implications of the material that they studied. Hence they travelled farther in seeking ways to explain historical processes.

If we look at the Aegean from the north, through the eyes of our four scholars, then economic relations between north and south begin to look very different from southern ones looking northwards. The hinterland does not consist simply of a narrow coastal strip, but extends deep into the continental interior. The organization not only of agricultural resources and their by-products, but equally the exploitation of minerals, and the development of overland routes, are central to understanding how the landscape contributed to wealth and revenues beyond subsistence level. Recent methodological trends that focus on the mutual interdependence of urban and rural communities, and the networked patterning of human dynamics in these historical societies, reinforce the need to look at the whole Balkan region and its Aegean coastline as an interrelated area. The chapters that follow explore the kind of evidence that can be marshalled to investigate these postulates and discuss how we might interpret the results in economic terms.

2

Herdsmen with golden leaves—narratives and spaces

COMPOSING A NARRATIVE

The limits of political narratives

Although the grand narratives of classical history, particularly those of Herodotus, Thucydides, and Polybius, refer to the north Aegean region repeatedly, on occasion extensively, the stories that they contain do not provide a ready means of understanding the socio-economic history of Macedonia, Thrace, and their adjacent coastal neighbours. Even if any or all of these authors had chosen to take a much closer interest in these areas, it is unlikely that a historical narrative of this kind would provide a contemporary reader with the sort of material that would help him or her to construct a convincing or satisfying picture of economic behaviour. To begin with, ancient historical narratives deal primarily with political topics (which might have some economic content), but their main focus was not what we would today consider to be economic issues. This is not because people in antiquity were not interested in, or did not understand economic matters; but rather that economic preoccupations were subsumed, in these broad syntheses, under a more abstract meta-narrative, involving time and the fate of states or empires. These meta-narratives have been preserved and copied, where other works, whether local histories or technical treatises, however valuable for their specialist content, simply did not enjoy wide currency and have disappeared, except for the occasional title as evidence.[1] Political narratives do undoubtedly include much useful economic material; but, whilst offering some necessary foundations, they cannot (as we have seen in Chapter 1,

[1] Clarke 2008 on local histories, esp. 181–93.

in the case of Rostovtzeff's *SEHHW*) provide a sufficient basis for economic analysis. There may be other political narratives that could add a good deal to our understanding of economic relations. Narratives relevant to the present book are the stories that explain how coastal and offshore communities developed conversations with the indigenous herdsmen, miners, and farmers, in order to give themselves a bit of longer-term security. Examples might be those about the Parian adventurers on Thasos, or the Tean settlers of Abdera, or the motley bunch of Megarians, followed by other neighbouring Peloponnesians, who set a foothold on the Golden Horn that was to become Byzantion. These stories have to be pieced together from various disparate kinds of evidence—inscriptions that overwhelmingly commemorate individuals, not social groups; occasional public decrees that reflect various institutional practices; a palimpsest of local tales, whose origins remain intractably obscure; and an expanding canvas of residual material culture.

The five hundred or so years that are reviewed here provide a broad enough canvas to evaluate the development of long-term assets, as well as short-term tactics, in a rapidly changing cultural and economic environment. In the first decades of the fifth century BC, Macedonia and Thrace could be thought of as regions, but also as kingdoms within regions. Before 500 BC, there is virtually no formal information about either kingdom, whether in terms of origins, area, or constituents. True, the major narrative histories of the period insert occasional digressions about the north into the larger canvas of international affairs. One of the most notorious examples is Herodotus' story about the Macedonian royal dynasty. In the middle of an exciting story about the behaviour of Alexander I of Macedon during Xerxes' invasion of Greece, Herodotus interrupts the narrative, just as Alexander is mounting his horse on his way to Athens, in order to relate the curious tale of how three brothers came to inherit the kingdom of Macedon (8. 137–138)—but the historian does not really tell the reader what the connection is between the story and the ruling dynasty. This is one of a number of 'origin myths' about the emergence of these kingdoms, which occupy a parallel, imaginative space alongside the demonstrably recent evidence of Herodotus' and Thucydides' near-contemporaries. The kinds of analyses which can be applied to contemporary information cannot be applied in the same way to these 'origin myths', which have a different status as narratives. The tale of Perdikkas and his brothers belongs to a recognisable folktale motif, in which inanimate objects or natural signs act as prophetic indications of future power. In the case of Perdikkas, the components of the story are a striking reflection of shared cultural motifs, rather than being historical echoes of actual events.[2]

Argead Macedonia and Odrysian Thrace emerged as neighbouring kingdoms in the second and third quarters of the fifth century BC, with parallel ruling dynasties, drawing on a range of capable immediate and more remote followers, whose exact identities are not easy to reconstruct. Both dynasties are associated with major public works at this time, including road building, the fostering of civic foundations, and even civic relocation in the case of Olynthos by Perdikkas II (Thuc. 1.58.2).[3] The Argeads were in early times associated with Aigeai, identified with Vergina, but at the turn of the fifth century Pella became the capital city of Macedonia, probably as a result of natural as well as planned relocation, and retained this status until the defeat of Perseus. In contrast, the Odrysian kings are not associated with any one specific centre, and Theopompos described the royal Odrysian court as an itinerant body (*FGrH* 115 F31), with the king conducting administration and dispensing justice at serial locations, as did many early modern rulers.[4] The social communities within territorial kingdoms such as Argead Macedon and Odrysian Thrace developed in rather different ways from the comparatively nucleated civic communities of mainland Greece and the islands, but have features in common with areas such as Thessaly, where regional administration emerged in concert with, but additional to, civic traditions.

Even this brief sketch is sufficient to show that the political narrative, such as our principal voices relate, conceals as much as it reveals. We want to know much more about the ways in which named communities developed and negotiated their resources with these new territorial hierarchies. We want to know how and why kingship was the mechanism that successfully united the heterogeneous communities within this region and what kinds of economic relationships made this mechanism work. The political narrative does not help to explain how material

[2] On the history of early Macedonia: Zahrnt 1984, 325–68; Sprawski 2010, esp. 131–4; Mari 2011a; Hatzopoulos (2003) accepts the 'historicity' of this passage, with some qualifications and repeats these ideas in Lane Fox 2011, 47; other scholars prefer to see in this story a more complex combination of tradition and renewal: Baragwanath 2008, 150 and n.81, discussing comparative examples; Greenwalt (1985); *idem* 1994; Sprawski 2010, 127–31; see further Ch. 5, for regional geography and ethnography.

[3] Road building: Thuc. 2.98.1 (Odrysian king Sitalkes); 2.100.1 (Archelaos of Macedon); cf. Thuc. 2.97.3–5 on Sitalkes' fiscal policies; Archibald 2000, 229–32; on the territorial definition of the early kingdom of Macedonia: *HM* II, 61–2; 65; Hatzopoulos 1996, 167–79; see further Ch. 4.

[4] Archibald 1998, 216.

resources were manipulated to these ends and how the material world was conceived as a canvas for imaginative possibilities. Gold was one example of a raw material that acquired special meaning. For the herdsmen who fattened their cows, sheep, and horses in the well-watered valleys of the south-east Balkans dressed their distinguished dead with gold leaf-like sheets. Indeed, gold is one of the examples of metal consumption that has a significant role in the economic history of this region. It had a social value in this context quite different from the one it later acquired when the same metal was converted into minted coins. This social value needs to be understood and explained, using approaches other than exclusively (or primarily) political ones.

A historical balance sheet

At the same time, it would be a mistake to imagine that we can draw up some kind of balance sheet of assets for a representative number of states in the north Aegean and use it as the primary basis for considering the economies of the region. Early modern and modern economies have usually been examined through the prism of the nation state. Assessments of revenue and expenditure are based on measurable income and taxes (expressed as GDP), with rather rough estimates for what cannot be measured. This is a good enough strategy for fiscal purposes, but fails to capture the wellsprings of individual economic motivation alongside behaviour. More significantly, perhaps, the pragmatic fiscal approach fails to capture the real wealth value of certain social and cultural assets, because we have no way of accounting for these in monetary terms. A contemporary analogy might illustrate the nature of the problem. There has been an attempt during the last decade to include heritage assets in the United Kingdom's overall state balance sheet. Titian's magnificent painting *Diana and Actaeon* was purchased in 2009 by the National Gallery, London, and the National Galleries of Scotland, on behalf of the British people, from the Duke of Sutherland, for the sum of £50 million.[5] The main reason for the inclusion of this picture in the 'national' balance sheet, drawn up for the UK's Treasury, seems to have been the ready availability of the figure for the picture's valuation and sale. As a report published in the *Financial Times* makes clear, the exclusion of many other material assets from the balance sheet, despite their considerable historical value, is a function of the cost of conducting

[5] 'Public sector accounting: How to treat treasures' by Adam Jones, *Financial Times*, 8 March 2012.

a complex valuation, which appears to exceed any benefit to be gained by the government from the figure that would be obtained. This reflection on contemporary material assets by a *Financial Times* journalist highlights an important aspect of historical perspectives on economies that most economists tend to ignore. For the economic journalist, the idea of putting a monetary value on Stonehenge or HMS Victory is evidently absurd, partly because accountants do not seem to know how to go about valuing this type of asset. For the historian, the long-term social value of monuments, the built environment, and cultural products, constitute a familiar set of elements in the economic landscape, albeit not as assets that would automatically attract a price tag.

Self defence

In recognizing that contemporary societies do not include everything that has economic significance within the discourse of budgets and fiscal accounting, we have an important lesson for historical economies. States and communities have a variety of assets, which include natural resources (both those exploited and those available for potential exploitation) and manufactured or constructed resources, such as transportation systems and the built environment. They also have resources of manpower and womanpower, as well as intangible assets, which in contemporary terms include licences, patents, trademarks, copyright, and other forms of intellectual, commercial, and technical expertise. In classical antiquity many of these assets (though not the more developed abstract mechanisms of exploitation) existed but were quite differently organized. States were, for the most part, equivalent to local or small regional units. In a world without policing mechanisms and international codes, the inhabitants had to be able to defend themselves. Most states could not defend territories spanning a distance beyond what could be reached by infantrymen in a day's march. If this is taken as *c.*30 km, then the territory of ancient Attica just about fits the model at *c.*2,400 km^2, with only a tiny number of independent city states exceeding this: Syracuse, Sparta, Pantikapaion in Crimea, and Cyrene in North Africa are the known examples.[6] There was no 'average' sized

[6] Hansen in *Inventory,* 70–3 for an analytical summary of the territories of classical *poleis*; Syracuse is estimated at *c.*12,000 km^2; Sparta at *c.*8,400 km^2 (before 371 BC); Pantikapaion at over 3,000 km^2; on Athens, Oliver 2007, 74–110, esp. 74–100, 109–10, for a recent re-evaluation.

classical state. 419 (66 per cent) of the 635 *poleis* or historically attested and spatially documented self-organizing communities listed in *An Inventory of Archaic and Classical Poleis* (2004) managed *c.*200 km^2 of territory or less, and 321 (50.5 per cent) of them controlled 100 km^2 or less. At various times in the second half of the first millennium BC such a territory might sustain between three and 50 people per square kilometre, and therefore theoretically between 300 and 5,000 people within the 100 km^2 area. In fact most population projections for this time-span bunch strongly at the lower end of this scale, because of the comparatively low density of people in the landscape of classical antiquity, with small population groups living in a highly dispersed pattern.[7] The main exceptions to this pattern were larger aggregates of land, which had accumulated or been merged through historical processes.

Thessaly: between north and south

The region of Thessaly is the most useful example of such an aggregate in the present context. The modern administrative district of Thessaly occupies *c.*14,037 km^2, just over ten per cent of the land area of the Greek state. The place name *Thessalia* was often applied as a rather loose geographical term, which could cover some or all of the area included in the modern *nome*, although in essence it refers to the four 'tetrads' that contributed troops to the collective army of 'Thessalia'. In this stricter sense it corresponds to the principal lowland plains, or some of the best agricultural land. These 'tetrads' were: Hestiaiotis and Thessaliotis in the north-west of the region, between the foothills of the Pindhos range and the tributaries of the upper Peneios River, the former on the northern reaches, the latter to the south; Pelasgiotis, the area between the lower estuary of the Peneios and the Larissaian Plain, which extends, in geological terms, as far as the Gulf of Pagasai; and Phthiotis, south-west of the Pagasitic Gulf. Two alleged fragments of Aristotle's *Constitution of the Thessalians* report the structure of military organization within the tetrads as consisting of subdivisions based on land units, each

[7] Fentress 2009, esp. 141–7 discusses Cosa, the well-studied urban nucleus of the third-century BC Roman colony, alongside data garnered in the Albegna valley survey (the hinterland of Cosa or *ager Cosanus*), as well as Jerba, Tunisia. The raw data from 839 sites in the *ager Cosanus* indicates 3.3 people/km^2, which might translate, if adjusted for missing sites, into 27/km^2 (p. 147); cf. Andreou and Kotsakis 1999, 39–40 (1.4 sites/km^2 in the Langadas survey) and Bintliff 1997, 3, 5 and fig. 3; 25–7; see now Price 2012. For further discussion see below and Chapter 3 on population matters.

contributing 40 cavalrymen and 80 infantrymen. This may well be a scheme introduced in the period after the Persian Wars, rather than at some time in the sixth century BC, as the fragments imply, but there are nevertheless sound reasons for thinking that a collective response mechanism, which allowed for a call-up of armed cavalrymen and infantry troops on a mutually agreed recruitment principle within the four tetrads, was operating in the sixth century BC.[8] At this time, certain leading families in the region, particularly the Aleuadai of Larissa, who are singled out by Herodotus and later authors as among the most proactive social groups, seem to have formed a focus for collective organization. Aleuas 'the Red' is the man named by Aristotle as having initiated the military 'reforms' that introduced the system that continued into his day (F498 Rose).[9] It seems most likely that the widespread consolidation of hoplite-type infantry warfare in Greece during the sixth century BC contributed to the form of collective action agreed upon in Thessaly. This may have started as a provisional scheme for mutual defence purposes, but it turned out to have other benefits in terms of social organization. Each of the Thessalian cities remained independent, having its own magistrates and decision-making bodies. What makes the region unusual is the mechanism for concerted action, which was embodied in the responsibilities of the *tagos*, the officer who acted as military coordinator. The fact that this post did not accumulate the kinds of sacred and secular duties of a monarch highlights one of the important ways in which Thessaly differed from Macedonia and Thrace. There were evidently years when the post was not filled (*Syll.*^{3} 55). This suggests that the communities contributing to collective initiatives were not keen on centralizing tendencies of any kind in civil matters. On the other hand, the combination of powerful landed families, with resources in horsepower as well as fixed property, and nucleated centres with their own self-governing apparatus, provides a useful comparative model with Thrace and Macedon.

[8] McInerney 1999, 155–85, 173–8; Stamatopoulou 2007, 315–19 with a synthesis of recent evidence and extensive bibliography.

[9] Arist. F497–498 (Rose) [*Constitution of the Thessalians*]; Helly 1995, 95–6, 175–99 (with arguments in favour of the early emergence of the scheme described by Aristotle); Sprawski 2009, 117–51 for arguments against an early date, including close study of artefacts illustrating weapons and fighting tactics; for further discussion of Thessaly and comparative material evidence, see also: Archibald 2000, 216–17, 226–31; Morgan 2003, 16–24, 79–105, 124–42; Stamatopoulou 2007, 313–37; Decourt et al. 2004, esp. 676–7, 691–707. The modern area calculations discussed above are drawn from <http://www.WolframAlpha.com>.

In important ways Thesssaly looked south, for Thessalian communities shared some key cultural traditions with other states in central and southern Greece. These notably included membership of the prestigious Amphictyony of Anthela, the body that effectively managed the affairs of Apollo's sanctuary at Delphi. Personal ties linked members of the most prominent families, the Aleuadai of Larissa, the Skopadai of Krannon, and others, to their peers, particularly among the wealthier families of states in central Greece.[10] However, material culture, increasingly visible as a consequence of rescue excavation in advance of recent development work, reveals ever more clearly those aspects of Thessalian cultural practice that link the leading families to their opposite numbers in Macedonia and Thrace, as well as to their peers in central Greece. These included the tastes for horse riding, for elaborate forms of individual burial and commemoration, and for membership of 'Orphic' cults, as well as features that are more obviously shared with many parts of the wider Greek world. Among the latter were traditional forms of temple construction, strong patterns of urban nucleation, and many of the associated forms of civic organization, including names of magistracies.[11] So Thessaly stands, Janus-like, between the world of central Greece and the north. The region was embedded in the nexus of central Greek political affairs, whilst at the same time it showed clear affinities, in other respects, with her more northerly neighbours. In later chapters, the cultural parallels between Macedonia, Thrace, and Thessaly will continue to provide illuminating evidence.

Economically, however, Thessaly was less closely connected to regions farther north in the period under consideration in this book. Time and again we will find economic connections that link the Thermaic Gulf

[10] Hdt. 5.63.3–64; 94.1; 6.127.4; cf. Paus. 10.16.8 (allegedly the earliest statue dedicated at Delphi was that of Echekratidas, of Larissa); personal ties: Stamatopoulou 2007, 316–19; 330–5 for victor lists with Thessalian names, including Olympia, Delphi, and local competitions; Delphic Amphictyony: Davies 2007, 47–69, assesses recent scholarship, the historicity of the stories surrounding the 'First Sacred War' and offers a suggested reconstruction of the emergence of the Delphic festival; Graninger (2010, 306–9, 323–4) discusses the early political and late classical or early Hellenistic cultural links between Thessaly and Macedonia.

[11] Morgan 2003, 63, 74, 87; Stamatopoulou 2007, 320–1 (temples at Moschato, Thessaliotis; Korope and Dendra, with figs 58–60; Mopsion and Gonnoi); Stamatopoulou 2007, 319–41 more generally on material culture; Hatzopoulos 1994a and 1994b, for cultural convergence in Thessaly and Macedonia; Archibald 2000, 212–33 on further cultural parallels between Thessaly, Thrace, and Macedonia; Decourt et al. 2004, 676–731 on the 76 identified urban centres and associated sites; for 'Orphic' gold sheets: Parker and Stamatopoulou 2004; Graf and Johnston 2007, nos. 25 (Pharsalos), 26a and 26b (Pelinna), 27–8 (Pherai); magistrates: Stamatopoulou 2007, 323 and n.103 for a survey of early epigraphic evidence.

with its eastern rather than its southern neighbours. These can partly be explained in historical terms and, to a lesser extent, in ecological or geographical terms. The interior of Thessaly had natural outlets to the sea along the Pagasitic and Malian Gulfs. It is true that mountain passes linked northern Thessaly with Macedonia, such as the Volustana Pass (between Elimeia and northern Perrhaebia), the Petra Pass (northern Pieria and northern Perrhaebia), and the Vale of Tempe, where the River Peneios has cut a channel between the massif of Mount Olympus to the north and Mount Ossa to the south. These were certainly used by military units as well as by herdsmen, and the ease of penetration into northern Perrhaebia may explain why the three cities of the 'Tripolis' (Doliche, Pythion, Azoros), as well as a more southerly outlier, Gonnoi, became effective Macedonian strongholds when central Macedonian authority was at its strongest in the third century BC.[12] Nevertheless, despite the political connections that brought Macedon and Thessaly closer together in the second half of the fourth and throughout the third century BC, and although there undoubtedly were artefacts and commodities that travelled through these passes, the general movement of commodities, whether in Macedonia or in Thessaly, was between inland areas and the Aegean coastline, rather than through the mountains that separated the two regions. The mountain passes were not the easiest routes of penetration. Patterns of ceramic exchange in the first half of the first millennium BC show that there are shared forms of certain everyday items, which reflect closely related technological traditions in lowland Thessaly and in lowland Macedonia, with some evidence of penetration through the Petra (and perhaps the Volustana) Pass.[13] Nonetheless, prevailing patterns of economic exchange in the fifth to first centuries BC seem to reinforce the framework of the narrative adopted here. Economic networks operated between inland and coastal districts, which reinforced west–east relations and those between Thessaly and its southern neighbours. Farther north the pattern of contacts was also predominantly, though by no means exclusively, between coastal and inland areas. In this south-easternmost corner of Europe, geography reinforced patterns of trade across language groups and across cultural boundaries, to enable those living inland to benefit from resources delivered by sea and, in turn, for coastal communities to make the most of resources to which they had no access on the sea shore.

[12] Graninger 2010, 323.

[13] Gimatzidis 2010, 272–3 with comments in nn. 973, 979, and references listed in the Appendix; see further discussion in Ch. 4.

The long shadow of the Greco-Persian Wars

Arguably the most significant events that affected the economic configuration of the north Aegean area (Fig 2.1) were the Greco-Persian Wars, as well as their physical and psychological aftermath. The presence of Persian armies and garrisons for over more than three decades along a wide strip of mainland along the north Aegean coast, between the Hellespont and the Vale of Tempe, exerted a powerful influence on the native peoples in this area. Communities that had lived as autonomous entities for centuries were suddenly and unexpectedly forced to comply with the demands of a huge invasion army and to divert their resources to this army's express needs. It was a bitter lesson in the disadvantages of being small, autonomous entities and few in number. The emergence of territorial kingdoms in Macedonia and central Thrace was one of the logical strategies in response to these experiences, although, as we have seen in the case of Thessaly, there was more than one kind of solution.

Let us first consider Macedonia. This kingdom had as its nucleus the regions of Pieria (including the middle and lower estuary of the River Haliakmon and the Pierian mountains) and Bottiaia (the lands drained by the River Loudias below Mount Bermion). As the authority and organizational capacity of the Macedonian crown expanded after the Persian Wars, so the territory under crown control expanded. To the west of Mount Bermion it came to include the adjacent districts of Elimeia and Eordaia, subsequently penetrating into the more distant neighbouring areas in the direction of Pindhos (Tymphaia, Parauaia, Lynkos, and Derriopos). It also expanded northwards, into Almopia, and eastwards, across the rivers draining into the Thermaic Gulf (Thuc. 2.99.3–6).[14] Such expansion was possible because the Argead rulers of this flourishing kingdom had everything to gain by being seen to be protectors of those who had been loyal to their policies in the troubled and ambiguous war years. In contrast, administrative control of the wider area around the eastern side of the Thermaic Gulf will have taken longer to develop. As I argue below, the territorial acquisitions of the Macedonian crown, including expulsions from Pieria, Bottiaia, Almopia, and other 'tribal' or 'ethnic' districts do not make sense unless the Argead rulers could justify such actions publicly in the wake of the

[14] Thuc. 2.99–101; 4.124–125 on Macedonian expansion, with S. Hornblower's 1991 *Commentary on Thucydides* 1, 391–2; Hatzopoulos 1996, I, 105–23, 167–79, with further references.

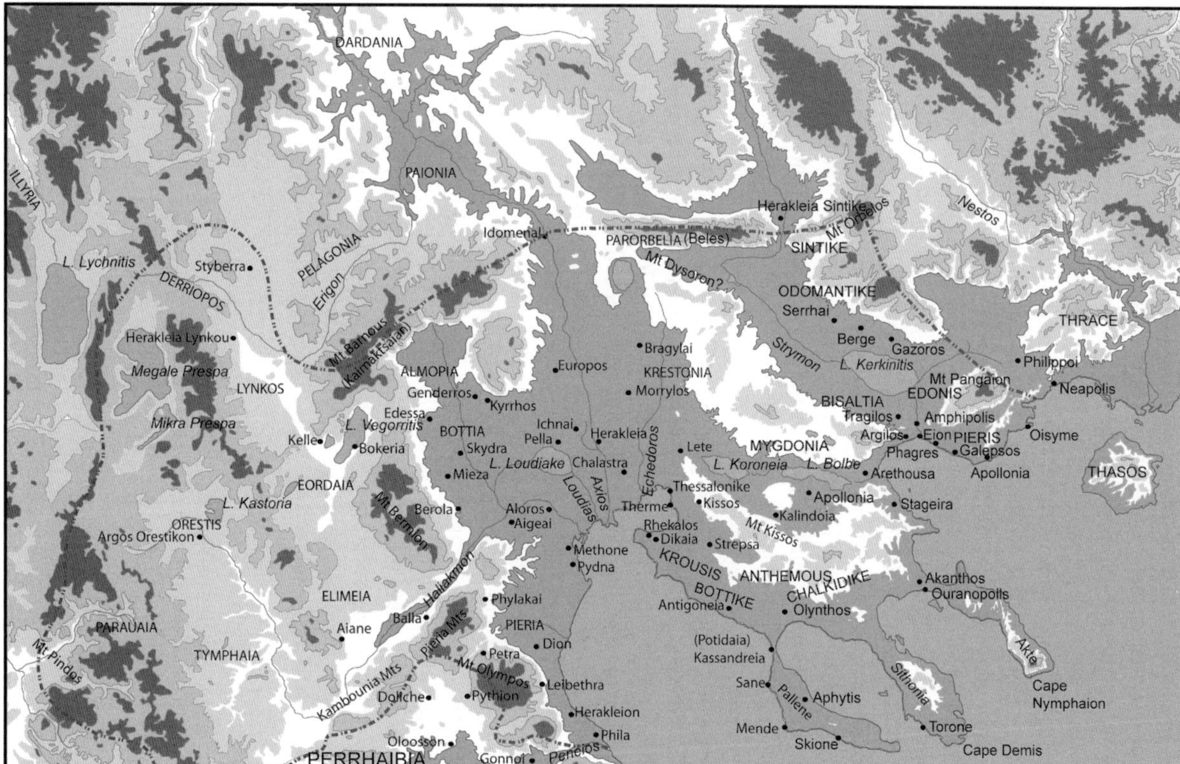

Fig. 2.1. Map of Macedonia from the sixth to second century BC.

Persian withdrawal. These were not simply acts of military opportunism, but of conscious adjudication.

In inland Thrace there was a similar process of territorial nucleation and expansion that paralleled events in Macedonia. Here, the Odrysian dynasty under its historic founder, Teres, established a substantial kingdom in the second quarter of the fifth century BC, focusing on the middle Maritsa (River Hebros) and Tundja (Tonzos), though royal power did not extend beyond Mount Rhodope at this time.[15] Initially we are ill-informed, since the political narrative of Thucydides, our principal source for this early phase, is almost entirely concerned with a highly localized situation in the 420s BC. More informatively, inscriptions that refer to formal inter-state agreements, particularly those between the Athenians and a succession of Odrysian princes in the first and second quarters of the fourth century BC, make clear that the rulers of the interior were not uninterested in the coastal zone of Thrace; they had, indeed, to be negotiated with, because they enjoyed 'traditional' rights.[16] We may not know much about the genesis of these rights. There is no reason to think that the recognition of these privileges at the time of the documented agreements was something new. Since these privileges were legally recognized, over several generations at least, according to surviving documents, the payment of money by the Athenians to the Thracian rulers is best explained in terms of economic relations. As we saw in Chapter 1, coastal sites acted as recipients and as exit points for commodities from the interior, and one of the things that rulers could provide was safe passage of goods, as well as the legal enforcement of property rights, without which the transport of any materials from outside local territory was problematic.

However, there was a wider issue as well. The demands for payment of money made by successive Thracian rulers throughout the Peloponnesian War, often alongside payments made by the coastal cities to the Athenians on behalf of the Delian League, suggest that such reciprocal

[15] Thuc. 2.29.2; 97.2–98.1; Archibald 1998, 79–90, 93–107; see further below.

[16] Archibald 1998, 112–25; Athenian agreement with Sitalkes: Thuc. 2.29.1–5; Ar. *Acharn.*145; Diod. 12.50.2; *IG* II[2] 21 & 22 negotiations between the Athenian Thrasyboulos and a Seuthes (Seuthes II?) with Archibald 1998, 124–5 and n.152 with further references; *RO* 47 (= *IG* II[2] 126: treaty between Athens and the Thracian kings, Berisades, Amadokos and Kersebleptes, 357 BC; at l.15: we read of the 'ancestral' tribute: *[. . pho]ron tom patrion*); ancestral privileges are also referred to in the earlier alliance with Hebryzelmis, 386/5 BC: *IG* II[2] 31 esp. l.9, see the discussion in Archibald 1998, 218–20 and Kellogg 2004/5, who associates the occasion of the honours granted to Hebryzelmis with his cooperation in the collection of the five per cent tax by Athenian ships, notwithstanding any perceived changes in the region that came about as a consequence of the 'King's Peace' in 387 BC.

arrangements originated in the aftermath of the Persian Wars, when there was a genuine motive for seeking protection from overwhelming alien troops. We are here face to face with the realities of the process of state formation, where theoretical arguments about the need for protection may be one thing but where tens of thousands of strangers, requisitioning food, fuel, and fodder, acted as a catalyst for state formation amongst communities that would otherwise have had no particular reason for acquiescing in the existence of a higher level of authority. Here in Thrace specifically, as in Macedonia, native communities conceded authority to those social groups who commanded a technical and strategic advantage that could be used to mobilize against a large invading force, namely horsepower. The cavalry horse was a vital strategic asset in an age when horses were the fastest form of transport and communication. Persian cavalry units constituted the state of the art until they were outfaced by Alexander the Great's Macedonian and allied cavalry units at the River Granikos and especially at the battles of Issus and Gaugamela.[17]

In this way the formation of kingdoms in Macedonia and Thrace reflected the same dynamic of community union that we find represented in the Aegean and central Greece with the formation of the Delian League. Whereas the Athenians and their Ionian allies opted for a naval strategy against the Persians from 479 BC onwards, the kingdoms of Macedonia and Thrace chose to develop cavalry resources and a corps of infantrymen who were lighter-armed than the traditional Greek hoplite. Even so, investment in collective defence required resource, and it is no accident that coined money appears in the north Aegean area in the final quarter of the sixth and the first decades of the fifth century BC.

Money and metals

This book explores the economies of the north Aegean in the second half of the first millennium BC, from the introduction of gold and silver coinages—largely to pay for military expenditure—until the introduction of the Tax Law of Asia and its striking preoccupation with the Hellespontine Straits; in other words, from the precocious emergence of coined money in the north Aegean to the incorporation of the north-east

[17] Bosworth 1988, 261–6 on cavalry figures and 74–85 on the Gaugamela campaign; Arr. *Anab.* 3.11.8; Diod. 17.57.1 (the 'Companion' cavalry or *Hetairoi*, numbered 1800 in the invasion army at the Hellespont in 334 BC; this excludes other cavalry groups, also recruited on a regional basis, including Paionians and Thracians as well as Thessalians and other Greeks); Sekunda 2010, 467–70. See further Ch. 4.

Mediterranean area into the fiscal structure of the Roman Empire. These financial measures, at either end of the chronological range examined here, were innovative economic mechanisms that had wide-ranging consequences in the whole region and provide a useful way of separating what came earlier from what came later.[18] The consequences of coined money at one end of this time span, and of a new, over-arching system of raising taxes at the other, were not confined to any one state or group of states, so it makes sense to look at the effects of money in the region as a whole.

The development of coinages does not follow a particularly logical pattern. A plethora of coastal cities, including Mende and Akanthos in the Chalkidic peninsula, Abdera farther eastwards, and a number of inland communities in and around Mount Pangaion, were among the pioneering entities that started minting coins in this area. The regal coinages seem to have begun later. The process of minting coins represents one of the ways in which metals, whether 'precious' metals (gold, electrum, silver), or 'base' ones (principally alloys of copper and iron), operated within north Aegean societies. Coined money was just one of the forms in which metals circulated, albeit a form that helped to speed up transactions. However, this effect of coinage would not have been appreciated at the time when the earliest series were being minted. So we need to distinguish between the reasons for the earliest issues, which were locally rooted, and the later strategies, elaborations, or modifications, which may have followed from different motives. Some coin series, notably the electrum staters of Cyzicus and Athenian tetradrachms, enjoyed a particular international reputation. Cyzicenes are well represented in Thracian coin hoards; Athenian tetradrachms are not. This requires some explanation. Perhaps relations between the Odrysian kings and Athenian representatives were rather more indirect than the series of formal treaties would have us believe; or mutual payments were made in bullion and are therefore harder to trace.

It is becoming increasingly apparent that one of the drivers of the production of money in the Aegean in the final decades of the sixth and the beginning of the fifth century BC was the emerging 'arms race' in the form of naval shipbuilding. Once the Persian kings had established control over the Levantine seaboard, and could thus dispose of the Phoenician fleet as they thought fit; and once they had also acquired

[18] There is a large bibliography on the coinage of the area; Howgego 1995, 46–51, 95–7, 99–100, for some introductory remarks; see esp. the contributions to Carradice 1987 and further, Chs 4 and 5 on coin issues; Cottier et al. 2008 for the 'Customs law' of Asia, esp. Mitchell 2008, 178–83.

effective control of Cyprus, and then neutralized the Egyptian fleet; then the Aegean became vulnerable to attack by Persian-led enemy fleets, as well as by land. The precise chronology of these events is far from certain, but the successful deployment of Phoenician ships, and the control of Cypriote ships and harbours, must have preceded and was certainly a prerequisite of Cambyses' successful occupation of Egypt in 525 BC. What is also clear is that the potential consequences of a Persian naval attack put those Aegean states with a serious interest in naval assets on their guard. The battle of Lade of 494 BC, in which an Ionian fleet evidently entirely composed of triremes (*triereis*: Hdt. 6.8.2–16), was beaten by a Persian fleet, similarly composed, was a key event in the development of civic fleets by a number of Ionian harbour cities. The investment by civic communities in triremes, rather than the older pentekonters, was 'a massive step-change in the naval armaments of the Eastern Mediterranean', and raised the costs of naval shipbuilding by at least an order of magnitude, as the demand for wood increased from *c.*10(?) to 25 tonnes, and of personnel from some 50 or more to 200 men, with appropriate increases in associated commodities, including hemp, pitch, and sailcloth.[19]

In the second half of the fourth century, a range of other coin types acquired particular potency in the north Aegean area. The gold, silver, and copper alloy denominations of Philip II and Alexander III of Macedon set new standards of production and volume that less powerful states could not and did not compete with. Instead, they became models for subsequent series by rulers and cities alike.

Our understanding of the connection between civic and regal coin issues on the one hand and the use of coins in commercial contexts on the other is still rather incomplete. Recent research tends to confirm the idea that major issues of silver and gold coins were primarily intended as troop payments. Yet small denominations, particularly fractional silver and copper alloy coins, were intended to provide 'small change', appropriate for market transactions. If we look at specific historical contexts, it becomes easier to see how given issues fit into the matrix of social affairs, with the exigencies of protection matched by the desire of civic authorities to benefit from commercial transactions by setting out the terms on which merchants and retailers could operate. A regional approach has

[19] The citation is from Davies (forthcoming 2013a), who also discusses the general increase in the unit costs of ship construction and personnel, citing Loomis 1998, 36–45, 42 n.40 for the cost calculation, and Gabrielsen 2008. Management and running maintenance costs, borne by the trierarch, also need to be factored in: Gabrielsen 1994, 49–50, 98–9, 118–25, 215–16; for the development of the trireme, see Wallinga 1993, 16–20.

the advantage of enabling us to look at the economic interconnections between neighbouring communities, since they were the most likely to exchange staples and raw materials, to use the same market facilities, to need each other's expertise and resources to construct public and private monuments, to transport commodities by land, and to cooperate in military conflicts.

If we want to construct an economic narrative, the agents we consider must include not just the various parties that feature in political dialogues, including the ruling dynasties of Macedon and Thrace; the coastal harbour towns of the north Aegean, the major islands (Thasos and Samothrace), and the topographical bottleneck of the Bosporus; but also the various communities of the continental interior.

Agents of change

The primary agents of economic change in the north were the indigenous inhabitants of the region. Previous studies of the northern Aegean in the Classical period have begun with historically-attested newcomers—the invading Persian armies at the turn of the fifth century BC, or the various Greek-speaking traders and settlers who had set up temporary staging posts along the north Aegean coastline between the seventh and fourth centuries BC. Here we have a major problem of information. Evidence of incoming traffic, often in the form of inorganic materials such as ceramics, has proved easier to identify and classify than more nuanced background information about local communities. Yet imports do not appear in a vacuum, since they represent one half of an exchange relationship and must be explained in terms of those who used them. Historical interactions may be better documented in treaties and written agreements, whether at regional or local level, but their existence can only be explained by becoming better acquainted with indigenous societies and with long-term changes in regional ecologies.

However, at first glance those indigenous peoples seem hardly visible. Such written evidence as survives is highly fragmentary. Only a tiny proportion of the written sources are of local origin. Even when we consider topographic information, which is the most accessible kind of data available to contemporary research, it is far from easy to interpret. We should begin with a defining example, namely the ancient city of Aigeai, south-east of the modern town of Vergina, which encapsulates many of the historical conundra that have made the study of northern settlement history, in Macedonia as well as Thrace and the Bosporus, such a complex one. The archaeological remains at Palatatsia (Heuzey's Palatitsa) are now generally accepted as belonging to Aigeai, but the literary testimonia are no earlier than the fourth century BC. Legend connected the foundation of Aigeai with the earliest kings, whether 'Perdikkas' or, from the fourth century BC onwards, 'Karanos', but the story that Herodotus gives of the Argead (or Temenid) royal origins does not refer to Aigeai (he refers instead to the 'gardens of Midas', allegedly below Mount Bermion). Moreover, all of these stories have a strong mythical or symbolic content, which makes it hard to judge what relationship they may have had, if any, with the historical evolution of the site itself.[20]

The earliest significant evidence identified to date comes from the Early Iron Age burials excavated by Andronikos. Remarkably, the royal burials of the successors to these founding figures occupy the same hallowed terrain as their early first millennium BC predecessors. Furthermore, despite the considerable chronological disparity between the latter and the former groups, the number of exceptional interments from the intervening period, particularly from the sixth century BC, is growing. There is a striking congruity between the style and customs displayed in these burials, which implies, at the very least, conscious continuities of practice throughout much of the first millennium BC.[21] As a result, one is now in a position to say that the strong cultural connections between the wealthier families of the middle and lower Haliakmon valley on the one hand, and the rulers of Macedonia on the other, do not, on the face of it, appear to be consistent with the historical-literary tradition that the Temenid, or Argead rulers of Macedonia (depending on which royal genealogy is accepted), originated in Argos. Many scholars do accept that tradition, since Herodotus and Thucydides were evidently willing to credit such stories, but the fact that early historians engaged with these genealogical conceits does not mean that they should be considered as scientifically proven. In fact the language of these genealogies resembles the content of praise poems, a genre in which both Pindar and Bacchylides composed for early Macedonian rulers, and we might expect

[20] Hdt. 8.137–139; Thucydides 2.99.3 cf. 5.80.2, accepts a connection with Temenus of Argos and his genealogical information resembles that given by Herodotus (see Greenwalt 1985); Hatzopoulos and Paschidis 2004, 798 no. 529, Aigeai, with testimonia and further references; Mari 2002, 136–52, 163–9, discusses the origin myths in the context of Philip II's interventions at Delphi; Greenwalt 1985 and King 2010, 373ff., esp. 376 for discussion of the separate putative genealogies (via Temenus or via Argeas, son of Makedon: Hes. *Eoae* F7); there is an important contribution to the debate about Macedonian origins in Hall 2001.

[21] See further discussion of this topic in Ch. 8.

references to the mythical forbears of their illustrious patrons, such as those exploited in poems for patrons in central Greece and the West.[22] There are, of course, other ways of explaining a historic Argive connection, such as a significant early royal marriage. A union between a scion of the Macedonian royal house and a distinguished Argive claiming Temenid descent would have produced the same tradition of an 'Argive' pedigree. Nevertheless, this sort of argumentation may be unduly literal. There is no need to assume that the ruling house was not indigenous; simply that it was well connected, as royal dynasties tend to be. The indigenous origin of the royal house seems also to be the view of archaeologists who have excavated within the cemetery at Aigeai, where a direct connection between the early burials and the historic royal tombs is now more usually assumed.[23]

If we now return from the debatably indigenous members of the royal house to the non-royal, but more certainly indigenous, inhabitants of the two kingdoms, they are thankfully now much more visible than they were. This is because the compilation of the *Inventory of Archaic and Classical Poleis* now provides historians with a broad-based resource, far wider in its scope than any previous attempt to map the relationship between historical communities and the territories they occupied. By deploying the expertise of a very large number of researchers in the compilation of data sets for regions outside as well as inside the areas covered by most historical accounts of Greek history, scholars can now see what has never been seen before—a pattern of urban and proto-urban units extending as far as the survey's own parameters were set. Not only can we see the historical agglomerations of the Greek mainland, the Aegean islands, and Ionia; we can also see how these compare with inland Sicily, or Epirus, Macedonia and inland Thrace, to select just some of the most relevant examples.[24] However, the enquiry that led to this compilation was in essence a literary rather than an archaeological one.[25] In consequence contributors have had to decide how far they

[22] Hornblower 2004, 180–1 on poems for the Macedonian dynasty; Pindar celebrated the 'namesake of the blessed Trojans . . . bold-counselling son of Amyntas' (Alexander I, the 'philhellene', son of Amyntas, *c.*498–454 BC) in a poem of which one fragment survives (F120). Bacchylides also composed a praise poem for Amyntas himself (F20b); King Archelaos won a four-horse chariot race at Olympia in 408 BC.

[23] See e.g. Drougou 2011, 251–5; cf. Saatsoglou-Paliadeli 2011, 272–3, 295.

[24] *Inventory,* 172–248 (Sikelia); 249–320 (Italia and Kampania); 338–50 (Epeiros); 794–809 (Makedonia); 885–99 (Inland Thrace).

[25] Hansen 2006, 33–47, 56–61. 'What follows is, therefore, about the Greeks' understanding of themselves, and in such an investigation the written sources must take centre-stage' (ibid. 56).

should include more specifically archaeological information about known habitation sites whose ancient name is unknown. The *Inventory* was intended to give priority to named Greek settlements, and the unwary reader has no means of knowing whether there are sites, albeit excluded from these lists, that could be relevant to a regional evaluation of the more peripheral areas. The progressive discovery of ever more new sites in Macedonia and Thrace, since the first forays of pioneering investigators in the middle of the nineteenth century, suggests that we should at least try to find out how many of them were significant population nuclei, and whether there are patterns of settlement in the north that indicate different approaches to land use from those familiar from more southerly parts of the Greek mainland.

Nicholas Hammond apart, historians have been reluctant to include archaeological evidence in their enquiries into the origins of the Macedonian kingdom. Thrace, on the other hand, has been studied by historians primarily as a Roman province, whose 'prehistoric' background has not been thought to have much relevance for students of classical antiquity.[26] In contrast to narrative accounts, material evidence offers an expanding source of new information that can be exploited in a variety of ways, particularly when we can cross-refer evidence on the ground to inscriptions as well as other types of written data. It therefore makes sense to begin with the material culture that tells us something substantive about the people, the herdsmen with golden leaves of this chapter's title, as well as places.

SETTLEMENTS, CITIES AND SANCTUARIES

Understanding settlement forms—*poleis* and related concepts

The modern history of the east Balkan region, as was explained in Chapter 1, has deeply affected the kinds of investigations that have been carried out at ancient settlement sites. Until the time of Andronikos's discoveries at Vergina in the late 1970s, fieldwork in Macedonia that was targeted to reveal evidence for the first millennium BC (rather than earlier periods) was limited to a small number of predominantly

[26] Ian Haynes's introduction to a new study of early Roman Thrace contains a map reproducing the principal military locations between the north Aegean and the Danube (fig. 1.1), whilst his text refers to Philippopolis, Seuthopolis, and Bizye (Haynes 2011, 6, 9–10); cf. Hawthorne, Varbanov, and Dragoev in the same volume; see further Chs 3 and 4.

urban locations. The urban landscape of ancient Thessaloniki is comparatively well known, thanks to documentation carried out by a string of scholars beginning in the nineteenth century, who bequeathed an archive of drawings, photographs, epigraphic transcriptions, and personal accounts.[27] Much of this material related to the Late Antique city, its fourth- to sixth-century monuments and extra-urban cemeteries. Nevertheless, pre-Roman remains, including public and private inscriptions, and parts of the Hellenistic urban plan, are accumulating. The rapid expansion of the contemporary city has triggered a wide range of rescue projects, which have yielded valuable data, though much of this is still unpublished.[28] The most important evidence of urban development in the area of the historic centre of Thessaloniki, prior to the civic amalgamation effected by Cassander (Str. 7 FF21, 24–5), is located in and around two *tells* (mounds): Toumba Kalamarias, north-east of the inner urban core of the modern city; and Karabournaki, still a prominent outcrop on a peninsula south of the main harbour.

The evidence from Toumba Kalamarias is still emerging from current investigations, but what has been revealed since these began in 1984 has proved to be unexpected and highly revealing. This mound, which was already inhabited in the Middle Bronze Age, was a very lively centre of high-quality craft production towards the end of the Late Bronze Age, when murex shells were used to make purple fabric dye and gold smithing was practised.[29] The latest dateable evidence on the mound is from the late sixth to the mid fifth century BC and is hard to evaluate because most structural material has been destroyed or eroded. These vestigial early classical remains directly overlie those of the final stages of the Late Bronze Age and the incipient Early Iron Age deposits that superseded them. Here there is no reason to believe in a cultural caesura such as took place in many other parts of the Greek mainland.

The low, flattened summit of Karabournaki hill was occupied from Late Bronze Age times until well into the Roman period. It flourished as a

[27] Vokotopoulou 1985 is a compilation of key texts, beginning with an extract from M. Cousinéry's description of the city, published in 1831, and includes a substantial architectural and epigraphic resource; Vacalopoulos 1963, 6–12, for a useful summary of economic and social history; Vokotopoulou 1986 summarizes a good deal of work carried out up to that date in the form of an exhibition catalogue. See now Adam-Veleni 2011, for a diachronic synthesis.

[28] Morgan 2000, 191–3; Archibald 2000, 220–6; regular reports of ongoing field investigations are provided in *AEMTh* and are summarized in *AGOnline* on behalf of the British School at Athens and the École française d'Athènes, available at <http://chronique.efa.gr/index/php/> and <http://bsa.ac.uk>.

[29] Andreou and Eukleidou 2007; see also *AGOnline,* ID828 with further references; 'complex B' phases 2 and 3 contained LHIIIC style ceramic sherds.

trading site with its own harbour installations during the sixth century BC.[30] This could have been Therme, one of the more prominent communities located around the gulf named after it. It was, according to the excavators, a mixed community of Greeks and indigenous 'Thracians', as well as traders, whose presence had a greater or lesser degree of permanency. The strong Ionian flavour of local ceramics, which are noticeably affected in form and design by imports, may well reflect the visits of Ionian tradesmen from north Aegean centres, particularly those supplying the numerous communities of the Chalkidic peninsula, from Thasos, and other north Aegean supply routes, although the same items could have travelled with various carriers. It is not easy to identify the range of merchants operating in these waters.[31]

Karabournaki is one, albeit perhaps among the most significant, in a string of coastal sites in the vicinity of the Thermaic Gulf and along the north Aegean coastline that witnessed an expansion of population into the continental interior during the first half of the first millennium BC. This pattern of population dynamics, which is connected to an expansion of pastoral resources and their seasonal accommodation within a wider landscape, does not correspond to the prevailing preoccupation among many, perhaps the majority of ancient historians, with settlement nucleation in the same period. The 'rise of the *polis*' remains one of the dominant templates used by contemporary scholars to examine this long historical phase. Nevertheless, for people in classical antiquity, abstract appreciation of the *polis* idea seems to have developed at a far faster rate than the physical concomitants, including public spaces and amenities, which we associate with the concept. 'The conclusion must be that an urban mentality and, indeed, ideology existed long before the typical Greek city had been conceptualized in a spatial sense.'[32]

The *polis* as an idea of community evidently existed for some time before it began to acquire physical dimensions that can be recognized two and a half thousand years later. A decade of intense research at the Copenhagen Polis Centre produced a wide range of thoughtful papers about the use of the term and its applications in time and space between the eighth century BC and the reign of Alexander the Great. The

[30] Tiverios et al. 2006; Tiverios 2009a; Tsiafakis 2010; Manakidou 2010.

[31] Flensted-Jensen 2004, 818–19, no. 552; Manakidou 2010; see further Ch. 5.

[32] Crielaard 2009, 369; cf. *Inventory*, 1376–1381, for lists of 'Political Architecture' and other built public amenities, where with few exceptions only temples predate the fifth century BC; Baralis 2010, 247–52 for settlement expansion in the first half of the first millennium BC.

Inventory that emerged as the Centre's crowning achievement has nevertheless concealed some of the more problematic aspects of the project's publication. The template applied to entries suggests a degree of homogeneity or equivalence about the sites referred to, which the evidence belies. Individual contributors to this tome have wrestled with intractable material that did not fit this template particularly well. The relationship between terms that often appear alongside references to *poleis,* including *emporion/emporia*, explored elsewhere under the Centre's aegis, has no place in the main compilation.[33] Although the editors recognize that *poleis* were found in many regions outside the Greek mainland, they have chosen to focus on Hellenic *poleis*, even though non-Greek *poleis* are referred to in *periploi* and other works describing Mediterranean topography and geography.[34] If the term *polis* could be applied to non-Greek sites, not just by narrative historians, but by geographers, including Hekataios, Strabo, and Ptolemy, as well as the authors of *periploi*, then the choice of terminology for non-Greek places becomes significant. Geographers were involved, by definition, in a task that demanded a more technical language and approach than did history writing, and one requiring cross-cultural comparisons that would be meaningful to contemporaries.

The reluctance of the *Inventory*'s editors to engage with the potentially broader cultural ramifications of the term *polis* becomes quickly apparent when we consider inland areas, on the one hand, which are much less well represented in surviving documentary resources than coastal ones; and, on the other, liminal regions of the Greek mainland. In simple numerical terms, coastal regions tend to score higher (in terms of the gross number of *poleis*) than inland areas (Fig. 2.2). Since the numbers only tell us about documented sites, (particularly, though not exclusively those known from ancient written records), the gross figures need to be scrutinized. A glance at the relative numbers of recorded *poleis* in different areas shows that the names are far from regularly distributed. There are 65 recorded in various written sources for the Chalkidic peninsula, excluding four that cannot be located on the ground. This contrasts markedly with the 17 that can be identified with some

[33] Notwithstanding the brief discussion in *Inventory*, 41.

[34] *Inventory*, 34–7 and 150–3 for the rationale of what has been included; objections to the unnecessarily restrictive cultural definition accepted by the Copenhagen Polis Centre (with partial but incomplete responses in *Inventory* 29, 35) are voiced by Davies 2000; Archibald 2000; Morgan 2000; Lomas 2000, esp. 173–85; for a more general critique of the narrow definition of *polis*, Vlassopoulos 2007, esp. 79–84 and P. J. Rhodes's qualifications in his review, *JHS* 125 (2005) 171–2. The final compilation thus excludes more detailed earlier discussion, such as Hansen's statement about non-Hellenic *poleis* (1996, 204), which is referred to below in Ch. 4.

Region	Named settlements not attested as *poleis*	Unidentified sites (ancient name unknown)	Named *poleis*
Macedonia	25		17 (Lower Macedonia)
Thrace, Axios to Strymon			
– Thermaic Gulf area	16+9		8
– Bisaltia			2
– Chalkidic peninsula			65 [+4]
Thrace, Strymon to Nestos	10	13	13
Thrace, Nestos to Hebros	7	8	11
Inland Thrace			6 [+39]
Thracian Chersonese	9		15
Propontic Thrace	14	2	9
Total	(90)	(23)	(189)

Fig. 2.2. Table showing comparative figures of documented *poleis* in the northern Aegean (unlocated *poleis* in square brackets).

confidence for Macedonia prior to the final third of the fourth century BC. The named locations all come from Lower Macedonia. None are listed from Upper Macedonia. There may be other, socio-economic, or ecological, as well as political reasons for the implied absence of *polis*-type agglomerations in Upper Macedonia, at least in the pre-Hellenistic period, to which I will return. Nevertheless, it is worth bearing in mind that among the 25 locations listed as 'pre-Hellenistic, not attested as *poleis*', there are at least half a dozen historically-attested sites in the Upper Macedonian regions (such as Aiginion, in Tymphaia, Alkomena, Bryanion, and Styberra, in Derriopos, Argos Orestikon and Keletron in Orestis, Euia and Greia in Elymeia or Eordaia), which, according to Hatzopoulos and Paschidis, whilst they 'did not enjoy the full prerogatives of the cities of Lower Macedonia, for these were reserved for the territorial units called *ethne* in our sources, which included both cities and villages,' can nevertheless be accredited with the higher status in other respects.[35]

A complex argument about the nature of royal administration, and of nested hierarchies of power within the Macedonian kingdom, has been abbreviated in the *Inventory* to a couple of paragraphs. In his 1996 monograph on Macedonian institutions under the Argead kings, Hatzopoulos developed a systematic rationale for the relationship between the

[35] Hatzopoulos and Paschidis 2004, 797.

Macedonian crown and the cities and territories that accrued under its authority.

The 'old kingdom', that is, the confines of the Macedonian kingdom up until the conquests of Philip II, included the districts of Bottiaia (comprising Emathia and Pieria); Amphaxitis, or the land between the Axios and Strymon rivers (comprising southern Paionia and Mygdonia); the semi-independent districts of Elimeia, Eordaia, and Orestis, on the left bank of the Haliakmon River west of Mount Bermion; and the remaining Upper Macedonian cantons—Tymphaia and Parauaia, south-west of the Haliakmon valley and extending as far as the high Pindhos mountains; and Derriopos, the cognate district to the north of the latter, encompassing the Prespa lakes and the adjacent uplands (Fig. 2.1).[36] The 'old kingdom', to use Hatzopoulos's term, becomes recognizable to historians in the aftermath of the Greco-Persian Wars, when Alexander I succeeded in acquiring new lands east of the River Axios in the wake of the Persian retreat, in addition to the nucleus of territory between Mount Olympos and the Axios valley. Both the main narrative accounts of this period, by Herodotus and Thucydides, present sketches of political affairs that focus almost exclusively on royal policies.

The fundamental problem for historians interested in the socio-economic history of Macedonia is to connect the substance of these accounts with the more detailed information that becomes available in the second century BC, through accounts of the Roman conquest of Macedonia; and in a range of inscriptions that span this rapidly changing political environment. An additional challenge is the hostile framework in which Macedonian affairs were resolved after the defeat of Perseus. The two key narrators of these affairs, Polybius and Livy, had every reason to disparage the policies and administrative achievements of Philip V and his son Perseus, and to enhance the benefits supposedly brought about as a result of the Roman settlement. Roman propaganda portrayed Perseus as a tyrant. Kingship was an easy target for the traditionally anti-monarchic sentiments of the Romans; but in addition to such latent sentiments was added the more serious and urgent pretext of sedition.[37] The inhabitants of Macedonian cities, towns, and villages were notionally offered

[36] Hatzopoulos 1996, I, 231–60, needs to be read alongside 167–216, where he develops his argument about the nature of royal and allied territories in more detail. More sceptical interpretations of Macedonian kingship and administration focus primarily on the biographies of Philip II and Alexander III, and have nothing specific to say about cities, or indeed any other form of settlement (e.g. King 2010, 374–5 and 390–1).

[37] Liv. 42.13.8–9; App. *Mac.* 11; Liv. 42.40.7–8; cf. Syll.[3] 643.21–24 (Roman decree at Delphi, 172/71 BC, a graphic and explicit series of accusations against Perseus); Champion 2007, 263–9, esp. 264; cf. also Walbank 2002a.

independence from royal authority in the settlement of 167 BC. In practice this was merely a preliminary gambit before the creation of provincial status for the region. The propagandist claims of the new imperial authorities must be stripped away if we are to gain any understanding of how these communities were constituted prior to 167 BC.

The 17 *poleis* listed in the *Inventory* constitute only the best-documented and the most intensely investigated sites: Aiane, Aigeai, Alebaia, Allante, Aloros, Beroia, Dion, Edessa, Europos, Herakleion, Ichnai, Kyrrhos, Leibethra, Methone, Mieza, Pella, and Pydna. Although much of the documentary evidence pertaining to some of these sites post-dates the Roman conquest of Macedonia, there are significant exceptions. Aigeai (Diod. 16.3.5; Theophr. Fr 5.27);[38] Alebaia (Hdt. 8.137.1); Allante/Atalante (Thuc. 2.100.3); Aloros (Ps.-Skyl. 66); Dion (Thuc. 4.78.6); Europos (Thuc. 2.100.3); Herakleion (Ps.-Skyl. 66); Ichnai (Hdt. 7. 123.3); Kyrrhos (Thuc. 2.100.4); Leibethra (Aesch. Fr. 83a.9); Methone (Thuc. 6.7.3); Mieza (Plut. Alex. 7.4); Pella (Hdt. 7.123.3; Thuc. 2.99.4); and Pydna (Thuc. 1.61.2), have a respectable pedigree as civic foundations.[39] The very idea of a historical pedigree reflects the self-conscious manipulation of community identities, a process that was continuously evolving throughout classical antiquity.[40]

One of the difficulties that we have in understanding and evaluating the kinds of sites that are not explicitly named *poleis,* or are acknowledged to have had their decision-making powers restricted in some way (according to Hatzopoulos's theory of Macedonian state administration), is the absence of any clear conceptual model for what the alternatives might be. For the editors of the *Inventory*, there is only one model, namely the 'Hellenic' *polis*. The absence of an explicit strategy for sites that are not obviously Hellenic is clear in ethnically mixed areas, such as Sicily, where there are 'twenty-nine noteworthy settlements which cannot be shown to have been Greek or "Hellenised" *poleis*'.[41] There is a lack of coherence in scholarly debates between the concept of regions as institutional units—with certain sites enjoying the privileges of constituting councils, sending out ambassadors, and concluding agreements with other, similar bodies in different regions—and the assumption that

[38] *Inventory*, 798–9 no. 529 with further references.

[39] *Inventory*, 797–806, no. 528 (Aiane); no. 530 (Alebaia); no. 531 (Allante); no. 532 (Aloros); no. 533 (Beroia); no. 534 (Dion); no. 535 (Edessa: attested on a 3rd century BC inscription from Delphi); no. 536 (Europos); no. 537 (Herakleion); no. 538 (Ichnai); no. 539 (Kyrrhos); no. 540 (Leibethra); no. 541 (Methone); no. 542 (Mieza); no. 543 (Pella); no. 544 (Pydna).

[40] Clarke 2008 esp. 169–230, 245–303.

[41] *Inventory*, 176.

only Hellenic institutions matter in understanding how any of these sites, whether Greek or non-Greek, operated in their own localities. In some inland communities, as in Sicily, or in southern Italy, and in Macedonia and Thrace, the majority of the inhabitants still spoke languages other than Greek in the fifth and fourth centuries BC, languages that continued to be spoken by a proportion of the population for many centuries thereafter. Yet Greek was the preferred language for inter-community negotiation in all these regions, partly because, aside from Punic, it was the principal language of commerce in the Mediterranean. Documents of an official character, with supra-local significance within the eastern Mediterranean, were written in Greek from the sixth century BC onwards, which is the time when documents first become archaeologically visible (principally in the form of lead letters, overwhelmingly of a commercial nature).[42]

In the absence of any strong institutional precedents, organized by territorial entities with the power to regulate the external relations of individual communities, it is likely that organizational practice in regions neighbouring Greece was progressively affected and shaped by inter-state custom in the eastern Mediterranean area as a whole. The territorial entities that are relevant in the east Balkan area, the kingdoms of Macedonia and Thrace, were institutional latecomers in the context of settlement histories. Sites like Toumba Kalamarias demonstrate that locations that cannot be shown to have been designated *poleis* in the pre-Hellenistic period were nevertheless operating as significant centres of production and exchange, with demonstrable inter-regional commercial connections, long before the term *polis* acquired currency. However we view the development of civic institutions in the north Aegean—and this process may have been a lengthy one—it had very deep roots.

If we consider the distribution of known Macedonian *poleis*, it is not irrelevant that many of the place names refer either to sites that had special regional functions (Dion as the most sacred focus of Macedonia; Aegeai and Pella as royal capitals), or operated as local central places (Aiane for Elimeia; Europos, Ichnai, and Allante in the lower Axios valley). As we proceed eastwards, the organization of populations is complicated by historical dynamics. The 65 sites in the Chalkidic peninsula include a few substantial sites, with longish histories (Aineia, Akanthos, Dikaia, Mende, Olynthos, Torone), and a longer list of rather modest place names, which happen to have featured in the Athenian Tribute Lists as named payers, but whose overall profile suggests that

[42] Harris (forthcoming) for a recent discussion.

they were decidedly minor players (e.g. Aioleion, Akrothooi, Alapta, Gigonos, Istasos, Othoros, Pharbelos, Piloros, Pistasos, Pleume). Others may well have had an ephemeral existence (Aige, Lipaxos). If we compare the named *poleis* in Chalkidike with the 72 listed in Caria, it becomes clearer that the Athenian Tribute Lists make prominent sites that might otherwise have disappeared from records.[43] Not all *poleis* listed in the *Inventory* can realistically be thought of as major towns, let alone as cities. Although in theory 'every *polis* town was the centre of a *polis* state',[44] the principle needs to be considered in its context. If we compare the 1,035 place names that are certainly or probably identified as *poleis* before *c*.330 BC alongside the 2,000 or so urban centres within the Roman Empire in the second century AD, when civic populations had manifestly multiplied, in many cases several times over (if not by an order of magnitude), then we must admit that many of the kinds of places referred to in this way were, with few exceptions, modest as 'urban' units.[45] Similarly, it is unlikely, as Hansen has claimed, that a third of the population of Greece lived in cities. If we look at comparative historical data, this proportion was achieved very rarely anywhere in the world before the nineteenth century.[46]

Greek and non-Greek sites

The 'liminal' areas of mainland Greece pose the more challenging conceptual problem. The editors of the *Inventory* admit that there were 'barbarian' *poleis*, but rather than seeing the investigation of 'barbarian' alongside Hellenic 'city-states' as an opportunity to highlight the defining characteristics that they seek to illuminate, a comparison between

[43] Inventory, nos. 557 (Aineia); 559 (Akanthos); 568 (Dikaia); 584 (Mende); 588 (Olynthos); 620 (Torone); 558 (Aioleion: paying 500dr in three separate years); 560 (Akrothooi: assessed but not listed as an independent tribute payer); 561 (Alapta); 572 (Gigonos); 574 (Istasos, paid 500dr in 422/1 BC); 590 (Othoros); 591 (Pharbelos); 593 (Piloros); 594 (Pistasos); 556 (Aige); R. Parker, ClRev 56 (2006) 382 on the relative distortion created by ATL.

[44] *Inventory*, 35.

[45] Clarysse and Thompson 2006, 2, 95: in the early Ptolemaic period the population of Arsinoe is estimated at 4,000, the *nome* as a whole housing between 85,000 and 90,000 people; the population of Crocodilopolis increased from *c*.4,000 in the second half of the third century BC to between 27,000 and 46,000 in the High Empire (ibid. 100); see now the contributions to Bowman and Wilson 2012.

[46] Maddison 2007, 42–3 and Table 1.7; cf de Callataÿ 2012, 68. Although Maddison's discussion of Roman urban populations may not be fully up to date, his international comparative data are well substantiated.

these entities is treated as subordinate to the compilation of Hellenic data. Evidence of 'barbarian' *poleis* must, apparently, be dismissed. 'Herodotos seems to assume that every Persian captain belonged to a *polis* and could be identified by his city ethnic' (= Hdt. 8.90.4); and again, 'the political structure of the Persian Empire is represented as a plurality of *ethne*, each consisting of a number of *poleis*' [= 7.96.2].[47] They reject Herodotus' way of describing Persian society on the grounds that 'the Greeks were notorious for reading their own names, terms, and concepts into foreign cultures.' Despite their reluctance to consider what social and political structures did underlie Herodotus' evaluation, the editors acknowledge a genuine difficulty in understanding what they call 'mixed' *poleis*, and for this purpose use examples from the north Aegean coast: 'the five *poleis* in Athos (Thuc. 4.109.4) and some of the *poleis* in the Thermaic Gulf, viz. Therme (Hecat. Fr. 146), Pella and Ichnai (Hdt. 7.123.3).'

Herodotus' terminology is taken more seriously in these cases. Therme is a particularly interesting case, because it was a major coastal *emporion*, and is variously referred to by different authors. Hecataeus' reference is interpreted as a *polis* 'in the urban sense', and his specific terminology (*polis hellēnōn Thrēikōn*) as a gloss for Greeks living in Thrace. Hatzopoulos prefers to interpret the distinction between *polis hellēnis* and *polis tout court* (applied by the author known as 'Pseudo-Skylax' in his *periplous* of the north Aegean coastline) as a political one, to nuance those communities that were politically dependent on the Macedonian crown from those that enjoyed autonomy.[48] Neither of these interpretations is wholly satisfactory. Both the cultural and the political explanations have some force, but either this term was not applied with any consistency, or some other nuance is required. The author who lies behind the sobriquet 'Pseudo-Skylax' was writing in the early fourth century BC, at a time of Macedonian political expansion, so the way in which he distinguishes some sites as specifically 'Greek' may have more to do with contemporary political tensions, in other words with competing bids for power in the region, rather than being a dispassionate geographical exposition.[49]

There was a time when Mogens Hansen took a different view of the inter-cultural nature of *polis* life and institutions: 'The orthodoxy takes it for granted that *polis* was a characteristic of Greek society and that in this

[47] *Inventory*, 36.

[48] *Inventory*, 818–19, no. 552 and 150–1 for the editors' interpretation of *polis hellēnis*; Hecat. F146 = St. Byz. 679.5–6; Ps.-Skyl. 66; Hatzopoulos 1996, I, 473.

[49] Shipley 2011, 140–7.

respect there was a gulf between the Greeks and the others. . . . But the gulf is rather between Aristotle and our other sources. In Herodotus, Thucydides, and Xenophon we hear about hundreds of barbarian *poleis*, often in the sense of city rather than state, but sometimes obviously in the sense of political community, and the terminology used by the historians does not convey the impression that the Greeks themselves felt *polis* to be one of the essential differences between Greeks and barbarians.'[50] It is altogether unclear why these insights were not ultimately translated into the form and composition of the *Inventory*. Perhaps the task may have appeared too complex and unmanageable, even with the large expert team brought in to put the individual chapters together.

Far from being a defining term, *polis* has become a slippery and diffuse word as a result of the Polis Centre's investigations. The *Inventory* has enormously enriched our knowledge of specific political units and the locations with which their names are associated. Nevertheless, it would be misleading to imagine that the information contained in these lists is representative of wider settlement patterns. Even in comparatively well documented areas, such as the Chalkidic peninsula, the socio-economic history of local communities needs to be understood in a dynamic fashion. Even over the period covered by the *Inventory*, some prospered, while others contracted. Beyond the coastal fringe, where Greek speakers were plentiful, stretched a landscape of other language groups—Thracians, Macedonians, and users of a plethora of dialects that can no longer be recognized or adequately characterized in terms of modern linguistic distinctions.[51] It is this linguistic divide that explains why we know so little about urban sites in the interior of Thrace and Macedonia. Greek monoglots relied on bilingual speakers for information about these areas, which automatically created a practical limitation. The fact that some Macedonian urban centres, not just on the coastline, but also inland, were recognized as *poleis* by Greek writers shows that self-conscious, autonomous cities did exist in the region. By the same token, and following the same logic, there would have been autonomous native civic centres in Thrace; this is what the evidence of pre-Macedonian urban foci indicates.[52]

[50] Hansen 1996, 204.

[51] Hatzopoulos refers to 'pre-Greek' populations and names (1996, I, 70–3, 77, 106, 182 n.5, 193 n.6, 195 n.8, 209–13, 232, 247.

[52] Archibald 2004; see further discussion below and in Chs 4 and 5.

Non-urban sites and the evolution of the 'dispersed city'

Not all large agglomerations, leave alone small towns, need necessarily have been recognized politically as *poleis,* a term that denotes significant legal as well as urban status. Some quasi-urban centres were evidently too small to be able to nominate a council. More importantly, those centres that did not have the capacity, or the authority, to make decisions on an international level lacked one essential characteristic determinant of autonomy. In Macedonia such centres were legally qualified as *politeiai,* meaning that they could own land and receive property, as well as enact legal decisions through an annually elected magistrate, but in other respects did not have the means or the mechanisms to deal with extra-territorial powers, whether in their own region or outside it.[53] Discussion of Aegean sites has focused rather too narrowly on the legally defined status of communities and on nucleated sites that can be identified with relative ease, either from inorganic surviving remains, or from some literary credentials. There has been far less interest in genuinely holistic descriptions of all the different kinds of settlement in a given environment. Most historical communities included a range of lesser and bigger sites, as well as functionally different components, including fortified towers, upland shelters, various kinds of processing facilities (around mines, workshops, harbours), and, particularly in regions such as the north Aegean, country estates, foresters' huts, and hunting lodges.

Intensive surveys are beginning to add an important and independent source of information about the large-scale pattern of anthropogenic sites of the first millennium BC, alongside Greek settlement nomenclature. Although such surveys are still available only for a limited range of locations, they provide good comparative data and a variety of site forms.[54] The Langadas survey, in the north-eastern hinterland of Thessaloniki, has produced evidence of a significant increase in site numbers during the first half of the first millennium BC, with a configuration of small settlements, alongside a few large ones (notably Lete). Sites were

[53] Hatzopoulos 1996, I, 80–1, referring to the decree of the Battynaioi (Rizakis-Touratsoglou 186, AD 193), together with the closely similar wording of a much earlier decree from Gazoros (Hatzopoulos 1996, I, 51–72).

[54] Langadas survey: Andreou and Kotsakis 1999, with further refs; Middle Strouma Archaeological Survey and Kazanluk survey: see note below; Tundja Regional Archaeological Project (TRAP) 2008–2011: A. Sobotkova and S. Ross, AIA/APA Annual Meeting, Philadelphia, January 2012 (preliminary report); Bintliff 1997 for comparisons with central and southern Greece.

nevertheless more dispersed in this rural part of lowland Macedonia, with a distribution of 1.4 sites per square kilometre. Crossing the ridge of mountains that separates the Langadas area and the Echeidoros valley from the River Strymon, surveys conducted since the 1970s have produced a slightly greater concentration of population—2.14 sites per square kilometre around Sandanski, just north of the Bulgarian–Greek border, 2.7 sites per square kilometre in the Blagoevgrad area farther north. This can be compared with a maximum concentration of 2–3 sites per square kilometre in sampled areas of central Bulgaria.[55] The statistics of ceramic scatters may translate into a range of historically documented locations, not all of which were necessarily habitation areas.

Any attempt to relate survey data with known historical place names, or with known types of site, is not particularly meaningful without some consideration of land use and local ecologies. The phenomenon of settlement mounds (referred to as *toumbas* or *tells*, depending on locality) is probably the most graphic illustration of fundamentally different ecologies in northern Greece and the east Balkans, compared with central and southern Greece. Such man-made mounds are still prominent topographic features, notwithstanding erosion over many centuries. These mound settlements, whilst being the most easily recognizable sites in the Bronze and Early Iron Ages, were by no means the only kinds of site identified from these periods, as rescue archaeology and intensive surveys have shown. Since the summits of these mounds are often eroded, leaving few clear traces of continuity into historical times, and there are usually few traces of related activity in their immediate vicinity, the challenge for researchers has been to try and understand how such compact, conservative patterns of community organization evolved into new organizational structures during the first half of the first millennium BC, and how these new forms of collective organization relate to the urban patterns discernible from the sixth century BC onwards. This challenge applies as much to inland and Aegean Thrace, as it does to lowland (and upland) Macedonia.[56]

[55] Śliwa and Domaradzki 1983 (joint Polish–Bulgarian survey of the middle Strymon valley); Domaradzki 2001; B. Athanassov et al., *AOR* 2009 [2010] 676–8; 2010 [2011] 555–8; AIA/APA Annual Meeting, Philadelphia 2012 (preliminary report); Kazanluk area survey: G. Nehrizov and J. Tsvetkova *AOR* 2008 [2009] 746–76; 2009 [2010], 144–6, 649–51; G. Nehrizov, J. Tsvetkova, A. Sobotkova, E. Bozhinova, *AOR* 2010 [2011] 571–4; Nehrizov and Tsvetkova, *AOR* 2011 [2012] 550–2.

[56] Baralis 2010, 248–50, 256 (on settlement dispersal along the north Aegean coastline).

Aigeai

In 2009 Angeliki Kottaridi published a summarized survey of the scope of archaeological enquiry over twelve years in the city of Aigeai, calling it a 'town in clusters'.[57] An area of some 50 ha (500,000 m^2) comprises the city's acropolis and the fortification wall around its inner core, including the royal palace, sanctuaries, residential areas, but also an extensive development outside the city's fortified area and cemeteries, including the mound burials of the Early Iron Age and the royal tombs that occupied much of the same collective space. Her purpose was to explain the extended layout in terms of civic and architectural development. Kottaridi compared the evidence that is emerging from the various areas sampled by archaeologists within this space to a number of ancient centres of the Greek mainland, including Athens, Thebes, Thespiai, and Pherai, where public and residential areas were disposed (in their early history at least) around a number of clusters, rather than concentrated in a single nucleus. At Aigeai the topography of the city below the acropolis was steep and broken into a number of deep channels cut by torrents, necessitating terracing operations to create larger open areas, whether for public spaces or for construction purposes. The organization of public and residential areas is still under investigation, but Kottaridi's instinctive evaluation of the style of urban development provides a helpful tool for understanding urban evolution at other sites in the northern Aegean area.

Amphipolis

The organization of private and public spaces in the pre-Roman phases of Amphipolis and Abdera is different from conventions in much of the Greek mainland, with multiple foci rather than progressive concentration around a central nucleus.[58] These sites have proved hard to investigate, precisely because of the extended nature of their topography.

Philippopolis

There has been a similar challenge at sites like Plovdiv in Bulgaria (ancient Philippopolis), where persistent evidence of long-term

[57] Kottaridi 2009, 773–80 and fig. 2; cf. also S. Drougou 2011, 243–56, who provides a preliminary assessment of the possible implications of the city's layout.

[58] Amphipolis: *Inventory*, no. 553; Abdera: *Inventory*, no. 640; cf. also Ioakeimidou et al., 2006.

settlement has been found in a number of separate locations, both on the acropolis of Nebet Tepe, and in the lower city at its foot. A configuration of multiple concentrations, which together amounted to a single collective, or a group of closely related local communities, would explain the persistent nature of this pattern and the apparently spontaneous emergence of a politically well-defined civic community when the earliest Hellenistic documents with which it can be associated become archaeologically visible.[59] The evidence that has accumulated makes clear that the centre of exchange focusing on the hilltop of Nebet Tepe was indeed an urban agglomeration, not just a loose collocation of residential districts. The dispersed nature of the sites identified does not conform to expectations of urban organization; but there is plentiful evidence of Early Iron Age and fifth to fourth century BC activity in and around the centre of Plovdiv. We need to rethink our ideas about urban planning in contexts where there was far less pressure on space, as compared with central and southern Greece. In the north Aegean area the challenge was the breadth not the lack of space.

Comparative research on urban planning can help us understand the implications of this type of spatial evidence. Students of urban planning have long recognized the operation of 'Zipf's law', namely the phenomenon that in human societies settlements fall into a natural hierarchy based on size, with a small number of genuinely large cities at the top of a progressively expanding logarithmic curve. This pattern of site sizes has recently been explored in the context of Roman imperial cities.[60] I suggested more than a decade ago that we should expect to see a similar pattern in pre-Roman settlement distributions in Macedonia, Thessaly and Thrace.[61] The comparative sizes of settlements are hard to evaluate in practice whilst so little is known about their overall spatial organization, whilst the 'dispersed' nature of some sites makes this task even more challenging. However, the well-founded principles behind Zipf's law offer a reliable way of thinking about sites in general. The majority of sites identified through current field investigation will have been small rural establishments, whether these were individual farms, hamlets, mining villages, or agricultural processing units (such as foresters' or charcoal burners' huts; and hunting lodges). Some will have been larger agglomerations, particularly those at road and river junctions, where natural routes crossed; and a few will have been much larger. The

[59] Philippopolis: *Inventory*, no. 655; see esp. Koleva et al. 2000, 103–21; Koleva and Katsarov 2009.

[60] See the contributions to Bowman and Wilson et al. 2012, esp. A. Marzano.

[61] Archibald 2000, 218–19.

presence of several larger, archaeologically identifiable settlements, within geographical districts that seem to have had genuine administrative status in this period, is some validation of the principles of Zipf's law. The wide distribution of substantial cemetery areas, either burial mounds or extensive flat cemeteries, which have a marked tendency to cluster around the largest habitation sites, is one of the clearest indications that some of the larger sites were also collective focal points. They include Aiani in Elimeia,[62] and Edessa in Bottiaia, whose urban pattern seems to reflect both concentrated areas of settlement and a penumbra of sub-urban sites, with a similar configuration around Alorus in Almopia.[63] In inland Thrace there is a particular concentration of sites with evidence of high-status material (analogous to the mortuary profile in the cemeteries at Aiani and Edessa) at the western end of the Thracian Plain, including the triangle of land between the foothills of Rhodope on the south, Strelcha and Krastevich on the north,[64] and the area between Plovdiv and Vasil Levsky, either side of the River Stryama, which includes some of the most spectacular funerary deposits from the region (Duvanli, Sarnegor, Chernozem, Starosel).[65] Apart from the metropolitan area of Plovdiv itself and Vasil Levsky, settlements in the area of Plovdiv have been registered but remain unexcavated, so the relationship between them and the pre-Macedonian site at Plovdiv cannot as yet be tested.[66] Similar patterns can be observed in other parts of Thrace, where distinct regional foci (often more than one) are noticeable in the vicinity of Chirpan,[67] in the lower Hebros valley, between the confluence of the Tundja (Tonzos) and the River Hebros, including eastern Rhodope and perhaps focusing on Kypsela,[68] as well as in the hinterland of Odessos.[69]

[62] Karamitrou-Mentessidi 2011 with refs.

[63] Chrysostomou 2006, 713–24; Chrysostomou 2008, esp. 32 fig. 9, showing the conservation area around the Southern Gateway, with traces of archaic structures; 57–9, figs 34–36 acropolis with high quality masonry; 63, fig. 43 (plan of HL/R houses); 76 fig. 72, farmhouse outside city walls; Chrysostomou 1994, 30, map 4 (Iron Age sites); 31, map 5, classical/Hellenistic sites; among these, the most significant are Nea Zoi and Aloros, naturally fortified hilltops.

[64] Krastevich and Strelcha: see Ch. 5, n.16.

[65] Duvanli, Sarnegor: Archibald 1998, 158, 317, 281; Chernozem: Kisyov 2005, 12–112; see also Ch. 8.

[66] Vasil Levsky: Kisyov 2004, 48–68; cf. Archibald 1998, 126, 141.

[67] Tonkova 2000, 133–40; Tonkova 2008; 2011.

[68] See esp. Nekhrizov and Mikov 2000, 161–80; Kypsela: *Inventory*, no. 645.

[69] Stoyanov 2000, 55–67; Minchev 2007, 7–80; Damyanov 2010, 265–76; see in general the contributions to *Pistiros et Thasos* for a wide-ranging regional perspective.

Maroneia

The recognition of 'dispersed' or dynamic forms of urban organization may help us to understand the history of Maroneia. One of the best known historical centres of the north Aegean throughout the second half of the first millennium BC, classical Maroneia has evaded investigators on the ground. Hellenistic and Roman inscriptions show that from the third century BC onwards, and probably from the fourth, Maroneia occupied the southern flanks of Mount Ismaros, long associated with the Ismarian wine echoed in a verse of Archilochos (fr. 2.2) at the hilltop named after Agios Charalambos. The oldest continuous activity in the area dating from the first millennium BC is on the acropolis of Agios Giorgios,[70] a fortified acropolis slightly to the east of Agios Charalambos. In a recent re-assessment of the topographical evidence for ancient Maroneia, Louisa Loukopoulou and Selene Psoma have underscored the fact that, of the known historical Greek communities between the River Nestos and Mount Ismaros, only Abdera and Hellenistic to Roman Maroneia have been securely located, whereas Dikaia, Stryme, and the pre-Hellenistic site of Maroneia have not. Their systematic revision of the evidence suggests that the urban concentration around Agios Charalambos reflects a later phase in the city's history, when this exceptionally rich community expanded from what may have been its original focus on the Molyvoti peninsula, separated from it by Lake Mitrikon (identified as Lake Ismaris), to include the hilltop of Agios Charalambos with the bay below it, and, in all probability, territory farther east, encroaching on the Samothrakian *peraia*.[71]

A number of different models of urbanization have historically been adopted in discussing territories north of the Aegean. Some of the best known examples, such as Olynthos, in Chalkidike (Fig. 2.3),[72] or Adjiyska Vodenitsa ('Pistiros'), or Seuthopolis, in eastern Thrace,[73] were the result of planned investments, involving the mobilization of royal and collective resources, although we know little about exactly how these rather remarkable developments were put into practice. Early Hellenistic cases of *synoikismos*, the merging of earlier, smaller social units, provide

[70] Loukopoulou and Psoma 2008b, 59–62, with bibl.

[71] Loukopoulou and Psoma 2008b, 69–81, 86 figs 9–12 (inscribed lead weights of Maroneia from Molyvoti); cf. Psoma 2008, 130–7, on the centres of Samothrakian *peraia*. Karadima and Psoma have presented the coin evidence from Agios Charalambos, which reinforces the interpretation postulated above (2007, 291–8).

[72] Cahill 2002 with refs.

[73] Adjiyska Vodenitsa as ancient Pistiros: see Ch. 1 n.19 and Ch. 5 nn.89–90; Seuthopolis: Dimitrov and Chichikova 1978; Stoyanov 2006, 85; K. Dimitrov 2011, 101–12.

Fig. 2.3. Much of central Chalkidike, especially the eastern half, is mountainous and has been heavily wooded since the early Holocene, despite a long history of human exploitation for fuel and construction purposes.

partial insights.[74] The need for significant investment is less evident in smaller towns, where we do see closely-packed urban settlement patterns, as in the Hellenistic phase of Agios Panteleimon, the lakeside town south-east of modern Florina.[75] The contrast between Aigeai, with its distributed plan and evidence of a number of successive alignments, and Pella, which was clearly intended to be an up-to-date capital, is telling.[76] Much of the city plan belongs to the early Hellenistic period, and far less is known about the city's organization in the fourth century BC.[77] Here, as at Edessa, Aigeai, and elsewhere in Macedonia, just as in Thrace, in coastal locations, such as Abdera and Maroneia, and in the interior, much of the evidence for systematic urbanization in terms of street planning and urban amenities begins to become visible, in material terms, from the third century onwards. That does not mean that these processes began only in Hellenistic times. On the contrary, there is plentiful evidence of urban beginnings, as we have seen; but the burden

[74] Teos and Lebedos *c.*303 BC, under Antigonos I: *Syll.*^{3} 344 = Bagnall and Derow 2004: 11–15, no.7 and Austin^2: no. 48 with further refs; Cohen 1995: 188–91.

[75] Adam-Veleni 1998, 19–46; M. Lilimbaki-Akamati and I. Akamatis, *AEMΘ* 19 (2005) [2007], 569–77.

[76] Akamatis 2006a, 615–26; Akamatis 2011, 393–408.

[77] Akamatis 2011, 394–5, 403.

of proof has been set in terms of later urban conventions, with fully paved street systems and extensive use of stone. The process of urbanization did culminate in such a pattern of advanced urban textures during the regional reorganizations effected under Roman rule, with cities acquiring large tracts of former rural land under Hadrian.[78] The analysis of districts and regions, as distinct from urban foci, in Thrace, as in Macedonia, suggests that regional structures played an important part in the articulation of settlement hierarchies. This is a topic to which we will return in Chapter 5.

Sanctuaries

The other main category of site that should be considered in a conspectus of sites is that of sanctuaries. In the central and southern Aegean, Iron Age votive offerings and cult activity, particularly in the form of residues of communal meals, have been documented at upland sites within and outside civic areas, in designated zones of settlements, and in independent locations, some of which became significant inter-communal sanctuaries. This pattern is also represented in the northern Aegean, although the forms of cultural elaboration adopted in particular locations show that there was a variety of approaches to the organization of sacred sites. Although the practice of depositing cult offerings and of feasting is common to north and south, the sort of investment made in public or collective activities seems to have been different in the north (notwithstanding some prominent exceptions). Sanctuary buildings tend to be of modest dimensions and without much architectural decoration, whereas burials were often complex procedures in their own right and accompanied by various forms of costly investment, both in terms of construction, ornamentation, and associated grave goods. This pattern is found throughout Macedonia and Thrace, but is also characteristic of many coastal cities, which might otherwise have been expected to follow the monumental traditions of Ionia. Poseidi, the location of the sanctuary to Poseidon on a promontory west of Mende, on Pallene, the westernmost finger of Chalkidike, and the shrine of Dionysos and Zeus Ammon at Aphytis, on the eastern side of the same peninsula, along with an Ionic temple, probably located at Therme, are the most striking exceptions.[79]

[78] Parissaki 2009, esp. 350–2.

[79] Christesen and Murray 2010 for a general discussion of cult building and Mari 2011b on Macedonian traditional cults; Poseidi: J. Vokotopoulou, *AEMΘ* 4 (1990) 399–410; 5 (1991) 303–18; 6 (1992) 443–50; 7 (1993) 401–12; Aphytis: Tsigarida 2011a, 143–5 and n.34;

'ROYAL' ECONOMIES—RAISING AND MAKING MONEY FOR A KING

Towards the end of Book 2 (2.97–98) in his *History of the Peloponnesian War*, the historian Thucydides describes the great invasion of Chalkidike conducted by the Thracian king, Sitalkes, which was to have been an invasion of Macedonia. He includes, by way of introduction, a number of remarks that define, in his view, the substance of the Odrysian kingdom. In addition to its geographical limits (a coastal border between the mouth of the Danube and Abdera, inland from Byzantion to the River Strymon), the historian refers to the tribute (*phoros*) raised by Sitalkes, from native districts and from Greek cities alike, as amounting to 400 Talents (T) of gold and silver, with at least as much, in the same metals, contributed as 'gifts' to the king, to various leaders (*paradynasteuontai*) and nobles (*gennaioi*) of the Odrysians. In addition to precious metals, these 'gifts' consisted of woven textiles, both 'plain and embroidered' (2.97.3). Three sentences thus provide the modern reader with a wealth of exceptional detail, not just about the kingdom and how it was organized, but also about the mechanisms used by its rulers to raise cash and capital. This brief but immensely informative historical resource is one that deserves to be explored from a variety of angles. At this point I want to focus on the public dimension of Odrysian royal taxation.

Taxes are an emotive subject in any society. The history of taxation in Western societies demonstrates the depth of popular resentment against taxes of any and every sort. Income tax has been among the most sorely resented measures introduced by governments; but the same resentment has applied equally to excise and other duties. In the United Kingdom peacetime income tax has formally been a temporary mechanism, since it was introduced by Sir Robert Peel in 1842.[80] Historically, universal public taxes have been closely connected with war chests, not with expenditure on public welfare and amenities. The proportion of government revenues devoted to military expenditure has fluctuated dramatically from place to place and from period to period. In classical antiquity, and in the early modern period, military expenditure formed a significant component of state expenditure, declining during the nineteenth century in the most industrially developed countries, and dwarfed by

Tsigarida 2011b; Misaïlidou-Despotidou 2009; Ionic temple, Therme: Schmidt-Dounas 2004; cult investment is explored further below, Ch. 8.

[80] Ferguson 2001, 71; Ch. 2, 'Hateful Taxes', 54–80.

welfare and other social payments in the twentieth, although the pattern in other parts of the globe has been different.[81]

Thucydides' description of Odrysian revenues presents a picture in which the relationship between payers and recipients is quite different from structures familiar in contemporary societies. He emphasizes the exceptional economic status of the Odrysian kingdom, second to none among European powers in its resources and its revenues, yielding to the Scythians only in the global numerical strength of its military.[82] The historian distinguished between formal 'tribute', using the same term, *phoros,* as he used in connection with the tribute paid by her allies to Athens.[83] What makes the account doubly interesting is the coexistence of what seem to be two parallel but different modes of operation—a formalized method of revenue raising, *phoros*, with a known gross threshold, expressed in silver talents, and a less formal system of 'gifts', which are not the same as 'tribute', but are nevertheless perceived by the historian as constituting income. Thucydides evidently wanted his readers to see both revenue sources as comprehensible parts of a single system, even if he thought that the 'gift-giving' was a less usual method of raising capital. The 'gift-giving' is something that the modern reader associates with the anthropology of Marcel Mauss and his seminal work, *Essai sur le don.*[84] Yet here Thucydides presents gift-giving as an alternative or additional source of income. The one form does not exclude the other. This parallelism is quite at odds with the polarity more usually identified by historians and anthropologists between money-based economies and gift-based systems. Thucydides implies nevertheless that the 'gifts' were, in a very real sense, revenue, not just presents; nor is there any suggestion that there was anything underhand or covert about the

[81] Ferguson 2001, 43–53, esp. Table 1; Goldsmith 1987, 22, 31, 48–51, 79.

[82] Thuc. 2.97.5: *ὥστε ἐπὶ μέγα ἡ βασιλεία ἦλθεν ἰσχύος. τῶν γὰρ ἐν τῇ Εὐρώπῃ ὅσαι μεταξὺ τοῦ Ἰονίου κόλπου καὶ τοῦ Εὐξείνου πόντου μεγίστη ἐγένετο χρημάτων προσόδῳ καὶ τῇ ἄλλῃ εὐδαιμονίᾳ, ἰσχύι δὲ μάχης καὶ στρατοῦ πλήθει πολὺ δευτέρα μετὰ τὴν Σκυθῶν.*

('This is how the [Odrysian] kingship came to have great power. Of the [states] in Europe between the Ionian Gulf and the Euxine, it was the greatest in terms of financial revenues and of all other forms of prosperity, although in the strength and number of its military forces it was decidedly behind that of the Scythians').

[83] Hornblower, 1991, 371; cf. also Papazarkadas 2009 for recent refinements of chronological problems connected to the epigraphic data; Loukopoulou 2002 on the Odrysian *phoros.*

[84] Mauss 1923–24; for a nuanced exposition of why 'gift-giving' in pre-modern societies may have been misunderstood by Mauss and others, see Wagner-Hasel 2006; Stronach and Zournatzi 2002, 335–9, explain how Odrysian tribute and gift-giving resembled Near Eastern practices (and why the heightened tensions of the Peloponnesian War may have inclined Thucydides to imply that there was something peculiar about these customs).

process. The different revenue streams, which would have amounted to a sum of the order of 800–1,000T per annum, can be considered alongside the 600T that the historian gives as annually accruing to Athens from her allies in the same period (2.13.3).[85] The most striking feature of the Odrysian revenue-raising system is its reliance on a commodity-based network that maximized a range of specialist materials.

There is no digression in Thucydides' work that could give us a comparable picture of Macedonian revenues in the fifth century BC. Most of our information, about financial, as about political matters, dates from a hundred or so years later. Philip II is said to have received 1,000T (*per annum*? Diod. 16.8.6–7), from a mine in the vicinity of Mount Dysoron.[86] This notorious anecdote marks a step change in Argead royal revenues, and gives little indication of what income the crown may have had in the previous century and a half at least. There are sound reasons for thinking that a system of royal administration had evolved in that time, which is partly reflected in the nomenclature of offices, surviving in distinctive dialect forms as indicators of earlier practice, once the Attic *koine* became progressively established during Philip's reign.[87] This administrative machinery was perhaps introduced, or expanded, to enable the collection of various taxes and tolls on behalf of the crown, a topic that will be explored more fully in the next chapter.

'Royal' economies are more difficult to manage that civic ones, according to the anonymous author of the pseudo-Aristotelian treatise on economic management, *Oeconomica* (1345b 13–15). He does not explain why there is a step change, in terms of complexity, between civic and royal administration. The reader is led to assume that this complication follows automatically from the kinds of decisions that have to be made in the royal chancery—about when to mint coins; about how expenses should be paid for (in coin or in kind); and about how to deal with revenues accumulating from regional sources (1345b 22–27). This

[85] Cf Xen. *Anab.* 7.1.27 (the overall revenues of Athens, from home and abroad, during the Peloponnesian War, amounted to no less than 1,000T). The sums presented in the Athenian Tribute Lists nevertheless do not indicate that annual tributes exceeded 400T. This base line (if that is what it was) dropped to 130T *c.*350 BC (Dem. 10.37–38) and reverted to the previous level as a result of the intervention of Euboulos; Lykourgos raised this to 1,200 or even 1,575 ([Plut.] *X orat.* 842F, 852B; cf Migeotte 2009, 53; Nixon and Price's (1990) pioneering exploration of the economic implications of variable amounts of the Athenian tribute has not been followed up (see further discussion below and in Ch. 5).

[86] For the possible location of Mt. Dysoron, see further discussion on mining and mines in Chs. 5 and 6.

[87] Hatzopoulos 1996, I, 431–42, on royal finances; 78–104, 482: on the offices of *skoidos* and *peliganes;* on the dissemination of Attic *koine* dialect in Macedonia: *idem* 1988a, 55–61; *idem* 1988b, 40–50; *idem* 1998, 79–80.

vivid sketch of economic management, which shines a torch-like beam onto contemporary economic ideas seems, on internal evidence, to have been written in the early third century BC, and provides the only panoramic insight into the management of territorial kingdoms from the period under consideration in this book.[88] The same anonymous author goes on to explain regional administration ('satrapal' management), principally in terms of the management of revenues; from land, first and foremost; from natural resources; from trade (port dues); from taxes and tolls (land and market taxes); from animals; and from the product of other activities ([Arist.] *Oec.* 1345b 33–1346a 5). The regional ('satrapal') account most likely derives from experiences garnered in the period of Alexander the Great's Successors in Asia Minor, when the Persian system of administration was still very prominent in local practice. The assumption seems to be that the balance of revenues would flow directly to royal coffers. We know very little about how these operations actually worked. Most of what we do know derives from the symptoms of decision-making in royal chanceries—particular coinages minted; particular letters sent by named rulers to named civic entities or individual landholders; Athenian forensic speeches (which give some idea of where political sensitivities lay), and various civic requests or royal responses to requests, gratefully commemorated by magistrates representing the recipients in stone inscriptions. Much of this information, though by no means all of it, refers to the kingdom of Macedonia. But there is also a similar, if smaller, range of material relating to the Odrysian kingdom of Thrace, which makes it easier to look at both of these territorial entities alongside one another and to find out whether they represent similar patterns of fiscal and operational behaviour. By examining these two states within the wider region of the north Aegean and east Balkans, a mesh of interconnected relationships becomes visible—between the royal courts and their rural retainers; between coastal cities and their hinterlands; between wealthy patrons and the communities that benefited from their largesse. The armies of the two kingdoms were among the most visible and dominant forms of human capital in the region. Nevertheless, these military assets need to be viewed in the context of regional economic relations, as well as the inter-regional tensions that dominate surviving political narratives.

Given the fragmentary state of information about fiscal measures, historians need to apply a model of sorts in order to get a realistic

[88] Van Groningen 1933; Descat 2003, esp. 155; Bresson 2005a, 45–50 for discussion of this author's interest in minting coins; Aperghis 2004, 117–79.

sense of how these ancient royal economies operated. Paul Millett has recently explored the role of plunder in the Macedonian economy, referring to the predatory powers of medieval European states as a stage in the evolution of fiscal mechanisms.[89] Plunder was certainly always an option, and one that delivered easy pickings, sometimes on a breath-taking scale—700T raised following the capture, by Philip II, of 180 Athenian grain ships at Hieron, on the northern approach to the Bosporus, in 340 BC (Theop. *FGrH* 115 F115; Philoch. *FGrH* 328 F162);[90] or 440T raised from the sale of prisoners, captured by Alexander III in the sack of Thebes in 335 BC (Diod. 17.14.1–4); and, most spectacularly of all, the 180,000T (equal to *c*.235 tons of gold and 2,350 tons of silver),[91] which is the sum of gold and silver acquired by Alexander III from the Persian treasuries and temporarily stored at Ecbatana. The sums recorded by historians were spectacular for the time, but their very notoriety made these monies hard to hide. Much of this revenue was sucked into the Roman treasury with the indemnities required by the Roman authorities after the defeats of Philip V, Perseus, and the Seleukid king, Antiochos III.[92] The military machine of the Argead kings, Philip II and Alexander III, was formidable, but it was not equivalent to the fiscal economy of the kingdom, or of the overall economy of classical and Hellenistic Macedonia, or of neighbouring areas. Here we must distinguish between regional economies and the revenues acquired by extra-territorial wars, even if part of those revenues did find its way back to the state treasury or to royal coffers. For many non-Macedonians, pillage may have been a prominent concomitant of Argead military endeavours, but it was not necessarily the most important or the most enduring one. John Davies has proposed that plunder should be subsumed under a

[89] Millett 2010, 503 n.119, citing Bonney and Ormrod 1999, 1–21, and Millett's general discussion of plundered revenue, 488–504.

[90] *HM* II, 576 n.3; Gabrielsen 2007; Archibald (forthcoming b/); see further Ch. 5.

[91] De Callataÿ 2012 has corrected the equivalent sum of 4,680T of silver, which would produce an unlikely gold-silver ratio of 10:1.

[92] Bresson 2005a, 56–66 for discussion; Alexander's acquisitions at Persepolis: de Callataÿ 1989 and de Callataÿ et al. 1993; Aemilius Paullus found 6,000T in Perseus' treasury but the overall sum acquired in booty was far greater: 120,000,000 sesterces (= 5,000T) according to Livy; 210,000,000 according to Velleius Paterculus (Plb. 18.35.4; cf. Livy, 45.40.1ff. (citing Valerius Antias) Vell. Paterc. 1.9.6); Plutarch, *Aemilius* 32.8 refers to 750 vessels, each containing 3T of coined silver (= 2,250T) as a component of the triumphal procession (de Callataÿ 2006a, 73 for detailed discussion); Antiochos III was ordered to pay 15,000 talents, 2,000 of which were spaced over twelve years, as part of the negotiations that resulted in the Treaty of Apamea (Plb. 21.17.1–6; 42.19–21; Liv. 37.45.4–21; 55.1–3; 38.38; App. *Syr.* 38–39), as well as 500,000 *medimnoi* of grain, which Bresson calculates as equivalent to the value of 333 1/3 T (Bresson 2005a, 60 and n.14; cf. Bresson, 195–6); de Callataÿ 2006a, 70–4, for a conspectus of triumphal booty.

more general label, namely 'command mode', one of four identifiable economic mechanisms operating in classical antiquity. 'Command mode' is taken to represent all those forms of revenue extraction that emanate from the exercise of power, including landlordism, tithes, and taxes. Plunder, according to this rationale, is a more extreme, possibly arbitrary form of requisitioning, at one end of a scale of centralized extraction that also includes legitimized forms, which may be rationally justified. The other three 'modes' according to this model are 'subsistence mode', 'market mode', and 'charitable mode'. A triple model, based on the first three of these 'modes', was formulated by Sir John Hicks as a succession of characteristic economic behaviours. In a joint paper, John Davies and I have applied this formula to Hellenistic kingdoms, arguing that these 'modes' should be envisaged as coexistent options, not as successive, or evolving, modes of operation.[93]

The gold and silver treasure accumulated for a full two centuries at Persepolis, drawn from the vast territories acquired by the Achaemenid rulers of the Persian Empire, and including some exceptional individual fortunes (such as that of Pythios the Lydian, which included 2000T of silver and 3,993,000 gold darics: Hdt. 7.28), represents a unique instance of capital acquisition, unparalleled until early modern times. Alexander capitalized probably 200,000T in all, a sum two orders of magnitude greater than the revenues of most contemporary states. Once put into circulation, the ordinary mechanisms of exchange seem to have ensured that this nest egg could not be reproduced. Alexander's Successors continued to exploit, but could not otherwise match this asset, despite various strategies for capital accumulation. François de Callataÿ has estimated, using the relative proportions of dies available for different producing centres over time, that Alexander's silver issues represented about half of all coins in circulation *c.*300 BC. At the same time, only a fraction, estimated at between 10 and 30 per cent of precious metals in circulation, was coined.[94] Antigonos Monophthalmos is said to have had an annual income of 11,000T (Diod. 19.56.5); Ptolemy II is supposed to have received 14,800T in money and 1,500,000 *artabae* of grain (St Jerome, *Commentary on the Book of Daniel,* 11.5). The equivalent annual expenditure on military pay in the early decades of the third century BC has been calculated at 8,000T, using an operating force of

[93] Davies 2009; Archibald and Davies 2011, esp. 3–11; Davies has added 'euergetistic or charitable mode' in an 'Afterword' to the new edition of Davies 2009 (Davies, forthcoming/b).

[94] De Callataÿ 2005a, 86–7 and Table 4.8 (size of selected early Hellenistic coin issues); on the proportion of monetized to non-monetized precious metals, De Callataÿ 2006a, 55–67; esp. 64.

100,000 mercenaries (including a field army, garrison troops, plus a fleet of 80–90 ships).[95] The Successors were obliged to continue finding sums of this order so as to carry on enforcing their authority and thereby justifying their right to rule over subject and would-be subject peoples.

Nevertheless, the bulk of the 200,000T released by Alexander III from the Persian treasuries and circulated by his Successors passed quickly into private hands.[96] The Asiatic campaign, and the Wars of the Successors, stimulated demand for all kinds of services in addition to purely military ones, and the availability of payment ratcheted up the quality of potential clients and candidates for these services. Much of the coined money ended up far away from the mints where it was issued. A great deal of it ended up in hoards, some in Asia Minor, much more in the east Balkans. The reasons for this dynamic, and the means by which the transfers came about, have not been fully explained. Martin Price, who made a special study of the coinage issued in the name of Alexander the Great, linked the burial of a number of hoards in inland Thrace with Celtic movements in the area during the third century BC. But he did not develop this explanation in any systematic way.[97] It is possible that the uncertainties caused by the presence of a number of Celtic irregular armies during the two middle quarters of the third century BC triggered the burial of various hoards, which were not subsequently recovered. Nevertheless, it does not explain why the coins buried in them found their way into these areas in the first place. The locations of hoards of precious metals is closely connected with the configuration of urban or quasi-urban foci, which suggests that the accumulation of money in these areas is linked to the presence of wealthy landowners in the vicinity and to commercial transactions. The silver and gold coins issued posthumously in the name of Philip II, on a lighter weight system, have been connected by George Le Rider with issues destined primarily for internal exchange within the region, whereas coins in the name of Alexander circulated widely and operated in effect as an international currency.[98] The owners of these hoards must be connected in one way or another

[95] The most recent calculation is by Le Rider and de Callataÿ 2006, 174 and n.3; cf. Archibald 2011, 48 and n.12; Bresson 2005a, 59–62 on early Hellenistic money supply; Aperghis 2004, 213–46 and Capdetrey 2004 for discussions of Seleukid fiscal policy.

[96] Cf. de Callataÿ 2006a, 51–4, 64.

[97] Price 1991, 47–9, 56–8, 66ff; the profile of Balkan hoards represents a different set of circumstances and quite different actual issues from the types of coins modelled on Philip II's issues struck by Celtic moneyers (see e.g. Dahmen 2010, 52 and n.45 for examples); see also Ch. 5 for further discussion of Balkan hoards (Rousseva 2002).

[98] Le Rider 1992 on the two-currency system, within and outside Macedonia, during the period 323–290 BC; Le Rider 1996, 294, 319, on issues of Philip II in the Balkans.

with the payment of services by the Successors, whether in the north Aegean region, or farther east.

The author of the pseudo-Aristotelian *Oeconomica* seems to be rather preoccupied with the mechanics of revenue-raising and minting, and rather less concerned than Aristotle himself was with the undesirable aspects of coinage for the purposes of exchange.[99] Whereas Aristotle took a rather detached view of exchange, focusing on the ethical dimensions of civic affairs, his anonymous pupil seems to reflect an age, or an environment, that was much more concerned with the technical aspects of minting. This is not surprising, considering the enormous transformation that took place in the scale and range of coin production on behalf of Philip II and Alexander III. These coinages did not just make a very great impression on contemporaries; they became the dominant regional and inter-regional media of exchange and some series continued to be minted long after the deaths of Philip and Alexander. The consistency and longevity of these issues has made them harder to date with precision. Philip introduced a bimetallic currency, with gold coins, later dubbed *Philippeoi* (Diod. 16.8.7 cf. Horace, *Epist.* 2.1.232–4), which were struck on the Attic standard, and were clearly meant for exchange outside Macedonia, while his silver issues were on the lighter standard, also used by the Chalkidian League and by other communities in the north Aegean region and sometimes referred to as 'Thraco-Macedonian'.[100] The series of silver tetradrachms that were issued in far greater quantities than any previous regal series probably began in 356 BC, at any rate some years into his reign. Most numismatists now accept that Philip's gold series did not begin until the 340s, perhaps around 348, perhaps a little later. Posthumous issues in Philip's name, using the same obverse and reverse types, continued to be struck during the reigns of Philip III Arrhidaeus and Alexander III. The principal coinage in the name of Alexander the Great (if we leave aside a short-lived series

[99] Arist. *Pol.* 1.1256b–7b; 1.1259a–b; *Nic. Eth.* 5.8, 1132b–1133b; Picard 1980; Bresson 2005a, 45–7.

[100] Le Rider, 1977, 354–5; Le Rider 1996, 21. Le Rider's original attempts to date Philip's and Alexander's series were partially revised by Price in his review of Le Rider's monograph of 1977 (Price 1979). A number of deeds of sale from Amphipolis refer to gold staters of Philip: Hatzopoulos 1996, II, no. 88 (dated 352/350 BC = Hatzopoulos 1991, 38–43, no. VII); *BullÉpigr* 1992, 321, ll. 7–9: '*stat| eron ch(r)yson philippei(o)n| dodek(a) hemist(a)terou*', when Hermagoras was priest and Spargeus was *epistates*; cf. also nos 89–91, with further references to payment in gold coin. The overall chronology of these references makes clear, however, that the term applies not to any specific coin issues, but to Macedonian gold coin in general (Hatzopoulos 1991, 82–7), so no conclusions can be drawn from these references about the introduction of 'Philippics'; C. C. Lorber, reviewing Le Rider 1996, provides a survey of the dating controversies, *SNR* 78 (1999) 205–9; cf. Dahmen 2010, 52.

showing Herakles and the eagle of Zeus), bimetallic, like his father's, began in all probability in 333/32 BC, after the battle of Issus, and continued to be struck at 26 mints throughout his reign, by many of his Successors, using the same face types, and by some civic mints, at intervals even into the second century BC.[101]

The mass of coinage struck for Philip and Alexander and the exceptional quality of the individual coins has enhanced the impression of their extraordinary status and their ubiquitous nature. Estimates of output do indicate that the silver tetradrachms of Alexander III represent the most numerous single types in circulation. De Callataÿ, building on detailed die studies of the output of certain civic mints, notably Athens, Rhodes, Lampsakos, Taras, and Maroneia, as well as of regal coins, and projecting these into estimates of (theoretical) annual issues of coins to supplement stock in circulation, has calculated the relative numerical relationships of different minting authorities. These projections suggest that there were six times as many tetradrachms of Alexander III in circulation during the later fourth and third centuries BC as there were silver coins of Philip II (or, in the second century, of Antiochos III), while Athenian silver coins, the most significant civic issues, represent an output of just under half the figure for Alexander tetradrachms. Although these projections are estimates, they do seem, on various criteria, to represent genuine proportionate relationships between different issuing mints.[102]

Perhaps the most surprising result of these estimated projections of minting output is the relatively limited level of overall monetization within these economies. The most consistent issuing authorities—those that do seem to have renewed the stock of their own coins in circulation on a comparatively regular basis—Athens, Rhodes, and Taras—were all states with exceptionally strong commercial interests. Athenian silver is known as having been exported as coin as well as bullion (Xen. *Vect.* 3.2); this could also have been true of other coinages. Royal mints, from the time of Philip II onwards, began to compete in output with these

[101] On the dating of the principal output: Price 1991, 27–9, 85–9; Troxell 1997, 48–50, 86–98; Le Rider 2007, 8–16; for the Herakles/eagle series, Wartenberg 1997.

[102] De Callataÿ 2005a, 80–8 and Tables 4.2–4.8; the author has calculated the average annual output of each of the different coinages examined using a common denominator of 'Attic drachm equivalent dies', based on an initial estimate of Rhodian didrachm-equivalent dies and Tarentine didrachm-equivalent dies, compared with Attic drachm-equivalent dies (80–3, Table 4.3), since these represent the most consistent minting history. The author makes clear that these are only estimated projections, involving a number of possible caveats. The actual numbers of surviving coin dies for any one type represents some fraction of the actual output of any one mint.

established trading giants. Yet, in terms of annual production, leaving aside the altogether exceptional production of coins in the name of Alexander the Great and the gold staters of Philip II, the numbers of fresh coins brought into circulation by other authorities, civic and royal alike, rarely reach anything beyond single figures. As de Callataÿ has emphasized, minting on these terms could easily be accommodated 'by a single craftsman using a single hammer'—if we accept that the ratio of coins to dies was a relatively constant one, a procedural matter that can neither be proved nor disproved. Notwithstanding the formidable needs of individual military rulers, including such exceptional figures as Antiochos III, their demand for capital, to cover military pay, appears on present evidence to represent a very modest amount in comparison with overall patterns of exchange over time, even if coin production was a well-developed mechanism, when compared with other periods and places.[103]

The idea that the defining characteristic of early Macedonian kingdoms, and those of their Hellenistic successors, was royal requisitioning for military purposes either needs to be quite differently conceived, or it represents only one aspect of royal economies. If it needs to be reconceived, then other commodities must be factored in, as well as coined money; and, if so, then other players must also be included. Booty, in the form of commodities, was a troublesome asset, because it needed guarding, transporting, and storing, if not conversion into liquid form. 'Liquid' form primarily meant ingots or scrap silver and gold. De Callataÿ has compared the relative amounts of different forms of booty recorded in Roman republican triumphs to calculate the general volumes of liquid precious metals as compared with coined money. The relationship between three forms of recorded booty appears to be relatively consistent. Ingots and similar forms of metal, termed *infecti* by Livy and other authors, represents the largest proportion, at around 70 per cent. Precious metals converted into plate consist of around 10 per cent of the total, while coined money forms the remaining 20 per cent.[104] These three categories refer only to the most compact and easily transferable resources, which are in any case a subset of the range of resources that could be drawn upon and utilized within the northern Aegean region. Our conception of royal economies needs to be enriched by a

[103] De Callataÿ 2005a, 86–7; [Antiochos III] 'the mean global activity for his entire kingdom represented the full productivity of a quarter of a single hammer in a single mint, i.e. a maximum of 1/48th of the available productivity (four monthly obverses per hammer and 12 mints)' (ibid. 87).

[104] De Callataÿ 2006a, 64–7 and Annexe 1, 70–4.

broader investigation of how the region's resources were perceived, exploited and applied. Human societies have used natural resources for a wide variety of reasons, which flow from perceived social needs or aspirations. A broader perspective on ancient economic behaviour in the north Aegean must take some account of what these social aspirations were and how they were connected to economic activities. So it is to the relationship between the social and the economic that these methodological reflections should now turn.

3

Societies and economies

THE SOCIAL AND THE ECONOMIC

> 'the new peace and the monarchical state, the shift of society's centre from the coasts to the hinterland—all these changes throttled ancient capitalism instead of causing it to flourish (as one might a priori expect).' (Max Weber, *The Agrarian Sociology of Ancient Civilizations,* 1909, tr. R. I. Frank, London and New York, 1976, 358)

Territorial centralization within the Hellenistic kingdoms was, according to Max Weber, the great undoing of the green shoots of 'ancient capitalism'. If we follow Weber's thought to its logical conclusion, then the formative role of Macedon was a key factor in this process of contraction, since the organizational practices of the kingdom were grafted onto and consolidated in all the kingdoms inherited by the Successors. The idea that territorial consolidation within a sovereign state should automatically precipitate a change in attitudes to capital, commercial enterprise, and economic performance seems an odd way of distinguishing between ancient kinds of 'capitalism' (if we accept this description with Weber) and more recent versions of capitalism. It needs more scrutiny.

Weber's evaluation of ancient economies is a useful starting point for thinking about the relationship between the social and the economic in classical antiquity. It is an interesting way of encapsulating the problem of economic changes, because it helps to connect monarchies with economic behaviour; and because Weber's approach to comparative historical economies, as illustrated here, was different in key respects from the arguments that have trapped debates about the economies of classical antiquity over the last half-century. Weber's long historical perspective was unusual among nineteenth- and early twentieth-century excursions into economic theory, in contrast to the great pioneers of the previous century.[1] Although his name is less frequently evoked today in the context of classical antiquity than it is in connection with medieval history and the 'Protestant ethic', Weber's endorsement of key concepts developed by some of his predecessors continued to have a profound impact on twentieth-century economic historians—the notion of the 'consumer city'; the 'rationalism' of certain industrial processes; and, above all, in the notion of a limited form of 'capitalism', limited, that is, by certain institutional and social phenomena, specifically the existence of slavery, and the breaks put on exports by the ideology of the propertied élite. Moses Finley approvingly underscored these aspects of Weber's analysis, although he was disinclined to use the term 'capitalism' in any form, however limited. According to Finley, 'the strong drive to acquire wealth was not translated [in classical antiquity] into a drive to create capital; stated differently, the prevailing mentality was acquisitive but not productive.'[2] He therefore argued forcefully that analogies with other, more recent historical periods of European history were misguided and wrong-headed. Yet that is precisely what Finley was doing himself, by emphasizing the supposedly profound differences between ancient subsistence patterns and 'modern' capitalism, to the virtual exclusion of any other theoretical approaches to historical economies.

During the course of the last century, there has been a great temptation, when thinking about exchange in the remote past, to imagine a world blighted by ignorance, primitivism, and lack of change. This is to apply criteria and expectations of progress appropriate mainly for the last two hundred years to all earlier periods, as if the process of industrialization explained ancient and medieval forms of subsistence as well as more recent ones. The historians of the late nineteenth and early twentieth century, who were most influential in formulating concepts about the economies of antiquity—Werner Sombart, Johannes Hasebroek, and subsequently Max Weber, Karl Polanyi, and Moses Finley—were mainly concerned with differentiating those characteristics that were considered to have formed the origins of modern capitalist economies from what came before them.[3] The context of these discussions was rooted in more

[1] Morley 2009, 31–9 for discussion of the historical context of Weber's approach; Nafissi 2005, 17–20 and 91–130, for a more detailed analysis of Weber's ideas about ancient economies; Hodgson 2001, esp. 178–231 for the 'ahistorical' turn from Talcott Parsons to John Maynard Keynes.

[2] Finley 1985 [1999] 144; Finley citing Weber approvingly: 26, 117, 122, 125, 138–9, 182, 192.

[3] Morris in Finley 1985[1999], ix–xxxii; cf. also I. Morris and J. G. Manning, 'Introduction', in Manning and Morris 2005, 1–44; W. Scheidel, I. Morris, and R. Saller, 'Introduction', *CEHGRW* 1–12; Bresson 2007, 8–26 with further analysis.

recent social and economic preoccupations, and particularly with the distinctiveness of Western 'modernity'. Historians and sociologists who took the long view of human history as their canvas were concerned with ways of explaining or elucidating the relationships, and the many intellectual and cultural facets, which connect 'antiquity' and 'modernity'; terms that became the twin components in a rhetorical reflection on the (largely unknowable) past.[4] What mattered most in such studies was the way in which classical antiquity served as a foil to 'modernity'. The authors were less interested in studying antiquity as a subject that deserved to be explored on its own terms.

The early inventors of theories about ancient economies retain an aura of authority, even though most of the ideas that they espoused no longer inform the assumptions that contemporary scholars of classical antiquity apply in their historical investigations. Historians today do not begin with the individual household as the primeval nucleus of ancient societies, as one of the most eminent founding theorists, Werner Sombart, did. The idea that all households and, by extension, whole communities, focused their energies on being 'autarkic', that is, not dependent on others, has been turned inside out by studies of Mediterranean ecologies (see further below). We no longer worry about whether ancient cities were primarily centres of consumption rather than production, whilst accepting that civic centres were the main loci of élite expenditure.[5] Nevertheless, there are other aspects of economic behaviour isolated by nineteenth-century historians that continue to generate intense debate. Members of the so-called German 'historical' school, such as J. K. Rodbertus and Gustav von Schmoller, justifiably objected to key aspects of 'classical' economic theory (as propounded by Adam Smith and David Ricardo). They were unhappy with what they saw as mechanistic processes, in which abstract 'market' principles were given free rein, without consideration of circumstances. Although some of the ideas developed by these late nineteenth-century historians have not stood the test of time (such as their notion of quasi-autonomous domestic economies, or about gratuitous gift exchange), their fundamental objections to impersonal economic drivers have gathered support from a variety of quarters and in some respects have become far more significant than the authors themselves could ever have imagined. Other topics explored by

[4] Morley 2009 provides a rich discussion.

[5] Finley 1985 [1999] 192–3 and cf. Morris, ibid., xvi–xviii; see the contributions to Parkins and Smith 1998; *CEHGRW* 82–3, 405–6, 546; 578, 669. For an extended analysis of Max Weber, Karl Polanyi, and Moses Finley, as well as their predecessors in the German 'historical' school, Nafissi 2005; Bresson 2007, 10–17.

early theorists remain important but contested. Among these perhaps the most under-rated phenomenon is the role of markets, a topic that deserves to be considered in more detail.

Ancient historians have tended to be conservative in their use of economic and sociological theories, following the lead set by modern historians and to a lesser extent by anthropologists. Archaeologists have adopted anthropological ideas much more readily, but have been less interested in the kinds of questions that historians are preoccupied with. This may explain why Moses Finley's 'minimalist' approach has had, and continues to have, an enormous appeal for students of classical antiquity, and why Finley's works are cited more frequently than Weber's. In his monograph *The Bücher-Meyer Controversy*, Finley retold the debates on economic questions of the late nineteenth century through a very particular lens, namely through the polarity of 'primitivist', or rather 'substantivist' and 'modernist' positions, with the 'primitivists'/'substantivists' cast as the angels, even though his own views about supposed 'modernists', notably Eduard Meyer, were far more complex, if not contradictory.[6] Finley adopted Bücher's 'substantivism' (the notion of the fundamental 'embeddedness' of ordinary economic relations in a social matrix), and adapted Weber's limited form of 'capitalism' by confining significant volumes of exchange, and significant economic development, to a small number of large cities, which, he argued, were effectively parasitic to the political structures that enabled exceptional variety and exceptional quantities of foodstuffs, exotic materials, and other manufactured commodities, to reach them.[7] The implication was that the wealthy élites—never sufficiently explored beyond Athens and Rome—preyed on the numerical majority of small farmers, tenants, and dispossessed, whether slave or free. This shrewd compromise effectively made Finley's views more elastic than his expositions imply, allowing subsequent studies to be measured up to his published evaluations, or contrasted with them. The tendency to measure up scholarly contributions to Finley's orthodoxy has given the discourse on ancient economic analysis a distinctly Manichean sense, with little recognition that Finley's attitude could, at worst, simply have been misconceived, or, at best, insufficiently nuanced.[8] The question whether Finley was justified in arguing that theories applied to the analysis of modern economies were irrelevant to the ancient classical world has in practice been evaded by

[6] Nafissi 2005, 203–8, 237–47.

[7] Finley 1985 [1999] 19–20, 23, 26–7, 32–3, 89, 106–7, 136–9, 144–6, 156–7, 192–3.

[8] The term 'Manichean' was applied by Andreau 2002 [1995] 34; Finleyan 'orthodoxy': see Morris in Finley 1985 [1999] xxiv.

ancient historians, although there has been a change of strategy during the last decade, albeit a change that has coincided with a new sense of doubt among contemporary economists.

During the last two decades, and particularly in the years since the financial downturn of 2008, economists have had to face up to an apparent gap between prevailing economic theories and the inescapable realities of economic crisis in many parts of the globe. For a number of historical analysts, the economic downturn has acted as a catalyst, clarifying existing doubts about the ways that contemporary capitalism is thought to work, rather than undermining established assumptions in a fundamental way. The re-evaluation of theories about contemporary economic phenomena has coincided with a renewed interest in the social dimensions of economic behaviour, in part due to the application of evolutionary theory to economic life, and partly as a result of experimental approaches, which suggest that people do not behave in the ways that theory predicts.

The principal problem faced by economic sociologists, and socially-inclined economists, has been, on the one hand, to make coherent connections between the thinking individual, who chooses how to live, and the broad matrix of society; and, on the other, to make sense of economies in holistic ways, whilst analysing trends, patterns, or outcomes. From Karl Marx to George Soros, analysts have sought to draw general principles from particular experiences; but the search for universal laws, or rules of economic dynamics, have proved frustratingly elusive. Analysis can capture something of the essence of economic patterns, or economic relations, but the process of simplifying ideas in order to understand what is going on has usually meant that other, possibly key, factors have been excluded in the process. This methodological difficulty awaits any economic analysis, whatever the period or place.

For much of the twentieth century, sociologists and economists adopted different routes and different methodologies towards the analysis of historical economies. In a defining article published in 1985, Mark Granovetter identified these parallel approaches as a tendency of some theories to be 'under-socialized' (a predominant weakness of classical economic theory), while sociologists have tended to produce 'over-socialized' models, giving an exaggerated importance to the influence of social mores on economic relations. The same sort of critique has been used to examine the kinds of models that have been applied to classical antiquity, although, as in the case of other periods and more recent contexts, there is little agreement among specialists about how these evaluations may lead to more holistic ways of approaching the economies of the past.[9] These debates involve far more than minor scholarly disputes. Differences of perspective result in part from different conceptual approaches, as well as ideological ones. So the discourse on historical economies cannot easily satisfy all those involved in the discussion. There will inevitably be aspects of complex social processes that will not be resolvable by adopting any single approach.

Yet without a theoretical perspective and a conscious methodology, no analysis can be achieved. How should historians organize research in order to explore economic behaviour? The lengthy discussions of the late nineteenth and early twentieth century brought about a measure of agreement among historians from the German, British, and North American traditions, namely that neither could the process of deduction from a body of accumulated data, nor the development of concepts based on specific cases (induction), be expected to produce appropriate ways of understanding historical economies.[10] As econometric techniques developed in the twentieth century, economists abandoned historical perspectives to historians and sociologists, in effect postponing the quest for long-term economic mechanisms or universal principles, even though many economists assume that long-term, if not universal economic patterns do exist.[11] The editors and some of the contributors to the new *Cambridge Economic History of the Greco-Roman World (CEHGRW)* have opted for one way of cutting this Gordian knot, namely by adopting the general approach of the 'New Institutional Economics', particularly the form in which these ideas are presented in the works of Douglass North.[12] Nevertheless, institutional approaches to historical economies are not particularly new. Thorstein Veblen's *The Theory of the Leisure Class* (1899) inspired several generations of sociologists and socially-minded economists, who wanted to allocate much more importance to social responses and to consumer attitudes. Although several chapters in the *CEHGRW* are devoted to consumption, their focus is overwhelmingly on the consumption of food, rather than of

[9] Granovetter 1985, esp. 481–93, 499–503; Morris in Finley 1985 [1999] xxviii–xxxii, with a discussion of Finley's ideas, which can be critiqued as 'under-socialized', as well as 'over-socialized'.

[10] Hodgson 2001, 79–177, with detailed discussion; cf. also the contributions to Rawski et al. 1996.

[11] Hodgson 2001, 232–57, 273–86.

[12] Scheidel et al., *CEHGRW*, 5–12 for a programmatic statement adopting the concepts of 'New Institutional Economics' (NIE) as applicable for the remote past of Eurasia; ibid. 113–43 for a fuller exposition of the potential value of NIE as a theoretical set of tools for ancient history by Frier and Kehoe; P. Bang's review, *JRS* 99 (2009), esp. 199–206 provides a broader context for these ideas and their applicability.

commodities or manufactured products, leave alone services. This makes it hard to evaluate the full applicability of the theoretical principles articulated in the introduction to the volume.

By adopting the ideas of 'New Institutional Economics', the editors of the *CEHGRW* have aligned themselves with the dominant thread of North American thinking about historical economies. An understanding of historical economies through institutions has proved to be a broad church, uniting historians as well as economists since the early 1900s (notwithstanding the kind of criticism of specific institutional arguments expressed by Mark Granovetter, for example).[13] The aspiration of many institutional historians within this tradition has been to focus on strong social uniformities and well-defined common institutional patterns, which provide suitable evidence for study and avoid the problems associated with the idiosyncrasy of subjective decision-making. The 'spirit of the age', a Hegelian concept made memorable by Max Weber, was no longer acceptable for a more scientifically-inclined era.[14]

The majority of North American theorists, from John Commons onwards, nevertheless took economic theory away from some of the key institutional ideas propounded by Thorstein Veblen at the turn of the nineteenth and twentieth century. Veblen was a brilliant thinker, but a cultural and social outsider among his academic peers.[15] Although he did not succeed in developing a systematically argued exposition of his ideas, some of his key concepts remain central to the future development of theories about long-term economic structures. Veblen was very interested in the role of knowledge in processes of production, particularly in the kind of knowledge that is acquired by habitual practices and cumulative experience. In place of the rationalistic, calculating *homo economicus* of classical, that is, eighteenth-century economic thought (and of its neo-classical, twentieth-century successors), Veblen wanted to put a human mind shaped by habits of thought and habitual practices, rooted in everyday experience. Among his closest intellectual colleagues and conceptual mentors were William James and Charles Sanders Peirce, who explored the idea of knowledge in terms of habitual propensities. Veblen understood that the principles of Darwinian natural selection had somehow to be factored into a historical understanding of human societies (unlike many of his associates and successors, who opted for a

[13] Granovetter 1985, 499–505, discussing Oliver Williamson's work on market hierarchies; see below for further discussion of markets.

[14] Hodgson 2001, 171, citing John Commons' direct criticism of Weber.

[15] Hodgson 1998; Hodgson 2001, 228, cites the distinguished economist Joan Robinson: [Veblen was] 'the most original economist born and bred in the USA.'

more mechanistic, Spencerian evolution of historical societies as quasi-homogeneous units).[16] Although ancient historians have begun to explore applications of natural selection at a metaphorical and at an abstract level,[17] Darwin's ideas have proved difficult to articulate in social contexts, since natural selection applies to the reproductive capacity of individuals, whilst simple biological models and metaphors of historical societies have consistently been found wanting. Nevertheless, Veblen's concept of habitual propensities provides a more flexible way of thinking about the origins and evolution of institutions than the rule-based definition adopted by North, whilst at the same time offering a direct connection to Pierre Bourdieu's notion of *habitus*.[18]

The instinctive sentiment of ancient historians for the ideas of the nineteenth-century German Historical School reflects a continuing appreciation of the close connection between social and economic factors in the ways in which ancient societies were organized. The labour-intensive character of the complete spectrum of activities associated with subsistence drove an overwhelming preoccupation with manpower (and womanpower), manifested in reproductive habits, the acquisition of servile labour, and the ordering of functional groups to maximize productive endeavour. The same drivers have powered other historical societies. In order to define the distinctive features of economies in the first millennium BC north Aegean, we need to take account of the ecological context of the societies located here, and of the specializations that they displayed.

ECOLOGICAL VARIABILITY AND INTER-DEPENDENT NETWORKS ACROSS THE AEGEAN

> 'No other city [other than Athens, that is,] has even two of these things: the same city does not even have timber and flax, but wherever there is flax in abundance, the land is smooth and timberless. There is not even copper and iron from the same city, but there is one product here and another there.' ([Xen.] *Ath. Pol.* 2. 12 tr. G. W. Bowersock)

[16] Veblen 1899, 18 and 20–69; Veblen 1919, 1–81 (on the role of scientific thinking and evolutionary thinking); 56-81 ('Why is Economics not an Evolutionary Science?' [1898]).

[17] See for example Morris 2009a and Scheidel 2009.

[18] Veblen 1899, 190; Bourdieu 1990, 52–65, 66–79, 107–09; Hodgson 1998; Hodgson 2001, 289–92.

The short and enigmatic constitutional treatise that found its way erroneously into the works of Xenophon, together with the genuinely Xenophontic *Ways and Means*, are probably the most useful and perceptive general statements about the world of inter-state commercial relations in the period between the second half of the fifth and the middle of the fourth century BC. Although the analytical value of these works has been denigrated,[19] most historians today see no reason why such writings should not be used alongside other types of evidence, whether literary, epigraphic, or material.[20]

Nineteenth-century historians of classical antiquity had a rather limited set of resources from which to speculate on ancient economic foundations, consisting mainly of literary works in Greek and Latin. Classical writers had few objective resources for reflecting on their own past and their Victorian readers lacked a convincing set of alternative data that could illuminate classical literature in independent ways. The study of inscriptions, and various classes of material evidence, some of which were also inscribed (notably trade *amphorae*) became increasingly available in the course of the twentieth century, but are only now being subjected to the kind of geographical and statistical analysis that will provide reliable data for economic purposes. The pioneering methodological studies have come from Romanists, who have produced a fundamental range of ceramic data sets.[21] Other types of material evidence, from identifiable settlements, to fish-processing vats and fulling workshops, are being subjected to spatial and volumetric analyses.[22] Leaving aside tombstones, epigraphic evidence does not lend itself at all easily to any kind of statistical analysis or to a clear methodological framework. Public inscriptions are simply too rare to provide more than sample data and are usually studied as independent documents, or classed with other documents of the same form, such as civic decrees or honours voted to

[19] Notably by Finley 1985 [1999] 19: 'In Xenophon, however, there is not one sentence that expresses an economic principle or offers an economic analysis, nothing on efficiency of production, "rational" choice, the marketing of crops.' Cf. ibid. 45, 73, and esp. 134–6, 236 n.39.

[20] In the *CEHGRW* Davies, Möller, and von Reden refer extensively to Xenophon's economic works (see esp. 339–48, 382, 466, 477 (Reger).

[21] David Peacock's seminal work on Roman *amphora* production and distribution (Peacock 1982) has inspired analogous work on Aegean and Black Sea transport fabrics (Whitbread 1995; Kassab Tezgör and Inaishvili 2010; Tzochev et al. 2011).

[22] Bowman and Wilson 2009, 12–84, setting out the principles of the project, *The Economy of the Roman Empire: Integration, Growth, and Decline;* Bowman and Wilson 2012; further volumes have been announced on the project's web pages http://oxrep.classics.ox.ac.uk/home

civic magistrates.[23] They are, nevertheless, invaluable as evidence of legally binding processes and procedures. This fact alone makes the appearance of public inscriptions in relatively remote parts of the north a matter of considerable interest. Almost every single example of a public document (and some private ones) from Thrace and Macedonia adds something unique and valuable to our knowledge of the local applications of what were, by the time such documents appear, widely established principles, not just in central and southern Greece and Ionia, but also in these neighbouring regions that are often excluded, consciously or unconsciously, from the 'Hellenic' cultural and political realm.

There are potentially knowable data sets of various material residues that can be examined scientifically (measured, dated, analysed); though what they mean in economic terms is debatable. Since economists and politicians debate the economic significance of various kinds of data even today, we should not be surprised that there are grounds for dispute about past economies. The existence of a debate does not invalidate the process of discussion; nor should it diminish the potential value of the data under discussion for determining economic relations or economic conclusions. The development of new theoretical frameworks in recent decades is making it easier to see how disparate data sets may nevertheless fit into a coherent pattern of exchange, which is consistent with the kinds of statements made by Ps.-Xenophon and Xenophon, as well as other ancient authors.

Finley believed that new material data, or larger quantities of material evidence, would not fundamentally affect the way we understand the underlying nature of ancient economies.[24] He conceived the ancient classical world as dominated by landowners of high status, although he was unwilling to define who was to be included and what proportion of the population was involved. The most glaring weakness of this assumption is not so much its emphasis on a particular status group, as the unchanging character of the underlying social framework. Since there is no evidence that landowners, however defined, controlled the means of production, there is no reason to think that the fundamental mechanisms of economic life were static. On the contrary, there are good reasons to believe that change was constant, though significant step changes can be demarcated in relatively restricted periods.

[23] See in particular Fröhlich 2004, 51–76 (aims of control and the vocabulary of civic control of magistrates); 113–15, 122–7, 147–52, 205, 265–6, 275–6, 292–3, 381–4, 400–1, 412–13, 429, 448; Hatzopoulos 1996, I, 371–429. See Index for individual documents.

[24] Finley 1985 [1999] 33, 59, 136–7, 138, 144–5, 146–7, 157, 193.

The static, caste-dominated view of ancient societies has been challenged from three directions—by a gradualist concept of state formation; by interactionist models of social intercourse, based on Network theory; and by the renewal of interest in ecological drivers of economic and social exchange. Ian Morris has argued, in a number of publications, and using separate data sets, that Aegean Greeks were consciously egalitarian in spirit and materially unremarkable, if comfortable, in the seventh and sixth centuries BC, while Athenian society changed during the fifth century from being markedly egalitarian towards the kind of stratified, top-loaded administrative and knowledge-based élite singled out by Ernest Gellner in his definition of an 'agro-literate' state. However, this analysis of Athenian society refers not to the territory of Attica alone, but to the wider network of overland resources acquired by a combination of alliance and brinkmanship.[25] Nevertheless, the focus of this analysis is on state formation, and Morris has redefined this process as one of progressive, dynamic stages, rather than a one-off development, which makes Gellner's original, and rather widely drawn definition of such societies look overly prescriptive and over-determined. Morris rejects the conventional label of 'empire' in describing Athenian power in the fifth century BC, in favour of the 'Greater Athenian State', emphasizing the institutions shared amongst the beneficiaries of Athenian power, which extended to a multitude of minor communities across the Aegean, including shared taxation, a shared coinage and a massive *emporion* at Piraeus.

Morris extends this highly dynamic conceptualization of Athenian state evolution, which gives predictable prominence to the formative role of military aggrandizement, to other states in the Aegean that acquired exceptional power amongst their peers, including Sparta, Thebes, Syracuse, and the Chalkidian League in the north. Peer competition among Greek communities has often been recognized as a political driver in Aegean history, but Morris's emphasis on demographic growth and responses to it in the form of egalitarian tactics has given this vector of success an added twist, by connecting demographic changes much more directly with socio-political emancipation.[26]

[25] Gellner 1983, 9–10; Morris 2009a, 136–9; Morris 2009b, 66–77; he contrasts the eye-watering wealth of the Lydian named Pythios, who lavishly entertained the Persian army and offered Xerxes his fortune of 2,000 silver talents and 3,993,000 gold darics (Hdt. 7.28–29), with the one Athenian of note, Kleinias, son of Alkibiades, who put out a trireme on his own account (Hdt. 8.17; Morris 2009b, 74). Morris builds his argument on a number of successive, detailed studies of funerary and residential data, particularly Morris 2005. This broad level of apparent material homogeneity is not inconsistent with real material disparities and real social tensions, as discussed by Rhodes 2000, esp. 126–36.

[26] Morris 2009b, 73–4; 2009a, 144–67; Morris 2005 for developing standards of living; cf. Nevett 2010, 52–4 and fig. 3.3.

This rationale of Greek state formation incorporates extra-territorial activities and acquisitions, but nevertheless focuses on the internal mechanisms of organizational development. Another aspect of the same process, namely the role played by social networks, has recently been explored in a series of conferences, some of which are now published.[27] Network theory is a tool with a great deal of potential for examining historical social interactions. As a method derived from physical and mathematical applications, it can provide greater clarity in understanding the effectiveness of a network in transmitting ideas, people, and goods. Networks do not generate exchange automatically, but rather undergo phase changes, when the relationships between individual links lead to the emergence of nodes and clusters of nodes. Events within networks can then generate more specific patterns. Experimental data shows that social networks do not correlate directly with other physical networks, since they display some memory-induced modifications. Whereas, in the physical world, networks often display power law distributions, with large numbers of poorly connected nodes and a few very well-connected 'hubs', networks in human societies are reinforced by memory and social institutions, which provide additional stability and continuity.[28] The network analogy is implicit in the narrative of Greek 'colonial' expansion in the first half of the first millennium BC, and Irad Malkin, perhaps more than any other scholar, has articulated the ways in which Greek overseas ventures reflect the dynamics of a 'small world' network, in which individuals, separated by varying geographical distances, may nonetheless be closely linked by virtue of shared interests or relationships. The potential weakness of this argument lies in the application of a very specific mechanism, designed to demonstrate the connectedness of historical individuals, to a diachronic set of data. In order to have explanatory value, a 'small world' network must be chronologically quite well defined, since the individuals who would have formed the nodes of the network were linked by personal ties of trust. Other kinds of networks than the 'small world' variety do not have to be personal ones; they can be organizational or functional networks. The current interest in social networks has spawned a great deal of research that is potentially relevant to the study of ancient societies too. It is clear, for example, that the psychological attitude of the

[27] See the contributors to *Networks;* Knappett 2011; Malkin 2011; also Dietler 2011; various contributors to *HellEc III.*

[28] Bak 1997, 183–98, 185–7, 'Real economics is like sand'; Watts 2003, 220–84; Ball 2004, 452–66; Collar 2009 provides a discrete exposition of the mechanical implications. The role of networks in the northern Aegean is developed in Chs 4, and 5.

participants in a network plays an active part in the effectiveness of information transmitted.[29]

In the north Aegean area, there is a wealth of data that can be exploited to understand how social networks developed in the second half of the first millennium BC. Coin distributions indicate the non-random pattern of economic networks, confirming literary and epigraphic references to commercial agreements between specified partners (see further Chapters 4, 5, and 6). This allows a more coherent view to emerge of those relationships that evolved as historic partnerships, with a marked degree of longevity. Among the longest-lived of these partnerships was that between the inhabitants of the island of Thasos and a wide network of contacts, Greek and non-Greek, across the east Balkans.

The recent spate of research on social networks has drawn attention away from ecological concerns, expressed most ambitiously by Horden and Purcell's *The Corrupting Sea*. Whilst being much quoted, this seminal study has been less influential on the historical analysis of individual regions than might have been expected.[30] The canvas is far larger than most historians and archaeologists are comfortable with, which has discouraged imitators.[31] Yet few commentators have acknowledged that Horden and Purcell's work has changed the way that historians conceive the ancient classical world as explicitly as Ian Morris has done.[32] Not all Horden and Purcell's concepts and arguments have been equally convincing. Their rejection of cities as subjects of analysis, and of concrete agglomerations in general, has been among the least persuasive of their theses, despite the important arguments that they have marshalled about the 'labile' urban fabric of much Mediterranean city life. This is a topic to which I will return below.[33]

Although they deny an 'interactionist' approach, there are aspects of Horden and Purcell's thesis that are entirely compatible with studies inspired by Network theory. The idea of 'dispersed hinterlands' and the notion of 'connectivity' itself belongs to the portmanteau of terms that

[29] Ball 2004, 466, commenting on Duncan Watts' repetition of the letter-posting experiment conducted by Stanley Milgram that demonstrated the 'six degrees of separation' between human subjects (Watts 2003, 130–9, 154–61).

[30] The most substantial engagement with Horden and Purcell's conceptual framework is by the contributors to Harris 2005. Among the many reviews I would single out are those of Shaw (2001) and Algazi (2005); see also my remarks in Archibald 2005a, 6–8.

[31] See now Broodbank (forthcoming).

[32] Morris 2003; idem 2009b, 79–80.

[33] Horden and Purcell 2000, 90–105, on the problems of defining settlement forms.

are subsumed under 'small world' networks.[34] 'Interaction' does not just apply to human communities. We also need a more systematic approach to human interactions with landscapes, flora and fauna. The value that Horden and Purcell ascribe to those aspects of Mediterranean ecologies that most ancient histories have eschewed—the role of marginal resources; of wetland environment, tree crops, textiles, and sedimentary history—is among the more significant and original contributions of their encyclopaedic study.[35]

EMERGING MARKETS

Markets, however, get modest recognition as vectors of exchange in Horden and Purcell's ecological history of the Mediterranean. 'The "market" is among those features of modernity whose presence or absence in the past is principally of interest from the progressivist point of view'.[36] Perhaps markets seemed to the authors an unattractively formal element, which disrupts their more fluid notion of 'redistribution', incorporating as it does commercial and non-market exchanges. Yet it is impossible to consider economic behaviour without clarifying the role of markets, which presuppose a set of important juridical concepts—concepts that participants in a market need to share for any exchanges, however modest, however informal, to take place. Not only must there be some mechanism for protecting the goods or commodities offered for sale (and of ensuring the quality of what was for sale), but there must also be recognition that property rights have been transferred from the seller to the purchaser. A widespread conviction by economists in the universality of 'the market' has meant that there has been surprisingly little investigation of how markets evolved and how they differ in historical and cultural terms.[37] If 'progressivism' is a fault, then the

[34] Horden and Purcell 2000, 115–22 (dispersed hinterlands); 123–72 (connectivity); cf. Watts 2003, 19–42, 159–61, 239–41, 299–301; Shaw 2001, 447; Archibald 2005a, 7–8; Malkin 2011, 15–64.

[35] Horden and Purcell 2000, 178–230 (margins and wetlands); 237–63 (the irrigated landscape); 298–341 (Mediterranean catastrophes). 'Here is where an ecological approach comes into its own, as accounts of culinary repertoires and agrosystems merge almost seamlessly into discussions of the socialized landscape and its transformations.' (Algazi 2005, 234).

[36] Horden and Purcell 2000, 149; see Algazi 2005, 243 for a spirited critique. Purcell has responded in the subject matter of the Sather Lectures, delivered in 2011.

[37] Granovetter 1985, 499–503 (critique of Oliver Williamson's *Markets and Hierarchies*, 1975); Hodgson 2001, 248–57, 249, 256, on the neglect of markets as institutions by

problem already has roots back in the remote past, in a revisionist argument criticizing Eratosthenes and Apollodorus for what Strabo took to be unjustified slurs by them on the geographical knowledge of Homer and the early Greek poets. The geographer refers to people who still know nothing about food storage or shopping, exchanging one commodity for another (*Geogr.* 7.3.7 (C300)). As it happens, the context is apposite, since Strabo places this critique in the midst of a discussion about knowledge of the Black Sea region, and of antique ideas about Thracians, Mysians, Getae, and peoples beyond them—Scythians, and the rather vague 'Hippemolgoi', 'Galaktophagoi', and 'Abioi' (Hom. *Il.* 13.5–6).[38]

Weber's identification of 'early capitalism' reflects his recognition of some developed forms of money transactions. Finley did not discuss the role of money in ancient economies and regarded markets as highly limited in scope: 'The typical "peasant market" was a place where peasants (and no doubt village craftsmen) met from a radius of five or six miles in order to fill gaps in necessities by exchange with each other; there were only a few things that a peasant could not produce himself—a metal ploughshare for example—when everything went well. The paucity of coin finds in genuinely rural areas is no accident'.[39] This echoes, in some respects, Plato's rather tongue-in-cheek description of an ideal society, in which life's simplicities are to the fore, with citizens walking about barefoot in summer, dining and drinking in garlands, eating home-produced food off leaves (*Resp.* 372a–c). Even Plato had to concede that a respectable society needed properly made agricultural tools, and a rational organization of buying and selling, if his philosophically inclined citizens were not to waste a lot of time hanging about (*Resp.* 370b–371c). His conclusion was that respectable societies needed specialists and needed to organize specialist activities in ways that would be socially useful (*Resp.* 2. 369b–370e). Xenophon reflects a more analytical response than his former academic associate, remarking on the profound

economists and historians alike. Harris 1989 [2006] on the legal mechanisms behind commercial exchanges in Athens. Veblen's reflections on markets are worth repeating: 'The course of market events took its passionless way without traceable relation or deference to any man's convenience and without traceable guidance towards an ulterior end. Man's part in the pecuniary world was to respond with alacrity to the situation, and so adapt his vendible effects to the shifting demand as to realize something in the outcome.' (1919, 141 [*Preconceptions of Economic Science II*, first published 1899]).

[38] Baladié (1989, 187–95) provides a nuanced framework of the ancient debates about Black Sea geography ad loc. 7.3.2–3, citing Poseidonios (*FGrH* 87 F104 = Edelstein-Kidd fr. 277a = Theiler F45) on the European origins of the Mysians and their vegetarian lifestyle.

[39] Finley 1985 [1999], 107.

differences in the division of labour between large and small towns (Xen. *Cyrop.* 8.2.5; cf. Xen. *Mem.3.* 10. 9–15: on the unique products of particularly gifted craftsmen). These remarks about particular kinds of goods for particular clients point to some specific ways in which the modern academic debate about ancient markets can be taken forward.

As economists have come to realize during the banking crisis of the last five years, even contemporary markets are hard to understand, because the reality of multiple transactions, in highly variable economic settings, cannot be subsumed under the formulae composed at the (necessarily simplified) abstract level. We may think of markets in terms of stocks and shares, or complex electronic flows; but the rules of formal inter-bank transfers are quite different, in substance as well as in kind, from the transactions made by individuals. If I want to pay for local services incurred during fieldwork in any southern European country (or in any predominantly rural part of the globe), I must pay in cash. Various international currencies are acceptable, but I may not pay by credit card. I can make an electronic bank transfer of credit from a UK bank account to a foreign bank account associated with overseas partners, but that must be done in a branch that has the designated authority to do so. The differences between these transactions reflect the non-compatibility of certain kinds of exchange. Similarly, the price of cup cakes at a charity event, or of second-hand items in a car boot sale, is determined by various locally determined criteria, not by the price of these items on the high street. As John Kay has argued, using many examples, from the price of Van Gogh's artworks to flower markets and Far Eastern commodities, there are many different markets and they operate according to different rules. Historical assets play a role in determining the range and robustness of markets in specific areas of the world, but social attitudes to consumption are at least as significant in determining how the cumulative effects of market transactions translate into national budgets.[40] We might expect ancient economies to display at least some of the same inconsistencies and incompatible transactions as in the contemporary world.

Recent work on banking, on the overall level of monetization in the Mediterranean, and on the range of denominations available in a large number of locations, shows that money in antiquity was not a rudimentary mechanism.[41] To admit this does not make ancient economies somehow analogous to modern ones. There is nothing particularly

[40] Kay 2003,14–36, 65–86.

[41] The contributions to Verboven et al. 2008 amply demonstrate the objective complexity of monetary practices, including credit transfers.

modern about the use of quantities of heavy metal as a medium of exchange. One of the most distinctive features of classical economies is the high social and economic value accorded to metals, whether coined or accumulated in other forms, notably as plate.

Another distinctive feature is the circulation of base and precious metals in numerous small denominations. Until recently, the very smallest copper alloy and silver coins were rarely discovered, because of their exiguous dimensions. The discovery of a large hoard of tiny silver coins from the vicinity of ancient Kolophon in Ionia (902 quarter and half obols, plus one obol), together with 77 pieces of worked and unworked silver metal, has done a great deal to change perceptions of how coined money was actually used. Such silver issues can be matched by similar small denominations of copper alloy coins from recent excavations, where dry sieving and flotation is regularly practised, as well as metal detecting. Such tiny copper alloy coins have been recovered from the Thracian *emporion* at Vetren, Bulgaria (ancient Pistiros) (Fig. 3.1).[42]

These tiny coins may have been discontinued once Roman-sponsored issues replaced these particular Greek denominations during the second half of the second century BC. There were two phases within this transition. The first began some time after the reopening of the Macedonian mines in 158 BC, (following their closure in 167), and the issuing of new denominations, with different face types from those of the defeated Macedonian monarch, Perseus. Bronze coins began to be issued under the authority of Roman administrators. The second phase is marked by a series of silver tetradrachms, showing a portrait head of Alexander the Great, and on the reverse the club of Herakles, together with the names of Roman magistrates, particularly Q. Braetius Sura and a man known only from this coin series as Aesillas.[43] The wide circulation of these issues, along with the 'New Style' large denominations of Thasos and Maroneia (which shadow the Athenian issues of this new form), is symptomatic of the wider economic changes that were affecting the whole east Balkan region. It is perhaps ironic that the whole area was more closely integrated, from an economic perspective, in this very period, than at any time before or afterwards, until the Ottoman era. The gradual replacement of Greek coins by Roman ones marks the economic transition from the forms explored in this book to the new economic order driven by Roman taxation. The most visible expression of this transformation is articulated in the regulations set out in the Tax Law of Asia, preserved in

[42] Kim and Kroll 2008 (Kolophon hoard); the copper alloy fractional money comes from the British excavation trenches at Vetren (unpublished; see Archibald forthcoming 2015).

[43] Touratsoglou 1993; Bauslaugh 2000; de Callataÿ 1997b; Dahmen 2010, 54–6, 59–61 with discussion.

(a)

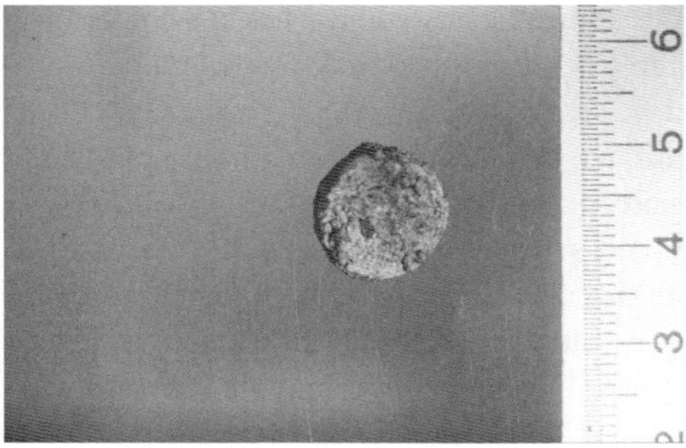

(b)

(c)

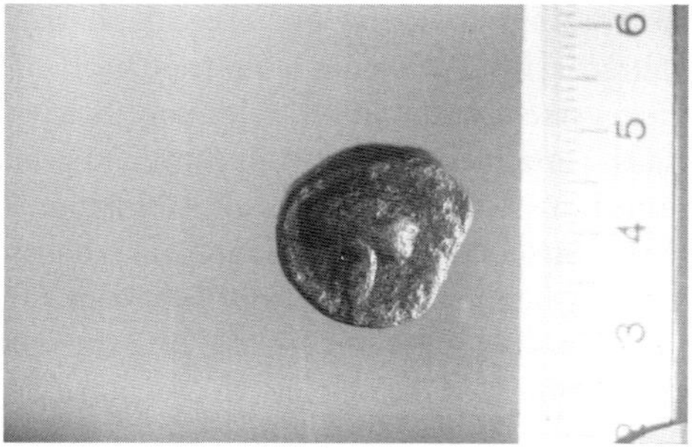

Fig. 3.1. (a–c) Bronze coins from Adjiyska Vodenitsa (ancient Pistiros), used as small change in local market transactions.

an inscription from Ephesus, by which the harbour dues emanating from the whole region of the Black Sea, the Hellespontine Straits, and the adjacent land masses, became subsumed under the imperial *portorium*.[44]

[44] Mitchell 2008, 198–201.

Before the introduction of the Asian Tax Law, we must assume that each community was entitled to raise its own taxes and to use the revenue therefrom for its own benefit. Harbour dues constituted one of the most lucrative resources for civic authorities, but also for territorial powers. The geographical or topographical foci of market centres made them targets for greater powers to exploit financially. Kotys I of Thrace could raise as much as 200 talents per annum from *emporia* in his territories (Dem. 23. 110). Philip II of Macedon redirected the harbour and market dues of Thessalian ports and other cities to his royal coffers (Dem. 1.22; Just. 11.3.2). That kings could and did intervene in the affairs of regions and individual civic communities is not in doubt. However, these occasional references to high-level intervention do no more than cast a strong but pin-like reflector on a very limited range of evidence. They tell us almost nothing about normal market operations.

Scholars of classical antiquity have been surprisingly reluctant to investigate the role of markets in inter- and intra-state affairs. Alain Bresson's collection of essays, *La cité marchande* (2000), was the first systematic attempt to engage with the commercial dimensions of Greek and non-Greek cities. Its publication coincided with that of Horden and Purcell's *The Corrupting Sea*, which may partly account for the comparatively limited influence that Bresson's book has had on recent historical approaches to markets.[45] The fluid notion of an undifferentiated kind of exchange has proved more amenable to the temperaments of many historians than a more prosaic look at money and markets. Markets have not been given due consideration by students of classical antiquity partly because of the long association in modern times between the idea of the market and industrialization. As a result, markets have become tainted with the notion of 'progressivism', as we have seen. If we dissociate markets from mass production, it becomes possible to see them in a different light. This topic will be explored further in Chapters 4 and 5.

How then might we set about reconstructing markets in the north Aegean region? We might begin with two approaches, one of which explores the kinds of essential equipment that an average inhabitant of our region would consider to form an inescapable investment for everyday life; or we might investigate the kind of evidence we dispose of for

[45] See however E. M. Harris's review of Bresson, BMCR (2001.09.40). Bresson contributed to Harris 2005 (Bresson 2005b), but Bresson's own oeuvre is not referred to by Purcell in his own chapter (Purcell 2005a); Bresson and Rouillard 1993 is fundamental to the discussion of inter-state exchanges in the first millennium bc; see also Descat 2000, 13–29 Archibald 2005a; and now *Tout vendre, tout acheter.*

markets which, in this particular area, are connected with quite a surprising variety of coin. Finley thought about essentials in terms of an imagined 'peasant', without recourse to the kind of everyday tools that constituted the minimum range to complete agricultural tasks. In his roundabout way, Plato conceded the importance of good quality tools. Iron tools are among the least considered items in the repertoire of domestic essentials.[46] The infrastructure of everyday life in the first millennium BC was unthinkable without such tools. The comparative invisibility of iron implements is largely due to the chemical structure of iron blades and thus the poor survival of this metal, not to its lack of importance to everyday subsistence. No farmer, herdsman, craftsman, or trader could survive for a day without iron tools. Such tools were not, admittedly, the kinds of artefacts that would be purchased often. This merely reinforces the natural periodicities of different kinds of exchange.

All markets were not of the same kind. Large purchases of grain, by designated officials, often called *sitonai,* on behalf of whole communities, took place typically once a year, although the timing of such exchanges could be planned to target particular harvests—the late spring or early summer harvests of Cyrene and Egypt, with the latest crop of all, available via the northern Black Sea ports, providing the ultimate back stop.[47] High value craft products, which needed a secure environment for buying and selling, were transmitted in circumstances where security could be ensured, both in terms of the physical environment, and in terms of due legal process. We might expect to find smiths operating from their own premises in an urban context, where craftsmen could assure purchasers of the quality of what they were proposing to buy.[48] Lower value, or perishable items, could easily be sold in temporary stalls, which leave few obvious traces.[49] Market transactions, then as now, may be quite informal arrangements, with home-made products, particularly fresh food, preserves, and second-hand goods, passing hands with minimal reinforcement or intervention by third parties, whereas specialist items and anything of value requires the ultimate sanction of a defined body of law. Once again it is Xenophon who provides a realistic spotlight on market exchanges. As the mercenary army, the remnants of Cyrus the Younger's Greeks defeated at Cunaxa in 401 BC, made its way towards

[46] Amouretti 2000; cf. Archibald (forthcoming c/).

[47] Bresson 2011, 77, discussing *SEG IX*, 2 (= *RO* 486–93, no.96), from Cyrene, early 320s BC.

[48] Cf. Tsakirgis 2005; Ellis Jones 2007.

[49] Demosthenes describes the mad rush to clear the stalls at Elateia in central Greece when Philip II suddenly appeared (Dem. 18.169).

the southern shores of the Black Sea the following summer, we are told that 'there was no market at hand' in that part of northern Bithynia close to Kalpes Limen, the bay midway between Herakleia and Byzantion, which Xenophon thought would make a good harbour town (*Anab.*6.4.16). A band of hungry men, between 9,000 and 8,000 strong at this stage of their journey (*Anab.* 6.2.16), is no ordinary sight, but in a period of endemic warfare, with numerous encounters in geographically disparate zones, groups of hungry or needy mercenaries, merchants, and other travellers, were not unusual. In the chapters that follow, we learn a good deal about how this band of battle-scarred adventurers planned to live off the land, if necessary, but were quite prepared to buy supplies when they needed them. There was a clear trade-off between the value of resource on the hoof, and the practicalities of transporting animals for the convenience of a ready food supply.[50]

In order to understand how these different kinds of markets worked in the north Aegean area, we also need to know what kinds of things had more than local value as commodities. Exceptional documents, such as the deeds of sale from Amphipolis, Philippoi, and elsewhere in Macedonia,[51] or the inscription naming Pistiros as one of a number of inland *emporia* in Thrace, where exchanges are guaranteed by the Odrysian prince exercising power during the 350s BC,[52] show the range and complexity of the social and economic infrastructure of market exchanges in the region before the expansion of inter-continental trade and traffic in early Hellenistic times. Such documents provide the necessary framework for discussing the exchange of commodities, which will be explored in more detail in the next two chapters. There is one other dimension that deserves a few methodological reflections, namely the social status of economic agents.

[50] Xen. *Anab.* 6. 4.23, 6.6.1, 6.6.3–4, 6.6.38, 7.1.19, 1.35, 7.56 (market sales planned or made by the mercenaries); 7.3.13 (plan to live 'off the land', a euphemism for theft, cf. 6.6.1); the story of the sheep captured from the countryside between Kalpes Limen and Chrysopolis, along with quantities of wheat and barley, wine, beans, millet, and figs (6.6.1, 6.6.5), later sold (6.6.37), to whom and where is quite unclear, on their way to Chrysopolis, reflects the different informal ways in which commodities exchanged hands, with and without money, and the ambiguities over ownership that such methods involved; Stronk 1995, 19–23 on fluctuating troop numbers. McInerney, discussing sanctuary economies, also emphasizes the very different demands and periodicities of sanctuary economies and their methods of managing herds (2010, 146–95, esp. 148–9).

[51] Hatzopoulos 1988b; 1991; and 1996, II, nos. 84–91 (Amphipolis); no. 83 (Philippoi); no. 92 (Mieza, with Hatzopoulos 2011a).

[52] Ch.1 n.19.

STATUS AND RANK

Finley's analysis of 'the ancient economy' stemmed from a number of unproven assumptions: that the propertied élites of antiquity were motivated mainly, if not exclusively, by a simple desire to maintain their inherited rank or status;[53] that these élites were in effect unchanging, stable social phenomena, with stable sources of revenue; that they effectively had an unchallenged control over negotiation in transactions; and that status or rank always trumped other ways of accruing or acquiring power, including new sources of knowledge and technology. Finley did not find it necessary to argue all these points in detail, whilst rejecting any alleged encroachment on the monopoly of economic power by non-élite groups, particularly in cities.[54]

It is not difficult to find examples of Roman exploitation, in view of the fact that Italy alone of the imperial provinces was free of tribute collection after 167 BC. Finley's chapter on 'Landlords and peasants' focuses on a select set of comparatively unusual landowners and their estates—that of Apollonios in the third-century AD Fayum; of the Apion family in sixth-century Egypt; or of Herodes Atticus in second-century AD Marathon. There was, he claimed, a progressively widening gap between smallholders and these sorts of big players. While the big players, including informative individuals, such as Cato the Elder, Columella, or Pliny the Younger, may have had all kinds of ideas about how to run estates, they

[53] Finley 1985 [1999] 35–61, esp. 41–7, 60; 144.

[54] Finley 1985 [1999] 59 (Lyons); 193 (Arezzo, Patavium, Marseille); 177–207, 'Further Thoughts'; cf. Finley 1980, 88: 'Without a sufficient cash-income, the Athenian élites could not have acquired the necessities for even their relatively low life-style, for their indispensable weaponry, or for the taxes which paid for public works, public festivals and public cults. None of this requires a revival of the Beloch-Meyer "modernism"; it requires merely an acceptance of some commodity production, in particular by the élites, and of the notion that members of the élites did not personally perform all the requisite labour, aided solely by members of their individual families.' Contra: Davies 1981, 73: 'That the liturgical class was not a caste is a truism. The evidence set out in *APF* [= *Athenian Propertied Families,* 1971] helps to make clear both the fact that its composition did change through the generations and the extent to which this change falls into a predictable pattern. Such change has two aspects, a family's biological continuity and the stability of its economic position.'... 'There is one family members of which are attested in the liturgical class for five generations; five families are attested for four generations; 16 families are attested for three generations; 44 families are attested for two generations; and no fewer than 357 are attested in a single generation only' (Davies 1981, 86). Davies goes on to explore the statistical evidence within the better-documented generations of the mid and late fourth century and concludes that, whatever the exact reliability of these surviving figures in relation to historical family histories, they seem consistent with the ephemeral nature of inherited wealth expressed by the author of [Dem.] 42.4.

lacked any calculated or systematic knowledge of rational accounting. This is one aspect of Finley's thesis to which there has been a huge academic response. There is plenty of evidence for 'rational accounting', particularly from Egyptian papyri, although evidence of accounting practices does not necessarily amount to strategies that used year on year figures as a basis for future agricultural plans. Accounts provided ledgers for recording private estate operations and dues owed by tenants, so were driven by annual rural dynamics. The productivity of estates is much harder to define and even harder to demonstrate. In many ways, historians may be aiming at the wrong sort of target. Attempts to quantify the best-documented case study, namely that of Ptolemaic and Roman Egypt, can most usefully be seen as heuristic devices. The process should not be seen as a data-generating mechanism; such an experiment amounts to no more than 'an ongoing, iterative exercise in the building of an open model that can be used by many scholars, experimenting with different values and incorporating new evidence as it becomes available' (in Roger Bagnall's definition).[55]

At the same time, Finley did not care to examine how the members of his prime Greek status group, namely the Athenian propertied classes, maintained their income, whilst paying for public liturgies; and what kind of effect such payments may have had on the revenues of individual families. Analysis of the Athenian liturgical class, that is of known individuals whose names can be connected with exceptional incomes, with direct payment of trierarchies, or of festival liturgies, or who qualified for the enlarged group of *(pro)eisphora* tax payers in the fourth century, indicates that only four hundred men in the fifth century, and

[55] Finley 1985 [1999], 95–122, esp. 97–109, 111–118; on accounting see esp. Macve 1985; contributors to Verboven et al. 2008 (especially, in this context, those of M. Faraguna, L. Migeotte, V. Chankowski, V. Gabrielsen, K. Geens, K. Vandorpe and W. Clarysse). There is now a substantial literature on the productivity of Roman agriculture and from a range of perspectives, none of which maps directly onto Finley's approach; see e.g. *CEHGRW*, 506–10 (J.-P. Morel, on Cato and second-century agricultural production, including wine exports, emphasizing some of the economic disparities that were beginning to cause profound social tension); 514, 523–8 (W. V. Harris: concentrates on some very significant fortunes in the early Empire; some degree of serious exploitation of slave labour, including women and children, but outnumbered by men); 550–9 (D. Kehoe: emphasizes various forms of evidence in support of crop diversification and rotation, all of which served to enhance crop yields; enhancements resulting from livestock rearing, the use of olive and vine presses; irrigation and other forms of technological investment; villa production for markets; different yields resulting from tenancies, especially under imperial legislation, the most notable examples being the *lex Manciana* and the *lex Hadriana de rudibus agris*, documented in the imperial estates of the Bagradas valley in north Africa). Cf. also Bowman in Bowman and Wilson 2009, 177–204, and Roger Bagnall's response, 205–9, with the citation above on p. 208.

three hundred in the fourth, could afford to pay the most demanding public liturgies, primarily the trierarchy. The enlarged group of twelve hundred individuals, brought forward by the law of Periander in 357 BC to cover the same naval bills, proved to be unworkable.[56] The payment of liturgies could and did win the benefactor public recognition, but the preferred forms of impressive expenditure favoured by the wealthiest Athenians evolved over the course of these two centuries, which points to changing perceptions, on the part of the wealthy, as well as the Athenian population at large, of what constituted valuable or desirable expenditure.[57] With the onset of Macedonian political domination of Athens, the mechanisms of private support for public works changed. These changes are probably the best indication of the discrete interconnection between private wealth and public benefits. Very little is known about liturgies in this period. The office of *agonothetes* replaced voluntary *choregoi*, and the main form of private taxation by wealthy citizens came from *eisphora*, based on a property assessment, and, from the later third century onwards, on a more flexible type of one-off payment, which could be raised from citizens and non-citizens, the *epidosis*.[58]

Many of the details of these changing methods of funding public services from private resources remain opaque; what they do reveal is a developing set of financial mechanisms, which indirectly point to different perceptions of what could and could not be afforded, as well as a continuing willingness, on the part of some wealthy individuals, to support the community. This is a more probing and more particularized story about Athenian economic affairs when compared with those approaches, more or less consciously 'substantivist' in form, which focus on much broader, longer-term relationships. The broader-brush analysis has more often sketched a thesis through the prism of landowning 'rich' and landless 'poor'. It has rarely picked out the inseparable link between public and private expenditure.

There are other ways of thinking about rank and fortune that broaden the scope of ancient Greek ideas about wealth and status. One new approach has been adopted by Ian Morris, building on recent research by a large number of scholars, including Nicole Loraux, Michael

[56] Davies 1981, 15–37; Isokr. 15.145; [Xen.] Ath. Pol. 3.4 (400 trierarchs per annum); Dem. 20.8 (one year's exemption permitted between liturgies, fourth century); Isaios 7.38 (two years' exemption); Dem. 14.16 (Periandros' law).

[57] Davies 1981, 93–114 (diminution in power of *gene*); 101–5 (the progressive diminution in expenditure on two- and four-horse chariot races, particularly in the fourth century BC); 114–22 (political ideology and political marriages); 122–31 (military and rhetorical skills as factors in power).

[58] Oliver 2007, 196–209; cf. Oliver 2006b on Athenian cavalrymen.

Jameson, David Cohen, Robin Osborne, and Lin Foxhall. Morris has identified what he terms a 'middling' ideology among leading groups within Athenian society, which shaped the way Athenians thought about themselves in the fifth and fourth centuries BC, and, by extension, the way in which other Greek communities of the mainland and Aegean islands perceived what they shared in common. This 'middling' ideology was much more than a shared set of ideas. It was, in Morris's view, a 'transactional order', that is, an abstract model of Athenian society that linked one generation to another and living communities to the cosmic order. 'The philosophy of the *metrios* was a useful democratic fiction, a structuring principle guiding behaviour.'[59] Athenian citizens shared the fact that they were men, that they all had the vote, that they had access to office, and that their opinions mattered. In many other respects, there were considerable differences between some citizens and others. The 'middling' ideology provided ways of embroidering connectedness despite these gulfs. Yet such evidence as we have suggests that the Athenians were a more equal society than many others, and much more equal than different parts of the Roman Empire would become. Morris has based this analysis, and subsequent elaborations of it, not just on the rhetoric of a 'middling' ideology, but also on different kinds of material evidence, including grave goods, the size of burials, and spatial relationships within housing units. He recognized that there was a public discourse in antiquity about wealth, just as there was a discourse about poverty. Wealth and poverty are not absolute categories; they rely on socially accepted standards of living, on attitudes to wealth differentials, and on culturally determined concepts of value.[60] In the idea of a 'middling' social ideology, Morris has tried to convey the particular tensions of Athenian society, where there were strong pressures to be, and to be seen to be, egalitarian. The psychological pressure to conform within a set of acceptable boundaries appears, in this analysis, to be reflected in certain

[59] Morris 2000, 116; 110–44; the concept of 'transactional orders' is derived from Parry and Bloch 1989, 26 (cited at Morris, 133): 'all these systems make—indeed *have* to make—some ideological space within which individual acquisition is a legitimate and even laudable goal; but... such activities are consigned to a separate sphere which is ideologically articulated with, and subordinate to, a sphere of activity concerned with the cycle of long-term reproduction.'

[60] Morris, 2000, 141, discusses the Gini coefficient for Athenian (fourth century BC) landholding at 0.39 (Foxhall) and 0.38 (Osborne); see further, ibid. 155–91, expanding his discussion of the development of a 'middling' ideology from the *c.*700–*c.*300 BC; Morris 2005, 107–26 (comparative housing units); Morris 2009b, 73–7 (various aspects of wealth and material culture).

aspects of everyday material culture; in the avoidance of ostentatious dress, funerary apparel, or grave markers.

This new reading of Athenian values can help us think in new ways about Athenian attitudes to societies of the north Aegean. Behind the anti-Macedonian rhetoric of Attic orators we catch a hint of a conflict of values.[61] Different values can also be detected in the social messages that northern societies projected. Unlike their southern counterparts, northerners shared distinctive attitudes to rank, social commemoration, and the treatment of deceased members after death. Macedonians and Thracians were still burying arms, armour, and favourite animals with their respected dead, when central and southern Greeks had long ceased to dispose of valued and valuable items in this way. Some of these cultural traits are also evident in Thessaly, so there is no clear cultural boundary between 'north' and 'south' in the distinctions elaborated here.[62] The liberal use of gold, in the form of hammered sheets in various shapes, jewellery, and dress attachments, has sometimes been interpreted as a bizarre sign of 'barbaric' wealth.[63] This is to misunderstand the social value of rank and the symbolic value of imperishable gold.[64] Gold has no intrinsic worth; its social value is driven by highly particular social rules. It is easy to assume that because we consider gold to be highly valuable, that past societies treated this rare metal in much the same way. The special role ascribed to gold by Macedonian and Thracian societies has arguably contributed to the metal's continuing value into modern times, through the creation of iconic pieces of jewellery, as well as through the issue of the Philippic gold coins, which in turn became models for Western European societies. These were later developments, however, which, as we shall see below, had a very different prehistory.

A factor that still constitutes a challenge to our understanding of exchange values is the degree to which certain commodities did not circulate in market conditions. Gold objects in Macedonia and other Balkan regions occupy a peculiar position in this regard. It is instructive to consider the significance of gold artefacts in these northern regions with what we know about the metal in early literary sources. Hélène

[61] See e.g. Badian 1982 for an exposition of the polarities between (southern) Greeks and Macedonians; Hall 2001 for a critical evaluation of contemporary approaches to ancient Macedonian identity; Hatzopoulos 2011b for a comprehensive review, comparing the relationship of ancient Macedonia to Greece with Prussia in relation to the rest of 'Germany' in the nineteenth century (73–4).

[62] On the historiography of 'north' and 'south' in the archaeology of Greece, Kotsakis 2009.

[63] Hammond, HM II, 186; cf. Hammond 1989, 43.

[64] Nicolet-Pierre 2006; Archibald 2012c.

Nicolet-Pierre has studied the social significance of gold in the Homeric poems. In the Iliad, in particular, we find a highly nuanced understanding of the gold talent: '[Il est . . .] . . . impossible de discerner une hiérarchisation dans les présents qu'énumèrent les vers cités. Les treize, les dix, les sept talents d'or font partie chaque fois d'un ensemble de cadeaux somptueux, témoignages de reconnaissance ou de générosité envers l'hôte, qui n'appellent pas de retour immédiat.' According to the author, gold is associated with aristocratic values and is not strictly speaking transferable, whether in exchange for other commodities, or in the form of a gift.[65] In the same publication, Raymond Descat followed up this investigation into archaic forms of exchange with a perceptive study of the concept of *multiple forms of money (monnaie multiple)*. In this scenario, a variety of commodities may be exchanged for some other good.[66] In some Mediterranean locations at least, this type of exchange may well have characterized certain transactions prior to (or independently of) market ones, when one commodity was exchanged for another, namely a given weight of metal.[67] The co-existence of such exchanges, in which commodities have a socially determined equivalence, together with a more limited and circumscribed circulation of specific materials, including gold, amber, and a range of manufactured weapons and vessels, seems to underlie the value system expressed in burials at a number of Macedonian and Thracian cemeteries. The relationship between these two forms of valuation did change over time, and evidently at different rates. Silver is comparatively rare in burials from the second half of the sixth century BC along the north Aegean coastline, just at the time when silver coinages were becoming established in the same geographical area.[68] Gold, on the other hand, continued to be used in high status burials over the next centuries, although the forms of the artefacts changed. Stamped foil sheets, which regularly appear in exceptional archaic burials, were increasingly limited to textile accessories.

An upper class

Rank was expressed in our northern societies through social groups that shared a distinctive lifestyle and training. A great deal of what we know about these groups is gained from funerary practices, which have an

65 Nicolet-Pierre 2006, 6 (citation above); 17.
66 Descat 2006, 25.
67 Descat 2006, 24–36.
68 Panagopoulou 2007 for the increasing use of silver as a commodity.

asymmetrical relationship to relations during life. The intense investment in mortuary arrangements—the treatment of the corpse; the disposal of the physical remains; the creation of specialized mortuary containers (caskets, coffins, burial chambers), are all part of a language of the dead that is palpably not the same as the treatment of the same individuals in life. At the same time, the conscious incorporation of ideas about rank in these contexts underscores the social dimensions of the dead; individuals and groups whose importance did not just matter to their nearest and dearest, but to the community of the living. This language of commemoration needs to be understood as part of the conscious allocation of resource for social as well as metaphysical reasons.

The '*paradynasteuontai*' and '*gennaioi*' of Thucydides' Odrysian leadership, like their opposite numbers in Macedonia, the cavalrymen who constituted the closest supporters of the Argead ruling dynasty, were not well-defined groups. None of our Greek or Latin narrative accounts provide much evidence for a dispassionate analysis of who belonged to these distinguished social circles. In Macedonia the term *hetairos* could refer to the king's personal friends, to those who assisted the king in his everyday duties, but also to a wider group of supporters. The terminology seems to conceal a chronological evolution in the application of this concept, with a narrower meaning in the fifth century BC, when it referred to the monarch's immediate entourage, and a broader application in the fourth, when the king needed a stronger sense of loyalty within a wider social network, exemplified in the extension of the term to his 'Foot Companions' (*pezhetairoi*).[69] Perhaps *hetairos* functioned as an aspect of the 'transactional order' in Macedonia, just as *metrios* did in Athens; but we lack the range of contemporary literary references to show how far the notion of *hetairos* was applied, and how it did come to be used, by extension, among serving Macedonian citizens at least.

The precise nuances of the term are hard to tease out, but there must always have been a more limited group of trusted individuals, who were the king's companions from his youth and who provided a pool of talent from which the king could choose those who would carry out particular

[69] *Pezhetairoi*: Harpokration s.v. *Pezhetairoi*, citing Anaximenes of Lampsakos (*FGrH* 72 F4); on the formation of a military elite: Hatzopoulos 1994a, 87–111; Savalli-Lestrade 1998, esp. Ch. 3, 'L'institution des *Philoi* royaux: du Compagnonnage à la formation d'une bureaucratie de cour', 289–307 (evolution of *hetairoi* in fifth- and fourth-century BC Macedonia); for the probability of a 'council' of *hetairoi*, Savalli-Lestrade 1998, 293, citing Hdt. 8.138; cf. Carlier 2000, 261–2.

functions. These men were the Macedonian 'nobility', the '*principes Macedonum*' referred to by Qu. Curtius, whose sons became royal pages, educated at court between 14 and 18 years of age, graduating to military training as ephebes from 18 to 20 years.[70] The social system of training royal companions seems to have survived into the kingdoms of Alexander the Great's Successors, although the 'King's Friends' or *philoi* of the early Hellenistic age were recruited from a much wider pool of talent than the *hetairoi* under the Argead monarchs had been. The deliberate change of term is therefore significant.[71] Prosopographical studies of surviving personal names suggest that those selected for key offices were hand picked, and were not necessarily limited to a narrow group of hereditary landowners in Macedonia, even in the fifth century BC.[72] The 800 *hetairoi* referred to by Theopompos as recipients of land grants in the reign of Philip II (Theop. *FGrH* 115 F224, 225), represent an overlapping social group with the 'noble' families, though distinct from them, not least because they included non-Macedonians. We are told that this group derived revenues from estates equivalent in size to those of '10,000 of the wealthiest Greeks' (F 225b). In numerical terms the group would represent the same proportion of 'rich' people per head of population as there were in the city of Athens, if the population of Macedonia in the fourth century BC amounted to *c.*500,000; a smaller proportion if the overall head count was substantially greater. At present there is no satisfactory way of deciding how realistic this figure is; it might even need to be doubled.[73] The fourth century BC was a period of immense social and demographic change in the north Aegean area,

[70] Curt. 5.1.42 (50 sons of Macedonian noblemen brought by Amyntas, son of Andromenes, to Alexander III at Babylon, to serve as a bodyguard): 'These act as the king's servants at dinner, bring him his horses when he goes into battle, attend him on the hunt and take their turn on guard before his bedroom door. Such was the upbringing and training of those who were to be great generals and leaders.' (Tr. J. Yardley); cf. 8.6.2–6. For similar accounts of the lifestyle of royal pages, cf. Arr. *Anab.* 4.13.1; Ael. *VH* 14.48; Diod. 17.65.1; Liv. 45.6.7–8.

[71] Savalli-Lestrade 1998, 291–306, 322–33, 355–68; Paschidis 2008; Ma 2011, 529–33.

[72] Paschidis 2006, 255–68; Mari 2002, 291–329; Karamitrou-Mentessidi 2011, 95–6 (on Elimiot *hetairoi*).

[73] Ellis 1976, 34 (*c.*500,000); Billows (1990, 202–4) would raise the population numbers to 1.5 million, using proxy data from nineteenth-century Macedonia. Hamilton (1999) follows Bosworth in arguing for a demographic decline after Alexander, but takes no account of field data. Faraguna accepts that this is feasible (2006, 133). However, his overall assessment rests heavily on the evidence of intensive surveys. The Langadas survey suggests a lower overall global population figure for Macedonia in the pre-Hellenistic period, if site numbers are compared with Ottoman ones (Andreou and Kotsakis 1999, 40–2, fig. 3.7). Bintliff (1997, 3; fig. 3, and discussion 28–33) suggests other ways of interpreting demographic change, which are explored further in Ch. 4.

although much of it was intra- rather than inter-regional change. In succeeding chapters, we will see that although there were quite a few prosperous towns in Macedonia (and in Thrace) in the period under consideration in this book, at least as much attention needs to be given to country estates when we consider the average standard of living of the region's inhabitants. This will, in turn, affect the way we can compare standards with other regions.

The Odrysian royal dynasty relied on a pool of 'noble' families in a manner similar to that of the Argeads. Hesychius includes in his Lexicon the term *Zibythides* as a term for noble Thracian men and women.[74] As in the case of the Macedonian 'nobility', very little textual evidence survives that provides specific information about this social group, or groups. Xenophon's writings provide a range of references of rather uneven quality. In the *Art of Horsemanship* (8.6), he refers to the Odrysian practice of racing downhill, like the Persians. Elsewhere his remarks are less complimentary and to some extent give a rather distorted view of who the Odrysians were. Xenophon refers on a number of occasions to Odrysians during the just over a month that he and his fellow mercenaries spent in the service of Seuthes, a regional prince and commander, who never aspired to the kingship. Although the author was not particularly concerned with the niceties of political relationships, he makes clear that those who carried out administrative roles were all Odrysians and that there was a clear structure of command between the central authority, which plays a rather minor role in the *Anabasis*, and regional administrators such as Seuthes, who is made in this narrative to have abused his authority (if the statement put into the mouth of one senior representative of king Medokos is at all trustworthy: *Anab.*7.7.3; 7.11). An unnamed ambassador of Medokos, described by Xenophon in a rather opaque way as a very powerful man coming from those who had come down from the interior (7.7.2), was brought in as a witness by Medosades, a lieutenant of Seuthes and a local landowner, to enforce the law of the central power. The logic behind Xenophon's story confirms the robustness of central administration. There is no evidence that regional dominions, such as Seuthes', somehow undermined the overall authority at the centre.[75] Individual self-appointed agents, such as Herakleides of Maroneia (who had no formal status with Seuthes), may

[74] Hesych. s.v. *Ζιβυθίδες. αἱ Θρᾷσσαι ἢ Θρᾷκες γνήσιοι.*

[75] Medokos: Xen. *Anab.* 7.2.33, 3.13–16; Odrysians: 7. 2.32, 5.1, 5.15, cf. Thuc. 2.97.3; Medosades: *Anab.* 7.1.5; 2.10, 2.23–25, 7.15–16; Medokos' patronage of Seuthes as a young man, and provision of cavalrymen to enable the restoration of Seuthes' inheritance: 7.2.32; Stronk 1995, 186, 269–73 for commentary; Archibald 1998, 122–5 on Seuthes (II); 123 and

have had personal aspirations that were at odds with those of regional administrators, and therefore tried to intervene in political relations, as he appears to have tried with the ambassadors from Parion that were on their way to Medokos with suitable presents (*Anab.* 7.3.16); but that does not equate with Seuthes' own policy. Xenophon, writing several decades after these events, was justifying his own conduct towards his peers, and responding to various criticisms that had evidently been made of his own behaviour and remuneration at the time. Much of the content of these books of the *Anabasis* consists of retrospective glosses on what was said and done, so as to show his own behaviour in a positive light. Seuthes' actions are thus given a less favourable spin.[76] The ambiguous profile of Seuthes in the *Anabasis* is different from the Seuthes of the same author's *Hellenika*, where he cooperated in 398 and 397 BC with the Spartan Derkylidas, operating first in Bithynia, then in the Chersonese, where the Spartan commander was following up the work of his predecessor in the area, Klearchos, who had launched a military campaign against unnamed Thracians in the area of the Propontis during his period as garrison commander at Byzantion (*Hell.* 3.2.2–5, 2.8–10; Diod. 14.38.6–7).

Diplomacy and power relations

These operations, on either side of the Hellespontine Straits, show events in which authorities from different cultural backgrounds, and with different political affiliations, cooperated closely in terms of regional policies. The action that took place in and around the Straits in the final years of the fifth and the beginning of the fourth century BC happened to be connected with the momentous events in the final years of the Peloponnesian War and its aftermath. As a result, the personalities and circumstances have acquired a little more colour and substance than formal agreements, decrees, or treaties usually provide. In this series of events Odrysian kings and princes were cooperating with Spartan commanders; elsewhere, and more usually, they were cooperating with Athenian officials, symptomatic of a long-term policy that is reflected in a series of honorary inscriptions for Odrysian rulers from Athens. These long-term policies of cooperation, however circumscribed

refs n.150 on the alleged breakdown of central authority (notably Tacheva 1988); see also Tacheva 1997, 97–149.

[76] Xen. *Anab.* 7. 5.16, 7.1–56 (Seuthes is presented in a distinctly ambiguous light, so as to enhance Xenophon's success in finally extracting the pay due to the mercenaries); Stronk 1995, 250–72, esp. 262–81.

their precise remit, belie the idea that the rulers of the Odrysian kingdom were traditionally opposed to Athenian interests in the north Aegean. There were instances where strategies did become polarized; but, in general, cooperation seems to have been driven by an awareness of mutual self-interest. Successive Athenian government officials recognized that dealing with the Odrysian kings and princes benefited Athenian interests, while Odrysian rulers also benefited from a benevolent approach on the part of the largest naval power in the Aegean.[77]

What was the reasoning behind these various diplomatic arrangements? Part of the answer lies in the vastly superior resources that the rulers of Macedonia and Odrysian Thrace could draw on. The Odrysians undoubtedly were the principal landward power east of the Strymon delta until the middle decade of the fourth century, when Macedonian control began to move eastwards, with the capture of Chalkidide, then Amphipolis and Krenides, which was to become Philippoi. Xenophon challenged Seuthes to pay him and the mercenary army 30T, for just over a month's pay (*Anab.* 7.7.25).[78] This was the kind of sum that the Athenians charged in annual tribute of the Thasians, twice the sum charged of the Byzantines (15.4300T to be exact), or of the Abderites (15T) in the previous half century.[79] The mining resources of the Thasians were evidently common knowledge. Herodotus describes revenues from those on the mainland that the Thasians also operated as 80T per annum, before these were wrested from them by the Athenians following the island community's revolt in 465–2 BC (Hdt. 6.46; Thuc. 1.100.2).

[77] Thuc. 2.29.1–5; Diod. 12.50.1–2; Ar. Acharn. 145 (Athenian treaty of 431 BC with king Sitalkes, with the mediation of Nymphodoros of Abdera, while Sitalkes' son Sadokos was made an Athenian citizen); Hdt. 7.137; Thuc. 2.67 (Peloponnesian delegation detained by Sitalkes at Bisanthe, 430/29 BC); Archibald 1998, 118–20 with discussion; *IG* II 2 21 (fragmentary inscription from Athens referring to an alliance with Seuthes (II?)) and 22 (alliance between Athens and Medokos, including *proxenia* for Medokos (?)) have usually been dated *c.*390/89 BC: see Archibald 1998, 125 and n.152 with references; see above, Ch. 2, n.16 for the treaty with Hebryzelmis (*IG* II2 31); *RO* 47 (= treaty between Athens and the Thracian kings, 357 BC); *RO* 53 (= alliance between Athens, Thracian, Paionian, and Illyrian kings, 356/5 BC); for relations between the Athenians and Kotys I, see Archibald 1998, 219–22; on the background of relationships between the communities of the Chersonese and Athens, Tzvetkova 2008, 172–83, 192–211 (and see further Ch. 5).

[78] Stronk accepts Roy's calculations of mercenary pay using Xenophon's figures at *Anab.* 7.7.25. Roy (1967, 320 and n.134), takes 1 Cyzicene as = 25dr.; if there were 5,250 men, then 5,250 + 1,750 = 7,000 Cyzicenes/month, which at 25dr/Cyzicene = 29.85T [Roy's figure], or if 26.66dr/Cyzicene = 31.84T [Stronk's figure]. Both sums are close to Xenophon's total, but the argument is circular, since it presupposes an army whose strength has been calculated on this basis. Xenophon is unlikely to have advertised in his memoir a sum that was less than the amount promised at *Anab.* 7.2.36.

[79] Nixon and Price 1990, 150, 152–8, and App. 166–70; Purcell 2005a.

The laconic phrases of both historians underplay the magnetic attraction of the north Aegean as a source of potential enrichment. In the aftermath of the Peloponnesian War, when the Athenians had drained their cash reserves, the continuing attractiveness of this zone was all too apparent to those, like Xenophon and his fellow mercenaries, whose strength in numbers terrified all but the most powerful states. The Spartan garrison force of Byzantion barred the city's gates against them (*Anab.* 7.1.12), and the subsequent irruption of mercenaries back into the city caused panic, a plan to call in the garrison from Calchedon, and severe terms for any mercenaries caught in the city (*Anab.* 7.1.19–20). An army not far short of 6,000 men running amok was a serious problem. Seuthes managed to negotiate his way out of Xenophon's challenge. This resolution focuses attention on the more vulnerable inhabitants of the region.

The capture of people for the purpose of ransom or enslavement is mentioned at various stages of the narrative. The 'Cyreans' are threatened with enslavement if they were to remain in Byzantion (*Anab.* 7.1.36). We later hear of 400 meeting this fate at the hands of the incoming governor, Aristarchos (7.2.6). The way in which innocent individuals might find themselves being enslaved is illustrated later in the narrative, when Xenophon and his mercenary hoplites, recently coming into the employ of Seuthes, captured some villages near the Strandja mountains.[80] Xenophon himself is quite relaxed about the idea that the local people should find themselves being enslaved (7.4.24), simply because some of the inhabitants of the village that the 'Cyreans' had attacked attempted to resist the destruction of their property (7.4.17–18). The historian uses different terms to describe people who were under the control of others; but the existence of people of unfree status in north Aegean societies is apparent, even if this status may have been different from people who found themselves being shipped out to other regions. Seuthes himself owned or controlled people, who could be reassigned as gifts to others, as if they were horses or cattle (7.2.2). However, the language of negotiation between Seuthes and Xenophon shows that the Greek historian's narrative abbreviates important social nuances about gender and about status. Seuthes offers Xenophon his daughter and

[80] Xen. *Anab.* 7.3.48 (about 1,000 captives, 1,000 oxen, and '10,000' other cattle); 7.6.26 (Xenophon speaks of the mercenaries' putative intentions of taking slaves and cattle from Thracian villages); 7.7.53 (one talent [in money? as ingots?], 600 oxen, 4,000 sheep and 120 slaves, part payment of mercenary pay by Seuthes); Stronk 1995, 221, 263, 280, *ad loc;* other references to captured individuals: 6.6.1 (*oiketes*); 7.2.2 (Kleanor and Phryniskos given a horse and a woman respectively by Seuthes); the more familiar term *andrapodon/andrapoda* appears at 6.3.3; 6.6.1, 38.

proposes to 'buy' a daughter of Xenophon's, should he have one (7.2.38). Seuthes implies the custom of bride price, and the discussion is part of a series of statements about friendship and loyalty, terms that re-emerge later in the narrative, when Medosades complains about the way that Xenophon and his men were treating villages in Medosades' control. He threatens to defend his territory against the depredations of the 'Cyreans', who had, by Xenophon's own admission, rampaged at will before they had become the 'friends' of Seuthes and his subordinates (7.7.3–5; cf. 7.16). In Xenophon's narrative, Seuthes, Medosades, and the unnamed senior Odrysian nobleman come across as circumspect and measured negotiators, more careful in their choice of words and diplomatic in their style of communication than the Spartan officials at Byzantion and other locations on either side of the Straits, who appear far more intolerant of the 'Cyreans' as a social force.

Subordinated people and peoples

The economic role of slaves in classical antiquity is still hard to specify, even though very large numbers of slaves (tens of thousands in second-century BC Italy),[81] are sometimes documented. Slaves were forcibly acquired, involved a degree of insecurity for their owners, and were expensive to maintain. Even if these hurdles were overcome, the realities of ancient slavery fall short of the Marxian definition of 'slave-owning societies'.[82] The biggest argument against such a radical claim is the

[81] Str. 14.5.2 (mid second-century Delos) with *CEHGRW*, 504–5 (Morel); 354–5 (Davies, citing Xen. *Vect.* 4.14–17: owners of 300, 600, and 1,000 slaves, hired out to mine contractors in late fifth-century Attica). Xenophon urged his fellow Athenians to buy three slaves for every citizen to expand production in the silver mines (*Vect.* 4.25). This would have produced perhaps 90,000 slaves—an unlikely figure; yet Hypereides talked of 150,000 slaves in the Attic mines (*Against Aristogeiton*, fr. 29, Jensen). Lauffer (1979, 124–8; 140) considers that there may have been some 35,000 slaves in the Laureion mines at its maximum period of exploitation in the fourth century. Fisher puts the overall number of slaves in fifth- to fourth-century BC Athens at 100,000–150,000 (Fisher 1993, 34–6; followed by Lewis 2011, 108). Andreau and Descat opt for a high figure of 200,000–250,000 slaves (although they reject the enormous number of supposed slaves, 400,000 [*oiketai*] quoted by Athenaeus, citing the historian Ktesikles [*FGrH* 245 fr. 2 = Athen. 10.445c], as a misunderstanding of the word *oiketes*, which by Athenaeus' own admission includes any householders, free or unfree: Athen. 6.267e); see further Oliver 2007, 80–6, for detailed analysis, and 74–100 for the broader demographic context, putting the global population of Attica at 200,000–300,000; Andreau and Descat 2006, 67–71, 115–28 on the employment of slaves in agriculture and production.

[82] Cf. Ch. 1 n.60; De Ste Croix 1981, 4, introduces the central importance of unfree labour, which in his view was responsible for the largest share of agricultural production (cf.

challenge posed by maintaining a constant supply of would-be slaves. In a recent survey of the topic, Jean Andreau and Raymond Descat have concluded that perhaps half the population of some of the larger, wealthiest ancient cities, including Athens and Rome, consisted of slaves, although this proportion was by no means stable. From the mid first century BC, the number of slaves in many Italian towns is estimated at between 30 and 40 per cent. However, most scholars now agree that the presence of slaves in different centres of population probably fluctuated quite markedly. Outside the major centres of slave consumption, their presence may well have been far smaller, in many places negligible. Slaves could provide useful labour; in the home, in the countryside, or in physically exhausting or unattractive production processes, including mining, tanning, fulling, pottery and other crafts. However, this required capital investment for the slave owner, an investment that could not be guaranteed, because of high mortality figures and the high variation in slave prices. Viewed in these terms, slaves represented an additional source of potential rent for the slave owner, rather than a source of productive endeavour.[83] Enslavement resulted from violent confrontation—usually in the context of military defeat or opportunistic kidnapping. There was always, therefore, a degree of exceptionalism about the circumstances for creating new slaves. The enslavement of foundlings and the fostering of children born to existing slaves were probably important alternative methods of generating new stock and are increasingly being recognized as mechanisms for satisfying demand.[84] Slavery and slave ownership were factors of economic and social interchange. They belonged to the money economy and the market, even if they were acquired by piracy or by other forcible means. So slaves belonged to accountants' balance sheets as much as they did to command structures.

Historians have often drawn attention to the origins of slaves in Thrace, so the significance of slavery in the economies of the north Aegean deserves particular consideration. Many of the slaves that feature in Attic comedy, and in fifth- and fourth-century BC Attic inscriptions, were called *Thraix* and *Thraitta,* implying an origin somewhere in Thrace. This is more than a stereotype; it is a conventional way of disguising genuine connections, whilst providing a plausible-sounding

ibid. 49–55, on direct forced labour; 71–9 on Aristotle's evaluation of labour; 140–204, slavery and 'unfree' categories of labour).

[83] Andreau and Descat 2006, 65–105 on slave numbers; 146–51 for the comparative attractiveness v. lack of attraction of slave ownership.

[84] Andreau and Descat 2006, 92–4; Lewis 2011, 109.

source.[85] A recent reappraisal of lists of slaves in Aegean inscriptions of the fifth and fourth centuries BC shows varying proportions of slaves identified as having a northern origin. The Attic *stelai* recording confiscated property following the profanation of the Mysteries in 415 BC list 45 slaves, of whom 19 (or 56 per cent), are given a Thracian or other northern origin, while a further 13 (36 per cent) have Asiatic or Near Eastern connections.[86] A naval inscription from the final quarter of the fifth or first quarter of the fourth century BC shows a somewhat different profile, with 11 (24 per cent) of the 45 ethnically identifiable names hailing from the north, while 31 (69 per cent) are of Asiatic or Near Eastern type.[87] Among the Thracians that appear on this list, one has a name that provides unexpected confirmation of the idea that some slaves were named after the place where they were bought: Pistyras.[88] Herodotus refers to a *polis* called Pistyros in the *peraia* of the Thasians, beside a lake full of fish and very salty water (Hdt. 7.109). The local geography in this part of Herodotus' narrative is rather imprecise, because the narrative moves towards a section located in the Chalkidic peninsula, where some more specific statements are made about the demands made by the Persian army on local resources. The lake and the ancient site have proved hard to identify in the local topography of the Thasian *peraia*, along the coastline west of Abdera as far as the estuary of the River Strymon. The locality called Pistyros by the historian is not referred to by any later author with reference to this coastline, including Pseudo-Skymnos. Nor did it appear in the Athenian Tribute Lists, which table even very modest communities, as we have already seen above. A coastal hilltop site that is consistent with the general indications given in Herodotus' text has been identified near the modern harbour town of Nea Karvali and the excavators have suggested that this could be Herodotus' Pistyros.[89] Only a small section of this fortified hilltop has been

[85] Andreau and Descat 2006, 85–7; Hdt. 2.134 (Thracian courtesan Rhodopis); Ar. *Ach.* 273 (Dicaeopolis' desire for his neighbour's Thracian slave girl); Ar. *Thesm.* 279–94; Ar. *Pax* 1138; Ar. *Vesp.* 828; Xen. *Anab.* 4.8.4 (former Athenian slave communicates with the Makrones near Trapezous); Xen. *Vect.* 2.3 (Athenian population full of Lydians, Phrygians, and other barbarians); Plb. 4.38 (slaves of the best quality from the Black Sea area); Velkov 1964; Velkov 1967, 1986; Avram 2007; Lewis 2011, 91 n.2, with further refs.

[86] Lewis 2011, 102–3, Table 1, App. pp.111–12 (= *IG* I^3 421–430).

[87] Lewis 2011, 112, App. Table 2 (*IG* I^3 1032 = *IG* II^2 1951).

[88] *IG* II^2 1032.136: *Πιστύρας*; Robertson 2008, 79–116; Lewis 2011, 96 n.20 and 112 no.42; cf. no. 33, a Triballian; Lewis 2011, 93–8, on what lies behind ethnic names; 95–6 on the association of names with the point of sale.

[89] Koukouli-Chrysanthaki, *A.Delt.* 27 (1972), Chr. 527; Koukouli-Chrysanthaki 1973; Isaac 1986, 12–3, referring to this site and neighbouring footholds in the *peraia*: 'Apart from Neapolis, none of these ever developed into substantial cities. They retained their archaic

investigated so far, and although most of the published evidence is more or less contemporary with the Persian Wars and their aftermath, with the kinds of ceramics that occur at various locations in the Thasian *peraia*, there is nothing to suggest that this was an international *emporion* later in the fifth century and thereafter. The hilltop is located south of the coastal road (which was later incorporated into the Via Egnatia). Another upland site, on a steeper acropolis on the northern side of the main coastal road, lying just east of the modern town of Akontisma, was heavily fortified with a masonry wall and towers in the period of Cassander (*c*.316–297 BC). Although the two hilltops are close enough to the coast and to the main east–west coastal access route, neither is especially well located for inter-regional commercial purposes. A slave market near Nea Karvali seems even less likely, given the fact that there was such a market at Abdera, less than 30 km away. An inscription found at Abdera, dating to the middle of the fourth century BC, provides clear evidence that Abdera was the main focus of slave sales in this period. It is unlikely that there would have been a rival centre of inter-regional slave exchange so close to Abdera.[90]

The organization of slave markets is still very imperfectly understood. The Abderitan text records a law concerning the sale of slaves (*andrapoda*) and pack animals—mules, asses, donkeys, cattle, and horses are all mentioned. Regulations were set out for the kinds of pledges or surety that should be made by the sellers to buyers concerning the health of those creatures being sold, with strict time schedules for the incubation of known diseases, including (with respect to human medical complaints) a year for epilepsy, ten(?) months for bowel diseases, four days for fever, and a variety of identifiable illnesses in cattle and horses, with corresponding periods of prior monitoring, listed in the damaged lower part of the text. Damage to the right-hand side of the text means that there is some ambiguity about the purpose of the security (*eggue*) that was required, presumably in case of the cancellation of a sale (ll. 4–5). This immensely interesting document suggests that there were regular sales of animals and, to a lesser extent, perhaps, people, in the agora of Abdera, and that consequently this law was introduced to regulate not just live sales, but to ensure that there was sufficient institutional provision for the kinds of problems that might arise when dealing with

character, modest agricultural communities, important to the Greeks because they gave access to the interior'. *Inventory*, 866–7, no. 638 (note proximity to the Vassova salt lake); M. Nicolaidou and I. Patera, 2005; Chankowski 2010, 245.

[90] SEG 47, 1026; *I ThrAeg* E3, 186–90 and pl.1; Chandezon 2003, no.23; Andreau and Descat 2006, 104.

vulnerable livestock and people. Animals and people were high-value items for exchange and therefore involved a higher risk for buyers and sellers. Healthy creatures meant healthy prices. Abdera had an *agoranomos*, a magistrate responsible for regulating market transactions, so the city was able to supervise the potentially complex kinds of sales that the law implies.[91] The Abderitans would have benefited from the proceeds of the market transactions through market taxes, so wanted to ensure that merchants were keen to bring their sales to their city and that purchasers did not go away with poor opinions that would damage the market's reputation. A passage in Plato's *Laws* (*Leg.* 915e–916c) and a reference to sale contracts and terms under which they might be cancelled in Hypereides' speech *Against Athenogenes* (7.1) show that the Abderitan law was in line with regulations elsewhere in the Aegean in this period.

The kinds of locations historically attested for slave markets include points of sale for captives from a wide range of origins, as in the case of Byzantion (Plb. 4.38), or Mylasa in Karia, and Ephesos in Ionia; as well as those where periodic markets provided opportunities for occasional sales, as in the case of Anaktorion, where the festival and associated *panegyris* of Apollo at Aktion was used by the Corinthians as an occasion to sell 800 prisoners from Kerkyra, all of whom were already technically slaves, according to Thucydides, in 431 BC.[92] In all these cases there were potentially various institutional mechanisms for ensuring that merchants who might be dissatisfied with their purchases could seek recourse to law. This kind of reassurance could not be given with much confidence in the case of a small roadside town like the one identified at Nea Karvali which, even if it were occupied in the middle of the fourth century BC, lacked the infrastructure of a civic centre with a range of appropriate officials who could enforce inter-state laws. At the time of the naval inscription already referred to, the Pistyros/Pistiros to which the slave name refers is more likely to have been the eponymous *emporion* mentioned on the so-called Pistiros inscription from inland Thrace, cut on a stone many hundreds of kilometres from the Aegean coast.[93] The inland site near Vetren provides a much more plausible focus of captives drawn from a wide hinterland beyond the Central Plain of Thrace, that

[91] SEG 30.662 (bronze weight from Abdera, early third century BC); *I ThrAeg*, p.189.

[92] Thuc. 1.55.1: 250 citizens of Kerkyra were well treated, on the other hand, with the aim of re-installing them at Kerkyra when circumstances changed; Andreau and Descat 2006, 102–4 on slave markets; *panegyreis* as opportunities for slave sales: Paus. 10.32.15 and Str. 12.5.3; Ephesos as a slave name: L. Robert, *BCH* 59/1 (1935) 453 col. B, l.11; Lewis 2011, 96 n.20; cf. Fraser 2000.

[93] See Ch. 1 n.19 with refs.

is, from outside the territories administered directly by the Odrysian princes who formulated the legislation guaranteeing the rights of merchants at Pistiros. At the same time, a slave named after this location carried with him some of the cachet of that international hub.

A SUMMARY OF THE NARRATIVE

The framing story of our account was shaped by the extraordinary demands made on the north Aegean communities by the Persian armies of occupation. The whole area explored in this book was affected by the Persian presence, even if large areas never saw a soldier from the occupying forces. Whatever the nature of Persian administration in the region, the Persian military monopoly of the Bosporus, the Hellespontine Straits, and the whole north Aegean coastline as far south as the Vale of Tempe, intercepted the natural patterns of communication linking Europe with Asia, and the inland parts of the east Balkans with coastal harbours. To be sure, this area was not occupied continuously by large armies; but from the time of Megabazos' campaign on the European mainland in 512 BC, following the expedition into the steppe region north of the Black Sea against the European Scythians, the patterns of traffic through the Bosporus began to be affected, then individual harbour cities were picked off, beginning with Perinthos (Hdt. 5.1–11), then Byzantion and Kalchedon (4.144), followed by the renewed attacks of Mardonios and other Persian commanders, in the wake of revolts by many of the cities in the Straits and Bosporus in 500 BC. Of greater long-term significance was the construction of an immensely ambitious programme of works, intended to create a permanent link between the Straits and Macedonia, in the form of a coastal road (Hdt. 7.115.3), with an extension through the forests of Perrhaibia (7.131), a canal across the Athos peninsula in Chalkidike (7.22–24), a bridge over the River Strymon, and, finally, a (temporary) bridge of boats, supported on flax and papyrus cables, across the Straits from Abydos to Sestos (7.33–36.5). The whole endeavour was supported by a logistical plan that involved the forward supply of the invasion armies with grain dumps at various points along the proposed route, at the 'White Cape' in Thrace, at Tyrodiza, at that time in the territory of Perinthos; at Doriskos, Eion, and unnamed locations in Macedonia (Hdt. 7.25.2).

Herodotus compared the consumption levels of the Persian forces with geomorphological processes. He describes how the pack animals of the armies drank dry the lake, full of fish, near the left bank of the

River Nestos, beside which was the *polis* of Pistyros (7.109.2). The Thasians had organized their communities on the mainland to provide billets for the Persian soldiers—a management feat in its own right. The people of Akanthos tried hard to respond positively to the political and economic demands, but many of them faced ruin. Antipater, son of Orgeus, claimed that the cost of providing the Persian king Xerxes and his troops with a meal cost 400T.[94] Herodotus cites the name of a reputable local man to indicate that this figure is not a sum plucked from the air. He does not tell us that money was raised, but rather that all the communities of the region were obliged to provide the wherewithal for the meal, and someone calculated the value in terms of the above global figure. Many local towns had to organize collections of grain and spent months milling barley and wheat flour, fattening cattle, poultry, and water fowls, as well as making suitable tableware in precious metals (7.118–119.2). The dinner for Xerxes is used to represent the kinds of demands that local people were expected to accede to. They went on paying the price of occupation for several years, until all the command centres along the road had been superseded by new, Greek-sponsored garrisons, who would require their upkeep from local inhabitants too. At the same time, the great works created by the Persians were a feat and a wonder. Even the workmen constructing the Athos canal had their own market (*agore*) and meeting place (*preterion*), to which grain, ready-ground, was directed from sources in Asia (7.23.4). All the inhabitants of the region, irrespective of language and cultural affinities, were equally affected. They were all made to provide supplies, to serve in the enemy fleet or the army. The experience of occupation by the Persian forces was something that united the inhabitants of the north Aegean area and the east Balkan region as no other factor could. It remained a model and an example of many different things that continued to shape regional practices for many years to come. The coast road, which was maintained by the local Thracians, was admired and honoured (Hdt. 7.115.3), terms that encapsulate the mixed emotions triggered by the phenomenon of Persian occupation.

The history of the twentieth century shows that wars create immense personal trauma. Yet wars are also a source of dramatic technological advances, as well as being the means by which territories come to be radically redrawn. The narrative of economies in the northern Aegean needs to accommodate the consequences of these different experiences of

[94] Balcer 1972; contributors to Carradice 1987, and Picard 2000, 247–52 on the local coinages of Chalkidike and the lower Strymon valley.

occupation. It must also accommodate the aspirations of people less directly affected by the logistics of military requisitioning. The vegetarian habits of the Mysians and their less well-known northern neighbours must find a place, as well as the cosmic preoccupations of the followers of Zalmoxis and other chthonic cult followers, which generated investment in funerary hardware. Whilst the lifestyles of country landowners distributed human investment in rural estates and their associated cult sites, the gradual nucleation of populations around some civic centres encouraged urban infrastructure. Urban centres of the pre-imperial age in the eastern Mediterranean were, with a very few exceptions, small by historical standards. The two territorial kingships of our story, Argead Macedonia and Odrysian Thrace, emerged as important political entities because there was a genuine demand, in the wake of the Persian occupation, for organizing mechanisms that could provide military and administrative support for communities that were widely distributed in substantial land areas, separated by forests, mountain ranges, and lakes. These royal authorities had to find ways of developing a discourse of kingship that would speak to the communities of the region, notwithstanding linguistic and cultural differences.

At the same time, the harbour towns of the north Aegean coast that had played such a significant role in the story of the Persian occupation began, from 479 BC onwards, to be drawn into a naval network with the states that founded the Delian League. Thus began the tension between two adversarial trajectories—a landward-orientated one, which sought to cement the infrastructure and articulation of neighbouring inland communities; and a maritime one, linked by naval communications. The coastal harbour towns of the north Aegean were organically linked to their hinterlands. They depended on inland resources for minerals, building materials, and transport. The communities that lacked coastal outlets were in turn dependent on the harbours and markets of their coastal neighbours for the supply of indispensable materials, which were determined as much by socially driven perceptions of appropriate lifestyles, as they were by perceived ideas of needs. Attempts by various powers to monopolize, whether partly or wholly, the maritime and landward networks—by the Argeads under Philip II and Alexander III; by Lysimachos and successive Ptolemaic, Antigonid and Seleukid rulers in the third century BC—were at best only partially successful. The economic wellbeing of the region depended on the free interchange of resources between coastal hubs and inland areas. The Roman authorities who negotiated peace terms with Antiochos III after the battle of Magnesia and with Perseus after his defeat at Pydna had evolved a strategy of separating key coastal cities, including Lysimacheia, Ainos, and Maroneia, from their hinterlands, in an attempt to find pretexts for intervention and footholds to future control of the region. Once Roman administration was established in the east Balkans, this policy had to be abandoned and the network of connections with inland areas resumed. Xerxes' coastal road became the basis for the Via Egnatia, and the cross-continental routes from Abdera to the Danube, and from Ainos and Byzantion northwards along the Black Sea coast, were reinvigorated.

The law on the sale of slaves and pack animals at Abdera provides a connecting link between the different economic drivers of this landscape. It is a technically demanding piece of legislation, requiring civic officials to make informed decisions about the physical health of people and animals to be put up for sale, and adjudicate in cases where sales were cancelled. Notwithstanding the serious import of the legislation, the content of this public document is reminiscent of the task placed on that shady character, Herakleides of Maroneia, on behalf of Xenophon's 'Cyreans', to sell the booty from the Thynian villages at Perinthos, which amounted to 1,000 captives, 2,000 cattle, and a great many small animals (Xen. *Anab.* 7.3.48, 4.2, cf. 5.2). Perinthos, like Abdera, was one of the leading harbour cities of the region. Even so, Herakleides was in effect supplying the livestock for a major regional sale in one go. The fact that this throughput of animals did not cause any significant problems at Perinthos gives us some idea of the level of commercial traffic for which this city was prepared. We need to think much more seriously about the productive capacity of the north Aegean region.

There is a telling expression of this productivity in a funerary stele found at Amphipolis, honouring Aulus Caprilius Timotheos, styled *somatemporos*, a term that echoes Strabo's description of the slave trade on Delos.[95] The Caprilii were among the prominent Italian families who established themselves in Macedonia after the creation of the Roman province of Macedonia. One member of this family, P. Caprilius Secundus, is the second in a long list of names on a *cippus*, discovered close to Herakleia Lynkestis on the Via Egnatia, and published by Léon Heuzey.[96] Timotheos was evidently a freedman of this *gens*.[97] Although the monument from Amphipolis commemorates a Roman slave dealer, whose power is illustrated in two registers below the main frieze in the form of two superimposed figure scenes, Timotheus chose to be represented in the

[95] Geogr. 14.5.2 (*σωματεμπορεῖν*); Duchêne 1986 and figs 1–3 (dated to the late first or early second century AD).

[96] Heuzey and Daumet 1876, 304–6; Duchêne 1986, 519.

[97] The dedication reads: *Αὖλος Καπρείλιος, Αὔλο[υ] | ἀπελεύθερος, Τιμόθεος | σωματένπορος*; Duchêne 1986, 518.

main scene in a manner more appropriate for an aristocratic landowner of the north Aegean region. The lowest register shows a group of eight slaves, chained together, led by a supervisor, and preceded by another man (perhaps the honorand himself?), whilst two women and two little girls follow at the rear. The middle frieze shows two pairs of slaves in tunics, each pair carrying a heavy, round-bottomed container on a pole (perhaps baskets of grapes, rather than cauldrons), while a fifth, on the far right-hand side, has a pointed *amphora* on his back and a jug in his left hand, undoubtedly alluding to wine. Hervé Duchêne, whose study of the *stele* includes photographs taken for the original publication in 1945, considers this scene to be the celebration of a new vintage, and wonders whether the juxtaposition of the new wine and the slave cordon was a conscious attempt to show not just the ways in which this freedman had made himself rich, but also to show the deliberate interchangeability of the one form of commodity for the other; wine for slaves, in the manner of Gallic traders, exchanging a barrel of wine for a single young slave (Diod. 5.26.3). He cites the traffic of wine, garments, and other 'civilized' products, in exchange for slaves and hides, at the *emporion* of Tanais, on the estuary of the River Don, where the nomads of Asia and Europe met merchants from Bosporus (Str. *Geogr.* 11.2.2). 'Amphipolis, sur la Via Egnatia et presque aux confins de l'Empire, n'est-elle pas de même une zone de contact entre le monde gréco-romain et la Thrace barbare?'[98]

My answer to this question is two-fold. First, the thesis of this book is that there was no such thing as a 'contact zone' between two compartmentalized worlds, the 'civilized' world and the 'barbarian' world, only many networks of exchange, commercial, cultural, and intellectual. The idea of a cultural divide may have existed at an abstract, intellectual level, but it did not exist in spatial terms. Places of exchange were quite common and determined by reasonable travelling distances. Far from being at the boundary of the civilized world, Amphipolis was a hub, on Xerxes' road and later the Via Egnatia, but also linked to its hinterland along the Strymon valley, the mining zone in the foothills of Rhodope, and thence to central Europe. Second, the exchange of one commodity for another is a form of exchange that we should expect to have been normal at any time in classical antiquity, though Diodorus' equation of one slave for a barrel (or an *amphora*) of wine is the kind of loose equivalence that belongs more comfortably at the anecdotal than the

[98] Duchêne 1986, 526.

evidence-based level.[99] The nature of ancient exchange depended on the evaluation of one commodity for an equivalent in weighed metal, usually silver. The relative price of weighed metal to other commodities is one of the distinctive characteristics of ancient exchange that deserves particular attention; the other is the impulse to create commodities. The instinct to create objects has not played a particularly prominent role in the discussion of ancient economies and is the subject to which we turn next.

[99] At 37.3.5 Diodorus gives 100dr. as the price of a jar of exclusive wine; in the Attic confiscation *stelai*, the price of some slaves is given as 173dr. and 179.5dr. respectively (Pritchett 1956, 278). So the unit prices are not perhaps quite so very different, although it is hard to find like-for-like equivalents in the documentary evidence.

4

The *longue durée* in the north Aegean

THE NORTH AEGEAN *LONGUE DURÉE* IN A NUTSHELL

This chapter explores the relationship that ancient north Aegean societies had with their material environment through the matrices of social groups and of everyday practical experience. The timescale examined here corresponds to the late Iron Age of southern Europe, which covers the second half of the first millennium BC. The long-term ecologies of the north Aegean region, which indigenous communities had co-created over several millennia since the start of sedentary agricultural village life in the Neolithic period (corresponding to the seventh through the fifth millennium BC in this region), formed the natural environment in which these societies emerged and in which new strategies for subsistence were developed. In other words, the kinds of choices that local Neolithic and Bronze Age groups made about where and how to live created the background, and set the parameters, for choices made in the first millennium. This applies, for instance, to the cutting back of forest cover in the vicinity of settlements; the creation of upland meadow for pasture; and the development of knowledge about the properties of raw materials.[1]

The distinctive characteristics of subsistence that emerged in the early first millennium BC are connected with the expansion of new forms of settlement, the dispersal of large numbers of people from the compact, closely spaced environment of Late Bronze Age mounds to a range of new locations, including smaller, more diversified lowland sites and various kinds of intermediate and upland foci, utilizing the full variety of ecological opportunities at different elevations in the landscape. This dynamic of dispersal was at least in part a function of enhanced

[1] Neolithic and Bronze Age: Chrysostomou et al. 2007; Grammenos et al. 1997; Misaïlidou-Despotidou 2008, 25–65 (Toumba Nares and Trapeza Nares, close to the River Gallikos).

agricultural and pastoral regimes. Palynological analyses show that forest cover in the mountain zone was still very dense. Some of the upland sites are easily identifiable by the dry stone circuits on their summits.[2] Enclosures afford a level of protection from other people, pens for flocks and herds, and act as wind-breaks. So enclosure does not automatically mean that people perceived dangers and uncertainty, and tried to defend themselves as best they could. If we look at the whole first millennium BC, and how settlement patterns changed over this period of time, then it becomes clear that defensive needs were often factored into the design, whether we are thinking of upland sites that look like small fortresses, or lowland farmhouses, whose most distinctive visual and planning feature was a multi-storey tower. The need for protection was not new, but communities in the north were evidently better able at this time (or had more flexibility) to protect those things as well as people that mattered most to them—their immediate families, kin, and social peers; the annual cereal crop and other stored produce; and manufactured goods that might be considered valuable.

The success of this process of social expansion into new ecological zones, in both upland and lowland locations, is reflected in a population increase, expressed in the overall number of sites registered as dating to the second half of the first millennium BC. As we have seen in Chapter 2, the intensification of field research in recent decades has multiplied the number of known sites, particularly the range of smaller locations. We can detect a new relationship in the landscape between traditional built structures—family farms and community-based facilities—and new forms of social investment, including sanctuaries and funerary monuments. These trends substantially contributed to the region's economic framework in the second half of the first millennium BC.

The pattern becomes less easy to comprehend in the third and second centuries BC, when urban centres grew at the expense of rural ones, but also became vulnerable to external pressures, in the form of aggression by new enemies. Attacks by Gallic soldiers are most frequently mentioned as the cause, particularly around the time of the large-scale Gallic attacks on Macedonia, Thrace, and the sanctuary of Apollo at Delphi.[3] Less often referred to, but probably of greater overall economic

[2] Gerassimidis 2000 on palynological data; Baralis 2010, 247–56, for a survey of Early Iron Age upland enclosures in Aegean Thrace; on the continued use of such upland sites, see Misaïlidou-Despotidou 2008; E. Bozhinova and A. Andonova, *AOR* 2008 [2009] 218–19; *AOR* 2009 [2010] 136–7, for fourth- to third-century BC activities at Dragoyna, Purvomay district.

[3] Plb. 4.45.9–46.4, 52.1–2; Liv. 38.16; Just. 24.4.5–6, 6.1.5, 8.9.16, 25.1–3; Paus. 10.19–23; see the contributions to Vagalinski 2010 for a recent reassessment of the Celtic presence in Thrace.

significance, was the disruption that these Celtic or Gallic incursions caused to traditional commercial relations between the continental interior of the east Balkan area and respective coastal nodes. In the following century and a half, the political policies of the Roman government, whose principal aim was to prevent the reigning monarchs of either Macedonia or the Seleukid kingdom from acquiring an effective hold on the 'bridge' to Asia (that is, territory on either side of the Hellespontine Straits), succeeded in isolating some of the key coastal ports along the north Aegean coast (notably Ainos and Maroneia) from their hinterlands. Similar policies pursued in relation to the major cities of the west Pontic coast also made the latter more amenable to Roman strategic objectives. From the first century BC onwards, the active support of regional *strategoi* in Thrace, drawn from some of the traditional aristocratic families, reflects a parallel and evidently effective strategy on the part of the Roman authorities of encouraging the development of governance in the Thracian regions, which had economic concomitants, visible at least at the level of coin circulation.[4] In Macedonia, the first century BC was a period when aristocratic families were much less visible among the ruling élite in the region.[5]

One of the most distinctive material characteristics of the first millennium BC is the development of a range of new mineral technologies, based on the manufacture of iron alongside cast and hammered bronze, as well as precious metals, to which were also added the techniques of core-formed and cast glass later in this period. Less visible, but no less important in economic terms, was the enhancement of organic products—the successful dyeing of textiles using a range of natural colourants and mordants, and the large-scale production of animal by-products: hides, furs, skins, and leather artefacts (boots and shoes, belts, harness equipment). Although the organization of production was on a lesser scale than we can assume for Roman imperial times, writers like Theophrastus make assumptions about the tanning and processing of different hides and skins, which imply that a range of specialized techniques was by now systematic. There is now evidence to support Theophrastus' views that leather was tanned as well as cured and used in the north Aegean area for a wide range of decorative as well as functional purposes.

The east Balkan landmass conceals a range of highly desirable resources, with important reserves of copper and iron, as well as precious metals and other minerals; crystalline rocks, providing high quality

[4] See further discussion in Chs 5 and 6.

[5] Sève 2005; Archibald (2012b).

building materials, and many kinds of timber. These could not easily be exploited. Not all of them were effectively investigated in antiquity. Successful exploitation required cooperation between technical specialists, who did not necessarily share a common language. This challenge explains why surviving historical narratives often contain a good deal of inter-community tension.

Materials used in the construction of the built environment traditionally composed, throughout prehistoric times, of clay, dry stone, and wood; from the fifth century BC onwards these came to include ashlar masonry, cut from granite, marble, limestone, or other, more restricted rocks, and (from the second half of the fourth century BC) fired bricks were used in eastern parts of the region.[6] The higher humidity and precipitation of northern areas favoured herds of horses and cattle, as well as sheep and goats, and therefore their respective by-products, particularly leather and wool. Whereas wool was also produced farther south, the greater availability of leather goods (for military and civilian purposes), and of meadows for horse-rearing, gave the northern margins of the Aegean important strategic advantages.

The mountains and river systems of the region have been subjected to phases of uplift, faulting and erosion since the Mesozoic era, with the formation (between 250 million and 65 million years ago) of intermediate lakes and rivers, creating varied and well-resourced local ecologies. The region lies within a geologically active zone, close to the interface between three tectonic plates: the Anatolian, the Eurasian, and the Aegean Sea plates, whose intersection overlies the Hellespontine Straits and runs south of two of the chief north Aegean islands, Thasos and Samothrace. The dynamic nature of the physical landscape has been reinforced by anthropogenic activity, in the form of forest clearance (for agriculture, mining and metallurgical processing, and route ways). These human activities have in turn generated levels of instability in the physical environment. They have induced changes in the surface patterning of the modern landscape, whose outward appearance (including urban conurbations, transportation networks, and other contemporary forms of intensive land use) partly conceals the earlier activities that characterized the region in classical antiquity. Alluvial sediments have left a thick layer of clays, gravels, and sand in the middle reaches of river valleys, particularly flanking large rivers with strong seasonal dynamic patterns, such as the Haliakmon, Loudias, Axios, Strymon, Iskur and Hebros, which have cut sinuous channels through lower-lying terrain

[6] Fired bricks: Archibald 1998, 291–3.

(Fig. 4.1). The lower estuaries of these river valleys, which are often the areas that have attracted the greatest interest of historians, have undergone substantial changes since antiquity. Strabo commented on the fact that in his day the River Nestos frequently changed its bed and flooded the surrounding countryside (*Geogr.* 7 fr. 443 (44)).[7] The area of the Thermaic Gulf has been particularly affected, but the coastal zone between the Chalkidic peninsula and the Straits has also been altered, with the shoreline receding progressively south and eastwards throughout the course of the first millennium BC. These natural processes coincided with various forms of intensive land management, including the partial draining of lakes and waterlogged terrain, activities that have been dramatically speeded up during the twentieth century.

Modern urban development has obviously played a key part in changes to the external appearance of the landscape, most notably in and around Istanbul, Thessaloniki and the western parts of Chalkidike. The construction of major motorway schemes is having a profound impact on our knowledge of past landscape use in the region as a whole, but is also changing traditional ways of accumulating environmental information using survey techniques, by making these areas much less amenable to pedestrian scholarly access (the Egnatia Hodos across lower Macedonia and Aegean Thrace to Istanbul; the A1/E80 between Sofia and Edirne for Istanbul; the new 'Trakya' and 'Maritsa' motorway routes in east-central Bulgaria; new gas plants in the same region; the Haliakmon Dam project in western Macedonia; new railway lines along the Pierian coast of Macedonia, and between Plovdiv and Svilengrad). Development often brings with it money for the investigation of past landscapes, which can be beneficial for our understanding of past societies. However, the pace and pattern of development rarely matches the needs of historical research. This means that the scope of our knowledge of the past is uneven and remains intractably unbalanced in favour of lowland, coastal zones, river valleys, and plains, at the expense of upland and marginal areas.

Any attempt to create a balanced portrait of past economies has to allow for such factors. Information tends to be highly abbreviated and fragmented in urban locations, more extensive but selective in extra-urban areas. Inevitably, regional analyses must work with samples that may not be fully representative and evidence that undoubtedly fails to

[7] Perissoratis and Konispoliatis 2003, on sea-level changes; Pavlopoulos et al. 2011 on uplift in the north-east Aegean and subsidence in the Thermaic Gulf; Chiverrell and Archibald 2009 for analysis of the fluvial geomorphology of one major river, the middle Hebros (Maritsa) during the first millennium BC.

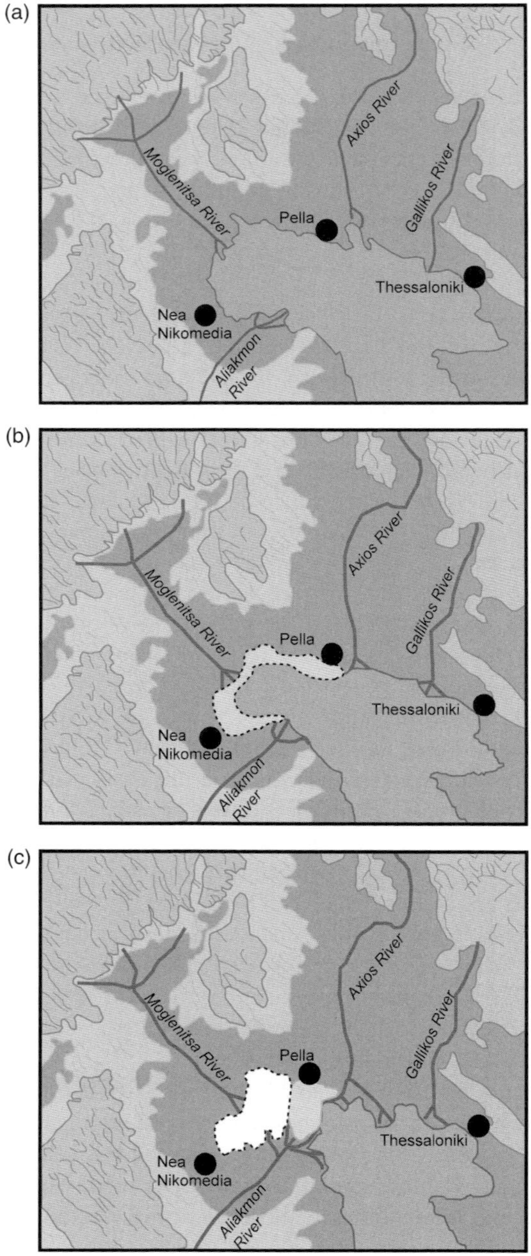

Fig. 4.1. Geomorphological changes in the Thermaic Gulf around the location of Neolithic Nea Nikomedia, Classical Pella and Hellenistic Thessaloniki; 4.1a shows the marine gulf *c*.4000 BC, with the main rivers (Haliakmon = Aliakmon, Moglenitsa = Loudias; Axios; and Gallikos = ancient Echeidoros) flowing into the Aegean sea. 4.1b shows how alluvial deposits around the estuaries of these rivers began to form lagoons during the second millennium BC, with the formation of a lake c.1600 BC (4.1c).

capture the full range of materials and assets that would have been relevant to the economies of classical antiquity in this region. Some historically attested places, as we saw in Chapter 2 in the case of the pre-Hellenistic city of Maroneia, have evaded modern expectations of what should have survived from the ancient past. Such examples remind us that the remote past is in some measure genuinely inaccessible or cannot be demonstrated to the satisfaction of the rationalist modern observer.

Essential commodities that circulated inland from coastal areas included salt, scarce minerals (alum, dyes, and pigments; building stone, glass, and tin), wine and other bulk foodstuffs, tiles and ceramic products. Wool, metal ingots and manufactures, hides, timber, cereals, and other foodstuffs travelled in the opposite direction towards coastal ports. A dense network of inland routes complemented long-haul maritime voyages and short-haul, more regular 'cabotage' along the north Aegean and western Black Sea coasts, while river traffic along the principal waterways, such as the Haliakmon, the Loudias and Axios, the Strymon and Hebros Rivers, was probably highly seasonal, making use of the higher water levels and calmer conditions of late spring and summer.

A COLLAGE OF LANDSCAPES

The Thermaic Gulf and Pella

The investigation of historic landscapes is a resource-intensive activity. In the nineteenth century, individual scholars could travel the countryside on mule or horseback, collecting notes and drawing inscriptions. Twentieth-century archaeological practice created the concept of the team project, with interdisciplinary objectives and specialist involvement from fields as diverse as engineering, botany, speleology, forensics, and veterinary science, as well as the more predicable collaborations with geographers, ceramic experts, zooarchaeologists, chemists, and analytic scientists. All of these fields of expertise have had an impact on the study of the north Aegean region and much of it has yet to be fully absorbed into the literature. Individual projects slice up the countryside to examine locations for defined research purposes. At the same time, modern development produces unexpected evidence that must somehow be coordinated with existing information. This breadth and variety of information makes it hard to evaluate what should be included in a study of the region's past economic potential. Almost everything is relevant in some way. A larger number of small, highly focused studies, driven by a variety of individual and institutional objectives, means that a historical synthesis must work with a collage of data sets that are not fully representative of the geographical space under discussion, but that do provide a very rich historical canvas.

It is appropriate to begin with a topic that has shaped a great deal of thinking about the pre-imperial history of Macedonia, namely the evolution of the Thermaic Gulf. Until the last decade, reconstructions of the ancient shore line of the Thermaic Gulf were founded on a combination of ancient accounts, particularly the brief but decisive evidence of the coastal locations of Pella and Ichnae in the Classical period (Hdt. 7.123.3; Thuc. 2.99.4), and the observations of nineteenth-century travellers, especially of the Frenchman Alfred Delacoulonche and the Austrian A. Struck, who both studied the Roman bridge at Klidi, dating from the third century AD, located on the southern side of the Gulf, which must once have spanned a river course, but is now buried some 5 km inland and is located north-east of the present bed of the River Haliakmon.[8] Struck concluded that much of the Gulf had become silted up by alluvial deposits in the period between *c.*500 BC and AD 500. Hammond took a rather different approach to the topography and hydrology of the area, believing that the changes in the geomorphology observed by Struck took place on a shorter time scale and were the result of marine intrusion, rather than fluvial dynamics.

This picture did not satisfy either historians or geographers, but a coherent reconstruction of the Gulf area has only begun to emerge since the completion of a major new geomorphological project, which has composed the first systematic map of the rivers and coastline, based on the analysis of cores from six boreholes, combined with data from satellite photographs. This new map shows the location of known prehistoric and early historic sites around the foothills of the main mountain massifs, Mount Paiko in the north, Bermion and the Pierian range in the south, with alluvial silts and gravels accumulating as cones at the junction with lower-lying terrain. According to the new data, the dynamic processes that caused the progressive silting of the river estuaries and the progradation of the coastline away from preferred settlement locations

[8] Ghilardi et al. 2008, 113 fig. 2, 115 fig. 3, with discussion of Struck and Hammond, *HM* I, 142–62; in Ps.-Skylax (66) Pella is linked to the sea by a channel of water, flowing out of a lake, Loudias, on the shore of which the city then stood. Cf. Str. 7 fr. 20 (the island of Phakos, where the Macedonian treasury was located, was connected by an island to the mainland and the city itself); Livy 49. 46 (refers to the *intermuralis amnis*).

began much earlier than most scholars had envisaged, in the third millennium BC, with riverine deposits gradually accumulating to form lagoons. A lake began to emerge in the later second millennium (*c.*1600 BC), so that by the fourth century BC, the Gulf had narrowed considerably (Fig. 4.2). The emphasis in this reconstruction on deltaic activity at river estuaries also provides a better foundation for understanding the topographic organization of roads around the edges of the lake.

This new framework for understanding local geography has been incorporated into one of the most detailed and ambitious new studies in the prehistory of the Gulf, at Angelochori, in the eastern foothills of Mount Bermion, and north-east of the later settlements at Lefkadia and Naoussa (Mieza).[9] Situated 1.5 km north-north-east of modern Angelochori is a low, ellipsoidal mound, with a natural core, currently 18.34 m asl. An area of 7,000 m^2 of the flat plateau was excavated between 1994 and 2003, revealing a Late Bronze Age settlement that relied on the freshwater lake created by the separation of channels of the River Haliakmon from the sea by a sand bar. The inhabitants of the plateau used unfired bricks to build their homes, in a style that closely resembles construction at other well known Bronze Age sites in lower Macedonia, including Assiros, Thessaloniki Toumba, Kastanas, and Angista Serres. Alongside the unbaked brick, post-built constructions are also found. The combination of different construction materials is typical of a range of contemporary sites in other parts of Macedonia and the east Balkan region. Angelochori can thus be inserted into a pattern that echoes wider regional characteristics with respect to the use of local materials and above all the tendency to focus settlement in the Late Bronze Age on hills that afforded natural protection.

Among the most valuable results of current research at Angelochori is the range of botanical evidence that gives a vivid and unusually detailed panorama of the local economy. The principal cereals, including two early varieties of wheat: einkorn (*Triticum monococcum*) and emmer (*Triticum dicoccum*), as well as spelt wheat (*Triticum spelta*), barley (*Hordeum vulgare*), and millet (*Panicum miliaceum*), represent some of the hardiest cereal types, which would tolerate variable climatic conditions. These cereals, together with a classic range of legumes (lentils: *Lens sp.*; bitter vetch: *vicia ervilia* L.; grass pea: *Lathyrus sativus*; Celtic bean: *Vicia faba* var. *minor*) were the staples of the whole east Balkan region in the prehistoric period and well into the first millennium BC, when the older forms of wheat appear as supplements to bread wheat

[9] Stephani 2010.

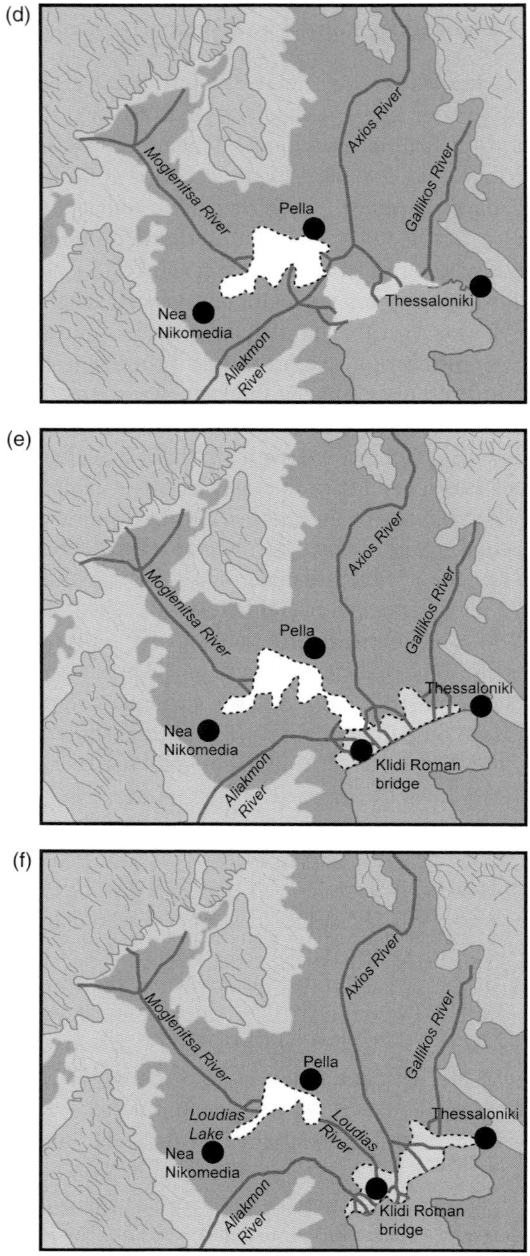

Fig. 4.2. Geomorphological changes in the Thermaic Gulf from the late classical period to the early twentieth century AD. 4.2d shows the narrowing of the plain, although river craft could still gain access to Pella via a narrow channel, *c.*400 BC. By the time that Macedonia became a Roman province, the harbour of Pella was silting up (4.2e); by AD 400, Pella was 28 km from the coast, while the Roman bridge at Klidi reinforces the eastward trend of communications in imperial times (4.2f).

(*Triticum aestivum*).[10] The vine (*vitis vinifera*) offered the commonest variety of fruit, and was equally well represented at other sites where sufficient samples have been collected. The presence of chaff suggested to the excavators that the cereals were stored in glume form and processed in batches when needed.

The domesticated animal species represented at Angelochori include cattle (*bos taurus*), sheep (*ovis aries*), goats (*capra hircus*), pigs (*sus domesticus*); dogs (*canis familiaris*), horses (*Equus caballus*), and donkeys (*Equus asinus*). Wild species included red deer (*Elaphus*), fallow deer (*Dama dama*), roe deer (*Capreolus capreolus*), hare (*lepus europaeus*), fox (*Vulpes vulpes*), badger (*Meles meles*), as well as finds of beaver tooth (*Castor fiber*), and wolf bone (*Canis lupus*). Sheep (12.3 per cent) and goats (5.4 per cent) were together the second most significant domesticates at this time after pigs (23.1 per cent), with cattle not far behind (10.3 per cent). Domesticates formed the largest proportion of animals recorded (69.7 per cent), including dogs (2.7 per cent), horses (1.9 per cent), and donkeys (0.7 per cent). Fallow deer were the commonest wild species hunted at 10.2 per cent of the total, followed by boar and hare. Pig was a crucial source of protein and evidently of major importance to the economy of Angelochori, with many animals slaughtered before they were a year old, while others were kept for up to two and a half years, which would enable a strong reproduction regime. Sheep and goats also seem to have been reared mainly for meat consumption, particularly the male animals, while females were retained for breeding purposes, and possibly milk. It is likely that cattle were used as draught animals, with which the large number of identifiable male bones would be consistent. Horses were also reared for draught and transportation, rather than for meat. The investigators assume that dogs were primarily used for hunting and herding.

How did life at Angelochori compare with other sites in Late Bronze Age and Early Iron Age Greece and the east Balkans? One of the ways in which economic behaviour has been tracked in these periods is through patterns of storage. How crops were stored provides an indication of consumption patterns and attitudes towards surplus resources. We lack a wide enough range of organic and faunal evidence from the conspectus of available known sites, but the well-studied *Toumbas* of Assiros and Kastanas, north of Thessaloniki, and Thessaloniki Toumba itself, had

[10] Stephani 2010, 171–97(archaeobotanical) and 199–220, 221–39 (zooarchaeological samples); cf. Valamoti 2004; Popova 2002, 289–97; Popova 2005; Popova and Marinova 2008, 500–6; Xenophon mentions millet (*Anab.* 7.5.12) as well as wheat and barley (*Anab.* 7.2.1) in south-eastern Thrace.

developed successful and rather specialized forms of storage in their Late Bronze and Early Iron Age phases, albeit slightly different in each case.[11] Cereals were stored in pits, ceramic containers, bins, and baskets. At Thessaloniki itself, the larger containers were also used for storing a variety of artefacts as well as natural produce. The topography of these hilltop sites makes it hard to distinguish private patterns of behaviour from what was publicly owned or publicly organized. So although we can be confident that these sites represent what look like rather socially stable environments, it is not yet possible to determine precisely how these forms of storage related to social units, whether individual families, or kin groups, or wider social networks.

The settlement on the plateau of Angelochori seems to have come to an end sometime in the early first millennium BC, but the evidence has been disturbed by later activity. The nearby site of Agrosykia, close to the corresponding northern foothills above the Thermaic Gulf, offers a broader chronological sweep to show how settlement developed in the area west of the River Axios. In the fifth millennium BC there was a community living here on a low hill below Mount Paiko, known as 'Peliti' Agrosykias. Early Iron Age burials have been discovered close by, distributed in the low-lying plain between 'Peliti' Agrosykias, the inhabited mound, and Leptokarya to the north of it. Both of these localities would later become suburbs of Pella.[12]

Pavlos Chrysostomou briefly describes the rural landscape of the area, which corresponds to the ancient district of northern Bottiaia.[13] We must imagine a landscape of densely wooded hills separated by well-watered valleys, providing an excellent environment for early communities, which would in principle have been for the most part self-sufficient. With the move of the capital to Pella, these areas became more closely integrated with the life of the new capital and its port, although many of the settlements located in the landscape remained small, independent farmsteads or villages throughout their history in classical antiquity. Expansion of the environs of Pella began in the late fifth century BC. The area around Pella saw the emergence of new sites and

[11] Margomenou 2008; Tsiafakis 2010, 382–3.

[12] *Inventory,* 850; Chrysostomou et al. 2007; A. Chrysostomou 2007, 210–79: post-Geometric pottery found without stratification including silvered and gold-tinged fabrics, pls III.1.2–4, resembling material from Kastanas, Thasos, and elsewhere; Gimatzidis 2010, 250 and fig. 75; the EIA cist tombs contained 8th–6th century BC material.

[13] Chrysostomou et al., 2007, 289–90; cf. P. Chrysostomou 1990, 205–31, reports on 34 sites added to the 17 known until then, comprising 16 Neolithic, 20 Bronze Age, 17 Iron Age and 22 classical/Hellenistic sites in the environs of Pella, covering *c.*18,000 ha.

the expansion of existing sites around the mid fourth century BC.[14] We know more about these rural sites than we do about the city of Pella itself in the fourth century BC, when it became the capital of Macedonia.

Rural country estates

The spatial coincidence of ancient with modern town sites and the difficulty of extrapolating from the limited evidence available from civic excavations means that isolated rural estates provide a more effective way of understanding agricultural production and consumption patterns. The estates around Pella provide a general sketch of how such farms operated over an extended period of time. The principal rural establishments were the property of wealthy landowners, who belonged to the leading aristocratic or otherwise distinguished families, and were located either in low-lying areas, close to rich farmland and meadows, or in upland, hilltop locations, with good views of the landscape, good sources of fresh water, and opportunities to exploit the wildlife. Rural farmsteads of Hellenistic, Roman, and early Christian date are located north and south of the River Platanos. These farmhouses have all the signs of well-established enterprises of some longevity. They were constructed of durable materials—including at least some ashlar masonry and a considerable amount of woodwork—and were roofed with Lakonian-type tiles.[15] Such estates benefited from the wide range of wild as well as domesticated species that could be reared or hunted in the vicinity. The range of domesticates includes a wider range of equids than those documented in earlier prehistory, with mules being the principal beasts of burden and farmyard fowls enriching the regular diet. A wealth of loom weights reflects substantial textile production for domestic use.

The expansion of road and rail development projects across Macedonia has greatly increased the number of recorded farmsteads of this type. A group of rural estates has recently been examined in the vicinity of Platamonas castle, which has been identified with the ancient city of Herakleion.[16] Platamonas castle was a key nodal point on the north–south coastal road between Tempe and Macedonia, overlooking the road at the point where the coastal strip is narrowest as it skirts the foothills of Mount Olympos. As in Bottiaia, the local environment—fresh water,

[14] *HM II*, 658ff; P. Chrysostomou 1990, 221; Akamatis 2011, 393–8.

[15] P. Chrysostomou 1995, 126, on the wealth of wildlife, vegetables, vines, and olives.

[16] Poulaki-Pandermali 2008, 'Krania-Herakleio', in Tsouna ed., 116–53, 154–7.

climate, and humidity—provides excellent conditions for stock raising and hunting. The area around the castle itself has yielded evidence of activity from at least the Early Bronze Age onwards, with workshops and other installations enclosed by a peribolos wall of dry stone at Krania, 370 m from the castle. In the second half of the eighth century BC, a large single-roomed structure, originally apsidal, later oval-shaped, with a single entrance on the long side, and a partially paved or pebbled floor, was built in a way that overlaps the Bronze Age enclosure and its terraces. This structure could have been the first Iron Age farmhouse in this area. Although the evidence for the next four hundred years is largely circumstantial (the late classical and early Hellenistic period is represented mainly by a potter's workshop), the Hellenistic phase saw a massive expansion. The castle was densely inhabited with domestic structures built of dry stone with multiple rooms. These were destroyed in the second century, presumably at the time of the transition to Roman authority, when there was a great deal of activity along the coast road. The fortification was eventually abandoned in the fourth century AD.

At a distance of 4 km from Platamonas castle was a very large rural villa at Tria Platania, which began life during the fourth century BC, was interrupted in the early third century BC (perhaps in connection with the Gallic invasion) and revived in the later third century BC, in the reign of Antigonos Gonatas, continuing into the time of Philip V. One of the special features of the Tria Platania estate is the evidence for the spatial organization of central tasks and storage arrangements for the preservation of wine and other foodstuffs (Fig. 4.3). The essential structures consist of a rectangular, almost square walled enclosure (55 m x 42.50 m), built of mud brick over foundations made of unworked stones, the floors on a thick substructure of stone and tile. The enclosure formed the external walls of a suite of rooms on at least three sides, facing onto a large open courtyard. The north and east wings also had a covered walkway, which may originally have extended on the remaining sides to create a regular, fully enclosed space. There was a tower in the centre of the courtyard, surrounded by a shallow trench. A pottery kiln was located west of the tower, circular in plan, with a central pillar and a stone-built fire chamber. A well was also located in the courtyard. Outside the farmhouse, there was a stone-paved path on the east and south fronts. This central building had been enclosed by a surrounding wall, *c.*1.20 m wide, extending from the north-east corner for a distance of 32 m northwards. Most of the associated finds were ceramic and provide a rich reflection of domestic equipment for the storage and consumption of wine, other liquids, and food. In the north-east corner of the complex was a storage room, a *pitheon*, containing ten ceramic

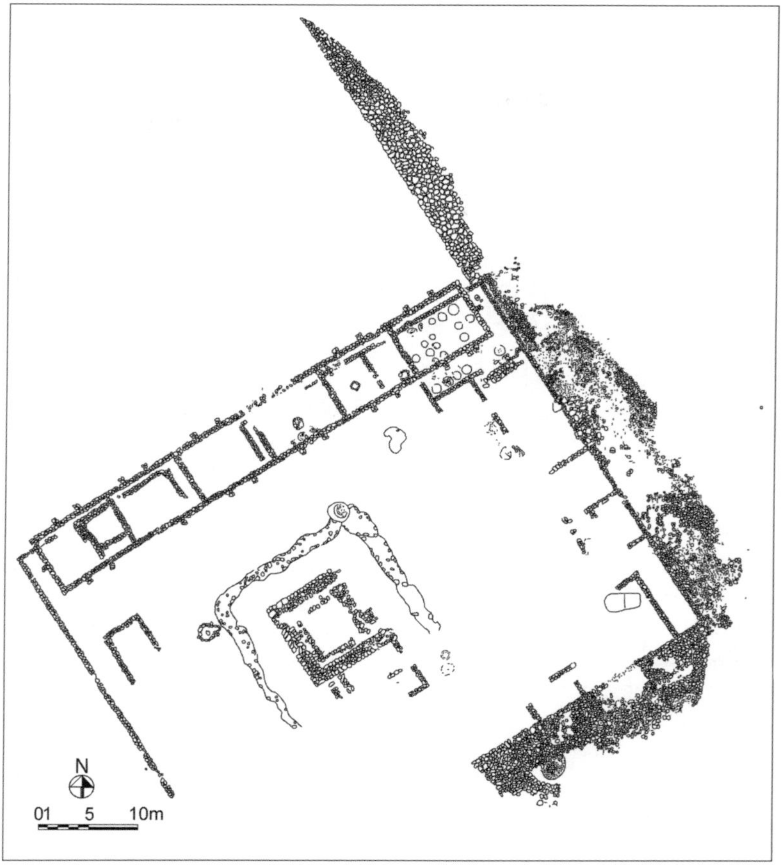

Fig. 4.3. Country house estate at Tria Platania, Macedonia, showing parts of the excavated complex that constituted the main residential and working quarters of the farmhouse, with a tower and ceramic kiln in the centre of the courtyard (late fourth to second century BC).

pithoi, and 16 pits that would have contained similar vessels.[17] The residues inside the storage vessels contained mainly grape pips, while others contained olives.[18]

The Tria Platania estate was not the only one in the area of Herakleion. The farmhouse at Komboloi (Fig. 4.4) was located on the east side of the main north–south road between the Vale of Tempe and Pieria, north of Herakleion and *c.*3.5 km south-west of the recently discovered acropolis

[17] Poulaki in Adam-Veleni et al., 2003, 56–60.
[18] Margaritis in Adam-Veleni et al. 2003, 61–2; Margaritis and Jones 2008a.

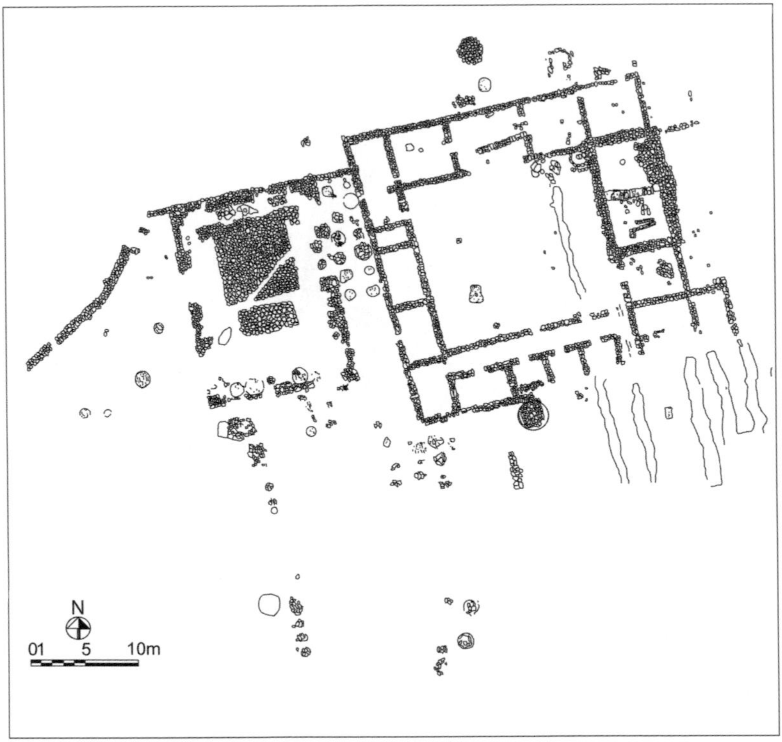

Fig. 4.4. Country house estate at Komboloi, Macedonia. The cellar, with strengthened walls, perhaps supporting a tower (in the middle of the east wing of the residential complex arranged around the square courtyard), seems to be the earliest structure. There is an area for agricultural processing on the west, around a paved coutryard, and there were other structures on the east side of the main residence, perhaps around another courtyard.

of Leibethra, another upland fortified site occupied between the eighth and first century BC.[19] The surviving remains of the country house were slightly smaller than that at Tria Platania (48 m x 28.5 m), but have many similarities with it in form and design. Only parts of the main structures were documented, consisting of a square residential complex with suites of rooms on four sides (28.5 m x 28.5 m), on a foundation of stone blocks with a clay mortar and an unbaked brick superstructure. The excavators

[19] Leibethra: E. Poulaki-Pandermali, E. Klinaki, 'Leibethra', *AEMΘ* 21 (2007) [2011] 161–9; Komboloi: Poulaki in Adam-Veleni et al. 2003, 63–70; Margaritis and Jones 2006 on the analysis of pressed grape remains.

suspected that there was a second complex around a courtyard to the east of the residential block, in which case the cellar with strengthened lateral walls (probably used for storing cereals, pulses, olives, and grape products, judging by the residues under collapsed beams and tiles) may well have supported a tower, which would then have been located in the centre of the estate. This wine cellar was evidently slightly earlier than the farmhouse itself. It seems that a vineyard already existed in the vicinity before the farmhouse was constructed. An earlier period of domestic use is suggested by a hearth, whose structural associations were evidently destroyed in the construction of the new complex.

A roofed corridor linked the store-room to the courtyard and house. Further store-rooms extended to the north and south of the investigated area, and the suspected second courtyard is to the east. On the west side of the residential block, there was a storage building, with a stone-paved courtyard, which seems to have been the main storage and processing area of the farm. In a regular space south of the courtyard, with a lowered floor covered with a lime plaster (5.30 m x 2.30 m), there were two pointed *pithoi* for storing wine, and a large quantity of grape pips.

The farm estate was the centre of a huge concentration of activity. Outside the main residential block, traces of roofing materials show that there were *stoas*, or covered corridors, used as workshop areas, with evidence of tools and equipment—a kiln and a hearth on the south side; numerous household ceramic vessels; iron tools, daggers, nails, loom-weights, and coins. The overall number of coins discovered in the farm complex was 232, dating from the reign of Philip II to the first quarter of the third century BC. This is quite an impressive number for a single property, but many of the recently excavated rural sites also produced coins. Both the estate at Tria Platania and at Komboloi show the same essential organizational template, consisting of a rectangular walled residential complex, with suites of rooms along each side; a scheme that could be repeated to provide subsidiary structures, catering for agriculturally related activities. Although there may in both cases have been other, more remote structures, including separate accommodation for retainers, the rationale seems to have been for the residents and their domestic assistants—whether employed retainers, relatives, or servants—to live in the main residential complex. The order of magnitude for these spaces implies that the inhabitants would have numbered in tens rather than hundreds.

Along the course of the Egnatia Odos farther along the coastline, in Mygdonia, a larger number of sites has been disclosed on the west bank of the River Strymon. Twenty-three separate sites, from various periods, have been registered. Among the most interesting for our purposes are the fortified complex at Vrasna, the property with an underground

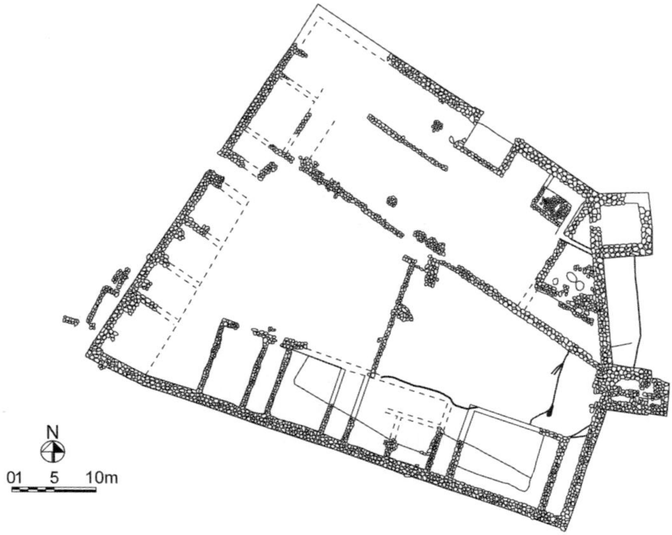

Fig. 4.5. Country estate at Vrasna, eastern Macedonia, consisting of residential and storage rooms enclosed by a fortification wall with three external towers (mid fourth century–168 BC).

stone-built pantry at the *Syndeterios* of the Egnatia Odos, and the country house at Asprovalta.[20] The property at Vrasna was protected by three external towers (Fig 4.5). This was an autonomous unit, with its own olive press and two stone mills, perhaps for grinding corn, and was evidently controlled by a local urban centre, since roof tiles carried the names of two officials (*astynomoi*): Thourippos son of Demetrios and Patrokles son of Proxenos. At Asprovalta, in the foothills of Mount Kerdylion, commanding the road east over the River Strymon, was a large farm complex extending over 0.35 ha. The earliest phase resembled the fourth-century BC Vari house in the Attic countryside, with a suite of rooms fronted by a porch and a courtyard in front. This design was transformed in the succeeding phase, when the walls of the porch were

[20] Adam-Veleni in Adam-Veleni et al. 2003, 114; Vrasna: 95–8; Syndeterios Egnatias: 99–100; Asprovalta: 101–7; Adam-Veleni 2009, 5–14; Adam-Veleni, 'Epigraphikes martyries apo ta Vrasna', *ArchMak* 6, 1–14.

doubled to enable the construction over it of a two-storey tower, around which corridors opened up on four sides, separating the tower from suites of rooms. Another courtyard was subsequently added on the north side, and later further buildings on the south side. Three stone kilns were added against the south wall, and a circular rubble construction, perhaps a threshing floor; but the most important activity in the final phase (the third quarter of the third century BC), was smithing, using ironstone mined from Mount Kerdylion.

The farmhouses discovered in Bottiaia, along the Pierian coastline, and in Mygdonia have provided detailed evidence of rural management on a lesser, but no less intensive scale, as compared with the larger units at Tria Platania and Komboloi. The similarities between these rural properties, particularly the fortified inward-facing units such as that at Vrasna, and some rural structures in inland Thrace such as the complex overlooking Lake Mandren near Burgas, point to the wider application of this kind of estate.[21] One of the most striking recent examples of a fortified rural residence is located below the peak of Kozi Gramadi (1,364 m), in the Sushtinska Sredna Gora range, north of the town of Starosel, and north-west of Plovdiv, which may have been a royal or princely hunting lodge, rather than a residence of any formal character (Fig. 4.6).[22] There is comparatively little evidence of subsistence. A hunting lodge would explain its location high up in the mountains, whilst at the same time showing evidence of close connections with the principal patterns of exchange. A surprising number of high value silver as well as copper alloy regal coins, belonging to Thracian and Macedonian rulers of the fourth century BC, as well as contemporary silver coins of Parion, the Thracian Chersonese, Thasos, and imitations of Thasian 'Silenos and nymph' types, may represent a relatively short period of occupation of the site itself. The fortified site at Kozi Gramadi may have been short-lived, but the area was by no means remote, as a hoard of late republican denarii demonstrates. One feature of the site does deserve special consideration, namely the masonry structure at the heart of this upland eyrie. The design of the central doorway, and the overall appearance of this structure, closely resembles tomb architecture from the second half of the fourth and early third century BC. If this structure were to have cult functions, it lacks many of the associated features, particularly votive offerings. So the resemblance may be a superficial one, simply because we lack suitable comparanda. On the other hand, it may

[21] Xen. *Anab.* 7.2.21; cf. 8.12–14; Balabanov 2000, 91–2 with further refs.

[22] Christov (2011, 180–7) argues that this exemplifies a periodic royal residence, but does not explain how the upland features resemble Theopompos' description of such periodic locations (*FGrH* 115 F31).

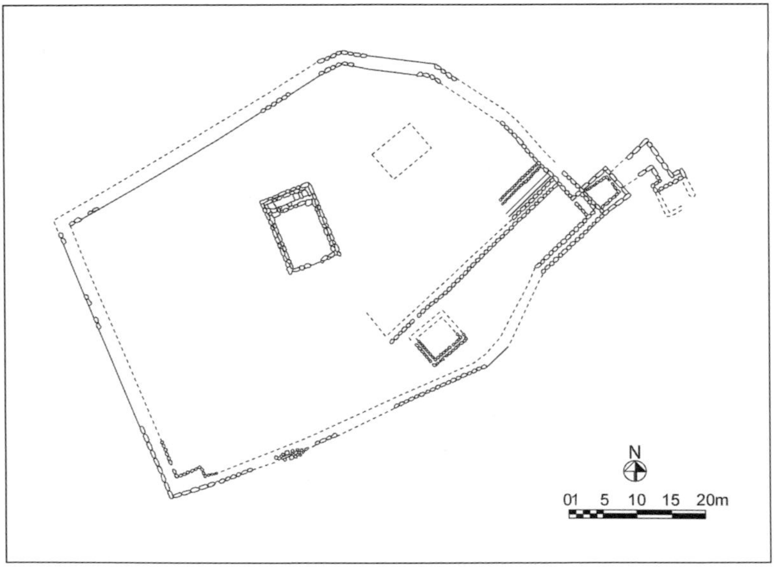

Fig. 4.6. Country estate near Kozi Gramadi, central Thrace, composed of a number of built structures enclosed by a substantial fortification wall (second half of the fourth century BC).

be that this ashlar structure was intended for cult purposes. If so, this was only one feature of the upland complex as a whole.

Country estates are well known in the landscape of Roman Thrace and survey in the region of Pautalia has revealed a network of such *villae rusticae*, set within a chessboard of villages or more substantial agglomerations, *c.*2–3 km apart. At 'Mramorite' near Borovetz, on the west bank of the River Strymon, a commemorative inscription and a mound cemetery close to a villa site with substantial architectural remains can be connected with a well-to-do family that acquired Roman citizenship, most likely in the late first century BC. Villa sites have also been identified at Kocherinovo and Krashevitsa, on the east bank of the middle course of the River Strymon, on the basis of architectural remains built to a high specification.[23] The settlement history of this part of the Strymon valley and the layout of such properties indicates a lengthy history of private estates that precedes the Roman political settlement. Very little research has been carried out to trace pre-Roman landholding of this type.

[23] Božkova 1994, 145.

The estates at Tria Platania and Komboloi represent two slightly different models of the type of large estate that must have been much more widespread in lower Macedonia, parts of Upper Macedonia, and central and Aegean Thrace during the Hellenistic period. Both provide ample evidence of dedicated storage facilities for wine and other agricultural products on a scale that significantly exceeds the needs of the putative inhabitants, as well as a range of subsidiary activities, including ceramic production for estate (and perhaps external) use and the manufacture of textiles and a variety of household products. These estates were centres of production in their own right, stored surpluses intended for commercial sale (as the numbers of coins found at these sites might demonstrate) and would have acted as centres of local employment for the wider rural population. The immediate household was involved in the centralized tasks connected with the storage of food supplies, the preparation of household meals, and the provision of textiles and equipment for the estate. The support staff probably also provided the workforce that produced the daily fruit, vegetables, and meat supplies of the inhabitants. It is less easy to demonstrate, on the basis of the central units alone, the role played by estate managers, the farming staff, those who looked after the estate's animals (riding, draught, and food stock), and any additional retainers, who would have been required to keep records, deal with tenants, and provide protection and suitable companionship for the female as well as the male residents.

Analysis of the botanical data from a number of farm sites is beginning to provide other ways of distinguishing between different forms of economic activity. Komboloi stands out on this count as an example of unusual surplus capacity. The range and form of plants represented shows that specialized viticulture was practised here and wine produced not just for internal consumption but also for large-scale market sale. Two of the large storage *pithoi* alone had the capacity of 170–204 *amphorae*.[24] The estate at Tria Platania, on the other hand, did not display anything like the same degree of specialized storage capacity, notwithstanding the size of the estate. Wine was probably made here for domestic consumption, but olives were particularly prominent as a foodstuff. The range of produce here was more consistent with its function as a self-sustaining enterprise. The presence of stamped *amphora* handles would indicate the presence of imported wines or other foodstuffs from among the main regional producing centres.

The footprints of Tria Platania and Komboloi were at the top end of the social scale in Macedonia. The area occupied by the residential block

[24] Margaritis 2006.

at Tria Platania (43 m x 56 m, *c.* 2,408 m^2), corresponds to two thirds of the size of the main court in the early Hellenistic palace at Demetrias (3,666 m^2); in the case of Komboloi, the area amounts to 22 per cent (between a quarter and a fifth) of the main court, the *anaktoron*, at Demetrias.[25] The palace at Aigeai, now attributed by A. Kottaridi not just to the second half of the fourth century BC but specifically to the reign of Philip II, occupied an area of 12,500 m^2; the western peristyle, which the excavator believes to have been among the earliest, if not the earliest construction belonging to the palace, measures 41.4 m x 41.4 m, or 1,713 m^2, which gives a useful comparative yardstick for evaluating the country houses of well-to-do Macedonians.[26]

The uneven incidence of documented rural establishments from the first millennium BC poses a significant challenge. How should we relate specific evidence from these kinds of sites, which can be characterized in some detail, with the broader spatial data, derived from surveys, whether extensive or intensive? Extensive survey in the *nomes* of Thessaloniki, Kilkis, and Chalkidike has produced a large number of recorded locations—144 pre-Iron Age sites in the *nome* of Thessaloniki alone.[27] The Langadas survey indicates a strong increase in the number of rural sites during the Early Iron Age, with a less well-marked, if sustained, profile in the succeeding Late Iron Age. Urban nucleations appear comparatively late and seem to belong to a surge in urban foci during the Hellenistic period. The same pattern has been assumed to have existed in the Thracian interior, particularly in the case of nascent urban centres in east central Bulgaria, as at Kabyle and Seuthopolis (Fig. 4.7).[28] Modern development work along the Bulgarian–Greek border; in east-central Bulgaria,[29] and in the environs of Istanbul,[30] has produced a rich haul of evidence that has yet to be fully analysed, published, and absorbed. In the rapidly changing commercial environment of south-eastern Europe, the kind of documentation currently available does not necessarily do justice to the quality of information being conveyed in preliminary

[25] Nielsen 1999, 268; see Davies 2005, esp. 121–3, for detailed discussion of putative unit costs of this and similar palace structures.

[26] Kottaridi 2011a, 304–5.

[27] Grammenos et al. 1997.

[28] Langadas survey: Andreou and Kotsakis 1999; Kabyle: *Inventory*, 893 no. 694; L. Getov, N. Handjiyska, I. Vulchev, *AOR* 2009 [2010] 417–19 for recent work in the Hellenistic *agora* of Kabyle; Seuthopolis: *Inventory*, 896, no. 657; for recent intensive survey in the Kazanlak area, see refs Ch. 2, n.55.

[29] Nikolov, Nehrizov, and Tsvetkova 2006; taking two seasons as examples, and only first-millennium BC sites, 17 were recorded under major road development projects in 2008 (*AOR* 2008 [2009] 137ff.); and a further 26 in 2009 (*AOR* 2009 [2010] 136–270).

[30] Özdoğan 1990; Crow and Turner 2009.

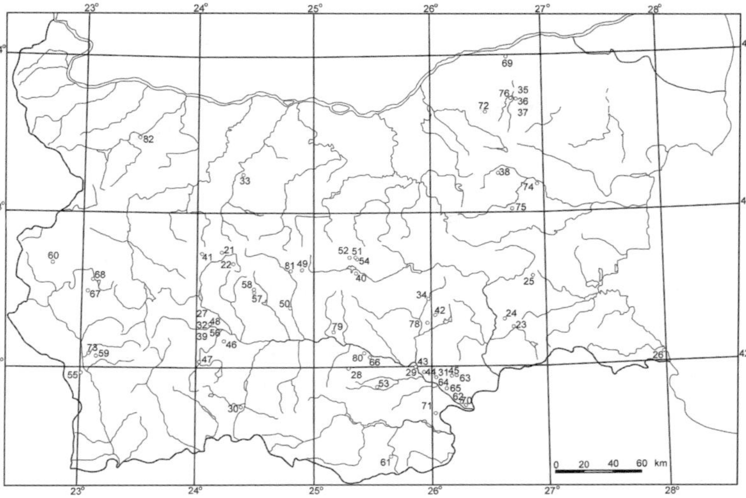

Sites and cemeteries dating to the first millennium*; sites and cemeteries from the fifth to first centuries BC**

21 Tumulus near Pirdop
22 fortified site near Smilovene, Koprivshtitsa**
23 Tumulus near Popovo, Bolyarovo district, Yambol region*, **
24 Tumulus near Stroino, Elhovo, Yambol region**
25 Tumulus no1, Krumovo Gradishte, Karnobat district
26 Tumulus near Sinemorets, Tsarevo district **
27 Adjiyska Vodenitsa, Vetren (ancient Pistiros)**
28 Dragoyna upland fortress, Dragoynovo, Purvomay district, Late Bronze Age
29 investigations near funerary mounds at Simeonovgrad, Plovdiv-Svilengrad railway development*
30 Tumular cemetery at Lilovo, Devin, Smolyan district**
31 Cult site at Semerchevo, Dosteevo, Harmanli district, Haskovo region*, **
32 Adjiyska Vodenitsa, Vetren (ancient Pistiros)**
33 Banunya, Bezhanovo, Lovech district (**)
34 Dyadovo tell, Nova Zagora district
35 Sboryanovo, Sveshtari, Isperih district, Razgrad region, 6 Hellenistic mounds**
36 Malak Porovets, Isperih, Razgrad region, four funerary mounds
37 Sboryanovo, Sveshtari (Byuven Kasab), Isperih district**
38 Tumulus no2, Ruets, Targovishte district**
39 Adjiyska Vodenitsa, Vetren (ancient Pistiros)**
40 rock sanctuary at Buzovgrad, Kazanlak district**
41 Tumulus at Mirkovo, Sofia district**
42 Golyamata Mogila, at Pet Mogili, Nova Zagora district**
43 Shihanov Bryag, Harmanli, site on motorway development AM Maritsa (**)
44 Shihanov Bryag, Harmanli, Haskovo region, Plovdiv-vilengrad railway development*
45 Two dolmens at Eshmedjika, Oryahovo, Lyubimets, Haskovo region*
46 Golyam Kosoman, Debrashtitsa, Pazardjik region, cult site**
47 Thracian cult site near Sveti Ilya, Velingrad**
48 Adjiyska Vodenitsa, Vetren (ancient Pistiros)**
49 Vasil Levsky, Karlovo district, settlement**
50 Razhevo Konare, Kaloyanovo, Plovdiv area, tumulus cemetery**
51 Tumulus on the property of the Arsenal company, Sheynovo, Valley of the Roses**
52 Tumulus cemetery near Yasenovo, Valley of the Roses**
53 Tumulus near Kelesheva Chuka, Konush, Haskovo region**
54 Tumuli near Sheinovo, Valley of the Roses**
55 Late Bronze Age features at Krasto, Pokrivnik, Blagoevgrad district
56 Adjiyska Vodenitsa, Vetren (ancient Pistiros)**
57 Krastevich, Hisarya region, settlement**
58 Krastevich, Hisarya region, cult site**
59 Tsarev Peak, Rila massif, investigations near the town of Bistritsa, Blagoevgrad district
60 Sveti Petar Peak, Dolna Sekirna, Breznik district*
61 Ada tepe, western slopes, Rhodope*, **
62 Early Bronze Age site and Early Iron Age ritual pits at Vaskovo, Lyubimets, Haskovo region*
63 Tumular cemetery near Bayamlaka, Vaskovo, Lyubimets*
64 Dana Bunar, Georgi Dobrevo district, Lyubimets, Haskovo region, Late Iron Age pits on the AM Maritsa motorway project**
65 Dana Bunar, Georgi Dobrevo, Lyubimets district, Haskovo region: Early Iron Age site*
66 site 11, near Krum, Dimitrovgrad district, Plovdiv-Svilengrad railway development
67 Two mounds at Vetrilnika, Staro Selo, Radomir district**
68 Three mounds below Golema Stoblenitsa peak, Studena, Pernik district (**)
69 Funerary mound near Tsarev Dol, Tutrakan, Silistra region
70 Kapitan Andreevo, Iron Age pits on the Plovdiv-Kapitan Andreevo railway development*
71 Late Bronze Age and Early Iron Age settlement at Kush Kaya, Vulche Pole, Lyubimets district*
72 Tumulus in the cemetery near Kaleto, Topchiy, Razgrad district**
73 Porominovo, Kocherinovo district, Kyustendil region, Tumulus
74 Tumulus near Salmanovo, Kyustendil region**
75 Tumulus 1 in a mound necropolis near Troshka Mahala, Vurbitsa**
76 Sboryanovo city **
78 Late Iron Age pits and Medieval site and cemetery in the former village of Gledachevo, Radnevo district **
79 Mound no1, cemetery of Bostanlaka, Orizovo, Bratya Daskalovi district**
80 Karabyulyuk, Yablkovo, 5th–3rd century BC site, on the Plovdiv-Svilengrad railway development **
81 Early Bronze Age cult features at Valinov Gorun, Dabene, Karlovo district
82 Malo Pole, Gradeshnitsa, Krivodol district

Fig. 4.7. Archaeological sites of the second and first millennium BC investigated during 2006 in the territory of Bulgaria (and reported in *AOR* 2006).

publications. As we will see in Chapter 5, a regional approach to this kind of information can give us a better sense of the relationships between different types of site, which can enhance what we do know in a variety of ways (Fig. 4.8).

The ecological environment provides the essential parameters within which our northern societies operated. If we want to get a clearer understanding of economic patterns beyond this preliminary sketch, then we need to develop concepts about the social mechanisms of decision-making and how these informed demand for certain commodities. We need to imagine a social matrix that provides a working model of the kinds of social constraints and social preoccupations that operated alongside the ecological givens in the northern Aegean of the first millennium BC. This involves interrogating material culture as well as the more usual narrative, numismatic, and epigraphic evidence. How does material culture speak about past societies and about the relationships between individuals and their social groups? This is where Thorstein Veblen and some current trends in anthropology provide useful points of departure.

THORSTEIN VEBLEN AND THE 'INSTINCT OF WORKMANSHIP'

How objects make subjects

In his seminal book, *The Theory of the Leisure* Class (1899), the economist Thorstein Veblen explored the concept of 'conspicuous consumption', a term that has since become a familiar item in the vocabulary of modern living. Yet Veblen's is not a household name in the same way that this perceptive phrase and others that he coined have become. In his own day, he was not fêted for the originality of his thinking and did not become a social guru. Veblen was a visionary, but some of the things he wanted to tell his contemporaries were not what people wanted to hear. He was critical of his own society, of North American business practices, and of received wisdom among his fellow economists, who responded by calling him 'not sound', or worse, 'not an economist', implying that he was no more than a social commentator. His technological approach to the grand sweep of history, and his low estimate of the role of politics, were deprecated by those of his academic contemporaries who made historical writing their business. Veblen's prescience about international

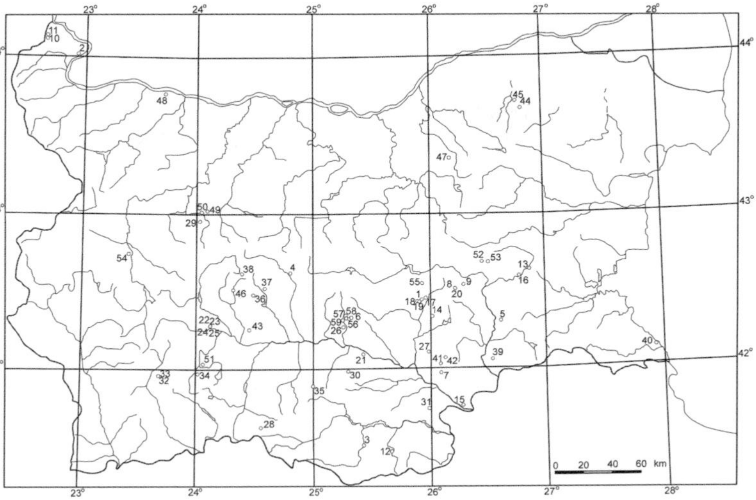

Bronze Age sites

1 Dyadovo tell, Nova Zagora region
2 Grindur, Vidin region
3 Sedlari settlement, Momchilgrad area
4 Balinov Gorun, Debene, Karlovo area, cult site and cemetery
5 Bailar Karyak' near Boyanovo, Yambol district, tumular necropolis
6 Malkata Momina Mogila', funerary and cult site, Bratya Daskalovi district
7 Yorgovite Mogili, Izvorovo, Harmanli district, tumular cemetery
8 Site 10, Lot 3, AM 'Trakya' (motorway development) Bikovo
9 Site 18A, Lot 3 along AM 'Trakya', Chokoba, Sliven district
10 Baley settlement near Orsoia, NW Bulgaria
11 Baley cemetery
12 Ade Tepe, Krumovgrad district, gold mines

Iron Age sites

13 Site 27 Lot 4, AM 'Trakya', Devetak village, Karnobat, Burgas district
14 Pet Mogili, Nova Zagora, site at Novata Cheshma
15 Svilengrad cult pits
16 Site 25, Lot 4, Malenovo, Straldza district
17 Site 20, AM 'Trakya' development project, Stoil Voyvoda, Nova Zagora district
18 Site 18, Lot 2, AM 'Trakya' development, Yorta, near Zagortsi, Nova Zagora district
19 Site 18A, Lot 2, AM 'Trakya' development, Yorta, near Zagortsi, Nova Zagora
20 Site 11, Lot 3, AM 'Trakya' development, Bikovo, Sliven district
21 Site 9, Plovdiv - Svilengrad railway development, Karabyulyuk, Yablokovo, Dimitrovgrad district
22 Emporion Pistiros (Adjiyska Vodenitsa), Vetren, Septemvri district
23 Emporion Pistiros (Adjiyska Vodenitsa), Vetren, Septemvri district
24 Emporion Pistiros (Adjiyska Vodenitsa), Vetren, Septemvri district
25 Emporion Pistiros (Adjiyska Vodenitsa), Vetren, Septemvri district
26 Halka Bunar, near Gorno Belovo, Bratya Daskalovi district, Stara Zagora region
27 Chengene dere', Pomoshtnik, Galabovo district, settlement
28 Gela upland fortress, Smolyan district
29 Site near the Church of Sveta Bogoroditsa, Osikovitsa, Pravets district
30 Dragoyna, Purvomay, settlement
31 Gluhite Kameni' rock complex, eastern Rhodope
32 Babyak, western Rhodope, Belitsa district, Blagoevgrad region, upland cult site
33 Babyak, 'Malkoto Vuzvishenye', Belitsa district
34 Ostrets peak, western Rhodope, 'sanctuary of Dionysos'
35 Belantash, Vrata, Asenovgrad district, rock sanctuary
36 Pamuk tepe, near Krastevich, Hisarya district, commercial settlement
37 Kozi Gramadi, Sushtinska Sredna Gora, royal residence
38 Smilovene' Koprivshtitsa, fortified site
39 Melnitsa, Elhovo district, Yambol region, rock sanctuary
40 Ahtopol, Black Sea coast

tumular cemeteries

41 Kayryaka, Bulgarska Polyana, Topolovgrad
42 Mangur tepe, Hlyabovo, Topolograd district, dolmen
43 Chernogorovo, Emerlin, Pazarkjik district, two tumuli
44 Arda Street no11, Isperih, tumulus
45 Sboryanovo, Isperih, Hellenistic necropolis
46 Strelcha, Panagyurishte district, investigations near Zhaba Mogila
47 Chamber tomb at 'Smoylan Punar' Gagovo, Popovo district
48 Tumulus near Kozloduy, Vratsa region
49 Laskovska Mogila, Ravnishte, Pravets district
50 Two tumuli at Vidrare, Pravets district
51 Tumulus at 'Stanilovets', Velingrad district
52 Krastava Mogila, Valley of the Roses
53 Ruschova Mogila, Valley of the Roses
54 Tumulus No1, Vrazhdebna, Sofia Airport
55 Funerary mound near Karanovo tell, Nova Zagora district
56 Vaulted chamber tomb in Momina Tumulus, Bratya Daskalovi, Stara Zagora district
57 Karakochova Mogila, Bratya Daskalovi, Chirpan district
58 Chitashka Mogila, Bratya Daskalovi, Chirpan district
59 Selskata Mogila', Bratya Daskalovi, Chirpan district

Fig. 4.8. Archaeological sites of the second and first millennium BC investigated during 2010 in the territory of Bulgaria (and reported in *AOR* 2010).

affairs during the First World War was little appreciated and his advice to politicians ignored.[31]

Nevertheless, Veblen's concepts still repay attention, even if the framework of his ideas was a nineteenth century one and his style not memorable. What makes Veblen's approach to material culture interesting is its anthropological dimension. For many historians, with Marx's 'fetishism of commodities' ringing in their ears, artefacts have evoked faint interest at best. It has been the role of anthropologists to remind us that objects matter and how far our understanding of and appreciation for others is shaped by the material objects with which we surround ourselves.[32] In his conclusion to a recent study of the domestic environment of a complete London street, the anthropologist Daniel Miller has reflected on the highly charged relationship that we have with everyday objects: 'An advantage of this unusual perspective [our relationship with objects] is that sometimes these apparently mute forms can be made to speak more easily and eloquently to the nature of relationships than can those with persons.'[33] Objects can speak more clearly, or more acutely, about our relationships with the material world, and with each other, than first person statements sometimes do. He goes on to say that 'objects create subjects much more than the other way round,' and that this realization should make us take material culture much more seriously than we do in practice.

Miller's conversations with the householders of Stuart Street are a live engagement with the kinds of abstract ideas coming out of anthropological enquiries that are providing students of material culture with a rich source for research. Veblen's critics were scornful of his focus on the importance of technology in history. Veblen himself was scornful of Karl Marx's evaluation of the history of technology, because he saw in Marx's world-view a Hegelian (or rather a Benthamite), crypto-optimistic philosophy, which had to be superseded by a Darwinian perspective on the complex organization of human societies.[34] Darwinian biology has been valorized a century after the publication of *On the Origin of Species*, but historians are still very uncertain about how to view Darwinian ideas in a cultural perspective. The intellectual exploration of the dynamic relationship between the human family and its material environment was

[31] See Max Lerner's Introduction to *The Portable Veblen,* 1–49, esp. 10–43; Hodgson 1998; Banta, Introduction to the Oxford World Classics 2007 edition, i–xv.

[32] Appadurai 1986, 6–16 on the 'fetishism' that Marx identified; 30–3 on Veblen's ideas.

[33] Miller 2008, 287.

[34] Thorstein Veblen, 'The Socialist Economics of Karl Marx', in Veblen 1919, 409–56 (originally published in 1906).

only just beginning at the turn of the nineteenth and twentieth century. The task of trying to understand how we relate to the material world was left mainly to anthropologists and archaeologists, who took some time to appreciate that this relationship is a genuinely reciprocating one. Human societies make things; but the built environment and artefacts also shape human societies.

Miller's research is primarily concerned with social relations and it is easiest to start with this aspect of our associations with the material. His simple-sounding statement: 'objects make subjects much more than the other way round' paraphrases the ways in which anthropologists are trying to express how the material world, modified by human interventions over millennia, informs relationships as well as providing the canvas on which we create life stories. Miller was able to compare how his subjects talked about their relationships with others and how objects and interiors narrated a kind of parallel version of these interpersonal relationships. He concluded that, notwithstanding the strong tendency to criticize 'materialism' and 'materialistic' tendencies of contemporary culture (a tendency that reaches back to the anti-materialistic values of Cynic philosophers, and of Mysians and Getae in our story),[35] the material objects that we choose to deploy in our homes and the material presentation that we create through our own persons reflect individual narratives that tell others who we want to be. In contemporary societies, these material configurations are not totally idiosyncratic choices; nor are they collective decisions, but something in between the idiosyncratic and the collective. We might say that they are customized choices—individual selections from within the broad pool of objects and styles, and shaped by a combination of social background, education, and personal experience.[36]

The fieldwork conducted by Daniel Miller and his researchers is the kind of fine-grained investigation that tries to understand choices at the level of the individual in society. In most historical situations, we do not have this option. There is an obvious practical dilemma in trying to make mute objects speak. Present experience and a wide range of historical texts show that the choices individuals make are constrained—by their experiences of everyday life; by their social position; by the context they

[35] Str. 7.3.3 (the ascetic practices of the Mysians, called 'pious men', who resemble those called *Ktistai* among the Thracians) citing Poseidonios; Baladié 1989, 188–9; cf. 193 ad 7.3.9 (C302–303); cf. also below on Lysimachos' capture by Dromichaites.

[36] e.g. Salganik and Watts 2009 provide experimental evidence, based on the responses of 2,930 participants in a web-based survey of reactions to new songs by emerging bands, which evidently confirm an earlier experiment by both authors.

live in; by specific aspirations; by limited knowledge or availability. The social constraints that operated in the north Aegean are not transparent from the material record. To the dispassionate observer, surviving artefacts present us with two quite specific methodological challenges to our understanding of ancient demand patterns (and this applies principally to what survives, which means, overwhelmingly, inorganic materials). One difficulty is the fact that, leaving aside recognizably exclusive objects (such as gold items, which as we saw in Chapter 2, were reserved for élite families and outside the normal circulation of commodities), much of the built environment and surviving movable objects that are found in excavations seem to offer a surprising degree of social comparability. There are, to be sure, many unique, exceptional artefacts, that represent bespoke commissions, often found as grave goods in the north Aegean area; but there are many more everyday objects, which do not seem to differ very much in typological terms. Presented with single examples of a given form, it is not easy to judge why one knife blade, or spearhead, or dress pin might have been chosen over another. In themselves, these items do not tell us very much about social differentiation. If anything, they imply that a large number of people had access to a good range of essential tools and ornaments. Outside some coastal colonies (Pontic Apollonia, Abdera, or Akanthos in Chalkidike), the apparent absence of large flat cemeteries, which could tell us something about broad social groups, makes it difficult to draw any general conclusions about the ways in which northern societies treated their ordinary members. Most funerary artefacts from the north come from discrete groups of objects, every one of which is slightly different from every other. The traditions of mound burial in particular disguise shared features of commemorative practice and emphasize instead the individual's uniqueness.[37]

We might conclude from the configuration of burials and grave goods that the language of social differentiation operated on at least two levels—the level of uniquely commissioned pieces, and the level of widely disseminated forms. This distinction seems to operate in relation to all types of objects and in different materials—metal, glass, and clay, and was probably echoed in organic items. This only refers to their method of manufacture, whereas there may well be other considerations at play in the application of ranking or other social distinctions, involving numbers of objects, or specific combinations. The high quality, bespoke items rank alongside the best that could be obtained anywhere in the Aegean. We know from Xenophon's recollections of Socrates that some metal smiths

[37] See Ch. 8 for further discussion of funerary consumption practices.

produced much sought-after (and hence expensive) arms, because they were, quite simply, made to a high specification.[38] When Plato talks about craftsmen (2. 369b–370e, 370e–371a, cf. Xen. *Cyrop.* 8.2.5), it is clear that purchasers in Athens had very high expectations, which less populous and less prosperous areas probably failed to match. Many writers tell us that the north was among the more prosperous regions of the Aegean. Thucydides is explicit about the general material *eudaimonia* of the Odrysian-controlled territories, while many of the tribute payers in the fifth-century Delian League, not just the big spenders, such as Thasos, Byzantion, Ainos, and Abdera, were among the higher-rated members of this Athenian-led maritime defensive network.[39] In the Macedonian and Odrysian kingdoms, demand for high-quality products was driven by élites whose interests and lifestyles made them gravitate to the countryside as well as to towns. The hundreds of élite burials that have been investigated across the east Balkan landmass show that quality craftwork was widely distributed in spatial, if not social terms.

The issue of the quality of human workmanship and its relationship to social groups will continue to be a preoccupation in the discussion that follows. The other, more intractable challenge posed by material data, namely the meanings that these objects had in their social settings, depends on some prior assumptions about social relations. Despite what has already been said about the semiotics of artefacts, we do not have any ready-made tools for 'reading' archaeological finds, which do, after all, constitute the largest reservoir of data about these northern societies. Although as modern observers we tend to see artefacts in an isolated way, they usually existed in a matrix of other objects and in defined settings. The very fact that we are distant from these material phenomena gives us an advantage; because we have less information, we can at least distinguish what is innovative from what is normal and routine.[40]

[38] Xen. *Mem.3.* 10. 9–15: 'why do you charge more for your breastplates than any other maker, though they are no stronger and cost no more to make? . . . the good fits are not the tight ones, but those that don't chafe the wearer?' Veblen puts a slightly different interpretation on serviceability: 'It is notorious that in their selection of serviceable goods in the retail market, purchasers are guided more by the finish and workmanship of the goods, than by any marks of substantial serviceability. Goods, in order to sell, must have some appreciable amount of labour spent in giving them the marks of decent expensiveness, in addition to what gives them efficiency for the material use which they are to serve.' (Veblen 1899, 188). This statement still rings true, notwithstanding large-scale industrial production of retail commodities.

[39] Thuc. 2.97.5 (see Ch. 2 n.57); on northern tribute payers: Nixon and Price 1990, 152–8.

[40] Latour 2005, 80–1.

Thorstein Veblen's 'anthropological' approach to *fin de siècle* material culture provides a useful complement to recent research by anthropologists and cognitive scientists, partly because of his acute observation of North American middle class *mores*, and partly because of his preoccupation with making things. It is useful even now because his reflections did not make the actors of the past less intelligent or less adept than they actually were. He nevertheless recognized that past societies were driven by semi-rational, often not fully articulated assumptions. Veblen moves with ease between the recent and the remote past, making connections that show how strong the attractions are of collective behaviour and how these collective forms reproduce hierarchical structures with social leaders setting the tone for the rest of society. There is a further reason for looking to Veblen that does not emerge directly from the scope of his reflections. His subject matter ranges freely in different historical settings but refrains from commenting on classical antiquity. His ideas are therefore free from the kinds of assumptions about cultural dominance that have played such a conspicuous part in evaluations of 'peripheral' European societies since the early nineteenth century if not earlier, and that have unconsciously continued to influence more recent paradigms of inter-cultural contacts. Michael Dietler has referred these tendencies as 'entangled ancient and modern colonialisms'.[41]

Veblen's analysis of conspicuous consumption begins with a reflection on manners. 'Manners, we are told, are in part an elaboration of gesture, and in part they are symbolical and conventionalized survivals representing former acts of dominance or of personal service or of personal contact. In large part they are an expression of the relation of status—a sublime pantomime of mastery on the one hand and subservience on the other.'[42] Here Veblen has encapsulated with considerable acuity the pattern of interpersonal dependence within hierarchical social groups and the behavioural traits associated with such formal relations. The context of his reflections, the final decades of the nineteenth century, coincided with the wealthy fictional North American dynasties of Henry James and the last flourish of the Victorian and Edwardian country house in the Anglo-Saxon world of northern Europe. Veblen's sensibility to the atmosphere of wealthy families and their dependants is one that few writers share today. He winds the clock of time backwards to an indistinct era when people could be owned just like fixed and movable material property. 'Women and other slaves are highly valued, both as an evidence of wealth and as a means of accumulating wealth. Together with

[41] Dietler 2009, 13–35; cf. Dietler 2011.

[42] Veblen 1899 [2007], 35–6.

cattle, if the tribe is a pastoral one, they are the usual form of investment for a profit.'[43] The style of generalization may be too sweeping and over-simplistic to contemporary ears. At the same time it has the merit of a broad model, which allows more detailed refinement. It is a good enough outline. The societies that we are looking at in the northern Aegean, whether those living inland, or along the coastal fringe, enjoyed climatic conditions that favoured investment in pastoral resources. Cattle, pigs, horses, and other equids are much more prominent in this region than they were farther south. In this landscape of pastoral exploitation, women have a prominence that can be read even from the scarce textual evidence that refers to them, while the material record speaks very clearly indeed. The accoutrements of female attire and ornament in the north Aegean, their representation in the ritual sphere, and their symbolic treatment in death, are all factors that point to quite specific narratives of female behaviour.[44] The visible spectrum of evidence may only apply to some women, a sample that very likely includes socially prominent females. Nevertheless, this language of representation does seem to emphasize the status of some women in a way that would be rather unusual in central and southern Greece at least. To this set of general observations we can add some specific clues. Strabo refers to the polygamous practices of wealthy Thracians and thus adds some extracts from lost plays by Menander to what Herodotus had already described in his digression on Thracian customs in the *Histories*.[45] The geographer seems to include this material partly because of its exotic value, and partly because it suits the moral argument, in this section of his work, about consumption and abstinence. Strabo's evaluation is not inconsistent with Veblen's broader-brush approach.

Veblen goes on to describe the progressive 'exemption' of personnel from productive employment, as domestic service replaced manual labour, and dependants indulged in 'vicarious' consumption, imitating the tastes and manners of their masters and mistresses.[46] He was talking about his own lifetime, but his understanding of the connections between social status and taste is applicable to other periods. The

[43] Veblen 1899 [2007], 39–40; see also Banta's comments on Veblen's revolutionary attitude to women's social roles in contemporary society, xxi–xxii.

[44] For the status of Macedonian women, see Carney 2010 and Archibald 2005b; Macedonian élite female burials: Archibald 2005b; élite female Thracian burials: Archibald 1998, 158–76; see further Ch. 8.

[45] Str. 7.3.3, citing Poseidonios and Menander (frs 794–795, Körte-Thierfelder = frs 547–548, Kock); 7.3.4 (C297), *Misogynes* (fr. 326, Körte-Thierfelder; fr. 326, Kock); Baladié 1989, 179–89 with comments; Hdt. 5.5.

[46] Veblen 1899 [2007], 35–7, 39–40.

tendency of the majority in any social group to follow trendsetters is an idea that we tend to take for granted. In classical antiquity it is well represented in perfume pots and votive offerings, but also in the frequent allusions to counterfeit goods. Attic comedy provides a wealth of examples of poor quality produce, dry and inferior products, and dubious imitations.[47]

Veblen's definition of 'leisure' makes a direct connection between social value and social employment. 'The early ascendancy of leisure as a means of reputability is traceable to the archaic distinction between noble and ignoble employments. Leisure is honourable and becomes imperative partly because it shows exemption from ignoble labour.'[48] This association of leisure with manifest lack of employment in servile or manual work was not only widespread in Greek aristocratic circles (and adopted vicariously by the citizens of Athens), but we find a particularly close example of Veblen's model in the lifestyle of the Thracian élite, when Herodotus draws attention to the conspicuous leisure of their horse-breeding warriors, with their distinctive martial ethos: 'To wear tattoos they [the Thracians] consider a mark of distinction; not to be tattooed a mark of low birth. The finest man is the man of leisure, while the one who works the soil is without respect. They consider the finest life to be one of martial pursuits and plunder.' (Hdt. 5.6) We find similar values among the Macedonian royal élite, with their tastes for hunting, training in war, and convivial feasts (Fig. 4.9).[49] Thanks to Veblen's analysis, we can view statements like those of Herodotus and Theopompos in the wider context of other 'leisurely' élites.

Veblen's argument tends to underestimate the genuine productive capacities of the 'leisurely' classes he was observing. But he had an important qualification when isolating those social groups whom he categorized as 'unproductive' in a literal sense. Conspicuous consumption is, in Veblen's model, balanced by what he calls 'the instinct of workmanship': 'Other circumstances permitting, that instinct disposes men to look with favour upon productive efficiency and on whatever is of human use. It disposes them to deprecate waste of substance or effort. The instinct of workmanship is present in all men, and asserts itself even under very adverse circumstances.'[50] Few sociologists and

[47] Foxhall 1998 and Archibald 2007 on perfume pots; Wilkins 2000, 156–201, for references to inferior imitations in Attic comedy.

[48] Veblen 1899 [2007], 64.

[49] See for example Theop. *FGrH* 115 F81, 224, 225, 236, 282; Sawada 2010. See also now the contributions to *Tout vendre, tout acheter*.

[50] Veblen 1899 [2007], 64–5.

Fig. 4.9. Olynthos (House A vi 3), dining room mosaic showing the mounted Bellerophon with his hunting dog.

anthropologists have paid as much attention as Veblen did both to the complexities of conspicuous consumption and to the reciprocal investment of effort and imagination in productive pursuits. The ubiquitous heaps of fired ceramic, the miles of defensive enclosures and paved paths, and the massed stone sunk to make breakwaters, are all silent witnesses to the same instinct in the north Aegean during the first millennium BC.

Carpets, textiles, and dress

For Veblen, aesthetic beauty and cost were closely related. But these were not stable quantities. What is more, objects that start off being desirable and rare might end up being considered essentials. 'As items which sometimes fall under this head, and are therefore available as illustrations of the manner in which this principle applies, may be cited carpets and tapestries, silver table service, waiter's services, silk hats, starched linen, many articles of jewellery and of dress.'[51] Again, many of these items, particularly carpets, tapestries, and silverware, feature prominently in the repertoire of socially desirable artefacts in the environment of the north Aegean. The suggestion that what starts off as a restricted commodity,

[51] Veblen 1899 [2007], 68–9.

but can then come to be considered a standard element of furnishing, is illustrated in the *Anabasis*, where Xenophon mentions Persian carpets in the hands of one of the 'Cyreans' (*Anab.* 7.3.18).[52] Carpets, it seems, were not the preserve of the social élite. They could be bought by anyone, so long as he had the resources.

This passing reference to what came into the possession of mercenaries is illuminating in other ways. Thucydides refers to textiles—not just any kind of tapestries, but different kinds of woven textiles, decorated and plain—*hosa hyphanta te kai leia* (ὅσα ὑφαντά τε καὶ λεῖα), as well as 'other kinds of manufactures' (*he alle kataskeue*), which were among the labour-intensive kinds of goods rendered as tribute to the Odrysian kings and paradynasts (2.97.3). Textiles and carpets feature on ancient and more recent lists of desirable commodities because these have always been among the most expensive to produce and the most evocative of private luxury. Handmade textiles, silverware and silk items continue to play a perennial and altogether exceptional role today as markers of distinction, and have upheld their high price, notwithstanding the arrival of new technologies. What matters about these choices, in Veblen's view, is whether such acquisitions contribute to the enhancement of a society's well-being.

In Strabo's day there was evidently a strong temptation, in some philosophical circles, to draw a sharp contrast between the modest lifestyles of some northern peoples on the one hand, and the perceived over-indulgence of city dwellers at the great hubs of the Mediterranean on the other. In Book 7 the geographer recounts the story of how Alexander the Great's general and successor in Thrace, Lysimachos, during a series of intense campaigns—at least two separate events can be identified—in the area of the Dobrudja and the Danube foreland during the 290s, was taken prisoner by the Getic king, Dromichaites.[53] The story has been retold by a number of different authors, who use the occasion to underscore the supposed frugality of the Getae with the ostentatious presentation of Lysimachos. The popularity of the story shows that it became a rhetorical *topos*. If this was the same man as the Dromichaetes mentioned by Polyaenus as being among the Thracian military associates of Antiochos II during a siege of Kypsela, in the

[52] Xen. *Anab.* 7.3.27 (Timasion owned a carpet worth 10 minas); Stronk 1995, 206.

[53] Diod. 21.12.1–6; Paus. 1.9.6; Polyaen. 7.25; Justin 16.1.19; Plut. *Demetr.* 52; *Mor.* 126e–f; 555d–e (= *De sera* 11); Str. 7.3.8 (C302); cf. 3.14; Baladié 1989, 192; Delev 2000, 390–3; 398–400, and Stoyanov 2006, 79–83 for the archaeological background of Sboryanovo, identified by both authors with Helis, Dromichaites' capital; Will, *Histoire Politique 1*, 89–94, 97–103, on the wider historical setting *c.*300–*c.*290 BC.

lower estuary of the Hebros, in 254 BC (Polyaen. 4.16), then it would appear that contemporary and later literary tradition could fashion rather different interpretations of Getic lifestyles, since Polyaenus attributes the reason for the defendants' decision to surrender themselves to Antiochos to the impressive character of the Thracian officers' dress. Military attire can rarely have had a more dramatic tactical effect. The story implies that not only was the Getic leader able to turn out creditably, but also that he was an impressive figure by international standards.

If Sboryanovo, the fortified upland city in a naturally defended promontory above a loop in the River Krapinets, *c.*40 km south of the Danube at Tutrakan and *c.*110 km from Odessos, is indeed the citadel of Helis, where Lysimachos was kept prisoner, then Diodorus, and Strabo after him, painted an over-generous contrast between the lifestyle of Lysimachos and that of Dromichaites. Lysimachos' power may in principle have been far greater than the Getic leader's. But Helis was a major civic centre, a *polis* according to Diodorus (in contrast to a range of sites that are variously designated *phrouria* or *choria*), with a defended nucleus of 20 ha and an overall area of *c.*100 ha, the focus of various craft industries, notably metallurgy, and a net importer of wines from Thasos, Herakleia, Sinope, and other Pontic centres.[54]

The sort of dress illustrated in contemporary Thracian tombs (such as Alexandrovo, Kazanluk Tomb and Ginina Mogila, Sveshtari) as well as other artwork, including engraved metalware and rings, echoes the best contemporary fashions in the Aegean, and is comparable to the kinds of dress depicted on the façade of the Agios Athanasios Tomb, *c.*15 km east of ancient Pella and *c.*20 km west of Thessaloniki, one of the best-preserved tableaux of images from the final decades of the fourth century BC.[55] The two large-scale figures flanking the doorway into the tomb chamber (1.45 m and 1.52 m respectively) offer a splendid representation of how we might expect a Macedonian soldier to be dressed, while the 25 figures on the frieze above the doorway illustrate the appearance of horsemen, distinguished diners, women musicians and

[54] Delev 2000, 396–401 and 400 n.90 for the author's proposal of the identification, which has since been accepted by the excavators (Stoyanov 2006, 87); see also Stoyanov 2002; Stoyanov 2006; Stoyanov et al. *AOR* 2006 [2007] 209–12; 2007 [2008] 211–17; 2010 [2011] 174–6; *Sboryanovo III* (forthcoming).

[55] Alexandrovo: Stoyanov 2008; Kazanluk: Zhivkova 1973; Ginina Mogila, Sveshtari: Fol et al. 1986; see also bibliography in Delev 2000, 396 n.73; on Thracian military dress, Archibald 1998, 204–6 with further refs; Agios Athanasios: Tsimbidou-Avloniti 2005, 109–49, pls 24–5, 27, 30–37; 172–82 with catalogue of Hellenistic painted tombs found to date in Macedonia; see also below on the warrior's dress from Malomirovo-Zlatinitsa.

attendants, as well as individuals serving.[56] Most of the figures on the frieze are clad in knee-length tunics and cloaks that reach below the knees. The tunics are of various colours: white, brown, purple, bright red, and blue. The colours used are of considerable interest in their own right.[57] The cloaks show a similar range of colours. Although it may not be realistic to imagine that the level of detail is entirely authentic, and bearing in mind the scale of the frieze itself (0.34–0.35 m high for a length of 3.75 m), the dress of these figures is designed with considerable care. If we compare the outfits of the frieze figures with the pair of cloaked soldiers 'guarding' the entrance either side of the doorway, then the care with which the frieze figures are depicted becomes even more apparent. The two large figures depict many of the same details of dress as the smaller ones on the frieze. Their cloaks have a characteristic design feature, with a broad vertical stripe at either end of what must be a rectangular piece of cloth, dyed in a contrasting colour to the main body of the garment, with a thin border in the same colour as the principal one. The bottom corners of the cloak are weighted, so that the lower edges drop straight down making the cloth less likely to obstruct movement.

The eight figures on the right-hand side of the frieze are soldiers, or soldiers and their batmen or orderlies. They are armed with the *sarissa,* Macedonian shields similar to those that appear on Antigonid coinage; two wear helmets and four have the *kausia*, which can also be seen on the heads of the two larger figures below the frieze. Many of the features of the frieze deserve attention in a discussion of furnishings. The couches on which the six central figures recline, listening to the two woman musicians, a kitharist and an aulos-player, are generously covered with red, white, and blue textiles. There are some fine side-tables with legs in the shape of feline limbs, and a magnificent sideboard, groaning with gold-coloured and silver chargers, which would not disgrace the *piano nobile* of a Renaissance *palazzo*.[58]

The images on the friezes at Alexandrovo, Kazanluk, Sveshtari, and other Thracian tombs can be analysed in a similar way. Where there are more figures for comparison, as at Alexandrovo and Kazanluk, periodicities and distinctions in dress are also noticeable. As we shall see in Chapter 8, this particular group of images from closely comparable mortuary contexts gives a convincing impression of what the Macedonian and Thracian landed élites also had in common in attitudes to

56 Tsimbidou-Avloniti 2005, 114–47, pls 27 and esp. 30–7.
57 See below and Ch. 7 for further discussion.
58 Tsimbidou-Avloniti 2005, 121, pls 33–34; Andrianou 2009, 61.

death, the afterlife, and commemoration. There are both subtle and more obvious distinctions between the Thracian, Getic, and Macedonian forms of dress, which suggest some of the ways in which local élites reinforced a sense of identity. The two large male figures on the Agios Athanasios façade have tunics with vertical, coloured stripes near the lateral margins, which suggest a particular connotation, perhaps a social as well as an aesthetic one. They wear fine leather boots with complex lacing, with straps plaited across the heel as well as over the front of the foot, a type of footwear that is also shown on the feet of the wreathed rider approaching the central scene from the left. Leather is a subject to which I will return below.

In overall terms, the figures on the façade of the Agios Athanasios tomb provide a wealth of evidence about appearance and dress in late classical and early Hellenistic Macedonia. There are visible distinctions among those represented—who does and who doesn't wear the *kausia*; who does and who does not wear boots; who has a cloak, who has other garments—that imply social nuances. Nevertheless, the easy familiarity of the figures in each other's company suggests that these distinctions were easily recognizable, but not particularly formal. Demetrios Poliorketes was evidently considered the most ostentatious of Alexander's successors. Even he preferred style, variety, and sheer luxury of design over social formality. Plutarch reports that Demetrios 'possessed an elaborate wardrobe of hats and cloaks, broad-brimmed hats with double mitres, and robes of purple interwoven with gold, while his feet were clad in shoes of the richest purple felt embroidered with gold. One of his robes had taken many months to weave on the looms: it was a superb piece of work in which the world and the heavenly bodies were represented. It was still only half finished at the time of Demetrius' downfall [288/7 BC], and none of the later kings of Macedon ever presumed to wear it, although several had a taste for pomp and ceremony.'[59]

North Aegean and Pontic grey wares

One example of the dynamics of social tastes in the north Aegean is represented by a class of grey-faced pottery that gradually became a ubiquitous phenomenon in the first millennium BC. Grey-faced wares represent one of the commonest and most widely diffused wheel-made fabrics throughout the east Balkan region (see Fig. 4.10). In most of the

[59] Plut. *Demetr.* 41 (tr. I. Scott-Kilvert).

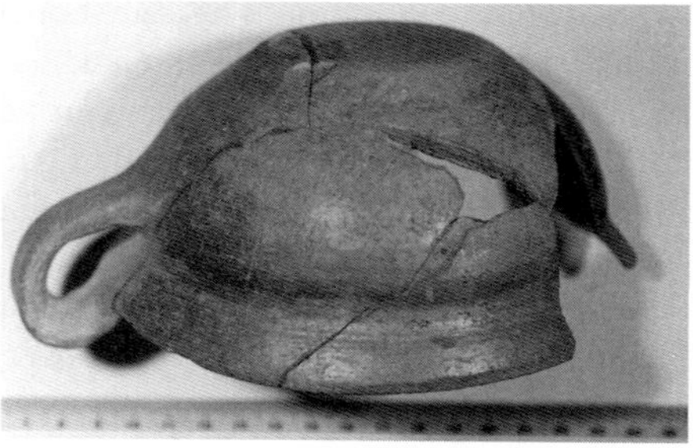

Fig. 4.10. 'Greyware' cup from Adjiyska Vodenitsa (ancient Pistiros), resembling a Greek skyphos.

localities in which they appeared, these were the first types of ceramics made on the fast potter's wheel known in these areas (this is certainly true north of Aeolis and the Hellespontine Straits). Single turn-tables, which require turning by hand, very likely continued to be used alongside the double kick-wheel; differently weighted wheels would in any case have been appropriate for different sizes of ceramic vessel. So this rather modest-looking pottery represents a significant technical innovation, which was probably accompanied by dietary innovations too. The new pottery includes fabrics with a black or grey lustrous slip, as well as those with a matt surface, and includes storage vessels as well as table wares, lamps, cooking wares, terracottas, and architectural ceramics.

A large range of local products has been identified, which broadly correspond to models known from sites in Ionia and Aeolis in Asia Minor, both in typological and technological terms. In overall appearance and technique this form of pottery resembles Aeolian *bucchero*, whose colour was the result of firing in conditions with reduced oxygen. The black-slipped forms do not seem to have travelled widely, whereas those without the black slip were extensively disseminated. The range and complexity of these different ceramic types means that issues of provenance, production, and distribution are best resolved through collaborative laboratory initiatives. A series of research projects, involving researchers from all the producing and recipient countries around the Black Sea, has resulted in advancing our understanding of this vast technological phenomenon during the last decade.

The study of grey-faced fabrics emerged in close connection with the investigation of Greek colonial sites along the northern and western shores of the Black Sea. Ceramics of local Balkan origin appear to outnumber, by a considerable margin, surviving examples of pieces imported from Anatolia. Local kiln evidence, as well as close typological similarities, means that the production of grey wares also needs to be viewed in connection with other types of ceramic outputs. Kilns at a number of coastal sites (including Istros) are comparatively well known but key-hole shaped or rectangular firing chambers of Aegean type have also been found at a number of inland locations, unrelated to Greek sites. A set of kilns has recently been investigated by M. Tonkova at Halka Bunar, near Chirpan, both for grey, reducing fabrics, as well as orange wares, produced in oxidizing conditions.[60] The products date to the second half of the fifth century BC. There is also a series of kilns at Adjiyska Vodenitsa, Vetren, dating to the second half of the fourth century BC.[61]

Study of these various fabric types has focused mainly on the classification of local products. The first monograph that attempted to put the various classifications into a more specific chronological framework was by Emil Moscalu (1983). Petre Alexandrescu produced a pioneering study of the regional distribution of forms originating from Asia Minor.[62] To these can now be added more specialized analyses of clays and production techniques, which have allowed a more nuanced and scientifically-based identification of imported and indigenous Balkan products.[63] Analyses of Histrian fabric types at the Lyon Laboratoire de Céramologie have allowed Pierre Dupont to isolate a specific profile for local products. This production appears to have got under way in the second quarter of the sixth century BC.[64] Closer collaboration between researchers from the east Balkans, south Russia, Ukraine, and Moldova is beginning to reveal relationships between these various production centres. In some cases local production merely reproduced, it seems, forms familiar from Anatolian metropolitan kiln works. The intermarketing of fabrics between these zones has yet to be fully elucidated. The geological homogeneity of the western Pontic coast as far as Dubrudja, and the northern coast as far as the Crimean peninsula, means that it is hard for ceramic specialists to differentiate between products

[60] Herries and Kovacheva 2007; Tonkova 2000; 2008; 2011.

[61] V. Taneva, *AOR* 2008 [2009] 252–4 (almost square chamber with clay walls, collapsed brick and tile from superstructure, and a brick-built bench-like supporting pillar opposite the firing chamber at the north end; clay kiln furniture and misshapen pots confirm the types of pottery made here, which included orange storage and tableware, tiles, and terracottas; dating is provided by a coin of Maroneia (second half of the fourth century BC) and by ceramic forms); *AOR* 2009 [2010] 205–7 (traces of an earlier kiln, with 17 pieces of kiln furniture and associated discarded pots, as well as bricks from the superstructure); Taneva 2011.

[62] Alexandrescu 1977; Alexandrescu 1999; cf. also Bouzek 1990.

[63] Dupont and Lungu 2008; Chichikova 2004; Božkova and Nikov 2009.

[64] Lungu 2009, 17.

from different origins; as a result, the detailed intra-regional pattern of technological dissemination remains opaque. Nevertheless, this research has opened up a new range of possible scenarios for the dissemination of advanced pyrotechnic methods.

Among the most popular and widely distributed shapes in this grey fabric were the inturned-rim bowl, a jug with a high, elevated strap handle, and the fish plate. The latter was evidently based on Attic models, while the jug with a strap handle (also called a mug, beaker, jug type 8) has otherwise been compared to a *kyathos* (a kind of dipper). It was widely disseminated along the northern and western Pontic coast, as well as in many inland locations. The wide, shallow, footed bowl, or *lekane*, with vertical handles fixed onto the horizontal rim, may ultimately be of Milesian origin. These are comparatively common at Apollonia, Mesambria, Callatis, Tomis, Istros, Orgame, Tyras, Pantikapaion, and occur in several different variants.

Comparatively few relevant fabrics of genuine Aeolian and Ionian origin have been studied at all closely.[65] Grey wares continued to be made at Troy in the eighth to sixth centuries BC, but the initiative for the dissemination of the new ceramics does not seem to be connected directly with that city. Actual Aeolian imports have been identified at Berezan, Istros, and Tariverde, alongside other imported ceramics, including Attic black figure. Milesian 'fruit stands' with moulded feet are also known from other Ionian sites, notably Samos. In Aeolis (as at Larissa) this form seems to derive from Bronze Age ceramic types. These particular forms do not seem to have been reproduced in colonial or more distant settings.

Perhaps the most striking result of these technical analyses of pottery is the absence of a linear set of connections between north Aegean models and Balkan imitations. The popularity of shapes in the recipient centres is different from those that were dominant in the putative originating communities. The vogue for 'inturned rim' bowls is one of the most recognizable regional characteristics of local tableware in the east Balkans. Another shape, the 'sessile' kantharos, a popular type of drinking cup known from Mytilene and other sites on Lesbos (although this form also had Attic, Boeotian, and Chiot variants), enjoyed a special significance in the Balkans and Black Sea area, and for a prolonged period of time.[66] The likeliest explanation seems to be that itinerant Greek potters may have provided the initial technical know-how for

[65] Principally Mytilene: see Dupont and Lungu 2008.
[66] Lungu 2009, 22 and refs nn.71, 72, 73.

producing batch samples in controlled firing conditions. The fact that some techniques and forms resemble native Early Iron Age pots suggests that in practice not only were the new methodologies changes of degree rather than kind, but also that knowledge of wider technologies was not altogether new either. Analysis of the ceramic production at Beidaud, a Getic oppidum *c.*30 km inland of Istros and halfway between Istros and another local centre of ceramic production, Orgame, shows the style and methods are distinctive and not directly derivative of either Istros or Orgame.[67] Similarly, a group of lustrous grey pots, together with Ionian bowls and a Corinthian-style *aryballos*, was found in the fill of a tumulus constructed in the mid sixth century BC at Prilep, near Karnobat, inland from the Black Sea coast in Bulgaria. Since this predates the general diffusion of wheel-made grey wares, it looks as if direct contacts were made with potters at or from Troy, Anatolian Larissa, or Antissa on Lesbos.[68] A related, but slightly different challenge is reflected in somewhat earlier ceramics in the east Carpathian region of the middle Dniester, where an earlier stage of ceramic borrowings has been postulated, belonging to a phase preceding the foundation of Greek trading settlements along the Black Sea coast.[69]

The relationship between Balkan and Pontic grey wares and north Aegean ceramic traditions implies that the associated technology was exchanged in a relatively unconstrained way during the seventh and sixth centuries BC and probably earlier. There was a similarly unconstrained pattern in the north-western Aegean, with Aeolian pottery from Lesbos being shipped to the indigenous Thracians on Thasos between the

[67] Dupont and Lungu 2010; 'Il n'est donc pas exclu que l'on puisse se trouver ici face à un atelier de l'intérieur (une telle éventualité avait déjà été envisagée par Mănucu-Adameşteanu 1992 . . .) dont il s'agira de déterminer si ses productions sont le fait de potiers grecs (itinérants ou sédentaires) opérant en territoire barbare ou bien de réalisations à mettre au compte d'artisans gètes initiés à la pratique de tournage et ayant adopté, tout ou partie, le répertoire de forme des ateliers grecs du littoral, comme dans le cas des potiers indigènes de Serra di Vaglio, imitant des terres cuites métapontines dès le milieu du VIe s.' (Dupont and Lungu 2010, 494).

[68] Božkova and Nikov 2009, 49: [re Prilep tumulus, mid or third quarter of the sixth century]: 'Cette date précède la période de grande propagation de la céramique monochrome dans la Thrace du Sud, tout en attestant d'une façon convaincante la présence de contacts anciens avec les centres maritimes et, vraisemblablement, avec Apollonia en particulier.' Tzochev (2011, 85) assumes that transmission was by the first generation of Apollonian settlers, but expresses surprise that commercial relations were established so quickly. Even if this were to be the case, it presupposes an earlier infrastructure for commerce with communities of the interior unconnected with the actual settlement at Apollonia.

[69] Levitski and Kashuba in Avram et al. 2009, 106–7 and figs 4–5; Daragan, in Avram et al. 2009, 130.

middle of the eighth and the early decades of the seventh century BC, as well as other ceramics originating from the Thermaic Gulf, including 'silvery'-slipped tableware and transport *amphorae*, the latter probably conveying wine from the mainland of Macedonia.[70] The single biggest attractor of imported pottery on the mainland was the best harbour facility on the Thermaic Gulf, and the associated Toumba Kalamarias (Thessaloniki Toumba), which has produced an exceptional range of ceramics from all over the Aegean; a sequence that seems to match the Late Bronze Age/Early Iron Age sites in the Chalkidic peninsula.[71] There was a visible surge in the volume of imports during the eighth century BC, notably of Euboian-style *skyphoi*, cup types that were appearing on Thasos at the same time. Just as a range of Aeolian and Ionian ceramics triggered a new level and variety of ceramic outputs in the east Balkan region, on a progressive scale from the seventh, and particularly from the second half of the sixth century BC onwards, so there was an elaboration of ceramic forms at the western end of the north Aegean in the same period, inspired partly by Euboian models, but also north Ionian ones. So there is something of an overlap in terms of popular forms between the north-western and the north-eastern trajectories of technological exchange in pottery manufacture. In the region of the Thermaic Gulf, the most popular forms were the *phiale* and various types of jug, with a preference for the indigenous jug with an oblique, 'cutaway' neck, but imported Ionian, Attic and Corinthian models were also copied.[72]

The wide popularity of a limited range of ceramic forms has given rise to the idea of a distinct regional set of preferences in what is now Central Macedonia. The 'silvery' pottery includes large storage vessels, as well as tableware, and is so called because of the mica-dusted slip that gives it a distinctive sheen. Pithoid-*amphorae*, deep bowls, water jars, shallow bowls (*lekanai*), and other shapes were decorated with lozenges, zigzags, and bands of waves, in a purplish coloured slip, using a multiple brush. These distinctive pots were made either at Sindos, close to Thessaloniki Toumba, or perhaps at multiple sites along the Thermaic Gulf.[73] Transport *amphorae* with 'sub-Geometric' decoration (multiple bands and concentric circles) may have been manufactured at Sindos, but there

[70] Muller 2010, 217. [71] Manakidou 2010, esp. 464–9.

[72] Panti 2008, provides a detailed conspectus of local fabrics, based on microscopic analysis of clays resembling those identified from fourth-century BC kilns located at Akanthos, including 'Ionizing' and other imitative forms, and Attic Black Figure and Corinthian fabrics (15–150); Karabournaki, 151–204; Sindos, 205–21; see esp. 234–5 [= Karabournaki] and 344–5. See also Chapter 6 for Euboian connections.

[73] Manakidou 2010, 465–6 and fig. 317; Gimatzidis 2010, 227, 251 fig. 75.

seem to have been multiple forms, which circulated widely in the north Aegean as far east as Troy, and which have been found inland as far as the southern foothills of Rhodope.[74] As with the monochrome tableware of the east Balkans and the various other styles circulating in the Thermaic Gulf, the transmission of ideas and technologies was not, it seems, a straightforward one. Referring to the geometric-type *amphorae* from Koprivlen, in southern Rhodope, Božkova comments: 'The . . . middle Nestos area . . . was integrated in the processes of commercial exchange current in the Aegean as early as the second half of the eighth or the beginning of the seventh century BC. This hypothesis supersedes the traditional opinion that until late Archaic times the privilege of acquiring, reproducing, and trading with products in the leading Greek pottery styles was restricted to the maritime settlements . . .'[75] This echoes what Pierre Dupont has already voiced in connection with ceramic innovation in the hinterland of Istros, at Beidaud. Božkova points to the dissemination of occasional Mycenaean ceramics and other, late second or early first millennium BC pottery in this area, which implies that there was an earlier network that continued to be exploited throughout the first half of the first millennium BC.[76]

Mining for metals and minerals

Apart from rather exceptional observers, like Theophrastus, few ancient writers had anything original to say about rocks and minerals. Historians were generally interested in people, not things, and least of all mute, shapeless, impenetrable masses of rock. Very occasionally, however, an incident provides an unexpected shaft of light. In the spring of 181 BC, Philip V of Macedon conducted a renewed campaign deep into the heartland of Thrace, following an invasion just two years earlier, in the summer of 183 BC, which was itself a partial re-staging of a great campaign as far as the Hebros, at Philippopolis and beyond to Kabyle, in 204 BC.[77]

[74] Gimatzidis 2010, 263; Catling 1998; Božkova 2005.

[75] Božkova 2005, 89.

[76] See now St. Bakardjiev, *AOR* 2009 [2010] 149–51, on Early Iron Age remains at Zavoy, Yambol district, including a bird bowl and rosette-decorated bowl (151 fig. 3, 1–2), evidently imported Ionian examples; these are surprisingly far inland at this date.

[77] Philip V's campaign in Thrace,183 BC: Plb. 23.8.3–7; Philip's campaign in Thrace, 181 BC: Livy (P) 40.21.1–2; 22.1; cf. Plb. ap. Str. 7.5.1; V's campaign in Thrace, summer 204 BC: Plb. 13.10, including a reference to *Καβύλη*, although the Polybian fragments make the precise details of this campaign unclear (Walbank, *Commentary,* II, 423).

In 184 BC Philip V had attacked Amadokos, the then king of Thrace, and had defeated and taken him prisoner. Polybius implies that these actions of Philip's also served Byzantine interests, because Thracian authorities had in effect superseded the Celtic ruler Cavarus as masters of the hinterland beyond Byzantion.[78] One of Philip's daughters was married to a Teres of Thrace (Diod. 32.15.7). These rather sketchy and very incomplete references from the lost books of Polybius' *Histories* offer no real leads in trying to understand Philip V's relationship with Amadokos, or with his Thracian neighbours in general. Frank Walbank interpreted Philip's strategy during the late 180s BC in Thrace as part of an attempt (along with his equally obscure negotiations with the Bastarnae in the area of the Danube, and with the Scordisci, also in the far north), to create the 'first Balkan empire'.[79] The complexities of this narrative and the syncopated nature of the events that survive from Polybius' account make it hard to understand exactly what the purpose of Philip's campaign was. Walbank was interested in the politics of Balkan relations, rather less so in the economic implications of Philip's strategy. Yet, although Philip's itinerary has only left brief references in later authors, it does offer an insight into what it was that political leaders knew and were interested in, as well as their general desires of aggrandizement.

Our principal source is Livy, drawing on the now unavailable books of Polybius, who tells us that in seven days, having marched from Stobi against the Maidoi in the Strymon valley, Philip reached the foot of a mountain called Haimos. He was responding, it seems, to reports that, on ascending this mountain, the Danube, the Black Sea, the Adriatic, and the Alps could all be seen. Attempts to identify which mountain, or range, Philip may have climbed have not met with great success.[80] This story seems to pick up some of the elements of a wider belief, circulating since the time of the historian Theopompos, if not earlier, in the extraordinary views that could be gained from climbing the highest Balkan peaks.[81] There is no mountain from which the Adriatic and the

[78] Philip's attack and capture of Amadokos: Plb. 22.14.12; Livy (P) 39.35.4; Walbank identified Amadokos either as a king of the Astai, or of the Kainoi (Walbank 1940, 237 n.5); Will, *Histoire Politique 2*, 252–3 for the general context; *HM III*, 468–71; Eckstein 2008, 350.

[79] Walbank 1940, 246.

[80] Livy refers to Mount Donax farther on (Livy (P) 40.58.2); Walbank, who thought that the identity of 'Haimos' should be determined by the distance from Stobi, opted for Mount Vitosha (= Skombros, also mentioned by Thucydides, 2. 96.4), following W. Leake.

[81] Thucydides makes the overland journey from Abdera to the Danube take eleven days by the shortest route (2.97.1–2); presumably he means a journey at speed on foot, but on horseback would have been preferable. Alexander the Great took ten days to reach the

Black Sea can be seen simultaneously. What this legend represents is a different kind of understanding of geography and topography from the scientific observation that we are used to. Livy may not have been curious about a mountain from which you could see half the known world; but for Philip, knowledge really did mean power. He could not afford not to know what others might know. Athenian philosophers may have downplayed technological know-how, but anyone with serious aspirations was bound to take the opposite view. The kings of Macedon were pioneers in the development of new military hardware, which promised to deliver real assets, but which also swallowed resource.[82]

Since the Roman settlement of international affairs in the Aegean at Apameia, following the defeat of Antiochos III at the battle of Magnesia, Philip had busied himself with enhancing his state revenues and the general prosperity of Macedonia.[83] This involved various infrastructure projects, such as road and bridge building in Thrace, as well as in Macedonian-administered territories, which might have military as well as civilian benefits.[84] These ambitious projects required resource, in terms of capital, manpower, and materials; thus money, metal, stone, and timber. Metals were critical to any and every operation. Philip's interest in existing, old, and new mines was not just a bit of useful enterprise, but a necessity. His acknowledged interest in Philip II as a model of kingship no doubt extended to his illustrious predecessor's success with the gold mines at Krenides-Philippoi, which proved to be so critical to the economic success of the Macedonian

Haimos range in spring 335 (Arrian *Anab.* 1.1.5), using seasoned troops. Theopompos apparently thought that a subterranean passage must link the Adriatic and Aegean seas (Strabo found this hard to believe: Strab. 7.5.9 = Theop. *FrGHist* 115 F 129).

[82] Cuomo 2007, 22–43, esp. 25–32 gives an acute analysis of the antipathy of philosophers towards technology; ibid. 41–76 on Macedonian military achievements. 'In sum, despite the persistence of voices that opposed the old way to the new, it can be said that the Hellenistic military revolution consisted at least in part of a change in mentality, attitude, or what we could call ethics—the military leader embraced characteristics usually associated with technical knowledge and expertise.' (ibid. 73)

[83] 'Not only did he increase the revenues of his kingdom by taxes on agricultural produce and by import and export duties [24.2: *vectigalia regni . . . fructibus . . . agrorum portoriisque maritimis auxit*]; he also restarted the working of old mines that had long been abandoned, and opened new workings in many places.' (Livy 39.24).

[84] 'When Lucius Scipio followed him [M. Acilius: in 190 BC] as consul, and had decided to take his army to the Hellespont by land, I did not merely give him the right to march through my kingdom; I also constructed roads, built bridges, and furnished supplies. This I did not only through Macedonia, but through Thrace as well, and there, besides everything else, I had to ensure that the local tribesmen would let him pass in peace.' (Livy 39.28).

crown in the second half of the fourth century and for the next two hundred years.[85]

Stone and timber can be identified and evaluated, even by those comparatively unfamiliar with the local geography of an area. Not so metals and minerals. These require specialist knowledge, first to identify the kinds of formations that could produce the desired minerals, and then to adopt an appropriate strategy for exploiting promising deposits. Even today, despite the existence of geological maps and data sets, mining is still a highly specialized activity, because theoretical knowledge can differ from practical experience. Ancient exploitation of minerals is connected with the exploration of mountain ridges and especially caves, whose early decoration and human appropriation reflects the dynamic relationship between people and rocks, rocks and people. The 'Cave of Polyphemos' at Maroneia is one recently studied example of long-term cave use in the north Aegean.[86]

Most of the specialist interest in early mineral exploitation in this region has come from geologists and mineralogists familiar with more recent extraction of metal deposits, rather than from archaeologists. So the synthetic studies of mines and mineral deposits by Georgiv on copper and Avdev on gold provide what might be considered 'maximalist' approaches to ancient knowledge about particular ore deposits, even though in many cases such locations have been confirmed by evidence of ancient tools in underground passages; or more directly by scientific analysis, such as the pioneering work of Chernykh and more recently by Pernicka and others on early copper in eastern Bulgaria.[87] Examination of slag accumulations, alongside evidence based on modern mineral deposits, has enhanced the resource base for archaeological study. Only the systematic scientific analysis of artefacts, in the context of what we know about local slag deposits (the most obvious evidence of past exploitation at particular ore sources), can actually demonstrate how particular metals were used in given localities.

[85] Krenides: Diod. 16.3.7; App. Syr. 105; Collart 1937, 39–71; Koukouli-Chrysanthaki 2011b, 438–9; Philip V and Philip II: Photios claimed that Philip V had Theopompos' *Philippika* abridged to 16 books, focusing on Philip II (176, p. 121a, 35).

[86] Cave of Polyphemos, Maroneia: A. Panti and M. Myteletsis, *AEMΘ* 20 (2006), 21–29 (Early Bronze Age to Byzantine use).

[87] Georgiv 1987; Avdev 2005, 23–70 and 37 fig. 16, 219–87, Appendix (known gold working sites); cf. Tonkova 2000, 138, map 2; Chernykh 1978; K. Dimitrov and I. Vajsov in *Durankulak 2* (Sofia 2002), 127–58, 159–76, respectively; see now the Bulgaro-German project on tracking ancient gold and iron mining activities, Chr. Popov et al., *AOR* 2008 [2009] 215–18; 2009 [2010] 133–5 (Ada tepe, Krumovgrad region, evidence for Late Bronze Age/Early Iron Age gold production); Craddock 2008, 96–108 on mining technology in the first millennium BC.

The mechanics of exploitation only provide a first step in understanding what the miners and those who supervised mining processes were trying to do. Philip V may have felt the intense pressure triggered by a geopolitical situation over which he had little control, and in which he was attempting to maximize his resource base using a range of approaches, including the outright acquisition of assets (one of the possible motives for his capture of King Amadokos of Thrace), as well as the exploration of possible new sources of revenue from new mines (a potentially lucrative strategy, but one that he could realize only by trial and error). The ways in which metals, mining, and smiths were perceived is rather more difficult for us to understand. The scientific understanding of pyrotechnology provides us with an explanation of how ores are turned into metal form. This contemporary understanding 'reveals' what has been understood for centuries as a magical process, with practitioners who were treated as magicians, capable of transforming nature by methods that defied explanation. Those who were interested in technology knew that there were 'recipes' for making particular substances and knowledge about such recipes was potentially a very powerful asset. Pliny's *Natural History* includes 'recipes' that were accessible to him in libraries and information was evidently exchanged amongst those who had certain technical interests in common.[88] In practice there was a huge gulf in terms of understanding, and of practice, between those who knew something about pyrotechnology and minerals, and those who did not. As we have seen in Chapter 2, around the time of the Persian Wars, gold was a socially exclusive metal. It was not in commercial circulation among indigenous groups and the minting of gold by the city of Abdera, as well as the circulation of some Persian electrum coin, is the first evidence of gold becoming a commercially available commodity. Nevertheless, these coinages did not change the socially driven value of gold in the north Aegean. Gold artefacts and ornaments continued to be deposited with socially distinguished individuals, notwithstanding the adoption of gold as a medium of exchange by Philip II and his successors.[89]

[88] 'What emerges from [Pliny's] selection of tests, often misunderstood by Pliny, and often obscure, even with our chemical knowledge, is a widespread habit of systematic discrimination, subject to a consensus of method and interpretation. This is by no means to be taken for granted in any period or community. It is easy to observe excellence of workmanship in surviving artifacts or to note the endurance of monuments, and to infer the skill of individual craftsmen or designers. What is less obvious is the way in which continuity of practice was ensured.' (Greenaway 1986, 158; Healy 1999, on Pliny's approach).

[89] See further Ch. 8; Abdera's gold coinage: Chryssanthaki 2002; Chryssanthaki-Nagle 2007; Kagan 2006; Persian gold in the North Aegean: Archibald 1998, 90 with M. Price, *CH*

Iron

Gold and silver represent only two aspects of the strategic armoury of available minerals. Iron, not silver or gold, was the fundamental metal of the first millennium BC. Every aspect of daily life and every kind of craft and specialized activity involved the use of iron tools. Despite the fact that iron was so essential to the organization of everyday life, not everyone, it seems, had equal access to iron instruments and weapons. Iron is among the commonest of minerals. Mineral ores containing iron, iron-bearing sands, and bog ores are widely distributed throughout the region. However, we do not really know how these ores were in practice identified and experimented with. The earliest iron artefacts from Macedonia and from several different parts of Thrace suggest a long period of experimentation in the early first millennium BC, when this metal seems to have been treated as a special kind of mineral, before it became an alternative to bronze, and then superseded bronze for making strong and sharp blades. Some of the earliest iron artefacts in the region come from Thasos, where iron succeeded copper alloys and early exploitation of gold, several centuries before the arrival of Parian settlers.[90] The knowledge of how to make iron blades sharp as well as strong was an asset of real strategic value, so it is perhaps not surprising that the techniques used to make iron blades were not widely disseminated, in contrast to the ceramic technologies involving grey-faced pottery. The highly unstable nature of early iron objects makes them difficult to conserve and most excavated iron artefacts corrode before they can be properly conserved. Few analyses of iron have been conducted in the north Aegean, but a recent study of finds from three separate origins provides evidence of significant differences between communities.

A type of steel, made either from carburized wrought iron, or by forging a bloom with high carbon content, was produced at a range of sites in the north Aegean from the fifth century BC onwards. A study area of 80 km x 50 km has produced a wealth of technological solutions to the challenges posed by the variety of iron ores available in the north Aegean, which display very different working properties (iron pyrites, manganese, copper-rich iron, oxides of iron, and iron-bearing sands). The technologies represented in the samples studied by Maria Kostoglou display little sign

2 (1976) 1: a hoard from 'Western Thrace'; Picard 2000 for a general survey of the early coinages in the region.

[90] Muller 2010, 216–19; cf. *HM* I, 13, 312–16 (iron deposits in Macedonia); Archibald 1998, 24, 66–71 on early iron-producing sites in lowland Macedonia and Thrace; Chernykh 1978 is still fundamental for comparative analysis of metal samples.

of radical change over the entire period investigated (sixth century BC to second century AD). Since particular technologies are linked to wider cultural patterns, there is no reason to believe that the social and economic structures of the extractive industries and associated smithing technologies, as well as the identities of the craftsmen involved in these processes, underwent any significant changes during the course of antiquity.[91]

Slags from iron working have been identified in a number of different zones between Rhodope and the north Aegean coast—north-east of Siderokastro, at Faia Petra; at Ano Vrondou and Panorama, two villages *c.*30 km north-east of Serres, and at Katafyto, 7 km north of Ano Vrondou, as well as other locations in the Vrondou valley and nearby at Vathytopos; at Domatia, 24 km south-west of Kavala; at Angistron, *c.*33 km north-west of Serres, close to the modern border with Bulgaria; at Kimmeria, 2 km north of Xanthi; at Thermes, close to the Greek-Bulgarian border; at Komaros, 5 km north of the ancient city of Zone (formerly known as Messemvria); on Mount Menoikion, near Nea Zichni (ancient Gazoros); and in and around Mount Pangaion. Although the slags at most of these sites have formerly been identified as of Ottoman date, metallurgical analysis of iron tools and weapons in the region makes it likely that some of them can be associated with much older exploitation from the first millennium BC, as well as from Roman imperial times. Some of the earliest iron products from the region were discovered in ninth-century BC dolmen burials at Roussa, in Rhodope, while an early sword was found at Vafeika, 1 km north of Xanthi.

Northern Greece and adjacent regions of the central and east Balkans are unusually rich in minerals, particularly metals. Gold, silver, lead, and copper are the most widely known deposits; but zinc, arsenic, iron, manganese, and nickel also occur, often in close proximity. The exploitation of radioactive magnetite-bearing sands has been documented on Thasos, in the Kavala area, and in the Vrondou mountains, as well as in the area of Alexandroupolis, and has also been recorded along the west Pontic coast of Thrace. The manganese-bearing ferrous ores of the Symbolon range represent a particular local technological variant. Haematite, one of the commonest iron-bearing ores, was more widely exploited.[92]

Kostoglou explored three case study areas, Abdera, Kalyva, and Zone, both in terms of the evidence that the physical remains at the three sites provided about the social character of these settlements and in terms of the scientific evidence that analysis of iron tools could offer. One of the

[91] Kostoglou 2008, 80. [92] Kostoglou 2008, 56–7.

most rewarding groups of iron objects analysed by Maria Kostoglou comes from Zone. Knives, scissors, spearheads and other weapons, axes, a saw, a plough share, strigils, keys, rings, bells, and other items were found in and around the sixth-century BC temple of Apollo on the eastern periphery of Zone. A set of iron spits and an elongated iron bar, of the type used as currency in continental Europe, were also among these presumed votives.[93]

Iron knives, spits, spearheads and arrowheads represent the commonest items at Zone. In the fifth century BC there was a wider range of knives and agricultural tools, such as billhooks and pruning hooks. Nevertheless, the scale of production appears to have been intended for local use. The concentration of industrial waste in the south-eastern part of the fortified area of the city probably indicates the location of smithing workshops. Kostoglou has emphasized the wide range of evidence that indicates a strong indigenous imprint at Zone—not only in the style of handmade pottery and funerary rites (dolmen and tumulus burial), but also in the selection of associated objects; the relative absence of certain characteristic classical Greek items, such as strigils, and the corresponding presence of distinctive types of iron spits and rings.[94]

Analysis of smelting and smithing slag, as well as artefacts, shows that a manganese-rich source of iron was used to manufacture tools, arrowheads, and spits, but copper-rich iron pyrites, probably from a nearby source at Kirke, is also identifiable. The usual method of producing iron objects in classical antiquity involved smelting the ores into a 'bloom', or bar, which could then be forged into an appropriate shape, a process that allowed modification of the metal's properties by carburizing the bar during the smithing process, thereby making it into a harder and more efficient blade. This is particularly true of the long, thin spit-shaped bars that were used to produce long blades, particularly swords. The close physical association of industrial waste and indigenous types of handmade pottery strongly indicates that indigenous miners and smiths were involved in these operations.[95]

The picture at Abdera was very different. Here there was no evidence of iron objects having been deposited in burials and there were few iron tools in the classical settlement. Furnace debris from iron and bronze production suggests that some of the pyrotechnic experience was shared

[93] Kostoglou 2008, 35–8, table 2 and fig. 14 (spits and currency bar [= MES21 AΠK351], 0.26 x 0.045 x 0.017 m, 615.6 g: table 7b, p.104); on obeloi, or currency bars: Strøm 1992 and P. Haarer, (2001), *Obeloi and iron in Ancient Greece*, unpublished PhD thesis, Department of Archaeology, Oxford.

[94] Kostoglou 2008, 42–3.

[95] Kostoglou 2008, 41–3, 57–66.

by specialists in both metals. The quality of the iron produced was lower than that at Messemvria-Zone and at the third study site, Kalyva. The knives lack carburized edges, so would not have been as effective to use. The blooms produced at Abdera came from iron oxides and sulphides, though it is not clear how the inhabitants obtained these, because the only sources of iron ores were outside the city's territory (perhaps from Thermes or Kimmeria, 30 km away to the north). The citizens would have had to negotiate with local miners for these ores, or would have had to obtain blooms produced by outside craftsmen.[96]

The final case study is a Macedonian fortress above the River Nestos, at Kalyva, with a circuit of masonry walls and towers constructed in the time of Philip II. Thracian ceramics of the early first millennium BC (and of the Roman imperial period), suggest that this was an upland strong point for the indigenous population that reverted to local control whenever any higher authorities had less influence on the area of the Nestos gorge above Xanthi. The surviving agricultural tools and weapons date principally to the imperial age, though the industrial waste suggests long familiarity with the iron oxides and pyritic ores, which were probably roasted in the vicinity from the local bog deposits at Potomaki, and then smelted into blooms and forged in the confines of the fortress. The production techniques indicate a good knowledge of how to manipulate the ores to produce the best results, but these smiths did not deploy the full range of metallurgical techniques potentially available in the region. They were simply producing what was required by the inhabitants of the fortress.[97]

Glass and pigments

A number of other minerals deserve mention alongside metals. One of the most interesting, if unexpected minerals, is natron, an essential component for the production of high-quality glass. Among the very few Mediterranean sources of this salt outside Wadi Natrun in Egypt is the marshy land near modern Pikrolimni, named after the salt lake that was once a more significant feature of the landscape of northern Chalkidike, and that has been identified with Lake Chalastra and the ancient city of Moryllos.[98] Despoina Ignatiadou has linked this salt with the unusually fine examples of a colourless type of glass found in a range of

[96] Kostoglou 2008, 43–8, 66–70.
[97] Kostoglou 2008, 48–50, 51, 70–4, 75.
[98] Ignatiadou 2002b; Ignatiadou et al. 2005; Hatzopoulos 1996, I, 53, 55; II. Nos 53, 54.

specialized products using glass inlays, notably the ornamental fittings of wooden funerary couches, which have been found at a number of major Macedonian centres, including Aineia in Chalkidike.[99] These items were intrinsically delicate, and unsuitable for long distance transportation. They are the kinds of products best made as close as possible to their place of use, so Ignatiadou's interpretation of these as locally made items is persuasive and the source of natron in the nearby lake certainly very plausible.

Techniques of glassmaking are also connected, albeit indirectly, to the manufacture of pigments. Many of the colours used in tomb painting, which provides the largest source of information about pigments in Thrace and Macedonia, are composed of earth colours—red and yellow ochres; charcoal or similar sources of carbon for black and grey tones; chalk and kaolinite for white. These are widely available, but would have been cleaned and prepared to a high concentration. The earliest 'synthetic' pigment was blue, whose purest form was Egyptian blue, made of copper and calcium silicate. The commonest form of this man-made mixture of minerals is blue glass, and was usually imported from Egypt.[100] Egyptian blue has now been identified in a large number of painted schemes in tombs of the north Aegean.[101] Blue appears in tomb decoration as an occasional colour, essentially a supplement to less expensive, more accessible earth tones. Blue was one of the most prized colours for Greek temple decoration alongside red, so the demand for blue was strong, widespread, and persistent, even if small quantities were used in individual locations. Blue ought therefore to be a trace element of exchange patterns.

Most of the colours used as pigments were applied in small quantities onto a lime or lime and chalk base-coat. Lime plaster was the commonest form of wall decoration, with or without additional colours. Lime is therefore likely to have been the commonest type of alkali available for general purposes and a lime compound was the most straightforward mordant for fixing the colours of textiles. Slaked lime (calcium hydroxide, $Ca(OH)_2$) was used for this purpose at a range of Bronze Age sites in

[99] Aineia Tomb I: fragments of glass and ivory (Vokotopoulou 1990, pl. 9a, especially the sheet and fragments of eye and leaf pattern, pl. 9γ, δ); Tomb II: (ibid. pls 18–20); Tomb III and pyre in the same mound: (ibid. pls 51–53, especially pls 51$\sigma\tau$ and 52γ; 83 fig. 43).

[100] Riederer 1997.

[101] Brecoulaki and Perdikatsis 2002; Brecoulaki et al. 2006, 309; Tsimbidou-Avloniti 2005, 199 (Egyptian blue mixed with 'bone black'); Ivanova 2011, 40–1, reviews evidence from tombs in the interior of Thrace with traces of Egyptian blue: (in chronological order) Ostrusha, Kran, Muglish, Kazanlak, as well as a fragment from Adjiyska Vodenitsa, Vetren, identified with Pistiros (ibid. 43 and pl. 6).

the Near East, Egypt and Europe and continues to be used today for enhancing the depth of indigo or woad.[102] Alum (hydrated potassium aluminium sulphate), which is a clear crystal refined from bauxite and a far rarer mineral than limestone, is nevertheless known in the region. In parts of the Mediterranean alum was used as a mordant for textiles, as well as an agent for finishing skins. In medieval times it was also used in the tanning of leather, but Pliny does not refer to it in that context, and alum has rarely been directly identified as a tanning agent in classical antiquity.[103] So the extent to which alum was used in the north Aegean, whether for fixing the colours of textiles, or in allied applications, is uncertain. The many colours used in textiles as they are represented in wall paintings, particularly the bright reds, orange, blue, green, and purple, would have needed a chemical mordant. Pliny (*NH* 35.184) and Dioscorides (*de materia medica* 5.106) both include Macedonia as a source of alum. Possible sources have not been identified, with the exception of Kypsela, which, though technically not in Macedonia, was referred to by Balducci Pegolatti in his treatise, *La pratica della mercatura*, of 1340. The traveller Pierre Belon visited the region and also referred to alum at Kypsela in ancient Thrace (1547). The solid geology of the region around Kypsela, where the presence of dacites, andesites, and ophiolithic rocks is recorded, suggests that the deposits close to the ancient city may well have been a source of the mineral in classical antiquity.[104] Pliny's reference to Macedonia nevertheless points to some degree of ancient exploitation, whether at Kypsela or at another, as yet unknown location.

Pastoral regimes in the northern Aegean

Animals, as two of the editors remind us in a recent volume of essays on the use and re-use of animal bones in historical settlements, are often both 'meal and symbol, related to everyday practice and ritual'.[105] Animals and humans have such a long history of interaction that we are prone to forget, in our increasingly urbanized societies, just how close this relationship has been, even in the very recent past. During the last

[102] Barber 1991, 237–43.

[103] Alum (KAl $(SO_4)_2$ $12H_2O$) as a mordant: 'In Cypro candidum et nigrius; exigua coloris differentia, cum sit usus magna, quoniam inficiendis claro colore lanis candidum liquidumque utilissimum est contraque fusissant obscuris nigrum' (Pliny, *NH* 35.184); Van Driel-Murray 2002, 260; Van Driel-Murray 2008, 485.

[104] Karadima-Matsa et al. 2005, 71 and 74 fig. 2.

[105] J. Lev-Tov and S. DeFrance in Campana et al., 2010, x.

half-century, many European societies have ceased to have a close working relationship with animals. Horse- and donkey-drawn vehicles are an occasional source of wonder; mules are even rarer, and even farmyard animals a curiosity. It needs an effort of the imagination to repopulate these landscapes with trains of mules, flocks of sheep and goats, and herds of cattle and horses, to say nothing of the lions, leopards, lynxes, panthers, and boars that Xenophon assured his readers were plentiful in Thrace at least (Xen. *Cyneg.* 11.1; cf. Pl. *NH* 21.17; Ael. *Hist. An.* 3.21). Xenophon did not mention bears, which still roam Mount Rhodope. Bears' teeth have certainly been found in the Thracian Plain at Adjiyska Vodenitsa, in the foothills of Rhodope.

The evidence from Angelochori, and from other sites in Macedonia and Thrace during the Bronze Age and Early Iron Age, shows that arable cultivation co-existed with pastoralism and the hunting of wild species. However, the evidence does not reveal how cultivation and pastoralism worked alongside one another. In principle animals may pasture on marginal land away from cultivated fields; but most scholars accept the existence of a symbiotic régime, in which animals moved across arable land after harvesting and made use of marginal or uncultivated resources farther away from cultivated areas when crops were growing.[106] If animals move across ploughed fields they consume the weeds of cultivation and their manure contributes to a more productive humus than is produced from a biennial fallow regime.

The nature of pastoral regimes in classical antiquity has aroused much debate over the last half-century. The scholarly focus during the late 1970s and early 1980s on pastoralism as the dominant regime of the Early Iron Age played a role in the formulation of Hammond's theories about the origins of the Macedonians. Nicholas Hammond used a model of extended transhumant pastoralism between Epirus and Macedonia to connect three elements that contributed to his understanding of the culture of Macedonia in the fifth and fourth centuries BC—Herodotus' story about the founding rulers of Macedonia (8.137–139); the closeness of the Macedonian dialect to north-west Greek; and Hammond's personal knowledge of the geography of Epirus and western Macedonia.[107]

[106] Hodkinson 1988; Forbes 1995, 332; Halstead 1996; Margaritis and Jones 2008b, 160–1.

[107] See Ch. 2 n.20 on Hdt. 8.137–39; Hammond, *HM I*, 415–16, 439; *HM II*, 28; cf. also Hatzopoulos 1996, I, 105: 'a group of transhumant shepherds, who for generations had tended their flocks on both the western and eastern slopes of the Pierian mountains, hardly distinguishing themselves from their Elymiot brothers across the Haliakmon, seized the old Phrygian settlement of Edessa, established their seat there, renaming it Aigeai, and became sedentary'; 'The peoples of upper Macedonia were ethnically, economically, socially,

The idea that a group of transhumant shepherds operating within the Pierian mountains 'settled down' at the site of Aigeai is not consistent with any reasonable interpretation of the archaeological data. There is no evidence and no theoretical basis for conceiving a social group without any connections to local farming regimes inserting itself into the fabric of lower Macedonian society in the seventh century BC. On the contrary, the close symbolic connections between the Early Iron Age burials at Aigeai and their historical successors makes this even less likely. There are more fundamental ecological and historical reasons for rejecting the notion of itinerant pastoralists in the Pierian hills. Chandezon argues that significant transhumant behaviour occurs on the margins of desert and temperate zones, not within the temperate zone as such. What is more, large-scale transhumance was not possible prior to the late Hellenistic period because of the complex pattern of land ownership in the east Balkan region, and the epigraphic evidence for the transmission of rights to pasturage, or *epinomia*, bears this out.[108] Despite the evidence of systematic diachronic studies of pastoral behaviour, which show very clearly that pastoral economies are closely integrated with arable ones, the idea that there were exclusively pastoral societies has not entirely been erased.[109]

Horse power

Most of the animal species that were present in classical times already belonged to the fauna of the Balkan peninsula in the Neolithic period. Horses are different. Levine has recently argued, on the bases of mitochondrial DNA testing, that mares from at least 77 separate lineages have contributed to the modern genetic pool—in contrast to the 'seven daughters of Eve' reputed to have been the female progenitors of anatomically modern human beings. The implication of the equid DNA is

culturally and politically more akin to the Epeirotic *ethne* than to the Lower Macedonians (or the Thessalians). Hammond has long since drawn attention to the fact that they were called Molossic *ethne* by the earliest writers, that like their Epirote brothers they practised transhumant pastoralism, that they did not live in cities but in open villages (κατὰ κώμας), and that they were organised in territorial units (ἔθνη)'. (Hatzopoulos 1996, I, 479).

[108] Chandezon 2003, 393 and n.15.

[109] In addition to the arguments presented by Chandezon 2003 (170–81, 333, 371, 377, 396 on *epinomia*) and the authors cited above, n. 106, see esp. Nixon and Price 2001, 401–3, for a systematic study of pastoral regimes on Crete; nevertheless, McInerney still envisages a division of pastoral and non-pastoral (?) societies, although he later assumes that pastoral practices were part of a mixed economy in ancient Greece (2010, 27–8, 71–2, 164–72).

that, as horse domestication expanded, wild horses were evidently added to the herds. Recent examination of the Early Bronze Age horse remains from two sites at Kanligeçit (Kirklareli), in Turkish Thrace, radiocarbon dated 2600–2300 cal BC, have been identified as work horses, for riding and for transportation. So they may have been used as pack animals, for traction, or simply for getting about the countryside.[110] Benecke thinks that these animals were imported from Anatolia, on the basis of metrical comparisons with some north-west Anatolian examples (although there were no horses at Troy until *c.*1700 BC). The domesticated horse is first attested in Mesopotamia and the Levant in the third millennium BC. At present the range of data sets within the whole region of western Asia is still unsatisfactory for a more precise model of the wider process of domestication, particularly in view of the genetic history of domesticated horses in Eurasia. Justin reports the incident in which Philip II brought 20,000 mares from his campaign against the Scythian king Atheas back to Macedonia specifically for breeding purposes (9.2.16). This explains how complex genetic patterns actually emerged.

Much of what we know about horses of the first millennium BC in the north Aegean comes from artefacts—coin obverses, funerary reliefs, painted images, and statuettes offer various facets of the everyday and the symbolic associations of equids and people in the north.[111] The range of these images testifies to the enormous social importance of horses in the whole of the north Aegean region. The subject deserves in-depth study in its own right and I can hardly do justice to it in a brief survey intended to highlight the economic dimensions of horse ownership. The climate, humidity, ample provision of rivers, and the availability of grazing land made the area an excellent one for horse-rearing (Fig. 4.11). Of the surviving horse skeletons recovered from excavation, the vast majority have come from burials and only a tiny proportion of registered finds have been subjected to any kind of scientific analysis. There has been no systematic study of all the available skeletal material and much of the evidence has yet to be published, even in preliminary form.[112] Perhaps the most detailed investigation has been applied in the

[110] Levine 2006; Kirklareli-Kanligeçit: Benecke 2006.

[111] See e.g. Prestianni-Giallombardo and Tripodi 1996 (Macedonian coin types); Zhivkova 1973, pls 1, 11–12, 22–3 (Kazanluk tomb paintings); Curtis and Tallis 2012, 108–54 with contemporary Near Eastern examples of Arab-type horses and harness equipment.

[112] Kouzmanov 2005, 143–4, summarizes the data from a wide number of Thracian burials. He notes that only a few of the specimens analysed exceeded 1.36 m in height (although the examples from Kaloyanovo, Sveshtari, and Zimnicea certainly exceeded 1.4 m; cf. Archibald 1998, 246–51, 288–97, for detailed discussion of contexts. Kouzmanov also

Fig. 4.11. Horse grazing, Septemvri, central Bulgaria.

context of the most intensively studied group of human burials from ancient Macedonia, namely the remains of four horses retrieved from the funeral pyre(s) of Tomb II at Vergina, along with an impressive range of other mammal bones.[113] Only some of the burnt horse bones, together with parts of their bridles, and bones from two dogs, some birds, and some fish, survived the fire of cremation and were recovered by archaeologists. The iron bit, presumed to belong to the male burial in Tomb II, was found complete with its bronze snaffle, on top of the vault above the tomb. It is similar to the bit shown on the horse of the frontally positioned rider in the centre of the painted façade of Tomb II. The bit was published by Faklaris before it became clear that there were horse bones amongst the species slaughtered and burnt on the same pyre. In addition to the published bit, the pyre contained parts of another full horse bit, most of a third set, and fragments of two further bits, all of iron, together with additional bridle parts, including bronze phalerae, each decorated with an eight-petalled rosette; fragments of leather straps with nails, both iron and bronze, adhering to them; 18–20 U-shaped iron strips, perhaps to cover the bridle straps; various other iron nails, and six copper alloy nails, with traces of leather, which may have belonged to the

notes the burial of partial horse skeletons, either of the head and limbs, as at Histria and Sveshtari; or of partial or complete skeletons without the head, as at Yankovo (mound 2), Zimnicea horse 8; and others: Kouzmanov 2005, 145.

[113] Antikas 2006, 206; see further discussion in Chs 7 and 8.

rider's sandals. There was also a pair of copper alloy spurs, semi-circular in shape, with a short, beak-like point. The range of items is reminiscent of the harness paraphernalia described by Xenophon.[114]

The associated material has proved to be more informative about the style and symbolism of the burial of royal horses than the heavily burned bones themselves have proven to be for our knowledge of cavalry or parade horses. In addition, however, Antikas refers to analyses of other horses' skeletons, recovered from a variety of contexts at Akanthos, Polymelos, Pydna, Therme, and Lagyna, all of which provide very useful information about their socio-economic functions.[115] Of the 9,052 human graves recorded in the cemetery at Akanthos, only twelve contained horses, although these would be considered highly unusual in other parts of classical and Hellenistic Greece, where horse burials are rare.[116] Bearing in mind the rather undemonstrative character of the human burials at Akanthos, the presence of the horse skeletons suggests close association with the social élites of the north Aegean, something that would not be apparent from personal grave goods, the form of human burials, or other features of the city's social life. The Therme horse was placed at right angles to the burial of a Macedonian 'hoplite', who was interred with two swords. The horse's head was laid on a stone on the western periphery of the man's cist tomb. Notwithstanding the dead man's other accoutrements, this was probably a cavalry horse, fifteen years old, with a standing height of 135–140 cm, which would indicate a relatively large specimen for this period. The skeleton of a horse recently excavated in a tomb of broadly the same period near Sedlare, in the Momchilgrad district of eastern Rhodope, was 146 cm in height, one of the tallest recorded skeletons from the region.[117] The Polymelos horse was found at a settlement site on the borders of Emathia

[114] Antikas 2006, 206–7 and figs 10–11; he refers to similar spurs found at Dodona and at Pella; Anderson 1961, 64–139 for Greek equipment in general.

[115] Akanthos (1994–97); Therme (1994); Polymelos (1996–99), Pydna (1996–2001): Antikas 2006, 205, figs 4–5 (Tomb 180, 2 horses); fig. 6: Therme horse; fig 7: Polymelos horse; fig. 8: Lagyna horses.

[116] Xen. *Hell.* 6.1.3 (Thessalian Polydamas of Pharsalos), 7.1.11, 3.2.5 (Thracian horse racing); Archibald 2000, 212 n.1 with further refs. Note the exceptional mid sixth-century BC tomb at H. Giorgios, Larissa, which contained eight wheel hubs and the metallic parts belonging to a vehicle or cart. The actual (?mule) carts had evidently been burned on a pyre prior to burial of the wheels (Tziafalias 1978, 156–81). Cf. also two 4-wheeled carts with their yoked horses found at Doxipara, near Alexandroupolis, Thrace (Triandaphyllos and Terzopoulou 2006).

[117] L. Ninov, *AOR* 2009 [2010] 271–3, reporting on faunal evidence from recent developer-funded projects, includes a brief description of the Sedlare horse, investigated by G. Nehrizov.

and Elymeia, during development work on the Odos Egnatia project. The bones of a foal were also found close by. The circumstances suggest an accidental deposit. The mare was about eight years old, the foal as many months. Again, these seem to have been horses reared for riding. Evidence of flooding, which may have destroyed the site, suggests how the two horses met their end. The first evidence of a team of work-horses from Macedonia comes from Lagyna, and their function is indicated by the particular pathology of the front legs, known as 'lower leg syndrome'. These examples provide some idea of the kind of information we can expect to get from surviving physical remains. They do give an indication of the frequency of horses in the northern Aegean. The future potential of such evidence is illustrated in the discovery of a cemetery at Lithochori, on the west bank of the River Nestos, with burials of horses, some of which included human as well as horse remains, extending in time from the fifth century BC to the fourth century AD.[118] Two burials (Tombs T26 and T27) contained pairs of steeds alongside the wheeled vehicles that they had drawn, as well as auxiliary mounts.

Animal products

Among the Greek inscriptions from the city of Augusta Traiana (modern Stara Zagora) is a fragmentary funerary altar that refers in its surviving portion to a bequest in favour of a society of tanners.[119] This is not the only inscription from Roman Bulgaria connected with leather craftsmen and this attests to their social prominence in the principal civic communities.[120] Tanners appear in Aristophanes' comedies at a time when their activities became generally more socially prominent. This prominence

[118] Poulios et al., 2007.

[119] *SEG* 47.1053 (second/third century AD); *IGBR* V, no. 5585; line 7: *tē technē tōn gnapheōn*; Sharankov and Tcherneva-Tilkiyan 2004, 83 and 97 fig.1.

[120] Plovdiv Archaeological Museum, dedication to Caracalla by the guild of leather workers: *IGBR* V, no. 5464. Text: (in the wreaths) a) *Ἡ βουλὴ* b) *Νεικα- εῖς καὶ ὁ δῆ-μος Ὀλυμπι- ασταί* c) *Νεικομ-* d) *ῥοπο- e) βυρσεῖς* 5 *ηδεῖς πῶλαι* (below the wreaths) *Φίλιππος Φιλίππου τῷ υἱῶι καὶ Παπιας Φιλίππου τῷ ἀδελ-φῶι Φιλίππωι ζήσαντι* 10 *ἔτη λ' μνήμης χάριν.*

Translation (L. Domaradzka): (a) The Council and the People. (b) [The community of] Nicaeans–Olympiasts. (c) [The community of] Nicomedians. (d) [The guild of] hawkers. (e) [The guild of] tanners. Philippos, son of Philippos—for his son, and Papias, son of Philippos—for his brother: Philippos, son of Philippos, who lived 30 years, in memory.

'The wreaths represent the communities which took part in the funeral, and of which the deceased and his relatives should have been members. The family of the deceased appears to have originated from Asia Minor, as shown by the presence of societies of Nicaeans and Nicomedians and by the name of one of the brothers, Papias.'

was evidently material as well as political, as two unusual inscribed stones from Athens, a dedication by Dionysios, which illustrates a cobbler's workshop, and another by Silon, showing a giant sandal, amply illustrate.[121] Shoemakers were among the most indispensable civic craftsmen in Plato's ideal state. Yet we know surprisingly little about the kinds of shoes that were worn at this time, or indeed about any other contemporary leather products.

Leather is the most familiar type of animal product. Edible animal products are the subject of Chapter 7. Inedible products included sinews; glue from boiled bones; horns and long bones used in decorative work; and the smaller foot and toe bones of cattle, ovicaprids, and pigs, particularly astragaloi, used for gaming and prophecy. By far away the most important inedible by-products were skins or hides. Polybius refers to cattle as among the key exports that were particularly desirable (to Aegean Greeks) from the Black Sea area, that is, amongst commodities travelling towards Byzantion and in transit (4.38.8–9). His statement could refer either to hides or to live animals, or it could in theory also mean preserved meat. As we shall see in Chapter 7, there are good reasons for thinking that live animals may have played a more significant role in this traffic than has usually been assumed. Here our focus is on cured and tanned hides.

Current research on leather and tanning practices has focused heavily on Roman military equipment, because most surviving examples of leather from temperate zones belong to this category. Although cured leather can survive in dry conditions, tanned leather has undergone a process that alters the collagen of skin chemically, making it resistant to water and bacteria. The development of curing and tanning practices is still rather mysterious. The kind of tanning manufactory excavated at Pompeii represents the culmination of experience that must have been rather more widespread in those areas where cattle and other contributing animals were common, and the demand from urban or military consumers high; we simply lack suitable evidence.[122] It is usually

[121] Camp 2004, 130, figs 9.1–9.3 (Agora I 7396, Dionysios, second quarter of the fourth century BC); 135 figs 9.6–9.7 (National Museum Athens, EM2565, Silon); Van Driel-Murray 2008, 490–1, is more sceptical about the economic status of cobblers (491).

[122] Van Driel-Murray (2002, 262, fig. 3; cf. Van Driel-Murray 2008, 484 fig. 19.1) shows a diagram of tanning procedures in Europe and the Near East, with cured leather common in Egypt, 'barbarian' and northern Europe sometime between 1000 and 500 BC, though southern Europe appears uncertain—there is no time line for cured leather, but tanned leather is identified as having begun there earlier than in Egypt (where it seems to be a development of Ptolemaic rule). Her evaluation is undoubtedly stronger on the Roman than the Greek evidence. Bravo and Trüpke (1970) 127–49, provide a comprehensive diachronic

assumed that the earliest method of curing hides in prehistory consisted of drying skins through smoking, or smoking combined with the application of layers of fat. Vegetable tanning is hard to detect, particularly if ancient samples were preserved in waterlogged conditions, where they might be subjected to secondary tanning. Intentional tanning involves bathing or submerging skins in tannin-rich vegetable infusions, including oak bark or galls, which contain very high concentrations of natural tannin. Theophrastus (*Caus. Plant.* 3.8.6) clearly knew about the properties of oak galls and refers in passing to their application in tanning. The kind of knowledge that his botanical descriptions display reflects a very good awareness of the tanning properties of these seemingly unlikely natural sources.[123] Very few leather fragments survive from the Aegean area, where conditions for the preservation of organic remains are far less common than in waterlogged or anaerobic conditions in northern Europe. However, a number of leather items have been noted in the course of excavations over the last century in central Thrace. A leather helmet was recovered from Golyamata Mogila, Duvanli, in the 1930s, and a leather jerkin, with an associated belt and thongs for a scabbard, from Lasar Stanevo, near Lovech, in the 1980s.[124] Nothing can be said about the methods by which these items were preserved, although the survival of large pieces of leather over almost two and a half thousand years speaks very positively for conditions that involved some level of dampness, even if the air in these contexts was sealed. In addition to this evidence, several fragments of leather and fur have recently been analyzed scientifically during the museum conservation process.[125] What is more, they provide some chronological parameters for understanding changing processes. Diana Nikolova studied fibres from earth samples recovered from a mound burial near Beliš, in the area of Troyan (northern Bulgaria), which contained pieces of Baltic amber, as well as a large collection of bronze ornaments. Red (made using madder, *rubia tinctoria*), dark blue (indigo), pink, and undyed fibres were detected in hemp or linen threads. A few purple threads were identified as murex–dyed. Leather straps, likewise dyed with extract of madder, and indigo (from an

survey of the classical sources and evidence from artefacts, with classical Greek contexts, including Homer and Herodotus, esp. I. 71, 171, 194, 202; 2. 86–8, 121, 141; 3. 9, 133; 4. 61–79, 89–92; 189; 5. 58; Theophr. *Caus. Plant.* 3. 8. 6; 9. 1; 14, 3; 18, 5; Leguilloux 2002, on the Pompeian manufactory.

[123] D. W. T. 'Oak galls in Theophrastus', *Nature* 139 (1937) 684–4.

[124] Archibald 1998, 199–201 with refs and 164 fig. 6.8; TPQ final quarter of the fifth century BC for the burial in Golyamata Mogila; the burial from Lasar Stanevo i slightly later.

[125] Nikolova, 2008, esp. 196–8.

unknown, but perhaps local plant source) were attached to the bronze belt fittings. Lipid analysis of the soil samples shows the presence of vegetable matter, which the author considers to have been used for curing the leather. The results demonstrate that the technology of leather production was of a high standard for the time (the tomb was dated by finds to between the eighth and seventh centuries BC). The deceased was laid out with a quite exceptional level of luxury and symbolic references for a period several centuries before any form of kingship has been recognized historically in the region.

Among the successors of this élite individual was the incumbent of a tumulus burial at Malomirovo-Zlatinitsa, in south-eastern Bulgaria, which is still undergoing investigation.[126] A fur strip made from lamb's hide was used to line the helmet from Zlatinitsa. This was dyed with alizarin (madder lake, or madder on a white substrate) and indigo, using vegetable extracts. A piece of purple fabric was also recovered, perhaps coloured using a combination of dyes (some purple from shell-fish, and some vegetable dye, such as madder). The fact that the leather had survived despite some evidence of degeneration shows, according to the author, that the curing process was achieved using tannins, perhaps from a combination of vegetable sources, such as acacia, oak, chestnut and other kinds of bark.[127] Lamb's hide is considered to be especially suitable for caps. In this case, red dye was infused first, followed by the indigo, to give a purplish colour. Besides the lamb's hide, some *à jour* fragments of leather with impressed decoration were also recovered. One large fragment had been tanned using vegetable tannin. In addition, a fragment of textile with some silk weft threads and showing white figures on a purple ground was recovered from a bronze basin. Some threads of Mediterranean purple dye, derived from *murex trunculus*, *murex brandaris*, or a similar source, were also detected.[128] These findings indicate that we can be much more confident about assigning tanning methods to the north Aegean region in the fourth century BC, if not earlier.

The culture of creativity in the north Aegean

Close study of the activities that communities of the north Aegean chose to prioritize and specialize in during the second half of the first millennium BC reveals patterns in part shaped by specialization within the region since the Neolithic period (particularly in terms of the long co-

[126] Agre 2006, 139–42 and pls1–5. [127] Nikolova 2007a, 184, figs 1–7.
[128] Nikolova 2007b; Nikolova 2010, figs 1–8.

existence between humans and animals, domesticated and wild), and partly by strong interactions with people from peripheral areas. This is apparent in the case study of grey-faced and Ionian-banded pottery styles, which became ubiquitous in the eastern and southern parts of the region from the late sixth century BC onwards, but were preceded by a more limited pattern of earlier imports and technologies stimulated by external contacts with other parts of the Aegean. A similar pattern of cross-currents between the western parts of the region and the islands of Thasos, Euboia, and more distant parts of the Aegean is apparent in the Thermaic Gulf.

Scientific analyses of leather, particularly the use of dyes, suggest a close connection between the techniques of wall decoration and other craft activities. Wall painting and leather decoration used many of the same pigments, whilst the copper-based pigments shared materials with metal smiths. The large-scale consumption of wood for pyrotechnology produced surplus bark, which, along with lime, would have been in demand by leather workers. We might expect there to have been practical synergies between these different crafts. We still have much to learn in terms of the spatial organization of these various activities; how they were integrated with residential structures; and how special skills were disseminated. The investigation of country estates is providing a different way of thinking about production and distribution and will help us to understand more clearly the inter-connectedness of sites across the landscape.

When we consider social relations, Veblen's idea of an 'instinct of workmanship' helps to focus attention on the range of objects that constituted the material environment. Even the most prosaic everyday objects, such as household and cooking wares, roof tiles, and shoes, were made in small workshops, at the domestic or local level, or on country estates. Dress, as pictured in tomb paintings, provides one way of evaluating social distinctions that bring social hierarchies together. The hats and cloaks of the better-off do have something in common with the ostentation favoured by Demetrios Poliorketes, a style that was not shared by many of his peers, according to Plutarch.

5

Regionalism and regional economies

EXPLORING THE NORTHERN AEGEAN AS AN ECONOMIC 'SUPER-REGION'

The northern Aegean as an axis of exchange and as an interface

Given that the landmass explored in this book is divided between three modern states (Greece, Bulgaria, and Turkey), and that it was not unified politically at any one time within the second half of the first millennium BC, in what sense can we consider it to have operated as an economic region or regions? It is not a contention of this book that the land area discussed here was in any sense a unity; it was not. If, however, we accept that complex societies of the European Iron Age did rely on a network of supplies, at varying distances from the consumers, and accept the overall applicability of the concept of Mediterranean 'connectivity' as a structural component of socio-economic relations, then it ceases to be necessary to think of ancient economies in an 'essentialist' manner, and in terms of well-defined geographical spaces. It was the economic interconnections between the different communities of the north Aegean that gave their economies a specific character in classical antiquity. It was the social expectations of the inhabitants, and the networks of exchange to provide them with specific commodities, that created the interconnections linking the various geographical spaces explored here. In a purely local and geographical context, 'the northern Aegean region' might simply refer to the islands of Thasos, Samothrace, Lemnos, and perhaps Lesbos and Chios, with the adjacent coastlines of the Thermaic Gulf, Chalkidike, and Thrace as far as the Chersonese; but as soon as we expand the frame of reference beyond the local and the geographical, then the scope of enquiry has to embrace more distant partners and different ecologies. The space under consideration includes a number of different 'regions' in the physical and administrative senses (whether we are thinking of ancient or more recent geographical or administrative divisions). This is why I refer to the area as an economic 'super-region'.

In Chapter 1, I suggested some of the ways in which the term 'north Aegean region' can be applied to the interlinked economies of two major territorial powers (Macedon and Thrace) and their coastal neighbours, who enjoyed a high degree of political independence from these kingdoms. The next chapter developed the theme of the Greco-Persian Wars as a defining stage in the history of the region, a period that catalysed the emergence of the two main territorial states. Macedon and Thrace became socio-economic magnets that refocused patterns of exchange between coastal and inland parts of the east Balkan peninsula. At the same time, a significant economic distinction began to emerge at the turn of the sixth and fifth centuries, with the development of new naval technologies by those Aegean states that had a vested interest in competing with the leading naval power of the era, namely the Phoenician and Egyptian fleets of the Persian Empire.[1] From an economic point of view, the accessibility of key strategic resources for shipbuilding, not just timber, but also hemp, iron, and copper, made it highly desirable for states that needed to expand their supplies in these resources to establish or develop effective connections with partners in appropriate areas who could provide them, or to get resources by direct territorial acquisition. The northern Aegean, particularly the mainland coast, provided one of the principal areas explored for these possibilities from the final decade of the sixth century BC onwards, if not earlier, as we will see in Chapter 6.

Geography still plays an important role in the ways that 'regions' are conceptualized by historians and economic geographers. The physical geography of localities, together with climate, soils, and precipitation, has had a powerful effect on the parameters of local cultures. There is a close identification between people and the landscapes they live in. The north Aegean sea is ringed by mountains—the northern Pindhos (effectively the western boundary of our region, in terms of local ecologies and historical connections);[2] the outliers of Pindhos to the east of the main range, Mounts Barnous and Bermion (Figs. 2.1 and 5.1), respectively west and east of Lake Vegoritis; the Pierian range as far as Olympos;

[1] Wallinga 1993, 130–44; Davies (forthcoming 2013a); on Mediterranean 'connectivity': Horden and Purcell 2000, 123–72.

[2] As the contributions to the periodic colloquia on Illyrian history and archaeology make clear, the western half of the Pindhos was mainly, though by no means exclusively, orientated towards the Ionian Sea (see e.g. the contributions to Cabanes and Lamboley 2004 and Antonetti 2010); Hatzinikolaou 2009 provides a survey of upper Macedonian historical geography up until the imperial reorganization: Livy 45.29.5–9, with Hatzopoulos 1996, I, 231–60, on 'the Districts' of Macedonia, esp. 231–40.

Fig. 5.1. Bridge over the River Haliakmon near Vergina (the ancient city of Aigeai)

Mount Boras/Voras, west of the River Axios, and Kerkine, to the east of it, which belongs to the southern outliers of the extensive mountain range of Rhodope; beyond it, the west–east running chains of the Sredna Gora and the Balkan range itself (Stara Planina, the 'Old Mountain'); Strandja, the plateau region separating the east Balkans from the hinterland of Byzantion; the triple spine of Chalkidike and its outcrops, Thasos and Samothrace. The mineral diversity of this mountainous landscape and its wealth in timber and related resources has been one of its key long-term strengths. These assets, including both the renewable and the non-renewable resources, have determined some of the area's principal economic activities.

Landscapes are more than potential physical resources that are available to be tapped by human societies. They are the canvases on which people write their life stories, just as they are the substance of individual and collective survival strategies.[3] The kinds of materials that we use to build domestic structures, the range of staple crops and the repertoire of symbolic forms that structure our cultural languages all depend on a range of essential local resources. In a twenty-first century context, the

[3] For survey literature that is particularly relevant here, Doonan 2004, 93–118, on Sinop and its environs (especially timber); Bintliff 2009; Constantakopoulou 2007, esp. 20–8 (island connectivity); 38–60 (religious networks); 228–53 (islands and their *peraiai*).

framework of regional administration tends to conceal the ways in which a region's inhabitants embed specificity through habitual practice. Administrative mechanisms promote tourism and local commercial interests by reinforcing the perceived characteristics of regions in an oversimplified way—through typical culinary specialities, or the traditional forms of architecture. The language of regional promotion can mask the very processes of cultural production, presenting regional identity under a homogenized template of definitive forms, creating a sense of timeless cultural continuity, when the realities are more dynamic and more varied.

The notion of 'regional economies' represents a different approach to conceptualizing a 'region' than what can be achieved by looking at geographical or cultural perspectives alone. Grounded as they are in specific physical environments, regional economies exist by virtue of the people who created them. Contemporary regional studies, whether of present or past landscapes, do integrate the ethnic and political dimensions of regions alongside geographic ones, whilst the links between geography and economic behaviour are the *raison d'être* of economic geography.[4] So geography is by no means irrelevant to the study of regional economies. Many modern niche industries arose because of specific synergies between a region and its inhabitants, and between the social drivers within that region and the demand for specific products. In terms of medieval and early modern industries, the textile producers of Prato, west of Florence, or the merchant traders around the Golden Horn at Istanbul, or the marble quarrymen of Thasos, all constitute examples of local skilled specialists whose expertise evolved as a result of synergies between social demand and local resources, and which developed over a long period of time.[5]

Regional studies of contemporary cultures offer other insights that can usefully be applied to economic questions about past societies. We might, for example, consider supply chains as indicators of economic networks. Another obvious case study might be the relationship between procurement zones for the exploitation of minerals, the specialists who extracted

[4] Elton and Reger 2007, 11–15; Reger 2011, 371–8; Reger 2013a and 2013b; Oliver 2006a; Constantakopoulou 2007, 245–52; see above Ch.1, 'The geography of north Aegean economies'.

[5] Prato: Horden and Purcell 2000, 94, 148; Golden Horn: Matschke 2002, 467, 471–2 (streets with dedicated crafts, including boot-makers, belt-makers, and furriers; the hunters' district [τῶν κυνηγῶν] near St John's Gate, money-changers, warehouses, craftsmen, and vegetable sellers); Thasian marble: there are nine contributions (covering different periods) in Part I of *Thasos, Matières Premières*, 'la Pierre', 15–126; cf. also Vavelidis et al. 2006; more generally on geography and innovation, see Archibald 2012a.

these minerals, the different user groups who transformed the mineral into a more accessible form, those who bought this form on behalf of end users, and the end users themselves. Iron production, as discussed in Chapter 4, involved a supply chain linking remote parts of Rhodope with cities on the Aegean coastline. This is a relatively straightforward pattern, because the trace elements in the ferrous ores can be followed in the artefacts and tools used in places within a 30 km radius of the mining areas.[6] There was a limited number of miners and smiths with the requisite knowledge to extract the metal in the first place, and an equally restricted number who knew how to manipulate these particular ores so as to produce workable tools. The distances are not large and the mechanisms of the supply chain were located within a small geographical area, as in the three cases explored in Chapter 4—the hinterlands of Zone, the fort of Kalyva, and Abdera. The situation is more complicated when we consider either more complex networks, with multiple potential suppliers and a more opaque process of supply or transmission (as in the case of grey-faced pottery, discussed in the same chapter), or more complex distribution patterns of objects, such as silver bowls inscribed with royal names and what appear to be places of origin.[7] Distribution maps of coins that originated in a given civic centre, or were minted by certain rulers, are one of the well-known ways of demonstrating particular kinds of economic outreach. Gary Reger has recently explored the regional significance of Milesian silver and copper alloy coins, minted in the later third and early second century BC, in this light, as well as other Milesian issues such as the gold and silver 'Alexanders', which are usually thought to reflect payments made to retiring war veterans.[8]

The most obvious and the most widely researched investigations of economic connections within the east Balkan area are those associated with the delivery of substantial quantities of wine and olive oil to many inland locations.[9] These were not merely mechanical patterns of bulk transmission of stock. As we saw in Chapter 1, transportation is not to be divorced from consumption and conscious patterns of demand. The capillary movement of wine and oil *amphorae* was complemented by evidence of other cultural traits that match the consumption of these two key foodstuffs—in the culinary field, the use of specific types of tableware and *haute cuisine*; in architecture, the adoption of ashlar masonry for

6 Ch. 4 n.91.

7 See Ch. 4 for grey-faced pottery; silver *phialai*: see below, n.56.

8 Reger 2011, 378–83.

9 Tzochev 2010 and other contributions in Kassab Tezgör and Inaishvili 2010; Tzochev 2011; Tzochev (forthcoming).

public amenities and of terracotta roof tiles. These material enhancements are visible throughout the region and on an increasing scale over the five-hundred-year period examined here, although there were marked fluctuations in the dissemination of specific artefacts and commodities.

Economic connections resulted from specific historical initiatives, which were driven by social or political imperatives, but they were also related to perceived ecological variability—the scarcity of certain minerals, and the need for shipbuilding timber, for instance.[10] Those seeking resources developed in our region included distant partners such as the Athenians, as well as partners from the region itself, such as coastal harbours in need of metal ore. The targets of significant external bulk trade were mainly located in lower Macedonia and north of Rhodope, although some of the coastal towns along the north Aegean periphery were also net consumers of wine in particular, from Thasos, Chios, Kos, and Rhodes, whilst Pontic producers (mainly Herakleia Pontika, Sinope, and Chersonesos) competed with the former on an increasing scale in the final three centuries BC, albeit primarily to satisfy consumption within the Black Sea region and adjacent inland sites. The apparent impenetrability of Rhodope is largely the result of modern national border administration; distributions of archaeological material within the mountain region do not support the idea that trade did not cross upland terrain.[11] In addition to the relatively well-known pattern of exchange between Aegean or Black Sea producers and Balkan consumers, new trading connections have recently been detected, delivering products from hitherto unknown producers in the east Balkan region (notably in Mesambria during the middle decades of the third century BC) to clients inland and to overseas destinations.[12] These kinds of network connections reinforce the robustness of the regional network envisaged here.

It has been apparent to researchers that significant fluctuations did occur in the demand and supply patterns between major consumer centres and major suppliers over three centuries (that is, between the early fifth and the late third or early second centuries BC). These fluctuations have been hard to understand, beyond the curves and dips shown on charts and graphs from different consumer centres. The quantities of

[10] See below, n.33.

[11] Archibald 1998, 49–52, 126–35; Nekhrizov and Mikov 2000, 161–70; see further below on the Pistiros inscription and its implications for movement across Rhodope.

[12] See esp. Stoyanov 2011 and other contributors to Tzochev et al. 2011.

Fig. 5.2. Vineyard in the east Balkan region

residual ceramic data are enormous; even ceramic experts have difficulty connecting the pottery with known sources and the results of classification have not been easy to analyse with respect to historical events. This complex picture has nevertheless been transformed by a range of scientific analyses of fabrics and of clay sources, and also by a valuable re-assessment of major known classes of pottery.[13] The vast majority of eastern Mediterranean centres that produced wine and oil for export seem to have had a rather restricted outreach. They were primarily involved in satisfying demand within their own immediate regions (Fig. 5.2). This remained true of most producers throughout the time-scale under consideration here. A proportion of producing centres seems to have made larger quantities of containers, but either there is no recognizable pattern in the observable distributions, or consumption was primarily regional. From an economic point of view, the regionally focused patterns are consistent with an established tradition of

[13] Lawall (2005) discusses problems of quantifying *amphorae*; Lawall (2011) explores the challenge of identifying *amphora* contents; Tzochev (forthcoming) and Panagou (forthcoming) present recent work based on the archive of Virginia Grace in the American School of Classical Studies, Athens, as well as a wide range of published data.

consumers, and with a regular rhythm of communication, probably connected with other transportation needs. These regionally orientated producers included Ilion, Corinth, Miletos, and Samos, and in the northern Aegean, Ainos, Oisyme, and Samothrace. Sites that seem to have developed particularly close or intense relations with given entrepôts on a larger scale included Akanthos and Mende in Chalkidike, and the island of Peparethos, just north of Euboia. Only a small number of producers, no more than four in all (Thasos, Kos, Knidos, and Rhodes) can be said to have had truly large export distribution patterns, with continuous production throughout this period.[14]

The proportion of this export trade that was shipped to different localities did vary over time, however. The output of Thasian wine *amphorae* has been studied in terms of the volume of jars produced at known production sites on the island, as well as in terms of the numbers of stamps that have been recovered at recipient centres. Although stamps represent an unknown proportion of the gross output of wine jars, there are various ways of estimating the relationship between stamps and unstamped jars. Some 28,000–30,000 Thasian stamps are available for study and the comparative incidence of Thasian stamps at different recipient centres, particularly when shorter episodes can be juxtaposed, does provide useful information for the full course of the island's output.

The earliest Thasian wine *amphorae* did not travel very far. During the course of the fifth century, this pattern of local exchange began to expand. In the later fifth century, between 70 per cent and 90 per cent of Thasian jars were exported outside the island's immediate hinterland (the island's *peraia*, or mainland possessions), primarily to consumer centres along the western and northern Black Sea coast, a proportion of which penetrated to dozens of known locations in the Thracian and Macedonian interior. There were intermediate *emporia*, along the main river arteries, at various distances from the coast, through which *amphorae* were trans-shipped to sites farther inland. These included Pella, on the River Loudias, in Macedonia (Fig. 2.1); a large penumbra in the hinterland of Odessos and in the Valley of the Roses, much of it probably river-borne; a number of sites between Edirne and Dimitrovgrad in the middle Hebros valley (Fig. 4.7);[15] Adjiyska Vodenitsa, near Vetren, in the Thracian Plain (Fig. 4.7, nos 27, 32, 39, 48, 56; Fig. 4.8, nos

[14] Panagou (forthcoming) identifies 58 potential centres of *amphora* production in the eastern Mediterranean, of which 51 have been located with reasonable confidence.

[15] Archibald 1998, 116–17 and fig. 9.5, for a preliminary analysis of sites; Triandaphyllos 2007 (middle Hebros valley finds); Balkanska and Tzochev 2008 (Seuthopolis); Tzochev 2010 (southern Thrace).

22–25); and sites at more distant locations farther north in the foothills of the Sredna Gora chain, such as Krastevich (Fig. 4.7, no. 36), and Vasil Levsky, near Karlovo (Fig. 4.7, no. 49).[16] The evidence for the dissemination of *amphorae* is represented by consumption at particular sites. So distribution patterns emerge rather from the overall range within which the products are represented. The commonest wine jars in the east Balkan interior at this time were Thasian, and, to a lesser extent, Chian ones. During the fourth century BC, the more distant entrepôts retained a significant share of the market (with Kallatis outstripping Istros, for example, in the volume of demand), but a larger proportion than previously was consumed by the principal urban foci of the north Aegean mainland, including Amphipolis, Abdera, and Maroneia.[17] Study of kiln sites seems to confirm that the number of potters on Thasos increased in the fourth century BC to satisfy this increased demand; but a significant drop in the take-up of wine exports by the more remote markets followed in the late fourth century (perhaps as a result of disruption in trading patterns during Lysimachos' reign, though it is also worth considering the indirect role of changing patterns of demand, brought about by demographic and social changes at this time). A further slump in Thasian exports succeeded this dip, during the third century.

At present it is not yet clear whether this was a progressive decline in Thasian imports to the region as a whole, or an abrupt change at a number of sites, including Seuthopolis.[18] Neutron Activation Analysis has allowed the complex group of vessels formerly labelled the 'Parmeniskos' Group (identified as technically related by Virginia Grace) to be dis-aggregated, revealing at least two production centres, one of which was probably in Chalkidike (since some samples have formerly been identified as from Mende, including examples from Pella); the other perhaps at Ainos, close to the estuary of the River Hebros. The samples used in the study were drawn from a number of key consumer centres of the east Balkan interior: Adjiyska Vodenitsa (Pistiros), Sboryanovo, Odessos, Kabyle, and a configuration of sites between the Bay of Burgas

[16] For Pella and Adjiyska Vodenitsa (Pistiros), see further below; Krastevich: M. Madjarov, D. Tancheva, *AOR* 2007 [2008] 217–20; 2008 [2009] 195–8, 197 fig. 3 for plan, 240–3; 2009 [2010] 200–1; 2010 [2011] 189–90; 2011 [2012] 166–8; Vasil Levsky: K. Kisyov, *AOR* 2008 [2009] 237–40; cf. also Archibald 1998, 126, 141, 226–9, for earlier literature.

[17] Avram 1996 (Istros); Conovici 2005 (bulk imports at Istros, Tomis, and Kallatis compared); Debidour 2008 on the commerce of Thasian *amphorae*; Tzochev 2010 and forthcoming; cf. Panagou (forthcoming) and Lawall (forthcoming).

[18] The end date for Thasian imports of *c.*275 BC comes from a revised study of the material from Seuthopolis by Balkanska and Tzochev (2008).

and the middle Hebros. Stoyanov used this data as a basis for a focused research programme in the vicinity of Mesambria Pontika, to determine whether the high concentration of related finds was symptomatic of production in Mesambria. This identification seems to be confirmed both by clay analyses and by the coincidence of at least two names on *amphora* stamps with those of magistrates at Mesambria.[19] The production of Mesambrian *amphorae* is particularly well represented at Kabyle and in the hinterland of Mesambria during the second quarter of the third century BC.

Thasian wine jars disappeared from the Balkan region after the second quarter of the third century BC, conceding to Rhodian, Koan, Mesambrian, and Pontic producers. Tzochev attributes the changing patterns in the export of Thasian wine to broader changes in the configuration of political (and hence economic) power in the Aegean and more generally in the eastern Mediterranean, beginning with the diminished role of the Athenians under Macedonian rule. The export of bulk commodities such as wine or oil was not unconnected to the export of other bulk products, particularly in cases where ship-owners collaborated in financing long-distance voyages, hedging their investments with a succession of mixed cargoes, aimed at multiple destinations—documented most famously in the journey between Athens, via Mende or Skione in Chalkidike, and the northern Black Sea grain ports, as described by the speaker of Demosthenes' speech *Against Lakritos* (35.10–13). In this case, 3,000 jars of Mendean wine (whose containers have been identified at a wide number of sites in the north Aegean) were pledged for a return cargo, which would probably have consisted of grain. Surviving fragments of wine jars give the perhaps false impression of large and consistent patterns of imports. The speech *Against Lakritos* reflects the kinds of single transports that can also sometimes be documented from wrecks of merchantmen. Although wine jars probably did travel mainly in irregular, seasonal transports to the major coastal outlets, albeit often in smaller vessels, the quantification of *amphora* sherds by context at least suggests that consumption was regular at recipient centres, so the supply of wine within given localities seems to have been stored in sufficient quantities to

[19] Kuleff et al. 2007 (INAA analysis); Stoyanov 2011, esp. 192–5 for magistrate Melseōn, whose name alludes to the mythical founder of Mesambria, Melsas, and is also the name of a coin issuer at Mesambria between 275 and 225BC (*IGBR* 1^2 308 (6)), as well as the middle name of a strategos, one of a group of six civic magistrates who dedicated an altar in the late second century BC (*IGBR* V, 5104).

satisfy the demand.[20] On the other hand, documents like the speech *Against Lakritos* show that major transports were potentially vulnerable to erratic changes at the supply end, if investors or ships' captains decided, for whatever reason, not to put up capital (in the case of the former), or not to chance a distant voyage (in the case of the latter). It is by no means clear which of the possible causes may have triggered the shift in traffic away from the underlying vector of Aegean trade in the Classical period (when Athens-based finance was linked to north Aegean products and Pontic grain), in the direction of the axis fuelled by Rhodian finance and shipping, bringing Rhodian wines, as well as other southern Aegean commodities, to the northern Aegean and Balkan region. The demise of the Piraeus played a part, as did the reduction in Athenian grain demand.[21]

There seems to have been a series of major discontinuities in the vectors of trade across the region. One is represented by the disruption to commerce that occurred at the time of Macedonian expansion eastwards under Philip II and Alexander III. The disappearance of Attic fine wares, which were very widely disseminated up to the end of the fourth century BC, is probably connected, first of all, to the occupation of Mounychia hill by a Macedonian garrison after 322 BC, and then, in 295 BC, with Demetrios Poliorketes' blockade of Piraeus, which prevented the supply of essential commodities to Athens by that route and, by the same token, of Athenian exports. Third-century BC Athenian exports, particularly tableware in the 'West Slope' style, are much less well represented.[22]

The brief appearance and subsequent disappearance of imported *amphorae* (with other evidence of a direct Greek presence) at Krastevich, deep in the foothills of the Sredna Gora mountains of central Bulgaria, testifies to the uncertainties experienced by merchants, who explored this new opportunity in the first half and probably into the third quarter of the fourth century BC, only to retreat thereafter.[23] At Adjiyska Vodenitsa, Vetren, there is evidence of a series of destructions, *c.*300 BC, when the fortified tower above the Eastern Gateway collapsed and was never

[20] Wrecks of wine *amphorae*: Gibbins 2001; Lawall 2011 and forthcoming; see Ch. 7 for further evidence of consumption patterns and quantification by context at Pistiros.

[21] Oliver 2007, 49–68, esp. 48–55 (Piraeus); 86–100 (population changes in the late fourth and third century BC).

[22] Rotroff 2005, 13–28.

[23] Krastevich: see above n. 16; I am grateful to the excavator, Mitko Madjarov, for his current interpretation of the data accumulated up until 2012.

rebuilt,[24] and in the period around 280–278 BC, when a hoard of Macedonian coins was concealed. This last evidence has been connected by the excavator, Jan Bouzek, with the historically-attested Celtic incursions at that time.[25] The period between the principal Celtic incursions in the Balkans and the war between Rhodes and Byzantion in 220 BC (Plb. 4.37.8; 45–52), presents a complex and confusing picture, since we have few precise facts on which to reconstruct a plausible understanding of the opaque tensions between, on the one hand, the cities of the western Black Sea coast and those near the Hellespontine Straits and, on the other, the various communities of the interior.

Alexandru Avram has provided an ingenious argument to explain why the invasion of Thrace staged by the Seleukid king Antiochos II during the later 250s BC was the ostensible sign of a larger confrontation between the Seleukid king and Ptolemy II of Egypt. Ptolemy bestowed a number of benefactions on the city of Byzantion, probably in the early 270s BC, and continued to provide support for the city, and for a closely connected alliance, which included Herakleia Pontika and Kios. Antiochos II besieged Byzantion, probably in 255 BC, at the time of the so-called 'Monopoly War' between Byzantion on the one hand and Istros and Kallatis on the other, for control of the *emporion* at Tomis.[26] Avram

[24] Domaradzki in *Pistiros I*, 30–1 (coins of Philip II, Alexander III and early issues of Lysimachos show traces of fire damage; examples of Lysimachos' final series do not); Katinčarova in *Pistiros III*, 36–7, confirming this chronology on the basis of three separate road surfaces in stone and the material between them); on trade *amphorae* at Adjiyska Vodenitsa: Bouzek et al. 2007; Tzochev in *Pistiros III*, 187–9; Y. Garlan in *Pistiros IV*, 246 (addenda and corrigenda); Tušlová et al. 2010 (dating imported *amphorae* at this site between the later fifth and end of the fourth century BC). However, among the samples analysed by Kuleff et al., there are examples with handles stamped *ΜΑΤΡ/ΟΔΩΡΩ* and *ΑΝΤΙ/ΦΙΛΟΥ* that belong to the 'Parmeniskos' group, formerly attributed either to Thasos or Mende and the cluster that includes the *ΜΑΤΡΟ/ΒΙΟΥ* stamps, identified by Stoyanov as products of a Mesambrian workshop from the end of the first quarter and mainly from the second quarter of the third century BC (Kuleff et al. 2007; Stoyanov 2011). The stamps in this series are typologically close to Thasian series X, dated by Tzochev 274–59 BC.

[25] J. Bouzek, *Pistiros III*, 64 and pl. 18; 286 (434 drachms of Alexander III, Lysimachos and other early Hellenistic Successors; 115 tetradrachms of Philip II, Alexander III, Demetrius Poliorketes, and Seleukos I; 3 gold staters of Alexander III); on the Celtic presence in the east Balkans and western Asia Minor: Mitchell 1993, 13–20; Chaniotis 2005, 220–1, 228, 230, 235–40; see also the contributions to Vagalinski 2010.

[26] Antiochos II and the siege of Byzantion: Memnon *FGrH* 434 F15; Polyaen. *Strat.* 4.16; Will, *Histoire Politique 1*, 247–8; Draganov 1993 on the coins minted at Kabyle; Avram 2003, 1184–9, 1201–2; civic inter-relations: 1193–1200; he also identifies *IGBR* I^2 388 as a decree of Mesambria, not Apollonia, though it honours an Apollonian benefactor; 'Monopoly War': Memnon *FGrH* 434 F13, with Avram 2003, 1187–8, 1211–12, and Gabrielsen 2011, 223–6, emphasizing the city's specialized control of fish stocks.

has explained the coincidence of these two events in terms of a polarization of interests. Ptolemy II was continuing a policy that allowed him a degree of power in the Straits and beyond, into the Black Sea. His support of Byzantion was a conscious component of this policy. Antiochos II, on the other hand, chose to court the cities of Apollonia, Kallatis, Istros, and probably Mesambria, perhaps using some of these as bases for operations inland, particularly for assaults on Kabyle (whose coinage was subsequently overstruck in his name), and perhaps Seuthopolis. A number of honorific inscriptions indicate cordial relations between Apollonia, Kallatis, and Istros at this time, while the distribution of coins in the name of Kavaros (the Celtic leader whose notoriety rests mainly on his threats to Byzantion), suggests that he operated from a base in the hinterland of Odessos, perhaps at the fortress of Arkovna.[27] Although, as we shall see, Kavaros appears in Polybius' account of the history of Byzantion as an aggressive threat to the city's interests, the circulation of his bronze issues, clearly intended for minor transactions, fits rather smoothly into the pattern of regional commercial relations, alongside the bronze coins minted by the city of Mesambria. A very similar pattern of connections emerged in the late second and first half of the first century BC, when regal issues minted by one Mostis were succeeded by those of the 'Sapaian' dynasty, based at Bizye. The most prominent of these were large issues of Rhoimetalces I, sponsored by the Emperor Augustus, and his successors in the region, Rhoimetalces II and III.[28] Such events highlight the changing form and nature of economic relations in the region, with an increasing focus on the Pontic seaboard and the Straits. Contrary to the impression of immense tension portrayed in the narrative sources, the coins issued by various authorities within the region, by civic magistrates, by local rulers, and by incoming powers such as Antiochos II,

[27] Lazarov 2010, 99–105 with further bibl.

[28] Karayotov 1994, a key survey of numismatic evidence from the environs of Mesambria, beginning with a hoard of Cyzicene electrum and a Persian gold stater among the earliest coins, continuing with the Kocharitza hoard of 101 Macedonian bronze issues (89 of Philip II, 10 of Alexander III, 2 Mesambrian helmet *en face*/wheel with 4 rays, META + head of Melsas and/or shield); bronze of Philip II and Alexander III from Bilka, Rouen and Goritza; Sredna Mahala: a hoard of Apollonia tetrobols and others from Rouen, Bilka, and elsewhere; third-century BC hoards of Athena Alkis types of Mesambria; Aitos: second-century hoard of third-century BC Mesambrian tetradrachms; second century: Sadievo (42 tetradrachms of Byzantion [Lysimachos] + 3 Thasian 'new style' as well as one of Kavaros); Aitos, Rudnik, and Burgas hoards of Mesambrian tetradrachms and those of Odessos and Byzantion. He notes the rarity of Adaios issues and Odessitan bronze. From the end of the second century BC, there is a hoard of Byzantine and Thasian coins from Debelt (286). Karayotov 2002, 431–7 on second- and first-century BC regal issues of Mostis and the Sapaian dynasty.

point to a high degree of interaction between the different agents operating in the region. The common occurrence of shared coin designs (such as the reverses with an owl on a spearhead on coins of Agathopolis, Bisanthe, and of the ruler Adaios, dating to the second quarter of the third century BC) and common countermarks, such as the bronze of Antiochos II countermarked at Kabyle, or the six- or eight-pointed star that appears on the reverse of Byzantion's earliest bronze issues (dated 240–220 BC) and contemporary coins of Adaios, show a closely interconnected web of commercial relations.[29]

The emergence of monopolistic behaviour, linked to control of the physical bottleneck constituted by the Straits, will be re-examined below in connection with the extraordinary rise of Byzantion. The internal picture of the east Balkans over the period *c*.300–100 BC indicates great prosperity on the one hand and substantial disruption of overland trade links on the other. The Celtic incursions of the early 270s BC are linked to rural destructions in lower Macedonian farm estates, as well as cities, such as Aigeai and Pistiros. At the same time, most of the coastal cities of the Aegean and west Pontic coast, the chief cities of lower Macedonia and central Thrace, experienced the first significant period of urban expansion in their histories, with the emergence of public squares, buildings, and various civic amenities. What is more, the archaeological evidence for the 'Celtic' presence in the region does not indicate a well-differentiated social entity.[30] This confirms the notion that there was far more to the conflict between Byzantion and its neighbours than a simple case of greed (on the part of neighbouring communities). The web of connections was interrupted by the advent of Roman troops in response to the activities of Mithridates VI of Pontus (132–63 BC). This is the point at which the configuration of the networks begins to change to the new order, based on bilateral treaties with Rome. The lead here seems to have come from Kallatis, as early as 106–101 BC.[31]

Cross-cultural exchange

More subtle but no less penetrating than bulk transports, and the coin distributions that seem to follow the same dynamics as the bulk produce, were other socio-cultural features of economic life that seemed to move in step with the demand for bulk commodities, particularly those

29 Jourukova 1994, 261–5, on Agathopolis and related issues.
30 See esp. Emilov 2010.
31 Avram 1999; Minchev 2011, 21–2.

associated with urban living, such as the appointment of market officials; the use of publicly approved coins, weights, and measures; the regulation of sales in general, and the collection of taxes. Should we expect the organization of market transactions to map directly over the kinds of commodities exchanged? This is a more complex question, which deserves deeper investigation. As the discussion of markets and market-type exchange revealed in Chapter 2, and as we will see further below, there is a variety of assumptions within the scholarly community about the infrastructure of exchange across cultural boundaries.[32] These assumptions are linked to ideas about the nature of socio-economic structures on the one hand and to site classification on the other. The socio-economic questions are concerned with the control of market-type and non-market transactions. Were territorial powers, like the kings of Macedon and Thrace, all-powerful in economic as in social matters? How might these forms of authority have affected transactions and demand at a local level? Were the kingdoms of Macedon and Thrace more like the Persian Empire, in terms of attitudes to money and markets, than to mainland Greece? In Chapter 2 I argued that 'royal economies' should not be taken at face value, namely as command mechanisms, driven mainly or simply by aspirations towards military aggrandizement. So there is no reason to assume that any and every transaction took place only with the express approval of the authorities. In fact, there are strong reasons for thinking that a good deal of exchange was unconstrained, as we saw in the case of grey-faced pottery in Chapter 4.

The unconstrained exchange of ceramic technologies amongst a range of locations in the north-east Aegean beginning in the mid sixth century BC (and in some cases mid seventh or even earlier) on the one hand, and various coastal and inland centres of the east Balkan peninsula on the other, suggests that there were no formal restrictions on inter-cultural exchange and that these exchanges operated rather effectively. The production patterns observed in the early stages of this technological process did not change significantly in the fifth and fourth centuries BC, when we might expect to see differences, if royal or princely decisions really did affect what could and could not be exchanged in fundamental ways. The general osmosis of commodities, reflected most clearly in the widespread consumption of imported fine pottery from Corinth, Ionia, and particularly Athens, seems therefore to have continued much as before; but the specific legal and social forms of economic mechanisms

[32] See in particular the discussion below about Pistiros in Thrace.

that enabled these kinds of transactions are still emerging from current research.

Royal monopolies

What was certainly new about the organization of commodity exchange under the monarchies was the introduction of a system of royal monopolies, reflecting a hierarchy of power, albeit one that had constantly to be reaffirmed. The royal monopolies over timber suitable for shipbuilding,[33] and over gold and silver mines, at Dysoron in Macedonia from the early to mid fifth century BC onwards[34] and at Krenides-Philippoi from the middle of the fourth century,[35] are simply the best known examples. Viewed alongside these royal prerogatives, the mining rights of the historian Thucydides, evidently located on the mainland opposite Thasos, begin to look much more socially distinctive than historians of Athens have generally allowed. These were not just perquisites of power.[36] The peculiar social significance of leaders in the societies of the northern Aegean at the time of the ancestral marriage between the Philaid Miltiades the Younger and Hegesipyle, the daughter of a Thracian landowner called Oloros (after whom Thucydides' own father was named) elevated to a new status the Philaidai, who had ruled the Chersonese since the Elder Miltiades had established an enclave of power among the Dolonkoi of the Chersonese in the 540s BC. The historian tells us that he had inherited mining rights in gold mines (4.105.1), which meant, according to his own account, that he had considerable influence among people of standing there. For local societies, the value of gold lay in its timeless symbolic qualities. The leaders of

[33] *RO* 12; Hatzopoulos 1996, II, no.1 (alliance between Amyntas III and the *koinon* of the Chalkidians, early fourth century BC); Borza 1987, 32–52; Millett 2010, 472–3.

[34] Hdt. 5.17 (Alexander I of Macedon received one silver talent every day from the Dysoron mines); located in the Philippoi Plain: Faraguna 1998, 375–8 (identifying Dysoron with Mount Menoikion, on the basis of *SEG* 34. 664B, in line with the topographical interpretation of L. Missitzis; Hatzopoulos 2008a, 14–35, for full bibliography and detailed discussion of the topography of the lower Strymon; Kremydi 2011, 160–1; see also Ch. 6 for other interpretations of this evidence.

[35] Krenides (and Daton)—Isokr. 8.24; Theop. *FGrH* 115 F43; Ps.-Skyl. 67; Str. 7. 331 frs 34, 41, 43—attracted the attention of Philip II of Macedon, who seized Krenides, which was subsequently renamed Philippoi, and became the most significant centre associated with the mining area (Str. 7.331 fr. 34). He famously drew 1,000 talents (presumably *per annum*) from these mines (Diod. 16.8.6).

[36] Thucydides' mining rights: 4.105.1; Plut. *Cim.* 4.1; *Mor.* 205c; Markell. *Vita Thuk.* 14, 40; Miltiades the Younger and Hegesipyle: Hdt. 6.39.2; *PAA* 653820; Miltiades the Elder: *PAA* 653685; Archibald 1998, 113–14, 117; see also Ch. 6.

society, female as well as male, were marked out with gold in death, to represent the link between their responsibilities in decision-making and action on behalf of their communities and the duties that they owed as a result in the metaphysical sphere.[37] The sheet-gold work that forms such a prominent component of sixth-century Macedonian burials came from a mine or mines that have not yet been identified. The Odrysian kings also had exceptional access to gold and silver reserves. The coincidence of known mines and gold artefacts, made from a similar, high-carat gold, in the river valleys at the western end of the Thracian Plain, indicates a close connection between mining and the consumption of gold and silver around Strelcha and Panagyurishte on the northern tributaries, Assenovgrad and the far western parts of Rhodope and the southern tributaries of the River Hebros, singled out by Pliny for gold mining (*NH* 33.66; cf. Luc. *Fugitivi*, 24: πολὺς χρυσὸς ἢ ἄργυρος ὀρύττεται, referring to the area of Philippopolis). These resources are less prominent in the works of ancient authors, because they were not the locus of inter-state competition.[38]

The cumulative evidence about gold mines and how they were exploited suggests that it would be incorrect to view mining rights exclusively in terms of kings, but rather to see a gradual evolution of rights of access in relation to how gold was used by northern societies. In the sixth century BC, gold and silver retained their significance as markers of élite social identity. In the course of the fifth century, the intense interest in gold and silver resources by many different users within the lower Strymon area and in the Pangaion district seems to have provoked a change in social practices too. Gold continued to be used in élite burials, but it was no longer deployed in the quantities that had been used in the past.[39] The lack of response to Thucydides' expectations of support from local peers may nevertheless be more apparent than real. The historian did retire to this region. There is every reason to believe that he did benefit from these dynastic connections. As we shall see in Chapters 6 and 8, the aristocratic circles of the later fifth century BC in the Strymon, Nestos, and Hebros valleys were still embedded in a social matrix that recognized the validity of hereditary roles, epitomized in the wearing of gold-sheet jewellery. The external use of the metal began to change only gradually in the more competitive environment of this period. The further intensification of the exploitation of precious

37 See further Ch. 8.

38 See Archibald 1998, 22–3 and fig. ix; Tonkova 2000, 138 map fig. 2, for gold and silver reserves in Thrace.

39 See Ch. 8.

metals under Philip II and his successors served to enhance the monetary value of gold at the expense of its social significance.

The competition for resources in the lower Strymon area, to which we will return in Chapter 6, has usually been explored in terms of rival Greek claims in the region, rather than from inter-cultural perspectives. One reason for the reluctance to consider these broader, inter-cultural connections is a widespread assumption that culturally, as well as politically, the region combined very different partners, comprising not only the kingdoms of Macedon and Thrace, but also a number of independent Thracian 'tribes' and the coastal Greek cities.[40] For a region to be recognized as an economic entity does not require *prima facie* cultural or ethnic unity. Reger has drawn attention to a number of examples where cultural differences are no barrier to regional convergence: 'the Native American tribe of the Maricopas, who speak a completely different language from their neighbors the Akimel O'odham and moved into the [Sonoran] desert in the 1700s, adopted cultural practices virtually identical to the Akimel O'odham, to the point that the two groups merged and now share a reservation in the US state of Arizona'. These south-western American communities share a very similar ecological environment, and have adapted to it using similar agricultural and seasonal practices, festivals, and housing.[41] Cultural and ethnic congruence may play a part in the manner in which economic patterns emerge and develop, but we need not assume that the absence of these common features constituted barriers to economic relations. On the contrary, it is a key argument of this book that cultural differences contributed to the economic space of east Balkan social and commercial culture in the second half of the first millennium BC.

Nevertheless, there is a well-embedded assumption about the cultural distinctiveness and separateness of the partners involved in commercial transactions that has complicated our understanding of how economic life was articulated. Since economic relations cannot be dissociated from social ones, as we saw in Chapters 2 and 3, it is appropriate to return at this point to the historiography of the region in order to comprehend

[40] e.g. Hatzopoulos 2002, 272 n.43, citing Mihailov 1989, 55: 'the principle of royal power in Thrace brought it closer to the political régime in Persia and opposed it to the Greek city-state (polis), but it should be borne in mind that this country was located between two different worlds, and served as a bridge between them in many aspects of life' (although this strikes a different note from Mihailov's earlier thoughts on urban development, esp. Mihailov 1986). Cf. Hatzopoulos' own remarks, 2002, 266–70.

[41] Reger 2011, 374; cf. also Reger's remarks on the legal application of the notion of 'homelands' to New England states.

how far modern perspectives have helped to frame the notion of cultural, political, and economic separation.

The historiography of economies in the east Balkan landmass

When Velizar Velkov started the series of symposia on 'Settlement life in Thrace' in the late 1970s, his aim was to refocus attention on a key aspect of antiquity that had become opaque as a result of the increasing trend in Bulgarian historiography, in the post Second World War period, to develop an abstract discourse about the Thracians. Whilst Michael Rostovtzeff's oeuvre on the Hellenistic world (*SEHHW*) had attempted to integrate the 'fringe' areas of the Mediterranean into his main narrative about classical antiquity, a new generation of post-war Bulgarian scholars was consciously drawing a boundary on the one hand between the Thracians as a cultural and historical phenomenon, and the Greco-Roman world on the other. Among the leading proponents of this new trend was Alexander Fol, who was inspired, initially at least, by the Marxist concept of the 'Asian mode of production', and whose conception of ancient Thracian society consisted of a tight, hierarchical ruling class, epitomized by Thucydides' description of Odrysian princes and paradynasts, whilst the population at large was in essence a cipher, a shadowy presence, whose relevance did not really feature in a theory preoccupied by the ritual dominance of priest-kings. It is one of the strange ironies of the Communist era in Bulgaria that the ordinary people of the ancient world were in practice ignored by contemporary scholarship. In parallel with this trend was the comparative lack of interest in the nature of citizenship, or of the collective status in general, of the inhabitants of Macedonia, who were dismissed as 'sub-citizens' or 'serfs'. This assumption is still active. 'It seems inherently unlikely that rural egalitarianism would prevail in a society where hierarchy was so much in evidence elsewhere'.[42]

Central to the ideas propounded by Fol, and adopted by a large number of sympathizers, was the inalienability of land. In Fol's view, the Thracian kings owned all land, so the concept of private ownership did not exist in Thracian territory. Fol's ideas were sketched out in a number of papers that examined the terminology of Thracian settlements in Greek and Latin authors; but the underlying theoretical

[42] 'Sub-citizens': Ellis 1976, 27; serfs: Billows 1995, 9–10, 136–7; cf. Millett 2010, 478, for the citation and further refs n.21.

principles of his approach were not fully explored.[43] In particular, Fol did not explain how it came about that kings acquired unassailable power, and how this was exercised in practice, when such evidence as we do have about the political history of the Odrysians points rather to a fluctuating control over specific geographical areas and little explicit information about the scope of royal authority. Xenophon is not an altogether objective guide to Odrysian regional power—as a mercenary he and the surviving Cyreans in the employ of the prince Seuthes, for just over a month during the winter of 400 BC (Xen. *Anab.* 7.1.5, 2.36), needed to keep their distance from native Thracians against whom they were fighting—but Xenophon nevertheless observes how an unnamed Odrysian officer from the central administration joined the local paradynast, Medosades, when it seemed that the behaviour of Seuthes and the Greek mercenaries was becoming ambiguous, and the rights of local people were not being upheld. Xenophon's unwitting testimony appears to contradict the idea that absolute power was exercised by Thracian kings; Medosades and other high-ranking officers owned land of their own. Xenophon was promised various pieces of land, including the town of Bisanthe, in return for services to Seuthes.[44]

Margarita Tacheva, who adopted the essential principles of the 'Asian mode of production' in her analysis of Thracian society and economy, was prepared to recognize that there was evidence in Thrace during the second half of the first millennium BC of the early signs of class structure, but she was critical of those historians who wanted to see in Thrace the emergence of a 'pre-*polis*' or *polis*-type society.[45] Tacheva took the view that territorial powers, including the kingdom of the Odrysians, were characterized by royal ownership of land and royal control over the means of production, which entailed the redistribution of commodities amongst the king's subjects. The coastal communities, in her interpretation, were socially and economically distinct from the Thracian population of the interior, because the former recognized private ownership of property and market exchange, using coinage. There was, in her view, a 'dialogue' between Greek coastal communities and the Thracians,

[43] Fol 1965; 1972, 73–5; 1975, 77–83; Tacheva 1997, 96–149, with discussion.

[44] Xen. *Anab.* 7.1.5, 2.10, 2.23–25, 7.15–16: Medosades; 7.2.32, 4.21, 5.1: other high-ranking Odrysians; Seuthes' promises of land, including the town of Bisanthe, to Xenophon: 7.2.38, 5.8, cf. on Bisanthe, Thuc. 2.61; Hdt. 7.137; Nep. *Alcib.* 7.4; Plut. *Alc.* 36.3; Stronk 1995, 140 and fig. 9.

[45] Tacheva 1997, 96–144, esp. 97; at 101 she discusses Xen. *Anab.* 7.7.29–32 as potential evidence of early class structure.

mediated by aristocratic individuals who owned slaves and other property.[46] In this interpretation, ancient references to economic 'enterprise', such as the Pseudo-Aristotelian anecdote concerning rural workers being urged to sow cereals for export to coastal towns, were interpreted in a similar light, as evidence of control over subject populations rather than as a partnership between the king and his subjects, which is, nevertheless, an equally valid understanding of the same passages.[47]

At the western end of our 'super-region', there has been a marked increase, during the last twenty-five years, in the number of epigraphic documents dealing with land sales—mainly, but by no means exclusively in the 'new' provinces of Macedonia, east of the River Axios. These deeds of sale, which date from the fifth to third centuries BC, provide some explicit evidence of land prices, as well as details about the mechanisms of sale.[48] In fourth-century BC Macedonia, royal power and prerogatives coexisted with independent, private sales and community transactions. There does not seem to be any incompatibility between the allocation of resources to royal appointees, as occurred, for example, at Amphipolis after its appropriation by Philip II, and the sales instigated by private landowners in the same city, whatever the immediate motives.[49] The implications of the evidence on land sales in Macedonia and the 'new' territories east of the Strymon have yet to be applied to Thrace. Tacheva's radical distinction between Macedonian and Greek forms of landholding on the one hand, and Thracian practices on the other, was based on an interpretation of Macedonian institutions that no longer has the support of many scholars of the region.[50]

The dominant post Second World War trend in Bulgarian scholarship on Thracian society and economy has also been under fire from archaeologists. The principal excavator of the early Hellenistic city of Seuthopolis,

[46] Tacheva 1997, 99–101.

[47] Archibald 1998, 226; [Ar.] *Oec.* II.26 1351a 26 refers to an incident involving the Athenian general Iphikrates, who was short of pay for his mercenaries and set them to sow three *medimnoi* of corn seed; another similar anecdote is recorded by Polyaenus (7.32), in which a king Seuthes provided five *medimnoi* of seed per farmer, within a group of farmers, with a view to selling the proceeds 'on the coast' for a large sum of money. The very similarity between these stories belies a significant gulf in economic mechanisms between Iphikrates' men and Seuthes' farmers.

[48] Hatzopoulos 1988b; 1991; 2011a.

[49] See esp. Hatzopoulos 2011a and his discussion of property in Mieza.

[50] Hatzopoulos has been the leading exponent of a less rigid and doctrinaire view of Macedonian society, but his views are founded on a growing body of epigraphic evidence; see Hatzopoulos 1988a; 1988b; 1991; and esp. 1997; 1999b; Faraguna (1998; 2006) and Mari (1999; 2002; 2011a) accept his interpretation; King 2010 for a more sceptical position regarding royal power (though the evidence of land sales is not in question).

D. P. Dimitrov, developed the theory that Seuthopolis may have aspired to the status of a contemporary Greek *polis* (as the topographical content of the inscription found there, now dubbed the 'oath of Berenike', indicates: *IGBR iii.2*, no. 1731; Velkov 1991, 7, no.1); but in practice this was a 'royal residence', a type of settlement identified with the fortified residences described by Xenophon in Thrace and north-west Asia Minor (Seuthes' residence: *Anab.*7.2.21; Asidates in Mysia: 7.8.12–14). Seuthopolis is, on this reading, a socially restricted type of settlement, with room for no more than some 40 aristocratic families. This social interpretation of Seuthopolis might equally, however, be applied to the spacious residences at the heart of Pella, or even to the generous accommodation at Olynthos, if we use the evidence of house forms and artefacts as direct reflections of societies. If these comparisons are valid, however, perhaps the spacious style of accommodation should be seen as a regional preference, rather than an ethnic one.[51]

Moreover, Stoyanov has criticized D. P. Dimitrov's evaluation of the social hierarchy at Seuthopolis, arguing that the excavator was too ready to dismiss the evidence for the extramural population of the city as poorly housed and indigent. Long-term archaeological investigations at Sboryanovo (identified with ancient Helis), where there are several extramural sectors, show that tiles may sometimes be the only evidence we can point to of domestic structures, other than portable artefacts; but these investigations show no significant differences between the kinds of everyday objects found inside the urban walls, as compared with similar material found outside.[52] If there are social distinctions to be drawn inside Thracian settlements, these cannot be made on the basis of the types of residential structures discovered so far.

Proponents of the 'Asiatic mode of production' in Thrace have had difficulty in accommodating the burgeoning evidence of commercial activities inland of the coastlines. Tacheva has argued that the rights accorded to Maronitan merchants and traders from other cities at the *emporion* of Pistiros were in effect forced on a puppet ruler, a successor of Kotys I, put in place by Philip II of Macedon, who was thereby obliged to renege on his exclusive rights. 'Urbanization [in Thrace during the second half of the fourth century BC] was very late due to the strong royal power and its economy, which prevented producers from participating

[51] Dimitrov 1958, 683–99; Dimitrov and Chichikova 1978, 10–11, 48–64; K. Dimitrov 2011, 101–12, with recent bibliography and detailed re-investigation of many of these arguments, even if his conclusion is that Seuthopolis, whilst having many of the essential features of an early Hellenistic city, did not have 'citizens'.

[52] Stoyanov 2006, 85; K. Dimitrov 2011, 101.

in the market by distributing their production and gaining the resulting profit, which was expropriated by the Odrysian rulers'.[53] No specific evidence, historical, literary, or epigraphic, is adduced to demonstrate how royal powers were asserted. Nevertheless, the capacity of rulers to implement their policies is perhaps ultimately less significant to economic analysis than the denial of community autonomy at any level. The idea of 'royal cities' is an attempt to square the application of royal power with the manifest evidence of urban nuclei, notably at Adjiyska Vodenitsa, near Vetren, at Philippopolis, Seuthopolis, Kabyle, Sboryanovo, and elsewhere.[54] Nevertheless, the relationship between the inhabitants of these 'royal residences' and the central power has not been examined. Porozhanov has identified sites as different as Kypsela, Doriskos, and Ganos as 'royal residences'.[55] The history of these sites shows that they underwent various changes over the course of their history and a single designation does not cover the changing dynamics of the region.

One independent source of information about place names in inland Thrace has been the series of inscriptions on silverware, particularly silver bowls. The find spots have a rather localized distribution in northern Thrace and include the hoard found at Rogozen, in northwest Bulgaria, of 165 gilded silver vessels now usually thought to have been among the items stolen from the baggage train of Philip II by the Getae, in the wake of Philip's Scythian campaign in 339 BC.[56] Hatzopoulos used these place names (some of which coincide, as we have seen, with Porozhanov's 'royal residences'), to argue that there were no politically autonomous civic communities in Odrysian Thrace: 'À l'intérieur du royaume, Pistiros, siège des *emporitai* grecs, n'était pas plus une *polis* que Béos, Apros, Sauthaba, ou Ergiskè, qui figurent toujours sur la vaisselle d'argent sous forme toponymique, en tant que localités, et jamais sous forme d'ethniques, témoignant de l'existence d'une communauté civique. Le royaume odryse manquait la culture politique qui eût permis l'éclosion des communautés civiques en son sein et à plus forte raison qui lui eût donné l'occasion de fédérer les *poleis* déjà existantes'.[57]

53 Tacheva 2007, 593. 54 See eg. Porozhanov 2009.

55 *Inventory,* no. 645, Kypsela; pre-Hellenistic sites not attested as *poleis*: *Inventory*, 871, Doriskos, called a *teichos basileion* and a *Perseōn phrourē* by Herodotus at 7.59.1; 913, Apros, Ergiske, Ganiai, Ganos.

56 Just. 9.3.1–3; G. Mihailov, *BullÉp* 1988, 259; 528); Archibald 1998, 121 fig. 4.4 (distribution of named sites), 237–9 on the incident with the Triballians, 265–8 for discussion of the hoard; Loukopoulou 2008, 139–69, esp. 158–63. The association with Triballian booty was first proposed by M. Hatzopoulos in 1987 and Loukopoulou has developed this thesis.

57 Hatzopoulos 2002, 267.

A number of different arguments have here been combined. First is the status of Pistiros, which, along with Beos, Apros, Sauthaba, and Ergiske, is negatively assessed in terms of political autonomy. The author does not explain why the Odrysian kingdom was 'incapable' of giving birth to autonomous communities, whilst the kingdom of Macedonia evidently was. The argument is based on assumptions that have not been fully articulated and the notion seems rather to rely on the kinds of cultural polarities that have aroused strong criticism from Rollinger and others (as we will see in the section that follows). The arguments that have dominated the discourse on 'the *polis*' are recognizable once more. Irrespective of where it was located in spatial terms, Pistiros qualifies as a *polis* in terms of the criteria defined by the Copenhagen Centre.[58] As to the other locations, the likeliest explanation of their appearance on silverware is as an indication of the mustering points for tribute or payment collection from coastal communities, who were not subjects of the Odrysians.[59] The inscriptions do not provide any evidence for or against the type of community that these represented. Judging by the ways in which places like Ganos (a *teichos* in Xen. *Anab*. 7.5.8; a *chōrion* in Aesch. 3.82), Ergiske (a *chōrion* in Dem. 7.37; 18.27), and Apros (a *polis* in Theopompos *FGrH* F160) are described in contemporary Greek sources, whether partial and opinionated or not, this was a heterodox group of places, selected for organizational convenience, perhaps.

Assumptions about the monopolizing nature of Odrysian power are not confined to those scholars who retain the ideological foundations of a Marxian dichotomy between 'Asiatic' and 'classical' state structures. Thucydides' analysis of Odrysian revenues has been interpreted by François Salviat in a way that shows full accord with such assumptions. The 'oligarchie clanique' of the Odrysians relied on *emporia* to supply rich Thracians with wine, in exchange for cereals, cattle, and slaves.[60] We can observe, in Salviat's understanding of the Odrysian economy, a similar social divide to that presented in the work of Fol, Tacheva, and others. Nor is it dissimilar to common scholarly attitudes regarding Macedonian social relations, as we have seen. This brief survey of the

[58] *Inventory*, no. 656.

[59] Archibald 1998, 121 fig. 4.4; *Inventory*, 913, listed as 'Pre-Hellenistic Settlements not Attested as *Poleis*'; Loukopoulou 2008, 148–53, drawing attention to the *patrios phoros* claimed by the Odrysian kings.

[60] 'Les *emporoi*, devenus par domiciliation *emporitai*, apportent argent monnayé, vins dont les Thraces riches usent parfois sans discrétion, produits de luxe; ils emportent céréales, du bétail, et aussi des esclaves. Les *emporia* sont un facteur essential de la prospérité économique du royaume. Aussi le pouvoir odryse promet-il franchises et stabilité' (Salviat 1999, 273).

socio-economic literature for parts of our 'super-region' reflects an impasse in attempts to understand the relationship between the holders of power and the territories in their possession. A look at territorial divisions, as we will see later below, provides one way of getting around this impasse.

DESCRIBING A REGION—THE ANCIENT GEOGRAPHY OF THE EAST BALKANS

Another way in which modern historiography has sought to distance and polarize the different parts of the east Balkan–north Aegean economic region has been to define Thracian royal practices in terms of Persian ones, whilst approximating Macedonian practices to those of the wider Greek world.[61] There are methodological as well as historical difficulties with this approach. Whilst it is perfectly legitimate to consider whether long-term historical connections with neighbouring cultural groups on the Asiatic side of the Bosporus had an impact on the organization and articulation of socio-economic practices on the European side, whether or not a relatively small kingdom, namely Odrysian Thrace, with a short institutional history, can legitimately be compared with a large territorial entity, the Achaemenid kingdom, whose institutional roots lie as much in centuries-old Babylonian and Assyrian practices as they do in the more recent innovations of the Achaemenid kings themselves, is a different kind of argument altogether. The trend of Macedonian historiography has been to compare Macedonian and Greek institutions. Whilst many Macedonian practices can be assimilated comfortably with Greek traditions (and recent research has done a great deal to illuminate these common traditions), there has been less scholarly enthusiasm to explore what made Macedonia regionally distinctive. It is even less clear why Thrace, a culturally related and neighbouring area, should be assumed to have been organized in ways that were structurally and politically fundamentally different from those of Macedonia, despite the shared experience of the Greco-Persian Wars. The ephemeral ambitions of Persia in southern Europe during the first three decades of the fifth century BC deserve a closer look if we are to evaluate the nature of the Persian legacy in economic terms.

[61] Hatzopoulos 2002; Zournatzi 2000; for different nuances on Thracian and Persian tribute, Stronach and Zournatzi 2002.

Herodotus, as we have seen at the end of Chapter 3, has quite a lot to say about the economic consequences of the Persian presence in Thrace and Macedonia; but the historian's focus is largely on the territories south of Rhodope, unless we follow the view that one of the three columns of Xerxes' Persian troops went much farther inland in 480 BC.[62] What the historian has to say about these peripheral areas of his narrative is partly shaped by the underlying spatial pattern of his account; that is, Herodotus' approach to the 'ethnographic geography' of the Greco-Persian Wars.[63] Herodotus' way of thinking about ethnography has been analysed in terms of a division of the known world into three parts, which were applied to his three continents—the ordered and familiar centre, the intermediate zone, and the unfamiliar fringes. He was dependent for information about the most remote areas on travellers' tales, but interpreted these according to his three-fold classification. Thrace and Macedonia are not well defined within this scheme. In some respects, both regions are assumed to belong to the familiar sphere of settled communities, built houses, and comprehensible rites. In other ways they offered interesting material for his audience, notably in the stories about Macedonian royal origins and Thracian élite attitudes to agricultural work (5.6), religious ideas, and funerary practices (5.4–7). Farther away to the north, there was more exotic value in the Getic stories about Zalmoxis.[64] Inland Thrace is more clearly defined (compared with Macedonia) as part of the 'intermediate' zone, between the familiar world of Greek-speaking farmers and the unfamiliar fringe of nomadic pastoralists.

Herodotus' detailed narrative of military preparations and encounters merges with his ethnographic construction, which creates a texture of bright, colourfully sketched spaces, separated by deep shadow. The shadowy areas include much of the north Aegean region, particularly south-eastern Thrace, the Thermaic Gulf, and Rhodope. This is because they do not play a significant enough role—either in the war narrative or in his three-fold ethnographic scheme—not because they did not deserve objective treatment in some other memorial.

Persian documents provide a wholly different way of approaching 'ethnographic geography'. In a recent review of the evidence for Greeks in the Persian Empire and Persians in the Aegean, Robert Rollinger has criticized the scholarly tradition that studies relations within the

[62] Salviat 1999, 267–71; on the Persian presence in the north Aegean, Archibald 1998, 79–90; Tuplin 2003.

[63] Karttunen 2002, esp. 457–66, 472–4.

[64] See Ch. 8.

geographical space of the Aegean and Near East in a dualist manner, that is, in terms of 'Greeks' and 'non-Greeks'. The combined evidence from Greek and Persian sources, particularly the archive documents from Persepolis, reveals 'intense and multi-faceted cultural interaction, which was able to prevail, largely unaffected by geo-political friction'.[65] The discourse that polarizes interactions into a dialogue between Greeks and non-Greeks does justice neither to the agents revealed by the archive documents, nor to the nature of broader historical phenomena. Rollinger's conclusions are based on new research that illuminates more clearly the identities of various workers listed in the Persepolis archive documents. One case relevant to the north Aegean region is the name 'Skudra', which has usually been taken to refer to the territories captured by Darius and Xerxes on the European side of the Straits.[66] Achaemenid historians are now inclined to think that the 'Skudraioi' referred to in the Persepolis Fortification Tablets lived in north-west Asia Minor, not in European Thrace or Macedonia.[67] So long as the word Skudra seemed to be applicable to the territories of the northern Aegean coastal areas that came under Persian rule from 513 BC, it was possible to refer both to 'Skudra' and to the Persian 'satrapy' in Europe, as if they were more or less synonymous. It now seems more likely that the inhabitants of the north Aegean coast should be among the various groups of 'Yaunā' referred to in the Persian documents. There is no obvious or apparent way of distinguishing amongst the various 'Yaunā', those of the

[65] Rollinger 2006, 212.

[66] According to Henkelman and Stolper (2009, 316–22), Skudrians cluster in a number of areas around Persepolis, including 300 *kurtaš* in the central region, around Fahliyān, north-west of Persepolis, 220 at Rakkan, 46 'stone cutters/polishers' at Tikraš; where *c.*1,000 are known—flour/barley and/beer received on behalf of various Skudrians, male and female. There is a northern cluster in towns and villages along the road from Media to Karaš/Gaba(e), in the direction of Taṁukkan and the Persian Gulf coast. Travelling Skydrians form a separate group, which includes women travelling some considerable distances, under supervision, to Persepolis, with authorization from the satrap of Arachosia-Gandara. Activities associated with the rations include wine producers, grain storers, servants (though sealed orders indicate more specialized functions), stone cutters/polishers, report-makers/supervisors, grain producers, and grooms; but the activities carried out were probably varied.

[67] Henkelman and Stolper 2009, 295: 'Even if Macedonian *Σκύδρα* was once a Thracian town, and even if this region was brought under Persian control in 513, it would still seem inexplicable why the Persians picked an ethnonym from the far west to denote the Thracians, many of whom they had encountered earlier during the Scythian campaign and probably before.' Their solution is to identify Skudrians with a mixed ethnic group of Asiatic Thracians = Bithynians, now better attested around Daskyleion/Ergili. This seems more plausible, especially as Scutari = Üsküdār, (*Σκουτάριον*) and several other toponyms in Bithynia show further parallels, as well as Uscudama = Edirne (Amm. Marc. 14.11.15, Detschew (1976 [1957], 349).

'mainland', those who 'dwelt by the sea', or those 'beyond the sea', in the terms familiar from Greek accounts—Ionians, Athenians, or others, indeed between these and Karians, or Lydians, or Thracians. 'Yaunā refers to an *ethnos* or a conglomeration of peoples, who lived at the western fringes of the empire and possibly beyond.'[68]

Bearing in mind this rather fluid categorization of peoples, both the 'ethnographic' distinctions made by Herodotus and the apparent lack of ethnic differentiation in Persian documents, we may understand why references to 'Thrace' in fifth-century BC documents and in later authors, including Strabo, are so imprecise and wide-ranging.[69] 'Thrace', as it appears in Athenian documents, is a handy umbrella concept, which was applied unsystematically by Greek agents and writers. As a result, the territory to which the term was applied did not fit logically and consistently over the peoples who in practice occupied the designated terrain. Athenians still talked about 'Thrace' in the fifth century BC when referring to areas that were already being subsumed into the expanding kingdom of Macedonia. Meanwhile, other parts of 'Thrace' were being divided up—by the peers and rivals of the Macedonian kings—farther east and north. Stories circulating in the Aegean about distant peoples were not keeping up with what was actually happening there.[70]

If we now consider the suggestion that the Odrysian treasury was copying or continuing Persian royal custom through the practice of inscribing royal names on silverware,[71] then the evidence is not quite what it seems. The inscriptions that appear to refer to geographical locations (Apros, Beos, Ergiske Sauthaba, perhaps Geiston)[72] are puzzling, precisely because the names are all concentrated in a small area of south-eastern Thrace, while the find spots are without exception located north of the Balkan mountains, in other words outside the

[68] Rollinger 2006, 205; 213 Table 11.1 ('Greeks' in the inscriptions of the Achaemenid kings).

[69] '[Thrace] Ce nom désigne dans Strabon, et dans l'antiquité en général, la partie de l'Europe où prédomine une population thrace; c'est en gros l'angle S.-E. de la péninsule balkanique. Ses limites sont au nord le Danube ... à l'est l'Euxin et le Bosphore, au S.-E. et au sud la Propontide, l'|Hellespont, l'Égée au S.O. la Macédoine où la frontière fut le Strymon d'abord, puis après Philippe II et Alexandre, le Nestos—étant entendu qu'il resta dans les limites de la Macédoine des enclaves et un fonds de la population thrace.' (Baladié 1989, 331 with copious text refs.) See e.g. F25 (Bermion, formerly occupied by Bryges, a Thracian people, some of whom crossed to Asia).

[70] See the discussion in Archibald 2010, 326–7 with further refs.

[71] Zournatzi 2000, 689–702.

[72] Loukopoulou 2008, 153–63, suggests that the formula [*Κότυος*] *ΕΓΓΕΙΣΤΩΝ* should be read *ἐκ/ἐγ λειστῶν* or *ληιστῶν* (with comparanda, 158–9); this is possible, though not entirely convincing (see Avram, *RÉG*122 (2009) = *BullÉp* 2009, 489–90).

territory of the Odrysian kingdom proper. Louisa Loukopoulou has restudied the inscriptions preserved on some of the vessels in the Rogozen hoard and has suggested that not only did these items come originally from the treasury of the most powerful Odrysian monarch defeated by Philip II, namely Kersebleptes, but that they were originally acquired as booty, and ended up as divided-up booty in élite burials of northern Thrace, having been stolen by the Triballians from Philip and parcelled out amongst local leaders.[73] She concedes that the Odrysian royal treasury probably contained a heterodox collection of items acquired in a variety of ways, including tribute, gifts, and as war booty. Individual inscribed silverware, or groups of silver, such as the set of rhyta from Borovo, Rousse, does not really fit the interpretation that all the items north of the Balkan range were acquired by theft. Examples like Borovo are still best interpreted as gifts, even if the inscriptions reflect an earlier 'treasury note'.[74]

So it is difficult to use these inscriptions as a basis on which to speculate about the methods used for documenting items that came into the Odrysian royal treasury. Notwithstanding the number of items preserved at Rogozen, the silverware it contained represents only some of the kinds of silverware in circulation. Precious metalwork that has survived into the twenty-first century was buried below ground, so that it could not easily be violated by robbers. Many of the fifth- and fourth-century BC tombs in central and southern Thrace were above-ground masonry structures, vulnerable to interventions. So far fewer of the gifts granted by Odrysian kings to their immediate followers survive.[75] There may be a broad similarity between Odrysian and Persian methods of inscribing ownership on silverware, but in Thrace the inscriptions include at most, besides the royal name, weight marks alongside the apparent place name in the genitive case, but without any additional information relating to manufacture, to royal treasuries, or to the 'king's house', as Achaemenid ones might. Plate that found its way into funerary contexts may have had texts added for other, more

[73] Loukopoulou 2008, 158–63; see also 162–3 for the weight inscription on a cup and *oenochoe* from Golyamata Kosmatka tumulus, attributed to Seuthes III, which refers to Seuthes in the genitive, as on the Rogozen and other inscribed vessels, but add weights in drachms, including Alexander drachms (cf. *BullÉp* 2008, 102).

[74] Borovo, Rousse: Archibald 1998, 160–1, 327 on gift-giving; see also Miller 2010; 867, 871–4, on Achaemenid echoes in Macedonian and Thracian silverware.

[75] Archibald 1998, Chs 6, 11, and 12; Kisyov 2005, for the unlooted tombs at Chernozem; cf. Delemen 2006. See also now the huge collection of (unprovenanced) plate in the Bojkov Collection, including more examples of the heterodox styles in circulation, although not all the items in the collection need have come from Thrace and some belong to distinctly different traditions, unknown on the European side of the Bosporus (Marazov 2011).

metaphysical purposes.[76] Stronach and Zournatzi have argued that the point of Thucydides' contrast between Thracian and Persian practices of gift-giving (2.97.3–4) was motivated by contemporary war-time pre-occupations with Persian money (during the later part of the Peloponnesian War), rather than being an intended ethnographic comment. At any rate, Xenophon adds an important gloss to Thucydides' statement about Thracian gift-giving: 'Then one Gnesippos, an Athenian, arose and said that it was an ancient and most excellent custom that those who had possessions should give them to the king for honour's sake, and that to those who had nought, the king should give, "that so", he continued, "I too may be able to bestow gifts upon you and do you honour".[77]

We are entitled to conclude, on the basis of these different perspectives, that current research on Persian administrative archives suggests that we have even less reason than may previously have been thought to imagine an Achaemenid administrative area, a 'satrapy' on the European side of the Bosporus; that comparisons between Persian and Thracian administrative practice seem to have little substance, beyond broad regional and general structural resemblance; and that categorical claims about the ways in which rulers (Macedonian as well as Thracian) exercised power over their subjects are not substantiated. Royal powers were qualified in various ways—by social practice, as well as by traditional loyalties. What is more, analyses of social relations have tended to underestimate how the intensification of commercial interactions modified social practice, as the region became increasingly more accessible to a wider range of interest groups.

THE INFRASTRUCTURE OF REGIONAL TRADE

Salt

The infrastructure of trade relies on a substructure of subsistence and social practice. One of the most fundamental products that needed to be brought inland was salt. Under the peace terms negotiated by Aemilius Paullus, salt was banned as an import to Macedonia, although the

[76] Zournatzi 2000, 693–8, admits (695) that the common feature is the inscription of ownership; Archibald 1998, 318–35, App. 2; cf. SEG 47.1061, with several alternative, metaphysical interpretations of inscriptions from Duvanli, including *ΔΑΔΑΛΕΜΕ* δᾶ δάλε με = 'earth protect me'.

[77] Xen. *Anab.* 7.3.28 (tr. Stronk); Stronach and Zournatzi 2002; Miller 2010, 870–2; 874–8; Aperghis 1999 on Persian storehouses.

Dardanians of Upper Macedonia were allowed access to salt from the coast, which was taken to Stobi in Paionia (Liv. 45.29.12–13) for redistribution farther afield. The fact that Paullus put a price on it immediately suggests that there were revenue implications, so perhaps a tax on salt, or a monopoly on the sale of salt, had become a customary royal practice under the Argead kings.[78] Salt is an essential component of diet, although we need very little of it in practice to satisfy the basic biological requirement. Nevertheless, the distribution of salt represents one of the principal drivers of the increase in intra-regional exchange in Late Bronze Age continental Europe, a process that underwent a significant step change in the first millennium BC, when there was a veritable explosion in the demand for salt and salt products, which included preserved fish, particularly in the most highly populated parts of southern Europe and the Mediterranean.[79]

The salty 'limans' of the Pontic coast were among the major producers of salt and salted products for export and we have already seen how this specialization probably lay at the heart of the 'Monopoly War' between Kallatis and Byzantion over Tomis. However, not all domestic salt was produced from the evaporation of seawater. In inland areas of the east Balkan peninsula, toponyms that include the name 'Slatina' may hold further clues about sources of salt from brine springs.[80] On the north Aegean coast the lagoons east of Abdera created a number of interior lakes, including at least one salt lake, associated in Herodotus' account with the site of Pistyros (Hdt. 7.109.2).[81]

Rivers, routes, and roads

Besides salt, a great deal of bulk traffic, including building materials, mill stones, and cattle, as well as containers of wine, oil, nuts, and various dry

[78] Davies in *HellEc* I, 25; cf. Millett 2010, 482.

[79] This is the theme of Harding 2007 and Moinier 2007; Carusi 2007 and 2008 presents the Mediterranean perspective more systematically.

[80] Gaydarska and Chapman 2007 for Iron Age sources of salt in the east Balkan peninsula; 148 fig. 1 shows Slunchev Bryag, Obzor, Solnik, Mirovo and Topola as coastal sources; possible inland sources listed include: Slatino, Slatina, Biala Slatina (western Bulgaria); Rozovets, Goran Slatina, Maisko Lyubentsi, Ivanski, Malak Porovets (north-east Bulgaria); Gabrielsen 2011, 224–5 on salted products in the 'Monopoly War' of Byzantion; cf. Carusi 2008, 70–9, on Pontic salt; Byzantion as a chief centre for salt products: Str. 7.6.2 and Carusi 2008, 77–9 and nn. 82, 83, 84 [= Plb. 4.38.2–4].

[81] Carusi 2008, 67 (who uses this as evidence to deny the validity of Salviat's thesis that Pistyros and Pistiros were one and the same, but located in the interior of Thrace); Loukopoulou and Psoma 2008b, 67–71 on Lake Ismaris and the lagoons east of Abdera.

commodities, travelled by rivers. The availability of water transport is another of the key linking factors in our 'super-region'.[82] The Haliakmon and the Loudias Rivers, like the Axios, the Nestos, and the Hebros, were major arteries for goods travelling inland during the summer months, when the volume of water was sufficient for flat-bottomed boats and rafts, and quiet enough to make larger transports viable. The results of river traffic can often be recognized by extended distribution patterns, with distinct concentrations following their course and those of major tributaries.[83] What began perhaps as a system of regular boatloads of salt to particular regional nodes, distributed therefrom to other destinations, developed an increasingly varied range of components, as the existence of reasonably predictable consignments made it feasible to plan for other commodities that could travel with them.

Current research is beginning to illuminate the kinds of routes and roads that emerged during the first millennium BC prior to the expansion of metalled roads under Roman administration, which begins in the Balkans with the Via Egnatia. Most of the information acquired so far relates to the course of these roads, rather than to their structure and appearance. Paved surfaces are found in urban centres. Away from these foci, there is likely to have been a variety of surface materials, depending on terrain. Pre-Roman roads seem to have lacked a uniform character. In central and southern Greece, there are extensive traces of cart roads with parallel lines of stone.[84] In northern Greece, Yannis Pikoulas has expanded a project begun in the Peloponnese with an ambitious programme in the Pindhos range, using upland fortresses built in the time of Philip II as a primary set of orientation points, on the basis of which he has explored a series of six separate routes across the high Pindhos west of Grevena, to link up with the lowland roads more readily identified during archaeological surveys, particularly around Edessa and in the

[82] Chiverrell and Archibald 2009 on seasonal flows; see above, Ch. 4.

[83] Vardarski Rid: Mitrevski 2001; a river galley is shown on a Philippopolitan coin of Antoninus Pius: Mushmov no. 5115; the river god Hebros is a common reverse image on the city's bronze coins of the imperial period: Mushmov nos 340 (Domitian); 5065, 5067, 5116–120; 5125 (Antoninus Pius); 5177 (Hadrian); <www.wildwinds.com/moushmov/philippopolis.html>.

[84] Most recently Pikoulas in Korres 2009, 244–8, on roads for wheeled traffic—parallel rails/rail-like arrangement of slabs, 1.4 m apart; see also, in the same volume, A. Matthaiou, 22–33, epigraphic evidence on roads; on the road system of Attica, G. Steinhauer, 34–73, including a detailed description of roads, photographs from recent excavations, and consideration of construction techniques and historical value; see esp. 44–5, figs. 3.4 and 3.5: road Athens–Acharnai; 50–1 and figs 3.11–3.12, road to Marathon and adjacent buildings; 55, fig. 3.15, ancient road between Spata and Loutsas, running alongside the modern road.

environs of Pella.[85] Pikoulas has also investigated roads in the area of Mount Pangaion, partly for comparative purposes, including the possible routes of the Persian 'royal road'.[86] East of the Strymon, more than a century of work on Roman roads in the east Balkan area has been collated and developed by Mitko Madjarov, whose synthesis includes important remarks about routes throughout the region prior to the Roman network. In the Thracian Plain, as in Rhodope, there is plentiful evidence of the kinds of routes that preceded the formal planning of the Roman network. In the central plain, there is in many cases a close enough correspondence between the location of Iron Age sites and the lines of Roman roads to indicate the probable routes that existed, even when actual roads cannot be identified with certainty, particularly in view of changes in the bed of the River Hebros (Maritsa) dating to this very period.[87]

In Rhodope, there were three principal road routes to the Aegean, which have been studied with considerable confidence on the ground—a western one, from Bessapara (Sinitovo), west of Philippopolis, to Dospat, branching thence either westwards to Nicopolis ad Nestum and south to Philippoi, or south via Dospat in the direction of Drama; a central road, due south of Philippopolis, passing the Persenk peak (2,074 m), through modern Smolyan to the Drama plain; and an eastern road, through Assenovgrad and the Topolovo defile, past the peak of Sini Vruh (1,537 m), where it bent westwards in the vicinity of the Iron Age sites of Pavelsko and Luki, to resume a southerly course through Momchilgrad, in the direction of Abdera. All of these roads superseded earlier Iron Age routes through Rhodope.[88] In the higher mountain ranges these undoubtedly became mule tracks rather than roads.

Perhaps the most intriguing questions about roads focus on the references to the waiving of taxes on road traffic, as stipulated in the Pistiros inscription found as Asar dere, near Vetren, central Bulgaria (ll 20–21: *τέλεα κατὰ τὰς ὁδοὺς μὴ πρήσσειν*), and to the granting of safe conduct for the goods transported, with the *emporitai* having sole right to open and close their vehicles (*τὰς ἁμάξ/[ας] καὶ ἀνοίγειγ καὶ κλείειν*).

[85] Pikoulas 2007; cf. Pikoulas 2001; Edessa: Chrysostomou 2008; Pella: P. Chrysostomou 1990, 220 and fig. 226.

[86] Pikoulas 2001, 190–2; see further Ch. 6.

[87] Madzharov 2009, 87–124 (Bessapara to Augusta Traiana, via Philippopolis and Karasura); cf. Tonkova 2000, 140–2; for changes in the geomorphology of the River Hebros: Domaradzki in *Pistiros I,* 32–3 and fig. 1.18; Chiverrell and Archibald 2009.

[88] Madzharov 2009, 256–320 with numerous illustrations, esp. 265–9 for pre-Roman routes; cf. Bouzek in *Pistiros et Thasos*, 41–4 and fig. 3; Nekhrizov and Mikov 2000, 161–70; the eastern route has been identified with that taken by Alexander the Great in 335 BC.

The passage is opaque and requires some imagination to make sense of it. But the two components of the sentence must be understood as parts of a single statement—in other words, the phrase about taxation on roads is to be understood in direct connection with the statement about vehicles being opened. The gesture implied by this way of understanding the text, as Alexandru Avram has explained, would have been a key element in enabling commodities to make what amounts in this document to a guaranteed 'extra-territorial' journey 'to Maroneia from Pistiros, or from other *emporia*, or from Maroneia to Pistiros, or to the *emporia* Belana of the Prasenoi' (ll. 21–25), the first known instance of formal international commodity transportation.[89]

It is hardly surprising that the location of Pistiros has aroused so much discussion. Can it really have been located deep in central Thrace? Would it not make better sense if it were located somewhere in the Thasian *peraia,* nearer the coast of the Aegean? How can there be a *polis* in the heart of the continent of Europe?[90] These are the kinds of questions that have been asked about the place name itself, irrespective of where the stone was discovered. The arguments about status once again resemble wider discussions about *poleis.* One of the best analogies to Pistiros is Naukratis in Egypt, which was also a large trading centre within a kingdom. Naukratis became a *polis* in the fourth century BC.[91] On the other hand, Pistiros is unlike Egypt, because there were many historic links that encouraged institutional parity amongst trading partners. The long-term proximity and interactions that are implied by networks of exchange from the Bronze Age onwards in south-eastern Europe make it much more likely that the kinds of distinctions contemporary historians make amongst the ethnic communities of the

[89] Avram 1997/98, 41; Chankowski and Domaradzka 1999, for the revised text, and Domaradzka in *Pistiros II*, 339–42 for further addenda.

[90] For a discussion of the various arguments, see *Dossier Pistiros;* (Fr. Salviat argues that the findspot of the inscription requires us to locate the Pistyros referred to by Herodotos (7.109) in central Thrace, rather than along the north Aegean coastal strip (*BCH* 123, 270), and even attributes membership of the Delian League to the same community by identifying it with the 'Kystirioi' of the Tribute Lists). B. Bravo and A. Chankowski, on the other hand, affirm that the epigraphically attested Pistiros is a *polis*, but deny that it has anything to do with the archaeological remains at Adjiyska Vodenitsa (*BCH* 123, 275–317). The other contributors to the volume, V. Chankowski and L. Domaradzka (247–58), K. Bošnakov (319–29), O. Picard (331–46), L. Domaradzka (347–58), and L. Loukopoulou (359–71), accept the identification of the latter with the epigraphic Pistiros. Salviat was not aware of some more recent investigations of Persian movements in Thrace when he compiled his article (e.g. Archibald 1998, 79–90); Archibald 2002a; Archibald (forthcoming a/; Chankowski 2010.

[91] Bresson 2000, 74–84.

region have more to do with modern preoccupations about identities than they do with ancient institutional practice. Ancient perceptions of differences between Greeks and non-Greeks in the north refer mainly to those aspects of cultural practice where differences were much more specific, such as attitudes to authority and commemoration, not in terms of representative bodies or in exchange mechanisms.

Markets and currencies

Since commercial transactions during the first millennium BC were normally bilateral, confirmed by signs and symbols of 'ritualized' friendship,[92] what we would expect to find is evidence of reciprocal relations and this is what the variety of coin types at major hubs seems to represent. At Nebet Tepe, the hilltop sanctuary and trading centre in the middle of Plovdiv (ancient Philippopolis), there are silver coins from various cities of Chalkidike, the lower Strymon valley, and beyond, as far as the Straits. The earliest issues of the late sixth to fourth centuries BC read like a roll-call of the main coastal trading harbours of the region: Akanthos; the 'satyr and nymph' issues of Thasos and Thasian imitations; coins of Neapolis; Dikaia by Abdera; Abdera itself; Maroneia, Orthagoreia, Ainos, Selymbria, the Thracian Chersonese, Parion, Kyzikos, Amisos; and beyond, Thebes, Athens, Aegina, Apollonia Pontika, and Istros. In the later fourth and third centuries BC, these were joined by numerous coins of Macedonian monarchs, by Pantikapaion, Kallatis, Histiaia, and the various 'new style' second-century BC issues of Athens, Thasos, Mesambria, the First Macedonian district, the magistrate Aesillas, and Mithridates Eupator, reflecting the progressive transformation of the economic drivers from the Aegean powers to Rome.[93] This panorama of contacts reflects the rather complicated structure of exchange, requiring specific agreements between specific community agents in order for transactions to be validated. The range of coins enumerated at Nebet Tepe is indicative of the general trend, rather than being a full reflection of transactions.

The finds consist almost entirely of silver and some gold coins, supplemented by a number of copper alloy ones. The proportions do not correspond to what we would expect in a commercial centre, but rather to the tastes and priorities of collectors. There are far too few copper alloy issues in proportion to silver ones. The reasons are not hard

92 On *xenia*-type friendships: Gauthier 1972; Herman 1987.

93 Kisiov et al. 1998, 10–33; Philippopolis: *Inventory*, no. 655.

to find. Gold and silver coins have value today and stimulate interest. Copper alloy coins have, historically speaking, rarely been attractive to collectors and certainly not to the same degree as precious metals. On the other hand, the presence of relatively large denominations suggests that the kinds of transactions taking place were connected with significant quantities of the commodities exchanged. The evidence from Nebet Tepe seems to reflect periodic visits by merchants, who were interested in big transactions.

The value that might be derived from this kind of evidence in the northern Aegean has so far been explored in a rather limited way, despite good evidence of widespread distribution patterns and other indicators of economic relations, extending in time and space during the period covered by this book. Figure 5.3 shows the distribution of coins in the east Balkans emanating from the Thracian Chersonese.[94] The hemidrachms of the Chersonese have been found as far north as Botevgrad and Loukuvit, well north of the Balkan range; and as far west as the headwaters of the Hebros, as well as a large number of places in between, along the middle Hebros valley. They often occur alongside similar denominations from Parion. We know that ambassadors from Parion were busy courting king Amadokos in 400 BC (Xen. *Anab.* 7.2.7, 3.17). So it is perhaps no surprise to find coins from these two cities so widely distributed. Three examples of markets present us with a range of possible scenarios for market-type transactions.

Pella

The first example is Pella. The *agora* at Pella provides a wealth of information about public and commercial activity over considerable periods of time, although these were brought to an end abruptly (by an earthquake, according to the excavators) because of the interrupted character of final activities—the quantities of terracotta statuettes 'ready for sale', as well as moulds and tableware in a destruction layer that evidently represents structural damage.[95] The *agora* consisted of an almost square piece of ground (261.7 m x 238 m), built over sloping terrain with an

[94] Archibald 1998, 126–35, with Table 5.1, figs. 5.1–5.2, 312–13 and fig. 13.1, for a preliminary assessment of numismatic finds; cf. Taneva 2000 (coins from excavations at Adjiyska Vodenitsa); Nekhrizov and Mikov 2000, 161–70, with cognate issues in eastern Rhodope.

[95] Lilimbaki-Akamati and Akamatis 2003, 40–51; Akamatis 2006a, 615–26; Akamatis 2011, 402–3; Akamatis 2012, 49, with full references; 49–59, with a more detailed exposition.

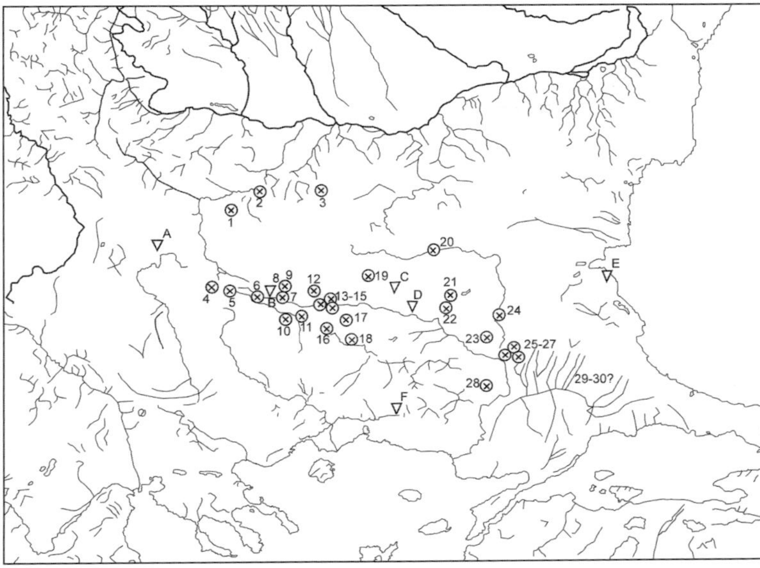

settlements

A	Pernik
B	Pistiros
C	Malko Trunovo
D	Yablkovo
E	Apollonia
F	Lenos

hoards

1 Botevgrad	CHVIII, No.136
2 Lyukovit	IGCH 393
3 Lovech	IGCH 392
4 Raduil	IGCH 737
5 Kostenets	CH VIII, No.109
6 Vinogradets	IGCH 743
7 Boshulya	Yourukova 1982, 62
8 Pamidovo	IGCH 735
9 Pamidovo	IGCH 736
10 Bratsigovo	Yurukova 1985, 58
11 Rozovo	Yurukova 1985, 58
12 Syedinenye	IGCH 750
13 Plovdiv	IGCH 749
14 Plovdivsko	CH VIII, No.171
15 Plovdivsko	Dimitrov 1989, 26
16 Gorni Voden	IGCH 748
17 Mominsko	IGCH 741
18 Dolnoslav	Dimitrov 1989, 26
19 Gorno Novo selo	IGCH 751
20 Dabovo	IGCH 757
21 Troyanovo	IGCH 753
22 Obruchishte	Draganov 1981, 36
23 Sladun	IGCH 740
24 Granitovo	IGCH 761
25 Edirne	CH III, No. 17
26 Edirne, environs	IGCH 744
27 Edirne	IGCH 745
28 Didymoteicheion	IGCH 739
29 Thrace	IGCH 738
30 southern Bulgaria	IGCH 746

Fig. 5.3. Distribution of coins from the Thracian Chersonese (second half of the fourth century BC).

inclination from north-east to south-west, which necessitated terracing of the structures behind a central piazza, which measures 200.15 m by 181.76 m. There was a Doric colonnade on the south wing, faced by a line of stone piers on the north wing. Shops and offices lined the back of the colonnades, built of unbaked bricks on stone foundations, liberally roofed with timber and Lakonian-type tiles, some of which are stamped *ΒΑΣΙΛΙΚΟΣ* or *ΠΕΛΛΗΣ*, although other stamps have also been recorded. An elaborate system of pipes and drains carried waste water under the walls and surrounding roadways, while fresh water was supplied from wells.

Study of particular areas of the *agora* suggests medium-term association between certain crafts and certain areas or structures. Pottery manufacture and sale was concentrated on the southern part of the east wing, while farther north were stalls selling terracottas. The southern wing seems to have been reserved for fresh food, particularly liquid products; stalls for butchers and fishmongers have also been suggested. The southern part of the west wing housed imported pottery and lamps. Metalworking, including some evidence of work in precious metals, judging by the presence of litharge (from cupellation of lead), was practised on the outskirts of the precinct, where moulds and slag have been found at the east end of the south wing. A large section of the wing seems to have been occupied by stores of dry goods, including grains and flour. Wells in the southern wing contained waste material from pottery, metalworking, and food, including olive pits, walnut shells, chestnut husks, grape pips, and various seeds.

The north *stoa* evidently housed the main administrative quarters, including a hall with a Doric colonnade in the centre, where a large statue base occupied a prominent position, and at least one inscription listing the names of civic magistrates was on display, as well as various offices and cult chambers to either side. Clay seals from papyrus documents, bearing a club and an eight-pointed star, and inscribed (of) PELLA/(of the) POLITARCHS (*ΠΕΛΛΗΣ/ΠΟΛΙΤΑΡΧΩΝ*), point to what must have been the city's principal administrative archive. In addition to this northern suite of rooms with administrative functions, there was a separate building in the south-west corner of the *agora*, which may have been a purpose-built headquarters for the city's commercial magistrates. It had a central peristyle, supported by Doric columns and Ionic piers. Within the destruction layer from the collapsed rooms facing the colonnade was a collection of clay sealings, showing a grazing cow, some of which also bore the inscription *Pellis/emporiou*, or the names of civic magistrates. Besides the sealings there were writing materials, including ink-wells and pens, as well as a stone stamp seal and fresh clay.

The excavators have so far provided a vivid portrait of the most distinctive features of the last days of Pella's main commercial hub and full publication will provide us with a more complete understanding. What is interesting about this manifestly purpose-built complex is the close proximity of workshops (metalsmiths, coroplasts), with sellers of fresh food. Stone masons, timber merchants, charcoal sellers, tanners, and similar insalubrious crafts are more likely to have been located farther away from the *agora*.[96] The products of commerce recovered from the excavation of the *agora* itself are closely tied to the period immediately preceding the market's destruction: trade *amphorae* from Rhodes, Knidos, Kos, Thasos, Akanthos, and Chios predominate among Aegean imports, alongside others from Brindisi, Latium, southern Italy, and North Africa. Akamatis' earlier examination of the proportions of stamped *amphora* handles produced a rather different distribution profile at Pella, with 32.8 per cent of the total represented by Rhodian vessels, 23 per cent Thasian, 20 per cent from the 'Parmeniskos' group (whether these originated in Mende or elsewhere in Aegean Thrace); and 12.5 per cent Knidian.[97] The coins associated with the ceramic and other metal finds in the *agora* included a substantial number of copper alloy issues, both those issued by Macedonian kings, and a wide range of civic issues; while among the silver money coins, issues in the names of Philip II and Alexander III predominated, with some in the name of the Paionian king, Audoleon. Among the latest coins were Roman issues and a hoard of 'new style' Attic tetradrachms, dated in the late 90s BC. The range of civic issues may well tell us more about the specific commercial links between Pella and merchants or trades people from other Aegean and east Balkan communities. The data published so far merely hints at these.

The sealings at Pella depict a cow—the manifest sign of one of the area's most prominent forms of livestock, and projected in another of the city's names, *Βούνομος*, or *Βουνόμεια* (St. Byz. 515.7–8). Where then was the cattle market? Presumably this, like the 'dirtier' activities already referred to, was located farther away from the residential streets. The high level of planning in the city's centre underscores the abstract importance of the *agora*—as a focus for civic expertise and strategic planning. Surely the *agora* was not built for the sale of cakes and terracottas? The scale of the square's architectural elaboration implies that it served political as well as commercial purposes, managerial ones, rather than the quite modest retail functions of its latter years.

Pistiros and Krastevich

The people of Pistiros, the Pistirenoi, are referred to in an inscription carved on granite and found reused at the Roman *mansio*, known from

[96] Billot 1992 on tanners in Athens.

[97] Akamatis 2000, 193–213; Akamatis 2012, 57–8, for chronological evidence of the *agora*'s destruction in the late 90s BC.

Fig. 5.4. Adjiyska Vodenitsa, identified with ancient Pistiros: approach to the eastern gateway from inside the city (looking north-east). The square external tower is behind the western threshold slab of the city gate in the centre, the roadway on its right, and the northern stretch of the fortification wall on the centre left

late antique itineraries as Bona Mansio, 2 km north–east of the river port at Adjiyska Vodenitsa (Hadji's water mill), near Vetren, a small, picturesque, modern town in the foothills of the Sredna Gora (Fig. 5.4). The local geography of the western end of the Thracian Plain in central Bulgaria has been altered by radical changes in the riverbed of the Maritsa (Hebros) River, which have resulted in a flat alluvial plain. This gives little hint of the ancient activities that took place on its banks. The late antique *mansio* was positioned on a spur overlooking the Roman road between Byzantion and Serdica, on the northern bank of the river. Below these foothills, successive braids have formed when the river has cut a new course. These successive cuts have destroyed ancient riverside structures, including much of the pre-Roman settlement at Adjiyska Vodenitsa, whose remains continue to be eroded by the river.[98] The surviving traces of an urban centre are preserved on either side of the eastern gateway, together with adjoining sections of a

[98] Chiverrell and Archibald 2009.

powerful two-faced masonry fortification wall, which protected a dense concentration of structures, including one (Building no. 1) that evidently had administrative functions, rather like the south-west building in the *agora* at Pella. Large numbers of coins, especially copper alloy but also silver coins, lead weights, and commercial scales were found there. Many structures had tiled roofs. Some of the tiles were locally made, whilst others (including tiles stamped with the letter 'A') were shipped upriver from south-eastern Thrace. Commercial *amphorae* from Chios, Thasos, Herakleia, and the centres producing vessels of the so-called 'Parmeniskos' group were certainly intended for local consumption, but others were evidently distributed to centres north of the Hebros that were not accessible by river. Relative percentages, as at Pella, are based on stamped handles rather than quantified ceramics, and the period in question spans the second half of the fifth to the second half of the third century BC.[99]

Imported ceramic provides an indicator of consumption in the first place, but it is also one sort of yardstick, albeit an indirect one, of commercial patterns. At Adjiyska Vodenitsa trade patterns are reflected in many other ways too. Metallurgical waste, as well as moulds, tools, and finished metal items, in precious as well as base metals, indicates the production of a wide variety of articles on-site, of which at least some were intended for sale and export. The unusual range of artefact styles suggests that there was a ferment of creativity at the heart of this exchange centre.[100]

Graffiti from Adjiyska Vodenitsa show that the inhabitants came from a variety of backgrounds. There are Greek names of broad geographical distribution, Ionian, Macedonian, and Thracian names.[101] The range of coins found here points to a similar variety of visitors and local or regional agents, with local representatives identifiable behind the Thracian regal issues, the most regular visitors shown by Thasian, Parian, Maronitan, and Chersonesian issues, which are among the commonest in silver and bronze. More occasional issues, such as those of Ainos, Kypsela, Sermyle, Kardia, Lysimacheia, Apollonia, and Mesambria

[99] Tušlova et al. 2010, 205–9; cf. also Bouzek et al. 2007; Tzochev 2007 on Pontic *amphorae* at Adjiyska Vodenitsa; Lawall 2005 on the problems of using statistics based only on *amphora* stamps; Taneva 2011 summarizes the evidence from the extra-mural ceramic kiln.

[100] See esp. Lazov, *Pistiros II*, 243–8, on bronze *toreutics*; Domaradzki in *Pistiros II*, 249–54, on 'Celtic' type *fibulae*; Bouzek in *Pistiros IV*, 221–2, for a distinctly 'northern' bronze appliqué of a lion; Archibald 1998, 138–41 (Adjiyska Vodenitsa) and more generally, 222–26, 260–81 for further comments about styles and tastes.

[101] Domaradzka 2002; 2005; 2007; Domaradzka and Domaradzki 1999.

Pontika, point to other commercial travellers.[102] As I have argued above, the mechanisms for ensuring the supply of any commodity meant that every community had to look after its own interests. For periods after the mid fourth century BC, when Macedonian coins progressively became available and widely disseminated, it becomes harder to connect specific users and to map their activities spatially. Individual coins can, of course, only be interpreted as indirect evidence for the movement of people. Yet, as we have seen, we can detect in the countermarks on coins the financial decisions of various authorities operating in the hinterland of Byzantion during the final two centuries BC, whether these were small civic entities or princes.

Apart from the hemidrachms of the Chersonese, which succeeded a not dissimilar, albeit less numerous, distribution of Cyzicene staters, one of the pre-Macedonian coin types that enjoyed a particularly wide outreach were the 'satyr and nymph' silver staters and drachmae of Thasos, or imitations of them. Examples have been recovered not just at sites in relative proximity to Thasos, but also from known, but comparatively distant centres of exchange, such as Vardarski Rid, near Gevgelija, FYROM, considered by its investigators to be one of the chief centres of Paionian authority, and Krastevich, a Thracian settlement and sanctuary in the foothills of the Sredna Gora, east of Strelcha.[103] Visual and scientific analyses of selected coins show that some, perhaps many, were not made on behalf of Thasians. Imitations could be copied to boost the supply of particularly popular monetary media; they might also be deliberate attempts to copy good coins using a different alloy. How imitations should be evaluated as valid media of exchange depends on whether rival issues were acceptable to different authorities. In modern contexts, the deliberate falsification of coinage is treated as a criminal offence, in order to discourage crime and to protect the monopolies of issuing authorities; but a moderate level of falsification is tolerated, in the case of coined money at least. At Athens the acceptance of false coins masquerading as Athenian ones by the official responsible for verifying coinage was a punishable offence, not least because of the well known

[102] Taneva 2000; the range and number of coins have increased appreciably since this publication, with the current total close to 2,000 coins, of which the hoard of *c.*280–78 BC comprises 552. De Callataÿ's table of published coins from excavations provides a broad scale of comparison, with Athens at the top (12,676 coins). The combined figure for Olynthos is 4,992 coins and Seuthopolis 1,305. Most published coin catalogues from excavated Greek sites have produced less than 1,000. De Callataÿ discusses the variable rate of survival over time (2006b, 179–91).

[103] Cyzicene staters: Archibald 1998, 126–35, for distribution and further refs; Picard 2000 for Thasian types; Vardarski Rid: Husenovski 2002; for Krastevich, see above n.16.

purity of Attic silver money. However, this does not mean that false coins were not accepted in other transactions. The existence of the regulations strongly suggests that false coins circulated freely.[104] The wide dissemination of 'imitation' Thasian issues reflects the widespread acceptability of the types, but does not tell us who made them. What matters is that they were acceptable as a medium of exchange and the occurrence of such coins in limited quantities, over a wide area, seems to be consistent with such an interpretation.

Investigations at Krastevich, a fifth- to fourth-century BC settlement nestling in the foothills of the Sredna Gora mountains, has, in the space of a few excavation seasons, produced surprising and unique features that force us to rethink what was happening deep in the interior of southern Europe. The investigations have focused in two locations, a terrace above the River Pyasechnik (Pamuk Tepe), and a hilltop (Sekiz Harman), *c.*1 km to the north-east, high above it. At Pamuk Tepe, and in an area *c.*50 m by 90 m, a number of structures with rubble stone foundations have been revealed, including two large multi-roomed building complexes, at least one of which had very well-built outer walls and inner staircases to an upper floor level (Fig. 5.5). The overall

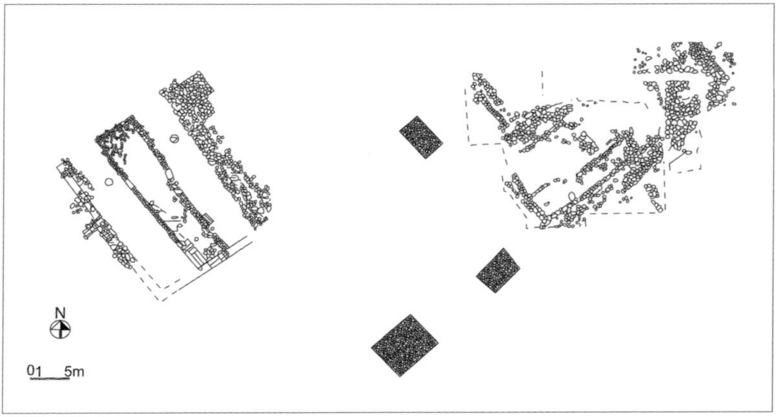

Fig. 5.5. Krastevich, near Strelcha, Bulgaria, plan of part of the town, showing the storage complex (left).

[104] Van Alfen 2005, 322–38, on Nikophon's law in Athens (SEG 26.72) and imitations of Attic coins; he distinguishes issues in terms of 'prototypes', 'artistic imitations', 'marked' imitations (those with an obvious distinguishing mark or countermark); perfunctory imitations, plated or debased coins and, finally, counterfeit coins. Most of these categories can be identified in the east Balkans.

plan of this building, with three long, narrow rooms and a stone waste-water channel (perhaps associated with industrial processes), resembles a well-protected storage block. Finds of storage *amphorae* and non-local coins (late fifth-century BC tetradrachms of Ainos and a pot hoard, containing silver coins of Thasos, Kyzikos, and Aegean Neapolis; issues of Apollonia and Mesambria), likewise indicate strong external commercial relations. The quality of the moveable finds, including metal ornaments and imported Attic fine ware, reinforce this impression. Yet none of these features prepares us for what was constructed on the hill above (Fig. 5.6). A limestone stylobate of almost square form, made up of well-finished ashlars, supported a stone colonnade, carved from cylindrical drums. The excavator, Mitko Madjarov, interprets this as the foundation for a sanctuary. It evidently had two phases, with a granite foundation of large masonry blocks in its refashioning. This does look like a temple, or temple-like structure. Although there are carved columns inside funerary monuments in various parts of the region, nothing in pre-Roman Thrace resembles this highly ambitious plan, which is hard to reach even now. Why such a monument was built high up in the hills above the Thracian Plain is one of the questions that future research at this site will grapple with.

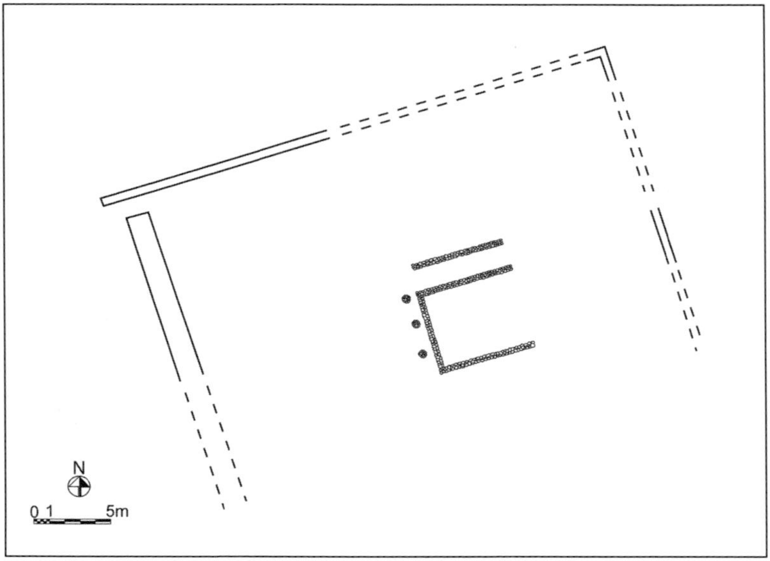

Fig. 5.6. Krastevich, near Strelcha, Bulgaria, plan of the upland sanctuary.

If merchants really were travelling so far inland, what were they hoping to take back in the opposite direction? The most plausible explanation is refined or bar metal. As I have argued in Chapter 4, the extraction of metals was a highly specialized skill, while mining and metallurgy were among the activities that indigenous groups had invested in over many centuries. The hills on the north-western margins of the Thracian Plain, north of Plovdiv, are rich in metals and the rivers are gold-bearing. Local place names reflect these prominent resources, particularly those referring to gold and iron. Besides these high-value items, cattle, or cattle products, particularly pelts, skins, and leather, might also have been added from a region well stocked with herds, as well as other foodstuffs. The northern tributaries of the River Hebros provided a ready means of transportation of bulk goods during the summer months, though an alternative overland route also existed to Adjiyska Vodenitsa and other sites along the Hebros, and thence either downstream or through Rhodope.

The whole region created by the triangle of land between the Sredna Gora range, the Klisoura defile (at the western end of the Thracian Plain) and the middle valley of the River Hebros around Plovdiv constitutes an intense concentration of high-value, prestige monuments and moveable artefacts in the period between the fifth and third centuries BC. These forms of local consumption reflect the products of inter-regional exchange patterns on a substantial scale. There are similar concentrations in the Valley of the Roses, in south-eastern Thrace (in the area around Kirklareli),[105] and in the combined regions of Emathia and Pieria, in lower Macedonia. All these particular regional concentrations coincided with the principal seats of princes and kings. The physical manifestations of significant consumption partly reflect the exploitation of regional resources and in part the concentration of royal and princely funds.

Byzantion—a major hub of northern commerce

Our third example is Byzantion (Fig. 5.7).[106] The irresistible rise of this city, long before it was chosen as the New Rome by the Emperor Constantine, has somehow escaped the kind of attention from classical historians that its wealth and strategic importance surely deserve. Almost all histories of Constantinople begin with Constantine, not with the city

[105] See further Ch. 8. [106] *Inventory* no. 674, pp. 915–18.

Fig. 5.7. Istanbul, view of the Bosporus from Topkapi palace, the heart of the ancient city of Byzantion.

of Byzantion itself and no monograph on Byzantion has been written since V. P. Newskaja's, originally published in Russian in 1953.[107] The scholarly and comparative evidence collected in the *Inventory of Archaic and Classical Poleis* helps to redress this strange imbalance. Byzantion can, as a result, resume its place among the truly exceptional city-states of the fifth and fourth centuries BC, alongside Athens, Sparta, and Syracuse. The territory controlled by the city of Byzantion in this period (estimated by Loukopoulou and Łajtar as *c.*1500 km^2), extended from a north-western frontier on Lake Derkos, a famous fishing lake in close proximity to the Black Sea coast, to the River Athyras (Kara Su), and along the Athyras lake (Büyükcekmeçe) in the south.[108] How and when the city acquired such extensive territory is not certain. According to Ps.-Skymnos (722–23), Byzantine territory included the locality Phileas, or Philia, in the north, on a promontory extending into the Black Sea. To the north it bordered land controlled by Thracian dynasts (Plb. 4.45.1);

[107] Newskaja 1955; Loukopoulou and Łajtar (2004) provide an up to date point of reference, but Isaac's chapter on Byzantion (1986, 215–37) is still a useful account and commentary; Robinson 2011, 146–9, reconsiders the city's constitutional structure with reference to Aristotle's statements (and their economic dimensions) about democracy at Byzantion.

[108] Str. 7.6.1, p. 319 and fr. 56; Pl. *NH* 4.46; Pompon. 2.24; Isaac 1986, 232–3 on territorial matters.

to the south-west, Byzantine land bordered that of Selymbria.[109] Most of the ancient sources that provide specific details belong to the city's post-classical history. There are sufficient pointers, nevertheless, in pre-Hellenistic sources to indicate just how significant the city had become by the time it was besieged (unsuccessfully) by Philip II of Macedon.[110] Xenophon's sojourn in the hinterland of Byzantion provides only incidental details that fail to emphasize the city's real territorial capacity. Moreover, its reach extended not just inland, but (periodically, at first) across into Asia. The city took possession of Kalchedon in the middle of the fourth century (Dem. 15.26).

In the fifth century, the city's fortunes were variable. The Hellespontine region was perceived as a major asset by the Persians, who hoped, perhaps, to hang on to it after their retreat from most of the European mainland (Hdt. 9.101), but were in the end forced out, step by step, at the hands of the Delian League. In the middle of the fifth century BC the city had liquidity problems and created a range of new sources of revenue by leasing sacred land and land belonging to private associations, selling off shop spaces, or fishing and salt-collecting rights, as well as offering citizenship for 30 minas to those with one citizen parent ([Ar.] *Oec.* II.3c, 1346b).[111] In the *Politics* (1291b 21), Aristotle talks about the high proportion of fishermen amongst the population of the city, a factor that, in the philosopher's view, affected the political climate of Byzantion, much as the rowers of the Athenian fleet affected that city's politics. Theopompos, on the other hand, talked about the propensity of the inhabitants of such a major *emporion* to gravitate in the direction of the market place and the harbour, lingering in the wine shops.[112]

The propensity of Byzantines to focus their energies on activities in and around the harbour reflects the importance of the Golden Horn as a centre of transhipment as well as regional exchange and, at the same time, the capacity of any authority located there to exploit the unique opportunity to extract revenues from those passing through the channel between the Bosporus and the Hellespontine Straits. Nothing illustrates this more vividly than the capture of the Athenian grain fleet in 340 BC by Philip II of Macedon, whilst he was besieging the city of Byzantion. This consisted of 180 ships, the dominant part of a convoy of 320 vessels, evidently transporting various other goods—incidentally a useful

[109] *Inventory*, no. 679.

[110] Diod. 16.76.3–4; 77.2; Justin 9.1.2–4; Dem. 8.14, 18.88–92; 244; Plut. *Phoc.* 14.3–7; Gabrielsen 2007, 295.

[111] Isaac 1986, 233–4; Nixon and Price 1990, 153–4; Robinson 2011, 146–9.

[112] Theop. *FGrH* 115 F62 = Athen. 12.32, p. 526 D–F.

indication of the level of trade in other commodities along this route. The convoy was assembled at Hieron, a harbour on the Asiatic shore at the northern end of the Bosporus.[113] Hieron provided the principal shelter at the entrance to the Bosporus, allowing ships passing out of the Black Sea to wait for favourable winds for the southward passage. It was never much more than a harbour with a sanctuary. Control of the harbour was exercised primarily by warships, which were at this time under Athenian control.[114] Philip not only seized the ships, but sold their cargoes—the grain, hides or live animals, timber, and other materials—whose value realized the eye-watering sum of 700T in cash for the Macedonian king.[115]

The incident was as significant in local terms as it was in international perspectives. Although Philip's success was the result of a ruse, it demonstrated that the size of the Athenian navy was no longer effective in setting the terms on which the transit trade operated through the Bosporus. After 340 BC the Athenians effectively ceased to be competitors for naval supremacy of the north-east Aegean.[116] This left the commercial control of the Bosporus almost exclusively to the Byzantines, although the shores and channel itself continued to be a focus for occasional military confrontations.[117] It is not easy to appreciate what this meant in terms of shipping. There is little surviving information directly relating to the city's naval capacity. The putative beneficiaries of the convoy seized by Philip would have included the Athenians, Byzantines, Rhodians, and Chiots.[118] During the third century BC, the Byzantines were reluctant to get involved in inter-state encounters outside the Bosporus and the Hellespontine Straits. Byzantine naval vessels are mentioned in the battle of Chios against Philip V of Macedon, alongside Rhodians and other, unnamed ships.[119]

[113] Theop. *FGrH* 115 F292; Philoch. *FGrH* 392 F162; Just. 9.1.1–6; Front. *Strat.* 1.4.13; *HM* II, 576; Bresson 2000b, 132–3, 277–8; Gabrielsen 2007, 295–6; 306–7 Moreno 2008, 668–9; the most specific and nuanced explanation of what occurred is contained in Didymus' *Commentary on Demosthenes,* 11.1, cols 10.34–11.5 (= T22 in Moreno 2008, 688–9).

[114] Moreno 2008, for a detailed discussion of the topography and history of the site.

[115] Gabrielsen 2007, for detailed discussion of the sums, esp. 295–7.

[116] Oliver 2007, 68–73, 169–71, 194–7, on Athenian naval activities in the Aegean during the third century BC.

[117] Such as occurred between Antigonos I's admiral, Nikanor, and Polyperchon's naval commander, Kleitos (Polyaen. *Strat.* 4.6.8 = Moreno 2008, 696, T38).

[118] Bresson 2000b, 131–3, discusses the composition of the grain fleet of 340 BC.

[119] Dumitru (2006, 147–52, esp. 148) discusses the passage in Plb. 16.1.10, where Byzantine vessels are included amongst the 65 enemy ships ranged against Philip V in the battle of Chios. There may have been about 20–25, perhaps 30 Rhodian vessels

The Aegean scope of Byzantine activity gives little indication of where the city's naval strength really lay. In order to understand this, we must get behind the story of Philip's capture of the convoy of ships through the Bosporus. The combined evidence of the different Greek historical and forensic sources on this incident, which are given particular coherence by a relevant passage in the *Commentary on Demosthenes* of Didymus, make it clear that ships were regularly convoyed through the channel and the Hellespontine Straits, in order to avoid the kind of arbitrary seizure along this route that Philip's capture in 340 BC represented. Gabrielsen has argued that the *sitopompeia,* the convoying of grain and other commercial transports, had become a more or less regular way in which ships crossing the Straits and Bosporus to the Black Sea arrived at Byzantion, particularly if they had to wait for favourable winds before proceeding northwards from there.[120] Similarly, convoys gathered at Hieron on the return leg of the journey, to be escorted back into the Hellespont.[121] The duty of escort was undertaken by Athenian ships in the fifth and fourth centuries. Thereafter, Byzantion probably took over the same kinds of functions. The cost of such protection came to be built into the budget of bottomry loans (Dem. 35. 10–13). The forensic speeches of Demosthenes contain frequent references to the hindering of merchant vessels (*ta ploia kōluein*) and the actual commandeering of merchant ships to unplanned harbours.[122] The passage from the Hellespontine Straits to the Bosporus became a bottleneck for ships, which were obliged to follow the winds and currents peculiar to these shores. In Chapter 43 of Book 4 in his *Histories,* Polybius describes how the currents flow in a zigzag manner from the Bosporus in the direction of Byzantion, making it easy for ships to stop off at the latter and difficult to dock at Chalkedon. The historian's account at this point of his narrative is entirely focused on the behaviour of waves, currents, ships, and natural features of the shoreline. He refers to the sanctuary of Zeus (Ourios) at Hieron and to the Hermaion on the European side, north of Byzantion. These more contextual details are woven into a reflection on the gradual silting up of the shorelines adjacent to the Black Sea and Maiotic Sea (the Sea of Azov), which diverts from the principal subject in this part of Book 4, namely the extraordinary success of Byzantion and its highly

(Dumitru 2006, 147 with further refs). The role of the Byzantine ships is otherwise unknown, although a number of Byzantine sailors, perhaps including an admiral, were voted honours at Athens; Dittenberger and others have dated these in connection with the events at Chios: Dittenberger, *SIG* ^{2} II, 580 = *IG* II^{2} 884 (ibid. 150).

120 Gabrielsen 2007, 299–311.

121 Moreno 2008, 646–70.

122 Dem. 17.19–21 (337 BC); Gabrielsen 2007, 311–13, with discussion.

advantageous position (Plb. 4.38.1–8). The strong maritime focus of Polybius' account, as well as its nice political perspectives, would suggest that he was drawing directly on a Rhodian source.[123]

The historian, who is here referring to the situation some one hundred years later, *c.*220 BC, goes on to say that if the Byzantines had allied themselves in the past with the Gauls, or, at the present time, with the Thracians, then they (the Byzantines) would not be, as indeed they were, the benefactors of all the Greeks. Polybius was being economical with the truth. The sort of control created by the Byzantines over the Straits was a benefit to merchants but at significant cost. The market-based economy of the import and export trade in grain and other commodities through the Straits represents only one aspect of the investment costs for merchants and ships' captains, who were also obliged to pay the 'protection' costs of the predatory arm of this exchange process, which operated in strict synergy with the commercial one.[124]

The origins of the predatory component in these relationships lie in the measures set up by Athenian officials in the aftermath of the Greco-Persian Wars, in order to secure the Straits for the Greek allies. The Byzantines were among the 'big spenders' amongst Athens' allies. The tribute that they paid to the Athenians on behalf of the League in the fifth century BC varied, but it was never less than 15T (the amount paid in 450/49 BC), whilst in 430 BC this tipped 21T. If we add to this the sum paid to the Athenians for tolls through the Hellespont, collected by local tax-farmers, then this could have raised the overall amount paid to Athens up to between 41T and 50T.[125] When such tolls came into existence is obscure. The evidence for tolls rests on the ten per cent tax, the *dekate*, referred to in the so-called first Kallias decree (IG I^3 52A = ML *GHI* 58A.7, variously dated to 434/3 or 431 BC), and in any case earlier than the similarly-named tax in Xenophon's *Hellenika*.[126] Xenophon describes how Alkibiades sailed to Chrysopolis in 410/9 BC, then a locality in the control of Kalchedon, on the coast opposite Byzantion (identified with modern Üsküdar), fortified it, and set up a toll station (*dekateuterion*). Gabrielsen argues, persuasively, that there was an earlier toll, operating in a similar way, originally located at Byzantion. But when the city fell into Spartan hands, in 411 BC, the Athenians lost control of their toll-raising powers until the city was regained as an Athenian

[123] Will *Histoire Politique II* ^{2}, 47.

[124] Gabrielsen 2007, 297.

[125] Loukopoulou and Łajtar 2004, 916, collect the evidence; Gabrielsen 2007, 296, with detailed discussion.

[126] Xen. *Hell.* 1.1.22 (for 410/9 BC); cf. Diod. 13.64.2–3; Polyb. 4.44. 3–4.

dependency by the same Alkibiades, in 408 BC (Thuc. 8.80.3; Xen. *Hell.* 1.3.15). Not so Kalchedon, which, save for the year when Alkibiades kept control of that part of the Asiatic coastline, passed into Spartan control. References to the *dekate* reappear in early fourth-century BC sources, but it is not clear whether they refer to the Hellespontine toll, or to other revenues raised in a similar way.[127] At any rate, the Hellespontine *dekate* was the best known toll of this kind (Dem. 20.60; 23.177), while the need to provide protection for ships in the Straits was already apparent at the time of the Greco-Persian Wars, and recognized by the Athenians in the appointment of 'guards', the *Hellespontophylakes*, who acted as military policemen, based at Byzantion.[128]

In the third century BC, Rhodes became the city's dominant Aegean partner. So the attempt to reintroduce the toll at the Bosporus, which the Rhodians interpreted as a direct blow to their commercial interests, became the lightning rod for a declaration of war in 220 BC. There are several separate but inter-related aspects of this conflict between two former partners. Polybius, as we have seen, uses the incident to explore Byzantion's unique position, which enabled the Byzantines to set terms for ships and merchants wanting to trade in the Pontic area. They had further strengthened their territorial position by the recent purchase of Hieron and were in the process of acquiring territory in Mysia, on the Asiatic shore of the Bosporus.[129] Stephanos of Byzantion refers to Astike,

[127] There may already have been a number of different technical applications of this term. The Athenian Grain Tax Law of 374/3 BC (*Agora I* 7557) actually mentions two *dekatai* (Stroud 1998, 4 ll. 59–61; pp. 27, 31, 81–4). Stroud speculated that the 'twin' *dekatai* referred to twice in *Agora I* 7557 (ll 59 and 61), may represent the toll going into the Bosporus and the second charge for the return trip (83). But he recognized that the intervening period between the Athenian control of Chrysopolis and the reference to Charidemos of Oreus collecting taxes in 357 BC (*dekátas lambánein ... toùs dekatēlógous ... axiōn toùs hautou tōn telōn ... kuríous eínai* [under the control of his own custom house officials]: Dem. 23.177), was one of major disruption in the Straits and Bosporus. See also *RO* 26, and commentary, 122–9. Rhodes and Osborne follow E. Harris in seeing the 'two tenths' as down-payments for that particular year, rather than monetary taxes raised from tolls, although they admit difficulties with the reference to the previous year's *dekatai.* Bresson noted the similarities between Agyrrhios' decree and the law from Samos (*Syll.*[3] 976, ll. 25–6, where the *eikostē* from Anaia is referred to), which seems the clearest parallel for a grain tax (Bresson, 207–8). A more wide-ranging investigation of the law is now available in Magnetto et al. 2010, esp. 243–44 for the text and 246, 248, for new translations by R. Stroud and U. Fantasia. No additional clarification emerges for ll. 59–61 as far as the 'twin *dekatai*' are concerned. Harris's interpretation of the down-payment does seem to answer the context of *Agora I* 7557 convincingly, and shows that the *dekate* was a concept that was acquiring a number of applications, in addition to the one associated with the Athenian toll station at Bosporus.

[128] Rubel 2001; Gabrielsen 2007, 294, 310–11.

[129] Byzantion's purchase of Hieron: Plb. 4.50.2–3; Dionysios Byz. *Anaplous* fr. 58; Byzantine sanctuary of Zeus Ourios, on the east side of the Bosporos, opposite the entrance

the region between Apollonia Pontika and Perinthos, as being part of Byzantine territory. The likeliest period of the city's expansion into these areas coincides with Polybius' account, and helps to explain the heightening of tension on the landward, European side of the Bosporus, as well as in the Straits.

Byzantion had for many years paid a ballooning tribute to the Galatian enclave at Tylis in south-eastern Thrace.[130] At the same time, Byzantion's territorial claims were being challenged. The Byzantines are compared by Polybius with Tantalos: they could see the fruit of their labours but not enjoy them, as 'their' crops were being either damaged or appropriated by the local Thracian inhabitants (4.45). The city expanded territorially because it was economically successful. Nor was this success due simply to brinkmanship in the extraction of protection money for ships passing through the Bosporus. The Byzantines had developed an expertise in organizing monopolies. The attempts to raise civic revenues through the sale or leasing of certain rights, including fishing and salting, show how this kind of expertise may have emerged. In the third quarter of the third century BC, the Byzantines progressively created a monopoly of control over Bosporan trade, which, with the purchase of Hieron, and consequently the city's complete dominance of the channel, was in danger of stifling the very partners who helped to make this a success story for Byzantion. This critical juncture masks a different kind of monopolistic activity, manifested in the city's protest, in *c.*255 BC, at the creation of a more remote monopoly, namely at the western Pontic harbour town of Tomis, by its near neighbour, Kallatis.[131] If Kallatis could have created a situation (by monopolizing Tomis) in which the city had a critical advantage in the pricing of salted fish, then this would have had a direct effect on the goods that Byzantion specialized in selling, namely salt and preserved fish (Plb. 4.38.4–5). The convoying of Black Sea grain transports made Byzantion a major clearing house for grain and other regional produce that often travelled alongside cereals—slaves, cattle (and hides), honey, and wax. Much of this arrived at the city's

to the Black Sea: Diod. 20.111.3 fr. 302; Plb. 4.50.3; territorial acquisitions in Mysia: Phylarchus *FGrH* 81 F8; Plb. 4.50.4, 9; Str. 12.8.11.

[130] Gabrielsen speculates that the Celts of Tylis had a reasonably accurate idea of what they could extract from Byzantion in the form of tribute (they demanded 80T per annum in *c.* 220 BC: Plb. 4.46.3–4). If the capacity of an average vessel was 3,000 *medimnoi* of grain, and the price of grain 5 drachmas a *medimnos*, this would deliver a toll of 15,000 drachmas per ship (Gabrielsen 2007, 295, 316; Bresson, 278 and n.66). For a recent review of the kingdom of Tylis, see the contributions to Vagalinski 2010.

[131] Memnon of Herakleia, *FGrH* 434 F13 (Photios 228a–b); Avram 2003, 1187–8; Gabrielsen 2011, 223–7.

markets by sea, but by no means all. As I have argued in Chapter 4, large quantities of live animals on the hoof and cured hides, as well as finished products, descended on Byzantion from Thracian centres in the interior, to supply the wide range of demand that the harbours of the city attracted.[132]

The Byzantines were forced to back down when their Asiatic possessions were occupied by the ruler of Bithynia, Prusias I, who encouraged the Thracian assaults on their back yard. In 217 BC, the old configuration of allies re-emerged after the impasse of three years before, when envoys from Byzantion, Chios, Rhodes, and Ptolemy IV offered to negotiate between Philip V of Macedon and the Aitolians (Plb. 5.100.9–11). Having, in all probability, attacked and then made peace with Byzantion in 200/199 BC, Philip V maintained good relations with the city in his later career, as did his son Perseus.[133] The extraordinary success of the city of Byzantion was in part the result of shrewd use of natural advantages; in part a consequence of regional specialization, backed by a 'sheltered' monopoly;[134] and partly the fruits of a flexible strategy of negotiation and networking, at one time with the Delian League, at another with its regional neighbours, and with its principal trading partners, particularly, but by no means exclusively, with Rhodes. When Roman officials set about organizing a tax-collecting regime in the region in the early first century BC, Hieron and Chrysopolis continued to form important nodes in their own network of toll stations. All cities and regions, without exemption, were obliged to pay the *portorium* and the Bosporus was considered among the most lucrative sources of revenue. The extension of the Via Egnatia as far as Byzantion may well have helped to provide the physical means of putting into effect this economic pincer movement.[135]

REGIONAL DIVISIONS

The division of the old kingdom of Macedonia into four republican states, as a result of Roman intervention, never found favour with its

132 See also Archibald (forthcoming/c).

133 Philip V in 200/199 BC: Will, *Histoire Politique* II, 45–6; Dumitru 2006; in 184 BC: Plb. 22.14.12; Livy 39.35.4; Perseus: App. *Mac.* 11.1 & 7; Livy 42.13.8; 40,6; 42.4; *HM III*, 497.

134 Gabrielsen 2011, 220–46, for an in-depth discussion of ancient and modern monopolies.

135 Mitchell 2008, 211; Walbank 1985; Walbank 2002a; Lolos 2009, 266.

inhabitants; they quarrelled among themselves because, says Polybius (31.2.12), 'they were unaccustomed to democratic and representative government ... they preferred of course the more primitive institutions of their own monarchy and the Macedonian people at arms.' This may have been what Polybius thought of Macedonian regional administration; but it is a view that singularly fails, not only to illuminate how Macedonia was organized under the kings, but why Macedonians liked the former regional structures created under their Argead and Antigonid rulers. Polybius 'never shows any *understanding* of what mattered to a Macedonian, he judges Macedonian policy invariably in terms of Achaean advantage.'[136] Frank Walbank's admission of the ancient historian's blind spot deserves serious reflection, because regional organization is crucial to an understanding of how the monarchies of Macedonia and Thrace operated in practice, and how we should view the links between central and local decision-making. Polybius, like Athenian orators such as Demosthenes and Demades, could only see kings as autocratic figure-heads. They failed to see how kings could also be managers and coordinators in regions where the distances between one major population centre and another, and especially between one lowland area and another, could be substantial, separated as they were by mountains, forests, and lakes. The effective exploitation of such regions was necessarily different from the experience of central and southern Greeks, inured to intense competition over territorial resources. The clearest indication of these royal coordinating functions is reflected in the Pistiros inscription, whose regulations are predicated on the existence of inter-regional roads, tolls (and, what is more important, the remission of tolls), as well as legal mechanisms, the overall coordination of which can only have been put in place by supraregional authorities, in this case, the Odrysian princes. Kings could underwrite major infrastructure projects, such as roads and ports, including riverside installations. The implementation of royal enactments fell to regional subordinates. Regional administration was the key component to the success of any central organization. Far from being rivals to power, regional administrators were the real force behind crown authority. Kings might circulate within their kingdoms, but regional administrators were the day-to-day decision-makers, policemen, and dispensers of justice. The scarcity of documentary evidence is not a sufficient reason for doubting that this echelon of power existed. Regional power was autocratic and seigneurial, emerging from the princedoms of the archaic

[136] Walbank 1970, 305 [2002a, 105], 306–7 [2002a, 106].

age. We glimpse this caste in the late archaic coinage of the Pangaion area, where rulers' names appear on coin legends alongside ethnic ones (notably Getas of the Edoni; Bisaltai, Tyntenoi, Oreskioi, Zaielioi, and others); and to some extent in regional prosopography (Arrabaios, king of the Lynkestians: Thuc. 4.79.2, 83.1). The persistence of regional names—Emathia, Pieria, Almopia, Amphaxitis, Eordaia, Tymphaia, Lynkos, Elimeia, and others, including those east of the River Axios: Mygdonia, Krestonia, Anthemous, shading into similar ethnic names in Thracian-speaking areas, the land of the Odomantians, Sintians, Bessoi, and Odrysians—in short, all the regional levies called up by King Sitalkes in 429 BC, and the Macedonian levies that responded, provide ample evidence of how regional organization was articulated.[137] The marriage between Sitalkes' nephew Seuthes to King Perdikkas of Macedon's daughter Stratonike, the diplomatic resolution of this invasion, illustrates the critical role of princes and princesses in government. This was the upside of dynastic diplomacy, even if factions and feuds were the downside.

Hatzopoulos has attempted to sketch the evolution of Macedonia's regional infrastructure, which eventually emerged as four districts, probably from the time of Philip II, although the nature of these four divisions remains problematic.[138] If these really were similar to the Roman divisions, as he suggests, then it is hard to see why Livy goes to such lengths (45.29.4–9) to describe how the new regions were to be arranged, and Polybius' remarks about the negative response of Macedonians to these divisions demand some explanation. There was undoubtedly novelty in the two easternmost districts, where parts of Thrace and Paionia were to be incorporated. We have much to learn about how the regal *merides* operated over time.

Maria Gabriella Parissaki has recently reviewed the districts of Thrace, the *strategiai*, that are documented in a range of late republican and early imperial inscriptions, principally dedications, which show how the preconquest Thracian élite was incorporated into the new Roman administrative machinery that came to constitute the foundations of Roman provincial administration.[139] One of the difficulties that has beset students of Thracian *strategiai* is the fluctuating number of these regional divisions. The reordering of epigraphic alongside historical data has enabled Parissaki to propose a new hypothesis about regional organization in Thrace. The earliest system that can be discerned from the

[137] Thuc. 2.99–101; Archibald 1998, 107–11.
[138] Hatzopoulos 1996, I, 231–60. [139] Parissaki 2009.

dedicatory inscriptions indicates a regional organization of fifty units (Pl. *HN* 4.40). Exactly how these regional units might be reconstructed in terms of actual modern topography is still unclear. Nevertheless, this prior system was superseded, at some point in Vespasian's reign, by a reduction to fourteen regional units (Ptol. 3.11.8–10).[140] The fifty divisions that are variously recorded in the earliest inscriptions of the late republican period reflect the deep roots of regional administration in the days of Odrysian rule, when territories were organized along 'tribal' lines. By the first century BC, the fulcrum of royal authority had moved from the middle Hebros and Tonzos river valleys to Bizye/Vize, in south-eastern Thrace (Pl. *HN*. 4.47), where the princes of the Sapaian dynasty had created an impressive civic centre, regional capital of the Astai, with a theatre and other civic amenities.[141] The intensity of economic activities in and around the Bosporus may well have contributed to this relocation of the centre of power in the south-east Balkans. The kinds of predatory relationships that existed between Byzantine 'protectors' and the ships whose security they protected were paralleled by predatory relationships from the landward side, represented most vividly in the tribute demanded of Byzantion by Galatians from their enclave in south-eastern Thrace. Nevertheless, coinage circulating in the region shows that market relations also operated between the different political entities of the interior, on both sides of the Bosporus, with coin types and counter marks signalling the acceptability of specific issues. The very success of Byzantion made its buying power a magnet for many social and ethnic groups in the northern Aegean. The city's economic success and dominance of the Black Sea trade also enhanced its political stature. Byzantion found itself among the key partners in major international negotiations, as we have seen in the case of Philip V of Macedon. The Ptolemies had courted Byzantion from the 270s BC onwards. This international dimension gave the city further assets, which the formerly dominant landward powers—the Odrysian kings of Thrace, the Antigonid kings of Macedon—and would-be powers, such the Galatians on either side of the Straits, could no longer compete with.

[140] Parissaki 2009, 337–50.

[141] Dawkins and Hasluck 1905, 175; Parissaki 2009, 324–6, 1/4–1/7, dedicated by Apollonios, son of Eptaikenthos, of Bizye, strategos in the environs of Anchialos.

6

The lure of the northern Aegean

BOUNDARY CONDITIONS

The previous chapter began by looking at broad commodity flows throughout the east Balkan and north Aegean 'super-region' and ended with the very specific conditions in the commercial bottleneck of the Bosporus, which enabled Byzantion to change from being one of many communities along the channel of water between the Aegean and Black Seas into an extremely powerful regional economic agent in her own right. In practice, this change took a long time to become apparent, which explains why reactions from amongst the city's neighbours also took time to evolve. We know very little about the physical appearance of the pre-imperial city of Byzantion. Its remains are buried under its more illustrious late Roman, Byzantine, and Ottoman monuments.

The terms that the Byzantines set for escorting ships entering and leaving the Black Sea were initially based on the terms determined or negotiated by the Athenians, whose main purpose had been to exercise a level of military control in the Hellespontine region. This was, in turn, driven by security considerations in the wake of the Persian retreat from Europe. What began as a defensive measure with the operations of the 'guardians' of the Hellespont, the *Hellespontophylakes*, intended to separate Persian-dominated territory from those who had emancipated themselves from Persian control, became a tool of extraordinary economic power in the hands of the Byzantines, not just because many Aegean communities, with the Athenians at the top of the list, had developed a strong taste for Pontic bread wheat,[1] and many east Balkan

[1] Sallares 1991, 331–2, 341–68, esp. 331 and n.133 with further refs; 341–54, 369–72, with Theophr. *Hist.Pl.* 8.4.5; see also Sallares in *CEHGRW*, 32. Sallares emphasizes the deep ecological roots of cereal distributions in the Mediterranean, which did not alter simply because of changing dietary demands, but were the results of gradual natural and human adaptations.

peoples had built up a thirst for Aegean wines and oil; but also because the east Balkan–north Aegean 'super-region' had become economically much more integrated. Changing social relations, gradual adaptations in the regular movements of basic commodities, such as salt and seasonal foodstuffs, and the parallel demand for a variety of extra-regional products had led to the increased coordination of road and riverine transport routes. For those times when economic relationships intensified within this region, and the number and pace of transactions accelerated, the enhanced numbers of ships passing through the Straits and Bosporus need to be factored into the equation.

Can we and should we attempt to calculate the volume of ships passing through the Straits in an average season? Gabrielsen has estimated that the revenue from convoying services (or from a more formal toll) that could have accrued per ship was *c.*15,000 drachmas (for an average cargo of 3,000 *medimnoi* of grain, if the price of grain was five drachmas a *medimnos*).[2] Naturally, the price of grain varied.[3] This applies to ocean-going, long-distance vessels, the most prominent in the scholarly literature, but probably the least numerous in terms of overall numbers of boats. The celebrated convoy caught in Philip II's trap in 340 BC, which numbered in excess of 230 ships, provides a convenient order of magnitude. The grain convoy in question gathered together those cargoes that resulted from the sale of grain in Pantikapaion, following the late summer harvest in the Crimean region.[4] Other traffic through the Straits was not determined by this particular seasonal factor. Grain ships were the container vessels of antiquity—large, easily spotted, easily taxed. No ship-owner who commissioned such a vessel is likely to have taken on any additional risks (getting such a cargo to its destination was risky enough). It was easier for tax collectors to be assiduous about these kinds of clients, who could deliver predictable revenue, than to chase up more nimble craft. So we need not assume that all ships were subjected to these same kinds of protection services.

The vulnerability of ships in the narrow passages of the Straits and the Bosporus is already apparent in the earliest narratives about the area (Herodotus describes how Histiaios of Miletos, using Byzantion as his

[2] See refs Ch. 5 n.130.

[3] Von Reden 2010, Ch. 6, 141–55 and App. I, Tables 4–7, for a recent review of data on cereal prices (fifth–first centuries BC); 5 drachmai is a comparatively conservative price for the Aegean (though approximately twice the price of Egyptian wheat). The author takes 5–6dr. as a 'normal' price, whilst acknowledging that inter-annual variation must be taken into account (Von Reden 2010, 154–5).

[4] Bresson 2011, 77 (and more generally for a discussion of the timing of harvests in different locations within the eastern Mediterranean).

headquarters, seized merchant ships exiting the Straits: 6.5.26). Yet, at the start of the period covered in this book, the northern Aegean offered singular opportunities to various people, which outweighed the evident risks of maritime mishaps. The north lured southerners because of its rich potential in terms of land, timber, and mineral resources. The recent publication of a corpus of nearly two hundred graffiti on pottery, including fine wares as well as transport *amphorae*, almost all of the period *c.*725–680 BC, from a huge pit of unknown purpose on the akropolis of Methone, situated just south of where the River Haliakmon would have flowed into the Aegean Sea at that time, gives an unexpected insight into the scale of maritime exchange before we have any narrative descriptions of such contacts.[5] What is more, not one but two cases of inscriptions in Carian script have been identified at Karabournaki/Mikro Karabournou, on the Thermaic Gulf, dating either to the late sixth or early fifth century BC.[6] One of these examples consists of three Carian names, or parts of names, on three fragments of a closed vessel, while the other is a piece of roof tile, inscribed with what appear to be numbers in an acrophonic system. We have seen how merchants from a wide variety of originating centres penetrated deep into the north Aegean landmass. They went because they discovered opportunities. Yet the success of these later adventures is not something that could have been anticipated from what we know about conditions in the coastal regions in the sixth and early decades of the fifth century BC.

The success of Byzantion was exceptional because the convoying of ships through the Straits and Bosporus was a valuable service to maritime traders, and because the recipients of these services were prepared to pay the additional costs that had to be factored into the risks of sea travel. Real expertise was required to manoeuvre in the winds, tides, and natural bottleneck created by the Straits. Nevertheless, the risks inherent in longdistance travel meant that the gatekeepers needed trusted networks to provide a steady stream of reliable clients during the convoying season. If we consider the willingness of agents to cooperate from a purely pragmatic angle, then the prerequisite for a trusted string of clients was an asset not shared by those outside the network. One such asset was the remission of tolls—*ateleia*. The Rhodians enjoyed *ateleia* in all Seleukid ports and operated as the 'most favoured' partners of the Byzantines. The remission of tolls was built into their assumptions about Black Sea exchange and is a prominent aspect of the provisions set out

5 Besios et al. 2012.

6 Adiego et al. 2012; Baralis (2008, 110–12) discusses theories of Phoenician settlement; see now Muller (2010, 218–19) and further below.

for traders in the Pistiros inscription, as we have seen in Chapter 5. The mechanism of bilateral trade agreements made it easy to offer such advantages to some clients and not to others. *Ateleia* shored up existing networks of trust. We should expect to see more evidence of these kinds of trust-based contracts, which in effect operated in much the same way as a 'sheltered' monopoly did, in other words, where the agents are protected from potential competition.[7]

Individual bilateral relations were the building blocks of exchange in the north Aegean 'super-region' as they were elsewhere in the Mediterranean. In any larger locality there would have been many such agreements. Individual agreements delivered specific results. Since different suppliers had access to a limited stock of resource, multiple suppliers were needed to provide a reasonable range of stock. The Pistiros inscription particularly favours traders from Maroneia (ll 21, 23, 27–28). Maroneia's prominent role in exchange here is not immediately apparent. Why did this community offer Thracians of Rhodope and the Thracian Plain advantages that they would not have had by trading with merchants of Thasos, who are among those given various advantages at Pistiros and other *emporia* in the Odrysian realm, including the remission of tolls. But the road connections that are singled out as being toll-free are those between Maroneia, the named and unnamed *emporia*. There is undoubtedly a connection between Thracian regal bronze issues and contemporary ones of Maroneia; and Maroneia's bronze circulated widely within and north of Rhodope.[8] Perhaps Odrysian princes were playing off Thasian against Maronitan merchants, to prevent quasi-monopolistic situations from arising amongst the competing merchants; or perhaps there was a particular historical reason for Maroneia's preferment. Maroneia's production of substantial quantities of bronze coins in three separate denominations (chalkoi, quarter obols, and hemiobols), from the beginning of the fourth century BC onwards, does imply a conscious attempt to provide liquidity for small transactions, while the

[7] Gabrielsen 2011, 224 and n.26 (citing Plb. 5.89.8, 21.43.17 on *ateleia* granted to Rhodian merchants or those based on Rhodes by Seleukos II); Plb. 5.88.7 and Diod. 26.8 (*ateleia* granted by Hieron II to grain-bearing ships destined for Rhodes); 221 ('sheltered' monopolies); Oliver 2007, 30–41, on Athenian grants of *ateleia* to merchants shipping grain to Athens and the special privileges granted to Kings Satyros, Leukon, Spartokos and Pairisades of Bosporus for facilitating grain transports destined for Athens and reducing the cost of these cargoes by remitting the tax of one fiftieth. Bilaterial treaties are explored in Gauthier 1972; Bresson 2000a and taxes at various gateways by Purcell (2005a).

[8] Nekhrizov and Mikov 2000, 161–72, with figs. 1–3, showing find spots; Schönert-Geiss 1987; see now Psoma et al. 2008, with a systematic study of Maronitan issues. De Callataÿ's comparative study of die numbers implies that Maroneia was a 'medium sized' producer of coin (de Callataÿ 2005a, 82–3 and Figs 4.4 and 4.6).

larger denominations were intended for major expenditure. The same kinds of agreements must also have existed with the Macedonian kingdom. We simply do not have an equivalent commercial agreement.[9]

One of the difficulties in trying to understand the changing nature of economic interactions is the difficulty of distinguishing between broad, quasi-evolutionary patterns of behaviour, with different agents gradually adapting their ways of doing exchange in response to wider practices, and significant events that had a marked impact on these processes. We do not know, for example, whether the Athenian agents in the Hellespontine region, the *Hellespontophylakes*, adopted a shrewd policy of taxing ships passing through the Straits soon after the Delian League was formed in 479 BC, or whether this was a somewhat later response to observations of commercial traffic. Rubel believes that the imposition of a two per cent tax could have begun as early as the 470s BC.[10] This question is connected to broader ones about how the Delian League operated over the course of the two middle quarters of the fifth century BC. Scholarly perceptions of the economic and political effects of this union have changed quite markedly over a century of research.[11] The economic role of the Straits, in the fourth and third centuries BC in particular, becomes easier to comprehend when we include in any putative scenario what was happening on the landward, European and Asiatic shores, as well as at sea. The narrative of Byzantine expansion makes better sense if we allow for a wider range of processes that affected events in the Bosporus. In principle, these processes could be traced further, in a series of infinitely regressing acts, with factors further afield having some impact on events along the coast, like waves moving progressively towards the sand. In practice, it may be more straightforward to adopt the concept of 'boundary conditions', a tool used by mathematicians and scientists to determine the circumstances in which certain values are considered to be valid.[12] This is not an attempt to introduce a false, mechanistic model into our thinking about economic processes. On the contrary, the concept of 'boundary conditions' is here conceived as a purely abstract, heuristic device, to help re-imagine what

[9] The agreement between Amyntas III for the Macedonian crown and the Amphipolitans, Bottiaians, Akanthians, and Mendaeans (RO 12), shows the same kinds of bilateral mechanisms in operation as in the Pistiros inscription, with the ruler representing one half of the agreement, with the other signatories as recipients of privileged access to timber resources in this case.

[10] Rubel 2001, 49.

[11] See esp. the contributions to Ma et al. 2009, for a wide-ranging review.

[12] Boundary conditions: <http://www.mathworld.wolfram.com/BoundaryConditions.html>.

should be included in an economic landscape of the remote past. Reflecting on what may have been the boundary conditions in any situation allows us to think more carefully about the kinds of assumptions we make about a historical context and to incorporate these in an explicit way in the scenario we want to use.

Recent research in the coastal zone south of Rhodope has shown that close study of the rural landscape can be very revealing when we want to gain a better understanding of how different social entities responded to each other's presence. Below we will look at Abdera, Thasos, and Samothrace, which together offer quite different perspectives on local interactions and allow the idea of 'boundary conditions' to be explored in specific ways. The evidence, documentary and material, about the two separate waves of newcomers at Abdera; about the changing relations of the nucleated community, its neighbours, and more distant partners alike, tells us a good deal about this community's relative success over the whole of our five hundred year period. The arrival of Parian settlers on Thasos, the progressive integration of native Thracians into the new Thasian polity, and the joint development of enterprises on the mainland opposite, provide the most complete model for understanding how communities that were initially peripheral to the region managed to develop such successful economic relations over a huge slab of territory. Samothrace is different from either of the former, with its focus on the Sanctuary of the Great Gods and a less visible, but no less penetrating relationship with the mainland. The modern historiography of the north Aegean has been and in many ways continues to be dominated by the paradigm of colonization, despite the fact that colonization and its close cognate, 'colonialism', have been ascribed to a 'a myopic reading of ancient literature, a long-sighted failure to discern the patterns which archaeology [has] revealed'.[13] The concept of 'boundary conditions' involves a wholly different way of thinking about socio-economic relations from the one-sided paradigm of colonization. Historical events do indeed feature in this enlarged canvas, but so do other kinds of singularities. Rule-based parameters, such as those created through formal agreements, naturally find their place, but so do natural processes, whether climatic, geomorphological, or biological. Only some of these were dominant at particular moments in time and our three contexts provide a variety of case studies. Horden and Purcell adopted the twin terms 'intensifications' and 'abatements' to cover a wider range of events and processes that can be discerned from ecological perspectives of Mediterranean history, terms that are compatible with what I propose here.[14]

[13] Purcell 2005b, 134. [14] Horden and Purcell 2000, 263–70.

ABDERA—A CAUTIONARY TALE?

The story of Abdera is a lesson about social choices. The first inhabitants of what was to become the archaic and classical city in the middle of the north Aegean coastline comprised a group of Klazomenians from north-west Asia Minor, who arrived *c.*650 BC. The evidence derived from excavation of the nucleus around the sea shore, particularly analyses of the skeletal remains of 235 burials (of the 309 recorded in all), presents a rather grim tale. These pioneers onto new territory simply failed to thrive. They seem to have had relatively restricted commercial connections with their former kin in northern Ionia. What is more, the anatomical data set shows a distinct reduction in the quality of their diet, exacerbated, perhaps, by the deleterious effects on infants of the marshy, malarial environment. Herodotus tells a rather different story. According to the Ionian historian, the Klazomenian pioneers were sent packing by local Thracians.[15] There is no *prima facie* case for this, judging by what can be recovered from archaeology; but we cannot expect material evidence to transmit nuances about social relations over an extended period of time. The sudden arrival of a sizeable alien group of Ionian settlers may well have triggered local anxieties (and not just among indigenous Thracians—other Greek settlers may not have been particularly welcoming either).[16] We can do no more than speculate about local fears or curiosity, as we can about how the newcomers responded to the local situation. The 'boundary conditions' for the Klazomenian newcomers involved the need to adapt to local ecological circumstances. The biological history of this new community suggests that this process of adaptation exceeded its members' capacities.

The experience of the Klazomenians may have been extreme. The second Abdera, set up, according to tradition, by a more intrepid group, or groups, from Teos, was ultimately more successful. The usual explanation for these two successive ventures is a combination of push and pull. The political situation in Ionia was becoming problematic during the second and third quarters of the sixth century BC, as first the Medes, then the Lydians and finally the Persians began to put political and economic

[15] Hdt. 1.168; Plut. *Mor.* 812a, Solinus 10.9–10; Koukouli-Chrysanthaki 1986; Parissaki 2002, 463; Skarlatidou 2010. Parissaki (2002) claims that the Bistones and Paiones strongly resisted successive waves of Greek colonists (citing Pindar's Second Paian and Apollod. *Bibl.* 2.5.8, Diomedes in the eighth labour of Herakles). The relationship between myth and historical events may well be much more complex than is offered by a literal projection of myth. The testimonia are briefly presented in *Inventory* no. 640. Picard 2007, 464–7, retains the idea of polarized cultures.

[16] Baralis 2008, 115–17.

pressure on the coastal cities of Ionia. At least, that is how Herodotus presents the situation, within the context of the impending Greco-Persian Wars. Herodotus' own narrative, however, reveals the kinds of mixed motives behind the complex decisions of the various parties involved.

The Abderitans had difficulty finding a good source of metal for their iron tools and weapons, as we saw in Chapter 4. The city's coinage, however, is one of the earliest and finest series of silver (and gold) coins from anywhere in the Aegean. Where did the Abderitans get the metal to make these coins? The ready availability of silver and gold seems to be the main message of the city's coin issues (and is the opposite of what the iron tools seem to be telling us). Since there are no reserves of silver and gold anywhere in the vicinity of Abdera, the inhabitants must have negotiated access to reserves with one or other indigenous group. More pretentious graves from the classical city's cemetery contain gold ornaments. The main sources were some distance away—either from the area of Mount Pangaion, or from the western parts of the Thracian Plain, where gold panning from the River Pyasechnik continues to produce some of the highest quality metal even today; or from the mined reserves in eastern Rhodope, perhaps a more plausible as well as accessible location of available deposits.[17] The consistent quality of Abdera's coinage suggests that the source of the metals was reliable for the whole of the city's pre-Roman history. Yet our principal sources give no indication whatever of who provided access to the metal. The Abderitans are conspicuously absent from among the various groups competing in the Pangaion district. So the assumption has to be that they negotiated successfully with the Thracian princes. Surviving coin issues in themselves provide only limited information about transactions. No Odrysian regal issues have been found at Abdera until the late fourth century BC and Abderitan issues are comparatively rare in the interior of Thrace until round about the same time. Chryssanthaki-Nagle has studied 2,925 coins found in the excavations at Abdera. Among them there were no Odrysian coins before those of Seuthes III. Spokes, evidently a local ruler, minted coins that are contemporary with hoards of Abderitan coins from the last quarter of the fourth century BC. She compares the relationship of Spokes' output to that of another individual who is commemorated

[17] Archibald 1998, 117–31 and Table 5.1; Nekhrizov and Mikov 2000, 162, map fig. 1, nos 1 (Startsevo) and 5 (Kurdjali), hoards containing Abderitan issues; Kagan 2006 for an early hoard of Abderitan silver containing minor denominations, including 5 didrachms, 2 drachms, 2 hemidrachms, 2 obols, and 18 hemiobols; Chryssanthaki-Nagle (2007) has dated the start of the silver coinage *c.*520/515–500 BC; see also Ch. 4 n.87 with further refs to mined reserves in eastern Rhodope.

exclusively in coins, namely Saratokos, whose bronze issues follow the minor bronze of Thasos.[18]

Visible, demonstrable connections between Thracians of the interior and Abdera emerge in the reign of Rhoimetalces I. Coins of the Sapaian royal house are plentiful at Abdera, in contrast to Odrysian issues, notably those of Rhoimetalces I (10 BC–AD 12). The gradual closure of second-century BC civic mints, including those of Thasos, Maroneia, the Macedonian districts, and the Successor kings, meant that liquidity problems could arise. Augustus was a patron of Rhoimetalces I and coins struck in his name in effect operated as proxy Roman issues. Abdera and Maroneia did not strike under Augustus. The variety of denominations enabled both large and small transactions.[19]

There is no particular reason to think that there was a change in the economic relations (or the boundary conditions) between Abdera and its neighbours. The paradigm of cultural isolation, with the Abderitans facing off hostile natives, simply does not account for the realities, not just of survival, but of real economic success. It seems more likely that the Abderitans had to pay for commodities with coin, in return for commodities by weight. The beauty and quality of their issues gave the Abderitans a valuable asset in the wider context of the Aegean as well as Thrace, but one that had first to be acquired with some other asset, whether cultural or material.[20] Maronitan bronze coins have been found to contain a comparatively high proportion of lead to copper. There are examples of coins from centres of exchange in the Thracian interior, imitating a variety of civic issues, including those of the Thracian Chersonese and the Thasian 'satyr and nymph' types of archaic form, which have a copper core covered with a thin layer of silver foil. Coin hoards do not usually contain these kinds of counterfeit or imitation issues.[21] Maroneia may have used a higher proportion of lead in its copper-based coins to counteract the effects of metal dilution. The wide circulation of these coins, which were not quite what their face value suggested, indicates that the 'boundary conditions' of exchange were flexible

[18] Chryssanthaki-Nagle 2007; Picard (2006, 278) wants Saratokos to be an independent ruler; cf. Peter 1997, 99–104.

[19] Chryssanthaki-Nagle 2007.

[20] Nymphodoros of Abdera, brother-in-law of King Sitalkes: Thuc. 2.29.1; 4; 67; Hdt.7.137.

[21] Psoma in Psoma et al. 2008, on the Maronitan issues; Taneva 2005, 29 (imitations of the Thracian Chersonese); Ivanova 2005, 43–5 (scientific analysis of 'satyr and nymph' types from Adjiyska Vodenitsa); cf. Picard in Grandjean and Salviat 2000, 305; cf. also Picard 2006, 467: 'Les découvertes de Pistiros laissent penser qu'une partie au moins de ces pièces fut frappée sur ce site'.

enough to allow for such media. Historical anecdotes, such as those about the emergency copper alloy issues of Timotheos at Olynthos in 362 BC and the emergency bronze issues of Perdikkas III of Macedon, show that such innovations, aimed at enhancing liquidity for immediate transactions, were accepted.[22] In these cases the proximate reason for minting a different alloy was the temporary lack of sufficient silver. These coin types operated in a restricted area, consistent with the notion that they were produced in specific circumstances and that there were limits to their acceptability, particularly in terms of exchanges beyond the immediate circle of networks that were reinforced in other ways.

THASOS AND ITS *PERAIA*

The dominance of Thasian wine imports in the whole east Balkan—north Aegean region throughout the fourth and for much of the third century BC was a prevailing theme of Chapter 5, while the Thasian silver coins of the late second and early first century BC dominated the region in the period when Mithridates VI of Pontus was at large.[23] These material symbols of the island's contemporary economic vibrancy (or, in the case of the late silver issues, former economic robustness), have often been interpreted as a logical extension of the well-known statements made by Herodotus (6.46–47) and Thucydides (1.100.2, 101.3) about the economic ambitions of Thasos on the mainland opposite.[24] The challenge has been to understand exactly what these authors meant by the island's power on the mainland. In what sense did the Thasians have power outside their island territory? What were the *emporia* of the Thasians?[25] Should these be understood literally, as physical spaces, or

[22] Psoma 2000, commenting on Polyaen 3.10.14 (Timotheos in alliance with Perdikkas of Macedon); cf. 4.10.2 (emergency bronze coin of Perdikkas); [Ar.] *Oec.* II.24 (Timotheos' emergency coinage); cf. Polyaen. 3.10.1 (Timotheos' emergency copper issues in Attica); Psoma 2000, 134 on the poor quality of Pausanias', near-contemporary, regal issues; for the coincidence of regal Macedonian and local civic issues in the late fifth/early fourth century BC, see also Pavlovska 2006 (part hoard from the environs of Negotino, containing tetrobols of Perdikkas II, the Chalkidian League, and Akanthos).

[23] Prokopov 2000.

[24] Grandjean and Salviat 2000, 14, 24–31, 177–92 (territory, outreach and economic activities of Thasos); Isaac 1986, 285; Archibald 1998, 25, 32, 55, 74, 77, 88, 114–17, 127–39, 217–18, 225–6 (Thasian relations with Thrace); Picard 1994, 1997, 2006; Brunet 1997, 2000; Pébarthe 1999.

[25] Hdt. 6.46.2: *ἡ δὲ πρόσοδός σφι ἐγίνετο ἔκ τε τῆς ἠπείρου καὶ ἀπὸ τῶν μετάλλων* '[the island's] revenues came from the mainland and also from the *metalla*'; Thuc. 1.100.2:

should we think of *emporia* in a more abstract way, as commercial operations, or access to wider and more distant markets?

These questions were reviewed by Pébarthe in an important paper that probes these concepts more deeply than previous attempts to grapple with the ancient texts have attempted to do. Pébarthe argues that the Thasians drew revenues from their dependencies on the mainland, including Oisyme and Galepsos, in the form of taxes on various commodities, including metals, mined on behalf of various Thracian communities of the area. The Thasians had negotiated or acquired specific rights at Skapte Hyle, from where, Herodotus tells us, they drew 80T a year (6.46.3)—considerably more than they could expect from mining revenues accruing from the island's mines—out of a total annual revenue of 200T, which could even rise to 300T. This provides a remarkable sketch of Thasos's economic potential in the late sixth and first half of the fifth century BC. Among the fundamental strategic assets developed at this time was the commercial harbour.[26] The city had expanded its monumental appearance in a number of sanctuaries within the wider civic environment of the city's immediate territory, particularly around the Artemision, the sanctuary of Herakles, and the sanctuary of Apollo Pythios, which was later among the precincts that marked the limits of the city's fortifications (Fig. 6.1).[27]

Pébarthe emphasizes that only at Skapte Hyle did the Thasians have direct involvement in the proceeds of the mines. Elsewhere in the region their profits were acquired indirectly, by the provision of exchange facilities, or places of exchange (the *emporia* referred to both by Herodotus and by Thucydides).[28] Herodotus makes clear (7.113) that the gold and silver miners of the Pangaion region were the Odomantoi, the Pieres and especially the Satrai, who, in the previous paragraph, are associated by the historian with the oracular shrine of Dionysos in the high mountains of Rhodope. Pikoulas's fieldwork in the lowland region between

περὶ τῶν ἐν ῇ ἀντιπέρας Θρᾴκῃ ἐμπορίων καὶ τοῦ μετάλλου ἃ ἐνέμοντο: '(later the Thasians revolted from them [= Athens and her allies], having been in dispute) over the *emporia* and the *metallon*, which they managed.' Ps.-Scylax, whose text is usually dated in the mid fourth century BC, refers to *poleis* of the coast of Thrace, including Amphipolis, Phagres, Galepsos, Oesyme, 'and other *emporia* of the Thasians' (67).

[26] J.-Y. Empereur and A. Archontidou, *BCH* 111 (1987) 622–6; J.-Y. Empereur and A. Simossi, *BCH* 112 (1988), 736–42; J.-Y. Empereur and A. Simossi, *BCH* 113 (1989) 2, 734–40; 114 (1990) 2, 881–7; 115 (1991) 2, 712–20; 116 (1992) 2, 721–6; 117 (1993) 647–52; Grandjean and Salviat 2000, 52–7.

[27] Grandjean and Salviat 2000, 82–7, 89–91, 99, 111–13, 142–3, 196–7; Muller 2010, 219–23.

[28] Pébarthe 1999, esp. 132–5.

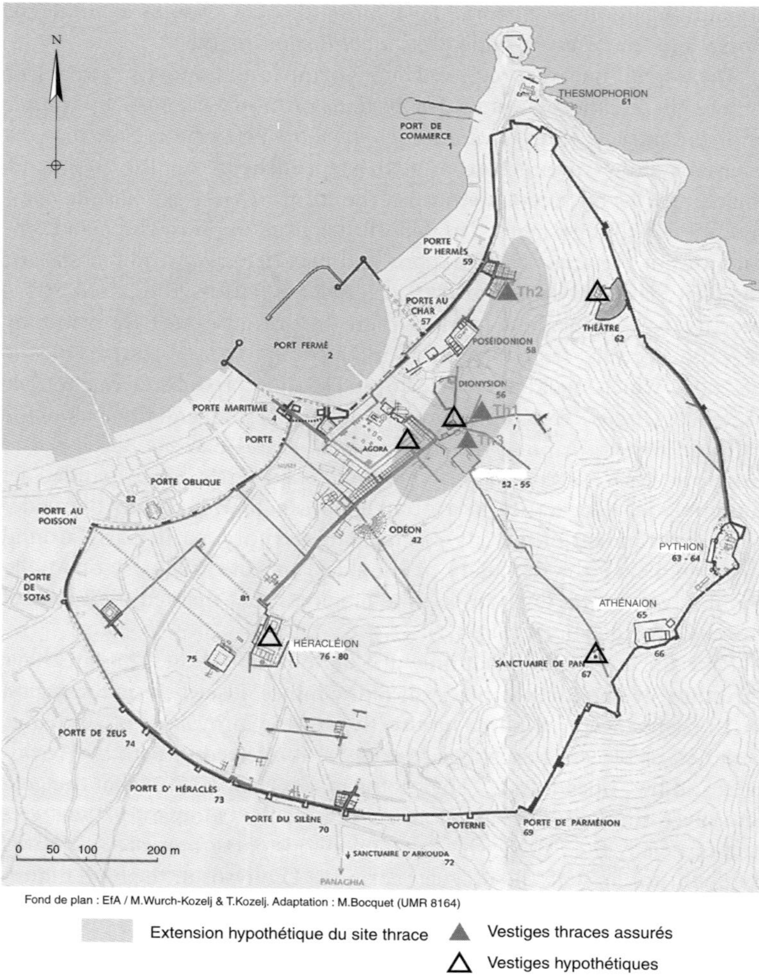

Fig. 6.1. Thasos, plan of the city area, showing evidence of Thracians in the area of the early city.

Mount Pangaion and Mount Symbolon, which faces the coastal plain, has revealed a plethora of hitherto largely unknown sites, which can perhaps be associated with the Pieres. The detailed investigation of roads and sites in this area shows the great potential of fieldwork for discovering new settlements, most of which are unnamed in the historical record. On the other hand, Kostoglou's fieldwork and scientific analysis of iron artefacts has underscored the strong continuity of mining and smelting technology along the entire Thracian coastline.[29]

The change of perspective reflected in Pébarthe's discussion arises from a number of developments in the study of the area between the lower estuaries of the Rivers Strymon and Nestos. The discovery at Neos Skopos, south of Serres, on the eastern bank of the River Strymon, of an inscription that refers to a grant or lease of land by the city of Berge to one Timesikrates (the text dated by letter forms *c.*470/460 BC), confirms the location of Berge at Neos Skopos, rather than at Vergi, on the western bank.[30] The presence of Thasians in this area, 12 km north of Amphipolis, shows that the idea of *emporia* probably needs to be applied more flexibly than simply to assume that Thasos operated an export trade via its coastal harbour towns. The evidence for Thasians much farther inland, indeed many hundreds of kilometres from the coastline, at Adjiyska Vodenitsa, and perhaps at places such as Krastevich, or Vardarski Rid, shows that the idea of Thasian *emporia* does need to be understood more broadly and flexibly than traditional approaches have allowed for.

When Thasian revenues attracted the attention of the Athenians, in the mid 460s BC, a three-year siege resulted in the Thasians having to pay penalties to Athens, razing their fortifications, giving up their fleet, paying a fine and thereafter a regular tribute, and having to give up their assets at Skapte Hyle (Thuc. 1.103.3).[31] This much is clear enough. What is less clear from Thucydides' own account, and from other evidence, is how the Thasians evaded further censure and regained their former assets, or something equivalent, on the mainland, and reasserted their commercial interests more successfully and vigorously than ever before, although the demise of Athenian naval and military influence in the northern Aegean from 412 BC onwards did provide the right conditions for a return to former clients. We do know that Neapolis acted as a loyal ally of the Athenians, even when Thasian politics underwent a series of political turnovers over the next few years. There is little ostensible evidence to go on apart from coinage. The second, post-archaic series of Thasian silver coins was widely imitated in the

[29] Pikoulas 2001, 45–109, with a catalogue of 81 sites and associated epigraphic documents; Kostoglou 2008, 77–80; 'All the evidence examined supports continuity that is evident in settlement patterns, burial practices, handmade pottery, and in iron technology' (ibid. 80).

[30] See most recently Bonias 2010, 237 and fig. 161; *Inventory*, no. 628, Berga; Picard 2006, 273–5; Hatzopoulos 2008a, 15, 31.

[31] Pébarthe 1999, 136–45 with discussion; Isaac 1986, 1–51, for a full review of the territory involved.

interior of Thrace.[32] Other cities along the north Aegean continued to mint at a time when Athenian tetradrachms were superseding other issues in the Aegean and well beyond it. Trying to fit the minting practices of cities along this north coastline, including Akanthos, Amphipolis, Abdera, Maroneia, and Ainos, into a coherent scheme around the political vicissitudes of the Peloponnesian War, and the much-discussed Athenian decree imposing the city's coinage, weights, and measures on all its allies in the Aegean, is not only difficult but a thankless task. There is a real danger of circularity in any argument where the evidence of anomalous minting can be explained away or shifted quite arbitrarily upwards or down the chronological scale.[33] Coins were not issued on a regular basis, but when money was needed for state payments. This also applies, at least partly, to bronze issues, as we have seen, even though bronze coinage was the medium for retail sales. Different copies of the decree on coinage, weights, and measures imply several versions of the text, which might indicate a developing strategy. Lisa Kallet's suggestion that these measures could be linked to the introduction of the *eikoste*—the twentieth, or five per cent tax—from 413 BC onwards offers a plausible rationale for the changes.[34]

Apart from the ambiguous witness of irregular coin issues, there is indirect evidence of north Aegean, possibly Thasian, workmanship in the fortification of Adjiyska Vodenitsa (Pistiros). Perhaps this was the work of Thasian exiles after the defeat by Athens in 463 BC.[35] If we consider the emergence of Pistiros (and accepting the identification with Adjiyska Vodenitsa), then the development of an urban plan, which current excavation indicates dates from the earliest evidence of significant activity around the eastern gateway, may have taken several decades in the third quarter of the fifth century BC, when we can least account for what Thasians were doing. Various explanations have been suggested to account for the fluctuations in tribute collected on behalf of the Delian

[32] Picard in Grandjean and Salviat 2000, 303–6; see also Ch. 5, refs in n. 23 and n.103 above.

[33] The Athenian decree enforcing weights and measures (ML45 = Fornara 97, variously dated 450–6, 425/4, and 414 BC) continues to arouse controversy; see most recently the contributions to Ma et al. 2009, esp. Kallet (50–8); Papazarkadas (72; arguments in favour of a low chronology, in the 420s); and Kroll 2009, on the volume of Athenian tetradrachm issues and putative connections between the decree and local minting in the northern Aegean. Archibald 1998, 114–20; Picard 2000, 249–52, on the relationship between Delian League tribute and numbers in circulation in the Asyut hoard as evidence of continuing economic robustness after 479 BC; Picard 1999, 36–9; Picard 2007, 466–7.

[34] Kallet 2001, 217; see also Kallet 2012; cf. Kroll 2009, 201–2.

[35] Bouzek 1996, 44–5; Picard 2007, 467.

League by Athens from Thasos and from its dependencies on the mainland. Thasos paid an enhanced tribute from 443 BC onwards, moving from payments of 3T to 30T.[36] These tend to imply, perhaps justifiably, a kind of 'stick and carrot' approach on the part of Athenian officials. The profile of coins discovered on the island suggests that Athenian politics certainly ruled the economic climate in the third and part of the fourth quarter of the fifth century BC, with a veritable panorama of coins from the 'Thracian district' of tribute collection.[37] However, the larger frame of reference is that of the north as a whole. An overwhelming number of coins found on Thasos hail from the kingdom of Macedon, including silver from the time of Amyntas II and the more numerous bronze issues (bronzes of Philip II and Alexander III dominate here, as elsewhere in the region); and from issuing centres of Thrace, both civic and ethnic coinages, representing a sizeable component from the late sixth to the early third century BC onwards. Abdera (130 out of 650 'northern' coins, of various periods), Maroneia (80 coins), and Krenides-Philippoi (90 coins) take the lion's share. There is some evidence from certain idiosyncratic coin types that the island of Thasos was sympathetic to anti-Macedonians at Olynthos and at Krenides.[38]

There are two principal factors that help to explain the nature of Thasian economic relations with its mainland hinterland or *peraia*. One is a gamble that failed; namely, Athenian attempts to plant a full-blown colonial settlement upriver from their naval base at Eion. The historian Thucydides, who knew much more than he was prepared to elaborate in his history of the Peloponnesian War, nevertheless presents a graphic and rather specific account of the failure, first of Aristagoras of Miletos, at the time of Darius' expedition to Greece; then of an Athenian venture that included 10,000 would-be colonists, which coincided with the siege of Thasos; and finally the expedition to found Amphipolis, under Hagnon, in 437 BC. The first attempt was defeated by the Edonians; the second by Edonians and other Thracians; and the third by the Spartan Brasidas, exploiting a variety of local anti-Athenian sentiments (4.102–109, cf. 1.100.3). Thucydides did not live to see the city's later history and eventual Macedonian capture. He may have been exiled by the Athenian demos as a result of his own role in the loss of Amphipolis

[36] Pébarthe 1999, 139–49 (restoration of mainland sources of revenue); cf. Brunet 1997, 229–42 (mainland influence regained only in 410–407 BC); Thuc. 8.64.2–5: restoration of Thasian fortifications, the fleet and financial autonomy).

[37] Pébarthe 1999, 146–50 on tribute to Athens; Picard 1999, 37, for Thasian coinage of this period.

[38] Picard 1999, 34–5, 39.

to Brasidas, but he was not necessarily sorry. He could live out the rest of his days as a tax exile in the Thasian *peraia*, or close by, a fact that in itself tells us something significant about the limitations of Athenian influence on the mainland. Athenian tetradrachms are conspicuous by their absence in Thrace, so perhaps Athenian traders were not welcome here, or had some difficulty establishing a network of reliable acquaintances.[39]

Thucydides' comfortable retirement on the mainland is particularly striking when we consider the ways in which Athenians were establishing themselves or acquiring property on Thasos in the third quarter of the fifth century BC. The Attic *stelai* recording the confiscations of those who defiled the Herms in the Athenian *agora* in 415 BC include two vineyards owned by Adeimantos, (one of perhaps of 8–10 ha, supervised by a slave, and which yielded 22 *pithoi* of wine for the auction of confiscated property; the other yielded 93 *pithoi*, a wine press, and a basin, suggesting a property of at least 30 ha.[40]

The second factor that helps explain Thasian economic power is connected to the first. The close coexistence, indeed cooperation, between the Thracian inhabitants of Thasos and the Parian settlers is one of the most interesting aspects of recent research into the island's history and archaeology (Fig. 6.2).[41] This cooperation extended to mining and processing operations, as well as physical coexistence in the area of the later civic space, in the sanctuaries of Artemis and Herakles, and that of Pan. Angeliki Kottaridi's description of Aegeai as a 'town in clusters' can be applied equally well to the first two centuries of Thasos town. This cooperation across a range of activities and specialisms, which reflects a creative synergy between the experience of mining and metallurgy among the island's indigenous population and the seagoing experience of the Parians, explains why the Thasians were so much more successful on the north Aegean mainland than some other Greek settlers. They could share the same networks as their indigenous peers and explore new options much deeper into the continental heartland.

The geography of the Thasian *peraia* still presents challenges to research. One of these concerns the nature of mining activities. The lack of a comprehensive geomorphological study of the Strymon valley,

[39] *Inventory* no. 553 (Amphipolis); Thucydides: Plut. *Cim.* 4; Marcell. *Vita Thuc.* 14; Isaac 1986, 34; Archibald 1998, 116–17; Picard 2007, 467: 'les chouettes ne circulent pas en pays thrace, alors que les trésors contiennent des monnaies de Thasos'.

[40] Stele VI, ll. 54–6, Fornara no. 147, p.173–4; Grandjean and Salviat 2000, 182; Brun 2004, 93–4 and fig. p. 93.

[41] Owen 2009, 87–95; Muller 2010, 216–23.

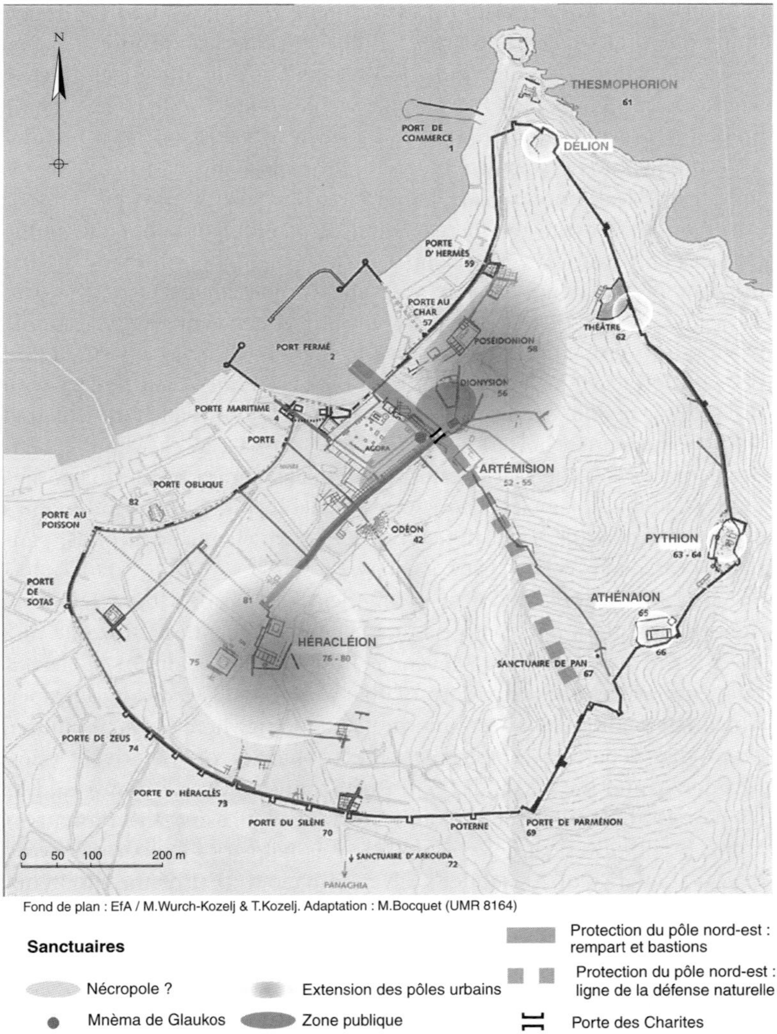

Fig. 6.2. Thasos, plan of the civic area in the sixth century BC, showing the persistence of districts within the confines of the later city.

comparable to that conducted in the Thermaic Gulf, means that evaluations of this region's mineralogical exploitation are based mainly on selective area studies and on comparatively late documentary evidence, which does not necessarily reflect earlier relations. Investigation of the slag deposits and mining evidence in the Pangaion region have focused particularly on the eastern end of the Pangaion massif and the much more plentiful evidence on the southern slopes of Mount Lekane, between ancient Neapolis and the western bank of the River Nestos, where Chaido Koukouli-Chrysanthaki would locate Skapte Hyle.[42] These preliminary explorations have not yet been followed up on a broader scale and by more systematic analyses of the surviving evidence. There is still a great deal more to learn about Pangaion's early history.[43] Herodotus refers not just to the Pieres, Odomantoi, and Satrai, but also to the Doberes and Paioplai (5.16), who are associated with a lowland area at the foot of the mountain, an area once called Phyllis. According to Thucydides, the Pieres originally lived farther west, in Macedonia proper, but were compelled to move to the Pangaion area by the kings of Macedon (2.99.3). Various authors connect Phoenician traders with the mining region.[44] Euripides associated Pangaion with Orpheus and with the horseman-hero, Rhesus (*Rhesus* 921–922; 972); while Apollodorus makes this the seat of another mythical Thracian ruler, Lucurgus (3.5.1). Latin and Greek authors were equally inspired by the mountain's evocative landscape, its distinctive wildlife, which included lions, panthers, bears, and lynxes,[45] and its snowy peaks.[46]

A key topographic problem is the identification of Mount Dysoron, the origin of the mine that generated such an exceptional income of a silver talent a day for King Alexander I of Macedon (Hdt. 5.17). Herodotus emphasizes the proximity of this location to Macedonia proper, which has traditionally been interpreted as somewhere in the mountain chain that separates Amphaxitis, the tributaries of the River Axios, Mygdonia, and the Chalkidic peninsula from the River Strymon and its tributaries. This physical proximity of Macedonia and the mountains above Bisaltia, west of Lake Kerkinitis, has helped to explain the typological similarity of Alexander's silver coinage to that of the Bisaltians, which evidently served as a model.[47] The restoration of the name 'Dysoron' on the decree of Alexander III concerning the territory of

[42] Gale et al., 1980; Photos et al. 1989; Koukouli-Chrysanthaki 1990, 500–14 and fig. 2.

[43] Pindar *Pyth.* 4.180; Aesch. *Persae* 494; Hdt. 6.46, 7.112 ([Arist.] *De Mirabilibus Auscultationibus*, 45). Theophrastus refers to its metal-bearing springs, whose mineral concentration raises the temperature of the water (Theophr. F159 = Athen. 2.42b); Pikoulas 2001.

[44] Pl. *NH* 7.197; Clem. Alex. *Strom.* 1. p. 307B; [Ar.] *Mir. Ausc.* 45.

[45] Pl. *NH* 21.17; Xen. *Cyneg.* 11.1; Ael. *Hist. An.* 3.21.

[46] Verg. *Georg.* 4.462; Lucan, 1.679f.; 7.482; Sil. Ital. 2.73f.; 4.776f.; 9.465; Val. Flacc. 1.575, 598; 4.631.

[47] Hammond, *HM* I, 92, 181–2; *HM* II, 74–91, 101; Borza 1990, 46–7; Hammond 1997; on the Bisaltian models of Macedonian coins, Kagan 1987, 22–3; Archibald 1998, 86, 88, 116; Picard 2000, 242–7; Picard 2006, 270–2.

Philippoi has recently persuaded a number of scholars to relocate Mount Dysoron to the mountains on the eastern margins of the Serres Plain, rather than to those to the west of it.[48] The inscription does not refer to a mine, but to forest (*hyle*: l.10), just after reference to land in Seiraike and Daineron (l.8). We might expect the first to be connected to the area of Serres. Even if the restoration of the word Dysoron is correct in this inscription, it does not mean that Mount Dysoron should be relocated from the western side of the Strymon valley to its far eastern margins. However imprecise Herodotus' geography of the Strymon estuary may be, such an interpretation effectively contradicts what the historian says about the limits of Macedonian power, the location of Bisaltia, and the technological proximity of Bisaltian and Macedonian regal coins.

The Thasian law on the wine trade should be viewed in the context of the island community's pervasive links with the mainland.[49] The 'très grand cru' of Thasos was protected from competition with other wines by a law, introduced *c.*410 BC, which imposed strict penalties on any ship owner or captain who should be carrying 'foreign' wines in the area between the Athos peninsula and Cape Pacheie (l.9). Commissioners of the *ēpeiros* (control of the taxation regime now being restored), were to supervise the traffic of commercial shipping and to impose fines. They were themselves liable to twice the fine if they failed to proceed against an

[48] Hatzopoulos 1996, II, no. 6, pp. 25–8; the attribution of Mount Dysoron to the vicinity of Philippoi was first made by L. Missitzis. This was not widely shared until the theory was revived by Faraguna (1998, 374–6) and Picard (2006, 271–5), and has been since elaborated by Hatzopoulos (2008a, 14–33, with further bibl.). This new interpretation departs from this author's earlier views, but the chief points that convinced him of a different position have not been answered in the new thesis; see esp. Hatzopoulos-Loukopoulou 1992, 15–25: based on the evidence of Hdt. 5.17.1–2, Thuc. 2.99.3–6, and two hoards containing significant quantities of coin originating in the Pangaion area, the Asyut and Dekadrachm hoards, the authors concluded that up until 480 BC, the Macedonian kingdom reached as far as the River Axios. 'Lower Paionia', that is, the area on the east banks of the Axios, extending into the west bank of the lower Strymon valley, remained outside the kingdom (24). Thereafter, Alexander took possession of this area briefly, in the wake of the Persian retreat (as suggested in the so-called 'Letter of Philip II' (= [Dem] 12.21). Alexander I only managed to expand farther eastwards, into Anthemous, Krestonia, and Bisaltia, in *c.*460 BC. Cf. also Hammond, *HM II*, 102, 114, 120, 138. 'Ce n'est que vers 415, après peut-être un premier intermède entre 445 et 434/3, que la Bisaltie fut solidement attachée au royaume, au moins jusqu'à la fin du règne d'Archélaos. Cela explique pourquoi Thucydide, écrivant sous son règne, parle des peuples dont ils (les Macédoniens) "occupent encore *aujourd'hui* les pays" '. (Hatzopoulos-Loukopoulou 1992, 25, italics are Hatzopoulos's).

[49] Pouilloux 1954, 212–13; Salviat 1986, 147–54; Brunet 1993; *SEG* 47 (1997) no. 1339; Grandjean and Salviat 2000, 182–5.

indicted felon, and informers were encouraged to provide information in return for a reward of half the penalty.[50]

SAMOTHRACE

Compared with its larger neighbour Thasos, Samothrace was more remote from mainland connections, and from some of the principal commercial contacts that typified the western end of the north Aegean coastline. A fragment from Antiphon's speech, *On the Samothracian tribute* (F50, Thalheim), contains claims about the island's alleged poverty.[51] Like Thasos, however, the island's multi-ethnic origins have been illuminated by recent research. Early Iron Age pottery at Vrychos, an upland defended site south of the sanctuary of the Great Gods, nearer the centre of the island, indicates close connections between Samothrace, Thasos (Kastri IIB2), and the north Aegean coastline, including sites like Kastanas, while the presence of megalithic tombs at Vrychos and at other island locations (Gialomandra, Sellada, Vigla) suggests cultural links with the mainland opposite. The native population seems to have been progressively Hellenized, in linguistic terms at least, with the advent of Samian settlers. The preponderance of non-Hellenic graffiti in the Sanctuary of the Great Gods between the seventh and fifth centuries BC was gradually replaced by Greek ones thereafter, even though the overall profile of the population remained relatively stable.[52] The cult of the Great Gods provides evidence, on this modest island, of a bold sociocultural initiative in what appear to be rather unpromising circumstances, while the elaboration of the sanctuary by external patrons, most notably by Macedonian and Ptolemaic rulers, shows how well connected the cult's administration actually was. The earliest identifiable marble-decorated structure, now called the Hall of the Choral Dancers

[50] *IG* XII, Suppl. 347, 2; Salviat 1986, 181–7; Grandjean and Salviat 2000, 185 (French translation), 183–4 for the other two decrees (figs. 123–4); the earliest fragment *c.* 480–70 BC, imposes confiscation of wine and vinegar in the event of an illegal product (= *ÉtThas.* III, 7); the second, *c.*425–410 BC, forbids the purchase of wine or mast before the first day of the month Plynterion (*IG* XII, Suppl. 347, 1).

[51] Constantakopoulou 2007, 102, 133, 237–9; *Inventory*, no. 515.

[52] Matsas 2009, 230 and fig. 7 (table comparing indigenous to Greek graffiti, sixth to fourth centuries BC); Matsas 2010, 32–4 and fig. 3.2a–d, for clay sealings with 'Linear A' pictograms, demonstrating a wide network of connections in the Middle Bronze Age; Matsas 2010, 35–8, summarizing the revised chronology of sanctuary structures to the Kabeiroi.

(formerly the Temenos), is thought to have been dedicated by Philip II *c.*340 BC, in recognition of his personal devotion to the cult. An open-air sanctuary has also been identified at Madul–Panaghia, on the south-western slopes, and another, dedicated to Kybele, at Kerassouda, on the southern slopes of the mountainous summit. The movement of Gallic mercenaries is thought to have caused considerable disruption to the island's mainland possessions, with the flight of prominent landowners, including a former *proxenos* and benefactor of Thasos, to that island.[53]

When arguably the most powerful ruler of the Hellenistic world in the late third century BC, the Seleukid King, Antiochos III, attempted to put his own stamp on the northern Aegean, through an ambitious campaign along the coast of western Asia Minor as far as the Hellspont, and on into the Thracian Chersonese, he was making a rhetorical and political bid to succeed Lysimachos as King of Thrace, his own predecessor Antiochos II, and, most recently, Attalus I. Notwithstanding his strategic panache and serious legal claims, the boundary conditions did not favour Antiochos. He was not familiar with the region; he lacked the sort of local network connections enjoyed by the Macedonian kings and the Ptolemies; and his ambitions happened to clash with those of influential Roman officers. His passage northwards ended in a compromise agreement at Lysimacheia in the Thracian Chersonese.[54]

[53] Psoma 2008, 121–37 (decree in favour of Polyaratos, son of Histiaios, *c.*290–280 BC).

[54] Ma 1999, 19–27; Plb. 4.48.7–10; 18.51.3 (claims of Antiochos III over European territory had no rival); conference at Lysimacheia: Plb. 18.51; App. Syr. 3; Liv. 34.58.

7

Dining cultures

MACEDONIAN AND THRACIAN ROYAL DINNERS

> 'But nowadays, as Theopompus records in the first book of his *Philippika*, there is no one even among those of moderate prosperity who does not set out a costly table, who does not possess cooks and many other servants and who does not spend more on daily requirements than used to be spent at festivals and sacrificial rites.'
>
> (Athenaeus, *Deipnosophistai* [*Sophists at the Banquet*] 6.275b)

The historian Theopompos was probably one of the authors who made a significant contribution to the notion of Macedonian dinners as spectacular occasions of conspicuous consumption and, incidentally, to the prevailing moralistic tone of much of the ink spilt on the subject of dinners in antiquity (judging by the kinds of snippets cited by other authors). When he compared Macedonian with Greek dinners, Athenaeus was not making an implicit comment about the culture of Macedonians in general, but rather confronting the ostentatious dining at royal courts with the various non-courtly traditions of dining elsewhere in the Greek-speaking Mediterranean.[1] His breathless race through the cultural celebrities of the ancient world, men (it is an account almost entirely preoccupied with men, and occasional unnamed, scantily clad females) whose notoriety made the repetition of their names an excuse for a tasty anecdote here, a salty quip there, is a collection of ill-assorted indicia of dining habits sandwiched between other gossipy behavioural eccentricities.

[1] Athen. 4.127d (comparing Macedonian and Greek dinners); Dalby 2000, 372–94, on Macedonian dinners described by Hippolochos of Macedon and Lynceus of Samos, dating from the late fourth and early third century BC; on Athenaeus as an author, see the contributions to *Athenaeus and his World*; Pelling's comments on Theopompos' fragments in Athenaeus are particularly apposite here (Pelling 2000, esp. 177–80).

Without Athenaeus, however, we would be deprived of the atmosphere of dining and the social connections between dinners, guests, dining environments, and dishes. The association in the above quotation between eating and the personnel needed to assure elegant dining proves the point. In the lifetime of Theopompos, which coincided with the two middle quarters of the fourth century BC, if not beyond, average lifestyles in the Aegean became more comfortable, at the very least, and for some, positively luxurious.[2] Olynthos, the town on the western margins of the Chalkidic peninsula, is often taken as typical of this period. The spacious houses documented in the excavations conducted by Johns Hopkins University have not been closely duplicated in the major civic centres of the Aegean, at least, not until the later fourth century BC. Since many residential properties were used for a variety of practical as well as productive purposes, comparison is by no means straightforward.[3] The most striking impression, from the perspective of the twenty-first century, is the comparative absence of kitchens and fixed amenities related to cooking. The evidence from excavated properties of the fifth to second centuries BC implies that meals were cooked in a range of locations, using portable hearths, rather than fixed ovens, with minimal fixtures.[4] This is particularly relevant when we come to consider the amenities of the better-off, and especially the organization of royal palaces.

Renewed investigations of the palace at Aigeai, and new excavations at the later and larger palace at Pella, are still in progress, so interpretation of functions and amenities in particular interiors is necessarily provisional.[5] Nevertheless, the complex at Aigeai has a striking arrangement of dining rooms, which seem to have been designed as key parts of the main north, west, south, and east wings. The pattern is clearest on the south wing, where there are two dining rooms, with distinctive raised borders to accommodate couches, in two pairs of rooms (H, G and E, D) either side of a connecting room (F). The arrangement of an ante-room, or connecting room, opening onto twin dining rooms, is repeated in the south-east corner (A with A1 and A2); the north-east corner (twin

[2] Von Reden 2007, 385–406, for a broad review.

[3] Cahill 2002; Ault 2007; Ellis Jones 2007; see the contributions to Westgate et al. 2007.

[4] Foxhall 2007; Cahill 2002, 80–1 on the 'kitchen complex', when recognizable, and passim (esp. 111, 115, 119, 126, 138–40; 152–69, 204–5); and 282–8, where the economic implications of the house plans and surviving contents are discussed.

[5] Kottaridi 2011b for the most up-to-date description of the palace at Aigeai; see also Kottaridi in Galanakis (ed.) 2011, 233–6; Étienne 2006, 106–13, with observations on Aigeai and Pella; Saatsoglou-Paliadeli and Kyriakou 2006; Saatsoglou-Paliadeli 2007; Akamatis 2011, 399–401, with further refs 399 n.20.

rooms: R, S; with symmetrical reconstructions beside P, leading into Q1 and Q2; mirrored in N5; with twin rooms (N1) and the north wing (N3) either side of N2 on the north wing). The largest set of dining rooms identified is the pair on the west wing (M1, M3), either side of M2.[6] The design of rooms in triplets is repeated using three different dimensions, with the smallest sets (A, A2, A3; P, Q1, Q2) occupying the same footprint as the middle-sized rooms (N1–3; R, S), exceeded only by the largest set of all (M1–M3). Each of these last rooms occupies a surface area of *c.*267 m^2, which could in principle accommodate 30 couches. Should we imagine the palace at Aigeai acting as a 'giant *andron*'?[7]

The identification of dining rooms seems relatively secure on the southern and eastern wings (R, S); less so on the northern and western sides. Accommodation is one thing; the provision of actual meals for large numbers is something quite different. The accounts of Alexander's banquets on campaign may refer to hundreds of guests in a common hall, but these descriptions also refer to the supporting environment—ante-chambers, bathrooms, bedrooms.[8] Athenaeus predictably includes memorable anecdotes about dinners hosted by Alexander the Great soon after the acquisition of the Persian royal household. He cites Ephippus of Olynthos, who wrote a book entitled *On the Death of Hephaistion and Alexander*, in which there was a description of the park in which banquets took place, with a gold throne for Alexander and couches with silver legs for distinguished guests, but more striking are the references to Alexander declaiming from memory a scene from Euripides' Andromeda, and his adoption of sacred vestments (12.537d–e). Elsewhere Athenaeus cites a scene from Chares' *Histories of Alexander*, in which a banquet was held for a hundred guests with ninety-two bridal chambers nearby for his friends (*FGrH* 125 F4 = Athen. 12.538c).

Whatever the packaging that Athenaeus intended to give his anecdotes, the impression gained from these near-legendary royal stories is the interconnection between dining and other activities, and other purposes. Athenaeus underscores the connection between pleasurable activity and the modelling of style and behaviour. He cites Herakleides of Pontus: 'Tyrants and kings, being in control of the good things of life, and having had experience of them all, put pleasure in the first place, since pleasure makes men's natures more lordly' (12.512a). Athenaeus includes a number of references to Thracian kings and princes that

[6] Kottaridi 2011a, 322–8.

[7] Étienne 2006, 109, with a perceptive discussion on the basis of publications prior to the restudy of the site in 2009.

[8] Curt. 6.10.21; 6.9.9; Étienne 2006, 109–10 with discussion.

connect them directly with Macedonian kings and princes. In one story, a letter had just arrived for Philip II from King Kotys, which triggered a humorous story whose exact purpose has been lost in the retelling (6.24e).[9]

However memorable, these were either exceptional events (not least because of their prohibitive costs), exceptional expenditure that found its way into the record books precisely for being out of the ordinary; or the cost includes maintenance for a much larger group of people.[10] The price for feeding some 60 or 70 royal friends of the Macedonian king is put by one writer, Ephippus, at 100 *mnai* a day, which indicates a cost 'per cover' of 143dr, as compared with 160dr for reports about the Persian royal house, where the sum was apparently intended to feed retainers as well as the individually honoured recipients. For the writers who recorded these grand feasts, the sums spent by a king, whether Persian, Macedonian, or other, were grist to an intellectual mill.[11] They were not the least, it seems, interested in how these sums were arrived at, and how resources may have affected what was on offer as refreshment at different times and places. Yet this is precisely what we need to know, if we are going to evaluate the consumption of royal households.

If we compare the dining habits of northern Aegean royal households with those of early modern princes, then the size of a household living from the proceeds of a country estate, royal, princely, or just wealthy, is unlikely to have numbered much over a hundred. Only the very wealthiest households of the last five centuries numbered 300 or more, drawing on resources from extensive territorial estates, often with additional income from a range of other assets.[12] Since these numbers represent

[9] The story is attributed to Hegesander of Delphi, to whom a number of other stories about Philip II are ascribed (Athen. 14. 614d; 260b). Athen. 12. 536d–e: 'Isanthes, king of the Krobyzi, surpassed all his contemporaries in luxury. He was rich and handsome,' (citing Phylarchos' *Histories*).

[10] The King of Persia might spend 400T on feeding 15,000 men at table (or 160dr a head): Ktesias *FGrH* 688 F39 and Deinon *FGrH* 690 F24, ap. Athen. 4.146c (Ephippus *FGrH* 126 F2), in the same passage of Athenaeus, records Alexander feeding 60–70 of his friends); Theop. *FGrH* 115 F113 ap. Athen. 4.145a (20–30T paid by a subject as a form of taxation to cover dinner for the Great King and his entourage); all cited by Davies 2005, 128–9 and n.19. Lenfant (2007) explores Athenaeus' references to Persian luxury in the enlarged context of the Hellenistic kingdoms. Lane Fox (2007, 287 with n.145) believes that it was Athenaeus himself who equated the cost of dinner for one Macedonian (Ephippus ap. Athenaeus) with a sitting for 15,000 Persian court followers.

[11] Phylarchus (*FGrH* 81 F41) and Agatharchides (*FGrH* 86 FF2–3) claimed that Alexander the Great's dinners exceeded the price of Persian jewel-encrusted treasures such as the gold plane tree, but these are broad-brush evaluations; Lane Fox 2007, 287.

[12] Davies 2005, 129 with further refs, nn.24, 25: Girouard 1978, 15: 'in the later Middle Ages, at any rate, the normal household for a peer or great prelate varied between 100 and 200 people'; cf. ibid. 15–17, 84, 111.

the people who were directly involved in the running of country estates and daily services to the owner, they suggest some organizational limits on the social units centred on wealthy European landowners of premodern times. Other retainers might be called upon for other part-time services, including military service. We do not have a concrete yardstick for such a household in classical antiquity. What we can say is that royal households in Macedon or Thrace did not adopt the Persian system of rations, allocated to individuals, who then provided for a range of other dependents.[13] These European courts operated on a different principle. It has always been clear that kings retained a close relationship with individual communities, an aspect of royal administration that remained highly characteristic throughout the final three centuries BC. This is what made it possible for Roman officials to interpose themselves as rival bidders for the interests of specific communities, a system that could not have emerged had there been a stricter administrative hierarchy along the lines of Achaemenid satrapies. Neither in Macedon, nor in Thrace, was there a well-defined distance between rulers and ruled, articulated by a distinct intervening stratum of regional administrators, responsible for tax collection and military authority, with their own retainers and satrapal courts, echoing the style and protocol of royal palaces.

Judging by the dinner held by the Odrysian prince Seuthes, Thracian rulers dined, on an everyday basis, like their Macedonian peers, facing their guests in a circular or near-circular plan. Distinguished native guests were invited, alongside visiting Greeks and others, with the king or prince offering unleavened bread and meat to whoever he wished, whilst keeping his own portion modest (Xen. *Anab.* 7.3.21–24).[14] The etiquette described here reinforces the idea of the prince as facilitator as well as benefactor—the individual with the pre-eminent capacity to redistribute food—for the benefit of the community as a whole. Food distribution thus acts as an archetype for the dissemination of other goods and services. Dinners, whether in tents or in the open air (Theop. *FGrH* 115 F31 ap. Athen. 12.531e), were perhaps much more common than formal assemblies in halls and purpose-built chambers, not least

[13] Lane Fox (2007, 287 and further refs n.146), cites Polyaen. 4.3.32, where Alexander is said to have destroyed a bronze pillar at Persepolis, bearing a list of contributions to the king's dinners; cf. Lane Fox 2011, 365: 'Philip introduced no complex Persian "ration system" at court, no secluded style of dining, no *chiliarch*, no ushers armed with whips, no graduated *proskynesis*'. The closest we come to a direct statement about Thracian redistribution is Gnesippos' statement in Xenophon's *Anabasis*, who talks of royal 'gifts' that might have included food, since the context is a meal (see Ch. 5 n.77).

[14] Stronk 1995, 208–11.

because more ambitious social events might be linked to hunting expeditions, when feasts were in any case more easily managed close to the scene of the kill.

Any assessment of dining practices drawn from such evidence as Athenaeus' tall tales is frustratingly tentative. There is surprisingly little detail about what was actually consumed in surviving narrative accounts of Macedonian and Thracian dinners. Athenaeus refers, for example, in Book 4, to the wedding banquet of Kotys I's daughter to the Athenian general Iphikrates, as portrayed in Anaxandrides' play *Protesilaos* (4.131b–c), but focuses mainly on the atmosphere and humorous possibilities of the incident—the purple rugs contrasted with the 'butter-eating' *hoi polloi* and Kotys himself tottering about with a golden jug. There is implied distance between the epic content of the poetry with musical accompaniment and the unrefined behaviour of the principals, but the reader has no way of knowing how Athenaeus selected and compressed his source material to produce this rather bizarre portrait, followed by an even more bizarre extract from a list of wedding presents for the groom—the herd of chestnut horses; the herd of goats; the golden sack; the limpet-shaped vessel; the jug of snow, for cooling liquids; the pot of millet; the cellar of onions; and the hecatomb of octopuses. The selection reads like a collage of deliberately chosen polarities, with a strong dose of predictable comic exaggeration. What is more, the cultural polarity that Anaxandrides may have adopted to reinforce his comic effects is strikingly absent from Xenophon's description of a dinner party. This merely underscores the extent to which Athenaeus' anecdotes, which play such a significant role in most historical evaluations of northern dining, are the product of conscious, fictive strategies.

STORAGE AS A PROXY FOR FOOD CONSUMPTION?

In order to understand the economic role of dining in the northern Aegean we must move beyond these syncopated anecdotes. Students of literature have rarely attempted to integrate literary references to diet and recipes with what can be known from other types of evidence. Historians, on the other hand, tend to look at broad patterns of consumption. 'Consumption' is integral to any contemporary evaluation of economic performance, whether at state, national, or local level. Yet consumption is neither a predictable nor a mechanical process. How we use resources is highly dependent on cultural patterns of behaviour. Consumption per head of population, and household consumption as a component of GDP, is not just dependent on aggregate national or household income, but also on attitudes to work and leisure, and to a variety of abstract cultural or social factors.[15] Although the idea of using consumption as a tool for studying social behaviour has been criticized as offering an unduly narrow focus for social analysis, the information gained about patterns of recent and contemporary behaviour has proved highly revealing as indications of collective, albeit complex, social responses (as we have already seen in Chapters 3 and 4).[16]

Studies of ancient consumption patterns have focused either on agricultural exploitation at selected sites, and usually in limited periods (as we saw in Chapter 4), or on the nutritional needs of given populations. However, it is one thing to postulate that most individuals, whether male or female, consumed between 150 kg and 230 kg of cereals per annum.[17] It is quite another to ascertain how diets were made up in practice, particularly in the continental parts of the northern Aegean, where there was readier access to a wider range of natural resources than there was in the land-hungry parts of central and southern Greece, including foraged foods, wild game, fish from lakes and rivers, as well as marine fish and molluscs. Finding food was integrated into other activities and preoccupations, which are much harder to discern and evaluate. Understanding cultures through diet is a comparatively new research direction for students of classical antiquity. The kind of research into northern diet that is currently in progress is necessarily exploratory in nature; it allows at least for some preliminary thoughts on how we might begin to interpret the behavioural patterns that are emerging from new studies of diet in the northern Aegean. The kinds of social ideas that drove these behaviours are sketched out in the final chapter.

Before considering the ephemeral traces of what was consumed at meals, it may be helpful to start with the evidence for the storage of dry and liquid foodstuffs. Even food that has been consumed can be identified, at least in part, from surviving residues, whether faunal remains, carbonized seeds, pips, or shells; containers and receptacles for storage

[15] Kay 2003, 31–6; 'Few of these correlations are simply causal: they are the product of a mixture of factors associated with higher productivity. Our economic lives are embedded in our social and political lives. . . . Different cultures have made different choices about the ways in which the capacities of their economies are reflected in the economic lives of their citizens' (ibid. 36).

[16] The literature on consumption is extensive; I have found Bourdieu 1984; Miller 1995 and 2008; Douglas and Isherwood 1996; Miracle and Milner 2002, particularly useful in this context.

[17] Cahill 2002, 226–7 and nn.19–20; Von Reden 2007, 403 with discussion and further bibliography.

can include traces of such residues, but also provide direct evidence of how food was consciously stored up and preserved. The space allocated for food storage offers indirect evidence of private and collective strategies to ensure the availability of essential and desirable resources.

The investigation of a range of country houses in Macedonia and Thrace is beginning to reveal how these establishments operated as centres of storage and consumption. The first and perhaps the most important impression that is gained from preliminary analyses of the organic remains at country houses is their lack of uniformity. Each establishment operated in a unique way. At Komboloi, south-east of Mount Olympus (Fig. 4.4), in the original estate house dating from the end of the fourth and early third century BC, there were many standardized pyriform storage *amphorae*, stacked in the living quarters and in the porticoes, and plentiful archaeobotanical evidence of grapes, raisins, olives, and figs. The large quantities of grape pips, together with a range of *pithoi* in a dedicated store room, are indicative of wine production on a scale that comfortably exceeded the domestic needs of the householders. The combined range of activities, tools, and facilities seems to point not just to storage, but to specialized production of wine.[18] Whether the wine produced on this estate was intended for the consumption of estate inhabitants and their guests only, or, as seems more likely to the excavators, for sale, cannot be determined from the incomplete state of the investigation, which did not explore the whole estate, but only one section of the built-up area. The provision of a separate complex, designated for storage, is in itself significant. The ceramic remains include a wide range of storage and tableware, pointing to a level of dining of some distinction, with equipment to provide for a household with high expectations and, it can be assumed, a varied diet to match these.[19]

[18] Poulaki in Adam-Veleni et al., 2003, 63–70; detailed analysis and discussion in Margaritis (2006, 34–5, 92–3, 111); the wine-processing plant was a lockable facility. Two of the large *pithoi* at Komboloi had capacity equal to 170–204 *amphorae* (Margaritis 2006, 113); one of these contained 8,000 grape pips. The Attic *Stelai* refer to vessels with much lower capacity: *phidakne*, a storage vessel with the capacity of 12 *amphorae*; and *pithoi*, with the capacity of 20 *amphorae*. Whatever the size of *amphora* in question, the vessels at Komboloi were an order of magnitude larger (Amyx 1958, 170–3; Cahill 2002, 227, gives the capacity of a storage *amphora* at Olynthos as typically 15–25 litres, the largest some 70 litres (ibid. 229). Salviat estimated that the first vineyard belonging to the Athenian Adeimantos on Thasos might have produced between 220 hl and 400 hl (= 2,200 litres) per annum; the second *c.*930 hl (= 9,300 litres), from a dozen hectares and *c.*30ha, respectively (1986, 151; cf. Brun 2004, 94). The order of magnitude seems to be correct (see further below and n.22).

[19] The ceramic data has yet to be published. There are short reports by Poulaki 2003, 63–70, and Margaritis 2006, 113.

The growing number of country estates investigated in advance of development work provides a panorama of larger and smaller establishments and a useful comparative perspective for the wealthier country houses like Komboloi. The geographical spread of these kinds of estates is expanding as modern development work joins remote areas more closely to existing conurbations. The discovery of successful, if comparatively remote, properties suggests that such establishments were widely distributed to exploit different ecological niches more effectively and were not necessarily concentrated in close proximity to towns (even if discoveries along the new Egnatia Odos show strong concentrations of late classical and early Hellenistic country houses around Thessaloniki, with imperial successors). Among the most recent discoveries is the farmhouse at Aghios Konstantinos, in the district of Grevena, dating between the third and second centuries BC.[20] The Komboloi and Tria Platania houses have yielded generous supplies of tableware—*skyphoi, kantharoi*, plates, *olpai*, *askoi*; as well as mortars and strainers for food preparation, suitable for a well-to-do family and their immediate adherents. Provision for storage at sites like Vrasna, east of Thessaloniki (Fig. 4.5), or at Asprovalta, another military establishment with a similar history, this time on the slopes of Mount Kerdylion, was more than adequate, but not nearly on the same scale, nor with the expansive style and internal furnishings of the former. This seems to be in keeping with the defensive or policing functions of these roadside facilities.[21] A fourth-century BC farmhouse on the hillside above Thasos town, at Marmaromandra, consists of two properties, a residential unit and a storage building, the latter containing *pithoi* set into the ground surface. It can be compared with the two vineyards on Thasos owned in the later fifth century BC by the Athenian Adeimantos and supervised by a slave, comprising respectively a minimum of 22 storage *pithoi* in the first and 93 on the second piece of land, which were collectively listed as quite respectable marketable property.[22]

[20] Karamitrou-Mendesidi 2009, 114–26; the structures cover an area of 750 m^2, with 11 rooms around a central courtyard, 12.5 x 12.5 m = 156.25 m^2; p. 115 fig. 2, and esp. 116 fig. 3, for the plan; 121 fig. 11, Room *Δ*, contains *pithoi* = in a dedicated *pitheon*, sunk into the floor. At least nine are visible on the reconstruction drawing of the house, 125 fig. 4. Construction of a rectangular kiln, which involved partial destruction of the southern external wall, indicates the end of use of the house, or parts of it.

[21] Adam-Veleni et al. 2003, 101–7; and Adam-Veleni 2009, 1–14, for a review of the evidence of country houses along the Egnatia Odos; See Ch. 4, nn. 15–20.

[22] Marmaromandra: Z. Bonias, *AD* 41 (1986) B', 168–71; Adeimantos' vineyards: Ch. 6, n.40; Grandjean and Salviat 2000, 182; cf. also Y. Garlan, *BCH Suppl.* XII (1986) 221–5 (Kalonero estate and *amphora* workshop, Thasos, owned by a well-known island family, including Aristagoras and his son Demalkes).

We do not need to assume that the larger estates were operated by gang slave labour, although slave-operated facilities may have developed in the late Hellenistic and early imperial period, when estates owned by prominent Macedonians were confiscated by Roman officials and numerous indigenous people became suddenly enslaved and available within the region.[23] At Olynthos, unusual concentrations of domestic equipment are consistent with a slave presence, although accommodation and equipment would indicate slave numbers per household unit in double figures at most.[24] Most of the known properties in Macedonia and Thrace dating from the pre-imperial age appear to be family-owned estates or facilities run by small groups of specialist personnel, with small numbers of free or slave hands, rather than intensively exploited investments owned by absentee landlords.

The best known model for domestic storage patterns in an urban context is Olynthos (Fig. 7.1), where the ceramic *pithos* was the most characteristic type of storage container, used for dry and liquid foodstuffs, although baskets, textiles, and clay-lined pits could also be used.[25] If an average family needed thousands of litres of cereals and hundreds of litres of wine to assure self-sufficiency, then the very large *pithos* in House A vii 4, room g, with capacity for 190 litres, could feed a household of six persons for a little more than one month.[26] Room g in House A vii 4 corresponds to about a quarter of the main store room in the Villa of Good Fortune in dimensions, but one fortieth the storage capacity of the latter. In case we might be tempted to think that the presence of more generous storage facilities in the villa section at Olynthos and the comparative absence of such storage arrangements on the North Hill point to economic disparities between the occupants of these two districts, there is strong evidence that houses close to the agora on the North Hill were better appointed and more valuable, in resale terms, than the villas.[27] Cahill is surely correct to see in these very different approaches to storage a set of variant economic strategies. There is an almost complete spatial disjunction between, on the one hand, residential accommodation close to the agora, which constituted higher value real estate, yielded more

[23] This is the thesis of Adam-Veleni 2009; for the historical context, Rizakis 2002.

[24] Cahill 2002, 263–5; cf. Xen. *Oec.* 7.25–38; 8.2–19; Chandezon 2011 for a review of personnel involved in estate management.

[25] Cahill 2002, 227 (three of five *pithoi* in the Villa of Good Fortune, Room j, contained olives, straw (cereals), and pine bark (wine?), respectively; and 227–30 for discussion of average consumption requirements and further refs.

[26] Cahill 2002, 232–3.

[27] Cahill 2002, 233–5; 277–81 with figure 49 and App. 2, 294–9, for the epigraphic evidence of property sales.

Fig. 7.1. Olynthos: view from the South Hill towards the Toronaean Gulf, with olive groves.

coins, and offered much less extensive food storage facilities; and, on the other, spacious villa units in the south-east part of the town, with plenty of storage containers, but fewer indicators of 'urban' features. Cahill emphasizes the complementary relationship between the two areas. Household 'industries', whether those associated with food production, such as cooking, baking, and fishing; or textile production, coroplasty, and weapons manufacture, tended to occupy locations closer to the centre of town; but general storage, for those without residential capacity or other communal facilities, could have been located elsewhere.[28]

So it would be simplistic to connect storage capacity alone with greater economic means. The capacity to store foodstuffs does not mean that the better-off piled up food, while the more vulnerable went without. At Olynthos some of the wealthier citizens, or non-citizen inhabitants, chose not to store food inside their residential walls. However, the owners of rural properties, like the country estates already discussed, had very different aspirations, and probably very different expertise from town-dwellers. The great modern wine vintages of Italy, France, Iberia, south-eastern Europe, California, Australia, and New Zealand, came

[28] Cahill 2002, 236–88 and plate 4.

about through the profitable combination of good soils and carefully selected vines with managerial expertise and, thereafter, careful nurturing of selected recipes according to a practised method. Something analogous must have been taking place in the rural properties of the northern Aegean. Rural estates are much more likely to have been the environments in which experiments could be conducted to improve the quality and preservation of foodstuffs, including wines and other liquids (such as perfumed oils). There is no reason why town dwellers should not have expressed a similar curiosity and experimented with wines and oils; but activities in and around the *agora* cluster around administration, retail, and other forms of exchange. The atmosphere of the *agora* was less conducive to resolving technical and logistical problems connected with the preservation of larger quantities of liquids and dry foods.

Even such a well-investigated site like Olynthos has not produced much specific evidence of bulk storage of cereals and other dry foodstuffs for communal use (if we exclude the pits on South Hill that may have been used for grain storage during the Persian occupation).[29] Underground storage is a traditional form of dry food preservation in the east Balkan region and this practice seems to have continued well into the second half of the first millennium BC. The best evidence for large-scale storage of this type has emerged during development work in rural parts of Bulgaria, although such pits, sometimes numbering not just in dozens, but in hundreds, have often been identified as having a ritual purpose because of their ultimate contents. Originally many of these pits were used for storing grain, as the evidence of special clay linings indicates.[30] The same phenomenon has been documented in Iberia, where fields of pits have been identified and have since become known as 'champs de silos' or 'campos de silos'.[31] Two aspects of the Iberian parallel are particularly helpful for evaluating the evidence from the northern Aegean. One is the fact that the phenomenon of underground storage is not universal in the region, but largely restricted to two areas, western

[29] Cahill 2002, 235.

[30] Margomenou 2008 for evidence from the early first millennium BC; Tsiafakis 2010, 382–6 (Karabournaki, domestic *pithoi* and semi-subterranean pits); a survey of the Bulgarian sites where large numbers of pits have been found is provided by Hawthorne et al. 2011, although these authors have tended to assume that all pits were located in the open air and have not pursued the relationship between the spatial evidence of pits and settlement data (for which see e.g. Archibald 2002b and 2002c).

[31] Dietler 2007, 257–8, nn.84, 85, with further bibliography; the capacity of individual silos ranged from 300 litres to 10,000 litres. Burch, Nolla, and Sagrera 2010, for a recent reappraisal of silos in Catalonia, in the vicinity of Emporion, covering the second half of the first millennium BC.

Languedoc and Catalonia. Second, the concentration of large numbers of storage pits in and around Emporion reinforces the link between trading networks and the provision of large numbers of grain-storage silos. The progressive expansion of storage capacity in these silos between the fourth and second centuries BC, independently of the life of the individual settlements with which the silos were associated, indicates a robust network of producers and distributors, and a continuing history of exchange. The investigators have assumed that cereals were regularly exported for the profit of the various urban and rural centres in Catalonia. Until the second century BC, these were indigenous landowners and tenants. Thereafter, and until the dissolution of the storage system, when eastern Iberia became more closely integrated with central Roman planning, Roman officials increasingly appropriated the proceeds of agricultural exploitation.[32]

The pit phenomenon has not been researched systematically in Macedonia and Aegean Thrace, but in Bulgaria there is a less distinct but nonetheless identifiable pattern of pit complexes in the hinterland of the Black Sea littoral; along the main rivers flowing towards the Aegean—the Hebros, Tonzos, Strymon, Nestos, and in eastern Rhodope, south of Kurdjali; but with a very marked concentration in the eastern half of the Thracian Plain, converging on the lower Hebros estuary.[33] The tradition has its origins in the Neolithic, but the number of sites where such pits have been identified was most numerous in the period *c.*600 BC until the reign of Augustus, although the acme of storage corresponds to the period *c.*600–200 BC, providing an intriguing parallelism with Catalonia. The hypothesis needs to be examined in detail; perhaps there was a similar overall pattern in the dynamics of cereal production and distribution. After all, an international grain market did emerge with the rise of large concentrations of population and with changes in socio-economic strategies, such as those identified among the town-dwellers at Olynthos, who chose not to store grain and other foodstuffs.[34] If so, then storage capacity in continental districts provides a new way of gauging the export of cereals from these areas to the Aegean.

Underground storage provides excellent anaerobic conditions for dry foodstuffs, such as grain, for limited periods. Annual storage of harvests and seed corn was a realistic strategy, but once opened, these pits had to be unsealed and emptied, or the grain stored temporarily in sealed, dry

[32] Burch et al. 2010, 399–400.

[33] Hawthorne et al. 2011, 60 and fig. 2 (distribution map); cf. 59 fig. 1 (timeline, 4500 BC–AD 500).

[34] Bresson 2011 on the international grain market; see above Ch. 1.

containers. At Adjiyska Vodenitsa, near Vetren (ancient Pistiros), locally made *pithoi* were used alongside underground pits. The ceramic containers would have provided more flexibility for shorter-term storage. The use of large ceramic containers in forms that originated along the Aegean seaboard also suggests that the taste for imported wines and oil-based products was itself a vector of change in forms of storage.[35] Ceramic *pithoi* from excavated sites in the north Aegean region have been dated in the fourth and third centuries BC. More research is needed to determine whether these replaced other containers, or whether the large-scale import of ceramic *amphorae* from wine producing centres, such as Thasos, Chios, and Mende, stimulated new methods of bulk storage by some clients at recipient centres.

NORTHERN AEGEAN DIET AND CUISINE

Cereals, legumes, and fruit

Was there a distinctive diet in the northern Aegean? Soultana-Maria Valamoti thinks that there was. Her investigations of prehistoric diets, like those of other archaeobotanists, suggest that the farming traditions of the Neolithic and Bronze Age laid the foundations of what was to become the underlying pattern of subsistence in the first millennium BC. The essential outline of a north Aegean dietary regime was introduced in Chapter 4, in connection with sites like Angelochori and Agrosykia in the Thermaic Gulf. Prehistoric archaeologists have begun to distinguish between a 'southern' and a 'northern' Greek diet, using a number of variables, which tell us different things about the relationship between 'north' and 'south', in cultural as well as ecological terms. The specific emphases within the range of available domesticates is one of these variables; but the method of preparing food—the balance between boiled and baked foods—as well as the range of communal and individual dishes in which it was served, are no less important in identifying what constitutes a particular cuisine.[36]

Scholars interested in the dissemination of domesticated plants have tended to focus research on the early history of cultivation. Changes that

[35] Lazov 1999; Archibald 2002b; 2002c.

[36] Urem-Kotsou and Kotsakis 2007 for comments on the range of (relatively undistinguished) communal vessels and highly distinctive individual cups in northern sites of the Neolithic period.

came about in the first millennium BC have only begun to attract the same level of scientific sampling and analysis during the last two decades. Valamoti has identified einkorn, one of the early varieties of domesticated wheat, together with the grass pea, as the distinctive staples of the northern diet, with a marked distribution in Macedonia and Thrace during the Neolithic and Bronze Age. Spelt wheat, the Celtic bean, and other legumes, as well as the opium poppy, were added to the repertoire of cereals and legumes over the course of the Bronze Age (through contacts with more northerly continental peoples), while millet made an early appearance in northern regions and became widespread in the Late Bronze Age. Valamoti has postulated a common origin for millet alongside domesticated horses. Perhaps riders helped to disseminate the new cereal.[37]

The archaeological and archaeobotanical evidence from Tria Platania, Komboloi, Krania, and a number of other country houses in Pieria and along the Aegean coast of Thrace presents a much clearer idea of how dietary regimes developed in the second half of the first millennium BC. In contrast to the intensive production of wine at Komboloi, at Tria Platania the dominant stored foodstuff was olive oil or preserved olives, although grapes and wine, pulses (lentils, peas, and beans), hulled barley, and pine nuts were also stored. Archaeobotanical samples were particularly well represented in the north wing of the complex at Tria Platania. The dominant cereal remains included durum wheat (*Triticum aestivum*), spelt wheat (*Triticum spelta*), oats (*Avena sativa*), and rye (*Secale cereale*).

It is not clear whether the presence of einkorn and emmer, which were dominant earlier in prehistory, but had been superseded by free-threshing durum-type wheat variants during the first millennium BC, represent 'contaminants' or weeds, or were simply fodder material. The range of pulses—lentils (*Lens culinaris*), peas (*Pisum sativum*), Celtic beans (*Vicia faba*), bitter vetch (*Vicia ervilia*), and grass pea (*Lathyrus sativus*)—can be matched at other sites in the east Balkans where similar evidence is forthcoming, which seems to confirm the continuing existence of a distinctive 'northern' dietary mix.[38] Bitter vetch is a nutritious plant but toxic when eaten raw. The seeds have traditionally been used as animal fodder, which probably explains their presence at the estate, whereas the other pulses may well represent a major component source of regular nutrition alongside cereals. The legumes had to be soaked and

[37] Valamoti 2007, 98–102.

[38] Tria Platania: Margaritis 2006; Popova 1996; and Popova 2002 (Adjiyska Vodenitsa, Vetren); 2005 (Koprivlen, near Gotse Delchev).

boiled, but would have enhanced the blandness of any cereal dish with a richer taste. Olives were evidently processed elsewhere, rather than in close proximity to the house, but olives were among the principal identifiable foodstuffs stored on the estate.

Since neither of the two estates could be fully investigated, and the associated finds have yet to be fully published, the preliminary evidence has to be considered in qualitative terms. There can be little doubt that the standard of living at the country house sites was high. The use of exceptionally large storage containers at Komboloi points to an ambitious plan for quality stored foods within the management strategy of the estate, while the range of plant residues at Tria Platania indicates a diet enriched with alternative cereals (hulled barley, rye, oats) and legumes, and laced with fruits and nuts—sesame (*Sesamum indicum*); blackberry (*Rubus fruticosus*); vine and grape (*Vitis vinifera*); cornelian cherry (*Cornus mas*); pine nut (*Pinus pinea*); hazelnut (*Coryllus avellana*); almond (*Amygdalus communis*); walnut (*Juglans regia*); acorn (*Quercus*). Danewort (*Sambucus ebulus*) has poisonous berries, but the leaves have medicinal uses. Flax plants may have been used for their oil seeds as well as fibres, while poppies could have served in a range of recipes and stimulant drinks.[39]

In the second half of the first millennium BC, one factor that made the 'northern' diet distinctive was the wide availability of durum wheat, spelt, lentils, and grass pea, which would have provided a regular diet of bread and porridge-like recipes, with an admixture of fruit, nuts, and a variety of herbs. Pine nuts and figs provided nutritious and tasty additions. Though figs in particular occur naturally in Macedonia and the coastal parts of Aegean Thrace, they would have travelled easily to other parts of the region.[40] The northern Aegean had its own range of high quality wines, of which that from Thasos—a heady, dark wine, with a fine bouquet (Arist. *Lys.* 196) and a scent of apple (Athen. I, 29e)—was manifestly highly prized, as its southern as well as northern distribution demonstrates.[41] Mendean wines were also valued and widely disseminated.[42] Discoveries of significant regional centres of wine production, such as the country house at Komboloi, show that we should not underestimate the importance of local wines alongside imported

[39] Margaritis 2006, 45; Valamoti 2007, 94, 96, on pulses and stimulant substances.

[40] Margaritis 2006, 34–8, 101.

[41] Salviat 1986, 147–54; Brunet 1993, 201–11; Grandjean and Salviat 2000, 182–3 with refs; Brock and Wirtjes 2000, 561; Xen. *Symp.* 41: in Athens Thasian wine was a symbol of luxury and was evidently expensive there.

[42] Brock and Wirtjes 2000, 460, 464, with refs; See Ch.5, 193–248 and nn.14, 20.

vintages. This is also true of Thrace, where grapes were domesticated early and where the abundance of wine-related iconography seems to confirm the production of native wines.[43] By contrast, we know much less about the cultivation and distribution of olives. In Macedonia, olive production is demonstrable at country houses like that at Tria Platania and can be variously documented in Chalkidike (Fig. 7.1) and on Thasos.[44] Consumption of olives and olive oil north of Rhodope still awaits a serious study.[45] As the extract from Anaxandrides' play quoted by Athenaeus makes clear, Thracians were butter eaters. Somewhere north of Rhodope olive oil overlapped with milk products.

Where's the beef? Meat consumption in the northern Aegean

Surveying the role of meat, and beef consumption in particular, in ancient Greece, Jeremy McInerney has recently highlighted the practical challenges of supplying meat to the communities of central and southern Greece between the sixth and third centuries BC, a time when human populations were rising and suitable grazing land diminishing. This period coincides with the most prolific epigraphic evidence of special provisions, whether at sanctuary or state level, for obtaining sacrificial meat. Cows are deeply implicated in the Greek cultural mentality, a phenomenon that McInerney has called the 'pastoral *habitus*' or 'bovine idiom' in Greek societies.[46] Cattle, the largest domesticated species of ancient Eurasia and Africa, hold a special place in the cultural vocabularies of those societies that have put cattle at the centre of collective consumption. Thus bulls became metaphors for masculinity and cows were associated with goddesses of fecundity and queenly nurture.[47] The 'bovine idiom' certainly existed in the northern Aegean, but was

[43] Popova 2002, 292, 297; Stoyanov 2011, 200; Valamoti et al. 2007, on early grape domestication and wine production.

[44] Xen. *Hell.* 5.2.38 (olive groves in Chalkidike); Cahill 2002, 226, with further refs; Hatzopoulos 1996, II, no. 22 (grants of land by King Lysimachos to Limnaios, including '*plēthra gēs endendrou*, l.7, 18: the trees are most likely to be olive trees); Grandjean and Salviat 2000, 181–2.

[45] Brun 2004, 92–117, esp. 93–95; 100–101(evidence from sites in the northern Aegean). A doctoral dissertation by Natalya Ivanova (University of Nottingham, UK) that explores olive production north of Rhodope, alongside other kinds of agricultural production, is in progress.

[46] McInerney 2010, esp. Ch. 6 (131–45) on *Homeric Hymn IV to Hermes* and the *Hymn to Apollo*; 150–94 (sacred economies; the emergence of markets for sacrificial cattle); 244–9 (the 'bovine idiom' in Greek culture).

[47] McInerney 2010, 32–3, 42–7, 49–73, 244–9.

differently configured. The *Homeric Hymn III to Apollo* and the *Homeric Hymn IV to Hermes* both refer to Pieria as the place where Hermes stole the cattle of Admetos, king of Thessalian Pherai, from Apollo.[48] The linkage between the main focus of the two poems on the one hand (on festival performances at Delphi, and their overall preoccupation with locations and communities in central Greece), and cattle breeding in the north Aegean on the other, seems tenuous, but reflects active social networks with the communities or rulers of Pieria that are not otherwise particularly visible in the political record of Delphi, although it is perfectly possible that the royal and civic representatives listed there on inscriptions of the fourth and third centuries BC followed an established tradition, whose roots simply cannot be demonstrated.[49]

Leaving aside Thessaly, and parts of central Greece (particularly the Krisaian Plain, south of Delphi and the meadow land around Lake Kopais between the river valleys of the Kephisos and the Asopos), the scope for pasturing large herds is limited in the southern parts of the Greek peninsula; not so in the north and north-east (Figure 7.2). Cattle are still plentiful in the well-watered valleys of the great east Balkan river courses. Pella prided itself on its cattle herds,[50] as did many northern Aegean communities, if we consider their coin types alone.[51] The question we need to answer, therefore, is whether or not there was a religious regime in the northern Aegean similar to that farther south. McInerney has exposed the socio-economic nexus between sacred festivals and sacrificial beasts. Festivals were the *raison d'être* of sanctuaries. Sanctuary authorities had to find a way of providing sacrificial animals for slaughter at festivals. At Delphi the cultivable land of the Krisaian Plain was set aside from early in the sixth century BC to provide pasture for sacred herds, while on Delos and at other sites where sacred laws and decrees have survived, land was leased so that the tenants could provide such animals.[52] The pattern of consumption throughout the festival year was

[48] McInerney 2010, 138 and refs n.71, 142–5; for historical pasturing of Thessalian animals in the foothills of Olympos, albeit near the Vale of Tempe rather than Pieria, there is an inscription from Gonnoi (Chandezon 2003, no. 17, second century BC).

[49] Mari 2002, 291–302, listing Macedonian representatives at Delphi.

[50] Pella also named *Βούνομος* or *Βουνόμεια* (Steph. Byz. 515.9–10); cf. Ch. 5, and nn.95, 97.

[51] Carradice 1987, Plate I, 1–4 (Fried: octadrachms of the Bisaltai); I, 5 (octadrachm, Getas of the Edoni); cf. Plate VIII 1–2 (Jessop Price: octadrachms of the Bisaltai); VIII, 4 (octadrachm of the Derrones).

[52] McInerney 2010, 152: 'there is a close connection between sacred land and sacred herds'; 146–72 (citing documents from Delphi, Delos, Kalaureia, Ilion, and particularly an exceptionally informative text from the sanctuary of Artemis Elaphebolos in eastern Phokis: *IG* IX 1.87.20–75, with translation p. 159 and discussion, 159–62). 'it is important to notice

Fig. 7.2. Cows and herdsmen near Strelcha, central Bulgaria.

irregular, but the challenge for sanctuaries in rural areas was not nearly as critical as it was for urbanized districts, particularly the city of Athens, with very little scope for nurturing stock in the vicinity. The Athenians could not boast a sacred herd, but had to find alternative ways of providing the enormous quantities of meat, particularly beef, required for civic festivals. If we take the public provision of sacrificial meat as literally as it is described by the 'Old Oligarch', then citizens could indeed expect a generous dose of meat ([Xen.] *Ath. Pol.* 2.9), perhaps as much as half a kilo per man, at the Panathenaic festival.[53] There were between forty and forty-five occasions throughout the Athenian festival year when meat was potentially available in large quantities for public consumption. In practice, however, it is much less clear how many people, including dependent family members, benefited from these handouts,

the recurring feature of sanctuary regulations: they are usually not concerned with piety or even ritual actions, except insofar as visitors continue to provide the god with his sacrifice and his priests with their perquisites' (with reference to the Amphiareion at Oropos: McInerney 2010, 171).

[53] McInerney 2010, 174–6, with detailed discussion; the estimate is based on 60 head of cattle at the Lesser Panathenaia (*IG* II² 334 B, fourth century BC, from Oropos); the half kilo portion would result from deme-based distributions, for men only; if women and children were to be included, the quantities would be proportionately much lower; McInerney 2010 187–8, on the numbers of sacrifices in the festival year.

and how much they received. The larger the event, the less likely was the chance that all who were eligible would receive a portion of any size.

The simple answer to the question posed above, regarding sacrificial regimes in the northern Aegean, should be yes—with one caveat. Although there is no document from the north comparable to those from Athens, Delphi, Delos, and other mainland sanctuaries which would illuminate the connection between sacred lands and sacrifice, festivals analogous to those that existed farther south took place, probably following an annual pattern that resembled better-known civic calendars. An inscription from Beroia, dating from the second half of the third century BC, refers to sacrifices, *thusia*, and the revenues accruing therefrom to the priests of Asklepios.[54] This is the closest we get to a process that echoes the increasingly lucrative nature of sacrificial beasts.[55] The letter of Andronikos to the sanctuary of the Egyptian gods in Thessalonike, conveying the *diagramma* of Philip V, which guarantees the rights and property of the sanctuary, refers to money (*chremata:* ll. 12, 24) and to treasuries (*thesauroi:* l.22), but not to land as such. Nevertheless, if we accept the logic already described about the nexus between sanctuaries and sacrifices, then the processes of sacrificial consumption can be assumed to have been much the same and the revenues for the Egyptian gods would have resembled the revenues of other priesthoods, with hides playing a significant role among the personal perquisites of priests and priestesses.

The caveat that should be added to this hypothesis concerns the part played by other sources of meat in northern diets. McInerney is convinced that although benefactors did contribute to the supply of sacrificial beef, little of this came from private sources, in Athens at least.[56] If he is right, and the demand for festival meat at Athens—beef in particular—did create a need to find suitable animals from far afield through commercial methods (because other avenues, including making maximum use of dependent territories, had already been pursued), then the market for beef was just as insistent (albeit for cultural rather than biological reasons), in the major conurbations of southern Greece (Athens, Corinth, in particular), as was the demand for cereals to supplement local production. The appearance of liberal quantities of meat in front of a bunch of hungry mercenaries must have come as a particularly welcome surprise to Xenophon's soldiers, at a dinner laid on by prince Seuthes, which was nothing particularly out of the ordinary;

[54] Hatzopoulos 1996, II, no. 82; I. Beroia, no. 16.
[55] McInerney 2010, 182–94.
[56] McInerney 2010, 179–82.

certainly not a festival dinner. We should look afresh at the herds of animals handed over to Xenophon's men as part-payment for their services, which explicitly included yokes of oxen (Xen. *Anab*. 7.2.36), while the 600 cattle that were part of the final payment suddenly look much more interesting than the historian was prepared to admit (Xen. *Anab*. 7.7.53).[57] Six hundred quality cattle, offered for sale at Byzantion, would have solved the sacrificial needs of a gargantuan consumer such as the city of Athens at a stroke, while the price could be negotiated to suit the seller.

In order to get some idea of meat consumption in these better-provided parts of the north Aegean, we can consider the evidence that is now accumulating about the deposition of animal waste at Adjiyska Vodenitsa (ancient Pistiros), in central Bulgaria. Animal bones have been recovered in a good state of preservation, in quantities well in excess of a metric tonne by weight, from an excavated area *c*.3000m^2, or one third of a hectare. A broad survey of 25–30 per cent of the tens of thousands of bones recovered up to the year 2000 showed that most of the material belonged to domesticated species, but also included some wild animals. The use of underground storage pits for the deposition of animal waste has enabled the investigators to identify 'consumption events', which can be distinguished from general patterns of animal waste disposal within accumulated layers of soil, particularly in the vicinity of the fortification wall, where there seems to have been a tendency to dump larger animal parts (Fig. 7.3, Sample 1).[58] A lined pit, which had also been recut (grid square D19/21), contained at its base a burnt offering, including charcoal lumps, around the base of a grey wheel-made bowl. Associated with the grey bowl were several butchered animal parts, including hare, dog, and domestic fowl. Shells of freshwater mussels were also present. As well as the scarcer species, the remains of at least one suckling pig, a similarly young lamb or kid, and half the skull of a puppy were found. A worked astragalus of a sheep or goat was also recovered.

Another similar pit, D19/02 (Fig. 7.3, Sample 3), which, like D19/21, contained a large quantity of ceramic and some metal finds, also yielded a butchered cattle skull and another mandible, perhaps belonging to a pair rather than a single beast, and three articulating lower limbs from a cow, perhaps the same cow. Although the cattle skull belonged to a youngish, perhaps castrated bull, the mandible was from a mature animal and the lower limbs cannot be assumed to come from either of

[57] See Ch. 1 and n.33.

[58] Stallibrass 2010, 58 Table 4.1, and 58–63 for discussion; cf. also Archibald 2002b; 2002c.

	Sample 1	(Sample 2)	Sample 2	Sample 3	comparison
Grid Square:	**B23**	**A9**	**A9**	**D 19**	**B21**
Context:	**VI planum**	**[952]**	**[952] K/1960**	**Pit 19/02 [1021]**	**48, 58, 122, 146, 151**
Context Type:	**Horizontal Layer**	**Pit**	**Basal layer in pit [952]**	**Pit layer**	**Horizontal Layers**
Cattle *Bos*	95 *50%*	35 *12%*	8 *4%*	70 *43%*	135 *44%*
Sheep/goat *Ovis/Capra*	57 *30%*	181 *61%*	127 *69%*	69 *43%*	123 *40%*
Pig *Sus*	22 *12%*	52 *17%*	28 *15%*	5 *3%*	33 *11%*
Dog *Canis*	12 *7%*	-	-	7 *4%*	9 *3%*
Horse *Equus*	2 *1%*	3? *1%*	3? *2%*	-	1 ~
Red Deer *Cervus*	-	2? *1%*	2? *1%*	-	2 + ?1 *1%*
Hare *Lepus*	-	4 *1%*	1 *1%*	1 *1%*	2 *1%*
Birds *Aves*	3 *2%*	21 *7%*	15 *8%*	11 *7%*	3 *1%*
Total identified	**191**	**298**	**184**	**163**	**309**
Others	49	448	209	214	685
Total recovered	**240**	**746**	**393**	**377**	**994**

Fig. 7.3. Table showing relative proportions of wild and domestic species in selected contexts at Adjiyska Vodenitsa, Vetren (ancient Pistiros).

these. In this pit there was also a sheep's skull, which could have been deposited fleshed; some mature sheep's limb bones, parts of a large dog, a red deer antler, and occasional bones of hare and domestic fowl. Despite the presence of individual artefacts that seem to have particular symbolic or cultic significance, the faunal remains in the pit relate to the 'non-meaty' parts of the respective larger animals. There seems here to have been a combination of 'ordinary' domestic-type animal waste on the one hand, and waste from the skinning process, rather than food consumption, on the other; in all, a palimpsest of different processes connected with the consumption of animal products.

By contrast, another pit, located at the back of Building No.1, a public structure alongside the main east–west road of Pistiros (Fig. 7.3, Sample 2), contained the complete heads and articulating joints of several sheep, after butchering, as well as 'ordinary' waste from the consumption of cattle, sheep, goats, and pigs. Analysis of the entire bone assemblage indicates that there were at least four and perhaps seven complete sheep and/or goats (five sheep and one goat can be identified securely). The sheep seem to have been selected in pairs; three were mature individuals and three were juveniles, slaughtered in their second year. These animals were slaughtered in a very similar way to other animals butchered elsewhere on this site, but here the remains of a collective meal can be identified more confidently. In addition, the discovery of a very deep pit, outside the fortification walls, containing dozens of complete animals, including cattle as well as sheep and pig, illustrates more ambitious 'consumption events', the waste of which probably had to be accommodated well beyond the principal residential areas of the settlement.[59]

What can we learn from the residues of meals at this inland site on the middle Hebros? The anecdotes filleted out of his various sources by Athenaeus do not map over the material found in the small selection of rubbish pits explored here; nor does the general epigraphic evidence surveyed by McInerney for civic sacrifices cover the same ground. At present there is a lack of comparative evidence, which might give us some idea of whether the consumption profile at this inland site is at all typical of the northern Aegean, although it may be close to the norm.[60] Perhaps the most significant element that emerges from the systematic study of faunal remains at Pistiros is the category deemed 'ordinary' waste. 'Ordinary' waste implies regular, non-festival, domestic meals, and includes residues of cattle, sheep, goat, pig, hare, chicken, occasional wild birds such as heron, molluscs, river fish, wild boar, and even bear. 'Ordinary' implies meat available for commercial purchase or small hunted animals. The references to markets for animals in Xenophon's *Anabasis* imply that animals of different sizes were bought and sold regularly, and there is no reason why there should not have been a cattle market in central Thrace. This does not mean that a sacrifice did not take place before the slaughter of the animals themselves. The general treatment of carcasses implies that slaughter was always framed in terms of ritual procedures, although disposal only sometimes was. The appearance of 'associated bone groups', or the reassembly of bones into joints

[59] The material was briefly surveyed by Sue Stallibrass in 2012.

[60] MacKinnon 2007 offers a survey of the range of evidence from Aegean sites in pre-Roman times.

prior to disposal, is a phenomenon known more widely in continental Europe.[61]

Marine fish and molluscs played a larger role in coastal areas, and included langoustine (Athen. 7.325e) as well as octopus (Athen. 7.318f), which could find its way inland as a special delicacy, as we have seen in the case of Iphikrates' marriage to Kotys I's daughter. The quantities were evidently impressive, if not the hecatombs of comic exaggeration. Preserved fish from Thasos had a reputation abroad that at least matched that from Ainos and Byzantion.[62]

The least well-understood dietary component—and not just in the northern Aegean—is the role of wild animals. Hunting has often been studied in terms of the associated cultural metaphors, rather than the economic value that may have accrued from the quarry. The cultural ramifications of hunting extend beyond the scope of this book, although the eschatological dimensions will be examined more closely in the next chapter. The discovery of a magnificent painted frieze depicting the capture of multiple large animals, on the front of Tomb II at Vergina, reopened the debate about what was true of Macedonian royal practice in the painting and what may have belonged to an imaginary landscape. One principal problem in understanding the images has been the possibility that the iconographic repertoire was acquired from Near Eastern sources, which would locate the painting and its content in a context after the Asiatic conquests of Alexander the Great, and therefore involve possible contamination of indigenous experiences with exotic ones from the east. Pierre Briant rejected this style of argumentation, arguing that big game hunting appeared in royal iconography much earlier in the fourth century BC and owed little to eastern precedents. In fact, as Greenwalt has suggested, similarities between Odrysian royal imagery, which also involve hunting scenes, may be more apposite than Near Eastern prototypes.[63] The Vergina painting is a complex image, with major and minor elements combined in a way that is by no means easy to reconstruct, notwithstanding the painstaking work of conservators. As many as six animal quarries have been identified, which include at least one stag, one boar, one lion, and one bear, surrounded by ten huntsmen and nine dogs. The choice of animals was evidently intended to be

[61] Stallibrass 2010, 62–3 with refs.

[62] Other notable fresh fish from Thasos and the northern Aegean: Athen. 2.105d (scorpion fish); 7.321a (mullet); preserved fish: Grandjean and Salviat 2000, 181; Ar. *Acharn.* 671; Athen. 4.164e; 7.329b; see also contributions to Bekker-Nielsen 2005, esp. Højte, 133–60, Lund and Gabrielsen, 161–9.

[63] Briant 1991; cf. also Greenwalt 1993, 515–16; Étienne 2002, 253–8.

symbolic as well as realistic, although scholars have tended to focus on the possible significance of human portraits rather than the meaning of the animal representations.[64] The iconography of hunting, which occupies a key role in Macedonian royal coinage, plays an even more prominent role in Thracian toreutics, particularly on horse gear, with boars, stags, bears, and other less easily identifiable creatures.[65]

The repertoire of hunting allusions on the walls of a vaulted tomb at Alexandrovo, near Haskovo, is one apposite example. This late fourth- or early third-century series of tomb painting echoes features of contemporary Macedonian funerary art, whilst retaining distinctive local elements. The circular burial chamber has two friezes, an upper one showing hunters pursuing four quarries (two stags, or a stag and a hind, and two boars); while the lower frieze is less well preserved but includes a scene of seated and standing figures (diners and those serving them) around at least two tables piled with vessels and food, but between the figures is the carcass of a bull.[66] The hunting scene shows independent figures, arranged serially, against a white background, rather than juxtaposed—four hunters on horseback with raised spears, four hunters on foot, and the four quarries beset by dogs. So the scene is intentionally much more symbolic than real, even if real prey is represented here, as in the dining scene below it.

CONCLUSIONS

The traditional cuisine of the east Balkan region, consisting of cereals, pulses, fruit, and nuts, a diet which had evolved over several thousands of years, was still the basis of diet in the second half of the first millennium BC. There is quite a lot of circumstantial evidence that suggests meat from domesticated species including sheep, goats, pigs, and cattle may have been consumed by a proportion of the population at least quite frequently. If Athenian citizens were eating meat on average once a week, through festival fare, then consumption in the northern Aegean is likely to have been at least as common and probably more so.

64 Saatsoglou-Paliadeli 2011, 282–4, summarizes the different views of who the protagonists were intended to represent; Briant 1991 and 1994a; Étienne 2000 and Étienne 2002, 253–8, explore the zoomorphic vocabulary.

65 Archibald 1998, 249–51; Marazov, 2011.

66 Kitov 2001; Kitov 2004, 43 fig. 3; cf. Stoyanov 2008, 58; this tomb has not been fully published. The details of the surviving images are difficult to verify.

This is hard to demonstrate, because more work needs to be done on faunal evidence to provide data comparable to what is now available from sites like Adjiyska Vodenitsa. Access to wild and marine species provided additional variety to what was already a relatively broad menu, while local wines coexisted with more highly valued imported ones. The evidence from country houses suggests that their owners took a great interest in the creative possibilities of food and food preparation, while houses at Olynthos show that specialization in foodstuffs, as well as non-food resources, was already well developed. The creative urge is also recognizable in the cultural semantics of food preparation, so aptly illustrated in Theopompos' remarks about dining fashions with which this chapter opened.

8

Continuity and commemoration

MONUMENTS, THE SACRED, AND SACRED LAND IN THE NORTH AEGEAN

As Jeremy McInerney has underscored in his recent study of cattle in Greek culture, sanctuaries were, first and foremost, *temene*; lands 'cut out' from other ground, not least to ensure the maintenance of sanctuary assets (including sacrificial animals), but also to distinguish sacred land from other kinds, whether we call them profane, collective, or private land.[1] The evidence for north Aegean sacred spaces is rather more opaque than what we know of sanctuaries in central and much of southern Greece. One of the unexpected discoveries about social behaviour in the pre-imperial northern Aegean is the variety of monumental structures that have a sacred character. Burial sites and sacred areas do not seem to have the distinct typologies in the north that they had in central and southern Greece. This has implications for how we think about the application of the term *temenos* in these regions, but also how we consider the abstract understanding and use of resources in these northern societies.

In the northern Aegean the historical mechanisms by which land was designated 'sacred' are both similar to and different from other parts of the Greek peninsula. The problem of sacred land is rendered more complex than elsewhere in the Aegean because there was a relationship between, on the one hand, sacred places intended for collective assembly and performance, and, on the other, those associated with mortuary structures. What is more, tombs often look like cult buildings and are consciously grounded in particular landscapes. The custom of building earthen mounds for the dead was a process that united them with the land in a unique way. Mounds occupy many times more space than a simple earth-cut pit or cist and construction took this space out of agricultural use. Surviving

[1] McInerney 2010, 147.

Fig. 8.1. Vetren, tumulus 2: mound in the fields between the archaeological remains at Adjiyska Vodenitsa and the town of Vetren, in the foothills of the Sredna Gora, west of Plovdiv, central Bulgaria.

examples are often located in arable fields (Fig. 8.1) which emphasizes how vulnerable such monuments are to erosion through the normal processes of land use. Intensive cultivation has denuded landscapes of many such constructions over more than two millennia, so ancient statistics for the original provision of mound burials can only be guessed at.

Even when such monuments were located in more marginal areas, on hills or scarps that made them yet more prominent features of the landscape, they nevertheless involved the concentration of exceptional resources—in terms of the manpower required to raise the mound; the stone to build the cist or tomb, sometimes an elaborate masonry structure; as well as a wide range of subsidiary and decorative materials, alongside all of which we should include grave goods. Tombs of this type were designed and built to a noticeably higher specification than private residential structures and therefore occupied a more significant role in regional economies than, for example, residential units. In terms of resource intensity, funerary monuments will often have attracted a cost much closer to that of cult buildings.[2] Many built tombs, whether

[2] See above, Ch. 4 and n.25; the theoretical price range is potentially enormous, with the Parthenon at 1893.9 Attic drachmae/m^2, at the high end, and a workshop adjacent to the

enlarged cists or actual chambers, were constructed of marble, granite, or at the very least a fine-grained limestone. Since one of the functions of these regional kinds of tombs seems to have been to make a cavity free of soil, so that it could be decorated in a special way on the inside, good quality ashlar masonry was the best method of ensuring that the pressure of the surrounding earth, whether below or above ground, could be resisted. Archaeologists usually connect mound burials with social exclusivity, and certainly with conscious social distinction. In classical Athens, a series of earth mounds in the Kerameikos cemetery was reused for prominent graves from the final quarter of the fifth century BC. Along with the burials in *periboloi* (walled enclosures), the graves in and around the Kerameikos mounds, and similar monuments in other Attic cemeteries, represent perhaps ten per cent of the population of fifth- and fourth-century BC Athens.[3]

In the northern Aegean monumental tombs were often located at some distance from urban concentrations, if not actually in rural areas. In larger peri-urban cemeteries, as at Edessa, or Aiani, Pella, or Abdera, or in the Pontic coastal harbour towns, graves are heterogeneous, with monumental constructions interspersed among pits and cists.[4] Outside major urban centres, monumental graves tend either to be isolated features in the landscape or arranged in clusters. Many of the vaulted or painted Macedonian tombs that have been investigated were not closely connected to any urban nucleus and the majority of Thracian monumental tombs were likewise sited in scattered, rural locations (see Fig. 4.7, nos. 21, 22–26; 30, 35–36, 38, 41, 42, 50–55, 67–69; 72, 74–75, 79; and Fig. 4.8, nos 41–59). This makes it likely that the choice of site was determined by social or dynastic considerations. The incumbents were buried, in all likelihood, on their own estates. Did the land in and around burial monuments become 'sacred land' as a result? The 'penumbra' of mounds around urban centres such as Seuthopolis, Sveshtari, Adjiyska Vodenitsa, and Philippopolis resembles the concentrations of

temple of Asklepios at Epidauros, calculated as 14.28 Attic drachmae/m^2, at the low end (Davies 2005, 120–1, with further refs). In terms of what has already been said above about equivalence to cult structures, the unit cost would have been somewhere in between these two extremes, but somewhat nearer the top end rather than the lower one.

3 Morris 1992, 128–38.

4 Edessa: Chrysostomou 2008, 41–7; Aiani: Karamitrou-Mentessidi 2006a; 2011; Pella: Chrysostomou and Chrysostomou 2000; 2001; 2002; 2007; Lilimbaki-Akamatis 2009; Nea Philadelphia, Thessaloniki: Misaïlidou-Despotidou 2008, 24–65; Sedes, Thessaloniki: Skarlatidou 2009; Oisyme and Galepsos: Koukouli-Chrysanthaki 2006; Abdera: Skarlatidou 2010; Amphipolis: Malamidou 2006a; 2006b; Apollonia Pontika: Hermary et al. 2010.

monumental tombs on the outskirts of Aigeai.[5] In these peri-urban or suburban areas, the expansion of modern residential accommodation and of rural pursuits has made it hard to identify whether the graves were located on land that was designated in some way, by markers, to separate it from other uses. The construction of earthen tumuli is itself a process of marking off ground, and where the stages of construction can be identified as coherent and consecutive acts, a funeral pyre formed the initial event, succeeded by a burial and covering of earth, although subsequent burials could be made by cutting into the fill. This is the sequence documented, for example, at Prilep, near Karnobat, in a mound containing early forms of the 'greyware' discussed in Chapter 4 (cf. Fig. 4.10).[6]

The prevailing pattern of mortuary structures throughout the northern Aegean area was of localized diversity. Even the highly distinctive barrel-vaulted Macedonian tombs display a considerable diversity of design, as well as a wide variety of subsidiary features. In inland Thrace, every built tomb is conceptually and structurally unique, even though some structural solutions or certain superficial features do recur. This means that the ideas about how to build monumental tombs operated on a different socio-economic model from those that determined the exchange of portable commodities. The design of tombs was therefore in all likelihood driven by a combination of available (or bespoke) technological skills and locally sourced materials (although, as we shall see below, the abstract concepts that tombs embodied are also difficult to trace in terms of social networks). During the second half of the fourth and early third century BC in Thrace, fired bricks partially replaced stone in areas like the Valley of the Roses, where suitable building stone was less accessible. This wholly new construction technique seems to appear independently of external stimuli, although comparable bricks were being made in a small number of other Aegean locations around the same time, including Olynthos.[7] Experimental evidence shows that fired bricks made to this specification have a high capacity to absorb moisture, so make an excellent backing material for painted plaster. Everything about the design and appearance of monumental tombs implies that the architects were working at the cutting edge of contemporary building

[5] Rural distributions of monumental tombs: Archibald 1998, 242–50 and figs. 10.2, 10.4; Sveshtari and Seuthopolis: Stoyanov 2000; 2002; 2006; Adjiyska Vodenitsa: Philippopolis: Koleva et al. 2000; see below for Aigeai.

[6] Georgieva and Momchilov 2003.

[7] Gerding 2006, 354–6 and figs. 1–2; there are unpublished fired bricks at Adjiyska Vodenitsa, from the city excavations, not from funerary contexts.

Fig. 8.2. Zhaba Mogila, Strelcha, view of the entrance to the tomb chamber. The carved embrasure of the doorway has relief bands of egg-and-dart on the lintel slab and around the lateral blocks, with a Lesbian kyma added just below the top of the lintel slab.

technology (Figs 8.2 and 8.3). Many of the Thracian tombs have corbel vaults, applying various methods of narrowing the roof space by improving on traditional methods. Barrel vaults were the first true self-supporting domes, although the structural properties of this phenomenon were not fully appreciated when they were first applied in funerary contexts. Elsewhere we can detect common features within the same locality, which suggests the development of specific local expertise, perhaps stimulated by a particularly successful solution, as in the case of the corbel-vaulted tombs at Kirklareli in Turkish Thrace, or the brick-built beehive tombs at Koprinka, near Seuthopolis. Otherwise the most striking thing about monumental graves is the fact that no tomb is much like any other.[8]

The monumental elaboration of funerary structures makes them hard to distinguish from cult buildings and perhaps this was a conscious

[8] Archibald 1998, 282–303; Rousseva 2000; Kitov 2003a; 2003b; 2005; Delemen 2006.

Fig. 8.3. Tumulus of Starosel: masonry krepis surrounding the earth mound (second half of the fourth century BC).

intention; many tombs resemble cult monuments in form, with temple-like exterior or interior decoration. There are some examples of monumental stone temples, which approximate much more closely to Aegean 'norms' of sacred architecture, particularly on the Kassandra peninsula of Chalkidike.[9] These are, nevertheless, exceptional. The principal foci of collective worship, whether at civic centres such as Pella or at the pan-Macedonian sanctuary of Zeus and the Muses at Dion, have not yielded large temples. On the contrary, and notwithstanding the patronage of Argead kings at Aphytis, or Samothrace, where significant buildings that conform to contemporary Aegean structural models arose, the pattern within Macedonia and in Thrace seems to have favoured small cult buildings, which look rather modest by wider Aegean standards (Fig. 8.4).[10] The distinction between expensive, monumental ashlar

[9] Tsigarida 2011b (temple of Zeus Ammon, Aphytis; the author proposes that the temple of Zeus was built by Philip II or a close successor, and destroyed by an earthquake at the end of the fourth century BC or slightly later); see also Ch. 2, n.79 (for Poseidi, ancient Mende, and the archaic Ionic temple in Thessaloniki). The structures identified at Krastevich in the Sredna Gora have not yet been fully revealed, but current excavations in any case indicate an original design without close parallels in the Aegean (see Ch. 5 n.16).

[10] Lilimbaki-Akamatis 1990; Akamatis 2006b, 627–39; 631 fig. 3, area of sanctuary of Darron and ?Thesmophorion); Akamatis 2011, 404–5, with further refs (sanctuaries at Pella); Christesen and Murray 2010, 436–8, 'Tombs not Temples'; 'The relatively minimal amount of resources expended on temple building stands in stark contrast to the enormous

Fig. 8.4. Dion, Macedonia: fourth-century BC temple foundations (centre right); two shrines built of ashlar masonry with columned entrances (Doric-style in antis) replaced late sixth-century predecessors in unbaked bricks.

structures in 'pan-Hellenic' sanctuaries, on the one hand, and small shrines in indigenous sites on the other, is hard to understand. Why should it have been acceptable to expend very large sums of money on the sponsorship of structures in sites of wider Aegean significance, including more distant sanctuaries like Delos, and not to devote the same resources in one's very own sanctuaries?[11]

The explanation may lie partly in the realm of international politics and partly in different ways of understanding human–divine interactions. A significant factor is the religious dimension of relations between rulers and their subjects. Leaders, whether at the level of kingdoms, regions, or localities, in Macedonia as in Thrace, held a special, cultic significance, which had no direct equivalent in the rest of the Aegean. It is tantalizingly reflected in the deification of Macedonian kings by a range of northern civic communities, as we can see in a series of inscriptions

investment that Macedonians made in tombs. . . . Early archaeological remains from non-mortuary contexts in Macedonia are notoriously poor, which makes the amount of wealth invested in the burials at Sindos [and similar cemeteries] all the more remarkable' (ibid. 438); Mari 2011b, 458–64; for Argead dedications on Samothrace, see now the contributions to Palagia and Wescoat 2010.

[11] Bringmann and von Steuben 1995, with a conspectus of Macedonian royal dedications on Samothrace, 261–6 [cat. nos 233, Philip III and Alexander IV–236]; Delos, 187–200 [cat. nos 117, Krateros–141, Perseus]; for regional munificence, cat. nos 110 (Perseus' dedication to Artemis Tauropolos at Amphipolis); no. 111 (Philip V dedicates stoas to Athena, Beroia); no. 112 (Alexander III, statue groups at Dion); cf. also Bringmann 2001.

that name particular kings alongside the names of gods.[12] Far from being cynical attempts to ingratiate themselves with their Macedonian overlords, these acts of public respect, offered by regional communities of the northern Aegean, are indicative of a regional understanding of the cultic role of leaders in society.

This cultic role may originally have developed (before the emergence of the historic kingdoms of Macedon and Thrace) because leaders of communities that were often geographically isolated could assure supplies of meat at collective gatherings. We have seen in Chapter 7 that feasting was a key way in which kings, princes (and, by analogy, local leaders) cemented trust amongst their peers and subordinates. Hunting dramatized the role of leaders as facilitators of supplementary meat resources. The managerial role of kings in the organization of hunting expeditions is reflected in a royal letter concerning the revenues of the sanctuary of Herakles *kynagidas*, patron of hunting and of young men in Beroia,[13] and also in the duties and privileges of different age classes during hunting episodes.[14] The close relationship between the Macedonian king and the young men who provided personal assistance to him as part of their training was paralleled by the king's dedications to Herakles, and Herakles' patronage of the young *kynegoi* (hunters). Here we can see how cult reinforced the social roles of the participants, but also gave the king himself a decisive role in the young men's wellbeing.

Civic and other types of community cult provided opportunities for collective dining in much the same way that they did elsewhere in Greece.[15] In principle the kinds of pressures on land resources that were exerting tension on the magistrates of growing populations in southern Greece were less relevant in the northern Aegean, where pasture land was plentiful and collective anxieties focused on the danger

[12] Mari 2007, and p. 385, Table 1 (Amphipolis; Berga; Kassandreia; Maroneia; Nikiti; Oreskeia; Philippoi; Philippopolis; Pydna; Thasos). These northern expressions contrast with the understanding of 'divine' status in more southerly communities, such as Athens (Christesen and Murray 2010, 441–3, with earlier bibliography).

[13] Hatzopoulos 1994a, 102–4, *I. Beroia* no. 3 (= Hatzopoulos 1996, II, no. 8; 248 bc, three letters of Demetrios, son and co-regent of Antigonos Gonatas, the first of which refers to *kynegoi* (l. 2), to priests of Herakles (ll. 4–5), and to *prosodoi* (l. 5), SEG 43.379); Hatzopoulos 1994a, 103–11, argues that *kynegoi* were the equivalents of *ephebes* in Macedonia.

[14] Plb. 31.29.3–5 (*kynegoi basilikoi* drafted into Scipio's reserve forces after the battle of Pydna); Ar. *Pol.* 1324b (referring to a former Macedonian law requiring men who had not yet killed an enemy to wear a halter in place of a belt); Hegesandros ap. Athen. 1.18a (Kassander forced at the age of 35 to sit at table, and at his father's feet, because he had yet to kill a boar without nets); Hatzopoulos 1994a, 87–111 with discussion; Carney 2002, 59–66.

[15] McInerney 2010, 184–95.

of attacks by wild animals, rather than the scarcity of sacrificial beasts. The need to provide protection for comparatively isolated inland communities, separated from one another by forests, explains the central importance of training a corps of young men in horsemanship and country pursuits. Funerary images and artefacts in graves strongly reflect the social significance of those who bore responsibility for protecting settled populations engaged in other pursuits. Besides providing protection from scavengers and occasional large predators, leadership carried the more basic duty of affirming social order and encouraging cordial relations. Michael Dietler has explained how alcoholic beverages could have reinforced positive social messages in southern Gaul, and more generally among south-western and central European societies, particularly when these came into contact with Phoenician and Greek traders. Commensality, or collective dining, was one of the key ways in which members of ancient communities affirmed mutual ties, but also cemented new ties, whether with merchants or with other visitors.[16] The mass adoption of various forms of drinking equipment was partly motivated by the recognition that exotic vessels, as well as the beverages for which they were designed, enabled social relationships to be seen in new ways. Royal, princely, and communal dinners put an onus on leaders as hosts, but these investments bore fruit when communities thrived as a result. Funerary furniture and decoration in the northern Aegean is much preoccupied with dining. In part this refers to the imagined dinners of an otherworldly afterlife; but the afterlife is imagined using the artefacts that the deceased would have been familiar with.

What concerns us here is the economic significance of those acts of mortuary differentiation between rulers and their ilk on the one hand, and other inhabitants, whether citizens or subjects, on the other. The social distinctions that put some individuals into special categories and not others did not just apply to kings. Queens, princes, senior officers, priests, and priestesses should also be included among those accorded distinctive obsequies. Age classes might also be expected to feature in some way in the grammar of mortuary practice, in the same way that their status was recognized in different forms of dress, footwear, and headgear in life. In this respect, Thracian rulers and others in Thrace fulfilling important public roles, female as well as male, enjoyed a similar social distinction to that held by their Macedonian peers. Mortuary rituals therefore deserve closer attention.

[16] Dietler 1990; 1999; 2009; 2011; Dietler and Herbich 2001.

ALL-CONSUMING DEATH

Among the uncommon finds that are on display in the museum constructed over the royal tombs under the 'Megale Toumba' (Great Tumulus) at Vergina are the conserved and reconstituted remains of the funeral pyre which was raised over Tomb II. Preliminary analysis of the faunal material includes cattle, dog, goat, sheep, bird, and fish bones. More than 3,000 mammalian bone fragments were recovered, mixed with those of birds and fish. They had all been exposed to high temperatures.[17] Archaeologists managed to retrieve some of the burnt horse bones, belonging to four riding horses, together with parts of their bridles, and the partial remains of two dogs, some of the birds, and fishes. This residual material gives at least a partial idea of the kinds of sacrificial offerings considered appropriate for accompanying the remains of a king to the afterlife. Complete horse skeletons have been recovered from dozens of Thracian tombs belonging to the landed élite, whether cavalrymen from the armies of Odrysian and other Thracian principalities, or simply country landowners. Dogs are also known; birds and fish are rather more surprising, if only because we lack comparable evidence.[18]

The ritualized burial of horses with their owners is comparatively unusual in Greece, perhaps because horse owners were rather uncommon. In the northern Aegean the practice of horse burial is especially marked in the fourth and third centuries BC, but examples such as those recently recovered near Lithochori, where a multi-period cemetery has been found on the west bank of the River Nestos, north of the new Egnatia Odos motorway, show that the tradition of horse burial, whether as single steeds, as pairs, or horses yoked to carts, was deeply embedded in the region, even if some periods happen not to be represented here.[19] The implication of these particular types of burial is that horses were

[17] Antikas 2006, 206, 207 fig. 13 (goat, dog, bird, and ?marine fish). The faunal evidence has not been published in a full scientific report; it is included as a very useful contextual component to Antikas's report on the horse bones. See above, Ch. 4, 'Horse power', for horse burials.

[18] Ph. Columeau provides an interesting recent report on the small faunal assemblage (*c.*200 bone fragments) from the Franco-Bulgarian excavations at Apollonia Pontika, where bones of at least one young goat, a minimum of two adult sheep and two lambs, parts of a pig and a very young piglet, domestic chicken, and some fish bones, were recovered from a funerary pyre excavated in 2004. All had been heavily burned and are assumed to have been consumed in a meal at the tomb (Hermary 2010, 173; the editor favours a different interpretation: 'un sacrifice non consommé': ibid. 165).

[19] Poulios et al. 2007 (with a range of burials from the fifth century BC to the fourth century AD, although there is a gap between the third century BC and the first century AD); Archibald 1998, 296–7, and Kouzmanov 2005 on horse burials from inland Thrace. See also

killed when their personal masters died. That is a clear enough message from the faunal evidence above Tomb II at Vergina, and the incidence of pet dogs as well as favourite horses in some Thracian tombs reinforces the connection between owners and their particular animals. To modern observers, such behaviour looks extravagant at best. These were not animals that had come to the end of their useful lives.

Scholarly interest in the Argead kings has focused attention on the most spectacular and exceptional monuments, particularly the barrel-vaulted chamber tombs. The earliest of this form, at Aegeai at least, appears to be the 'Tomb of Eurydike', close to the so-called 'Rhomaios' tomb with an Ionic façade (Fig. 8.5), dated by the excavators to the 340s BC.[20] A recent review of painted tombs of all forms lists 25 of the barrel-vaulted type, of which 13 have been identified at Aigeai alone, frequently

Fig. 8.5. Vergina, tomb with Ionic façade (*c.*300 BC), known as 'Rhomaios' Tomb', after the archaeologist Konstantinos Rhomaios, who first investigated it in 1937.

Ch. 4, above; Galanakis (ed.) 2011, 100 fig. 88 and cat. no. 203 (miniature iron cart; further examples are discussed below).

[20] 'Tomb of Eurydike', *c.*340 BC: Ginouvès and Hatzopoulos, eds, (1993), 156–61, and 161–91 for the principal tombs at Vergina and Levkadia; Tsimbidou-Avloniti 2005, 175 no. 8, with bibl.; Saatsoglou-Paliadeli 2011, 288–90; Drougou 2011, 252–6, on the cemeteries of Aigeai; Kottaridi in Galanakis (ed.) 2011, 131–52; Andronikos 1987 is still fundamental for study of the Great Tumulus; Hatzopoulos 2008b and Lane-Fox's introductory chapter in Lane-Fox 2011 provide full discussions of the dating of Tomb II, with arguments in favour of an identification of the occupants with Philip II and princess Meda (cf. also Archibald 1985); favouring Philip III Arrhidaios and his wife Eurydike/Kynna: Borza and Palagia 2007. The skeletal evidence points decisively to Philip II and Meda (Musgrave et al. 2010).

occurring in clusters; one rock-cut tomb (at Marina, Naoussa); three chamber tombs without barrel vaults (at Aghios Athanasios near Thessaloniki, Vergina/Palatatsia (Heuzey's Palatitsa), and Katerini), and 22 cist-type tombs, enlarged cist burials, or sarcophagi, from Makrygialos in Pieria to the lower Strymon valley and Amphipolis.[21] The painted tombs seem to correspond to the monuments on which the greatest amount of resource had been expended. Some of these may well have belonged to members of the king's immediately family, but many of the incumbents were from non-royal, élite families. Excavators have identified recognizable clusters of tombs, which logically belong to dynastic groups.

The range and distribution of burials at Aigeai provide an insight into the organization of mortuary practices in and around the city. More than a thousand burials have been investigated to date, but the wealth and complexity of this material has yet to be fully analysed. Although the quantitative data is limited, the extraordinary quality of some of the available information provides significant insights. These insights help to delineate the distinctive character of northern mortuary traditions, but also to define the economic dimensions of these rituals. The oldest burials, on the east side of the city, partly overlap with classical ones, although most of the archaic and classical tombs were located in the north-western sector. Sixth-century BC burials reflect clear connections, in the style and choice of grave goods as well as the material selected, with Early Iron Age traditions at Aigeai on the one hand, and later, more ostentatious expressions of similar style on the other. The 'Temenids' cluster' of burials on the south-western periphery of the field of Early Iron Age tumuli contained a number of cremation pyres close to burials dating to the two middle quarters of the sixth century BC. Male burials frequently contained quantities of weapons, sometimes armour, and drinking equipment. Female graves show an abundance of ornaments and vessels. The 'lady of Aigeai', perhaps a queen of the later sixth century BC, was buried with an elaborate set of sheet-gold ornaments, some of which probably decorated her shroud, as well as gold jewellery and a selection of metal and clay vessels.[22] From the third century BC onwards, the city's fortification walls created a visible division between the civic environment and those peripheral areas that continued to be used for burial. Tumuli are dominant in the plain north of the city, the

[21] Tsimbidou-Avloniti 2005, 172–84; on Macedonian built tombs, see also Miller 1993, 95ff.; Huguenot 2008, I, 37–51; II, 29–38.

[22] 'Lady of Aigeai': Galanakis (ed.) 2011, 53, 55 fig. 39, 237 fig. 720, cat. nos. 328–414; Early Iron Age burials at Aigeai: Andronikos 1969: Kottaridi 2009; Kottaridi 2011c, 141–2; cf. Kottaridi 2011c, 93–126.

area first investigated by Léon Heuzey (after whom one of the tombs is named) and sporadically elsewhere in the north and north-east. Mounds were, of course, only one form of burial style. Pits and cists represent most of the 'lesser' interments.

Aside from the royal burials, a number of non-royal graves are worth exploring more closely. One recently investigated grave complex provides unusually rich evidence of mortuary practices. The 'Stenomakri' Toumba at Vergina is a burial mound named after its elongated, 'oblong' shape. It lies in the north-west part of the cemetery area of ancient Aigeai, some 200 m from the 'Great Tumulus', and, when surveyed by archaeologists, was still the second largest tumulus in the vicinity after the former (43.70 m x 23.40 m). It was first investigated in 1981 by Chrysoula Saatsoglou-Paliadeli, still under the watchful eye of Andronikos, and re-investigated by A. Kyriakou in 2003–5. Like the 'Great Tumulus', it is composed of a number of separate burials with their own earthen fill, which have merged into a single, cumulative structure. The earthen surround did not, however, protect the contents from pillage, perhaps during the historical attack of the Gauls on Vergina in 274 BC (Plut. *Pyrrh.* 26), as well as in subsequent centuries. Despite these onslaughts, the complex of up to four burials is among the most interesting as well as the most complete Macedonian funerary inventories dating to the fourth century BC.

Three of the burials were of men, all equipped with weapons, all evidently senior military officers, judging by the associated artefacts found in two cases (Tombs B and *Γ*) in funerary pyres above the roof of a limestone ashlar cist; in one case on a mortuary bed. The interior of the first cist (Tomb B), which was not big enough to contain an extended human skeleton (1.42 m x 1.04 m x 1.00 m), was painted with red, white, and blue pigments, with a plain scheme except for a frieze of ribbons and garlands, hanging from imaginary and real iron nails. It was otherwise empty. Among the finds that eluded looters was a set of (now fragmentary) polychrome water jars, of which there must have been at least ten in all, together with a range of iron weapons—the blade of a sarissa, a spear head, two or more javelins, an iron sword with a composite handgrip, upwards of nine iron strigils, a gilded bronze wreath of myrtle leaves and florals, an iron horse bit, and three iron pins, associated with what is thought to have been a wooden chest intended to contain the cremated bones of the deceased. After the remains were put in place, an earthen mound some 20 m in diameter was raised over the grave. The excavator considers this tomb to date some years before the middle of the fourth century BC.[23]

[23] Kyriakou 2008.

The second cist grave (Tomb *Γ*), like its predecessor, was a stone box with a painted interior, of slightly smaller dimensions (1.21 m x 0.87 m x 0.70 m). This time the decoration consisted of a white background with a red frieze. The bones of the second man were probably placed in a metal box. Again, most of the information about the associated grave goods comes from the remains of a pyre. There was another collection of polychrome *hydriai*, perhaps fifteen, as well as some painted pottery (of the kind more usually associated with women's burials: four oil flasks, a jug, and an *amphoriskos*), a silver *kalyx* cup, three iron swords, the butt of a sarissa, two spear heads, nine javelins, fragments of a horse bit, multiple iron strigils, two silver and at least four iron pins, a gilded bronze myrtle wreath, and the iron lid of a leather vessel. In addition, there were fragments of a bronze wreath of oak leaves; attachments, perhaps made of ivory, for a wooden box; ivory attachments for a bed, and clay gilded terracotta reliefs. Perhaps a man and a woman were buried here. A third man, around 35 years old, was later buried in a pit grave that was inserted into the composite mound. His body was laid on a wooden bed, with a spearhead, an iron sword with a silver foil-decorated handle, an iron knife, two strigils, and a gilded bronze wreath. This man had evidently been a horseman for much of his life. The mound fill contained horse's teeth, while the pyre associated with Tomb *Γ* yielded dog, goat, and sheep bones.

Despite the looting of the Stenomakri tumulus, the quantities of hardware concealed in the three identifiable graves is astonishing, particularly when compared with the vast majority of burials of this date from central and southern Greece, where grave goods were generally modest.[24] The tendency to mortuary modesty is also sometimes apparent in the north, when we compare the 405 graves excavated at Akanthos with flat cemeteries at Aiani, or Archondiko, near Pella. Just over 40 per cent of the graves at Akanthos had some goods and, notwithstanding the city's manifest levels of wealth, there was a very limited range of largely ceramic items, in striking contrast to the frequent and varied grave goods in the Macedonian and Thracian interior. Similarly, at Apollonia Pontika there is a complete absence of arms, a dearth of any metal objects, and a

[24] Morris 1992, 118 (on Athenian burials of the fifth and fourth centuries BC): 'It is not just that precious metals are virtually absent from burials; pottery too was used sparingly. . . . I would suggest that we should not see pots as symbolic substitutes for more valuable materials, but on the contrary should take the buriers' parsimony as having a positive message about abstention from display.' Cf. Morris 1992, 123–5, on the infrequency of metal and ceramic artefacts in domestic contexts, and the reluctance to parade wealth in Athens; 174–99 for a nuanced analysis of family graves at Vroulia, Rhodes.

limited range of ceramic items among the 56 tombs excavated by the Franco-Bulgarian team between 2002 and 2004.[25] The preference for modest tomb inventories is more characteristic of coastal 'colonial' sites than of indigenous northern ones. Many coastal communities, whose funerary traditions were more closely tied to wider Aegean practices, display a greater preference for simple burial or cremation in pits or cists, while the principal social emphasis was on standing memorials. Funerary *stelai*, with simple inscriptions of a name and patronymic, or the same accompanied by a short text, are the commonest memorials from coastal settlements. The more pretentious have carved relief sculpture. Memorial stones were beginning to become fashionable in fifth-century BC Macedonia, but at Aigeai there was a preference for painted rather than carved *stelai*.[26] Funerary monuments of the *stele* form were comparatively rare in inland Thrace before the Macedonian conquest and the earliest surviving specimens may have belonged to visiting merchants.[27]

The sheer proliferation of mortuary evidence from inland tombs and cemeteries has become ever more apparent as research has developed in the last half century, and as new burial sites have been discovered in advance of planning and development projects. Many of the built tombs have been looted much more thoroughly than the Stenomakri tomb, making it hard to evaluate what the original mortuary ritual involved. Comparison between looted and intact burials in inland Thrace suggests that looters were mainly interested in gold and silver vessels, which could easily be melted down, rather than bronze or iron utensils; although weapons and, to some extent, complete pieces of ceramic fine ware vessels may also have been an attraction for collectors.[28] Sheet bronze and iron rarely survive well below ground, so the prodigal amounts of good quality metal that were put out of use in the burials of leading individuals, as exemplified in the Stenomakri tumulus, is significant.

Recent discoveries have enlarged the range and quality of known tomb finds in significant ways. Painted sarcophagi and a greatly enlarged range of gilded silver vessels are among the notable finds, although the extraordinary portrait head of Seuthes III represents one of the most unusual

[25] Hermary 2010, 143–65.

[26] Saatsoglou-Paliadeli 1984 for a conspectus of *stelai* recovered from the fill of the 'Great Tumulus'.

[27] Domaradzka 2005, 24 fig. 9 (*stele* of Antiphanes, son of Herandros, from Parvenets, near Plovdiv, dated to the late fifth–early fourth century BC by the author).

[28] Archibald 1998, 241 and fig. 10.1 (bar chart of contents of 75 selected tomb inventories).

mortuary finds of recent years.[29] Mortuary rites represent a significant aspect of social practice with an important public dimension in the practical construction of tombs and mounds, and in the organization of sacrifices; there is also some evidence (albeit rather ambiguous), that group rituals were conducted in and around tombs when these were opened up for successive visits or burials. Unlike funerary regulations in central and southern Greece, there seems to be no evidence of sumptuary legislation to restrict particular commemorative forms or acts.[30] Where known, Greek sumptuary laws seem to have been intended to restrict the capacity of certain sections of society to spend wealth in ways that were judged ostentatious and socially injurious. The implication of significant expenditure on mortuary processes in the northern Aegean seems to be that these considerations did not apply. Either this form of conspicuous consumption was approved of by wider groups within northern societies, or objections to such expenditure (if any) were ignored. If approved, then the selection of tomb forms and grave goods was not primarily, or exclusively, a matter of wealth, and distinction was based at least partly on substantive social roles, not just on power relations.

Burial in the northern Aegean was not therefore just a matter of rites of passage, aimed at severing the ties of the living from the dead. It was much more than this. The inclusion of sacrificial animals, both hunted and domestic species; furniture, and textiles, as well as plate, washing utensils, and dining equipment in the more generously appointed graves (in Macedonia as well as Thrace), implies a specific set of ideas, perhaps a spectrum of ideas, about the nature of life and death and about an afterlife, as well as concepts of what was meet and appropriate for persons of different status. Tomb paintings provide a wide range of ideas and images that cannot be conveniently subsumed into a single narrative or conceptual framework. There are, undoubtedly, images that seem compatible with Orphic, Pythagorean, or related eschatologies; and gold sheets, sometimes inscribed with a few words, echo ideas that

[29] Kisyov 2005, 16–74 (Tumuli I and 3, Chernozem, which most closely resemble the élite burials at Duvanli); Marazov 2011 (material in the Vassil Bojkov Collection, some of which is likely to come from burials in central Thrace, esp. nos 42–66, 92–7, 99–108, 110–17, 120–31, all of which have analogies in central Thrace; Kitov 2001; 2003a; 2003b; 2005. The portrait head of Seuthes III has been displayed in a recent exhibition at the Royal Academy of Arts, London (*Bronze*, ed. D. Ekserdjian, Royal Academy of Arts, 2012, no. 26).

[30] Examples of this type of sumptuary legislation include Solon (Plut. *Sol.* 21.6) and Demetrios of Phaleron in Athens (Cic. *Leg.* 2.64–66); or the Twelve Tables in Rome (X. 1–4); Morris 1992, 128–55 for an incisive discussion of mortuary fashions; on the use of Zhaba Mogila, Strelcha, and the Ostrusha tomb for successive events, Archibald 1998, 288–91.

belong within this spectrum.[31] The images offer a wider set of references and narratives, the most enduring of which are the eternal banquet and the metaphysical hunt. Both images appear in Thrace, as in Macedonia, and had an extended afterlife into imperial times, as the *stele* commemorating Aulus Caprilius Timotheos, *somatemporos* at Amphipolis, demonstrates.[32]

BURIALS AND NORTHERN SOCIETIES

The most representative sample of Macedonian mortuary data comes from the west cemetery of Archondiko, the site that preceded Pella. Of 330 burials subjected to preliminary analysis, 86 (or 26 per cent) dated from the Early Iron Age. These were mainly pit graves, with some stone-lined cists. The majority were inhumations, although there were also some pot cremations. Most of the sampled graves belong to the Archaic age (174 graves, or 53 per cent), with the remaining 70 (21 per cent) dating from the Classical or early Hellenistic period.[33]

The analysis published by Anastasia and Pavlos Chrysostomou, the excavators of Archondiko, was specifically concerned with evidence of ranking in the inventories of the archaic male burials. They interpreted the choice of grave goods in this sample from the western cemetery as an expression of the social status of the deceased. If we leave aside the ten per cent of burials that were affected by later interventions, the remaining tombs reflect clear differentiation along gender lines. Men's heads were arranged to face north or westwards, females east or southwards. The range of grave goods is as wide, if not wider, than those of other known Macedonian cemeteries of the period. Men and women

[31] Hatzopoulos 2006 for a rationalization of the concepts; Galanakis (ed.) 2011, 152 fig. 171 and cat. no. 169 (gold lip-shaped sheet from Aigeai, inscribed 'Philiste, to Persephone, rejoice'; Edmonds 2011, 16–50: north Aegean examples are found in his Group D, *lamellae* with Dionysos and Persephone: Amphipolis 320–280 BC; Group E: *lamellae*-like mouth pieces, with the '*chaire*'-formula to Pluto and Persephone: Aghios Athanasios, third century BC; Group F: *lamellae* and mouth pieces with the deceased's name only or the word *mystes* (Methone, *c.*300 BC; Pella, *c.*300 BC*; Pydna, *c.*336–300 BC; Europos *c.*300 BC*; Pella *c.*300 BC; Dion *c.*300? BC); NB: *glass eyes also included; in principle all these tomb groups contain some evidence of pretention, e.g. other gold, evidence of biers, ivory; bronze or clay wreaths, figurines; some glass vessels.

[32] Ch. 3 and refs n.96; for another dimension of shared mystical traditions, namely to the Great Gods of Samothrace, see Dimitrova 2008, 52–3, 59, 71–3, 94–121, 130–50, 242–3 (initiates from Macedonia, Thrace, and the Hellespontine region).

[33] Chrysostomou and Chrysostomou 2007.

alike were equipped with imported pottery vessels (Rhodian *bucchero*, Korinthian, Ionian and Attic) and regionally produced bowls and cups; clay statuettes showing a well-defined range of gods and goddesses; bronze trefoil jugs, *lebetes* and *phialai*, as well as the distinctive miniature iron vehicles first encountered at Sindos.[34]

The excavators subdivided the contents of the male graves according to the presence or absence of arms. A minority of male burials in the sample (11 out of 77, or 14 per cent) lacked weapons altogether. Of the remaining 66 individuals, 24 (36 per cent) were equipped with a spear and knife, 29 (44 per cent) with a sword, spear or spears and knife, and 11 (17 per cent) with a helmet, sword, spear, and knife. Finally, there are two burials containing in both cases a bronze shield, as well as a helmet, sword, spears, and knives. Each of these groups had a corresponding set of ceramic equipment, with the lowest ranking group accompanied by pottery drinking sets, or narrow-necked vessels containing aromatic oils. The higher ranking groups, beginning with the sword burials, were accompanied by bronze drinking sets and dress ornaments (iron and some silver *fibulae*; silver and bronze rings), as well as mouth pieces made of thin silver or gilded sheets, in some cases made of sheet gold. Typically, a pair of spears was laid on either side of the head of the deceased, with the sword placed diagonally across the chest.

The highest-ranking group displayed the highest degree of individuality in terms of active selection. The occupant of Tomb 9, for example, was equipped with a bronze Illyrian-style helmet, laid on one side of his head, an Ionian *kylix*, an iron spear head, a gold diadem decorated with geometric patterns, and a gold ring on one finger of his right hand. An iron sword, the hilt of which was decorated with gold foil, was laid diagonally across his chest. A second spearhead was located near his right leg. He had been laid in the grave wearing garments decorated with sheet-gold strips and other gold stamps bearing rosettes. In addition, he was accompanied by several iron knives, the iron felloes of a miniature two-wheeled cart, with lead fittings and miniature furniture, together with an assortment of clay statuettes of animals, including a lion's head and a dog, bronze and clay drinking vessels, and two *aryballoi*, probably containing perfumed oils. This was but one of a small group of tombs that were exceptionally rich and varied in their contents (including Tombs 83, 131, 145, 189, 194, and 239).[35]

[34] Despini et al. 1995.

[35] Chrysostomou and Chrysostomou 2007, 120–9 with detailed descriptions of contents.

The occupant of Tomb 194 was evidently a young man, below the age of thirty, and was buried around the middle of the sixth century BC. In addition to the kind of weaponry already described above for Tomb 9, this man had a large trapezoidal gold sheet with stamped decoration on his chest, together with a smaller gold sheet, both having originally been attached, in all probability, to a leather cuirass. Similar sheets, with analogous functions, are known from two other burials from the western cemetery of Archondiko (Tombs 131 and 239), and have been documented at Sindos. Such equipment is also known from at least one fifth-century burial at Duvanli in central Thrace.[36] The main chest ornament given to the man in Tomb 194 at Archondiko was decorated with vegetal and geometric patterns and heraldic lions, similar to examples from sheet-gold work in archaic burials at Vergina, Aiani and Trebenishte, Illyria. In addition, the same young man had a stamped gold sheet in the shape of a human hand, placed on his left hand. This is another feature that has analogies in the archaic burials at Trebenishte.[37] One of the best-preserved and elaborate female interments from Archondiko (Tomb 262, dated 510–500 BC) contained a necklace of gold, glass and amber beads; a gold diadem; a gold face mask; a gold bracelet, and three pairs of gold and silver pins. Her dress and shoes were covered with gold sheets. She was provided with several iron knives, a generous set of bronze vessels (a *lekanis*, an *oinochoe*, two *lebetes*, ten *phialae*), two fine decorated imported clay cups, six female figurines, a bronze miniature vessel, and a miniature iron cart.[38]

Comparisons from inland Thrace could be chosen from among the justly renowned fifth-century BC tombs at Duvanli, Brezovo, or Dulboki.[39] These are matched by recently discovered intact graves, such as the enlarged sarcophagus that contained the skeleton of a mature man, cut into the ground below Tumulus I at Chernozem. Like many of his Macedonian peers, and the male incumbents from a galaxy of mounds at Duvanli, Brezovo, and Dulboki, the man from Chernozem Tumulus I was armed and provided with a high-quality drinking set. He had body armour (a bronze breastplate, neck guard of iron plates, and a leather belt or strap for his quiver); two groups of bronze arrow heads (many of whose wooden shafts were partially preserved), two iron spear heads and one butt, and a large sheet-gold chest ornament, decorated

[36] Despini et al. 1995, nn.89, 117, 217; Chrysostomou and Chrysostomou 2007, 122 and n.32; Archibald 1998, 199 and nn.19–22 with further refs.

[37] Chrysostomou and Chrysostomou 2007, 125 and nn. 30, 35, 36, with further refs.

[38] Chrysostomou and Chrysostomou, *AEMΘ*, 2003, 17, 505–16.

[39] Archibald 1998, 135–45, 151–76.

with Medusa's head—repeated in gold foil on the breastplate—and a procession of wild animals. The drinking set shows taste, sophistication, and intriguing intellectual preoccupations; there was a bronze *hydria*, a shallow-footed washing basin, a silver *kylix* with a gold foil *tondo*, showing Bellerophon killing the chimaera; a silver *patera*, and two very rare items, a silver strainer and a silver spoon. Among the ceramic items was a red figure *hydria*, showing a domestic scene with eight women, one of whom sits in the centre playing a lyre.[40]

The liberal use of sheet gold, whether as foil attachments for textiles, decorated plaques on the neck, chest, or mouth of the deceased; as covering for limbs; or as face masks, has emerged as a specific regional custom in the northern Aegean, with examples from Aiani, Sindos, Aigeai, and at related dynastic burial grounds such as Trebenishte, near Lake Ochrid.[41] In lowland Macedonia and in Thrace, these customs were not restricted to a narrow ruling élite, but, as the evidence from Archondiko shows, were accorded to a broader range of individuals. Variable wealth or status was expressed in the range of additional goods, while the gold strips and sheets proclaimed the social and symbolic prominence of the incumbents. In other words, social status did not always match economic capacity.[42] The herdsmen with golden leaves included priests and priestesses, educators, trainers, and administrators.

The graves at Archondiko were organized in family groups, judging by the combinations of adults and immature individuals, sometimes congregating around a central grave. Further analysis will help to show how the ranks identified by male inventories compare with familial graves. The quantities of gold found in later sixth- and fifth-century BC burials did not continue on the same scale in later periods. Over the course of the fifth century BC, gold was becoming available as a commodity and its symbolic value diminished as a result. The contents of monumental tombs built in the fourth century BC and later, seem to distinguish individuals more readily on the basis of wealth than of social status.[43] Nevertheless, the theme of the afterlife, and the status of the deceased in this metaphysical state, continued to be the chief preoccupation of those who designed these tombs.[44]

[40] Kisyov 2005, 16–59 and pls I–XVIII.

[41] Theodossiev 1998; Archibald 1998, 167–76 (mortuary customs); 172–3 and figs 6.10–6.11 (gold sheets); 252–9; 318–35, catalogue of metallic vessels; Chrysostomou and Chrysostomou 2007, 128–9.

[42] See e.g. Borisova 2005, 131 and fig. 7 (three gold sheet appliqués, associated with a few pots, from the rubble-built cairn, from one of 17 tumuli investigated near Kalugerovo, Sofia district, between 1988 and 1993).

[43] Guimier-Sorbets and Morizot 2006.

[44] Hatzopoulos 2006.

REASSEMBLING NORTHERN AEGEAN ECONOMIES

I have left the subject of mortuary data to the end of this book. Graves are problematic as sources of information about living societies, because they incorporate partial, consciously reconstituted data, not a panorama of everyday life; and because we do not really know how to relate the sample evidence that survives with the past societies to which the incumbents belonged. On the other hand, burials show us how resources were consumed on behalf of individuals in a way that no other cumulative evidence can.

Much of the content of this book has been concerned with networks of exchange within the east Balkan landmass. Exchange only forms one component of economic behaviour; but neither the depth nor the complexity of inland exchanges, reaching far into the east Balkan landmass, have been explored before and deserve exposition in their own right. Since the documentary evidence rarely extends beyond Greek-speaking communities, it is not easy to appreciate the scope of overland transactions in a region that is still comparatively unknown to classical scholars. In Chapter 1 I proposed that the argument used by Corinthian representatives in Thucydides' narrative of the outbreak of the Peloponnesian War—namely, that people living inland need to pay attention to those with harbours and ships (Thuc. 1.120.2)—applies just as well to the northern Aegean landmass as it does to the Peloponnese. The capillary-like movement of storage *amphorae* from the harbours of Thasos' mainland ports, and from other 'gateway' locations along the north Aegean and west Pontic coastlines, suggests a combination of riverine and overland traffic. The residual distribution of such containers can only act as a broad-brush indication of the directions of travel. Distribution maps of artefacts rarely show any kind of straightforward traffic patterns. What they do show, however, is something about the dynamics of travel, the preferred routes, and the sort of infrastructure (upland tracks, roads, inland harbours) that repeated traffic entails.

The generous provision of artefacts as grave goods in the northern Aegean reveals how local and non-local resources were combined to create new meanings. If Hatzopoulos is right about the connection between status and particular forms of dress and equipment among Macedonian men and youths, then the choice and range of weapons or other accoutrement in burials was intended to signal the military and social achievements of the deceased.[45] The highly specific range and

[45] Hatzopoulos 1994a, 87–111.

numbers of military equipment in inland Thracian tombs may well have been animated by similar protocols, based on age classes. Like the male burials at Archondiko, it is possible to discern distinctions based on the presence of a pair of spearheads; or spearheads, a sword, and body armour; or some combination of these. The fact that such burials are widely distributed in space does not detract from the grammar of mortuary practice that these graves evidently display.[46] Women's graves, like men's, also show traces of a mortuary grammar, although no systematic study has yet been attempted. It is in mortuary habits and practices of consumption that we see the closest cultural similarities between Macedonian and Thracian societies, and where the economic rationale for linking the two kingdoms is clearest. Tomb construction was perhaps the most resource-intensive activity, requiring scores of individuals for the preparation of terrain, materials, and building; but the spectrum of activities involved in mortuary procedure, including the hunting of sacrificial animals; processions to the burial site; the cremation of the human remains, along with grave goods; or the inhumation of the body on a bier or funerary bed; the disposal of further artefacts, and the consumption of funerary meals, were elaborate and time-consuming procedures.

The consumption of imported plate and pottery has attracted much scholarly attention. From an economic point of view, the truly exotic items deserve at least equal value. The amber beads found in Tomb 262 at Archondiko can be matched at Aigeai.[47] Andrew Sherratt's insistence on the 'big picture' of ancient exchange, incorporating continental Europe as well as the Mediterranean, has been vindicated. Amber has been discovered at many Aegean sanctuary sites,[48] but, as we have seen earlier, it is also found in inland Thrace, which shows that overland routes from the Baltic to southern Europe must have been operating in this period.[49] The story of the Hyperborean maidens,

[46] Archibald 1998, 151–76, 240–59.

[47] Galanakis (ed.) 2011, 109 fig. 101 and cat. no. 414 (Aiani cemetery, grave *c.*470–60 BC); it is not clear why Kottaridi believes the necklace must have travelled via the Po valley to Macedonia (ibid. 110).

[48] Kilian-Dirlmeier 2002, 73–5, 'Gegenstände aus Bernstein' (= 750–575 BC), 75 fig. 7 and p. 274–5, 'Liste 133' (Olympia, Sparta, Perachora, Pherai, Idaian Cave, Psykro, Arkades, Lindos; Phana, Chios; Emborio, Chios; Delos, Artemision; Siphnos; Ithaka; Ephesos, Artemision). The Philia examples resemble those from Ithaka, Perachora, and Chios, made of a porous mass, which sometimes shows a reddish pigment at the centre. The author does not speculate on routes or networks; however, she does provide a pie-chart, p. 225, and discussion pp. 223–9, on native and external votives. Baltic amber plays a modest part, less than 25 per cent, but more than one eighth of votives are 'Balkan' objects.

[49] Nikolova 2008; see above, Ch. 4, n.125.

and their Delian connections, does not connect directly with the amber route, but it is animated by an awareness of these links (Hdt. 4.32–36). The other exotic material that needs to be explained is the pigment Egyptian blue, which is found in a surprising number of tombs and in rural locations.[50]

Devotion to the activities associated with the mortuary process, despite looting within a short time of death, is one of the most intriguing aspects of northern cultures. How should we imagine this shared connection between cultures that were separated by language, geography, and political considerations? Bruno Latour has offered an escape from conventional sociological approaches to cultural groups in his Actor-Network theory, which dissolves the quiddity of 'the social' and of 'societies' in favour of something more nuanced, but also more dynamic. His impatience with hard-edged social theories has something to contribute to our perceptions of societies in the northern Aegean because it allows for change, as we have seen it taking place, several times over, between one radical time period, the Greco-Persian Wars, and another—the intervention of Roman authorities in the economies of the region. Latour argues that theories of the social need to be sensitive to the dynamics of human behaviour. Interactions do not happen in the same way in different places, but they are triggered by a complex pattern of consecutive causes that have different origins. Particular social environments do not operate automatically, but need individuals to come together to bring about a shared event.[51] Therefore, we do not have to argue that the same kinds of processes or activities were at work everywhere. On the other hand, we do need to create a narrative that animates the chain of interactions that we want to study. My narrative has been about the consequences of invasion and the reactions of the populations along the northern Aegean to a historic threat that affected the region as a whole. The adjustments that followed created new forms of consumption based on the cavalry class that provided military defence. It is not clear how these societies modified their behaviour once Roman political power began to affect their resource base directly, but the ostentatious mortuary practices that are so visible until the third century BC underwent significant changes. This implies that whole populations were obliged to adjust their consumption patterns to the new situation by modifying some of their most fundamental social expressions of life

[50] Brécoulaki 2006, 55–8; Brecoulaki and Perdikatsis, 2002; Brecoulaki et al. 2006; Tsimbidou-Avloniti 2005, 198–99; 202–3, Table 1; Kisyov 2005, 66; Ivanova 2011.

[51] Latour 2005, 175–220.

and death. These adjustments undoubtedly affected the demand for technical and specialist skills, and for exotic materials. The economic patterns of the final two centuries BC in the northern Aegean should be 'reassembled', to use Latour's term, to reveal what were to become new expressions of these deepest of cultural motives.

Bibliography

Abulafia, D. (2005), 'Mediterraneans', in W. V. Harris (ed.), *Rethinking the Mediterranean,* Oxford, 64–93.

Adam-Veleni, P. (1998), *Petres of Florina*, Thessaloniki.

——(2003), 'Mygdonia – Gulf of Strymon.' in P. Adam-Veleni et al., *Ancient Country Houses on Modern Roads*, Athens, 91–114.

——(2009), 'Farmhouses in Macedonia: the beginnings of "feudalism"?', in *20 Chronia* AEMΘ, 1–14, Thessaloniki [Greek with English summary].

——(2011), 'Thessalonike', in Lane-Fox (ed.), 545–62.

——, Poulaki, E., and Tzanavari, K. (2003), *Ancient Country Houses on Modern Roads*, Athens.

Adams, C. (2007), *Land Transport in Roman Egypt. A Study of Economics and Administration in a Roman Province*, Oxford.

——(2012), 'Transport', in W. Scheidel (ed.), *The Cambridge Companion to the Roman Economy*, Cambridge, 218–40.

Adiego, I. J., Tiverios, M., Manakidou, E., and Tsiafakis, D. (2012), 'Two Carian Inscriptions from Karabournaki/Thessaloniki, Greece', in *Stephanèphoros*, 195–202.

Agre, D. (2006), 'Vladetelski grob ot mogila mezhdu selata Malomirovo i Zlatinitsa, Elhovski (Yambolski oblast)' [A ruler's tumulus grave between the villages of Malomirovo and Zlatinitsa, Elhovo (Yambol district)], in *Settlement Life in Ancient Thrace* IV, 139–42.

Akamatis, I. M. (2000), *Ensphragistes laves amforeōn apo tēn Agora tis Pellas. Anaskaphi 1980–1987. Hoi homades Parmeniskou kai Rodou. Symboli sti meleti tis hellinistikis epigraphikis*, Athens.

——(2006a), 'Panepistēmiake anaskaphe agoras Pellas, 2006' [The Excavation of Aristotle University in the Agora of Pella, 2006], *AEMΘ* 20, 615–26.

——(2006b), 'To programma ton diadromon ston archaiologiko choro tis Pellas. Ta nea archaiologika dedomena', *AEMΘ* 20, 627–39.

——(2011), 'Pella', in Lane-Fox (ed.), 393–408.

——(2012), 'L'agora de Pella', in *Tout vendre, tout acheter*, 49–59.

van Alfen, P. (2005), 'Problems in Ancient Imitative and Counterfeit Coinage', in *HellEc II*, 322–54.

Algazi, G. (2005), 'Diversity Rules: Peregrine Horden and Nicholas Purcell's *The Corrupting Sea*', *Mediterranean History Review* 20/2, 227–45.

Allen, R. E. (1983), *The Attalid kingdom. A constitutional history*. Oxford.

Alexandrescu, P. (1977), 'Les modèles grecs de la céramique thrace tournée', *Dacia* N. S. 21, 113–37.

Alexandrescu, P. (1999), 'Les modèles grecs de la céramique thrace tournée', *L'aigle et le dauphin*, Bucharest, 138–93.

Amandry, M. and Hurter, S., in collaboration with D. Bérend (eds) (1999), *Travaux de Numismatique grecque offerts à Georges le Rider*, London.

Amouretti, M. Cl. (2000), 'L'Artisanat indispensable au fonctionnement de l'agriculture,' in F. Blondé and A. Muller (eds), *L'Artisanat en Grèce ancienne. Les Productions, les Diffusions, Actes du Colloque de Lyon (10–11 décembre, 1998)*, Univ. Charles de Gaulle–Lille 3, Lille, 147–64.

Amyx, D. A. (1958), 'The Attic Stelai, Part III. Vases and Other Containers', *Hesperia* 27, 255–310.

Anderson, J. K. (1961), *Ancient Greek Horsemanship*, Berkeley and Los Angeles.

Andreau, J. (2002), 'Twenty Years after Moses I. Finley's *The Ancient Economy*', in W. Scheidel and S. von Reden (eds), *The Ancient Economy: Recent Approaches*. London and New York, 33–49 (first published as: 'Vingt ans d'apres *L'Economie antique* de Moses Finley', *Annales: Histoire, Sciences sociales* 50 (1995) 947–60).

——(2010), *L'économie du monde romain*, Paris.

——, Briant, P., and Descat, R. (eds) (1994), *Économie antique. Les échanges dans l'Antiquité: le rôle de l'État*, Saint-Bertrand-de-Comminges.

——and Chankowski, V. (eds) (2007), *Vocabulaire et expression de l'économie dans le monde antique*, Études 19, Bordeaux and Paris.

——and Descat, R. (2006), *Esclave en Grèce et à Rome*, Paris.

Andreou, S. and Eukleidou, K. (2007), 'Η ανασκαφή στην Τούμπα Θεσσαλονίκης το 2006 και το 2007', *ΑΕΜΘ* 21 [2011], 255–262.

—— and Kotsakis, K. (1999), 'Counting People in an Artefact-Poor Landscape: The Langadas Case, Macedonia, Greece', in J. Bintliff and K. Sbonias (eds), *Reconstructing Past Population Trends in Mediterranean Europe, The Archaeology of Mediterranean Landscapes, 1*, Oxford, 35–43.

Andrianou, D. (2009), *The Furniture and Furnishings of Ancient Greek Houses and Tombs*, Cambridge.

Andronikos, M. (1969), *Βεργίνα* I. *Το νεκροταφείο των Τύμβων*, Athens.

——(1987), 'Some reflections on the Macedonian Tombs', *BSA* 82, 1–16.

Antikas, T. (2006), 'Symbols of heroism: horse burials in royal and common Macedonian tombs', in M. Mashkour (ed.), *Equids in Time and Space, Papers in honour of Véra Eisenmann*, Oxford, 203–9.

Antonetti, Cl. (ed.) (2010), *Lo spazio ionico e le comunità della Grecia nord-occidentale. Territorio, società, istituzioni*, Venice.

Aperghis, G. G. (1999), 'Storehouses and Systems at Persepolis. Evidence from the Persepolis Fortification Tablets', *JESHO* 42, 2, 152–93.

——(2004), *The Seleukid Royal Economy: The Finances and Financial Administration of the Seleukid Empire*, Cambridge.

Appadurai, A. (1986), *The social life of things. Commodities in cultural perspective*, Cambridge.

Archibald, Z. H. (1985), 'The gold pectoral from Vergina and its connections,' *OJA* 4/2, 165–85.

——(1998), *The Odrysian Kingdom of Thrace: Orpheus unmasked,* Oxford Monographs on Classical Archaeology, Oxford.

——(2000), 'Space, hierarchy and community in Archaic and Classical Macedonia, Thessaly and Thrace', in *Alternatives to Athens*, 212–33.

——(2001), 'Away from Rostovtzeff: a new SEHHW', in *HellEc I*, 379–88.

——(2002a), 'The Odrysian river port near Vetren, Bulgaria, and the Pistiros inscription', *TALANTA* 32/33 (2000–2001), 253–75.

——(2002b), 'A River Port and *emporion* in Central Bulgaria: An Interim Report on the British Project at Vetren', *Annual of the British School at Athens* 97 (2002), 309–51.

——(2002c), 'Underground deposits: Pit no. 9 and the "field" of pits', in *Pistiros II*, 46–58.

——(2004), 'Inland Thrace', in M. Herman Hansen and T. Heine Nielsen (eds), *An Inventory of Archaic and Classical Poleis,* Oxford, 885–99.

——(2005a), 'Markets and Exchange: the Structure and Scale of Economic Behaviour in the Hellenistic Age', in *HellEc* II, 1–26.

——(2005b), 'Officers and gentlemen (or gentlewomen): exploring Macedonian élites in the Classical and early Hellenistic periods', in K. Nawotka and A. Łoś (eds), *Elite in Greek and Roman Antiquity*, Wrocław (= *Antiquitas* 28), 13–25.

——(2006), 'The Central and North Balkan Peninsula' in K. Kinzl (ed.), *A Companion to the Classical Greek World,* Malden Mass. and Oxford, 115–36.

——(2007), 'Contacts between the Ptolemaic kingdom and the Black Sea in the early Hellenistic Age', in V. Gabrielsen, J. Lund, and T. Madsen (eds), *Regional and Interregional Connections in the Black Sea*, Aarhus, 253–71.

——(2010), 'Macedonia and Thrace', in Roisman and Worthington, 326–41.

——(2011), 'Mobility and innovation in Hellenistic economies: the causes and consequences of human traffic', in *HellEc* III, 42–65.

——(2012b), 'Agoranomoi in Macedonia', in C. Hasenohr (ed.), *Institutions des marchés: Agoranomes et édiles 1, Atelier de recherche GDRI, Les Marchés dans le monde antique: espaces, pratiques, institutions,* Bordeaux, 109–19.

——(2012c), '"What female heart can gold despise?" Women and the Value of Precious Metals in Ancient Macedonia and Neighbouring Regions', in *Stephanèphoros*, 25–30.

——(2013a), 'Innovation and the transmission of knowledge in Antiquity: a look at current networking models', in F. de Angelis (ed.), *Regionalism and Globalism in Antiquity,* Colloquia Antiqua 7, Leuven, 21–38.

Archibald, Z. H. (forthcoming 2013b), 'Joining up the dots: making economic sense of pottery distributions in the Aegean and beyond', in A. Tsingarida and D. Viviers (eds), *Pottery Markets in the Ancient Greek World (8th–1st Centuries BC) Proceedings of the International Symposium held at the Université libre de Bruxelles, 19–21 June 2008*, Brussels, 133–57.
——(forthcoming a/), 'Moving upcountry; ancient travel from coastal ports to inland harbours', in K. Höghammer and A. Lindgren (eds), *Ancient ports—the geography of connections. International conference at the department of Archaeology and ancient history, Uppsala University, 23–25 September, 2010*, Uppsala.
——(forthcoming b/), '"Connectivity", Polybius, Byzantium and the evolution of south-eastern Thrace', in M. Sayar (ed.), *Eleventh International Congress of Thracology, Istanbul, 8–12 November 2010*, keynote address, Istanbul.
——(forthcoming c/), 'Tegeas from Torone and some truths about ancient markets', in G. Oliver and Z. H. Archibald (eds), *The Power of the Individual in Ancient Greece. Essays in honour of Professor J. K. Davies*, Stuttgart.
——(forthcoming 2015) (with contributions by Mark Adams, Richard Chiverrell, Matthew Ponting, and Sue Stallibrass), *Pistiros: a Late Iron Age River Port in south-eastern Europe, the Liverpool project, 1999–2005.*
——and Davies, J. K. (2011), 'Introduction', *HellEc III*, 1–18.
Audoin-Rouzeau, Fr. and Beyries, S. (2002), *Le Travail du cuir de la Préhistoire à nos jours: Actes des Rencontres 18–20 octobre 2001*, Antibes.
Ault, B. A. (2007), '*Oikos* and *Oikonomia*: Greek houses, housholds, and the domestic economy', in R. Westgate, N. Fisher, and J. Whitley (eds), *Building Communities. House Settlement and Society in the Aegean and Beyond*, BSA Studies 15, London, 259–65.
——and Nevett, L. C. (1999), 'Digging Houses: Archaeologies of Classical and Hellenistic Greek domestic assemblages', in P. M. Allison (ed.), *The Archaeology of Household Activities*, London, 43–56.
——and Nevett, L. C. (eds) (2005), *Ancient Greek Houses and Households, Chronological, Regional, and Social Diversity*, Philadelphia.
Austin, M. M. (1986), 'Hellenistic Kings, War and the economy', *CQ* 36, 450–66.
Avdev, St. (2005), *Istoriya na zlatodobiva po Bulgarskite zemi*, Sofia.
Avram, A. (1996), *Les timbres amphoriques. Vol. 1 (= Histria viii)*, Paris.
——(1997/98), 'Notes sur l'inscription de l'emporion de Pistiros en Thrace', *Il Mar Nero* iii [1999], 37–46.
——(1999), *Der Vertrag zwischen Rom und Kallatis. Ein Beitrag zum römischen Völkerrecht*, Amsterdam.
——(2003), 'Antiochos II Théos, Ptolémée II Philadelphe et la Mer Noire', *CRAI* 2003, 1181–213.

——(2007), 'Some Thoughts about the Black Sea and the Slave Trade before the Roman Domination (6th–1st Centuries BC)', in V. Gabrielsen and J. Lund (eds), *The Black Sea in Antiquity: Regional and Interregional Economic Exchanges*, Black Sea Studies 6, Aarhus, 239–52.

——, Buzoianu, L., Chera, C., Custurea, G., Dupont, P., Lungu, V., and Nastasi, I. (2009) (eds), *Pontic Grey Wares, International Conference Bucarest–Constanza, September 30–3 October 2008*, Pontica 42, Supplementum 1, Constanța.

Badian, E. (1982), 'Greeks and Macedonians', in B. Barr-Sharrar and E. Borza (eds), *Macedonia and Greece in Late Classical and Early Hellenistic Times*, Washington D.C., 33–51.

Bagnall, R. S. (1976), *The administration of the Ptolemaic Possessions outside Egypt*, Leiden.

——(1997), *The Kellis Agricultural Account Book*, Dakleh Oasis Project, Monograph 7, Oxford.

——and Derow, P. (2004), *The Hellenistic Period. Historical Sources in Translation*, Oxford.

Bak, P. (1997), *How nature works*, Oxford.

Balabanov, P. (2000), 'Méchanismes de commerce à l'époque hellénistique dans les environs de Messambrie et d'Apollonie Pontique', in *Pistiros et Thasos*, 87–99.

——(2010), 'The origin of amphorae with englyphic stamps', in Kassab Tezgör and Inaishvili (eds), 19–22.

Baladié, R. (1989), *Strabon. Géographie, Tome IV (Livre VII)*, Paris.

Balcer, J. M. (1972), 'The Persian Occupation of Thrace, 519–491 BC. The Economic Effects', in *Actes du II Congrès International des Études du Sud-Est Européen*, Sofia, 241–58.

Balkanska, A. and Tzochev, Ch. (2008), 'Amphora Stamps from Seuthopolis—Revised', in D. Gergova, A. Božkova, Chr. Popov, and M. Kuzmanov (eds), *Phosphorion. Studia in Honorem Mariae Čičikova*, Sofia, 188–205.

Ball, P. (2004), *Critical mass, how one thing leads to another*, London.

Baragwanath, E. (2008), *Motivation and Narrative in Herodotus*, Oxford.

Baralis, A. (2008), 'The Chora Formation of the Greek Cities of Aegean Thrace. Towards a Chronological Approach to the Colonization Process', in P. Guldager Bilde and J. H. Petersen (eds), *Meetings of Cultures Between Conflicts and Coexistence*, Black Sea Studies 8, Aarhus, 101–30.

——(2010), 'Habitat et réseaux d'occupation spatial en Thrace égéenne: l'impact de la colonisation entre Grecs et Thraces', in Tréziny (ed.), 247–64.

Barber, E. J. W. (1991), *Prehistoric Textiles*, Princeton.

Baud-Bovy, D. (1921), 'The Mountain-Group of Olympos: an Essay in Nomenclature', *The Geographical Journal* 67/3, 204–13.

Bauer, A. A. (2011), 'Life is Too Short for Faint-Heartedness: The Archaeology of Andrew Sherratt', *Journal of World Prehistory* 24, 99–105.

Bauslaugh, R. A. (2000), *Silver Coinage with the Types of Aesillas the Quaestor,* New York.

Bearzot, C., Landucci, F., and Zecchini, G. (eds) (2003), *Gli stati territoriali nel mondo antico,* Milan.

Beck, C. W. and Bouzek, J. (eds) (1993), *Amber in Archaeology, Proceedings of the Second International Conference on Amber in Archaeology, Liblice, 1990*, Prague.

Bekker-Nielsen, T. (ed.) (2005), *Fishing and Fish Processing in the Black Sea Region*, Black Sea Studies 2, Aarhus.

Benecke, N. (2006), 'On the beginning of horse husbandry in the southern Balkan peninsula—the horse bones from Kirklareli-Kanligeçit (Turkish Thrace)', in M. Mashkour (ed.), *Equids in Time and Space, Papers in honour of Véra Eisenmann,* Oxford, 92–100.

Besios, M., Tzifopoulos, G. Z., and Kotsonas, A. (2012), *Μεθώνη Πιερίας: Επιγραφές, Χαραγματα και εμπορικά σύμβολα στη γεωμετρική και αρχαϊκή κεραμική από το 'Υπόγειο της Μεθώνης Πιερίας στη Μακεδονία*, Thessaloniki.

Billot, M. F. (1992), 'Le Cynosarges, Antiochos et les Tanneurs. Questions de Topographie', *BCH* 119, 119–56.

Billows, R. A. (1990), *Antigonos the One-eyed and the creation of the Hellenistic state.* Berkeley, Los Angeles, and London.

——(1995), *Kings and Colonists: Aspects of Macedonian Imperialism,* Leiden.

——(2007), 'Rebirth of a region: Ionia in the early Hellenistic period', in H. Elton and G. Reger (eds), *Regionalism in Hellenistic and Roman Asia Minor,* Études 20, Bordeaux, 33–43.

Bintliff, J. (1997), 'Demography and the Rise of Complex Societies in the Ancient Aegean: core-Periphery, Neo-Malthusian, and Other Interpretive Models', *Journal of Field Archaeology* 24, 1–38.

——(2009), 'Catchments, settlements, chambers, and demography: case studies and general theory in the Greek landscape from prehistory to "Early Modern Times"', in F. Favory and L. Nuninger (eds), *Archaeodyn. 7 Millennia of Dynamics: Settlement Pattern, Production, and Trades from Neolithic to Middle Ages*, Dijon, 107–11.

——(2010), 'Classical Greek urbanism: a social Darwinian view', in R. M. Rosen and I. Sluiter (eds), *Valuing Others in Classical Antiquity,* Leiden, 15–41.

Boivin, N. (2008), *Material Cultures, Material Minds,* Cambridge.

Bonias, Z. (2010), 'L'importance de la plaine du Strymon comme voie de contacts culturels et commerciaux entre Grecs et Thraces', in Tréziny (ed.), 235–9.

Bonney, R. and Ormrod, W. M. (1999), *Crises, Revolutions, and Self-Sustained Growth: Essays in European Fiscal History, 1130–1830,* Stanford.

Borisova, T. (2005), 'Trakiyski mogilen nekropol kray selo Kalugerovo, Sofiyska oblast', in G. Kitov and D. Dimitrova (eds), *Zemite na Bulgariya. Lyulka na Trakiyskata Kultura, Vtori Tom*, Sofia, 129–32.

Borza, E. N. (1982), 'Athenians, Macedonians, and the Origins of the Macedonian Royal House', in *Studies in Attic Epigraphy, History, and Topography presented to Eugene Vanderpool,* Hesperia Supplement 19, Princeton, 7–13 (= *idem,* in C. G. Thomas (ed.), *Makedonika* Claremont, 1995, 125–33).

——(1987), 'Timber and Politics in the Ancient World', *PAPS* 131, 32–52 (reprinted in C. G. Thomas (ed.), *Makedonika,* Claremont, 1995, 85–112).

——(1990), *In the Shadow of Olynthus. The Emergence of Macedon*^{2}, Princeton.

——and Palagia, O. (2007), 'The Chronology of the Royal Tombs at Vergina', *JDAI* 122, 81–125.

Bosworth, A. B. (1988), *Conquest and Empire, the Reign of Alexander the Great,* Cambridge.

Bourdieu, P. (1984), *Distinction: a social critique of the judgement of taste*, London.

——(1990), *The Logic of Practice*, London.

Bouzek, J. (1990), *Studies of Greek Pottery in the Black Sea Area*, Prague.

——(1996), 'The position of the Pistiros fortification in the development of the ancient poliorcetics and stonecutting techniques', *Pistiros I,* 43–6.

——, Rückl, Š, Titz, P., and Tsochev, Ch. (2007), 'Trade amphorae', *Pistiros III,* 133–86.

Bowman, A. and Wilson, A. (eds) (2009), *Quantifying the Roman Economy. Methods and Problems,* Oxford.

——and Wilson, A. (2012), *Settlement, Urbanization, and Population*, Oxford Studies on the Roman Economy, Oxford.

Božkova, A. (1994), 'Notes on the settlement pattern in an area of the city territory of Roman Pautalia', in *Settlement Life in Ancient Thrace* IV, 144–7.

——(2005), 'A pottery group with Geometric decoration from a Thracian site at Koprivlen in southwestern Bulgaria', in Bouzek and Domaradzka, 85–90.

——(2009), 'Un complexe de céramique monochrome des environs de Simeonovgrad, dans la vallée du Hebros', in A. Avram et al. (eds), *Pontic Grey Wares, International Conference Bucarest–Constanza, September 30–3 October 2008,* Pontica 42, Supplementum 1, Constanța, 223–44.

——(2010), 'Le commerce des sites indigènes entre Odessos et le Danube aux IIIe et IIe s. av. J.-C. selon les timbres amphoriques', in Kassab Tezgör and Inaishvili (eds), 103–6.

Božkova, A. and Nikov, K. (2009), 'La céramique monochrome en Thrace et ses prototypes anatoliens. Problèmes de chronologie', in P. Dupont and V. Lungu (eds), *Les productions céramiques de Pont-Euxin à l'époque grecque*, Actes du Colloque international, Bucarest, 18–23 septembre 2004, *Il Mar Nero* 6, 47–55.

——and Vasileva, D. (2009), 'Un complexe de céramique monochrome des environs de Simeonovgrad dans la vallée du Hebros', in A. Avram et al. (eds), *Pontic Grey Wares, International Conference Bucarest–Constanza, September 30–3 October 2008*, Pontica 42, Supplementum 1, Constanța, 223–44.

Braudel, F. (1982), *The Wheels of Commerce. Civilization and Capitalism, volume 2*, London.

Braund, D. (2008), 'Scythian Laughter: Conversations in the Northern Black Sea Region in the 5th Century BC', in P. Guldager Bilde and J. H. Petersen (eds), *Meetings of Cultures Between Conflicts and Coexistence*, Black Sea Studies 8, Aarhus, 347–67.

Bravo, G. A. and Trüpke, J. (1970), *100,000 Jahre Leder*, Basel and Stuttgart.

Brécoulaki, H. (2006), 'La peinture funéraire en Macédoine', *Rois, Cités, Nécropoles*, 47–60.

——, Fiorin, E., and Vigato, P. A. (2006), 'The funerary *klinai* of tomb 1 from Amphipolis and a sarcophagus from ancient Tragilos, eastern Macedonia: a physico-chemical investigation on the painted materials', *Journal of Cultural Heritage* 7, 301–311.

——and Perdikatsis, V. (2002), 'Ancient painting on Macedonian funerary monuments, IV–III c. BC: a comparative study on the use of color', in M. A. Tiverios and D. S. Tsiafakis (eds), *Color in Ancient Greece, the Role of Color in Ancient Greek Art and Architecture 700–31 BC:* proceedings of the conference held in Thessaloniki, 12–16 April, 2000, organized by the J. Paul Getty Museum and Aristotle University of Thessaloniki, Thessaloniki, 147–54.

Bresson, A. (1993), 'Les cités grecs et leur *emporia*', in A. Bresson and P. Rouillard (eds), *L'emporion*, Paris, 163–226.

——(2000a), 'Aristote et le commerce extérieur', in Bresson, 109–30 (reprinted from *REA* 89, 1987, 217–38).

——(2000b), 'L'attentat de Hiéron et le commerce grec', in Bresson, 131–49 (reprinted from J. Andreau, P. Briant, and R. Descat (eds) (1994), *Économie antique. Les échanges dans l'Antiquité: le rôle de l'État*, Saint-Bertrand-de-Comminges, 47–68).

——(2005a), 'Coinage and money supply in the Hellenistic Age', in *HellEc II*, 44–72.

——(2005b), 'Ecology and Beyond: the Mediterranean Paradigm', in W. V. Harris (ed.), *Rethinking the Mediterranean*, Oxford, 95–114.

——(2007), *L'économie de la Grèce des cités, I. Les structures et la production*, Paris.
——(2011), 'Grain from Cyrene', in *HellEc III*, 66–95.
——, Ivantchik, A., and Ferrary, J.-L. (eds) (2007), *Une Koinè Pontique, Cités grecques, sociétés indigènes et empires mondiaux sur le littoral nord de la mer noire (viie s.a.C. - iiie s.p.C.)*, Mémoires 18, Bordeaux.
——and Rouillard, P. (eds) (1993), *L'emporion*. Paris.
Briant, P. (1991), 'Chasses royales macédoniennes et chasses perses: le thème de la chasse au lion sur la chasse de Vergina', *DHA* 17, 212–55.
——(1994a), 'Sources gréco-hellénistiques, institutions perses et institutions macèdoniennes: continuités, changements, et bricolages', *Achaemenid History* VIII, 283–310.
——(1994b), 'Prélèvements tributaires et échanges en Asie Mineur achéménide et hellénistique', in J. Andreau, P. Briant, and R. Descat (eds) (1994), *Économie antique. Les échanges dans l'Antiquité: le rôle de l'État*, Saint-Bertrand-de-Comminges, 69–81.
——and Chauveau, M (eds) (2009), *Organisation des pouvoirs et contacts culturels dans les pays de l'empire achéménide*, Paris.
Bringmann, Kl. (2001), 'Grain, timber, and money: Hellenistic kings, finance, buildings and foundations in Greek cities', in *HellEc I*, 205–14.
——and von Steuben, H. (eds) (1995), *Schenkungen hellenistischer Herrscher an griechische Städte und Heiligtümer*. Teil 1, *Zeugnisse und Kommentare*, Berlin.
Brock, R. and Wirtjes, H. (2000), 'Athenaeus on Greek Wine', in *Athenaeus and his World*, 455–65.
Brodersen, K. (2006), *Aristoteles: 77 Tricks zur Steigerung der Staatseinnahmen, Oikonomika II*, Stuttgart.
Brun, J.-P. (2004), *Archéologie du vin et de l'huile de la préhistoire à l'époque hellénistique*, Paris.
Brunet, M. (1993), 'Vin local et vin de cru. Les examples de Délos et Thasos', *BCH* Suppl. XXVI, 201–11.
——(1997), 'Thasos et son Épire à la fin du Ve s. et au début du IVe s. avant J.-C.', in P. Brulé and J. Oulhen (eds), *Esclavage, guerre, économie en Grèce ancienne, Hommages à Yvon Garlan*, Rennes, 229–42.
——(2000), 'Thasos: structure du territoire et fonctionnement économique de la cité', in *Pistiros et Thasos*, 183–90.
Burch, J., Nolla, J. M, and Sagrera, J. (2010), 'Le système de stockage en silos sur le territoire ibérique aux environs d'Emporion', in Tréziny (ed.), 391–401.
Burnett, A., Wartenberg, U., and Witschonke, R. (eds) (1998), *Coins of Macedonia and Rome: Essays in honour of Charles Hersh*, London.

Cabanes, P. and Lamboley, J. L. (eds) (2004), *L'Illyrie méridionale et l'Épire dans l'Antiquité IV, Actes du IVe colloque international de Grenoble (10–12 octobre 2002)*, Paris.

Cahill, N. (2002), *Household and City organization at Olynthus,* New Haven and London.

Callataÿ, F. de (1989), 'Les trésors achéménides et les monnayages d'Alexandre: espèces immobilisées et espèces circulantes', *REA* 91, 259–74.

——(1997a), *Recueil quantitatif des émissions monétaires hellénistiques*, Wetteren.

——(1997b), *L'histoire des guerres mithridatiques vue par les monnaies*, Louvain-la-Neuve.

——(2004), 'La richesse des rois Seleucides et le problème de la taxation en nature', in V. Chankowski and F. Duyrat (eds), *Le roi et l'économie: Autonomies locales et structures royales dans l'économie de l'empire séleucide.* Actes des recontres de Lille (23 juin 2003) et d'Orléans (29–30 janvier 2004). *TOPOI*, Supplement 6, Lyon, 23–47.

——(2005a), 'A quantitative survey of Hellenistic coinages', in *HellEc II*, 73–91.

——(2005b), 'The Graeco-Roman Economy in the Super Long-Run', *JRA* 18, 361–72.

——(2006a), 'Réflexions quantitatives sur l'or et l'argent non monnayés à l'époque hellénistique (pompes, triomphes, réquisitions, fortunes des temples, orfèvrerie et masses métalliques disponibles)', in *Approches*, 37–84.

——(2006b), 'Greek Coins from Archaeological Excavations: A Conspectus of Conspectuses and a Call for Chronological Tables', in *Agoranomia*, 177–99.

——(2012), 'Le retour (quantifié) "du miracle grec"', in *Stephanèphoros*, 63–76.

——, Villaronga, L., and Depeyrot, G. (eds) (1993), *L'Argent monnayé d'Alexandre le Grand à Auguste*, Travaux du Cercle des études numismatiques 12, Brussels.

Camp, J. (2004), 'Athenian cobblers and heroes', in S. Keay and S. Moser (eds), *Greek Art in View. Studies in honour of Brian Sparkes,* Oxford, 129–37.

Campana, D., Crabtree, P., Defrance, S. D., Lev-Tov, J., and Choyke, A. (eds) (2010), *Anthropological Approaches to Zooarchaeology. Complexity, Colonialism, and Animal Transformations,* Oxford.

Capdetrey, L. (2004), 'Le *basilikon* et les cités grecques dans le royaume Séleucide: modalités de redistribution de la richesse royale et formes de dépendance des cités', in V. Chankowski and F. Duyrat (eds), *Le roi et l'économie: Autonomies locales et structures royales dans l'économie de l'empire séleucide.* Actes des recontres de Lille (23 juin 2003) et d'Orléans (29–30 janvier 2004). *TOPOI*, Supplement 6, Lyon, 105–29.

Carlier, P. (2000), 'Homeric and Macedonian Kingship', in *Alternatives to Athens*, 259–68.

Carney, E. (2002), 'Hunting and the Macedonian élite: sharing the rivalry of the chase', in D. Ogden (ed.), *The Hellenistic world: new perspectives*, London, 59–80.

——(2010), 'Macedonian Women', in Roisman and Worthington, 409–27.

Carradice, I. (ed.) (1987), *Coinage and Administration in the Athenian Empire: the Ninth Oxford Symposium on Coinage and Monetary History*, BAR IS 343, Oxford.

Carusi, C. (2007), 'Le commerce du sel dans l'Antiquité grecque', in D. Monah et al. (eds), *L'Exploitation du sel a travers le temps*, Piatra-Neamt, 221–33.

——(2008), *Il sale nel mondo Greco (VI a.C.—III d.C), Luoghi di produzione, circolazione commerciale, regimi di sfruttamento nel contest del Mediterraneo antico*, Bari.

Casson, S. (1926), *Macedonia, Thrace and Illyria: Their Relations to Greece from the Earliest Times down to the Time of Philip Son of Amyntas*, Oxford.

Catling, R. (1998), 'The Typology of the Protogeometric and Subgeometric Pottery from Troia and its Aegean Context', *Studia Troica* 8, 151–87.

Champion, C. (2007), 'Empire by Invitation: Greek political strategies and Roman Imperial Interventions in the Second Century BCE', *TAPA* 137, 255–75.

Chandezon, Chr. (2003), *L'élevage en Grèce (fin ve–fin 1er s. a.C.) L'apport des sources épigaphiques*, Bordeaux.

——(2005), 'Il est le fils de l'âne: remarques sur le mulet dans le monde grecque', in *Les Équidés*, 207–17.

——(2011), 'Some aspects of large estate management in the Greek world during Classical and Hellenistic times' in *HellEc III*, 96–121.

Chaniotis, A. (2005), *War in the Hellenistic World*, Malden Mass.

——(2011), 'The impact of war on the economy of Hellenistic poleis: Demand creation, short-term influences, long-term impacts', in *HellEc III*, 122–41.

Chankowski, V. (2010), 'Pistiros et les grecs de la côte nord-égéenne: problèmes d'interprétation', in Tréziny (ed.), 241–6.

——and Domaradzka, L. (1999), 'Réedition de l'inscription de Pistiros et problèmes d'interprétation', *BCH* 123, 247–58.

——and Duyrat, F. (eds) (2004), *Le roi et l'économie: Autonomies locales et structures royales dans l'économie de l'empire séleucide.* Actes des recontres de Lille (23 juin 2003) et d'Orléans (29–30 janvier 2004). *TOPOI*, Supplement 6, Lyon.

Chankowski, V. Gotzev, A., and Nehrizov, G. (2004–5), 'Pistiros', *BCH* 128–129, 1227–53.

Chernykh, E. V. (1978), *Gornoe delo i Metalurgiya v drevneyshey Bolgarii*, Sofia.

Chichikova, M. (2004), 'Trakiyskata keramika rabotena na kolelo (VI–IV v. pr. Khr.)', *Annual of the Archaeological Museum Plovdiv* 9/2, 194–211.

Chiverrell, R. and Archibald, Z. H. (2009), 'Flooding and river evolution: implications for human occupation and activity at Vetren, central Bulgaria' *Géomorphologie: relief, processus, environnement*, 4, 287–302.

Christesen, P. and Murray, S. C. (2010), 'Macedonian Religion', in Roisman and Worthington, 428–45.

Christov, I. (2002), 'Mountainous Thrace—1st millennium BC. Problems and Trends of Investigation', in *Thrace and the Aegean*, 231–36.

——(2011), *Kozi Gramadi, Prouchvanye na Odriska vladetelska rezidentsiya i svetilishta v Sredna Gora, Tom I Kozi Gramadi, Studies of an Odrysian Ruler's Residence and Sanctuaries in Sredna Gora Mountain, 8th–1st centuries BC, volume 1,* Sofia.

Chrysostomou, A. (1994), *Ancient Almopia*, Thessaloniki.

——(2006), 'Anadeixi—diamorphōsi archaiologikou chōrou Edessas' [The Enhancement and development of the Archaeological Site at Edessa, 2005-2006], *AEMΘ* 20, 713–24.

——(2008), *Αρχαία Έδεσσα*, Thessaloniki.

Chrysostomou, P. (1990), '*Η τοπογραφία της Βόρειας Βοττιαίας. Η Πέλλα, η αποικία της Πέλλας και οι χώρες τους*' [Topographie du Nord de la Bottiée—le territoire de Pella], in Mnimi Lazaridi, 205–31.

——(1995), 'Anaskaphe sti romaiki kai Byzantini Pella', *AEMΘ* 9, 117–136.

——(1997), '*Βασιλικοί δικασταί και ταγοί σε μια νέα επιγραφή με ωνες από την κεντρική Μακεδονία*', *Tekmeria* 3, 23–45.

——, Aslanis, I., and Chrysostomou, A. (2007), *Agrosykia, Enas oikismos ton proistorikon kai istorikon chronon,* Verroia.

——and Chrysostomou, A. (2000), '*Τα νεκροταφεία του Αρχοντικού Πέλλας*', *AEMΘ*, 14, 473–00.

————(2001), ''*Ανασκαφή στη δυτική νεκροπολη του 'Αρχοντικού Πέλλας κατά το* 2001', *AEMΘ*, 15, 477–88.

————(2002), 'Excavations in the West Cemetery of Arhondiko near Pella in 2002', *AEMΘ*, 16, 465–78.

————(2007), 'Τ*άφοι πολεμιστών των αρχαϊκών χρόνων από το Αρχοντικό Πέλλας*', *AncMac VII,* 113–32.

Chryssanthaki, K. (2002), 'Les rapports entre Abdère et les Thraces, vus par les documents monétaires', in *Thrace and the Aegean,* 421–30.

Chryssanthaki-Nagle, K. (2007), *L'histoire monétaire d'Abdère en Thrace (VIe s. avant J.C.–IIe s. après J.C.),* MELETEMATA 51, Athens.

Clarke, K. (2008), *Making Time for the Past. Local History and the Polis*, Oxford.

Cohen, G. M. (1995), *Hellenistic Settlements in Europe, the Islands, and Asia Minor*, Berkeley, Los Angeles, and Oxford.

Collar, A. (2009), 'Network Theory and Religious Innovation', in *Networks*, 144–57.

Collart, P. (1937), *Philippes, ville de Macédoine, depuis ses origines jusqu'à la fin de l'époque romaine*, Paris.

Conovici, N. (2005), 'The Dynamics of Trade in Transport Amphoras from Sinope, Thasos, and Rhodes on the Western Black Sea Coast: a Comparative Approach', in Vl. Stolbaand and L. Hannestad (eds), *Chronologies of the Black Sea Area in the Period c.400–100BC*, Black Sea Studies 3, Aarhus, 97–117.

Constantakopoulou, C. (2007), *The Dance of the Islands*, Oxford.

Cottier, M. (2012), 'Retour à la source: A Fresh Overview of the Persian Customs Register TAD C.3.7', in *Stephanèphoros*, 53–61.

——, et al. (eds) (2008), *The Customs Law of Asia*. Oxford.

Craddock, P. (2008), 'Mining and Metallurgy', in J. P. Oleson (ed.), *The Oxford Handbook of Engineering and Technology in the Classical World*, Oxford, 93–120.

Crielaard, J. P. (2009), 'Cities', in K. A. Raaflaub and H. van Wees (eds), *A Companion to Archaic Greece*, Malden Mass., Oxford, and Chichester, 349–72.

Crow, J. and Turner, S. (2009), 'Silivri and the Thracian hinterland of Istanbul: an historic landscape', *Anatolian Studies* 59, 167–81.

Cuomo, S. (2007), *Technology and Culture in Greek and Roman Antiquity*, Cambridge.

Curtis, N. and Tallis, N. (2012), *The Horse from Arabia to Royal Ascot*, London.

Dahmen, K. (2010), 'The Numismatic Evidence', in Roisman and Worthington, 41–62.

Dalby, A. (2000), 'Lynceus and the Anecdotists', in *Athenaeus and his World*, 372–94.

Damyanov, M. (2010), 'Greeks and natives in the region of Odessos', in Tréziny (ed.), 265–75.

Daragan, M. (2009), 'Grey pottery from monuments of the early Scythian period in the middle Dnestr region (western Podolian group of monuments)', in A. Avram et al. (eds), *Pontic Grey Wares, International Conference Bucarest–Constanza, September 30–3 October 2008*, Pontica 42, Supplementum 1, Constanța, 119–47.

Davies, J. K. (1981), *Wealth and the Power of Wealth in Classical Athens*, New York.

Davies, J. K. (1998), 'Ancient Economies: Models and Muddles', in H. Parkins and C. Smith (eds), *Trade, Traders and the Ancient City.* London and New York, 225–56.

——(2000), 'a Wholly non-Aristotelian Universe: The Molossians as Ethnos, State, and Monarchy', in *Alternatives to Athens*, 234–58.

——(2001), 'Hellenistic Economies in the Post-Finley Era', in *HellEc I*, 11–62.

——(2005), 'Linear and Nonlinear Flow Models for Ancient Economies', in Manning and Morris, 127–56.

——(2007), 'The Origins of the Festivals, especially Delphi and the Pythia', in S. Hornblower and C. Morgan (eds), *Pindar's Poetry, Patrons, and Festivals, from Archaic Greece to the Roman Empire,* Oxford, 47–65.

——(2009), 'Ancient Economies', in A. Erskine (ed.), *A Companion to Ancient History*, Malden Mass. and Oxford, 436–46.

——(forthcoming, 2013a), 'Corridors, cleruchies, commodities, and coins: the pre-history of the Athenian Empire', in A. Slawisch (ed.), *Handels- und Finanzgebaren in der Ägais im 5. Jh. v. Chr. — Trade and Finance in the 5th c. BC Aegean World*, BYZAS 18, Istanbul.

——(forthcoming/b), 'Afterword', in A. Erskine (ed.), *A Companion to Ancient History*², Malden Mass. and Oxford.

Dawkins, R. M. and Hasluck, F. W. (1905–06), 'Inscriptions from Bizye', *BSA* 12, 175–83.

Debidour, M. (2008), 'Peut-on parler d'un marché des amphores thasiennes ?' in Y. Roman and J. Dalaison (eds), *L'économie antique, une économie du marché? Tables Rondes de Lyon 2, 2004*, Paris, 87–09.

Decourt, J.-Cl., Nielsen, T. H., and Helly, B. (2004), 'Thessalia and adjacent regions', in *Inventory*, 676–731.

Delemen, I. (2006), 'An Unplundered Chamber Tomb on Ganos Mountain', *AJA* 110/2, 251–73.

Delev, P. (2000), 'Lysimachus, the Getae, and archaeology', *CQ* 50, 384–401.

——(2009), 'Profesor Velizar Velkov (18th May 1928–21 April 1993)', in Chr. Popov and A. Tenchova (eds), *Sbornik v pamet na Profesor Velizar Velkov,* Sofia, 9–14 [In Bulgarian].

Derow, P. S. (1989), 'Rome, the Fall of Macedon, and the Sack of Corinth', *CAH* VIII², 290–323.

De Ste Croix, G. E. M. (1981), *The Class Struggle in the Ancient Greek World,* London.

Descat, R. (2000), 'L'État et les marchés dans le monde grec', in E. Lo Cascio (ed.), *Mercati permanenti e mercati periodici nel mondo romano. Atti degli Incontri capresi di storia dell'economica antica (Capri 13–15 ottobre 1997),* Bari, 13–29.

——(2003), 'Qu'est-ce que l'économie royale?', in Fr. Prost (ed.), *L'Orient mediterraneen de la mort d'Alexandre a aux campagnes de Pompee,* Rennes, 149–68.

——(2006), '*Argyrōnetos:* Les transformations de l'échange dans la Grèce archaïque', in *Agoranomia*, 21–36.

Despini, A., Misaelidou, D., Tiverios, M., and Vocotopoulou, I. (eds) (1985), *Sindos. Catalogue de l'exposition,* Thessaloniki.

Detschew, D. (1976 [1957]), *Die thrakischen Sprachreste,* 2nd edn with bibliography 1955–1974, by Zivka Velkova, Vienna.

Dietler, M. (1990), 'Driven by drink: The role of drinking in the political economy and the case of early Iron Age France', *Journal of Anthropological Archaeology* 9, 352–406.

——(1999), 'Rituals of commensality and the politics of state formation in the "princely" societies of early Iron Age Europe', in P. Ruby (ed.), *Les Princes de la Protohistoire et lémergence de l'État: Actes de la Table Ronde international de Naples (1994),* Collection Centre Jean Bérard 17/Collection École française de Rome 252, Naples, 135–52.

——(2007), 'The Iron Age in the western Mediterranean', in *CEHGRW*, 242–76.

——(2009), 'Colonial Encounters in Iberia and the Western Mediterranean: Exploratory Framework', in M. Dietler and C. López-Ruiz (eds), *Colonial Encounters in Ancient Iberia: Phoenician, Greek and Indigenous Relations*, Chicago, 3–48.

——(2011), 'Feasting and fasting', in T. Insoll (ed.), *Oxford Handbook of the Archaeology of Ritual and Religion,* Oxford, 179–94.

——and Herbich, T. (2001), 'Feasts and labor mobilization: Dissecting a fundamental economic practice', in M. Dietler and B. Hayden (eds), *Feasts: Archaeological and ethnographic perspectives on food, politics, and power,* Washington D.C., 240–64.

——and López-Ruiz, C. (eds) (2009), *Colonial Encounters in Ancient Iberia. Phoenician, Greek, and Indigenous Relations,* Chicago and London.

Dimitrov, D. P. (1958), 'Za ukrepiteni vili i rezidentsii u Trakite v Predrimskata epoha' (Sur les villes fortifiées et les résidences chez les Thraces à l'époque préromaine), *Izsledvaniya v chest na Akad. D. Dechev,* Sofia, 683–99.

——and Chichikova, M. (1978), *The Thracian City of Seuthopolis,* BAR Supplementary Series, 38, Oxford.

Dimitrov, K. (2011), 'Social and Religious Aspects of the Royal City in Early Hellenistic Thrace. II.I. Seuthopolis: the City and the Society', *Seminarium Thracicum* 7, 95–119.

Dimitrova, N. M. (2008), *Theoroi and Initiates in Samothrace. The Epigraphic Evidence*, Hesperia Supplement 37, Princeton N.J.

Domaradzka, L. (1999), 'Monuments épigraphiques de Pistiros', *BCH* 123, 347–58.

——(2002), 'Catalogue of graffiti discovered during the excavations at Pistiros-Vetren (1988–1998). Part one: Graffiti on fine imported pottery', in *Pistiros II*, 209–28.

——(2005), 'Graeco-Thracian relations in the Upper Maritsa valley (5th to 4th century BC)', in Bouzek and Domaradzka, 19–26.

——(2007), 'Catalogue of graffiti discovered at Pistiros-Vetren (1988–2004). Part 2: Graffiti on pottery used in the household', in *Pistiros III*, 221–35.

——and Domaradzki, M. (1999), 'Population structure of Pistiros', *Ancient Macedonia, Sixth International Symposium*, I, 383–92.

Domaradzki, M. (2001), *Materiali za Archeologiya na Sredna Struma (The Archaeology of the Middle Struma region. Preliminary Investigations)*, Razkopki i Prouchvaniya (Excavations and Studies) 27, Sofia.

——(2005), 'The Archaeological Map of Bulgaria', in Bouzek and Domaradzka 2005, 261–66.

Doonan, O. P. (2004), *Sinop Landscapes, Exploring Connection in a Black Sea Hinterland*, Philadelphia.

Douglas, M. and Isherwood, B. (1996), *The World of Goods: towards and anthropology of consumption*, London and New York.

Draganov, D. (1993), *The Coinage of Cabyle*, Sofia.

van Driel-Murray, C. (2002), 'Ancient skin processing and the impact of Rome on tanning technology', in Fr. Audoin-Rouzeau and S. Beyries (eds), *Le Travail du cuir de la Préhistoire à nos jours: Actes des Rencontres 18–20 octobre 2001*, Antibes, 251–65.

——(2008), 'Tanning and Leather', in J. P. Oleson (ed.), *The Oxford Handbook of Engineering and Technology in the Classical World*, Oxford, 483–95.

Drougou, S. (1987), 'Το *ύφασμα της Βεργίνας*', in *ΑΜΗΤΟΣ, τιμητικός τόμος για τον καθηγητή Μ. Ανδρόνικο*, I, Thessaloniki, 303–15.

——(2006), 'Vergina 2006: additional work on the Macedonian Tomb with an Ionic façade', *ΑΕΜΘ* 20, 767–70.

——(2011), 'Vergina—the Ancient City of Aegae', in Lane-Fox (ed.), 243–56.

Duchêne, H. (1986), 'Sur la stèle d'Aulus Caprilius Timotheos, Sômatemporos', *BCH* 110, 513–30.

Dumitru, A. (2006), 'Byzance et les Philippe de Macédoine', *BCH* 119, 139–56.

Dupont, P. (2010), 'Les amphores "samiennes" et "proto-thasiennes" de Zeest: la piste nord-Ionienne ?', in Kassab Tezgör and Inaishvili (eds), 39–43.

——and Lungu, V. (2008), 'Plats milésiens à couverte noire de mer Noire', *Anatolia Antiqua* 16, 77–86.

———(2009), *Les productions céramiques de Pont-Euxin à l'époque grecque*, Actes du Colloque international, Bucarest, 18–23 septembre 2004, *Il Mar Nero* 6, Rome/Paris.

———(2010), 'Beidaud: un cas d'acculturation potière dans l'hinterland gète?' in Tréziny (ed.), 493–8.

Eckstein, A. M. (2008), *Rome Enters the Greek East. From ANARCHY to HIERARCHY in the Hellenistic Mediterranean, 230–170 BC*, Malden Mass., Oxford, and Victoria.

——(2010), 'Macedonia and Rome, 221–146 BC', in Roisman and Worthington, 225–50.

Edmonds, Radcliffe G. III (2011), 'The "Orphic" gold tablets. Texts and translations, with critical apparatus and tables', in Radcliffe G. Edmonds III (ed.), *The 'Orphic' Gold Tablets and Greek Religion*, Cambridge, 16–50.

Ellis, J. R. (1976), *Philip II and Macedonian Imperialism*, London.

Ellis Jones, J. (2007), '"Living above the shop": domestic aspects of the ancient industrial workshops of the Laureion area of south-east Attica', in Westgate et al. (eds), 267–80.

Elton, H. and Reger, G. (eds) (2007), *Regionalism in Hellenistic and Roman Asia Minor*, Études 20, Bordeaux.

Emilov, J. (2010), 'Ancient Texts and the Galatian Royal Residence of Tylis and the Context of La Tène Finds in Southern Thrace. A Reappraisal', in Vagalinski (ed.), 67–87.

Epstein, J. M. (2008), 'Why model?', Santa Fe Working Papers, 08-09-040, <http://www.santafe.edu>.

Errington, M. (1990), *A History of Macedonia*, Berkeley, Los Angeles, and Oxford.

Ekserdjian, D. (2012), *Bronze*, London.

Étienne, R. (2000), 'La chasse à l'ours', in A. Avram and M. Babeş (eds), *Civilisation grecque et cultures antiques périphériques. Hommage à Petre Alexandrescu à son 70e anniversaire*, Bucarest, 68–76.

——(2002), 'Macédoine entre Orient et Occident: essai sur l'identité macédonienne au IVe siècle av. J.-C.', in C. Müller and F. Prost (eds), *Identités et cultures dans le monde méditerranéen antique*, Paris, 253–75.

——(2006), 'Architecture palatiale et architecture privée en Macédoine (IVe–IIe s. avant J.-C.', in *Rois, Cités, Nécropoles*, 105–16.

Faraguna, M. (1998), 'Aspetti amministrativi e finanziari della monarchia macedone tra IV e III secolo a.C.', *Athenaeum* 86, 349–95.

——(2006), 'L'economia della Macedonia ellenistica: un bilancio', in *Approches*, 121–46.

Fasolo, M. (2003), *La Via Egnatia 1. Da Apollonia e Dyrrhachium ad Herakleia Lynkestidos, Viae Publicae Romanae, 1*, Rome.

Fentress, E. (2009), 'Peopling the Countryside: Roman Demography in the Albegna Valley and Jerba', in A. Bowman and A. Wilson (eds), *Quantifying the Roman Economy. Methods and Problems,* Oxford, 127–61.

Ferguson, N. (2001), *The Cash Nexus. Money and Power in the Modern World, 1700–2000,* London.

——(2008), *The Ascent of Money. A Financial History of the World,* London.

Finley, M. I. (1980), *Ancient Slavery and Modern Ideology,* London.

——(1985) [1999], *The Ancient Economy 2,* updated with a new foreword by Ian Morris, Berkeley and Los Angeles.

Firatli, N. (1964), *Les stèles funéraires de Byzance Gréco-Romaine,* avec l'edition et l'index commenté des épitaphes par Louis Robert, Paris.

Fisher, N. (1993), *Slavery in Classical Greece,* London.

Flensted-Jensen, P. (2004), 'Thrace from Strymon to Axios', in *Inventory,* 810–53.

Fol, A. (1965), 'Le développement de la vie urbaine dans les pays entre le Danube et la mer Égée jusqu'à la conquête romaine', *Études balkaniques* 2–3, 309–17.

——(1972), *Demografska i sotsyalna kultura,* Sofia.

——(1975), *Trakya i Balkanite prez rannoelinicheskata epoha,* Sofia.

——, Chichikova, M., Ivanov, T., and Teofilov, T. (1986), *The Thracian Tomb near the Village of Sveshtari,* Sofia.

Forbes, H. (1995), 'The identification of pastoralist sites within the context of estate-based agriculture in ancient Greece', *BSA* 90, 325–38.

Foxhall, L. (1998), 'Cargoes of the heart's desire. The character of trade in the archaic Mediterranean world', in N. Fisher and H. van Wees (eds), *Archaic Greece. New approaches and new evidence,* London and Swansea, 295–309.

——(2007), 'House clearance: unpacking the "kitchen" in Classical Greece', in Westgate et al., 233–42.

Fraser, P. (2000), 'Ethnics as Personal Names', in S. Hornblower and E. Matthews (eds), *Greek Personal Names: Their Value as Evidence,* Oxford, 149–57.

Fröhlich, P. (2004), *Les cités grecques et le contrôle des magistrats (ive–1er siècle avant J.-C.),* Geneva.

Gabrielsen, V. (1994), *Financing the Athenian fleet. Public taxation and social relations,* Baltimore.

——(2001), 'Economic Activity, Maritime Trade and Piracy in the Hellenistic Aegean', *REA* 103/1–2, 219–40.

——(2003), 'Piracy and the Slave-Trade', in A. Erskine *A Companion to the Hellenistic World,* Oxford, 389–404.

——(2005), 'Banking and Credit Operations in Hellenistic times', in *HellEc II,* 136–64.

——(2007), 'Trade and Tribute: Byzantion and the Black Sea Straits', in Gabrielsen and Lund (eds), 287–324.

——(2008), 'Die Kosten der athenischen Flotte in klassischer Zeit', in F. Burrer and H. Müller (eds), *Kriegskosten und Kriegsfinanzierung in der Antike*, Darmstadt, 46–73.

——(2011), 'Profitable partnerships: Kings, cities, and trade', in *HellEc III*, 216–50.

——(forthcoming), 'From Taxpayer to Moneylender: The Hellenistic Benefactor Revisited'.

——and Lund, J. (eds) (2007), *The Black Sea in Antiquity: Regional and Interregional Economic Exchanges*, Black Sea Studies 6, Aarhus.

Galanakis, Y. (ed.) (2011), *From Herakles to Alexander the Great, Treasures from the Royal Capital of Macedon, a Hellenic Kingdom in the Age of Democracy*, Oxford.

Gale, N. H., Gentner, W., and Wagner, G. A. (1980), 'Mineralogical and Geographical Silver Sources of Archaic Greek Coinge', *Metallurgy and Numismatics* 1, 3–49.

Game, J. (2008), *Actes de vente dans le monde grecque*, Lyon.

Gauthier, Ph. (1972), *Symbola: les étrangers et la justice dans les cités grecques*, Annales de l'est, Nancy.

Gaydarska, B. and Chapman, J. (2007), 'Salt research in Bulgaria', in D. Monah et al. (eds), *L'Exploitation du sel a travers le temps*, Piatra-Neamt, 147–60.

Gellner, E. (1983), *Nations and Nationalism*, Oxford.

Georgieva, R. and Momchilov, D. (2003), 'Nadgrobnata mogila kray s. Prilep—myasto za pogrebenye ili zhertvoprinoshenye?' in A. Fol (ed.), *Patyat. Sbornik nauchni studii posveteni na zhivota i tvorchestvo na dr. Georgi Kitov*, Sofia, 63–7.

Georgiv, V. (1987), *Poleznite izkopaemi ot vremeto na Trakite*, Sofia.

Gerassimidis, A. (2000), 'Palynological Evidence for Human Influence on the Vegetation of Mountain Regions in Northern Greece: The Case of Lilaias, Serres', in P. Halstead and Ch. Frederick (eds), *Landscape and Land Use in Postglacial Greece*, Sheffield Studies in Aegean Archaeology, 3, 28–37.

Gerding, H. (2006), 'The Early Use of Fired Brick in Hellenistic and Roman Architecture', in C. C. Mattusch, A. A. Donohue, and A. Brauer (eds), *Common Ground: Archaeology, Art, Science, and Humanities, Proceedings of the XVIth International Congress of Classical Archaeology*, Oxford, 355–8.

Ghilardi, M., Fouache, E., Queyrel, Fr., Syridis, G., Vouvalidis, K., Kunesch, S., Styllas, M., and Stiros, S. (2008), 'Human Occupation and Geomorphological Evolution of the Thessaloniki Plain (Greece) since mid Holocene', *Journal of Archaeological Science* 35, 111–25.

Gibbins, D. (2001), 'Shipwrecks and Hellenistic trade', in *HellEc I*, 273–312.

Gill, D. W. J. (2011), *Sifting the soil of Greece: the early years of the British School at Athens (1886–1919)*, BICS Supplement 111, London.

Gimatzidis, S. (2010), *Die Stadt Sindos. Eine Siedlung von der späten Bronze- bis zur Klassischen Zeit am Thermaischen Golf in Makedonien,* Rahden.
Ginouvès, R. and Hatzopoulos, M. B. (eds) (1993), *Macedonia, from Philip II to the Roman Conquest,* Princeton.
Girouard, M. (1978), *Life in the English Country House, A Social and Architectural History,* New Haven, Conn.
Glenny, M. (1999), *The Balkans, 1804–1999, Nationalism, War, and the Great Powers,* London.
Goldsmith, R. (1987), *Pre-Modern Financial Systems,* Cambridge.
Graf, F. and Johnston, S. I. (2007), *Ritual texts for the afterlife: Orpheus and the Bacchic gold tablets,* Princeton N.J.
Grammenos, D. B., Besios, M., and Kotsos, S. (1997), *Απο τους προϊστορικους οικισμόυς της Κεντρικής Μακεδονίας,* Thessaloniki.
Grandjean, Y. and Salviat, Fr. (2000), *Guide de Thasos*[2], Paris.
Graninger, D. (2010), 'Macedonia and Thessaly', in Roisman and Worthington, 306–25.
Granovetter, M. (1985), 'Economic Action and Social Structure: The Problem of Embeddedness', *American Journal of Sociology* 91/3, 481–510.
Greenaway, F. (1986), 'Chemical Tests in Pliny', in R. French and F. Greenaway (eds), *Science in the Early Roman Empire: Pliny the Elder, his Sources and Influence,* London and Sydney, 147–61.
Greenwalt, W. (1985), 'The introduction of Caranus into the Argead King List', *GRBS* 26/1.
——(1993), 'The iconographical significance of Amyntas III's Mounted Hunter Stater', *Ancient Macedonia V*, 509–19.
——(1994), 'A Solar Dionysos and Argead legitimacy', *AncWorld* 25, 3–8.
——(2010), 'Macedonia, Illyria, and Epirus', in Roisman and Worthington, 279–305.
Grigorova, V. and Prokopov, I. (2002), 'Les drachmes d'Apollonia et Dyrrachion en Illyrie dans la circulation monétaire en Thrace (IIe—Ier s. av. J.-C.)', Trésors et fonds de musées bulgares contentant des monnaies d'Apollonie et Dyrrachion', in *Thrace and the Aegean,* 651–81.
van Groningen, B. A. (1933), *Aristote: Le second livre de l'Économique,* Leiden.
Gruen, E. S. (1982), 'Macedonia and the Settlement of 167 B.C.', in Adams and Borza, 1982, 257–67.
Guimier-Sorbets, A.-M. and Morizot, Y. (2006), 'Construire l'identité du mort: l'architecture funéraire en Macédoine', in *Rois, Cités, Nécropoles,* 117–29.
Guldager Bilde, P. and Petersen, J. H. (eds) (2008), *Meetings of Cultures Between Conflicts and Coexistence,* Black Sea Studies 8, Aarhus.

Hall, J. M. (2001), 'Contested ethnicities: Perceptions of Macedonia within Evolving Definitions of Greek Identity', in I. Malkin (ed.), *Ancient Perceptions of Greek Ethnicity*, Cambridge Mass., 159–86.

Halstead, P. (1996), 'Pastoralism or Household Herding? Problems of Scale and Specialization in Early Greek Animal Husbandry', *World Archaeology* 28, 20–42.

Hamilakis, Y. (2000), 'The Anthropology of Food and Drink Consumption and the Aegean Archaeology', in S. J. Vaughan and W. D. E. Coulson (eds), *Palaeodiet in the Aegean*, Wiener Laboratory Monograph 1, Oxford, 55–63.

——(2007), *The nation and its ruins: antiquity, archaeology, and national imagination in Greece*, Oxford.

Hamilton, Ch. D. (1999), 'Macedonian migration and its effects', *AncMac VI*/1, 471–81.

Hammond, N. G. L. (1989), *The Macedonian State. Origins, Institutions, and History*, Oxford.

——(1997), 'The Lakes on the Lower Strymon and Mt. Dionysos,' *Ancient World* 28, 41–7.

Hansen, M. H. (1996), 'Aristotle's Two Complementary Views of the Greek *Polis*', in R. W. Wallace and E. M. Harris (eds), *Transitions to Empire. Essays in Greco-Roman History, 360–246 BC in honor of E. Badian*, London and Norman, Okla., 195–210.

——(2006), *Polis. An Introduction to the Ancient Greek City-State*, Oxford.

Harding, A. (2007), 'Salt in Late Bronze Age Europe', in D. Monah et al. (eds), *L'Exploitation du sel a travers le temps*, Piatra-Neamt, 191–8.

Harris, E. M. (1989) [2006], 'The liability of Business Partners in Athenian Law', *CQ* 38, 339–43 (reprinted in E. M. Harris, *Democracy and the Rule of Law in Classical Athens: Essays on Law, Society, and Politics in Classical Athens*, Cambridge and New York, 2006).

——(2001), 'Workshop, marketplace, and household. The nature of technical specialization in classical Athens and its influence on economy and society', in P. Cartledge, E. Cohen, and L. Foxhall (eds), *Money, Labour, and Land: Approaches to the economies of ancient Greece*, London, 67–96.

——(forthcoming), 'Were there Business Agents in Classical Greece? The Evidence of Some Lead Letters', in U. Yivtach (ed.), *Legal Documents in Ancient Societies (LDAS) I The Letter: Law, State, Society and the Epistolary Format in the Ancient World. Proceedings of a Colloquium held at the American Academy in Rome (28.–30.9.2008)*, Wiesbaden.

Harris, W. V. (ed.) (2005), *Rethinking the Mediterranean*, Oxford.

Hatzinikolaou, K. G. (2009), '*Συμβολή στη μελέτη της ιστορικής γεωγραφίας της Ανω Μακεδονίας*', *Makedonika* 38, 1–20.

Hatzopoulos, M. B. (1988a), *Une Donation du Roi Lysimaque*, MELETEMATA 5, Athens.

Hatzopoulos, M. B. (1988b), *Actes de vente de la Chalcidique Centrale*, MELETEMATA 6, Athens.
——(1991), *Actes de vente d'Amphipolis*, MELETEMATA 14, Athens and Paris.
——(1994a), *Cultes et rites de passage en Macédoine*, MELETEMATA 19, Athens and Paris.
——(1994b), 'Thessalie et Macédoine: Affinités et convergences', in *La Thessalie. Quinze années de recherche archéologiques, 1975–1990. Bilans et Perspectives*, 2, Athens, 249–54.
——(1996), *Macedonian Institutions under the Kings. I. A Historical and Epigraphic Study; II. Epigraphic Appendix*, MELETEMATA 22, Athens and Paris.
——(1997), 'L'état Macédonien antique: un nouveau visage', *CRAI*, 7–25.
——(1998), *Actes de vente d'Amphipolis*, Athens.
——(1999a), 'Le macédonien: nouvelles données et nouvelles théories', *Ancient Macedonia VI*, Thessaloniki, 225–39.
——(1999b), 'La Macédoine de Philippe II à la conquête romaine. L'apport des récents documents épigraphiques', in *XI Congresso Internazionale de Epigrafia Greca e Latina. Roma, 18–24 settembre 1997*, Rome, 257–73.
——(2000), '"L'histoire par les noms" in Macedonia', in S. Hornblower and E. Matthews (eds), *Greek Personal Names, their Value as Evidence*, Oxford, 99–117.
——(2001), *L'organisation de l'armée macédonienne sous les Antigonides. Problemes anciens et documents nouveaux*, Athens.
——(2002), 'La Thrace au carrefour des deux mondes', in *Thrace and the Aegean*, 265–72.
——(2003), 'Herodotos (VIII.137–138), the Manumissions from Leukopetra and the Topography of the Middle Haliakmon Valley', in R. Parker (ed.), *Herodotus and his world*, Oxford, 203–18.
——(2006), 'De vie à trépas: rites de passage, lamelles dionysiaques, et tombes macédoniennes', in *Rois, Cités, Nécropoles*, 131–9.
——(2008a), 'Retour à la vallée du Strymon', in *Thrakika Zetemata 1*, MELETEMATA 58, 13–54.
——(2008b), 'The Burial of the Dead (at Vergina) or the Unending Controversy on the Identity of the Occupants of Tomb II', *Tekmeria* 9, 91–118.
——(2011a), 'A list of sales from Mieza and the constitution of extensive landed properties in the Central Macedonian plain', *Tekmeria* 10, 47–69.
——(2011b), 'Macedonians and other Greeks', in Lane-Fox (ed.), 51–78.
——and Loukopoulou, L. (1992), *Recherches sur les marches orientales des Temenides (Anthemonte—Kalindoia)*, MELEMATA 11, vols I–II, Athens and Paris.

——and Paschidis, P. (2004), '*Makedonia*', in M. Herman Hansen and T. Heine Nielsen (eds), *An Inventory of Archaic and Classical Poleis,* Oxford, 794–809.

Hawthorne, K., Varbanov, V., and Dragoev, D. (2011), 'Thracian pit sanctuaries: continuity in sacred space', in I. P. Haynes (ed.), *Early Roman Thrace. New evidence from Bulgaria,* JRA Supplementary Series, 82, Portsmouth, Rhode Island, 59–83.

Haynes, I. P. (ed.) (2011), *Early Roman Thrace. New evidence from Bulgaria,* JRA Supplementary Series, 82, Portsmouth, Rhode Island.

Healy, J. F. (1999), *Pliny the Elder on Science and Technology,* Oxford.

Helly, B. (1968), 'Des lions dans l'Olympe!', *RÉA* 70, 271–85.

——(1995), *L'Etat thessalien: Aleuas le Roux, les tétrades et les tagoi*, Lyon.

——(2009), 'La Thessalie au 3e siècle av. J.-C.', in *Αρχαιολικο Έργο Θεσσαλίας και Στερεάς Ελλάδας* 2, 2006, I, 339–68.

Henkelman, W. F. M. and Stolper, M. W. (2009), 'Ethnic identity and ethnic labelling at Persepolis: the case of the Skudrians', in P. Briant and M. Chauveau (eds), *Organisation des pouvoirs et contacts culturels dans les pays de l'empire achéménide,* Paris, 271–329.

Herman, G. (1987), *Ritualised friendship and the Greek city,* Cambridge.

Hermary, A. et al. (ed.) (2010), *Apollonia du Pont (Sozopol), La nécropole de Kalfata (Ve—IIIe s.av.J.-C.). Fouilles franco-bulgaries (2002–2004),* Bibliothèque d'Archèologie Méditerranéenne et Africaine 5, Paris and Aix-en-Provence.

Herries, A. I. R. and Kovacheva, M. (2007), 'Using Archaeomagnetism to answer arachaeological questions about burnt structures at the Thracian site of Halka Bunar, Bulgaria', *Archaeologia Bulgarica* xi/3, 25–46.

Hersh, Ch. (1999), 'A 1992 Hoard of Bronze Coins of Philip II from Beroia in Thrace', in M. Amandry and S. Hurter (eds), *Travaux de Numismatique grecque offerts à Georges le Rider,* London, 161–5.

Herzfeld, M. (2005), 'Practical Mediterraneanism: Excuses for Everything, from Epistemology to Eating', in W. V. Harris (ed.), *Rethinking the Mediterranean,* Oxford, 45–63.

Heuzey, L. (1860), *Le mont Olympe et l'Akarnanie, exploration de ces deux régions*, Paris.

——and Daumet, H. (1876), *Mission archéologique de Macédoine*, Paris.

Hodgson, G. M. (1998), 'On the Evolution of Thorstein Veblen's Evolutionary Economics', *Cambridge Journal of Economics* 22, 415–31.

——(2001), *How economics forgot history, The problem of historical specificity in social science,* London and New York.

Hodkinson, S. (1988), 'Animal husbandry in the Greek *polis*', in C. R. Whittaker (ed.), *Pastoral economies in Classical antiquity*, Cambridge Philological Society Supplement 14, Cambridge, 35–74.

Hodos, T. (2010), 'Globalization and Colonization: A View from Iron Age Sicily', *JMeditArch* 23/1, 81–106.

Hoepfner, W. and Brands, G. (eds) (1996), *Basileia. Die Paläste der hellenistischen Könige*, Mainz.

Hornblower, S. (1991), *A Commentary on Thucydides I. Books I–III*, Oxford.

——(2004), *Thucydides and Pindar: historical narrative and the world of epinikian poetry*, Oxford.

——and Morgan, C. (eds) (2007), *Pindar's Poetry, Patrons, and Festivals, from Archaic Greece to the Roman Empire*, Oxford.

Howgego, C. (1995), *Ancient History from coins*, London.

Hoz, J. de (2010), 'L'écriture gréco-ibérique et l'influence hellène sur les usages de l'écriture en Hispanie et dans le sud de la France', in Tréziny (ed.), 637–57.

Huguenot, C. (2008), *Eretria XIX, La Tombe aux Erotes et la Tombe d'Amarynthos*, Lausanne.

Husenovski, B. (2002), *Srebrnyiot stater od tip "kentaur i nimfa" od numizmatičkiot fond na lok. Vardarski Rid, Makedonsko nasledstvo*, Skopje.

Ignatiadou, D. (2002a), 'Colorless glass in late Classical and early Hellenistic Macedonia', *JGS* 44, 11–24.

——(2002b), 'Erevna gia to Chalastraio vitro', *AEMΘ* 16, 241–8.

——, Dotsika, E., Kouras, A., and Maniatis, A. (2005), 'Nitrum Chalestricum: the natron of Macedonia', in H. Cool (ed.), *Annales du 16e Congrès de l'Association Internationale pour l'histoire du Verre*, Nottingham, 64–7.

Ioakeimidou, E., Kallintzi, K., Malama, V., Miza, M., Sarantidou, M., and Chrysaphi, M. (2006), 'Anaplisi—anadeixi archaiologikou chōrou Avdirōn' [Configuration—enhancement of the archaeological site of Abdera], *AEMΘ*, 20, 9–19.

Isaac, B. (1986), *The Greek Settlements in Thrace until the Roman Conquest*, Leiden.

Ivanova, E. (2005), 'Investigation and conservation of finds from various materials excavated at Pistiros', in Bouzek and Domaradzka, 37–46.

——(2011), 'Characterization of Pigments used at Emporium Pistiros (5th to 3rd century BC)', *Eirene* 47, 40–44.

Jourukova, J. (1994), 'Agathopolis—d'après les données épigraphiques et numismatiques', *Settlement life in Ancient Thrace IV*, 261–5 (see also Yourukova).

Kagan, J. H. (1987), 'The Decadrachm Hoard: Chronology and Consequences', in I. Carradice (ed.), *Coinage and Administration in the Athenian Empire*, BAR IS 343, Oxford, 21–8.

——(2006), 'Small change and the beginning of coinage at Abdera', in *Agoranomia*, 49–60.

Kallet, L. (1993), *Money, Expense, and Naval Power in Thucydides' History 1–5.24*, Berkeley, Los Angeles, and Oxford.

——(2001), *Money and the Corrosion of Power in Thucydides: The Sicilian Expedition, and its aftermath*, Berkeley, Los Angeles, and London.

——(2012), 'The Origins of the Athenian Economic Arche', *JHS* 132.

Karadima, Chr. and Psoma, S. (2007), 'The excavation coins of Maroneia: a preliminry report', in *Thrace in the Graeco-Roman World*, 291–8.

Karadima-Matsa, Chr., Blondé, Fr., and Picon, M. (2005), 'L'Alun de Macédoine', in Ph. Borgard, J.-P. Brun, D. Cardon, V. Forest, and M. Picon (eds), *L'Alun de Mediterranee*, Collection du Centre Jean Berard 23, Naples and Aix en Provence, 69–75.

Karamitrou-Mentessidi, G. (2006a), 'Aiane 2006: Research in the east cemetery', *AEMΘ* 20, 833–42.

——(2006b), 'Kozani prefecture: Polymelos, Keitos, Perdikkas, Mikrokastro, Aliakmon,' *AEMΘ* 20, 847–69.

——(2009) [2011], 'From the research at the Ilarion Dam (Aliakmon): The excavation at Megas Aï Girorgis and Aghios Konstantinos near Dimitra, Grevena', *To Archaiologiko Ergo stin Ano Makedonia* I, 109–29.

——(2011), 'Aiani- Historical and Geographical Context', in Lane-Fox (ed.), 93–112.

Karayotov, I. (1994), 'La *Χώρα* de Mesambria Pontika d'après les données archéologieques et numismatiques', *Settlement Life in Ancient Thrace* IV, 283–92.

——(2002), 'Les rois thraces de Bizye et le littoral Ouestpontique', *Thrace and the Aegean*, 431–37.

Karttunen, Kl. (2002), 'The Ethnography of the Fringes', in E. J. Bakker, I. J. F. de Jong, and H. van Wees (eds), *Brill's Companion to Herodotus*, Leiden, Boston, and Cologne, 457–74.

Kassab Tezgör, D. and Inaishvili, N. (eds) (2010), *PATABS 1—Production and Trade of Amphorae in the Black Sea, Actes de la Table Ronde international de Batoumi et Trabzon, 27–29 Avril 2006*, Istanbul and Paris.

Katinčarova, D. (2005), 'Die Metallerzlagerstätten im Pistirosgebiet', in Bouzek and Domaradzka, 31–6.

Kay, J. (2003), *The Truth about Markets, Why Some Nations are Rich but Most Remain Poor*, London.

Kellogg, D. (2004/2005), 'The Athenian Decree honouring Hebryzelmis of Thrace Reconsidered', *AJAH* new ser. 3–4, [2007], 58–71.

Kiderlen, M. (1996), 'Zum gesellschaftlichen Kontext und zur schichtspezifischen Zuordnung grosser Stadthäuser des 4. Und 3. Jhs. v. Chr.' in *Basileia*, 76–83.

Kilian-Dirlmeier, I. (2002), *Kleinfunde aus dem Athena Itonia-Heiligtum bei Philia (Thessalien)*, Mainz.

Kim, H. S. and Kroll, J. H. (2008), 'A Hoard of Archaic Coins of Colophon and Unminted Silver', *American Journal of Numismatics* 20, 53–104.

King, C. J. (2010), 'Macedonian Kingship and other Political Institutions', in Roisman and Worthington, 373–91.

Kinzl, K. (ed). (2006), *A Companion to the Classical Greek World*, Malden Mass. and Oxford.

Kisiov, K., Prokopov, I., and Dotchev, C. (1998), *Numismatic Riches of Archaeological Museum Plovdiv*, Sofia.

Kisyov, K. (2004), *Trakiyskata kultura v regiona na Plovdiv i techenyeto na r. Stryama prez vtorata polovina na I hil. pr. Chr.* Sofia.

——(2005), *Thrace and Greece in Ancient Times, Part 1. Classical Age Tumuli in the Municipality of Kaloyanovo*, Plovdiv.

Kitov, G. (2001), 'A newly found Thracian Tomb with frescoes', *Archaeologia Bulgarica* 2, 15–29.

——(2003a), 'The Valley of the Thracian Rulers—1', *Archeologiya* 44, 13–28.

——(2003b), 'The Valley of the Thracian Rulers—2', *Archeologiya* 44, 28–42.

——(2004), 'New observations in the Alexandrovo Tomb', *Archeologiya* 45, 42–51.

——(2005), 'Excavations at the Svetitsa tumulus, near Shipka', *Archeologiya* 46, 137–46.

Knappett, C. (2011), *An Archaeology of Interaction. Network Perspectives on Material Culture and Society*, Oxford.

Koleva, B. and Katsarov, G. (2009), 'Rescue excavations on the west slope of the Nebettepe hill in Plovdiv', *Annual of the Regional Archaeological Museum—Plovdiv* xi, 1–16.

——, Martinova, M., and Bospatchieva, M. (2000), 'Des données nouvelles sur l'histoire de Plovdiv', in *Pistiros et Thasos*, 103–21.

Korres, M. (2009), *Αττικης Ὀδοί. Αρχαιοι δρομοι της Αττικής*, Athens.

Kostoglou, M. (2008), *Iron and Steel in Ancient Greece. Artefacts, Technology and Social Change in Aegean Thrace from Classical to Roman Times*, BAR IS 1883.

Kotsakis, K. (2009), 'Communautés en transition: la Macédoine grecque du VIIe au 1[ier] mil. av. J.-C.', in G. Kourtessi-Philippakis (ed.), *La Préhistoire du Sud-Est européen: traditions et innovations*, Études Balkaniques 15, Paris, 229–55.

Kottaridi, A. (2009), '*Η έρεβνα στις Αιγές μία πόλη κατά κώμας*' [Research at Aigai, a Town in Clusters], in *20 Chronia AEMΘ*, Thessaloniki, 773–80.

——(2009), '*Η νεκρόπολη των Αιγών στα αρχαϊκά χρόνια και οι βασιλικές συστάδες*', *20 Chronia AEMΘ*, Thessaloniki, 143–53.

——(2011a), 'The Palace of Aegae', in Lane-Fox (ed.), 297–333.

——(2011b), 'The royal banquet: a capital institution', in Galanakis (ed.), 167–92.

——(2011c), 'Burial customs and beliefs in the royal necropolis of Aegae', in Galanakis (ed.), 131–52.

Koukouli-Chrysanthaki, Ch. (1973), '*Ειδησεις 'εκ της Θασίων 'Ηπειρώ*', *AAA* 6/2, 230–40.

——(1986), 'Abdera and the Thracians', *Thracia Pontica* III, Sozopol, 82–98.

——(1990), 'Ta 'metalla' tis Thasiakis Peraias', in *Mnimi Lazaridi*, 496–9.

——(2006), 'Les nécropoles de la Pérée thasienne: Oisymè et Galepsos', in *Rois, Cités, Nécropoles*, 169–84.

——(2011a), 'Amphipolis', in Lane-Fox (ed.), 409–36.

——(2011b), 'Philippi', in Lane-Fox (ed.), 437–52.

Kouzmanov, M. (2005), 'The horse in Thracian burial rites', in Bouzek and Domaradzka, 143–6.

Kremydi, S. (2011), 'Coinage and Finance', in Lane-Fox (ed.), 159–78.

Kremydi-Sicilianou, S. (2007), 'MAKE: Evidence for a Coinage under the Antigonids', *RN* 163, 91–100.

Kroll, J. H. (2009), 'What about coinage?' in J. Ma, N. Papazarkadas, and R. Parker (eds), *Interpreting the Athenian Empire*, London, 195–209.

Kuleff, I., Stoyanov, T., and Pernicka, E. (2007), 'On the origin of stamped amphorae from Thrace (Bulgaria)', *OJA* 26/1, 53–78.

Kyriakou, A. (2008), *Η Στενόμακρη τούμπα της Βεργίνας. ταφικές πρακτικές στη Μακεδονία του 4 αι*, Thessaloniki.

Landucci Gattinoni, F. (2003a), *L'arte del potere, Vita e opera di Cassandro di Macedonia*, Historia Einzelschriften 171, Stuttgart.

——(2003b), 'Tra monarchia nazionale e monarchia militare: il caso della Macedonia', in C. Bearzot, F. Landucci, and G. Zecchini (eds), *Gli stati territoriali nel mondo antico*, Milan, 199–224.

Lane-Fox, R. J. (2007), 'Alexander the Great: "Last of the Achaemenids"?', in C. J. Tuplin (ed.), *Persian Responses. Political and Cultural Interaction with(in) the Achaemenid Empire*, Swansea, 267–311.

——(ed.) (2011), *Brill's Companion to Ancient Macedon: Studies in the Archaeology and History of Macedon, 650 BC–300 AD*, Leiden.

Latour, B. (2005), *Reassembling the Social. An Introduction to Actor-Network-Theory*, Oxford.

Lauffer, S. (1979), *Die Bergwerkssklaven von Laureion*, Mainz.

Lawall, M. (2005), 'Amphoras and Hellenistic Economies: addressing the (over)-emphasis on stamped amphora handles', in *HellEc II*, 188–232.

——(2011), 'Socio-economic Conditions and the Contents of Amphorae', in Ch. Tzochev, T. Stoyanov, and A. Božkova (eds), *PATABS II, Production and Trade of Amphorae in the Black Sea, Acts of the International Round Table held in Kiten, Nessebar and Sredetz, September 26–30 2007*, Sofia, 23–33.

Lazarov, L. (2010), The Celtic Tylite State in the Time of Cavarus', in Vagalinski (ed.), 97–113.

Lazov, G. (1999), 'Pithoi from the excavations of the *emporium* Pistiros', in *Thasos, Matières premières*, 339–48.

Le Bohec-Bouhet, S. (2006), 'Réflexions sur la place de la femme dans la Macédoine antique', in *Rois, Cités, Nécropoles*, 187–97.

Leekley, D. and Efstratiou, N. (1980), *Archaeological Excavations in central and northern Greece*, Park Ridge, N.J.

Leguilloux, M. (2002), 'Techniques et équipements de la tannerie romaine: l'exemple de l'*officina coriaria* de Pompéi', in Fr. Audoin-Rouzeau and S. Beyries (eds), *Le Travail du cuir de la Préhistoire à nos jours: Actes des Rencontres 18–20 octobre 2001*, Antibes, 267–82.

Lenfant, D. (2007), 'On Persian *tryphē* in Athenaeus', in C. J. Tuplin (ed.), *Persian Responses. Political and Cultural Interaction with(in) the Achaemenid Empire*, Swansea, 51–65.

Le Rider, G. (1977), *Le Monnayage d'argent et d'or de Philippe II frappé en Macédoine de 359 à 294*, Paris.

——(1992), 'Les deux monnaies macédoniennes des années 323–294/290', *BCH* 116/1, 391–404.

——(1996), *Monnayage et finances de Philippe II. Un état de la question*, MELETEMATA 23, Athens.

——(2007), *Alexander the Great: Coinage, Finances and Policy*, tr. W. E. Higgins, Philadelphia.

——and De Callataÿ, F. (2006), *Les Séleucides et les Ptolémées. L'héritage monétaire et financier d'Alexandre le Grand*, Monaco.

Levine, M. (2006), 'mtDNA and horse domestication: the archaeologist's cut', in M. Mashkour (ed.), *Equids in Time and Space, Papers in honour of Véra Eisenmann*, Oxford, 192–201.

Levitski, O. and Kashuba, M. (2009), 'Early wheel made ware from east Carpathian region (on the basis of finds from Trinca – "Izvorul lui Luca" settlement)', in Avram et al. (eds), 93–118.

Lewis, D. (2011), 'Near Eastern slaves in Classical Attica and the slave trade with Persian territories', *CQ* 61/1, 91–113.

Lilimbaki-Akamatis, M. (1990), 'Iera tis Pellas', in Mnimi Lazaridi, 195–200.

——(2009), 'Archaeological work at Pella, 1987–2007', in *20 Chronia AEMΘ*, Thessaloniki, 169–82, Greek with English summary, 183–4.

——and Akamatis, I. (eds) (2003), *Pella and its environs*, Thessaloniki.

Lolos, Y. (2009), 'Via Egnatia after Egnatius: Imperial Policy and Interregional Contacts', in *Networks*, 264–84.

Lomas, K. (2000), 'The Polis in Italy: Ethnicity, Colonization, and Citizenship in the Western Mediterranean', in *Alternatives to Athens*, 167–85.

Loomis, W. T. (1998), *Wages, welfare costs and inflation in Classical Athens*, Ann Arbor.

Loukopoulou, L. (1989), *Contribution à l'histoire de la Thrace propontique durant la période archaïque*, Athens and Paris.

——(2002), 'The *"Prosodos"* of the Thracian Kings', in *Thrace and the Aegean*, 345–53.

——(2008), 'Les inscriptions des trésors nord-balkaniques', in Loukopolou and Psoma (eds), 139–69.

——and Łajtar, A. (2004), 'Propontic Thrace', in *Inventory*, 912–23.

——and Psoma S. (eds) (2008a), *Thrakika Zetemata I*, MELETEMATA 58, Athens.

————(2008b), 'Maroneia and Stryme Revisited. Some Problems of Historical Topography', in Loukopolou and Psoma (eds), 55–86.

Lozanov, I. (2010), 'On the import amphorae in Thrace (6th–3rd centuries B.C.): Reflections on some recent discoveries in the Middle Hebros Valley', in Kassab Tezgör and Inaishvili (eds), 85–96.

Lungu, V. (2009), 'Projet d'Atlas de référence des céramiques grises monochromes du Pont-Euxin à l'époque grecque', in Avram et al. (eds), 13–40.

Ma, J. (1999), *Antiochos III and the cities of western Asia Minor*, Oxford.

——(2011), 'Court, King, and Power in Antigonid Macedonia', in Lane-Fox (ed.), 521–43.

——, Papazarkadas, N., and Parker, R. (2009) (eds), *Interpreting the Athenian Empire*, London.

MacKinnon, M. (2007), 'Osteological Research in Classical Archaeology', *AJA* 111, 473–504.

Macve, R. H. (1985), 'Some glosses on G. E. M. de Ste. Croix's "Greek and Roman accounting", in P. Cartledge and F. D. Harvey (eds), *CRUX. Essays presented to G. E. M. de Ste. Croix on his 75th birthday*, Exeter, 233–64.

Maddison, A. (2007), *Contours of the World Economy*, Oxford.

Madzharov, M. (2009), *Roman Roads in Bulgaria, Contribution to the Development of Roman Road system in the provinces of Moesia and Thrace*, Veliko Turnovo [in Bulgarian and English].

Magnetto, A., Erdas, D., and Carusi, C. (eds) (2010), *Nuove ricerche sulla legge granaria ateniese del 374/3 a.C.*, Pisa.

Malamidou, D. (2006a), 'Les nécropoles d'Amphipolis: nouvelles données archéologiques et anthropologiques', in *Rois, Cités, Nécropoles*, 199–206.

——(2006b), 'Anaskaphika stoichoia gia tin parousia ton ellinon stin periochi ton ekbolon tou Strymona prin apo tin idrysi tis Amphipolis: Ennea Odoi kai Argilos', *AEMΘ* 20, 185–96.

Malkin, I. (2011), *A Small Greek World: Networks in the Ancient Mediterranean*. Greeks Overseas Series, New York and Oxford.

Manakidou, E. (2010), 'Céramiques "indigènes" de l'époque géométrique et archaïque du site de Karabournaki en Macédoine', in Tréziny (ed.), 463–80.

Manning, J. G. (2011), 'Networks, hierarchies and markets in the Ptolemaic economy', in *HellEc III*, 296–323.

Marazov, I. (2011), *Thrace and the Aegean. Vassil Bojkov Collection*, Sofia.

Margaritis, E. (2006), 'Olive and vine farming in Hellenistic Pieria: an archaeobotanical case study of settlements from Macedonia, Greece'. Unpublished PhD dissertation, Cambridge University.

——and Jones, M. (2006), 'Beyond cereals: crop processing and *Vitis vinifera* L. Ethnography, experiment, and charred grape remains from Hellenistic Greece', *Journal of Archaeological Science* 33, 784–805.

————(2008a), 'Olive oil production in Hellenistic Greece: the interpretation of charred olive remains from the site of Tria Platania, Macedonia, Greece (4th–2nd century B.C.)', *Vegetation History and Archaeobotany* 33, 393–401.

————(2008b), 'Greek and Roman agriculture', in J. P. Oleson (ed.), *The Oxford Handbook of Engineering and Technology in the Classical World*, Oxford, 158–74.

Margomenou, D. (2008), 'Food storage in Prehistoric Northern Greece: Interrogating Complexity at the Margins of the Mycenaean World', *JMA* 21/2, 191–212.

Mari, M. (1999), 'Potere centrale e poteri locali nella Macedonia dei re: realtà istituzionali e imagine letteraria', in *Mediterraneo Antico, Economia, Società, culture* 2/ii, 627–49.

——(2002), *Al di là di Olimpo. Macedoni e Grandi Santuari della Grecia dall'età arcaica al primo ellenismo*, MELETEMATA 34, Athens.

——(2007), 'The Ruler Cult in Amphipolis and the Strymon Valley', in *Thrace in the Graeco-Roman World*, 371–86.

——(2011a), 'Archaic and early Classical Macedonia', in Lane-Fox (ed.), 79–92.

——(2011b), 'Traditional Cults and Beliefs', in Lane-Fox (ed.), 453–65.

Marzano, A. (2012), 'Rank-Size Analysis and the Roman Cities of the Iberian Peninsula and Britain: Some Considerations', in A. Bowman and A. Wilson (eds), *Settlement, Urbanization, and Population, Oxford Studies on the Roman Economy*, Oxford, 196–228.

Mashkour, M. (ed.) (2006), *Equids in Time and Space, Papers in honour of Véra Eisenmann*, Oxford.

Matsas, D. (2009), '*Η Σαμοθράκη πριν την άφιξη των Ελλήνων αποίκων*' in *Z. I. Μπόνιας* and J. Y. Perreault (eds), *Έλληνες και Θράκες/Greeks and Thracians, Πρακτικά του Διεθνούς Συμποσίου 'Έλληνες και Θράκες στην παράλια ζώνη και την ενδοχώρα της Θράκης στα χρόνια πριν και μετά τον μεγάλο αποικισμό'/Acts of the International Symposium 'Greeks and Thracians along the coast and in the Hinterland of Thrace during the years before and after the great colonization', Thasos, 26–27 September 2009*, Thasos, 205–36.

——(2010), 'Problems in Island Archaeology: Towards an Archaeology of Religion on Samothrace,' in O. Palagia and B. Wescoat (eds), *Samothracian Connections: Essays in honor of James R. McCredie*, Oxford, 33–49.

Matschke, K.-P. (2002), 'The late Byzantine Urban Economy, Thirteenth to Fifteenth Centuries', in A. E. Laiou (ed.), *The Economic History of Byzantium: from the Seventh through the Fifteenth Century*, Dumbarton Oaks Studies 39, Washington D.C., 463–95.

Mauss, M. (1923–24), 'Essai sur le don. Forme et raison de l'échange dans les sociétés archaiques', *Sociologie et anthropologie*[9], [1985] Paris, 30–196.

McGing, B. (2010), *Polybius' Histories*, Oxford.

McInerney, J. (1999), *The Folds of Parnassos*, Austin.

McInerney, J. (2010), *The Cattle of the Sun. Cows and Culture in the World of the Ancient Greeks,* Oxford and Princeton.

Mee, C. and Renard, J. (eds) (2007), *Cooking Up the Past, Food and Culinary Practices in the Neolithic and Bronze Age Aegean,* Oxford.

Migeotte, L. (2009), *The Economy of the Greek Cities from the Archaic Period to the Early Roman Empire,* Berkeley and Los Angeles.

Mihailov, G. (1986), 'Le processus d'urbanisation dans l'espace balkanique jusqu'à la fin de l'Antiquité', *Pulpudeva* 5, 5–30.

——(1989), 'The Inscriptions', in A. Fol (ed.), *The Rogozen Treasure*, Sofia, 46–71.

Miller, D. (1995), *Acknowledging Consumption*, London.

——(2008), *The Comfort of Things,* London.

Miller, M. C. (2010), 'Luxury Toreutic in the Western Satrapies: Court-Inspired Gift-Exchange Diffusion', in B. Jacobs and R. Rollinger (eds), *Der Achämenidenhof. The Achaemenid Court. Akten des 2. Internationalen Kolloquiums zum Thema 'Vorderasien im Spannungsfeld klassischer und altorientalischer Überlieferungen', Landgut Castelen bei Basel, 23.-25. Mai 2007,* Wiesbaden, 853–97.

Miller, S. (1993), *The Tomb of Lyson and Kallikles,* Munich.

Millett, P. (2010), 'The Political Economy of Macedonia', in Roisman and Worthington, 472–504.

Minchev, A. (2007), *Odesos prez elinisticheskata epocha (kraya na IVv.pr. Chr.—nachalo na 1 v.sl.Chr.),* Varna.

——(2011), 'Greek traditions and Roman taste: continuity and change in Odessos/Odessus (3rd *c.* BC–3rd *c.* AD)', in Haynes (ed.), 15–39.

Miracle, P. and Milner, N. (eds) (2002), *Consuming passions and patterns of consumption*, McDonald Institute Monographs, Cambridge.

Misaïlidou-Despotidou, V. (2008), 'Nea Philadelpheia settlement installations and cemeteries in the hinterland of Thessaloniki', in K. Tsouna (ed.) 2008, 25–65.

——(2009), 'Aphytis 1997–2006', in *20 Chronia AEMΘ*, Thessaloniki, 221–236.

Mitchell, S. (1993), *Anatolia: land, men, and gods in Asia Minor*, Oxford.

——(2008), 'Geography, Politics, and Imperialism in the Asian Customs Law', in *The Customs Law of Asia,* 165–201.

Mitrevski, D. (2001), *Staromakedonskiot grad na Vardarski Rid*, Skopje.
Moinier, B. (2007), 'Éléments pour une géographie du sel dans l'Antiquité', in D. Monah et al. (eds), *L'Exploitation du sel a travers le temps*, Piatra-Neamt, 235–57.
Monah, D., Dumitroaia, G., Weller, O., and Chapman, J. (eds) (2007), *L'Exploitation du sel a travers le temps*, Piatra-Neamt.
Moreno, A. (2008), 'Hieron. The Greek Sanctuary at the Mouth of the Black Sea', *Hesperia* 77, 655–709.
Morgan, C. (2000), 'Politics without the polis: Cities and the Achaean Ethnos, c.800–500 BC', in *Alternatives to Athens*, 189–211.
Morgan, C. (2003), *Early Greek States Beyond the Polis*, London.
Morley, N. (2009), *Antiquity and Modernity*, Malden Mass. and Oxford.
Morris, I. (1992), *Death-Ritual and Social Structure in Classical Antiquity*, Cambridge.
——(2000), *Archaeology as Cultural History: Words and Things in Iron Age Greece*, Oxford.
——(2003), 'Mediterraneanization', *Mediterraean History Review* 18, 30–55.
——(2005), 'Archaeology, Standards of Living, and Greek Economic History', in *AncEcon*, 91–126.
——(2009a), 'The Greater Athenian State', in I. Morris and W. Scheidel (eds), *The Dynamics of Ancient Empires, State Power from Assyria to Byzantium*, Oxford, 99–177.
——(2009b), 'The Eighth Century Revolution', in K. A. Raaflaub and H. van Wees (eds), *A Companion to Archaic Greece*, Chichester, Malden Mass., and Oxford, 64–80.
——and Scheidel, W. (eds) (2009), *The Dynamics of Ancient Empires, State Power from Assyria to Byzantium*, Oxford.
Moscalu, E. (1983), *Ceramica traco-getică*, Bucarest.
Muller, A. (2010), 'D'Odonis à Thasos. Thraces et Grecs (viiie–vie s.): essai de bilan', in Tréziny (ed.), 212–24.
Müller, Chr. (2010), *D'Olbia à Tanaïs. Territoires et réseaux d'échanges dans la mer Noire septentrionale aux époques classique et hellénistique*, Bordeaux.
Müller, C. and Hasenohr, C. (eds) (1998), *Les Italiens dans le monde grec, Actes de la Table Ronde, Paris, 14–16 mai, 1998, BCH* Supplement 41.
Musgrave, J., Prag, A. J. N. W., Neave, R., Lane Fox, R., and White, H. (2010), 'The Occupants of Tomb II at Vergina. Why Arrhidaios and Eurydice must be excluded', *International Journal of Medical Sciences* 7, 1–15.
Nafissi, M. (2005), *Ancient Athens and Modern Ideology. Value, Theory and Evidence in Historical Sciences. Max Weber, Karl Polanyi, and Moses Finley*, BICS Supplement 80.
Nehrizov, G. (2006), 'Iron Age Pit Sanctuary and Early Bronze Age Settlement near the Town of Svilengrad (Summary)', in V. Nikolov,

G. Nehrizov, and J. Tsvetkova (eds), *Spasitelni archeologicheski razkopki po traseto na zhelezopatna liniya Plovdiv-Svilengrad prez 2004g.*, Veliko Turnovo, 397–501 [454–56].

——and Mikov, R. (2000), 'Relations commerciales dans les Rhodopes de l'est, 5eme–1ier siècles avant J.-C.', in *Pistiros et Thasos*, 161–80.

Nevett, L. (2010), *Domestic Space in Classical Antiquity*, Cambridge.

Newskaja, V. P. (1955), *Byzanz in der klassischen und hellenistischen Epoche*, tr. H. Bruschwitz, and ed. W. Hering, Leipzig.

Nicolaidou, M. and Patera, I. (2005), '*Ανασκαφική Έρευνα στα ανατολικά της Καβάλας*', *AEMΘ* 19 [2007], 25–34.

Nicolet-Pierre, H. (2006), 'Les Talents d'Homère', in *Agoranomia*, 1–20.

Nielsen, I. (1999), *Hellenistic Palaces.* Studies in Hellenistic Civilization V, Aarhus.

Nikolov, V. (2006), *National Museum of Archaeology, 100 Years from the opening of the first exhibition, 18.05.1905–18.05.2005,* Sofia.

——, Nehrizov, G., and Tsvetkova, J. (eds) (2006), *Spasitelni archeologicheski razkopki po traseto na zhelezopatna liniya Plovdiv-Svilengrad prez 2004g.*, Veliko Turnovo.

Nikolova, D. (2007a), 'Izsledvaye na ivitsa ot kozhucharska kozha ot archeologicheski razkopki kray s. Zlatinitsa, Yambolsko (5–4v. pr.n.e.)' [Investigation of a fur strip from the archaeological excavations by Zlatinitsa village, Yambol district (5th–4th century BC)], *Izvestiya na Natsyonalen Istoricheski Muzei* 18, 181–5.

——(2007b), 'Chimichen analiz na tekstilen fragment of mogilno pogrebenye kray s. Zlatinitsa, Yambolsko (5–4v. pr.n.e)' [Chemical analysis of a textile fragment from a tomb burial by Zlatinitza village, Yambol district (5th–4th century BC)], *Izvestiya na Natsyonalen Istoricheski Muzei* 18, 186–8.

——(2008), 'Analiz na organika ot Trakiyskoto mogilno pogrebenye kray s. Beliš, Troyansko (viii–vii v. pr. Chr.)' [Analysis of organic material from a mound burial near Belish, the Troyan district (8th–7th century BC)], *Izvestiya na Natsyonalen Istoricheski Muzei* 20, 192–9.

——(2010), 'Izsledvanye na fragment ot azhurni kozheni shiriti ot mogilno pogrebenye kray s. Zlatinitsa, Yambolsko (iv-iii v.pr.n.e.)', *Izvestiya na Natsyonalen Istoricheski Muzei* 22, 186–8.

Nixon, L. and Price, S. (1990), 'The Size and Resources of Greek Cities', in O. Murray and S. Price, *The Greek City from Homer to Alexander*, Oxford, 137–70.

——(2001), 'The diachronic analysis of pastoralism through comparative variables', *BSA* 95, 395–424.

North, D. C. (1990), *Institutions, Institutional Change, and Economic Performance,* Cambridge.

Oleson, J. P. (ed.) (2008), *The Oxford Handbook of Engineering and Technology in the Classical World,* Oxford.

Oliver, G. J. (2001), 'Regions and Micro-regions. Grain for Rhamnous', in *HellEc I*, 137–55.

——(2006a), 'Hellenistic Economies. Regional Views from the Athenian *Polis*', in *Approches*, 215–56.

——(2006b), '*Polis* Economies and the cost of the Cavalry in Early Hellenistic Athens', in *Agoranomia*, 109–24.

——(2007), *War, Food, and Politics in Early Hellenistic Athens,* Oxford.

Osborne, R. (2008), 'Reciprocal Strategies: Imperialism, Barbarism, and Trade in Archaic and Classical Olbia', in P. Guldager Bilde and J. H. Petersen (eds), *Meetings of Cultures Between Conflicts and Coexistence,* Black Sea Studies 8, Aarhus, 333–46.

Owen, S. (2009), 'The "Thracian" landscape of Archaic Thasos', in S. Owen and L. Preston, *Inside the Greek City in the Greek World, Studies of Urbanism from the Bronze Age to the Hellenistic Period,* Oakville and Oxford, 85–98.

Özdoğan, M. (1990), '1989 yili Trakya ve Marmara bölgesi araştirmalari', *Araştirma Sonuçlari Toplantisi* 12, 1, 345–75.

Palagia, O. and Wescoat, B. (eds) (2010), *Samothracian Connections: Essays in honor of James R. McCredie*, Oxford.

Panagopoulou, K. (2007), 'Between Necessity and Extravagance: Silver as a Commodity in the Hellenistic Period', *BSA* 102, 315–43.

Panagou, T. (forthcoming), 'Patterns of Amphora Stamp Distribution. Tracking Down Export Tendencies', in *Markets, Households, and City-States.*

Panti, A. (2008), *Τοπική κεραμική από τη Χαλκιδικη και το μυχο του Θερμαϊκού Κόλπου* (Ακανθος, *Καραμπουρνακι*, *Σινδος*), Thessaloniki.

Papazarkadas, N. (2009), 'Epigraphy and the Athenian Empire: Reshuffling the chronological cards', in J. Ma, N. Papazarkadas, and R. Parker (eds), *Interpreting the Athenian Empire,* London, 67–88.

Papazoglou, F. (1988), *Les Villes de Macédoine à l'époque romaine,* Paris.

Pare, C. F. E. (ed.) (2000), *Metals make the World Go Round. The Supply and Circulation of Metals in Bronze Age Europe,* Oxford.

Parissaki, M.-G. (2002), 'Greeks and ore-Greeks in the society of Abdera. The Evidence of Prosopography and Onomastics', in *Thrace and the Aegean,* 463–68.

——(2007), 'Prosopography and Onomasticon of Aegean Thrace', MELETEMATA 49, Athens.

——(2009), 'Étude sur l'organisation administrative de la Thrace à l'époque romaine: l'histoire des stratégies', *REG* 122, 319–57.

Parker, R., and Stamatopoulou, M. (2004), 'A new funerary gold leaf from Ferai', *ArchEph*, 1–32.

Parkins, H. and Smith, C. (1998), *Trade, Traders, and the Ancient City*, London and New York.

Parry, J. and Bloch, M. (1989), 'Introduction', in J. Parry and M. Bloch (eds), *Money and the Morality of Exchange*, Cambridge, 1–32.

Paschidis, P. (2006), 'The Interpenetration of Civic Elites and Court Elite in Macedonia', in *Rois, Cités, Nécropoles*, 251–68.

——(2008), *Between City and King. Prosopographical Studies on the Intermediaries Between the Cities of the Greek Mainland and the Aegean and the Royal Courts in the Hellenistic Period (322–190 BC)*, Athens.

Pavlopoulos, K., Kapsimalis, V., Theodorakopoulou, K., and Panagiotopoulos, I. P. (2011), 'Vertical displacement trends in the Aegean coastal zone (NE Mediterranean) during the Holocene assessed by geoarchaeological data', *Holocene* 22, 717–28.

Pavlovska, E. (2006), 'A Part of a Hoard of Tetrobols from the Numismatic Collection of the NBRM', *Folia Archaeologica Balkanica* 1, 277–84.

Peacock, D. S. (1982), *Pottery in the Roman World*, London.

Pébarthe, Chr. (1999), 'Thasos, l'empire d'Athènes et les emporia de Thrace', *ZPE* 126, 131–54.

Pelling, C. (2000), 'Fun with fragments. Athenaeus and the historians', in *Athenaeus and his world*, 171–90.

Perissoratis, C. and Konispoliatis, N. (2003), 'The impacts of sea-level changes during latest Pleistocene and Holocene times on the morphology of the Ionian and Aegean seas (SE Alpine Europe),' *Marine Geology* 196, 145–56.

Peter, U. (1997), *Die Münzen den thrakischen Dynasten (5–3. Jahrhundert v. Chr.)*, Berlin.

Petersen, J. H. (2008), 'Kurgan Burials from Nymphaion—a New Approach', P. Guldager Bilde and J. H. Petersen (eds), *Meetings of Cultures Between Conflicts and Coexistence*, Black Sea Studies 8, Aarhus, 215–35.

Philippa-Touchais, A. (1996), 'Le personnel grec de l'École française d'Athènes', *BCH* 120, 223–51.

Photos, E., Koukouli-Chrysanthaki, Ch., Tylecote, R. F., and Gialoglou, G. (1989), 'Precious Metals Extraction in Palaia Kavala, N.E. Greece', *Der Anschnitt, Beihaft* 7, 179–90.

Picard, O. (1980), 'Aristote et la monnaie', *Ktèma* 5, 267–76.

——(1994), 'Thasos et la Thrace: l'apport des monnaies de bronze', *Settlement Life in Ancient Thrace* IV, 266–76.

——(1997), 'Monnaies de fouilles et histoire grecque: l'exemple de Thasos', in K. A. Sheedy and Ch. Papageorgiadou-Banis (eds), *Numismatic Archaeology. Archaeological Numismatics, Proceedings of an International Conference held to honour Dr. Mando Oeconomides in Athens, 1995*, Oxford, Oxbow monograph 75, 29–39.

Picard, O. (1999), 'Le commerce de l'argent dans la charte de Pistiros', *BCH* 123, 331–46.

——(2000), 'Monnayages en Thrace à l'époque achéménide', in O. Casabonne (ed.), *Mecanismes et Innovations dans l'Anatolie Achéménide, Numismatique et histoire, Actes de la Table Ronde Internationale d'Istanbul, 22–23 mai 1997*, Paris, 239–53.

——(2006), 'Mines, monnaies et impérialisme: conflits autour du Pangée (478–413 av. J.-C.)', in *Rois, Cités, Necropoles*, 269–83.

——(2007), 'Esquisse d'une histoire des rapports économiques entre grecs et thraces', in *Thrace in the Graeco-Roman World*, 464–73.

Pikoulas, G. A. (2001), *H Chōra tōn Pierōn*, Athens.

——(2006), 'Apo tin Pindo ston Olympo. Apologismos kai schediasma', *AEMΘ* 20, 587–90.

——(2007), 'Oi diavaseis tis Pindhou kai o Philippos B', *AncMac VII*, 209–20.

Popova, Tsv. (1996), 'The archaeobotanic samples from the clay altar', in *Pistiros I*, 173–4.

——(2002), 'Studies of carbonised vegetation remains from Pistiros', in *Pistiros II*, 289–97.

——(2005), 'Palaeobotanical and anthracological analysis from the Koprivlen site (Gotse Delchev district)', in Bouzek and Domaradzka, 99–102.

——, and Marinova, E. (2008), 'Palaeoethnobotanical Data from South-Western Region of Bulgaria', in H. Todorova, M. Stefanovich, and G. Ivanov (eds), *The Struma/Strymon Valley in Prehistory, Proceedings of the International Symposium, Strymon Praehistoricus.* In the Steps of James Harvey Gaul vol. 2, Sofia, 499–508.

Porozhanov, K. (2009), 'The residences of the Odrysian rulers', *Thracia* 18, 255–70.

Pouilloux, J. (1954), *Études thasiennes, III*, Paris.

Poulaki, E. (2003), 'Country houses in the areas of Phila-Herakleion and Leiveithra, on Macedonian Olympus', in P. Adam-Veleni et al. (eds), 2003, 53–70.

Poulaki-Pandermali, E. (2008), 'Krania-Herakleio', in Tsouna (ed.), 2008, 116–53, with English summary, 154–7.

Poulios, V., Mengidis, D.-D., Kosmidou, E. (2007), '*Λιθοχώρι Καβάλας* 2007. *Σωστική ανασκαφή στη σύγχρονη Εγνατία οδό*', *AEMΘ* 21 [2011], 399–407.

Prestianni-Giallombardo, A. M. and Tripodi, B. (1996), 'Iconografia monetale e ideologia reale macedone: i tipi del cavaliere nella monetazione di Alessandro I e di Filippo II', *RÉA* 98, 311–55.

Price, M. J. (1979), 'The Coinage of Philip II', *NC* 139, 230–41.

——(1991), *The Coinage in the Name of Alexander the Great and Philip Arrhidaeus*, London and Zurich.

Price, S. (2012), 'Estimating Ancient Greek Populations. The Evidence of Field Survey', in Bowman and Wilson (eds) 2012, 17–35.

Pritchett, W. K. (1956), 'The Attic Stelai: part II', *Hesperia* 25, 178–325.

Prokopov, I. (2000), 'The Tetradrachms of the Thasos Island and of the Thasos type in coin hoards from Bulgaria', in *Pistiros et Thasos*, 217–29.

Psoma, S. (2000), '*Τας παλαίας πεντεδραχμίας*: un stratagème de Polyen et le monnayage d'argent des rois de Macédoine de 413 à 360 av. J.- C.', *RN* 155, 123–36.

——(2006), 'The "Lete" Coinage Reconsidered', in *Agoranomia*, 61–86.

——(2008), 'An Honorary Decree from Thasos (IG XII, 8, 267) and the Samothracian peraia during the Hellenistic period', in Loukopoulou and Psoma (eds), 121–37.

——, Karadima, Chr., and Terzopoulou, D. (2008), *Coins from Maroneia and the Classical city at Molyvoti. A Contribution to the History of Aegean Thrace*, MELETEMATA 62.

Purcell, N. (2005a), 'The Ancient Mediterranean: The View from the Customs House', in W. V. Harris (ed.), *Rethinking the Mediterranean*, Oxford, 200–32.

——(2005b), 'Colonization and Mediterranean History', in *Ancient Colonizations*, 115–39.

——and Horden, P. (2005), 'Four Years of Corruption', in W. V. Harris (ed.), *Rethinking the Mediterranean*, Oxford, 348–75.

Raaflaub, K. A. and Van Wees, H. (eds) (2009), *A Companion to Archaic Greece*, Chichester, Malden Mass., and Oxford.

Rawski, T. G., Carter, S. B., Cohen, J. S., Cullenberg, S., Lindert, P. H., Mccloskey, D. N., Rockoff, H., and Sutch, R. (1996), *Economics and the Historian*, Berkeley and Los Angeles.

von Reden, S. (2007), 'Classical Greece: Consumption', in *CEHGRW*, 385–406.

——(2010), *Money in Classical Antiquity*, Cambridge.

Reger, G. (1994), *Regionalism and Change in the Economy of Independent Delos, 314–167 B.C.*, Berkeley, Los Angeles, and Oxford.

——(2011), 'Inter-regional economies in the Aegean basin' in *HellEc III*, 368–90.

——(2013a), 'Networks in the Hellenistic Economy,' in S. Ager and R. Faber (eds), *Belonging and Isolation in the Hellenistic World*, Phoenix Supplement 51, Toronto, 143–154.

——(2013b), 'Economic Regionalism in Theory and Practice', in A. Tsingarida and D. Viviers (eds), *Pottery Markets in the Ancient Greek World (8th–1st Centuries BC) Proceedings of the International Symposium held at the Université libre de Bruxelles, 19–21 June 2008*, Brussells, 99–111.

Rhodes, P. J. (2000), 'Oligarchs in Athens', in *Alternatives to Athens*, 119–36.

Rhomiopoulou, K. (2006), 'Nécropoles macédoniennes du littoral et de l'arrière-pays', in *Rois, Cités, Nécropoles*, 301–8.

Riederer, J. (1997), 'Egyptian blue', in *Artists' Pigments. A Handbook of Their History and Characteristics*, vol. 3, Oxford, 23–46.

Rizakis, A. and Touratsoglou, I. (1985), *Ἐπιγραφες Ἄνω Μακεδονίας* I, Athens.

Rizakis, A. D. (2002), 'L'émigration romaine en Macédoine et la communauté marchande de Thessalonique: perspectives économiques et sociales', in C. Müller and C. Hasenohr (eds), *Les Italiens dans le monde grec, Actes de la Table Ronde, Paris, 14–16 mai, 1998, BCH* Supplement 41, 109–32.

Robertson, B. (2008), 'The slave names of *IG* I^3 1032 and the ideology of slavery at Athens', in C. Cooper (ed.), *Epigraphy and the Greek historian*, Toronto, 79–116.

Robinson, E. W. (2011), *Democracy beyond Athens: Popular Government in the Classical Age*, Cambridge.

Roisman, J. and Worthington, I. (2010), *A Companion to Ancient Macedonia*, Malden Mass. and Oxford.

Rollinger, R. (2006), 'The Eastern Mediterranean and Beyond: The Relations between the Worlds of the "Greek"' and "Non-Greek" Civilizations', in K. Kinzl (ed.), *A Companion to the Classical Greek World*, Malden Mass. and Oxford, 198–226.

Rotroff, S. (2005), *Hellenistic Pottery. The Plain Wares, The Athenian Agora, XXXIII*, Princeton.

Rousseva, B. (2002), 'Les philippes et les alexandres d'or en Thrace Ancienne', in *Thrace and the Aegean*, 501–12.

Rousseva, M. (2000), *Thracian Cult Architecture in Bulgaria*, Yambol.

Roy, J. (1967), 'The mercenaries of Cyrus', *Historia* 16, 287–323.

Rubel, A. (2001), '*Hellespontophylakes*—Zöllner am Bosporos? Überlegungen zur Fiskalpolitik des attischen Seebundes (*IG* I^3 61)', *Klio* 83, 39–51.

Ruseva, B. (2006), 'Monetni nachodki ot yamnoto svetilishte kray s. Yabalkovo' [Coins from the Pit Sanctuary near the Village of Yabalkovo] Summary, in V. Nikolov, G. Nehrizov, and J. Tsvetkova (eds), *Spasitelni archeologicheski razkopki po traseto na zhelezopatna liniya Plovdiv-Svilengrad prez 2004g.*, Veliko Turnovo, 234–43 [241].

Ruseva-Slokoska, L. (1993), *100 godini Natsionalen Archeologicheski Muzei*, Sofia.

Saatsoglou-Paliadeli, C. (1984), *Τὰ Ἐπιτάφια μνημεῖα ἀπὸ τὴ Μεγάλη Τούμπα τῆς Βεργίνας*, Thessaloniki.

——(2007), 'The Palace of Aigai: Preliminary Publication', *AEMΘ* 21, 127–34.

——(2011), 'The Arts at Vergina-Aegae, the Cradle of the Macedonian Kingdom', in Lane-Fox (ed.), 271–95.

——and Kyriakou, A. (2006), 'Excavation at the Palace and cemetery of Aigai', *AEMΘ* 20, 759–66.

Salganik, M. J. and Watts, D. J. (2009), 'Web-based Experiments for the Study of Collective Social Dynamics in Cultural Markets', *Topics in Cognitive Science* 1/3, 439–68.

Sallares, R. (1991), *The Ecology of the Ancient Greek World*, London.

Salviat, Fr. (1986), 'Le vin de Thasos', *BCH Suppl.* XIII, 145–96.

——(1999), 'Le roi Kersobleptès, Maronée, Apollonia, Thasos, Pistiros et l'histoire d'Hérodote', *BCH* 123, 259–73.

Samuels, W. J., Biddle, J. E., and Davis, J. B. (2003), *A companion to the history of economic thought*, Malden Mass. and Oxford.

Saripanidi, V. (2010), 'Local and imported pottery from the cemetery of Sindos (Macedonia)', in Tréziny (ed.), 471–80.

Savalli-Lestrade, I. (1998), *Les Philoi royaux dans l'Asie Hellenistique*, Geneva.

Sawada, N. (2010), 'Social customs and institutions: Aspects of Macedonian Élite Society', in Roisman and Worthington, 392–408.

Scheidel, W. (2009), 'Sex and Empire, A Darwinian Perspective', in I. Morris and W. Scheidel (eds), *The Dynamics of Ancient Empires, State Power from Assyria to Byzantium*, Oxford, 255–324.

Scheidel, W. and von Reden, S. (eds) (2002), *The Ancient Economy: Recent Approaches*, London and New York.

Schmidt-Dounas, B. (2004), 'Frühes Peripteraltempel in Nordgriechenland', *AM* 119, 107–39.

Schönert-Geiss, E. (1987), *Die Münzprägung von Maroneia*, Berlin.

Sekunda, N. V. (2010), 'The Macedonian Army', in Roisman and Worthington, 446–71.

Sève, M. (2005), 'Notables de Macédoine entre l'époque hellénistique et le Haut Empire', in P. Fröhlich and Chr. Müller (eds), *Citoyenneté et Participation à la Basse Époque Hellénistique*, Geneva, 257–73.

Sharankov, N. and Tcherneva-Tilkiyan, S. (2004), 'The life of ancient Philippopolis in Lucian's dialogue, "Runaways"', *Godishnik na Archeologicheski Muzei Plovdiv/Annual of the Archaeological Museum Plovdiv*, 9/2, 75–121.

Shaw, B. D. (2001), 'Challenging Braudel: a new vision of the Mediterranean', *JRA* 14, 419–53.

Sherratt, A. (1995), 'Reviving the grand narrative: Archaeology and long-term change', *Journal of European Archaeology* 3, 1–32.

Shipley, G. (2011), *Pseudo-Skylax's Periplous: the circumstances of the inhabited world: text, translation and commentary*, Exeter.

Skarlatidou, E. K. (2009), 'The cemetery of Thermi (formerly Sedes), Thessaloniki: 20 years of excavation', in *20 Chronia AEMΘ*, Thessaloniki, 329–42.

——(2010), *Το Αρχαϊκο Νεκροταφειο των Αβδηρων*, Thessaloniki.

Śliwa, J. and Domaradzki, M. (eds) (1983), *The Lower Strumesnica Valley in Prehistoric, Ancient, and Medieval Times*, Krakov.

Soueref, K. (2007), '*Μια πιθανή εισαγωγή στην αρχαϊκή Μακεδονία*' (*Mia pithane eisagoge stin archaike Makedonia: enotites chorou stin anatolike parathermaiki zone) ArchMakedonia* VII, 651–74.

Sprawski, S. (2009), *Tessalia, Tessalowie i ich sasiedzi*, Krakow.

——(2010), 'The Early Temenid Kings to Alexander I', in Roisman and Worthington, 127–44.

Stallibrass, S. (2010), 'Body Parts, Placements and People in an Iron Age Town in Bulgaria', in D. Campana et al. (eds), *Anthropological Approaches to Zooarchaeology. Complexity, Colonialism, and Animal Transformations*, Oxford, 56–64.

Stamatopoulou, M. (2007), 'Thessalian Aristocracy and Society in the Age of Epinikian', in S. Hornblower and C. Morgan (eds), *Pindar's Poetry, Patrons, and Festivals, from Archaic Greece to the Roman Empire*, Oxford, 309–41.

Stephani, E. (2010), *Αγγελοχώρι Ημαθίας. Οικισμός της 'Υστερης εποχής του Χαλκού*, 1. Thessaloniki.

Stolba, Vl. and Hannestad, L. (eds) (2005), *Chronologies of the Black Sea Area in the Period c.400–100 BC*, Black Sea Studies 3, Aarhus.

Stoyanov, T. (2000), 'Spatial patterns and economic development of the northeastern Thrace—7th–2nd centuries BC', in *Pistiros et Thasos*, 57–67.

——(2002), 'The Getic capital at Sboryanovo (NE Bulgaria)', *TALANTA* 32–33 [2000–2001], 207–21.

——(2006), 'Kabyle, Sevtopolis i Helis—Tri varianta na urbanizma v rannoelinisticheska Trakya', in *Settlement Life in Ancient Thrace* IV, 79–96 [in Bulgarian].

——(2008), 'On the pictorial programme of the Aleksandrovo tomb', *Archaeologiya* 49, 58–66 [in Bulgarian with English summary].

——(2011), 'New Evidence for Amphora Production in early Hellenistic Mesambria Pontica', in Ch. Tzochev, T. Stoyanov, and A. Božkova (eds), *PATABS II, Production and Trade of Amphorae in the Black Sea, Acts of the International Round Table held in Kiten, Nessebar and Sredetz, September 26–30 2007*, Sofia, 191–201.

Strøm, I. (1992), 'Obeloi of pre- or protomonetary value in Greek sanctuaries', in T. Linders and B. Alroth (eds), *Economics of cult in the ancient world*, Uppsala, 41–51.

Stronach, D., and Zournatzi, A. (2002), 'Odrysian and Achaemenid Tribute: Some New Perspectives', in *Thrace and the Aegean*, 333–43.

Stronk, J. P. (1995), *The Ten Thousand in Thrace, An Archaeological and Historical Commentary on Xenophon's* Anabasis, *Books VI.iii-vi–VII*, Amsterdam.

Stroud, R. S. (1998), 'The Athenian Grain-Tax Law of 374/3 B.C.', *Hesperia* Supplement 29, Princeton N.J.

Tacheva, M. (1988), 'Politicheskata detsentralizatsya v Odriskata durzhava ot poslednata chetvart na V v.pr.n.e. do vuztsaryavaneto na Kotys I (383–359g. pr.n.e.)', *Istoricheski Pregled* 44/12, 22–36.

——(1997), *Istoriya na Bulgarskite zemi v drevnostta prez elinisticheskata i rimskata epoha*[2], Sofia.

——(2007), 'The Pistiros Inscription: the mirror of a new Thracian society', in *Thrace in the Graeco-Roman World*, 588–95.

Taneva, V. (2000), 'Les monnaies de Pistiros', in *Pistiros et Thasos*, 47–53.

——(2005), 'The trade contacts of Pistiros during the second half of the 4th century BC', in Bouzek and Domaradzka, 27–30.

——(2011), 'The Potter's kiln found at Pistiros', *Eirene* 47, 25–8.

Theodossiev, N. (1998), 'The Dead with Golden Faces: Dasaretian, Pelagonian, Mygdonian, and Boeotian Funeral Masks', *OJA* 17, 345–67.

Tiverios, M. (2009a), 'Karabournaki: University of Thessaloniki excavations (1994–2008)', in *20 Chronia AEMΘ*, Thessaloniki, 385–96, with English summary, 396.

——(2009b), 'The double trapeza at Anchialos', in *20 Chronia AEMΘ*, Thessaloniki, 397–406, with English summary, 407.

——, Manakidou, E., and Tsiafakis, D. (2006), 'Excavations at Karabournaki in 2006: the Ancient Settlement,' *AEMΘ* 20, 263–70.

Tonkova, M. (2000), 'Sur le système des sites du Deuxième Age du Fer dans la region des Collines de Chirpan', in *Pistiros et Thasos*, 133–44.

——(2003), 'Late Iron Age pit-sanctuaries in Thrace: the contribution of the studies at Gledačevo', *Thracia* 15, 479–505.

——(2008), 'Trakiyski tsentar v m. Chalka Bunar, s. Gorno Belovo, obshtina Bratya Daskalovi, Starozagorska oblast', *AOR* 2007, 222–5.

——(2011), *Trako-rimski dinastichen tsentar v rayona na Chirpanskite vuzvishenya*, Sofia.

Touratsoglou, Y. (1993), *The Coin Circulation in Ancient Macedonia*, Athens.

——(2010), *A Contribution to the Economic History of the Kingdom of Ancient Macedonia (6th—3rd centuries BC)*, Athens.

Treuil, R. (1996), 'L'École française d'Athènes et la préhistoire/protohistoire du monde égéen', *BCH* 120, 407–39.

Tréziny, H. (ed.) (2010), *Grecs et indigènes de la Catalogne à la Mer Noire*, Bibliothèque d'archéologie méditerranéenne et africaine 3, Paris and Aix-en-Provence.

Triandaphyllos, D. (2007), 'Archaologikes martyries gia tin para ton Evro kai ton Arda chōra tōn Odrysōn', in *Thrace in the Graeco-Roman World*, 626–38.

Triandaphyllos, D. and Terzopoulou, D. (2006), 'Wagons and horse burials in the Roman Age tumuli in Greek Thrace', *Eirene* 42, 167–82.

Troxell, H. (1997), *Studies in the Macedonian Coinage of Alexander the Great*, Numismatic Studies 21, New York.

Tsakirgis, B. (2005), 'Living and working around the Athenian Agora: A Preliminary Case Study of Three Houses', in B. A. Ault and L. C. Nevett (eds), *Ancient Greek Houses and Households, Chronological, Regional, and Social Diversity,* Philadelphia, 67–82.

Tsiafakis, D. (2010), 'Domestic Architecture in the Northern Aegean: the Evidence from the ancient settlement of Karabournaki', in Tréziny (ed.), 379–87.

Tsigarida, B. (2011a), 'Chalcidice', in Lane-Fox (ed.), 137–58.

——(2011b), 'The Sanctuary of Zeus Ammon at Kallithea (Chalcidice)', *Kernos* 24, 165–81.

Tsimbidou-Avloniti, M. (2005), *Makedonikoí Táphoi ston Phoínika kai ston 'Agio Athanásio Thessaloníkis,* Demosieumata tou Archaiologikou Deltiou 91, Athens.

Tsouna, K. (ed.) (2008), Αρχαιολογικες *Τροχιοδρομήσεις από τη Θεσσαλονικη στον Πλαταμωνα*, Athens.

Tuplin, C. J. (2003), 'Xerxes' March from Doriscus to Therme', *Historia* 52, 385–409.

——(ed.) (2007), *Persian Responses. Political and Cultural Interaction with (in) the Achaemenid Empire*, Swansea.

Tušlovà, P., Kučovà, S., and Weissova, B. (2010), 'Greek and Black Sea Transport amphorae in emporion Pistiros. Quantified Analysis of Material Excavated until 2009', in *Pistiros IV*, 205–20.

Tziafalias, A. (1978), '*Ανασκαφικές εργασίες στον 'Αγιο Γεώργιο Λαρίσης*', *Athens Annals of Archaeology*, 156–81.

Tzifopoulos, Y. Z. (2011), 'Center, periphery, or peripheral center. A Cretan connection for the gold lamellae of Crete', in Radcliffe G. Edmonds III (ed.), *The 'Orphic' Gold Tablets and Greek Religion*, Cambridge, 165–99.

Tzochev, Ch. (2007), 'Black Sea Transport Amphorae', in *Pistiros III*, 187–9.

——(2010), 'Between the Black Sea and the Aegean: the diffusion of Greek trade amphorae of southern Thrace', in Kassab Tezgör and Inaishvili (eds), 97–101.

——(2011), 'Archaic Amphora Import from Thracian Sites around the Bay of Bourgas', in Ch. Tzochev, T. Stoyanov, and A. Božkova (eds), *PATABS II, Production and Trade of Amphorae in the Black Sea, Acts of the International Round Table held in Kiten, Nessebar and Sredetz, September 26–30 2007,* Sofia, 73–86.

——(forthcoming), 'The Export of Thasian Amphoras and Markets in the Black Sea Region', in *Markets, Households, and City-States.*

——, Stoyanov, T., and Božkova, A. (eds) (2011), *PATABS II, Production and Trade of Amphorae in the Black Sea, Acts of the International Round Table held in Kiten, Nessebar and Sredetz, September 26–30 2007*, Sofia.

Tzvetkova, J. (2008), *Istoriya na Trakiyskiya Chersones (ot Troyanskata Voyna do Vremeto na Rimskoto zavoyavanye) [History of the Thracian Chersonese (from the Trojan War until the time of the Roman Conquest)]*, Veliko Turnovo.

Urem-Kotsou, D. and Kotsakis, K. (2007), 'Pottery, cuisine, and community in the Neolithic of northern Greece', in C. Mee and J. Renard (eds), 225–46.

Vacalopoulos, A. P. (1963), *A History of Thessaloniki*, Thessaloniki.

Vagalinski, L. (ed.) (2010), *In Search of Celtic Tylis in Thrace (III BC), Proceedings of the Inter-disciplinary Colloquium arranged by the National Archaeological Institute and Museum at Sofia and the Welsh Department, Aberystwyth University, held at the National Archaeological Institute and Museum, Sofia, 8 May 2010*, Sofia.

Valamoti, S. M. (2004), *Plants and People in Late Neolithic and Early Bronze Age Northern Greece, An Archaeobotanical Investigation*, BAR IS 1258, Oxford.

——(2007), Traditional Foods and Culinary Novelties in Neolithic and Bronze Age Northern Greece: An Overview of the Archaeobotanical Evidence', in C. Mee and J. Renard (eds), 89–108.

Valamoti, S. M., Mangafa, M., Koukouli-Chrysanthaki, Ch., and Malamidou, D. (2007), 'Grape-pressings from northern Greece: the earliest wine in the Aegean?' *Antiquity* 81, 54–61.

Vanderspoel, J. (2010), 'Provincia Macedonia', in Roisman and Worthington, 251–75.

Vavelidis, M. and Andreou, S. (2008), 'Gold and gold working in Late Bronze Age northern Greece', *Naturwissenschaften* 95, 361–6.

——Chotzidis, A., and Melfos, V. (2006), 'Quarries and quarrymen in Thraki, from the antiquity to the present', *AEMΘ* 20, 41–9 [in Greek].

Veblen, Th. (1899), *The Theory of the Leisure Class: An Economic Study in the Evolution of Institutions*, edited with introduction and notes by M. Banta (2007), New York and Oxford.

——(1919), *The Place of Science in Modern Civilization and Other Essays*, New York; reprinted 1990 with Introduction by W. J. Samuels, New Brunswick, N.J.; New York, 2007.

Velkov, V. (1962), 'Les campagnes et la population rurale en Thrace au IVe – Ve siècle', *Byzantinobulgarica* I, Sofia, 31–66 (reprinted in Velkov 1988, 181–216).

Velkov, V. (1964), 'Zur Frage der Sklaverei auf der Balkanhalbinsel während der Antike', *Études Balkaniques* 1, 125–38; (reprinted in Velkov 1988, 113–26).

——(1967), *Robstvoto v Trakya I Mizya v Antichnostta,* Sofia.

——(1970), 'Über einige Probleme der sozialökonomischen und ethnischen Entwicklung im II – V. Jahdt. und des Übergangs von der Antike zum Mittelalter im VI – X Jhdt.', *Études historiques* V, Sofia, 13–55 (reprinted in Velkov 1988, 235–77).

——(1971), 'Bergbau und Hüttenwesen bei den alten Thrakern', *Jahrbuch für Wirtschaftsgeschichte* ii, Berlin, 175–92 (reprinted in Velkov 1988, 73–80).

——(1988), *Geschichte und Kultur Thrakiens und Mösiens,* Amsterdam.

——(1991), *Kabyle II,* Sofia.

——and Domaradzka, L. (1994), 'Cotys I (383/2–359av.J.C.) et l'emporion Pistiros de Thrace', *BCH* 118, 1–15.

Verboven, K., Vandorpe, K., and Chankowski, V. (eds) (2008), *Pistoi dia tèn technèn. Bankers, Loans, and Archives in the Ancient World,* Studia Hellenistica 44, Leuven.

Vlassopoulos, K. (2007), *Unthinking the Greek Polis*, Cambridge.

Vokotopoulou, J. (ed.) (1985), *Meletes gia tēn archaia Thessalonike: Thessalonikēn Philippou basilissan*, Thessaloniki.

——(with E. Trakosopoulou-Salakidou, M. Tsimbidou-Aulonitou, P. Adam-Veleni, and K. Sismanidis) (1986), *Θεσσαλονίκη, από τα προϊστορικά μέχρι τα Χριστιανικά χρόνια*, Athens.

——(1990), *Oi Taphikai Tymboi tis Aineias.* Dimosieumata tou Archaiologikou Deltiou 41, Athens.

Wagner-Hasel, B. (2006), 'Gift Exchange: Modern Theories and Ancient Attitudes', in S. Deger-Jalkotzy and I. S. Lemos (eds), *Ancient Greece. From the Mycenaean Palaces to the Age of Homer*, Edinburgh, 257–69.

Walbank, F. (1940), *Philip V of Macedon*, Cambridge (reprinted with new Foreword, Hamden Conn., 1967).

——(1957–79), *A Historical Commentary on Polybius*, 3 vols, Oxford.

——(1970), 'Polybius and Macedonia', *AncMac I,* 291–307 (reprinted in F. W. Walbank, (2002a), 91–106, Oxford).

——(1985), 'Via illa nostra militaris. Some Thoughts on the Via Egnatia', *Selected Papers: Studies in Greek and Roman History and Historiography*, Cambridge, 193–209.

Walbank, F. W. (2002a), *Polybius, Rome and the Hellenistic World, Essays and Reflections,* Oxford.

——(2002b), 'The Via Egnatia: Its Role in Roman Strategy', *Journal of Ancient Topography* 12, 7–18.

Wallinga, H. T. (1993), *Ships and sea-power before the Great Persian War*, Leiden.

Wartenberg, U. (1997), 'The Alexander-eagle Hoard: Thessaly 1992', *NC* 157, 179–88.

——and Kagan, J. (1999), 'Some Comments on a New Hoard from the Balkan Area', in M. Amandry and S. Hurter (eds), *Travaux de Numismatique grecque offerts à Georges le Rider*, London, 409–507.

Waterhouse, H. (1986), *The British School at Athens, 1886–1986: The First Hundred Years*, BSA Supplement 19, London.

Watts, D. J. (2003), *Six Degrees. The Science of a Connected Age*, London, Heinemann.

Westgate, R., Fisher, N., and Whitley, J. (eds) (2007), *Building Communities. House Settlement and Society in the Aegean and Beyond*, BSA Studies 15, London.

Whitbread, I. K. (1995), *Greek transport amphorae: a petrological and archaeological study*, London.

Wilkins, J. (2000), 'The Comic Agora', *The Boastful Chef*, Oxford, 156–201.

Yourukova, Y. and Domaradzki, M. (1990), 'Nouvel centre de la culture thrace—Vetren, la région de Pazardjik (notes préliminaires)', *Numizmatika* 24/3, 1–24 [in Bulgarian].

Zahrnt, M. (1984), 'Die Entwicklung des makedonischen Reiches bis zur den Perserkriegen', *Chiron* 14, 325–68.

——(2006), 'Macedonia and Thrace in Thucydides', in A. Rengakos and A. Tsakmakis (eds), *Brill's Companion to Thucydides*, Leiden, 589–614.

Zhivkova, L. (1973), *Das Grabmal von Kazanluk*, Recklingshausen.

Zournatzi, A. (2000), 'Inscribed Silver Vessels of the Odrysian Kings: Gifts, Tribute and the Diffusion of the Forms of the "Achaemenid" metalware in Thrace', *AJA* 104, 683–706.

Index of sources

2. INSCRIPTIONS

General index